POLAND

THE ROUGH GUIDE

THE ROUGH GUIDES

OTHER AVAILABLE ROUGH GUIDES

AMSTERDAM • BARCELONA • BERLIN • BRAZIL
BRITTANY & NORMANDY • BULGARIA • CALIFORNIA & WEST COAST USA
CANADA • CRETE • CZECH & SLOVAK REPUBLICS • CYPRUS • EGYPT
EUROPE • FLORIDA • FRANCE • GERMANY • GREECE • GUATEMALA & BELIZE
HOLLAND, BELGIUM & LUXEMBOURG • HONG KONG • HUNGARY • IRELAND
ISRAEL • ITALY • KENYA • MEDITERRANEAN WILDLIFE • MEXICO • MOROCCO
NEPAL • NEW YORK • NOTHING VENTURED • PARIS • PERU • PORTUGAL
PRAGUE • PROVENCE • PYRENEES • ST PETERSBURG • SAN FRANCISCO
SCANDINAVIA • SICILY • SPAIN • THAILAND • TUNISIA • TURKEY
TUSCANY & UMBRIA • USA • VENICE • WEST AFRICA
WOMEN TRAVEL • ZIMBABWE & BOTSWANA

FORTHCOMING
AUSTRALIA • CORSICA • ENGLAND • SCOTLAND • WALES

Rough Guide Credits

Text:	Chapters 1–4 Mark Salter, chapters 5 & 6 Gordon McLachlan
Text Editors:	Jack Holland, Miranda Davies and John Fisher
Series Editor:	Mark Ellingham
Editorial:	Martin Dunford, Jonathan Buckley, Greg Ward, Kate Berens, Jules Brown
Production:	Susanne Hillen, Andy Hilliard, Gail Jammy, Vivien Antwi, Alan Spicer, Melissa Flack
Publicity:	Richard Trillo
Finance:	Celia Crowley

Grateful acknowledgement is made for permission to quote from *All Played Out* by Pete Davies (Heinemann).

The publishers and authors have done their best to ensure the accuracy and currency of all the information in *Poland: The Rough Guide*; however, they can accept no responsibility for any loss, injury or inconvenience sustained by any traveller as a result of information or advice contained in the guide.

This second edition published July 1993 by Rough Guides Ltd, 1 Mercer Street, London WC2H 9QJ. Distributed by the Penguin Group:

Penguin Books Ltd, 27 Wrights Lane, London W8 5TZ
Penguin Books USA Inc., 375 Hudson Street, New York 10014, USA
Penguin Books Australia Ltd, 487 Maroondah Highway, PO Box 257, Ringwood, Victoria 3134, Australia
Penguin Books Canada Ltd, 10 Alcorn Avenue, Toronto, Ontario, Canada M4V 1E4
Penguin Books (NZ) Ltd, 182–190 Wairau Road, Auckland 10, New Zealand

Originally published by Harrap Columbus.
Previous edition published in the United States and Canada as *The Real Guide Poland*.

Typeset in Linotron Univers and Century Old Style to an original design by Andrew Oliver.
Printed by Cox & Wyman, Reading, Berks

Illustrations in Part One and Part Three by Edward Briant.
Basics illustration by Simon Fell. Contexts illustration by Tommy Yamaha.

592pp. includes index

A catalogue record for this book is available from the British Library.
ISBN 1-85828-034-6

POLAND
THE ROUGH GUIDE

Written and researched by

MARK SALTER
and
GORDON McLACHLAN

THE ROUGH GUIDES

ACKNOWLEDGEMENTS AND THANKS

Mark would like to thank Mia for her constant support, encouragement and patience, and the many friends and colleagues here and in Poland whose advice, warmth and hospitality helped make this book possible. In particular: in Gdańsk – Adam Gosziewski and family, Adam and Gosha, Grzegorz, Leszek, Joanna, Mr Andrzej Januszajtis and the staff of the COIT office; in Warsaw – Marek K, Jacek and Magda Czaputowicz, Ryszard, Krysza and Janek Litynski, Emily, Peter, Jacek and Radka S, Michał Cichy for help with the listings section, Christopher Bobiński of the FT, Jerzy Socała, Piotr Treda and colleagues at ORBIS; in Kraków – Jakub, Bogdan, Janina Pizło of COIT and above all Marek Czersky for answering all the questions.

Thanks are also due to many others: Jarek Putresza in Białystok; Franek Bachleda in Zakopane; Wiesław Szumiński in Suwałki; the Banachs in Sanok; Jan, Julia Doszna and fellow Łemkowie for memorable times in the Beskid Niski; Aldona, Arvid Kosa, and all the Griygoutis family for Lithuanian hospitality; Rob Humphreys, fellow author; the comrades of END; everyone at Svenska Freds in Stockholm; Maciej Z; Dominic Ziegler for nearly catching a Bieszczady trout; Anna Wolek of the *Economist* for much advice, humour and vodka; Geoff Patton and John Saville; Mark Ellingham for tireless and inventive rescue work; David Goldblatt for additional emergency work; to Jack Holland and Bob Ordish for additional material; and last but certainly not least, Piotr Cieplak for a decade of friendship . . . and argument.

For the **second edition** special thanks to Tim Burford for his hiking contributions, Adam and Anya in Gdańsk for advice, enthusiasm, and meals (as usual), Gosia in Warsaw (and the Suwalszczyna), Malgosia Chechlińska and Leszek Krzanik of TRIP, Zakopane for letting me beat up their Polski Fiat, Julia D. for music, fellow editor and friends at SIPRI for support, in particular Zdislaw Lachowski for Polish proofreading and all-round help: and last but not least Hannah, for being born.

At the **Rough Guides office**: Jack Holland for editing most of the new stuff, Miranda Davies and John Fisher for the rest; Susanne Hillen for heroic work on the maps; Mark E. and Jonathan B. for additional support – the League's yours for once!

Gordon would like to thank: Edward Giecewicz in Kłodzko, Erwin Piesch in Jelenia Góra, and especially Ireneusz Spychalksi in Wrocław; Paweł Domachowski; and Melanie Ellis, Jolanta Wieteska, Zdzisław Ciuk, Lucja Ginko, Małgorzata Raczkowska, Barbara Kowalczyk, Piotr Maniurka, Tadeusz Hanelt, Ilona Łabno, Ewa and Jerzy Kubski; Agata Mrocko, Tom Kolbusz, Ryszard Bryzek and Piotr Wilem at Pascal; Tim Dowd, Valerie Ibaan, Michele Tarnow and Perry Pederson of the Peace Corps; Karen Zietlow (and her pupils in Legnica), Jane and Piotr Kumelowski, Richard Blanke, Jean and Michael Fox, David Lindley, and Sebastian Olden-Jørgensen.

Both authors thank Margaret Doyle for proofreading and Sam Kirby for updating the maps.

Thanks to all those perspicacious readers of the first edition of the guide, who took the time and trouble to write in with updates, criticisms and helpful suggestions. Particular thanks go to all the US Peace Corps volunteers in Poland who sent us their comments – keep up the good work! The list (in no particular order) goes as follows:

Ann Rogers, Barry Dickens, David and Ellen Elliot, David Reene, John Woodhead, Nancy Maurer, Pamela Cook-Spinogle, Paul Clark, Philip Seitz, Robin Root, Sebastian Olden-Jorgensen, Simon Edwards, Sysse Engberg, Uta Protz, William Kennedy, Peter Hothersall, Suzi Kanyr Hagen, Elisabeth Cox, Stan & Janet Lanislaus, Amy Tonnessen, Suzanne Barfoot, Roben Flack, Peter Perkins, Andrew Stankiewicz, John Lyon-Maris, Gavin Gibb, Juliette Fraser, Michele Weaver, Alex Berland, Judi Morton, Jack Rosenbloom, Hans Belt, Roger Manser, Robert Swiderski, Evelyn Cibule, Jonathan Hill, Jeff Martin, Mary Gorecki, Lauren Stranneman, Valerie Ibaan, Michele Tarnow, Perry Pedersen, Jean Barclay, Helen Eldred, Virginia Brown, Colleen Healey, Markus Jung, Richard Lynch, Zbigniew Janiszewski, T Sidey, Patrick Chapman, Tim King, Anthony Wingate, Mike Wicksteed, Rosalind Rowe, Colin Mulcahy, Deborah Owen, Sean de Podesta, Karin Burns, SH McCombie, Mark Czerkawski, Siana Tackett, Edward Michalski, Denis and Janet Jackson, Betty Geisler, Mrs SE Cooper, Thomas Radice, Janet Hine, W Trio, Greg McColgan, John Theakstone, Gordon McMullen, Eddy Boutmans, Robert W Farquhar, John Barrett, Malcolm Hawkins and Christine Shefford, David Danisz, Hilda Simpson, ACB Hooper, Piotr and Jane Kumelowski, Ian Fraser, Sarah Williams, Alice Hannahs, Helen Giejgo, Betsy Green, Anthony Hadfield, Stan Skubisz, Richard Blanke, Peter Hide, Ian Bates and Sharon Hall, James Gilley, Martin Clark, Richard Bradbury, Michael Paduchowski, Mike Adkins, Teresa Rubkinowicz, Gill Manning-Press, Rachel Morley, Arnold Markowitz. Apologies to anyone whose name or signature we couldn't quite decipher.

CONTENTS

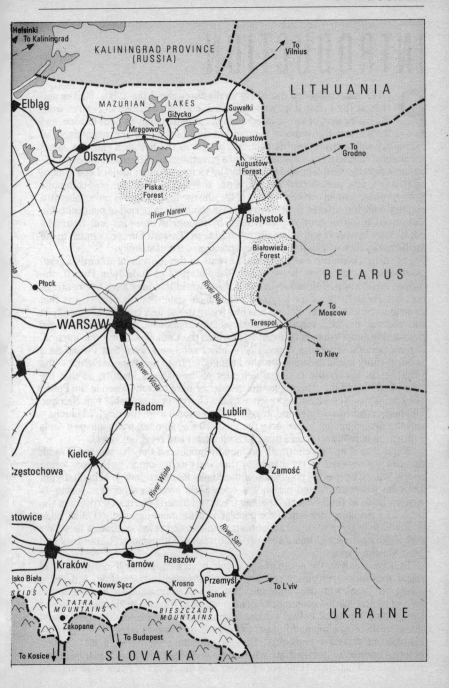

INTRODUCTION

P olish images flooded the world media throughout the 1980s. Strikes and riots at the Lenin shipyards of Gdańsk and other industrial centres were the harbingers of the disintegration of communism in Eastern Europe, and throughout the years of martial law and beyond Poland maintained an exemplary momentum towards political change. At the decade's end, the annus mirabilis of 1989 saw the establishment of a government led by the Solidarity trade union, a development followed in 1990 by the victory of union leader Lech Wałęsa in Poland's first presidential election since the 1920s. With the post-commuist political order now an established fact of life, the media spotlight is rather less on a country enjoying what is, by its own peculiar standards, a period of political calm. Compared to other countries convulsed by nationalist tensions and fratricidal ethnic wars in what is still habitually referred to as "Eastern Europe" – much to the locals' annoyance – Poland can at times appear an oasis of stability.

For many Poles, the most important events in the movement towards a post-communist society were the visits in 1979 and 1983 of Pope John Paul II, the former archbishop of Kraków. To the outside world this may have been surprising, but Poland was never a typical communist state: Stalin's verdict was that imposing communism on Poland was like trying to saddle a cow. Polish society in the postwar decades remained fundamentally traditional, maintaining beliefs, peasant life and a sense of nationhood to which the Catholic Church was integral. During periods of foreign oppression – oppression so severe that Poland as a political entity has sometimes vanished altogether from the maps of Europe – the Church was always the principal defender of the nation's identity, so that the Catholic faith and the struggle for independence have become fused in the Polish consciousness. The physical presence of the church is inescapable – in Baroque buildings, roadside shrines and images of the national icon, the Black Madonna – and the determination to preserve the memories of an often traumatic past finds expression in religious rituals that can both attract and repel onlookers.

World War II and its aftermath profoundly influenced the character of Poland: the country suffered at the hands of the Nazis as no other in Europe, losing nearly one quarter of its population and virtually its entire Jewish community. In 1945 the Soviet-dominated nation was once again given new borders, losing its eastern lands to the USSR and gaining tracts of formerly German territory in the west. The resulting make-up of the population is far more uniformly "Polish" than at any time in the past, in terms of both language and religion, though there are still significant ethnic minorities of Belorussians, Lithuanians, Ukrainians and even Muslim Tartars.

To a great extent, the sense of social fluidity, of a country still in the throes of major transitions, remains a primary source of Poland's fascination. A decisive attempt to break with the communist past as well as tenacious adherence to the path of radical market economic reforms adopted in the late 1980s have remained the guiding tenets of Poland's post-communist political leadership. Few would question the economic and human toll reaped by Poland's attempt to reach the eldorado of capitalist prosperity. Despite this, the Polish people, as so often before, continue to demonstrate what to the visitor may appear an extraordinary resilience and patience. Hope springs eternal in the minds of Poles, it seems, and for all the hardships involved in establishing a new economic order – an order to which the majority of Poles retain a remarkable, if grumbling, political commitment – individual initiative and enterprise of every conceivable kind is flourishing as almost nowhere else in the region. By 1993 the first tentative signs of the much hoped for economic recovery were beginning to make themselves apparent. Tourism is proving no exception to the general "all change" rule, but despite the continuing state of flux in the country's tourist infrastructure, it is now easier – if not, given the continuing alarming rise in crime, always safer – to explore Poland than anyone could have imagined only a few years back.

Encounters with the people are at the core of any experience of the country. On trains and buses, on the streets or in the village bar, you'll never be stuck for opportunities for contact: Polish hospitality is legendary, and there's a natural progression from a chance meeting to an introduction to the extended family. Even the most casual visitor might be served a prodigious meal at any hour of the day – usually with a bottle or two of local vodka brought out from the freezer.

Where to go

Poles delineate their country's attractions as "the mountains, the sea and the lakes", their emphasis firmly slanted to the traditional, rural heartlands. To get the most out of your time, it's perhaps best to follow their preferences. The **mountains** – above all the Carpathian range of the Tatras – are a delight, with a well-established network of hiking trails; the **lakes** provide opportunities for canoeing and a host of other outdoor pursuits; and the dozen or so **national parks** retain areas of Europe's last primeval forests, inhabited still by bisons, elks, wolves, bears and eagles. Yet you will not want to miss the best of the **cities** – Kraków, especially – nor a ramble down rivers like the Wisła for visits to Teutonic **castles**, ancient waterside towns and grand, Polish **country mansions**, redolent of a vanished aristocratic order. The **ethnic regions** offer insights into cultures quite distinct from the Catholicism of the majority, while the former centres of the **Jewish** community, and the concentration camps in which the Nazis carried out their extermination, are the most moving testimony to the complexity and tragedy of the nation's past.

Unless you're driving to Poland, you're likely to begin your travels with one of the three major **cities**: Warsaw, Kraków or Gdańsk. Each provides an immediate immersion in the fast-paced changes of the 1990s and a backdrop of monuments that reveal the complexities of the nation's history.

Warsaw, the capital, had to be rebuilt from scratch after the war, and much of the city conforms to the stereotype of Eastern European greyness, but the reconstructed Baroque palaces, churches and public buildings of the historic centre, the burgeoning street markets and the bright shopfronts of Poland's new enterprise culture are diverting enough. **Kraków**, however, the ancient royal capital, is the real crowd puller for Poles and foreign visitors alike, rivalling the Central European elegance of Prague and Vienna. This is the city where history hits you most powerfully, in the royal Wawel complex, in the fabulous open space of the Rynek, in the one-time Jewish quarter of Kazimierz, and in the chilling necropolis of nearby Auschwitz-Birkenau, the bloodiest killing field of the Third Reich. **Gdańsk**, formerly Danzig, the largest of the Baltic ports and home of the legendary shipyards, presents a dynamic brew of politics and commerce against a townscape reminiscent of mercantile towns in the Netherlands.

German and Prussian influences abound in the **north** of the country, most notably in the austere castles and fortified settlements constructed by the

Teutonic Knights at **Malbork**, **Chełmno**, and other strategic points along the **River Wisła** – as the Vistula is known in Poland. **Toruń** is one of the most atmospheric and beautiful of the old Hanseatic towns here.

Over in the **east**, numerous minority communities embody the complexities of national boundaries in Central Europe. The one-time Jewish centre of **Białystok**, with its Belorussian minority, is a springboard for the Soviet borderlands, where onion-domed Orthodox churches stand close to Tartar mosques. Further south, beyond **Lublin**, a famous centre of Hassidic Jewry, and **Zamość**, with its magnificent Renaissance centre, lie the homelands of Ukrainians, Lemks and Boyks – and a chance to see some of Poland's extraordinary wooden churches.

In the **west**, ethnic Germans populated regions of the divided province of **Silesia**, where **Wrocław** sustains the dual cultures of the former German city of Breslau and the Ukrainian city of L'viv, whose displaced citizens were moved here at the war's end. The other main city in western Poland is the quintessentially Polish **Poznań**, revered as the cradle of the nation, and today a vibrant and increasingly prosperous university town.

Despite its much-publicised pollution problems, Poland has many regions of unspoilt natural beauty, of which none is more pristine than the **Białowieza forest**, in the southeast extremity; the last virgin forest of the European mainland, it is the habitat of the largest surviving herd of European bison. A journey westwards from here, through the southern uplands, would pass through the wild **Bieszczady** mountains and the alpine **Tatras** before arriving at the bleak **Karkonosze** mountains – all of them excellent walking country, interspersed with less demanding terrain. On the opposite side of the central Polish plain, the wooded lakelands of **Mazury** and **Pomerania** are as tranquil as any lowland region on the continent, while the Baltic coast can boast not just the domesticated pleasures of its beach resorts, but also the extraordinary desert-like dunes of the **Słowinski Park** – one of a dozen National Parks.

When to go

Spring is arguably the ideal season for some serious hiking in Poland's mountainous border regions, as the days tend to be bright – if showery – and the distinctive flowers are at their most profuse. **Summer**, the tourist high season, sees plenty of sun, particularly on the Baltic coast, where the resorts are crowded from June to August and temperatures consistently in the high 70s. The major cities can get pretty stifling at these times, with the effects of the heat compounded by the influx of visitors; accommodation can be tricky in the really busy spots, but a good network of summer hostels provides a low-budget fall-back.

Autumn is the best time to come if you're planning to sample the whole spread of the country's attractions: in the cities the cultural seasons are beginning at this time, and the pressure on hotel rooms is lifting; in the countryside, the golden "Polish October" is especially memorable, the rich colours of the forests heightened by brilliantly crisp sunshine that's often warm enough for T-shirts.

In **winter** the temperatures drop rapidly, icy Siberian winds blanketing many parts of the country with snow for anything from one to three months. Though the central Polish plain is bleak and unappealing at the end of the year, in the south of the country skiers and other winter sports enthusiasts will find themselves in their element. By mid-December the slopes of the Tatras and the other border ranges are thronged with holidaymakers, straining the few established facilities to the limit.

AVERAGE DAILY TEMPERATURES (°F) & MONTHLY RAIN (mm)

		Kraków	Gdynia	Poznań	Przemśyl	Warsaw
January	Max	32	35	33	32	32
	Min	22	27	24	20	22
	Rain	28	33	24	27	27
February	Max	34	35	34	34	32
	Min	22	25	22	21	21
	Rain	28	31	29	24	32
March	Max	45	40	44	43	42
	Min	30	30	30	29	28
	Rain	35	27	26	25	27
April	Max	55	48	54	55	53
	Min	38	36	37	37	37
	Rain	46	36	41	43	37
May	Max	67	59	67	67	67
	Min	48	45	47	46	48
	Rain	46	42	47	57	46
June	Max	72	66	72	73	73
	Min	54	52	52	53	54
	Rain	94	71	54	88	69
July	Max	76	70	76	75	75
	Min	58	58	57	57	58
	Rain	111	84	82	105	96
August	Max	73	70	73	73	73
	Min	56	57	55	55	56
	Rain	91	75	66	93	65
September	Max	66	64	67	67	66
	Min	49	51	48	48	49
	Rain	62	59	45	58	43
October	Max	56	55	56	57	55
	Min	42	44	41	40	41
	Rain	49	61	38	50	38
November	Max	44	44	43	43	42
	Min	33	36	33	33	33
	Rain	37	29	23	43	31
December	Max	37	38	37	38	35
	Min	28	31	28	28	28
	Rain	36	46	39	43	44

PART ONE

THE

BASICS

GETTING THERE FROM BRITAIN AND EUROPE

There are regular services from the UK to Poland by air, train and coach. Flights are obviously the simplest option, with direct flights to Warsaw and connections to other major Polish cities; return tickets average out at £200–250. Trains are only marginally cheaper, unless you're under 26, in which case you can buy a discount *BIGE* ticket or the month-long InterRail pass. Coaches – which are run mainly for the benefit of Polish emigrés – are a long, slow haul, but a bargain, at around £100 return. Another option, if money is more a concern than time, is to fly to Berlin and continue from there by train. By car, it's a 1000-kilometre drive to the Polish border from the French coast – best covered in two or more days.

BY PLANE

From London (Heathrow) both *British Airways* and *LOT* (Polish Airlines) operate daily scheduled flights (more at peak periods) on the 2hr 30min run to **Warsaw**, with connections on to other major cities throughout the country. In most cases you'll arrive in Warsaw in time to catch the onward domestic flight, but you'll need to check this – for some cities you may end up having to spend the night in the capital. In addition, there are direct weekly flights from London (Heathrow) to **Kraków** (Fri) and **Gdańsk** (Sat), plus a direct summer service to **Szczecin**. In summer *LOT* also operate charters **from Manchester** and **Glasgow** to Warsaw and Gdańsk.

Early booking is always advisable, with flights filling up weeks in advance at peak times, particularly at Christmas when emigré Poles return home in force.

FARES AND AGENTS

The regular London–Warsaw **Apex fare** from *BA* or *LOT* is currently £289 in low season (Jan 16–May 31, Oct 1–Dec 15), £339 during the rest of the year. The usual Apex restrictions are in force: you must stay over a Saturday night, reservations must be made at least 14 days in advance and you're entitled to only a £50 refund for tickets cancelled before the 14-day deadline. Tickets are valid for three months and can be booked from either airline or most travel agents. For **under-24s** there's a return youth fare of £257 (low season) or £307 (peak periods), only bookable the day before and subject to availability.

The **cheapest** *BA* or *LOT* seats, however, are those sold by *Polorbis*, the official tourist office (see "Information and Maps"), and by *Fregata* and *Travelines*, two established Polish-run travel outfits. From these operators, one-month returns cost around £160–190 low season, £180–235 at

---

UK AIRLINE AND FLIGHT AGENCIES

British Airways, 156 Regent St, London W1 (☎081/897 4000).

Campus Travel, 52 Grosvenor Gardens, London SW1 (☎071/730 3402); plus branches nationwide.

Fregata Travel, 100 Dean St, London W1 (☎071/734 5101); 117 Withington Rd, Manchester M16 (☎061/226 7227).

GTF, 182–186 Kensington Church St, London W8 (☎071/792 1260).

German Travel Centre, 8 Earlham St, London WC2 (☎071/379 5212).

LOT, 313 Regent St, London W1 (☎071/580 5037).

Polorbis, 82 Mortimer St, London W1 (☎071/636 2217).

STA Travel, 86 Old Brompton Rd, London SW7 (☎071/937 9921); plus branches nationwide.

Travelines, 154 Cromwell Rd, London SW7 (☎071/370 6131).

peak periods. For students and under-26s there's a discounted version of the under-24 fare mentioned above – £166 low season, £176 peak periods. All three companies also regularly offer a number of short-break "specials" to Warsaw.

In summer, especially, it's worth shopping around for cheap flights from bucket shops and cut-price operators, too; though Poland is hardly a major **discount** destination, you can often find competitively priced offers in the quality Sunday papers, London free magazines, the *Evening Standard* and, most dependably, the travel section of the London listings magazine *Time Out*. Specialist agents like **STA Travel** and **Campus Travel** are often a good bet as well, with prices sometimes as low as £160 return.

VIA BERLIN

As a cheaper alternative you might consider flying **to Berlin** (return fares cost as little as £100), and continuing to Warsaw by train, an inexpensive eight-hour journey. In addition to agents like *STA Travel* and *Campus Travel*, it's worth contacting specialists such as **German Travel Centre** and **GTF** (see addresses above).

FLIGHTS FROM IRELAND

There are no direct flights from Ireland to Poland, so the easiest option is to **fly to London** and book a connection on from there. It's also worth checking out fares to **Berlin**, whence you can carry on relatively cheaply by train. The best people to consult are independent travel experts **USIT**, 12–21 Aston Quay, O'Connell Bridge, Dublin 2 (☎01/679 8833).

BY TRAIN

Travelling by train to Poland is an enjoyable way of getting there, allowing stopoffs along the way. You'll only really save money over the cost of a flight, however, if you're under 26.

The **ordinary return fare** (which is twice that of a single) is £214 for London–Warsaw, with a journey time of 31 hours on the fastest route (via the Hook of Holland, Hanover and Berlin). Trains leave London's Liverpool Street station in the morning from Monday to Saturday, arriving in Warsaw the following afternoon. Couchettes, if available, cost £12; the pricier sleeping berths are theoretically reserved for people going on to Moscow, but may be available if demand is low. Tickets, which you can buy from any British Rail

For details on how to take your **bike** to Poland, see p.24.

ticket office and most travel agents, are valid for two months and allow any number of stopovers.

Cheaper rates are available from specialist operators such as *Fregata* and *Travelines* (see above): *Travelines* quote £144 for the return trip to Warsaw, £169 on their special luxury carriage. It would be cheaper still to go to Szczecin (£133 return) and continue on by local trains.

Eurotrain offer under-26s a return **BIGE fare** on the same route for £149 (£77 single); again tickets are valid for two months, with unlimited stops en route. An extra £20 gets a pass for one week's unlimited second-class travel in Poland – worth doing if you plan any rail travel, just to save on the queues. Another option for under-26s is the **InterRail** pass. Costing £249, this gives one month's free travel on most European railways, plus around a third off rail travel in Britain and discounts on some ferries, including cross-Channel services. Inside Poland it gives you free travel on a rail system which connects all the major towns and rural areas – albeit painfully slowly in many instances. **Senior citizens** with a *Rail Europe Senior Card* can travel for £161 return (£81 single).

One **warning** about rail travel, however. There have been reports of numerous robberies on international night services into Poland, especially from Berlin and Prague. Some have involved entire compartments being stripped while their occupants are put to sleep by gas fed through the ventilation system.

MAIN UK RAIL TICKET AGENTS
British Rail European Travel Centre, Victoria Station, London SW1 (☎071/834 2345).
Eurotrain, 52 Grosvenor Gardens, London SW1 (☎071/730 8518).
Wasteels, 121 Wilton Rd, London SW1 (☎071/834 7066).

BY COACH

Coach travel is an arduous but cheap way to get to Poland, much favoured by impoverished Poles during the holiday seasons, and often packed as a consequence.

COACH OPERATORS

Bogdan Travel, 5, The Broadway, Gunnersbury Lane, London W3 8HR (☎081/992 8866).

Eurolines, 52 Grosvenor Gardens, London SW1 (☎071/730 8235).

Fregata Travel, 100 Dean St, London W1 (☎071/ 734 5101); 117 Withington Rd, Manchester M16 (☎061/226 7227).

New Millennium, 20 High St, Solihull, Birmingham B91 3TB (☎021/711 2232).

Tazab Travel, 273 Old Brompton Rd, London SW5 (☎071/373 1186).

Travelines, 154 Cromwell Rd, London SW7 (☎071/370 6131).

The most reliable services are operated by **Eurolines**, a division of the *National Express* coach company, in conjunction with **Fregata**. They run a regular service **from London to Warsaw** (via Ostend, Brussels, Frankfurt an der Oder and Poznań) and **to Kraków** (same route to Poznań, then via Wrocław, Opole and Katowice). These now run at least once a week throughout the year, departing on Sundays, with extra services at holiday times and up to three a week during the summer. The journey time for Warsaw is around 36 hours, a bit longer for Kraków: cost for both destinations is £90 return and £65 single, with £5 off for under-26s and reductions for senior citizens and children. Tickets can be bought at any *National Express* office in the UK, together with an add-on fare from any destination to London (no reduction on standard rates, though).

In addition, a number of other **Polish emigré-run companies** run "buses", which can turn out to mean anything from a double-decker Mercedes to a minibus. The best established of these is **Travelines**, who run coaches from London to Warsaw via Amsterdam and Poznań, and to Kraków via Amsterdam, Wrocław and Katowice. Prices are £65 single, £95 return from London. On all services there's a £5 discount for under-26s and senior citizens, and a £20–30 discount for children. **Tazab** operates similar services at similar prices, again aimed primarily at the Polish community in this country, as do **Bogdan Travel**, who also offer a service from London to Gdańsk via Szczecin.

Also well worth considering – and one of the better bargains in European travel – are the coach and accommodation packages offered by **New Millennium**. They do a weekly run **to Zakopane** from Dover (you make your own way there from London), leaving on a Friday morning and arriving at Zakopane on the Saturday evening. Current price, including a week's accommodation in Zakopane, is a remarkable £109 all-in.

BY CAR AND FERRY

Driving to Poland means a long haul of 1000km from Calais or Ostend to the border – and another 450–500km from there to Warsaw or Kraków. Flat out you could do the journey in a day and a half, but it makes more sense to allow longer, breaking the journey in northern Germany or Berlin.

The most convenient ferry crossings are the *P&O* services from Dover/Folkestone to **Calais or Ostend**, though an alternative favoured by Poles is to take the overnight boat from Felixstowe to **Zeebrugge**, allowing a bit of sleep before a solid day's driving. From any of these ports, the most popular and direct route is via Brussels, Düsseldorf, Hanover and Berlin.

An alternative which halves the driving distance is to catch the *Scandinavian Seaways* ferry **from Harwich to Hamburg** (20hr) and then drive down to Berlin. Costs are significantly higher, however, as they are for the most convenient ferry route from the north of England – the daily *North Sea Ferries* service **from Hull to Rotterdam** (14hr).

HITCHING

Hitching to Poland, your best bet is to follow the **Ostend–Berlin** route detailed above. It is well

FERRY COMPANIES

Scandinavian Seaways, Parkeston Quay, Harwich, Essex CO2 4QG (☎0255/243456), or 15 Hanover St, London W1 (☎071/409 6060).

P&O, Russell St, Dover, Kent CT16 1QB (☎0304/ 203388; phone reservations ☎081 575 8555).

North Sea Ferries, King George Dock, Hedon Road, Hull HU9 5QA (☎0482/77 177).

BORDER CROSSINGS

Following the breakup of the Soviet Union – and the split of neighbouring Czechoslovakia – Poland now shares **land borders** with six countries: **Germany**, the **Czech Republic**, **Slovakia**, **Ukraine**, **Belarus**, **Lithuania** and the **Russian Federation** (Kaliningrad region). Recent political changes have made the formalities of entering Poland from Germany, the Czech Republic or Slovakia pretty straightforward, though in summer long delays often build up at the busiest customs points, as the pitifully understaffed Polish customs force search for smuggled goods – a major and growing problem, owing to big-time cigarette-, alcohol- and drug-smuggling operations run by post-Soviet mafias.

Theoretically at least, entering or leaving Poland from **the east** via the former Soviet republics ought to be less difficult now than in the past. Despite the easing of travel restrictions, though, the actual state of affairs is pretty uneven: the mentality of many post-Soviet guards is very much "business as usual", and this, combined with the lack of properly functioning crossing points, means that the delays (by car especially) can be horrendous.

To keep locals up to date during the summer holiday season, Polish radio broadcasts "border reports" after the weather news, giving details of the length of the queues (up to 10km on a bad day) and expected waiting time (up to sixty hours). The opening of more border crossings features prominently in high-level discussions between politicians on all sides – indeed in some instances (Lithuania, for example) it can be taken as a litmus test of the state of relations between the two countries. To date, however, little substantial progress has been made, the tiny number of new or expanded crossing points being more than matched by the volume of people wanting to travel. In fairness though, money – or rather, the lack of it – is as much a problem as political will, and an issue which Western governments would do well to take seriously.

Current border crossings (open 24 hours unless specified) are:

The Czech Republic–Poland (west to east)
Habartice–Zawidów (Prague–Gorlitz).

Harachow–Jakuszyce (Prague–Wrocław route, via Jelenia Góra).

Kralovec–Lubawka (Prague–Wrocław route, via Wałbrzych).

Pomezni Boudy–Przełęcz Okraj (Prague–Wrocław route, via Wałbrzych).

Dolni Lipka–Boboszów (Prague–Wrocław route, via Kłodzko).

Mikulovice–Głuchołazy (Brno–Opole route).

Krnov–Pietrowice (Brno–Opole route).

Nachod/Slone–Kudowa (Prague–Wrocław route, via Kłodzko).

Česky Tesin–Cieszyn (Brno/Ostrava–Kraków route).

Bohumin–Chałupki (Ostrava– Katowice route).

Slovakia–Poland (west to east)
Trstena–Chyżne (Ruźomberok–Kraków route).

Sucha Hora–Chochołów (open 7am–7pm).

Javorina–Łysa Polana (Poprad–Nowy Targ route, via Tatra mountains).

Mnisek–Piwniczna (Poprad–Nowy Sącz route, via Beskid Sądecki).

Vysny Komarnik–Barwinek (Presov–Rzeszów, via Dukla).

Germany–Poland (north to south)
Linken–Lubieszyn

Pomellen–Kołbaskowo (Berlin–Gdańsk route).

Schwedt– Krajnik Dolny

Frankfurt an der Oder–Świecko (Berlin–Warsaw route).

Guben–Gubin

Forst–Olszyna (Berlin–Wrocław/Kraków route).

Bad Muskau–Łeknica

Görlitz–Zgorzelec (Dresden–Wrocław route).

Ukraine–Poland
Szeginie–Medyka (L'viv/Kiev route).

Jagodin–Dorohusk (L'viv/Kiev route).

Belarus–Poland
Briest–Terespol (Warsaw–Moscow route).

Brzugi–Kuźnica (Białystok–Grodno route)

Lithuania –Poland
Lazdijai–Ogrodniki (Warsaw–Vilnius route).

Kaliningrad Province–Poland
Gronono–Mamonowo (Elbąg–Kaliningrad route).

Bagrationowsk–Bezledy (Warsaw/Olsztyn– Kaliningrad route).

worth asking around on the ferry – you may strike lucky and get a lorry going through to Düsseldorf or beyond. An alternative is to contact the German *Mitfahrzentralen* organisations, who link up hitchers and drivers for a small fee plus something towards petrol costs. They won't get you to Poland, but for £35 you can make it to Berlin, a big chunk of the journey. One contact address for a Berlin *Mitfahrzentrale* is Kurfürstendamm 227, 1000 Berlin 15 (☎30/82 7606).

BY BOAT

For anyone happy with a slow journey by sea there's the option of travelling by **cargo ship** to Poland. A Polish freighter leaves **Tilbury** in Essex every Monday, going up to Middlesborough on Tuesday, and arriving in **Gdynia** on the Friday.

Accommodation (12 places in all) is in two-berth cabins. Cost is £160 single from Tilbury, £130 single from Middlesborough. For more details contact **Gdynia-American Lines**, 238 City Road, London EC1 (☎071/251 3389).

FROM SCANDINAVIA

A number of regular, all-year ferries also run from Scandinavia to Poland's Baltic ports. Routes are:
Helsinki–Gdańsk (37hr)
Ystad–Gdańsk (18hr)
Ystad–Świnoujście (7hr)
Copenhagen–Świnoujście (9hr)
Nynäshamm–Gdańsk (18hr)

The ferries are operated by *Polferries*; for details, again contact *Gdynia-American Lines* (see above) or their Swedish agents *Pol-Line AB* in Ystad Färjeterminalen, 27100 Ystad (☎0411/16010) and Nynäshamm Färjeterminalen, 14900 Nynäshamm (☎0752/17017).

ORGANISED TOURS

The number of foreign visitors on package tours continues to outweigh independent travellers. During the communist era, **Orbis**, the state tourist company, had unquestioned dominance of this market, with a couple of Polish emigré-run operators coming a distant second. However, over the past year or two small travel operations have mushroomed in Poland – a recent estimate was over 2000 – and a growing number of British and other western European travel companies have set up their own programmes, often in co-operation with local private operators.

ORBIS/POLORBIS

Orbis operate an extensive range of tours, which are retailed overseas through *Polorbis* agencies. The bulk of the tours are one- or two-week packages, their busy schedules taking in Warsaw and Kraków plus a combination of places such as Poznań, Wrocław, Częstochowa, Gdańsk, Lublin and the Tatras. At £425–495 for a week, £750–820 for two weeks, these are pricey options.

More interesting are some of their **specialist ventures**, such as a seven-day **Jewish tour**, taking in Warsaw, Kraków, Auschwitz and Lublin (good value at around £550), or the **Warsaw Opera weekends**, a long-weekend package starting at £255. *Polorbis* also offer hiking in the Tatras, horse-riding, steam railway tours, nature trails, and mountain/spa resort vacations.

OTHER SPECIALISTS

Few of the larger general operators feature Poland in their brochures: an exception is **Wallace Arnold**, who do a twelve-day trip centred on four nights in Kraków for £434; unfortunately, most of the time is spent getting there and back. **Shearings** do a fourteen-day tour to Zakopane, with a detour to Prague, for £379. **Fregata Travel** offer a range of packages along similar lines to *Orbis*: historic cities, theme tours such as "Chopin's country" and "In the footsteps of John Paul II", and hiking holidays. Prices too are similar to those of *Orbis*. They also operate a number of all-in **city breaks** to Warsaw, Kraków, and Gdańsk throughout the year (2 or 3 nights), starting from £194. **Travelines**, **Tazab** and **Bogdan Travel**, which, like *Fregata*, are run in Britain by Polish emigrés, also offer this kind of tour.

New Millennium offer packages to the Tatras base of Zakopane, starting at £109 for a return coach trip plus a week's accommodation in a pension. In winter they can arrange ski hire. Almost equally competitive prices, provided you book early, can be had from **Poland Tours** who have ten-day packages to either Zakopane or Krynica from £109. **Silesian Villas** have well-equipped chalets and villas in Warsaw, Zakopane and the Beskid Śląski – prices start at £110 per week for four people, making it a real bargain, but you need to arrange your own transport here. **Travel Guide Holidays** do an eight-day "Polish highlights" holiday for £485, plus a ten-day trip to the Jelenia Góra for £179, and an eleven-day trip to Zakopane for the same price; with the last two,

£30 extra gets you the luxury of a four-star hotel, rather than the guest houses usually offered in such packages.

Other UK-based specialists include **TEFS Railways Tours**, who do steam train trips; **Inter-Church Travel**, who run ten-day trips at Easter, Corpus Christi and the Feast of the Assumption, taking in Warsaw, Częstochowa, Zakopane, Kraków, Kalwaria and Wadowice; and **Exodus**

Expeditions, who offer a 15-day backpack through the Tatras and Beskid Sądecki, staying mainly in mountain refuges along the way, that costs £780.

Cycling enthusiasts could consider **Bike Events'** East European tour: this starts from Kraków, heading south through the Tatras into Slovakia, and ending up in Budapest. Tour price is £569, plus an extra £229 for the airfare.

SPECIALIST OPERATORS

Bike Events, PO Box 75, Bath BA1 1BX (☎0225/310 859).

Bogdan Travel, 5, The Broadway, Gunnersbury Lane, London W3 8HR (☎081/992 8866).

Exodus Expeditions, Dept RG, 9 Weir Rd, London SW12 0LT (☎081/675 5550).

Fregata Travel, 100 Dean St, London W1 (☎071/734 5101); 117 Withington Rd, Manchester M16 (☎061/226 7227).

Inter-Church Travel, Middelburg Square, Folkestone CT20 1BL (☎0800/300444).

New Millennium, 20 High St, Solihull, Birmingham B91 3TB (☎021/711 2232).

Poland Tours, 22 West View, Bedfont, MIDDX TW14 8PP (☎0784/247286).

Polorbis, 82 Mortimer St, London W1 (☎071/636 2217).

Shearings, Miry Lane, Wigan, WN3 4AG (☎0942/824824).

Silesian Villas, 42 Ickburgh Rd, London E5 8AD (☎081/806 6264).

Tazab Travel, 273 Old Brompton Rd, London SW5 (☎071/373 1186).

TEFS Railways Tours, 77 Frederick St, Loughborough LE11 3TL (☎0509/262 745).

Travel Guide Holidays, 10, St Mary's Place, Newcastle-upon-Tyne, NE1 7PG (☎091/221 0444).

Travelines, 154 Cromwell Rd, London SW7 (☎071/370 6131).

Wallace Arnold, Gelderd Rd, Leeds LS12 6DH (☎0532/310739).

GETTING THERE FROM AUSTRALASIA

There are at present no direct flights from Australia or New Zealand through to Warsaw, so there are two alternatives: either you fly to **London or another major European city** and shop around for a discount flight (or train) from there, or head for **Bangkok or Singapore** to connect with one of the *LOT* flights to Warsaw. For the latter, bucket shops will probably be able to undercut the Apex price of around Aus$3700 return.

Whether or not you qualify for **student or youth discounts**, it's worth enquiring first through an agent like *STA Travel*. They have more than twenty offices in Australia, including 1a Lee St, Railway Sq, Sydney 2000 (☎02/519 9866) and 224 Faraday St, Carlton, Victoria 3053 (☎03/347 4711). Their ten offices in New Zealand include branches in Christchurch, Palmerston North and Wellington, as well as the head office at 10 High St, Auckland (☎09/309 9723 for telephone sales).

GETTING THERE FROM THE USA AND CANADA

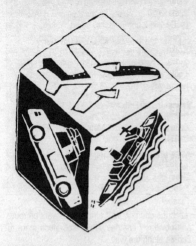

The easiest way to get to Poland from the US and Canada is to fly direct to Warsaw. Alternatively, if expense is a main consideration, you may consider flying to London or another good-value western European destination, and continuing by a combination of bus, train, and ferry. There are options to suit every schedule and sense of adventure.

BY PLANE

SCHEDULED FLIGHTS

LOT (Polish Airlines) flies **direct to Warsaw** from New York's JFK five times a week, once a week from Newark, New Jersey, and four times a week from Chicago's O'Hare airport. As a rule, tickets are not cheap – a low-season, round-trip Apex fare from New York or New Jersey will set you back $749, rising to $974 in the summer high period (flying from Chicago this increases to $799 in low season, and $1099 during high season). That said, *LOT* occasionally makes special offers, arranged though the formerly official travel agency **Polorbis** (see p.7), and flying midweek can also reduce fares to as little as $530.

Several other carriers, including *Delta*, *KLM*, *Swissair*, *Lufthansa*, and *Sabena* offer more reasonable fares to Warsaw **via other European cities**. *Sabena*, for instance, flies via Brussels and can run as low as $599 in low season, $748 in

high. *Delta* flies via Frankfurt for broadly similar fares. Once in Warsaw, *LOT* connects with most of the major Polish cities. April 1–May 31 is shoulder season (another good option if you're budgeting) when fares run about $650 midweek.

Most **Apex fares** to Poland require a minimum stay of seven days and a maximum of three months, and in the majority of cases must be booked at least 21 days in advance. The cheapest seats available are to be found by booking through *Polorbis*, who, though no longer nationalised, retain a special agreement with *LOT* and are able to sell **discounted tickets** on most flights. Other cheap flights can be found by booking through the *Polish American Travel Agency*, which specialises in handling Polish flights and tours, and *American Travel Abroad Inc*, essentially a charter firm but one which also sells individual flights on the major airlines (addresses for both these organisations are given on p.12). Specialist agents such as *STA* and *Council Travel* (see overleaf for addresses throughout the US and Canada) sometimes have special arrangements with the airlines and can offer cheap fares, especially if you're under 26. It's also worth checking the travel sections of the major Sunday papers to see what's on offer.

FLIGHTS VIA BERLIN

With cheap flights to Warsaw still something of a rarity, many travel agents suggest flying into Berlin and taking a train to the Polish capital from there – an inexpensive eight-hour journey (or half that to Poznan). *TWA* and *Lufthansa* both fly direct to Berlin, with round-trip, low-season fares of $618, rising to $718 in high season. Again, it's worth checking with the specialist agents before contacting the airlines.

FLIGHTS FROM CANADA

LOT flies direct to Warsaw from Montréal on Fridays, and from Toronto on Wednesdays, Fridays and Sundays. The cheapest fare they offer from Montréal is CDN$948 in low season, CDN$1285 in high. *LOT* also runs charters from Montréal: lowest fares run about CDN$799, highest CDN$1285. All the other major airlines fly to Warsaw as well, but you have to make a change in New York or western Europe in order to get a cheaper fare.

DISCOUNT FLIGHTS

You can bypass the airlines altogether and go straight to a **travel agent**, who will at least guide you through the maze of fares even if they can't offer anything cheaper, and they will often be able to match any special deals the airlines are offering direct. Check the Sunday newspapers' travel sections, which are always advertising discounted fares, or consult a **youth and student specialist** like *Council Travel* or *STA Travel*, who often have the best deals, and not just for students. Another option is to contact a **discount travel club** – organisations which specialise in selling off unsold seats of travel agents for bargain rates, often at up to half the original price, though you usually have to be a member to get the best deals. You could also try a so-called airline ticket **consolidator**, who sells unsold seats direct from airlines, though bear in mind that discounts are usually lower than with travel clubs and you may not get the exact flight you want.

TRAVELLING VIA BRITAIN

If you're travelling to Poland via Britain as part of a wider European tour, the simplest option is to take one of the daily scheduled **flights** to Warsaw, taking just 2hr 30min from London's Heathrow airport (see preceding pages for the full picture).

If you have the time, however, travelling onward overland can be an excellent way to reach the country, as it allows stopovers en route and obviously enables you to see much more of Europe along the way.

BY TRAIN

The fastest rail route from London to Warsaw takes you via the Hook of Holland, Hanover, and Berlin, in a journey time of around 33 hours. An **ordinary round-trip fare** on this route, however, will cost you £214 ($320). For this reason most vacationers make use of the variety of **railpasses** available.

Eurail (☎1-800/777-0112), organised through *STA* and *Council Travel*, offers a range of passes that are valid throughout the different European rail networks. Prices vary according to the duration of your trip and the distance you wish to cover.

In addition to their all-country youthpass ($508 for one month; $698 for two) which is available only to people under 26, they have a new *East European Flexi Railpass*, which has no age restrictions. Covering Poland, Czechoslovakia, Austria, and Hungary, this allows five days of travel out of a period of fifteen days for $169, or ten days within a month for $275. See also "Organised Tours" opposite for details of the *Polrail Pass*.

BY BUS

Another option, though few but the most budget-oriented traveller would consider it, is to take a cheap flight to London and continue from there by

DISCOUNT FLIGHT AGENTS AND CONSOLIDATORS

Access International, 101 W 31st St, Suite 104, New York, NY 10001 (☎800/TAKE-OFF). Consolidator with good East Coast and central US deals.

Council Travel, 205 E 42nd St, New York, NY 10017 (☎212/661-1450). Head office of the nationwide US student travel organisation. Branches in San Francisco, LA, Washington, New Orleans, Chicago, Seattle, Portland, Minneapolis, Boston, Atlanta and Dallas, to name only the larger ones.

Encore Short Notice, 4501 Forbes Blvd, Lanham, MD 20706 (☎301/459-8020 or ☎800/638-9278). East Coast travel club.

Interworld, 3400 Coral Way, Miami, FL 33145 (☎305/443-4929). Southeastern US consolidator.

Moment's Notice, 425 Madison Ave, New York, NY 10017 (☎212/486-0503). Travel club that's good for last-minute deals.

Nouvelles Frontières, 12 E 33rd St, New York, NY 10016 (☎212/779-0600); 800 bd de Maisonneuve Est, Montréal, PQ H2L 4L8 (☎514/288-9942). Main US and Canadian branches of the French discount travel outfit. Other branches in LA, San Francisco and Québec City.

STA Travel, 48 E 11th St, New York, NY 10003 (☎212/477-7166); 166 Geary St, Suite 702, San Francisco, CA 94108 (☎415/391-8407). Main US branches of the originally Australian and now worldwide specialist in independent and student travel. Other offices in LA, Boston and Honolulu.

Stand Buys, 311 W Superior St, Chicago, IL 60610 (☎800/331-0257 or ☎800/548-1116). Good Midwestern travel club.

TFI Tours, 34 W 32nd St, New York, NY 10001 (☎212/736-1149 or 800/825-3834). The very best East Coast deals, especially worth looking into if you only want to fly one-way.

Travac, 1177 N Warson Rd, St Louis, MO 63132 (☎800/872-8800). Good central US consolidator.

Travel Avenue, 180 N Jefferson, Chicago, IL 60606 (☎312/876-1116 or 800/333-3335). Discount travel agent.

Travel Brokers, 50 Broad St, New York, NY 10004 (☎800/999-8748). New York travel club.

Travel Cuts, 187 College St, Toronto, ON M5T 1P7 (☎416/979-2406). Main office of the Canadian student travel organisation. Many other offices nationwide.

Travelers Advantage, 49 Music Square, Nashville, TN 37203 (☎800/548-1116). Reliable travel club.

Unitravel, 1177 N Warson Rd, St Louis, MO 63132 (☎800/325-2222). Reliable consolidator.

Worldwide Discount Travel Club, 1674 Meridian Ave, Miami Beach, FL 33139 (☎305/534-2082).

---

bus to Warsaw. An arduous but cheap way to reach Poland, buses are much favoured by impoverished, UK-resident Poles during the vacation seasons, and are often packed as a consequence. The most reliable and the costliest services are operated by **Eurolines**, a division of the *National Express* bus company. This runs a regular service **from London to Warsaw** (via Ostend, Brussels, Frankfurt an der Oder, and Poznań) and **to Kraków** (same route to Poznań, then via Wrocław, Opole, and Katowice). For full details and prices, see p.5.

ORGANISED TOURS

With the opening up of Poland, independent travel is gradually becoming easier, but the **organised package tour** still remains the most popular method of seeing the country. During the communist era, *Polorbis* had unquestioned dominance of this market, and despite a recent growth in the number of small travel operators, most packages from the States will still be booked through them. They have an extensive selection, ranging from 6 to 21 days, including flights, accommodation, and most meals, but they're not especially cheap. A fifteen-day planned excursion called "Panorama of Poland", which takes in the main sights of the country, will cost around $2000, if travelling from New York; from Chicago and Los Angeles you'll need to add on extra for the airfare. "Southern Delight" is a ten-day tour of the country's southern provinces, starting in Warsaw and visiting Kraków, Zakopane, Częstochowa, Wadowice (birthplace of the pope), and Wola, before returning to Warsaw. From New York, this will cost you between $1520 and $1710, depending on the time of year: for (low) additional fares, you can fly from Chicago and Los Angeles.

In addition, *Polorbis* arrange tours with a wider scope, taking in other countries. A thirteen-day tour of Poland and Russia, visiting Warsaw,

Kraków, Moscow and St Petersburg between May and September, costs $2649 flying from New York, and $3038 from Los Angeles. Alternatively, an "Eastern Europe Highlights Circle" tour, visiting Warsaw, Kraków, Budapest, Vienna, Prague and Wrocław in fourteen days, costs $2960 flying from New York, $3150 from Chicago. This tour runs from the end of May through mid-September. Between the same dates there's also a "Capitals of Poland and Russia" tour covering Helsinki, Warsaw, Kraków, Auschwitz, Częstochowa, Moscow and St Petersburg. Prices run from $2829 to $2979.

Another major operator to Poland is *PAT (Polish American Tours)*. Their packages include the "Best of Poland", a twelve-day ten-night tour of Warsaw, Kracków, Auschwitz, Częstochowa, Zakopane, Toruń, Gdynia and Mrągowo. This costs between $1725 and $1985, depending on city of departure and time of year. *PAT* also feature several other themed packages,

including "Historic Poland" and "Southern Adventure" that offer good value for money.

Polorbis also run a separate tour company for those wishing to roam a bit farther afield, called *Orbis Independent Travel*. This arranges the minimum necessary and leaves exploring up to the individual, while organising day excursions, for instance to Polish castles and cathedrals, for those who want them. If you're considering this form of travel, bear in mind that rail tickets for journeys within Poland should wherever possible be purchased inside the country, as prices for tickets reserved abroad can be up to fifty percent higher. To bypass this problem, you can take advantage of the internal *Polrail Pass*, also arranged through *Polorbis*, which can cover any period from eight days up to a month and gives free travel on the entire rail network. An eight-day pass starts at $35 for second-class, or $50 for first-class travel, rising to $45/$67 for 21 days, $50/$75 for a month.

SPECIALIST TOUR OPERATORS

Amber Tours, 7337 W. Washington St, Indianapolis, IN 46231 (☎317/243-4561).

American Travel Abroad, 240 W. 57th St, New York, NY 10107 (☎212/586-5230).

Exotik Tours, Drummond Bldg, Ste 905 1117 St. Catherine Street West, Montréal PQ H3B 1H9 (☎514/284-3324).

General Tours, 245 W. 57th St, New York, NY 10016 (☎212/685-1800).

Globus Gateway/Cosmos, 95–25 Queens Blvd, Rego Park, NY 11374-4511; (☎800/221- 0090).

Kentours, 294 Queen Street West, Toronto, Ontario, M5V 2A1 (☎416/593-0837).

Love Holidays, 16000 Ventura Blvd, Suite 200, Encino, CA 91436 (☎818/382-7820).

Maupintour, 831 Massachusetts Ave, Lawrence, KS 66044 (☎913/749-0700).

Orbis Independent Travel Same address as *Polorbis*.

PAT Tours, 1053 Riverdale Rd, West Springfield, MA 01089; (☎413/747-7702 or ☎800/388 0988).

Pekao International Travel and Tours, 1610 Bloor St West, Toronto, Ontario M6P 1A7 (☎416/588-1988). This company runs many scheduled flights direct from Toronto to Poland.

Polish American Agency Inc., 799 Broadway, New York, NY 10003 (☎212/674-3673).

Polorbis, 342 Madison Ave, New York, NY 10173; (☎212/867-5011); 338 North Michigan Ave, Chicago, Illinois IL 60601 (☎312/236-9013).

Polish American Travel Agency, 123 Second Ave, New York, NY 10003 (☎212/475-5588).

Unitours, 411 W. Putnam Ave, Greenwich, CT 06830 (☎203/629-3900).

RED TAPE AND VISAS

Citizens of the UK, USA, Ireland and most EC nations require only a valid passport, which should have at least six months to go before its expiry, in order to enter Poland: they no longer require a visa of any type. However, nationals of many other countries – including Australia, New Zealand and Canada – still require a visa, which should be obtained prior to arriving in Poland. This situation will persist until the countries concerned come to reciprocal arrangements for their abolition.

The following information is pertinent to those applying for a visa in the UK: prices for visas are broadly similar at other Polish consulates and embassies worldwide, though notably cheaper in Canada.

Visas are issued for a definite number of days, with ninety the upper limit. As the duration of your stay doesn't affect the cost of the visa, you may as well apply for the maximum if you're unsure how long you'll want to stay. Although you have to state your intended date of arrival, there's no obligation to keep to this: visas are valid for any period in the six months following the issue date.

To qualify for a visa, you must have a **full** passport, valid for at least nine months beyond the date of your application and with at least one clear page for the authorisation stamp. The visa **application form** can be obtained (in person or by post) either from *Polorbis* or from a Polish consulate. *Polorbis* can also handle the transac-

POLISH EMBASSIES AND CONSULATES ABROAD

Australia: 10 Trelawny St, Wollahara, Sydney, NSW2025 (☎02/329816).

Canada: Toronto, 2603 Lakeshore Blvd W, Ontario MAV 1GS (☎416/252 5471). Montréal, 1500 Pine Ave O, Québec H3G1B4 (514/937 9481). Ottowa, 443 Daly Ave, Ontario K1N 6H3 (☎613/789 0468).

Denmark: Richlieu Alle 12, Hellerup, Copenhagen (☎627244).

Netherlands: Alexanderstraat 25, Den Haag (☎70/602806).

New Zealand: The Terrace, Wellington (☎04/712456).

Norway: Olaf Kyrres Plass 1, Oslo 2 (☎02/550208).

Sweden: Karlavägen 35, Stockholm (☎08/114132).

UK: 19 Weymouth St, London W1N 3AG (☎071/580 0476). Open Mon, Tues, Thurs & Fri 10am–2pm, Wed 10am–noon. 2 Kinnear Rd, Edinburgh EH3 5PE (☎031/552 0301). Open Mon–Fri 10am–2pm. The UK embassy should be used by Irish citizens, as Poland has no consular representation in Ireland.

USA: Washington, 2224 Wyoming Ave NW, DC 20008 (☎202/234 3800). New York, 223 Madison Ave, NY 10016 (☎212/889 8360). Chicago, 1530 N. Lake Shore Drive, Chicago, IL 60610 (☎312/337 8166).

POLORBIS OFFICES ABROAD

Netherlands: Leidsestraat 64, Amsterdam 1017 PD (☎20/253570).

Norway: 1 Biugata 0186, Oslo 1 (☎02/419140).

Sweden: Birger Jarlsgatan 71, Stockholm 11356 (☎08/235345).

UK: 82 Mortimer St, London W1 (☎071/636 2217).

USA: 342 Madison Ave, New York, NY 10173 (☎212/867 5011); 338 North Michigan Ave, Chicago, IL 60601 (☎312/236 9013).

tion on your behalf on payment of a handling charge, which at their London office costs £5.75. You should allow two weeks for delivery, though you can get it the next day (or over the weekend) on payment of a £5 supplement. Joint passport holders require separate forms, though accompanied children under 16 included on a parental passport do not. When it has been completed, the form should be presented along with your pass-

port, two passport-sized photographs and the appropriate **fee**. Currently this is £20 for a visa for a single entry into Poland, £30 for a double entry, £40 for a treble entry, and so on up to £70 for any number of entries. **Transit visas**, valid for 48 hours if you want to stop off in Poland on the way to somewhere else, cost £10 single entry, £15 double; if you want one you also have to submit any visa relevant to your ultimate destination.

HEALTH AND INSURANCE

Reciprocal arrangements between Poland and Britain (and most other European countries) mean you're entitled to free basic medical care in the country; there is, however, a charge for certain imported drugs and for some specialised treatments. It's important to carry your NHS card as proof of your entitlement to free treatment; without it you will probably end up paying the full cost. If travelling from the US, it's essential to get full insurance before you leave, since there are no reciprocal arrangements between the USA and Poland.

An alternative in the bigger cities is provided by the larger Western embassies, who run health clinics which nationals can attend for a fee. The UK offers this service at their Warsaw Embassy; other nationals should consult the relevant city listings for Warsaw, Kraków and Gdańsk.

Inoculations are not required for a trip to Poland. **Tap water** is officially classified as safe, but in the cities no one drinks it without boiling it first; mineral water is readily available as an alternative.

PHARMACIES AND HOSPITALS

Simple complaints can normally be dealt with at a regular **pharmacy** (*apteka*), where basic medicines are dispensed by qualified pharmacists, whom Poles consult over most everyday health problems. In the cities many of the staff will speak at least some English or German. Even in places where the staff speak only Polish, it should be easy enough to obtain repeat prescriptions (there may be a fee for Western medicines), if you bring along the empty container or remaining pills. In every town there's always one *apteka* open 24 hours; addresses are printed in local newspapers.

For more serious problems, or anything the pharmacist can't work out, you'll be directed to a **hospital** (*szpital*), where conditions will probably be pretty horrendous, with too many patients for the beds, a lack of medicines and often insanitary conditions. Doctors are heavily overworked and scandalously underpaid. If you are required to pay for any medical treatment or medication, remember to keep the receipts for your insurance claim when you get back.

INSURANCE

Given the exceptions to the free health-care arrangements, and the possibility of theft or injury on holiday, it's a good idea to take out some **private insurance**. Low-price insurance specialists like *Endsleigh* (97 Southampton Row, London WC1; ☎071/436 4451) can provide you with a month's basic cover for around £20 – and any bank or travel agency will sell you a policy.

If you have anything stolen while you're in Poland, **report the theft** to the police immediately and get a written report – without it you won't be able to claim back home. Be prepared for the process of form-filling to take hours.

US AND CANADIAN CITIZENS

In the **US and Canada**, insurance tends to be much more expensive and may be medical cover only. Before buying a policy, check that you're not already covered by existing insurance plans. **Canadians** are usually covered by their provincial health plans; holders of **ISIC cards** and some other student/teacher/youth cards are entitled to $3000 worth of accident coverage and sixty days ($100 per day) of in-patient benefits for the period during which the card is valid. **Students** will often find that their student health coverage extends through the vacations and for one term beyond the date of last enrollment. Bank and charge **accounts** (particularly *American Express*) often include certain levels of medical or other insurance, and travel insurance may also be included if you use a major credit or charge card to pay for your trip. **Homeowners' or renters'** insurance often covers theft or loss of documents, money and valuables while abroad, though conditions and maximum amounts vary.

Only after exhausting the possibilities above might you want to contact a specialist travel insurance company; your travel agent can usually recommend one. Travel insurance policies are quite comprehensive, anticipating everything from charter companies going bankrupt to delayed or lost luggage, by way of sundry illnesses and accidents. **Premiums** vary widely, from the very reasonable ones offered primarily through student/youth agencies (*STA*'s policies range from about $50–70 for 15 days to $500–700 for a year, depending on the amount of financial cover), to those so expensive that the cost for anything more than two months of cover will probably equal the cost of the worst possible combination of disasters. Note also that very few insurers can make on-the-spot payments in the event of a major expense or loss; you will usually be reimbursed only after going home.

None of these policies insures against **theft** of anything while overseas. (Americans have been easy pickings for foreign thieves – a combination of naivety on the part of the former, and an all-Americans-are-rich attitude among the latter – and companies were going broke paying claims.) North American travel policies apply only to items **lost** from, or **damaged** in, the custody of an identifiable, responsible third party – hotel porter, airline, luggage consignment, etc. Even in these cases you will have to contact the local police to have a complete report made out for your insurer. If you are travelling via London it might be better to take out a British policy (though making any claim may prove more complicated).

COSTS AND MONEY

Poland is currently one of the great travel bargains. The abolition of all compulsory exchange controls and the effective legalisation of the black market mean that most of the essentials of travel, such as food and drink, public transport and entrance fees are cheap for anyone with Western (hard) currency. Accommodation is priced on a different scale, but is still inexpensive as a rule. Note that prices are often much higher in Warsaw than in the rest of the country, and are similarly increased in places which see a lot of foreign visitors, such as Kraków and Poznań.

AVERAGE COSTS

Rampant inflation and the lifting of subsidies over the past couple of years have put severe economic pressures on Poles. However, for Western visitors, prices for most goods remain very low. You can **eat** and **drink** well for £5/$7.50 or less even at some of the country's best restaurants, though it's becoming increasingly easy to spend £10/$15 or more for a meal. In a more basic restaurant a meal can be had for not much more than £2/$3, and substantial hot meals can be had from milk and snack bars for much less than this – 40p/60¢ will often buy a main course. Coffee or tea with cakes in a café can be had for a similarly nominal amount.

Prices for **public transport** are little more than pocket money – even travelling across half the length of the country by train or bus only costs around £7/$10. Similarly, you never have to fork out much more than £1/$1.50 to visit even the most popular **tourist sights**, with 25–50p/40–75¢ the normal asking price.

Only if you go for expensive **accommodation** will your costs start to rise. Here at least there's plenty of opportunity to spend money, with international hotels in the main cities charging up to £150/$225 per night. On the other hand, if you stick to campsites, youth and tourist hostels or sports hotels, you'll seldom spend much more than £3/$4.50 on a bed. Budget on about twice as much for a room in a private house or in the cheapest hotels. In the most popular resort areas, full-board terms in pensions and holiday homes can generally be found for £7–10/$10–15.

CURRENCY

The Polish unit of currency is the **złoty** (abbreviated as zł), which is now fully convertible within the country. The dropping of the artificially high exchange valuation imposed by the communists made its value plummet against hard currencies; it has periodically stabilised, then had to be devalued. At the time of writing it stood at 24,000zł to the pound sterling, 16,000zł to the US dollar.

The złoty is now almost entirely a paper currency, but **coins** are gradually replacing the more worthless notes. There are **notes** of 50, 100, 200, 500, 1000, 2000, 5000, 10,000, 20,000, 50,000, 100,000, 500,000 and 1,000,000zł.

TRAVELLERS' CHEQUES, CREDIT CARDS AND HARD CURRENCY

Travellers' cheques, available at virtually all banks and financial institutions, are the easiest and safest way of carrying your money, being fully refundable should they be lost or stolen. The snags are that in Poland only **main banks**, *Orbis* **offices** and **hotels** will accept them, that the number of places providing the service is actually decreasing, and that the transaction can sometimes be a lengthy process. This is not a particular problem in major cities and tourist areas, but

cashiers in provincial towns are often so unfamiliar with the procedure that you can be kept waiting for hours. If travelling in such areas you really do need a supply of cash as a backup.

Credit and charge cards are more established than you might expect. *Access/Mastercard, American Express, Diners Club, Eurocard, JCB* and *Visa* are accepted by *Orbis* in payment for accommodation, meals, telephone and telex bills, transportation tickets, car hire and tourist services; you can also arrange a cash advance on most of these cards at their hotels and main offices, though you have to wait for an authorisation call to Warsaw. An increasing number of shops, particularly those dealing in hard currency, will also take your plastic.

Poland's desperate need for foreign currency is reflected in the ease with which it's possible to change money. In general, Poles tend to use the **US dollar** as their yardstick and this is the currency they're keenest to acquire; the **Deutschmark** is also in strong demand, the **pound** less so, though it should still be accepted quite readily. It therefore makes sense to take a supply of dollars, if only for contingency purposes.

EXCHANGE

As a rule the most competitive **exchange rates** are offered by the **banks** (usually open something like Mon–Fri 7.30am–5pm, Sat 7.30am–2pm), though you'll almost certainly be kept waiting at the desk. A flat commission of around 20,000zł per transaction is normally deducted.

Orbis **hotels** also have exchange desks, which are usually open round the clock; they tend to offer poor rates and charge hefty commissions, though these are not uniformly applied. The main *Orbis* **office** in each town is supposed to offer a full currency exchange service; this is usually quick and efficient, with a better rate than you'll get in their hotels. However, most offices now seem to be prepared to change cash only.

A whole host of **private banks**, designated by the names *kantor* or *walut*, have sprung up in all the cities, many run in tandem with another retail business and often open till late at night. All of these change **cash only**, and some may take dollars and Deutschmarks only.

The effective legalisation of the **black market** rate means that illicit currency transactions are definitely no longer worth the risk; the likelihood is that you'll be given counterfeit notes or swindled in some other way.

INFORMATION AND MAPS

There's no direct Polish equivalent to the national tourist boards found in most other European countries; as a result, the provision of information is diffuse, to say the least. Warsaw, for example, has no central tourist office, and tourist information is disseminated by a host of offices, shops and hotels bearing the sign *Informator Turystyczny* (IT). What follows is a guide to the country's various tourist organisations and the services they provide. As yet, they're still mainly geared to organised group visits, though the importance of independent travel is increasingly being recognised.

ORBIS

By far the largest tourist outfit in Poland is *Orbis*, usually known outside the country as *Polorbis*. Founded in the 1920s, it was turned by the communists into a vast organisation with an unusually wide range of functions. Presumably it will at some time be broken up into several parts, but there's no sign of that happening as yet, though some offices have been franchised off to the former management, while there's increasing competition from the new private agencies.

In Poland *Orbis* at present runs 55 international-type hotels and 160 offices. These offices sell air, rail, bus and ferry tickets, change money, arrange guided tours, car hire and special interest activities, make hotel reservations, organise bookings for sports and cultural events, and process visa extensions. Their responsibility for promoting

tourism in their own region is rather nebulous, though special offices for foreign visitors do exist in the largest cities, and many other branches are well clued-up on the tourist facilities in their area. Others, however, seem to have brochures on anywhere in the world except their own region. The addresses of the most important *Orbis* offices are listed in the appropriate sections of the Guide.

Abroad, the company acts both as the main agent for holidays in Poland and as the nearest equivalent to a state tourist office (see "Red Tape" for addresses). Even if you're intending to visit Poland under your own steam, it's well worth writing or going along to one of their offices to pick up free **promotional material** in English, which is often difficult to come by in Poland itself. In addition to a series of six glossy brochures covering the whole country, there are also a few booklets on specialist interests (music, architecture, folklore, activity holidays) and an excellent road map (£1.50).

OTHER TOURIST ORGANISATIONS

PTTK – which translates literally as "The Polish Country Lovers' Association" – has a rather more direct responsibility for internal Polish tourism than *Orbis*, administering information offices throughout Poland. In addition, it runs hostels in both city and holiday areas, and rents bungalows for family holidays in the lake regions. Its main foreign service department is at ul. Świętokrzyska 36, Warsaw (☎20-82-41).

Almatur is a student and youth travel bureau – and the obvious contact point for getting to meet young Poles. It arranges international work camps, special study, activity and hobby programmes, educational exchanges and, during the summer, accommodation in international student hotels, holiday centres and camps (*Baza Studentowa*). These are open to anyone under 35 on production of Almatur vouchers, which are available from their offices; rates are reduced if you have an ISIC card. Almatur's head office is at ul. Ordynacka 9, Warsaw (☎26-23-56); other addresses can be found in the Guide under the appropriate section.

Elsewhere, a number of **city or municipal based tourist offices** dispense information and run tours and excursions for their particular patch.

Among the best established of these are *Syrena* in Warsaw and *Wawel Tourist* in Kraków. A host of **local, private tourist agencies** have set up over the past year or two, as well, running a variety of trips and accommodation. See the appropriate parts of the Guide for addresses.

MAPS

The maps in this book should be sufficient for most purposes, though a detailed **road map** of the country is a useful extra. Easiest to follow is *Bartholomew's Europmap: Poland* (1:800,000), which is especially clear on rail lines. The *Orbis Poland: Roadmap* (1:750,000) is useful, too, and widely available in Poland; abroad it is available through *Polorbis* or in map shops, in modified form, as *Hildebrand: Poland*. PPWK, the state map company, produce an extremely good, though not easily available, *Atlas Samochodowa* (1:500,000), divided into regions, with supplementary schematic town plans. PPWK also produce the atlas as a series of 16 individual regional maps.

Should you need more detailed **city maps**, try to get hold of the appropriate *plan miasta*, available cheaply at local tourist offices, kiosks, street sellers and bookshops. These list all streets in A–Z format, and give exhaustive listings on bus and tram routes, places of entertainment, restaurants and cafés. In the past, they have often been out of print for long periods; the situation has improved enormously lately, but remains unpredictable and patchy. Most bookshops keep a reasonable national selection. Even more essential, if you intend doing any serious walking, are the **hiking maps** of the National Parks and other tourist areas. Known as *Mapa Turystyczna*, these cost only a nominal amount and are very clear and simple to use: although the texts are usually only in Polish, the keys to the symbols are in several languages, including English. They can be even harder to come by than the city plans, though again things have been better recently: if you see a map you'll need later on in your travels, snap it up rather than risk not being able to get it in the region itself.

MAP OUTLETS IN THE UK AND NORTH AMERICA

London *Daunt Books*, 83 Marylebone High St, W1 (☎071/224 2295); *National Map Centre*, 22–24 Caxton St, SW1 (☎071/222 4945); *Stanfords*, 12–14 Long Acre, WC2 (☎071/836 1321); *The Travellers' Bookshop*, 25 Cecil Court, WC2 (☎071/836 9132).

Chicago *Rand McNally*, 444 North Michigan Ave, IL 60611 (☎312/321 1751).

New York *The Complete Traveler Bookstore*, 199 Madison Ave, NY 10016 (☎212/685 9007); *Rand McNally*, 150 E 52nd St, NY 10022 (☎212/758 7488); *Traveler's Bookstore*, 22 W 52nd St, New York, NY 10019 (☎212/664 0995).

San Francisco *The Complete Traveler Bookstore*, 3207 Filmore St, CA 92123; *Rand McNally*, 595 Market St, CA 94105 (☎415/777 3131).

Seattle *Elliot Bay Book Company*, 101 S Main St, WA 98104 (☎206/624 6600).

Toronto *Open Air Books and Maps*, 25 Toronto St, M5R 2C1 (☎416/363 0719).

Vancouver *World Wide Books and Maps*, 1247 Granville St (☎604/687 3320).

GETTING AROUND

Poland has comprehensive and cheap public transport services, though they can often be overcrowded and excruciatingly slow. As a general rule, trains are the best means of moving across the country, as even the most rural areas are still criss-crossed by passenger lines. Rail buffs, in addition, will find Poland the most fascinating country in Europe: more than two dozen narrow-gauge lines are still in operation (identified in timetables by the word *wąsk*), and steam is used on some of these as well as on a few mainline routes. For information on the major train connections, consult the "Travel Details" section at the end of each chapter. The text of the Guide points out those places where it's preferable to take buses – which are usually better for short journeys or in the more remote areas.

Driving is also covered in the section following. You'll find car hire prices surprisingly high, but taxis are cheap enough to be considered for the occasional inter-town journey, especially if you can split costs three or four ways. Additional and enjoyable means of getting around include coastal and river ferries and, of course, walking in the Tatras and other mountain areas.

TRAINS

Polish State Railways (*PKP*) is a reasonably efficient organisation, though the number of its services, particularly on rural routes, has been butchered since the fall of communism and continues to be reduced at frequent intervals. *PKP* runs three main types of train:

● **Express** services (*ekspresowy*) are the ones to go for if you're travelling long distances, as they stop at the main cities only (although they are still extremely slow by western European standards, with the exception of a few recently introduced "named" trains). Seat reservations, involving a small supplementary charge, are compulsory; if you haven't understood the reservations system the ticket inspector will sell you one, albeit at a heavy supplement. Expresses are marked in red on timetables, with an R in a box alongside.

● So-called **fast** trains (*pośpieszne*), again marked in red, have far more stops, and reservations are optional.

● The **normal** services (*normalne* or *osobowe*) are shown in black and should be avoided whenever possible: in rural areas they stop at every haystack, while even on inter-urban routes it usually takes about an hour to cover 20km.

Fares won't burn a hole in the pocket of even the most impoverished Westerner. Even a long cross-country haul such as Warsaw to Wrocław, Kraków or Gdańsk will set you back little more than £5/$7.50. At these prices it's well worth paying the fifty percent extra to travel **first-class** or make a **reservation** (*miejscówka*) even when this is not compulsory, as sardine-like conditions are fairly common. Reservations can be made up to sixty days in advance, or ninety days for return trips.

Most long inter-city journeys are best done overnight; they're often conveniently timed so that you leave around 10 or 11pm and arrive between 6 and 9am. For these, it's best to book either a **sleeper** (*sypialny*) or **couchette**; the total cost will probably be little more than a room in a cheap hotel; the second-class sleepers are around £6/$9 per head. They sleep three to a compartment and offer comfortable bunks along with a washbasin, towels, sheets and blankets; first class has one bed fewer. Although preferable to sitting up, the couchettes (about £3.50/$5) are rather cramped, with six to a cabin.

TICKETS

Buying tickets is no problem in small places, but in the main train stations of the cities it can be a major hassle, due to the bewildering array of counters, each almost invariably with a long snaking queue. Make sure you join the line long before your train is due to leave; in the worst cases (eg Warsaw and Poznań), you may have to wait for a considerable while.

Tickets currently come in all shapes and sizes, but the only time you have to think for yourself is if you have an **undated ticket**, which you validate by sticking in a machine before departure. If you're going for a sleeper or couchette, major stations have special counters.

As an alternative to the station queues, you can buy tickets for journeys of over 100km at **Orbis offices**. The main branches of these are also the best places to book for **international journeys**.

Discounts are available for students (with an ISIC card), pensioners and for kids between 4 and 10; those under 4 travel free, though they're not supposed to occupy a seat. **Rail passes** for the whole network are available for periods of seven, fourteen or twenty-one days or for a whole month, but you'd have to take an awful lot of trains to justify the outlay.

STATION PRACTICALITIES

In the station, the **departures** are normally listed on yellow posters marked *odjazdy*, the **arrivals** on white posters headed *przyjazdy*. Due to the recent spate of cutbacks, some stations may only have makeshift arrival and departure boards listing the services currently in operation. Unfortunately, these give no indication of journey time.

If you're intending to do a lot of travelling in Poland, it would make sense to invest in the six-monthly network **timetable** (*rozkład*) which can be bought at all main stations – at least until stocks last. Otherwise, you may find yourself having to queue regularly at the information counters, which often have the longest lines of all.

Each **platform** (*peron*) has two tracks, so take care that you board the right train; usually only the long-distance services have boards stating their route, so you'll often have to ask. To make matters worse, it's fairly common practice for trains to be re-routed to a different platform at the last minute: if you don't understand Polish you should always keep a sharp look out for the sudden movement of people from one platform to another. Electronic departure boards are increasingly common, though as yet are confined to major cities.

The **main station** in a city is identified by the name *Główny* or *Centralna*. These are open round the clock and usually have such facilities as waiting rooms, toilets, kiosks, restaurants, snack bars, cafés, a left luggage counter and a 24-hour post office. Outside the main cities they're the only place where you'll be able to get something to eat after about 9pm. The Poles operate an eccentric system for **checking in luggage**. You have to declare its value to the attendant at the left luggage office (*przwerza bagażu*) and then pay one-hundredth of this sum as insurance on top of the basic storage charge. In practice, it's pointless offering a realistic estimate as chances of theft are minute. Only a couple of stations in the country have individual lockers.

Facilities **on the trains** are much poorer, though some have a buffet car (check on the departure board) and light refreshments are available on all overnight journeys. **Ticket control** is rather haphazard, particularly on crowded services, but it does happen more often than not. If you've boarded a train without the proper ticket, you should seek out the conductor, who will issue one on payment of a small supplement.

BUSES

The extent to which you'll need to make use of the services of **PKS**, the Polish national **bus company**, depends very much on the nature of your trip. If you're concentrating on cities, then the trains are definitely the better bet: **inter-city** buses are often overcrowded and slow and services less frequent and marginally more expensive. There are very few long-haul routes and no overnight journeys. However, in **rural areas**, notably the mountain regions, buses are usually the better means of getting around, scoring in the choice and greater convenience of pick-up points and frequency of service.

TICKETS

In towns and cities, the main **bus station** is usually alongside the train station. **Tickets** can be bought in the terminal building; in larger places there are several counters, each dealing with clearly displayed destinations. (In a few places the terminal is shared with the train station, so make sure you go to the right counter.) Booking this way ensures a seat, as a number will be allocated to you on your ticket. However, the lack of computerised systems means that many stations cannot allocate seats for services starting out

PUBLIC TRANSPORT IN CITIES

Trams (usually antiquated boneshakers) are the basis of the public transport system in nearly all Polish cities. They usually run from about 5am to midnight, and departure times are clearly posted at the stops. Tickets, which cost around 3000zł (about 12p/18¢), must be bought from a *ruch* kiosk; nearly all use an overstamp, meaning they can only be used in the city where they were bought. On boarding, you should immediately cancel your ticket in one of the machines; checks by inspectors are rare, but they do happen from time to time. Note that some tickets have to be cancelled at both ends (arrows will indicate if this is so): this is for the benefit of children and pensioners, who travel half-price and thus have to cancel only one end per journey. If you transfer from one tram to another you'll need a second ticket.

The same tickets are valid on the municipal **buses** (which are usually red, in contrast to the yellow favoured by *PKS*) and the same system for validating the tickets applies – but note that **night services** require two tickets. The routes of the municipal buses go beyond the city boundaries into the outlying countryside, so many nearby villages have several connections during peak times of the day.

When translated into Western money, the price of **taxis** is cheap enough to make them a viable proposition for regular use. In the new free-market economy, plenty of people have turned to taxi driving, and outside hotels, stations and major tourist attractions you often have to run the gauntlet of cabbies. Be wary of unmetered taxis (unless you agree the price in advance) and of drivers who demand payment in hard currency, and always ensure that the driver switches on the meter when you begin your journey. Because of the riproaring inflation of the past few years, what you actually pay is the meter fare times a multiplier, the current figure for the latter being displayed on a little sign; prices are fifty percent higher after 11pm.

Prices are also raised by fifty percent for journeys outside the city limits. However, costs are always negotiable for longer journeys, between towns, for example, and can work out very reasonable if split among a group.

from another town. In such cases, you have to wait until the bus arrives and buy a ticket – which may be for standing room only – from the driver.

The same procedure can also be followed, provided the bus isn't already full to overflowing, if you arrive too late to buy a ticket at the counter. With a few exceptions, it isn't possible to buy tickets for return journeys on board. Note too that a few routes are now run by private companies and generally leave from outside the bus station. As with the trains, *Orbis* offices are the best place to go if you want to book on an **international** route.

TIMETABLES

Noticeboards show **departures** and **arrivals** not only in the bus stations, but on all official stopping places along the route. "Fast" buses (which carry a small supplement) are marked in red, slow in black. The towns served are listed in alphabetical order, with the relevant times set against each, and mention made of the principal places passed on the way. This can be extremely confusing, as the normal practice is to list only services which terminate in that particular town, and not those which continue onwards. Thus you'll have to check down the "via" (*przez*) column to find additional departure times to your destination.

If in doubt, ask at the information counter, which will be equipped with the multi-volume set of timetables listing all *PKS* routes.

PLANES

The domestic network of **LOT**, the Polish national airline, operates regular **flights from Warsaw** to Gdańsk, Katowice, Koszalin, Kraków, Poznań, Rzeszów, Szczecin, Słupsk, Wrocław and Zielona Góra – all of which take about an hour. Some routes are covered several times a day, but services are sharply reduced on Sundays and during the winter months. Most of the cities mentioned are also linked directly to some of the others, but Warsaw is very much the lynchpin of the system. As a general rule, airports are located just outside the cities, and can be reached either by a special *LOT* bus or by a municipal service.

Tickets can be purchased from both *LOT* and *Orbis* offices, where you can also pick up free **timetables**. Prices are currently in the region of £40–45/\$60–70 one-way (there are no savings on returns). Kids up to the age of two travel for ten percent of the adult fare, provided they do not occupy a separate seat; under-12s go for half price.

BOATS

In summer, ferries and hydrofoils connect towns along the **Baltic coast**, notably around Szczecin and in the Gdańsk area where they connect the Tri-City of Gdańsk, Sopot and Gdynia with each other and with the Hel Peninsula. The main companies are: *The Szczecin Shipping Company*, Marine Terminal, ul. Jana z Kolna 7, Szczecin (☎225-918), and *The Gdańsk Shipping Company*, ul. Wartka 4, Gdańsk (☎311-975). If you're in Poland and want to book tickets for services onwards (say to Scandinavia), contact the *Polish Baltic Shipping Co.* head office: ul. Morska 2, 78–100 Kołobrzeg (☎252-11). The company also has offices in Świnoujscie and Gdańsk.

Inland, excursion boats also run along certain stretches of the country's extensive system of **canals** – most enjoyably from Augustów near Białystok and along the ingeniously constructed Elbąg canal – and short sections of the main **rivers**, such as the Wisła: additionally, a curious system of chain-haul car/passenger ferries – antiquated in the main – services the upper reaches of the Wisła and coastal surroundings.

DRIVING AND CAR RENTAL

Access to a car will save you a lot of time in exploring rural areas, and driving is relatively easy-going anywhere in the country. Poles are not – as yet – routine car owners and recent inflation has, if anything, cleared the roads still further.

CAR HIRE

Car hire in Poland is fairly pricey: costs vary but you should reckon on spending around £60/$90 a day, £400/$600 a week for a Fiat Uno or Peugot 205 with unlimited mileage – prices are often quoted and calculated in Deutschmarks. Cars can be booked through the usual agents in the West (see box) or in Poland itself: all the four major operators now have their own agents in all or most of the major Polish cities. Alternatively you can hire through the main *Orbis* offices (Gdańsk, Katowice, Kraków, Łódź, Poznań, Szczecin, Warsaw and Wrocław: see the relevant sections for addresses). Payment can be made with cash or any major credit card, and you can drop a car at a different office from the one where you rented it.

Cars will only be rented to people **over 21** who have held a full licence for more than a year. Anyone planning on **renting a car outside**

Poland and bringing it into the country needs to be aware that rising levels of **car theft** (see box opposite) have led several of the major rental companies to slap severe restrictions on taking their car eastwards.

Check the conditions carefully before renting anything – if you ignore a ban, it means you effectively accept the financial risk for the car's full value if it's damaged in an accident or stolen. Of the major companies *Hertz* currently seem to operate the least restrictive policies, but since they (like the other majors) have agents in Poland, you're better off renting inside the country.

PAPERWORK

If you're taking your **own car**, you'll need to carry your vehicle's registration document. If the car is not in your name, you must have a letter of permission signed by the owner and authorised by the AA or RAC. You'll also need your driving licence (international driving licences aren't officially required, though they can be a help in tricky situations), and possibly an international insurance green card to extend your insurance cover – check with your insurers to see whether you're covered or not. You're also required to carry a red warning triangle, a first-aid kit, a set of replacement bulbs and display a national identification sticker.

INTERNATIONAL CAR RENTAL RESERVATIONS

UK:
Avis ☎081/848 8733
Budget ☎0800/181 181
Europcar ☎081/950 5050
Hertz ☎081/679 1799

US:
Avis ☎1-800/331-1212
Budget ☎1-800/527-0700
Hertz ☎1-800/654-3131

Canada:
Avis ☎1-800/387-7600 from Ontario and Québec; ☎1-800/268-2310 from elsewhere.
Budget ☎1-800/268-8970 from Québec; ☎1-800/268-8900 from elsewhere.
Hertz ☎1-800/620-9620 from Toronto; ☎1-800/263-0600 from elsewhere.

RULES OF THE ROAD

The main **rules of the road** are pretty clear, though there are some particularly Polish twists liable to catch out the unwary. The basic rules are driving on the right; compulsory wearing of seat belts outside built-up areas; children under 12 must sit in the back; right of way must be given to public transport vehicles (including trams). Drinking and driving is strictly prohibited – anyone with a foreign number plate driving around after 11pm, however innocently, has a strong chance of being stopped and breathalysed.

Speed limits are 60kph in built-up areas (white signs with the place name mark the start of a built-up area, the same sign with a diagonal red line through it marks the end), 90kph on country roads, 110kph on motorways, and 70kph if you're pulling a caravan or trailer. **Fines**, administered on the spot, range from the negligible up to around £10/$15.

Other problems occur chiefly at night, especially on country roads, where potential disasters include horses and carts, mopeds without lights and staggering inebriated peasants. In cities, beware of a casual attitude towards traffic lights and road signs by local drivers and pedestrians.

Road conditions are generally pretty good, though in the east of the country especially things can get a bit bumpy once you start veering off the beaten track. Motorways are still confined to a couple of stretches in the southwest, although, with major new projects such as the proposed "Via Baltica" linking the whole southern Baltic coastline the subject of ongoing discussion, the picture could well change significantly by the end of the decade.

PETROL

For **leaded petrol** users at least, finding fuel is becoming less and less problematic. An increasing number of small-scale operators and privatised state fuel depots have added substantially to the number of service stations around. Many stations in cities and along the main routes are open 24 hours a day, others from around 6am to 10pm; almost all out-of-town stations close on Sunday. Fuel is often **colour coded** at the pumps:

- red: 98 octane
- yellow: 94 octane
- green: 86 octane

As a rule always go for the highest octane available: 86 octane is much too low for most Western cars. While **diesel** is usually available (the pumps have an ON sign), getting hold of **lead-free fuel** (*benzyna bezołowiowa*) is more problematic. Though the number of stations selling unleaded (either 91 octane or, for Western vehicles periously low, 82.5 octane) is gradually increasing, especially in the big towns, tourist resorts and along the major routes, finding the stuff can be a headache – a periodic-table **Pb** sign with a diagonal red line through the middle indicates a station which has unleaded petrol.

Carrying at least one fuel can permanently topped up is thus strongly advised, especially in rural areas where lead free is virtually unobtainable. If you can find it from a major station, there's a brochure that lists unleaded filling stations throughout the country.

BREAKDOWNS AND SPARES

The Polish motoring association *PZMot* run a 24-hour **car breakdown** service: for addresses and phone numbers, see the "Listings" section at the end of each main city account. The national HQ, which can provide some English-language pamphlets on their services, is at ul. Krucza 6/14, Warsaw (☎290-647 or ☎293-541). Anywhere else dial ☎954 at the nearest phone and wait for assistance. For peace of mind it might be worth taking out an **insurance policy** like the AA Five-Star

---

CAR CRIME

With **car-related crime** – both simple break-ins and outright theft – one of the biggest criminal growth areas in Poland today, and foreign-registered vehicles one of the major targets, it pays to take note of the following simple precautions: especially in big towns, always park your vehicle in a guarded parking lot (*parking strzeżony*), never in an open street – even daylight break-ins occur with depressing frequency. Never leave anything of importance – including vehicle documents – in the car. Guarded lots cost little (rarely more than £1/$1.50 a day) and in most towns and cities you can usually find one located centrally – the major hotels almost always have their own nearby. If you have a break-in, report it to the police immediately. They'll probably shrug their shoulders over the prospects of getting anything back, but you'll need their signed report for insurance claim purposes back home.

scheme, which will pay for on-the-spot repairs and, in case of emergencies, ship you and all your passengers back home free of charge. Though still dominant, the traditional national vehicle, a 1960s Fiat design, has now been joined by a welter of luxury and foreign imports. As a consequence, finding spares for major Western brands like Volvo, Renault and Volkswagen is much less of a headache than it used to be, at least in the cities: driving in through the suburbs you'll now see a welter of dealers' adverts pointing you to the nearest supplier. If it's simply a case of a flat tyre, head for the nearest sizeable garage.

HITCHING

A by-product of the previous scarcity of private vehicles in Poland is that **hitchhiking** is positively encouraged. PTTK have institutionalised the practice through their *Społeczny Komitet Autostop* (Social Autostop Committee), which sells a package comprising a book of vouchers for 2000km of travel, an ID card, maps and an insurance policy. The relevant number of vouchers should be given to the driver, who then qualifies for various prizes and is indemnified for any compensation claims. The Autostop packages are valid from May to September (nominal charge), and available to anyone over 17 from larger PTTK offices and some youth hostels; the head Autostop office is ul. Narbutta 27a, Warsaw (☎496-208).

Finally, note that the Polish convention is to stick out your whole arm – not just your thumb.

WALKING

Poland has some of the best **hiking** country in Europe, specifically in the fifteen areas designated as National Parks and in the mountainous regions on the country's southern and western borders. There's a full network of marked trails, the best of which are detailed in the *Guide*. Many of these take several days, passing through remote areas served by refuge huts (see "Accommodation" p.28). However, much of the best scenery can be seen by covering sections of these routes on one-day walks. Few of the trails are too strenuous and, although specialist footwear is recommended, well worn-in sturdy shoes are usually enough. For more on hiking in the mountains, and some important tips, see p.373.

CYCLING

Cycling is often regarded as an ideal way to see a predominantly rural country like Poland. Even on the back roads surfaces are generally in good shape, and there isn't much traffic around – anyone used to cycling in Western traffic is in for a treat. An additional plus is the mercifully flat nature of much of the terrain, which allows you to cycle quite long distances without great effort. You'll need to bring your own machine and a

POLAND'S NATIONAL PARKS

Babia Góra see p.350
Białowieża see p.226
Bieszczady see p.284
Gorce see p.363
Kampinoski see p.100

Karkonosze see p.411
Ojców see p.352
Pieniny see p.375
Roztoczański see p.265
Słowiński see p.490

Świętokrzyskie see p.360
Tatras see p.370
Wielkopolska see p.467
Wigry see p.207
Woliński see p.501

supply of spare parts: except in a few major cities like Warsaw and Kraków, and a number of southern mountain areas like the Bieszczady, bike rental and spare part facilities are still a rarity. In rural areas, though, bikes are fairly common, and with a bit of ingenuity you can pick up basic spares like inner tubes and puncture repair kits.

Taking your bike on **the train** won't present any problems: there's a nominal charge, and your bike normally goes in the luggage compartment. The same goes for hotels, which usually put your machine either in a locked luggage room or guarded parking lot. You need to exercise at least as much caution concerning **security** as you would in any city at home: strong locks and chaining your bike to immobile objects are the order of the day, and always try and take your bike indoors at night.

ACCOMMODATION

Accommodation will probably account for most of your essential expenditure in Poland, though you're by no means confined to the international hotels so heavily touted in most promotional material: almost everywhere, there are now plenty of cheap alternatives. Listings have been made as wide-ranging as possible to reflect the immense diversity of choice on offer: privately run hotels, pensions, hostels, workers' hostels, youth hostels, rooms in private houses and a good range of campsites.

ORBIS AND OTHER LUXURY HOTELS

Orbis run some 55 **international hotels** throughout Poland, which can be booked with a minimum of fuss before your departure. A few of these are famous old prewar haunts, but the vast majority date from the last twenty years and are in the anonymous concrete style favoured for business purposes the world over. This stock is now being supplemented by some even more luxurious establishments, often as joint ventures with well-known Western hotel chains. Needless to say, all such hotels are extremely pricey, but they do have consistently high standards. Minimum **rates**

are around £40/$60 single, £70/$100 double, rising to more than £150/$225 per head in the most exclusive addresses in Warsaw.

Even if this is way beyond your budget, it's still worth knowing about these hotels, as you're more likely to find staff speaking English and other foreign languages here than you are in any tourist office. Non-guests are also able to make use of their very Westernised **facilities**. Particularly useful are the 24-hour currency exchange, plus the telex and telephone services – often the easiest means of making an international call. In addition, these hotels have restaurants, cafés and bars, and may have other facilities such as a swimming pool, solarium, sauna, tennis court, hairdresser, hard currency shop, nightclub and disco.

Orbis also run a number of **motels** on the outskirts of major cities; these are usually a bit cheaper than their more central counterparts, but generally only practical if you've got your own transport.

OTHER HOTELS

Most other hotels have far more rudimentary facilities. They're graded on a **star system** (officially abolished but informally retained by the establishments themselves), but these are generously awarded: most four-star Polish hotels would be lucky to be graded as two-star anywhere else. It's harder to give guidance on prices here than in any other type of accommodation: some highly recommendable hotels charge less than £5/$7.50 for a double with bath, but you can easily land a tacky room without facilities for three or four times that price somewhere else. Faded old two-star places are the best value; even in the cities they only cost around £6/

$9 single, £10/$15 double. If you calculate on paying £10/$15 a day per head as an average, you should end up well in pocket. Generally speaking, savings are made the more people occupy a room, but these seldom amount to much. **Breakfast** is sometimes included in the room price, but more often is not. Always ask for prices with and without bath – there may be a substantial difference.

The cheapest of all hotel rooms are provided by **sports hotels** (*Dom Sportowy*), which generally charge around £3.50/$5 a head. These, however, exist mainly for the use of visiting sporting teams, which means they're likely to be fully booked for at least part of the weekend, and at other times deserted. They're also usually located in a park way out from the centre; they don't serve meals; and you may be asked to share a room with a stranger.

PENSIONS AND HOLIDAY HOMES

Some of Poland's best accommodation deals can be found in the **pensions** (*pensjonaty*) situated in the resort towns of major holiday areas such as the Tatras, the Karkonosze and the Kłodzko region. These are a particularly attractive option if you're travelling in a group, as triples and quadruples offer substantial savings over doubles; singles are extremely scarce. Half-board terms range between £8–16/$12–24 per head; it's sometimes posssible to get bed and breakfast only, but it would be a pity to miss out on the excellent regional cuisine that's usually provided. For reservations and further details, contact an *Orbis* office in the appropriate area.

Another possibility is to rent a **summer cottage**. Available between mid-May and the end of September, these are roughly analogous to the French *gîtes*. Intended for quiet breaks, with opportunities for cycling, rambling, angling and water sports, they are mostly located in secluded rural areas, notably the Mazurian Lakes, the Lubuska region and Western Pomerania, though there are also some along the Baltic coast. All have a living room with dining area, a bathroom with hot and cold running water, a fully equipped kitchen, a fireplace, and a patio or balcony. They have between one and five bedrooms, sleeping from three to eight people, and are priced accordingly. Obviously they must be booked in advance: for full details, contact *Polorbis* in London, or any *Orbis* office. *Silesian Villas* (see "Getting There") also offer a good selection.

A NOTE ON PRICES

The abolition in July 1990 of specially increased prices for foreigners has led to a state of flux in the price of rooms which, compounded by the runaway inflation afflicting the country – currently between 30 and 40 percent though hopefully now slowing down – means that it's near impossible to give accurate prices in złotys for rooms. However, as the złoty lessens in value, so the exchange rate improves, meaning that the prices we've quoted in pounds sterling will remain relatively stable. A rough idea of what you can expect to pay for different types of accommodation is given in the sections below and throughout the Guide, but be prepared for anomalies and fluctuations in price.

A recent addition to the holiday lodging scene are **workers' hostels** (often designated *FWP*), formerly run by unions and factories for their own employees but increasingly privatised and open to general trade.

PRIVATE ROOMS

You can get a **room in a private house** almost anywhere in the country. The disadvantages include sometimes shabby flats, which may be situated on the outskirts of town, but it's an ideal way to find out how the Poles themselves live.

All major cities have an office providing a room-finding service, usually known as the ***Biuro Zakwaterowania***. The charges don't vary much usually: £6–7/$9–11, and at least half as much again in Warsaw. You should be given a choice of location and category (from 1 down to 3); you register and pay for as many nights as you wish, then are given directions to the house where you'll be staying. You must arrive there before 10pm; there will probably also be a restriction on how early you check in (perhaps 1pm). In case you don't like the place you're sent to, it makes sense not to register for too many nights ahead, as it's easy enough to extend your stay by going back to the *Biuro*, or paying your host directly. Note that there's no scope under this setup for negotiating special rates: the host is obliged to inform the *Biuro* if you're staying on, or else is liable to have someone else sent by them to occupy your room.

Some ***Orbis* offices** also act as agents for householders with rooms available to let. These are often a little more expensive and may be subject to a minimum stay of three nights (or else a hefty surcharge). However, the administration is far less tight than with a *Biuro Zakwaterowania* and you can subsequently extend the length of your stay by negotiation with your host, who'll no doubt be happy to pass on in the form of a price reduction some of the substantial share of your payment that would otherwise go to *Orbis*.

At the unofficial level, many houses in the main holiday areas hang out **signs** saying *Noclegi* (lodging) or *Pokoje* (rooms). It's up to you to bargain over the price; £3/$4.50 is the least you can expect to pay. You may get a particularly good deal if you offer hard currency: one reason why you should carry a supply of Western cash. In the cities, you won't see any signs advertising rooms, but you may well be approached outside stations and other obvious places. Before accepting, establish the price and check that the location is suitable; the same comments about payment apply.

YOUTH HOSTELS

Scattered throughout Poland are some 200 **official youth hostels** (*Schroniska Młodzieżowe*), identified by a green triangle on a white background. However, a large percentage of these are only open for a few weeks at the height of the summer holiday period, usually in converted school buildings, and are liable to be booked solid, while most of the permanent year-round hostels are still very much in line with the hairshirt ideals of the movement's founders. Children under 10 are not allowed in, and preference is supposedly given to those under 26, though there's no upper age restriction. Make sure you bring a sheet or sleeping bag.

Two plus points are the **prices** (rarely more than £2.50/$4 a head, with £1.50/$2.50 a likely average) and the **locations**, with many hostels placed close to town centres. Against that, there's the fact that dormitories are closed between 10am and 5pm, that you must check in by 9pm, and that a 10pm curfew is usually enforced.

The most useful hostel **addresses** are given in the *Guide*, but if you need a complete list, either buy the official International Handbook or contact the head office of the Polish youth hostel federation (*PTSM*) at ul. Chocimska 28, Warsaw (Mon–Fri 8am–3.30pm; ☎498-354/498-128) for their own comprehensive handbook (*Informator*). It's best to buy an **IYHF** membership card before you go (see box below); current yearly charges are £4 if you're under 21, £7 otherwise.

OTHER HOSTELS

One reason the youth hostels maintain the accent on youth is that there's a network of adult **tourist hostels**, often run by **PTTK** and called either **Dom Turysty** or **Dom Wycieczkowy**. Found in both cities and rural locations, these are generally cheaper than any hotel, but are often a poor bargain at around £5/$7.50 for a bed in a small dorm with basic shared facilities.

In July, August and early September **Almatur** also organises accommodation in **university hostels** in the main university towns. Rooms have two, three or four beds; the charges including breakfast are around £4/$6 for students (proof will be required), £6.50/$10 for others under 35, which is the age limit. You can eat cheaply at the cafeteria on the premises, and there are often discos in the evenings. The location of these

---

YOUTH HOSTEL ASSOCIATIONS

Australia *Australian Youth Hostels Association*, Level 3, 10 Mallett St, Camperdown, New South Wales 2050 (☎02/565 1699).

Canada *Canadian Hostelling Association*, 1600 James Naismith Drive, Suite 608, Gloucester, Ontario K1B 5N4 (☎613/748 5638).

England and Wales *Youth Hostel Association* (*YHA*), Trevelyan House, 8 St. Stephen's Hill, St. Alban's, Herts AL1 2DY (☎0727/55215). London shop and information office: 14 Southampton St, London WC2E 7HY (☎071/836 8542).

Ireland *An Oige*, 61 Mountjoy St, Dublin 7 (☎01/304555).

New Zealand *Youth Hostels Association of New Zealand*, PO Box 436, Christchurch 1 (☎03/799970).

Northern Ireland *Youth Hostel Association of Northern Ireland*, 56 Bradbury Place, Belfast, BT7 1RU (☎0232/324733).

Scotland *Scottish Youth Hostel Association*, 7 Glebe Crescent, Stirling, FK8 2JA (☎0786/51181).

USA *American Youth Hostels* (*AYH*), PO Box 37613, Washington, DC 200013 (☎202/783 6161).

hostels can vary from year to year: contact an *Almatur* office (relevant addresses are given in the text) or *Polorbis* before you go.

In mountain areas, a reasonably generous number of **refuges** (*schroniska*), which are clearly marked on hiking maps, enable you to make long-distance treks without having to make detours down into the villages for the night. Accommodation is in very basic dormitories, but costs are nominal and you can often get cheap and filling hot meals; in summer the more popular refuges can be very crowded indeed, as they are obliged to accept all-comers. As a rule the refuges are open all year round but it's always worth checking for closures or renovations in progress before setting out.

CAMPGROUNDS

There are some 400 **campgrounds** throughout the country. The most useful are listed in the text; for a complete list, get hold of the *Campingi w Polsce* **map**, available from bookshops, some

travel bureaux or the motoring organisation *PZMot*. Apart from a predictably dense concentration in the main holiday areas, they can also be found in most cities: the ones on the outskirts are almost invariably linked by bus to the centre and often have the benefit of a peaceful location and swimming pool. As you'd expect, the major drawback is that most are open May–September only, though a few operate all year round. **Charges** usually work out at less than £2/$3 per head, a bit more if you come by car.

One specifically Polish feature is that you don't necessarily have to bring a tent to stay at many campgrounds, as there are often **chalets** for hire, generally complete with toilet and shower. Though decidedly spartan in appearance, these are good value at around £3.50/$5 per head. In summer, however, they are invariably booked long in advance.

Camping wild, outside of the National Parks, is acceptable so long as you're reasonably discreet.

FOOD AND DRINK

Poles take their food seriously, providing snacks of feast-like proportions to the most casual visitors and maintaining networks of country relatives or local shops for especially treasured ingredients – smoked meats and sausages, cheeses, fruits and vegetables. The cuisine itself is a complex mix of influences: Turkish, Russian, **Lithuanian, Ukrainian, German and Jewish traditions all leaving their mark. To go with the food, there is excellent beer and a score of wonderful vodkas.**

The best meals you'll have in Poland are likely to be at people's homes, if you get the invitation. However, with the moves towards a market economy, the country's growing number of **restaurants** – most of which specialised in ungarnished slabs of meat during the communist era – have been looking up. At their best, in fact, they are as good as any in central Europe, dishing out a spoonful of caviar for starters before moving on through traditional soups to beef, pork or duck dishes. And, like much else, they are cheap for Western tourists.

Drinking habits are changing. Poles for years drank mainly at home, while visitors stuck to the hotels, with such other **bars** as existed being alcoholic-frequented dives. Over the last couple of years, though, something of a bar culture has been emerging in the cities, supplementing the largely non-alcohol-serving cafés. Elsewhere, drinking is still best done at the local hotel or restaurant.

FOOD

Like their central and eastern European neighbours, Poles are insatiable **meat** eaters: throughout the austerities of the past decade, meat consumption here remained among the highest in Europe. Beef and pork in different guises are the mainstays of most meals, while hams and sausages are consumed at all times of the day, as snacks and sandwich-fillers. In the coastal and mountain regions, you can also expect **fish** to feature prominently on the menus, with carp and trout being particularly good.

Although a meal without meat is a contradiction in terms for most Poles, vegetarians will find cheap refuge in the **milk bars** (see below), whose dairy-based menus exclude meat almost entirely (continuing Jewish traditions). They have a very mixed reputation, popular on the whole with the young and with students, but often scorned by their elders. At the opposite end of the economic scale, the plusher restaurants normally carry a selection of **vegetarian** dishes (*potrawy jarskie*); if the menu has no such section, the key phrase to use is *bezmięsne* (without meat).

BREAKFASTS, SNACKS AND FAST FOOD

For most Poles, the first meal of the day, eaten at home at around 7am, is little more than a sandwich with a glass of tea or cup of coffee. A more leisurely **breakfast** might include fried eggs with ham, mild frankfurters, a selection of cold meats and cheese, rolls and jam, but for most people this full spread is more likely to be taken as a second breakfast (*drugie śniadanie*) at around midday. This is often taken in the workplace, but a common alternative for younger, city Poles is to stop at a milk bar or self-service snack bar (*samoobsługa*).

Open from early morning till 5 or 6pm (later in the city centres), **snack bars** are soup-kitchen-type places, serving very cheap but generally uninspiring food: small plates of salted herring in oil (*śledź w oleju*), sandwiches, tired-looking meat or cheese, sometimes enlivened by some Russian salad (*sałatka jarzynowa*).

Milk bars (*bar mleczny*) are even cheaper options, offering a selection of solid, non-meat meals with the emphasis on quantity. Milk bars and snack bars both operate like self-service cafeterias: the menu is displayed over the counter, but if you don't recognise the names of the dishes (the vocabulary section below will help) you can just point. Unfortunately, the milk bar seems to be becoming something of a threatened institution; many have closed down in recent years.

TAKEAWAY AND FAST FOOD

Traditional Polish **takeaway stands** usually sell *zapiekanki*, baguette-like pieces of bread topped with melted cheese; a less common but enjoyable version of the same thing comes with fried mushrooms. You'll also find **hotdog stalls**, doling out sub-Frankfurter sausages in white rolls, and stalls and shops selling **chips** (*frytki*); the latter are generally fat and oily, sold by weight, and accompanied by sausage (*kiełbasa*) or chicken (*kurczak*) in the tourist resorts and some city stands, or by fish (*ryby*) in the northern seaside resorts and lakeland areas.

More Western-style **fast food** is starting to take off, too, with pizza and hamburger joints opening up in every town of any size. Like much of the new private enterprise, quality is variable.

DO-IT-YOURSELF SNACKS

If the snacks on offer fail to appeal, you can always stock up on your own provisions.

Most people buy their **bread** in supermarkets (*samoobsługowe*) or from market traders; bakeries (*piekarnia*) are mostly small private shops and still something of a rarity, but when you do find them they tend to be very good, as the queues indicate. The standard loaf (*chleb zakopiański*) is a long piece of dense rye bread, often flavoured with caraway seeds. Also common is *razowy*, a solid brown bread sometimes flavoured with honey, and *mazowiecki*, a white, sour rye bread. Rolls come in two basic varieties: the more common is the plain, light white roll called a *kajzerka*, the other is the *grahamka*, a round roll of rougher and denser brown bread.

Supermarkets are again a useful source for **fillers**, with basic delicatessen counters for cooked meats and sausages, and fridge units holding a standard array of hard and soft cheeses. Street markets often reveal rather more choice – certainly for **fruit and vegetables**. Few market stalls supply bags, so bring your own.

COFFEE, TEA AND SWEETS

Poles are inveterate tea and coffee drinkers, their daily round punctuated by endless cups or glasses, generally with heaps of sugar.

Tea, which is cheaper and so marginally more popular, is drunk Russian-style in the glass, without milk and often with lemon. Cafés and restaurants will give you hot water and a tea bag (Chinese tea as a rule), but in bars it's more likely to be *naturalna* style – a spoonful of tea leaves with the water poured on top.

Coffee is served black unless you ask otherwise, in which case specify with milk (*z mlekiem*) or with cream (*ze śmietaną*). Most **cafés** (*kawarnia*) offer only *kawa naturalna*, which is a strong brew made by simply dumping the coffee grounds in a cup or glass and pouring water over them. *Espresso* and *capuccino*, usually passable imitations of the Italian originals, are confined to the better cafés or restaurants. In cafés and bars alike a shot or two of vodka or *winiak* (brandy) with the morning cup of coffee is still frequent practice.

CAKES AND ICE CREAM

Cakes, pastries and other sweets are an integral ingredient of most Poles' daily consumption, and the cake shops (*cukiernia*) – which you'll find even in small villages – are as good as any in central Europe. *Sernik* (cheesecake) is a national favourite, as are *makowiec* (poppyseed cake), *drożdówka* (a sponge cake, often topped with plums), and *babka piaskowa* (marble cake). In the larger places you can also expect to find *torcik wiedeński*, an Austrian-style *schlagtort* with coffee and chocolate filling, as well as *keks* (fruitcake) and a selection of eclairs, profiteroles and cupcakes. Wherever you are, go early in the day, as many cake shops sell out quickly, as do the cafés with their more limited selections.

Poles eat **ice cream** (*lody*) at all times of the year, queueing up for cones at street-side kiosks or in *cukiernia*. The standard kiosk cone is watery and pretty tasteless, but elsewhere the selection is better: decent cafés, and in particular the misleadingly named alcohol-free *cocktail bars*, offer a mouthwatering selection of ices.

RESTAURANT MEALS

The average **restaurant** (*restauracja*, sometimes *jadłodajnia*) is open from late morning through to mid-evening: all but the smartest close early, though, winding down around 9pm in cities, earlier in the country. Some don't open till 1pm due to the ban on the sale of alcohol before that time. Relatively late-night standbys include Orbis hotel restaurants and, at the other end of the scale, train station snack bars.

Officially restaurants are **graded** from *kat 1* (luxury) down to *kat 4* (cheap), categories which are displayed at the top of the menu; unless your funds are very limited, stick to the top two ratings only – 3 and 4 *kat* places can be dirty and dire. Many of the newer private places seem to have eluded this system, however, and categories may well be entirely redefined over the next year or two.

Except in the big hotels and poshest restaurants, **menus** are usually in Polish only; the language section opposite should provide most of the cues you'll need. While the list of dishes apparently on offer may be long, in reality only things with a price marked next to them will be available, which will normally reduce the choice by fifty percent or more. If you arrive near closing time or late lunchtime, the waiter may inform you there's only one thing left.

There are no hard and fast rules about **tipping**, but a common practice is to round the bill up to the nearest 1000 złotys, except in upmarket places, where leaving ten percent is the established practice.

SOUPS AND STARTERS

First on the menu in most places are **soups**, definitely one of Polish cuisine's strongest points, varying from light and delicate dishes to concoctions that are virtually meals in themselves.

Best known is *barszcz*, a spicy beetroot broth that's ideally accompanied by a small pastry (*z pasztecikiem*). Other soups worth looking out for are *żurek*, a creamy white soup with sausage and potato; *botwinka*, a seasonal soup made from the leaves of baby beetroots; *krupnik*, a thick barley and potato soup with chunks of meat, carrots and celeriac; and *chłodnik*, a cold Lithuanian beetroot soup with sour milk and vegetable greens, served in summer.

In less expensive establishments you'll be lucky to have more than a couple of soups and a plate of cold meats, or herring with cream or oil (*śledź w śmietanie/oleju*) to choose from as a starter.

In better restaurants, though, the **hors d'oeuvres** selection might include Jewish-style gefilte fish, jellied ham (*szynka w galarecie*), steak tartare (*stek tatarski*), wild rabbit paté (*pasztet z zająca*), or hard-boiled eggs in mayonnaise, which sometimes come stuffed with vegetables (*jajka faszerowane*).

FOOD AND DRINK GLOSSARY

Basics

Śniadanie	Breakfast	*Pieczyste*	Steak	*Jarzyny/*	Vegetables
Obiad	Lunch	*Desery*	Dessert	*warzywa*	
Kolacja	Dinner	*Drób*	Poultry	*Owoce*	Fruit
Nóż	Knife	*Potrawy*	Vegetarian	*Surówka*	Salad
Widelec	Fork	*jarskie*	dishes	*Cukier*	Sugar
Łyżka	Spoon	*Dodatki*	Extras/	*Sól*	Salt
Talerz	Plate		supplements	*Pieprz*	Pepper
Filiżanka	Cup	*Ryby*	Fish	*Ocet*	Vinegar
Szklanka	Glass	*Chleb*	Bread	*Olej*	Oil
Przekąska/	Starter	*Bułka*	Rolls	*Chrzan*	Horseradish
zakąska		*Masło*	Butter	*Ryż*	Rice
Jadłospis	Menu	*Kanapka*	Sandwich	*Makaron*	Macaroni
Zupa	Soup	*Jajko*	Egg	*Frytki*	Chips
Dania gotowe/	Main dish	*Mięso*	Meat	*Śmietana*	Cream
główne danie					

Soups, Fish and Poultry

Barszcz czerwony –	Beetroot soup (borsch)	*(zupa) Cebulowa*	Onion soup
z pasztecikem	– with pastry	*(zupa) Jarzynowa*	Vegetable soup
Barszcz ukraiński	White borsch	*Kołduny*	Dumplings
Bulion/rosół	Bouillon	*Śledź*	Herring
Żurek	Sour cream soup	*Pstrąg*	Trout
Krupnik	Barley soup	*Łosoś*	Salmon
Chłodnik	Sour milk and vegetable	*Karp*	Carp
	cold soup	*Węgorz*	Eel
Kartoflanka	Potato soup	*Makrela*	Mackerel
Kapuśniak	Cabbage soup	*Sardynka*	Sardine
(zupa) Owocowa	Cold fruit soup	*Kurczak*	Chicken
(zupa) Pomidorowa	Tomato soup	*Kaczka*	Duck
(zupa) Ogórkowa	Cucumber soup	*Indyk*	Turkey
(zupa) Grzybowa	Mushroom soup	*Gęś*	Geese
(zupa) Fasolowa	Bean soup	*Bażant*	Pheasant
(zupa) Grochowa	Pea soup		

Meat

Dzik	Wild boar	*Kotlet*	Pork	*Bekon*	Bacon
Sarnina	Elk	*schabowy*	cutlet	*boczek*	
Wątróbka	Liver with onion	*Wołowe*	Beef	*Salami*	Salami
Golonka	Leg of pork	*Befsztyk*	Steak	*Baranina*	Mutton
Wieprzowe	Pork	*Kiełbasa*	Sausage	*Cielęcina*	Veal

Vegetables

Marchewka	Carrots	*Pomidor*	Tomato	*Papryka*	Paprika
Kapusta	Cabbage	*Ogórek*	Cucumber	*Kapusta kiszona*	Sauerkraut
Ziemniaki	Potatoes	*Groch*	Peas	*Szpinak*	Spinach
Cebula	Onion	*Ćwikła/*	Beetroot	*Ogórki*	Gherkins
Czosnek	Garlic	*buraczki*		*Szparagi*	Asparagus
Grzyby/pieczarki	Mushrooms	*Kalafior*	Cauliflower	*Fasola*	Beans

Fruit, Cheese and Nuts

Banan	Banana	*Maliny*	Raspberries	*Bryndza*	Sheep's cheese
Śliwka	Plum	*Winogrona*	Grapes	*Oscypek*	Smoked goats'
Ananas	Pineapple	*Gruszka*	Pears		cheese
Jabłko	Apple	*Czarne jagody*	Blackberries	*Twaróg*	Cottage cheese
Kompot	Stewed	*borówki*		*(ser) Myśliwski*	Smoked cheese
	fruit	*Pomarańcze*	Orange	*(ser) Tylżycki*	Cheddar cheese
Cytryna	Lemon	*Czarne*	Blackcurrant	*Laskowe/orzechy*	Almonds
Morele	Apricots	*porzeczki*		*Orzechy włoskie*	Walnuts
Truskawki	Strawberries	*Czereśnie*	Cherries		

Cakes and Desserts

Tort	Tart	*Galaretka*	Jellied fruits	*Pączki*	Doughnuts
Ciastko	Cake	*Mazurek*	Shortcake	*Ciasto*	Yeast cake
Czekolada	Chocolate	*Sernik*	Cheesecake	*drożdżowe*	with fruit
Lody	Ice cream	*Makowiec*	Poppyseed cake		

Food Terms

Mielone	Minced	*Antrykot/wołowy*	Mixed	*Marynowany*	Pickled
Pieczeń	Roast meat	*Świeży*	Fresh	*Surowy*	Raw
Sznycel	Escalope/schnitzel	*Kwaśny*	Sour	*Gotowany*	Boiled
Szaszłyk	Grilled	*Grill/z rusztu*	Grilled	*Słodki*	Sweet
Kotlet	Cutlet	*Nadziewany*	Stuffed	*Smacznego!*	Bon appetit!

Drinks

Herbata	Tea	*Spirytus*	Spirits	*Napój*	Bottled fruit
Kawa	Coffee	*Wódka*	Vodka		drink
Woda	Water	*Piwo*	Beer	*Sok pomarańczowy*	Orange juice
Woda	Mineral water	*Wino*	Wine	*Sok pomidorowy*	Tomato juice
mineralna		*Koniak*	Cognac/brandy	*Miód pitny*	Mead
Mleko	Milk	*Sok*	Juice	*Wino wytrawne*	Dry wine
Cocktail	Milk shake	*Gorąca*	Drinking	*Wino słodkie*	Sweet wine
mleczny		*czekolada*	chocolate	*Na zdrowie!*	Cheers!

MAIN COURSES

The basis of most main courses is a fried or grilled cut of **meat** in a thick sauce, commonest of which is the *kotlet schwabowy*, a fried pork cutlet. However, Poland's stock of wild animals means that in better restaurants you may find wild boar (*dzik*) and elk (*sarnina*) on the menu. Two national specialities you'll find everywhere are *bigos* (cabbage stewed with meat and spices) and *pierogi*, dumplings stuffed with meat and mushrooms – or with cottage cheese, onion and spices in the non-meat variation (*pierogi ruskie*). Another favourite is *flaczki*, tripe cooked in a spiced bouillon stock with vegetables; also worth trying are *gołąbki* (cabbage leaves stuffed with meat, rice and occasionally mushrooms) and

golonka (pig's leg with horseradish and pease pudding). Duck (*kaczka*) is usually the most satisfying poultry, particularly with apples, while carp (*karp*), eel (*węgorz*) and trout (*pstrąg*) are generally reliable **fish** dishes, usually grilled or sautéed, occasionally poached. **Pancakes** (*naleśniki*) often come as a main course, too, stuffed with cottage cheese (*z serem*).

Main dishes come with some sort of **vegetable**, normally boiled or mashed potatoes and/or cabbage, either boiled or as sauerkraut. Fried potato pancakes (*placki ziemniaczane*) are particularly good, either in sour cream or in a spicy paprika sauce. Wild forest mushrooms (*grzyby*), another Polish favourite, are served in any number of forms, the commonest being fried or sautéed.

Salads are generally a regulation issue plate of lettuce, cucumber and tomato in a watery dressing. If available, it's better to go for an individual salad dish like *mizeria* (cucumber in cream), *buraczki* (grated beetroot) or the rarer *ćwikła* (beetroot with horseradish).

DESSERTS

Desserts are usually meagre, except in the big hotels and plush restaurants, where a selection of cakes and ice creams will probably be on offer. If it's available try *kompot*, fruit compote in a glass – in season you may chance upon fresh strawberries, raspberries or blueberries. Pancakes (*naleśniki*) are also served as a **dessert**, with jam and sugar or with *powidła*, a delicious plum spread.

DRINKING

Poles' capacity for alcohol has never been in doubt, and drinking is a national pursuit. Much of the drinking goes on in **restaurants**, which in smaller towns or villages are often the only outlets selling alcohol.

In the cities and larger towns, you'll come upon **hotel bars** (frequented mainly by Westerners or wealthier Poles), a growing number of **privately run bars** (*bary*), which mimic Western models, and the very different and traditional **drink bars**.

The last, basic and functional, are almost exclusively male terrain and generally best avoided: the haunt of wideboys and hardened alcoholics, they reflect the country's serious alcohol problems, caused in part by a preference for spirits rather than beer or wine.

BEER

The Poles can't compete with their Czech neighbours in the production and consumption of **beer** (*piwo*), but there are nevertheless a number of highly drinkable, and in a few cases really excellent, Polish brands.

The best and most famous **bottled beers** are all from the south of the country. Żywiec produces two varieties: the strong, tangy *Tatra Pils* and *Piwo Żywiecki*, a lighter smoother brew, ideal for mealtime drinking. The other nationally available beers are *Okocim* from the Katowice region, and *Leżajsk*, a strongish brew from the town of the same name near Rzeszów. There's also an assortment of regional beers you'll only find in the locality, *Gdańskie* and *Wrocławskie* being two of the most highly rated.

Draught beer (*ciemne*) is a rarity, though wooden barrels of local beer do occasionally crop up in the most unlikely places, particularly villages in the south.

VODKA AND OTHER SPIRITS

It's with **vodka** (*wódka*) that Poles really get into their stride. Such is its place in the national culture that for years the black market value of the dollar was supposed to be directly pegged to the price of a bottle. If you thought vodka was just a cocktail mixer you're in for some surprises: clear, peppered, honeyed – reams could be written about the varieties on offer. Ideally vodka is served neat, well chilled, in measures of 25 or 50 grammes (a *czysta* – 100 grammes – is common, too) and knocked back in one go, with a mineral water chaser. A couple of these will be enough to put most people well on the way, though the capacities of seasoned Polish drinkers are prodigious – a half-litre bottle between two or three over lunch is nothing unusual.

Best of the **clear vodkas** are *Żytnia*, *Krakus* and *Wyborowa*, valuable export earners often more easily available abroad than at home. A perfectly acceptable everyday substitute is *Polonez*, one of the most popular brands and the one you're most likely to encounter in people's houses and in the average restaurant.

Of the **flavoured varieties**, first on most people's list is *Żubrówka*, a legendary vodka infused with the taste of bison grass from the eastern Białowieza forest – there's a stem in every bottle. *Pieprzówka*, by contrast, has a sharp, peppery flavour, and is supposed to be good at warding off colds. The juniper-flavoured *Myśliwska* tastes a bit like gin, while the whisky-coloured *Jarzębiak* is flavoured with rowanberries. Others to look out for are *Wiśniówka*, a sweetish, strong wild cherry concoction; *Krupnik*, which is akin to whisky liqueur; *Lytrynówka*, a lemon vodka; and *Miodówka*, a rare honey vodka. Last but by no means least on any basic list comes *Pejsachówka*, which, at 75 percent proof, is by far the strongest vodka on the market and is rivalled in strength only by home-produced *bimber*, the Polish version of moonshine.

Other popular **digestifs** are *śliwowica*, the powerful plum brandy which is mostly produced in the south of the country, and *miód pitny*, a heady mead-like wine. Commonest of all in this category however is *winiak*, a fiery Polish brandy you'll find in many cafés and restaurants.

SOFT DRINKS

The commonest **soft drink** is *napój*, a bottled blend of fruit juice and mineral water, the most popular varieties being strawberry (*truskawkowy*) and apple (*jabłkowe*). They are tasty and refreshing, and always preferable to the sickly varieties of *oranżada* and *lemonada*. There are plenty of sweet Polish-style Pepsis and Cokes on sale, too, as well as the much higher priced originals, which are consumed with gusto by Poles keen to identify with the symbols of Western consumerism.

Sparkling **mineral water** (*woda mineralna*) from the spas of the south is highly palatable and available throughout the country; the commonest brand name is *Kryniczanka*. Considerably less recommended is *syfon*, the stringent carbonated water you get on train platforms and in some of the cheaper restaurants.

COMMUNICATIONS AND THE MEDIA

POST OFFICES AND THE MAIL

Post offices in Poland are identified by the name *Urząd Pocztowy* (*Poczta* for short) or by the acronym PTT (*Poczta, Telegraf, Telefon*). Each bears a number, with the head office in each city being no. 1. Theoretically, each office has a **poste restante** facility: make sure, therefore, that anyone addressing mail to you includes the no. 1 after the city's name. This service works reasonably well, but don't expect 100 percent reliability. **Mail** to the UK currently takes up to a week, to the US a fortnight, but seems to move twice as fast in the other direction. Always mark your letters "Par avion"; if you don't, they will almost certainly go surface – taking up to six weeks to the UK, several months to the US – even if you have paid the correct airmail postage. **Post boxes** are green, blue or red; these are respectively for local mail, airmail, and all types of mail. **Opening hours** of the head offices are usually Mon–Sat 7/8am–8pm; other branches usually close at 6pm, often earlier in rural areas. A restricted range of services is available 24 hours a day, seven days a week, from post offices in or outside the main train stations of major cities.

TELEPHONES

The antiquated **telephone system** bequeathed by the communists is one of the biggest obstacles to Poland's economic development. Frantic efforts, with a great deal of foreign help, have been made at modernisation, but the system is likely to be in transition for some time to come.

MAKING CALLS

At the time of writing, three types of public **pay phones** were in existence. The old grey machines with dials are still the most common; they're also very unreliable and can only really be used for making local calls. Gradually, these are being replaced by yellow push-button phones, which work much more efficiently. Finally, there are the brand-new blue machines which are best of all, but as yet confined to main post offices in the largest cities. These last are operated by a card, bought at a counter. The grey and yellow phones require *jetons* (*żetony*), which can also be bought at kiosks. These come in two types: the small **A** tokens (currently costing 600zł) are for **local calls**; the larger **C** tokens (currently

INTERNATIONAL CODES

UK	☎0044
Irish Republic	☎00353
USA and Canada	☎001
Australia	☎0061
New Zealand	☎0064

CODES FOR MAJOR POLISH CITIES

Częstochowa ☎034	Kraków ☎012	Toruń ☎056
Gdańsk/Gdynia/Sopot ☎058	Łódź ☎042	Warsaw:
Katowice	Lublin ☎081	6 digit nos ☎022
6 digit nos ☎032	Poznań ☎061	7 digit nos ☎02
7 digit nos ☎03	Szczecin ☎091	Wrocław ☎071

6000zł) for **long distance calls**. When dialling, place the *jeton* on the slide, but do not insert it until someone answers at the other end – otherwise you'll lose it and be cut off.

Local calls, and dialling from one city to another, should present few problems. The codes given below work from abroad (omitting the initial zero) and, for the most part, within Poland itself. However, the internal coding system is still subject to variations (and hence only local numbers are given in the *Guide*) and it's always better to ask at the post office before dialling. This is essential if calling from a large city to a small town, which can be a real headache. If necessary, you can get the operator to place the call for you; an expensive option, but it should solve all your problems. **Emergency calls** (police ☎997, fire ☎998, ambulance ☎999) are free.

Making **international calls** at least within Europe, is far less of a problem these days than it was. First dial the international code (see opposite), then wait (for anything up to a minute) for a continuous tone before dialling the rest of the number, not forgetting to omit the initial zero. Be sure to stock up with a good supply of *jetons*, as each lasts for less than a minute. For calls **outside Europe**, you'll probably have to rely on the services of the operator, and be prepared to wait. To speed up the process, ask for the call to be put through fast (*szybko*), but note that this will double the price. There's no facility for reversing the charges.

THE MEDIA

With the collapse of communist rule, the Polish media were transformed, leaving the party line and *samizdat* traditions behind in a sudden rush of legal, free expression. The free press that has flourished in the wake of communism's demise in Poland is arguably the most dynamic in the region: an indication of this is provided by a recent state press index, which listed almost 1000 registered publications, including 75 daily newspapers and 164 weeklies.

Things have moved rather slower in television and radio: it took until March 1, 1993 for the authorities to approve legislation dismantling the state monopoly on radio and TV, and the country's two state-run TV channels, four national radio stations, and a growing network of local TV and radio stations are still technically regulated by a hangover from the communist era, the powerful State Radio and Television Committee (RTVC), whose head is directly appointed by the prime minister. Overall though, the old adage of "Two Poles, Three Opinions" has now found expression in the diversity of new independent broadcasting.

NEWSPAPERS AND MAGAZINES

The Polish *samizdat* press of the 1980s was the most sophisticated and widely read in eastern Europe, forcing a degree of liberalisation on the official press through the necessity to compete for readers. The transition from an underground medium has been difficult, and articles are often long on argument and short on reporting; design and style have some way to go to match Western equivalents, with poor-quality paper, monotonous slabs of text, and poorly reproduced photographs the current norm.

The difficulties of the transition have been further compounded by the ex-communist party members' struggle to retain control over part of the media, as well as the protracted period of domestic political infighting and instability that continued throughout the early 1990s and which has only recently begun to show signs of abating.

Arguments about **ownership** continue to rattle on: one of the first things the country's first post-communist government did in 1989–90 was to liquidate the old party publishing company *RSW*. The problem was that the way the process was handled left the door open for smarter elements of the *nomenklatura* to retain effective control over significant parts of the existing press network, which they have duly done – an example of the so-called "enfranchisement of the *nomenklatura*" which has embittered ordinary Polish people.

Among **Polish-language daily newspapers**, most popular is the tabloid *Gazeta Wyborcza*, eastern Europe's first independent daily, set up in 1989. Forced to abandon the *Solidarity* logo from its masthead following a bitter dispute between its editor, veteran dissident and intellectual Adam Michnik, and Lech Wałęsa, the paper has gone from strength to strength, with a daily circulation (550,000) that puts it among the top ten selling European dailies. *Gazeta* is strong on investigative journalism, and has a mildly left-of-centre political stance.

Other national daily papers include *Rzeczpospolita*, originally the official voice of the communist government, now a highbrow independent paper with a strong following among businesspeople and government officials. *Zycie Warszawy* is a centrist Warsaw-based daily with a strong nationwide circulation: recent investments in state-of-the-art hi-tech printing equipment have given it the most Western appearance of all the dailies. *Trybuna*, once the official newspaper of the communist party, is still pursuing a leftist agenda. As in many countries, **local** rather than national papers are what most of the population read, a fact partly explicable by the delays in getting Warsaw-based dailies out to the country until the following day: though generally pretty unexciting, they're often useful for current events.

Weekly papers comprise a colourful mix of the specialist (women's magazines are the nation's best-sellers), the political and the sensationalist. Top sellers in the latter category include *Skandale*, which features the usual diet of sex, violence and pure invention ("NOW I'M PREGNANT WITH ADOLF HITLER'S CHILD", a recent headline, gives an indication of the tone); and *Nie*, edited by the flamboyant and outspoken Jerzy Urban, spokesman for the communist government throughout most of the 1980s.

Of the political organs, the theoretically inclined *Polityka* is another former communist mouthpiece (in this case for the liberal wing of the party), while the recently set up *Wprost* explicitly aims itself at Poland's new breed of yuppies. *Tygodnik Solidarnosc*, the original union weekly established in the heydays of the early 1980s and then banned until 1989, is now firmly in the hands of a faction within the declining Solidarity movement. Circulation of the once hugely popular *Tygodnik Powszechny*, a liberally minded Catholic weekly that used to be the country's only officially published independent newspaper, has declined rapidly of late following some rather misjudged forays into the political domain during the Mazowiecki government era.

There's only one **English-language newspaper**, the *Warsaw Voice*, a Warsaw-based weekly that's widely available throughout the country. Highly readable and informative, it's also a useful source for listings in the capital.

Western newspapers and magazines are now available the same day in the big cities. Most common are the *Guardian* International Edition, *Financial Times*, *Times* and *Herald Tribune*, plus magazines like *Newsweek*, *Time* and *The Economist*.

Ruch kiosks are the main outlets for papers and magazines. You can also find foreign newspapers in hotel lobbies, foreign-language bookshops and foreign press clubs (KMPiK) in the major cities.

TV AND RADIO

In addition to the Polish **TV channels**, anyone living in the east of the country can get Russian, Belarussian and Ukrainian stations, anyone in the south Czech or Slovak, and in the west, German. Many Poles consider these a useful supplement to the national network, whose standards (pedestrian news programmes, makeshift sets, lots of dubbed imports, shameful football coverage) are very slowly becoming more sophisticated. As political infighting within and between successive government administrations diminishes, some of the instabilities affecting domestic TV are levelling off, with attendant beneficial effects on the quality of programming. For increasing numbers of Poles **satellite**, and in the big cities **cable TV** are popular additions to the range of TV viewing options: the *Orbis* chain of hotels and a number of others now carry a selection of international cable/satellite channels, including CNN International, BBC World Service TV, MTV and Sky (in German).

The state **radio stations** also present a strange interim picture, broadcasting programmes imported from the BBC (in English and Polish) plus German- and French-language programmes amid the mix of local bulletins and shows. If you want to pick up the complete **BBC World Service** in English, you'll need a shortwave radio tuned to 12.095 MHZ (24.80 metres) or 9.410 MHZ (31.88 metres).

The Polish Radio 1 programme broadcasts news and weather reports in English on the hour from 9am–noon in summer. Wavelengths vary around the country – check the local press for details. In the major cities, such as Warsaw, Kraków and Gdańsk, privately run **local radio stations** are worth tracking down for their dynamic music programming and English-language news bulletins during the summer months.

OPENING HOURS AND HOLIDAYS

Most shops are open on weekdays from approximately 10am to 6pm. Exceptions are grocers and food stores, which may open as early as 6am and close by mid-afternoon – something to watch out for in rural areas in particular. Many shops are closed altogether on Saturdays, with others opening for just a few hours.

Other idiosyncrasies include *Ruch* **kiosks**, where you can buy newspapers and municipal transport tickets, which generally open from about 6am; some shut up around 5pm, but others remain open for several hours longer. Increasing numbers of **street traders** also do business well into the evening, while you can usually find the odd shop in most towns offering late-night opening throughout the week.

As a rule, *Orbis* **offices** are open from 9 or 10am until 5pm (later in major cities) during the week; hours are shorter on Saturdays, sometimes with closure on alternate weeks. Other **tourist information offices** are normally open Monday to Friday 9am to 4pm. All the large cities now have several grocery stores open round the clock; the most useful are listed in the *Guide*.

TOURIST SITES

Visiting **churches** seldom presents any problems: the ones you're most likely to want to see are open from early morning until mid-evening without interruption. However, a large number of less famous churches are fenced off beyond the entrance porch by a grille or glass window for much of the day; to see them properly, you'll need to turn up around the times for Mass, ie first thing in the morning and between 6 and 8pm.

The current visiting times for **museums** and **historic monuments** are listed in the text of the Guide. They are almost invariably closed on one day per week (usually Monday) and many are closed on another day as well; on the days remaining, many open for only about five hours, often closing at 3pm. Some of the museums in the major cities have managed to extend their opening times recently, but this has often been at the expense of having only one section open to the public at any particular time. Entrance charges are generally nominal.

PUBLIC HOLIDAYS

The following are national public holidays, on which you can expect most shops and sights to be closed:

January 1

Easter Monday (variable March/April)

May 1 (Labour Day)

May 3 (Constitution Day)

Corpus Christi (variable May/June)

August 15 (Feast of the Assumption)

November 1 (All Saints' Day)

November 11 (National Independence Day)

December 25 & 26

FESTIVALS AND OTHER ENTERTAINMENTS

One manifestation of Poland's intense commitment to Roman Catholicism is that all the great feast days of the Church calendar are celebrated with wholehearted devotion, many of the participants donning the colourful traditional costumes for which the country is celebrated. This is most notable in the mountain areas in the south of the country, where the annual festivities play a key role in maintaining a vital sense of community. As a supplement to these, Poland has many more recently established cultural festivals, particularly in the fields of music and drama. As well as a strong ethnic/folk music scene, contemporary music in Poland is intriguing, if a little inaccessible to outsiders.

RELIGIOUS AND TRADITIONAL FESTIVALS

The highlight of the Catholic year is **Holy Week**, heralded by a glut of spring fairs, offering the best of the early livestock and agricultural produce. Religious celebrations begin in earnest on **Palm Sunday**, when palms are brought to church and paraded in processions. Often the painted and decorated "palms" are handmade, sometimes with competitions for the largest or most beautiful. The most famous procession takes place at Kalwaria Zebrzydowska near Kraków, inaugurating a spectacular week-long series of mystery plays, re-enacting Christ's Passion.

On **Maundy Thursday** many communities take symbolic revenge on Judas Iscariot: his effigy is hanged, dragged outside the village, flogged, burned or thrown into a river. **Good Friday** sees visits to mock-ups of the Holy Sepulchre – whether permanent structures such as at Kalwaria Zebrzydowska and Wambierzyce in Silesia, or *ad hoc* creations, as is traditional in Warsaw.

In some places, notably the Rzeszów region, this is fused with a celebration of King Jan Sobieski's victory in the Siege of Vienna, with "Turks" placed in charge of the tomb. **Holy Saturday** is when baskets of painted eggs, sausages, bread and salt are taken along to church to be blessed and sprinkled with holy water. The consecrated food is eaten at breakfast on **Easter Day**, when the most solemn Masses of the year are celebrated. On **Easter Monday**, it's the people themselves who are doused, usually by gangs of children armed with buckets and sprays.

Seven weeks later, at **Pentecost**, irises are traditionally laid out on the floors of the house, while in the Kraków region bonfires are held on hilltop sites. A further eleven days on comes the most Catholic of festivals, **Corpus Christi**, marked by colourful processions everywhere and elaborate floral displays. Exactly a week later, the story of the Tartar siege is re-enacted as the starting-point of one of the country's few notable festivals of secular folklore, the **Days of Kraków**.

St John's Day on June 24 is celebrated with particular gusto in Warsaw, Kraków and Poznań; at night wreaths with burning candles are cast into the river, and there are also boat parades, dancing and fireworks. July 26, **St Anne's Day**, is the time of the main annual pilgrimage to Góra Świętej Anny in Silesia.

The first of two major Marian festivals on consecutive weeks comes with the **Feast of the Holy Virgin of Sowing** on August 8 in farming areas, particularly in the southeast of the country. By then, many of the great pilgrimages to the Jasna Góra shrine in Częstochowa have already set out, arriving for the **Feast of the Assumption** on August 15. This is also the occasion for the enactment of a mystery play at Kalwaria Pacławska near Przemyśl.

All Saints' Day, November 1, is the day of national remembrance, with flowers, wreaths and candles laid on tombstones. In contrast, **St Andrew's Day**, November 30, is a time for fortune-telling, with dancing to accompany superstitious practices such as the pouring of melted wax or lead on paper. **St Barbara's Day**, December 4; is the traditional holiday of the miners, with special Masses held for their safety as a counterweight to the jollity of their galas.

During **Advent**, the nation's handicraft tradition comes to the fore, with the making of cribs to adorn every church. In Kraków, a competition is held on a Sunday between December 3 and 10, the winning entries being displayed in the city's Historical Museum. On **Christmas Eve** families

ARTS FESTIVALS

January
WROCŁAW Solo Plays
WARSAW Traditional Jazz

February
WROCŁAW Polish Contemporary Music
POZNAŃ Boys' Choirs

March
CZĘSTOCHOWA Violin Music
WROCŁAW Jazz on the Odra
ŁÓDŹ Opera; Student theatre

April
KRAKÓW Organ Music
KRAKÓW Student Song

May
WROCŁAW Jazz on the Odra
ŁANCUT Chamber Music
WROCŁAW Contemporary Polish Plays (May/June)
KRAKÓW "Juvenalia" (student festival)
GDAŃSK "Neptunalia" (student festival)
ŁĄCKO (near Nowy Sącz) Regional Folk Festival
BIELSKO-BIAŁA International Puppet Theatre (every even-ending year – 1994, 96, etc.)

June
PŁOCK Folk Ensembles
KRYNICA Arias and Songs
OPOLE Polish Songs
BRZEG Classical Music
KRAKÓW Short Feature Films
KAZIMIERZ DOLNY Folk Bands and Singers (June/July)
MRĄGROWO Country and Western Festival

July
JAROCIN Rock Festival
STARY SĄCZ Old Music
GDAŃSK-OLIWA Organ Music

KUDOWA-ZDRÓJ Music of Stanisław Moniuszko
MIĘDZYZDROJE Choral Music
KOSZALIN World Polonia Festival of Polish Songs (every 5 years – next 1996)
RZESZÓW World Festival of Polonia Folklore Groups (every 3 years – next 1995)
ŚWINOUJSCIE Fama Student Artistic Festival

August
DUSZNIKI-ZDRÓJ Music of Frédéric Chopin
SOPOT International Songs
KRAKÓW Classical Music
ŻYWIEC Beskid Culture
JELENIA GÓRA Street Theatre
GDAŃSK Dominican Fair

September
WARSAW Contemporary Music
ZAKOPANE Highland Folklore
GDAŃSK Polish Feature Films
BYDGOSZCZ Classical Music
SŁUPSK Polish Piano Competition
TORUŃ International Old Music Festival
WROCŁAW "Wratislavia Cantans" (Choral Music)
ZAKOPANE Festival of Highland Folklore
ZIELONA GÓRA International Song and Dance Troupes

October
KRAKÓW Jazz Music
WARSAW Jazz Jamboree
WARSAW Film Week
WARSAW International Chopin Piano Competition (every 5 years – next 1995)

November
POZNAŃ International Violin Competition (every 5 years – next 1996)
WARSAW "Theatrical Encounters"

December
WROCŁAW Old Music

gather for an evening banquet, traditionally of twelve courses; this is also the time when children receive their gifts. **Christmas Day** begins with the midnight mass; later, small round breads decorated with the silhouettes of domestic animals are consumed. **New Year's Eve** is the time for magnificent formal balls, particularly in Warsaw, while in country areas of southern Poland it's the day for practical jokes – which must go unpunished.

MUSIC

Though less dynamic than some of its eastern European neighbours, Polish **folk music** nevertheless plays a noteworthy role in national cultural life. Traditional folk comes in (at least) two varieties: a bland, sanitised version promoted by successive communist governments and still peddled, with varying degrees of success, principally for foreign consumption: and a rootsier, rural vein of genuine and vibrant folk culture, which you chiefly find among the country's minorities and in the southern and eastern parts of the country. Thanks in part to Chopin, who was profoundly influenced by the music of his native **Mazovia** (*Mazowsze*), Mazovian folk music is probably the best known in the country, traditional forms like the mazurka and polonaise offering a rich vein of tuneful melodies and vibrant dance rhythms. Other regions with strong traditional folk musical cultures include Silesia, the **Tatras**, whose music-loving *górale* have developed a rousing polyphonically inclined song tradition over the centuries, and the **Lemks** of the Beskid Niski, whose music bears a tangled imprint of Ukrainian, Slovak and Hungarian influences. Among the notable showcases for Polish folk music of all descriptions are the tri-annual **Festival of Polonia Music and Dance** in Rzeszów which draws a welter of *emigracja* ensembles from the worldwide Polish diaspora, and the annual autumn folk festival bash in **Kazimierz Dolny**.

The nation's wealth of folk tunes have found their way into some of the best of the country's **classical music**, of which Poles are justifiably proud, the roster of Polish composers containing a number of world-ranking figures, including Chopin, Moniuszko, Szymanowski, Penderecki, Panufnik, Lutosławski and the recent runaway best-seller Henryk Górecki. The country has also produced a wealth of classical musicians, mostly in the first half of the twentieth century when pianists Artur Rubinstein and musician-premier

Ignacy Paderewski gained worldwide prominence. A cluster of Polish orchestras, notably the Polish Chamber Orchestra, the Warsaw and Kraków Philarmonics, and the Katowice-based Radio and TV Symphony Orchestra, have made it into the world league and are regularly in demand on the international touring circuit.

All the big cities have **music festivals** of one sort or another, which generally give plenty of space to national composers, the international Chopin piano festival in Warsaw (held every five years) being the best known and most prestigious of the events. Throughout the year it's easy to catch works by Polish composers since the repertoires of many regional companies tend to be oriented towards national music.

Jazz has a well-established pedigree in Poland: ever since the 1950s when bebop broke through in the country there's been a wealth of local talent, and a number of home-grown musicians, notably tenorist Zbigniew Namysłowski, violinist Michał Urbaniak and trumpeter Tomas Stanko, have made it into the international big league. The annual Warsaw *Jazz Jamboree* in October is well established as a major international event that always attracts a roster of big names. Jazz **club life** is still largely confined to a scattering of venues in the big cities, principally Warsaw, and until the economic situation improves significantly it's unlikely this will change much, though there are hopeful signs in a number of more out of the way towns like Zamość.

More than any of its eastern European counterparts Polish **rock and pop music** has always been open to and influenced by the latest Western trends. In the 1970s psychedelia and experimental rock held sway while in the 1980s punk and reggae came to the fore, the popularity of both due in part to their latent espousal of political protest – anything gobbing at authority or chanting down Babylon went down particularly well in post-martial law Poland, and every Pole understood exactly which incarnation of apocalyptic evil was being referred to. For every band like cult stars Dezerter that made it at the popular level (though not with the communist authorities, who remained suspicious of anything that smacked of cultural subversion) there were a hundred inventively named and obscure outfits such as the The Dead Pork Cutlets, and Millions of Bulgarians who enjoyed their brief moment of counter-cultural musical glory.

Into the 1990s a Polish **rap/house** scene has begun to develop, with hard-hitting artists like Tadzik gaining a strong following among Polish youth disaffected with the new-found joys of capitalism. From the wealth of Polish rock and pop only some of the music ever makes it onto disc, but especially in university areas and the youth-oriented city bars and clubs check out the fly-posters for up-and-coming gigs, which cover the whole spectrum from acid jazz combos to frenzied death metal outfits. The annual **Jarocin** festival (July) which started life in the mid 1980s as an explicitly alternative event has since broadened its base to include a range of more "respectable" acts, though you'll still find the defiantly prickly Polish chapter of "Crass" anarchists out in force among the more sober-jeaned characters that dominate the audience.

CINEMA

Cinemas (*kino*) are cheap and generally rudimentary – Dolby sound systems are just beginning to filter through to the cities – and can be found in almost every town in Poland, however small, showing major international films (especially anything American) as well as the home-produced ones. Many foreign films are dubbed into Polish, though of late a welcome trend towards using subtitles has begun to develop. This month's listings are usually fly-posted up around town or outside each cinema. Titles are always translated into Polish, so you'll need to have your wits about you to identify films like *Milczenie Owiec* as *The Silence of the Lambs* or *Tańczący z Wilkami* as *Dancing with Wolves*. (The film's country of origin is usually shown – WB means British, USA American, N German.)

Based around the famous **Łódź film school** postwar Polish cinema has produced a string of important directors, the best known being **Andrzej Wajda**, whose powerful *Człowiek z Żelaza* ("Man of Iron") did much to popularise the cause of Solidarity abroad in the early 1980s. As in all the ex-communist countries the key issue for Polish film-makers used to be getting their work past the censors: for years they responded to the task of "saying without saying" with an imaginative blend of satire, metaphor and historically based parallelism whose subtle twists tend to leave even the informed Western viewer feeling a little perplexed. In the case of Wajda and other notables like **Agnieszka Holland**, **Krzysztof Zanussi** and **Krzysztof Kieślowski**,

though, a combination of strong scripting, characterisation and a subtle dramatic sense carries the day, and all these directors enjoy high prestige in international film circles.

Into the 1990s the picture looks a little different, concerns over the censor now replaced by the more conventional film-maker's headache of securing funding (whatever else the communists did wrong, they did, as some directors ruefully recall now, guarantee a level of film financing) and responding to a profoundly changed political and social reality. Early post-communist efforts like Kieslowski's award-winning *Veronica's Double Life* and Wajda's *Korczak* suggest an artistically productive future for Polish cinema.

THEATRE

Theatre in Poland is popular and still cheap (though less so than it used to be), and most towns with a decent-sized population have at least one permanent venue with the month's programme pinned up outside and elsewhere in the town. The serious stuff tends to go on in the often sumptuous *fin-de-siècle* creations established by the country's trio of Partition-era rulers – Hapsburg opulence if you're in Kraków, Russian-tolerated classicism in Warsaw, Prussian austerity in Gdańsk. Aside from the odd British or US touring company, there's little in English, though the generally high quality of Polish acting combined with the interest of the venues themselves – Poles go as much for the interval promenade as the show itself – usually makes for an enjoyable experience.

Theatre's special role in Polish cultural life dates from the Partitions-era, when it played a significant role in the maintenance of both the language and national consciousness. In recent decades **Jerzy Grotowski**'s experimental **Laboratory Theatre** in Wrocław (disbanded in 1982 when he emigrated to Italy) gained an international reputation as one of the most exciting and innovative trends in theatrical theory and practice to emerge since Stanislavsky's work in Moscow in the early part of this century. Theatre companies like the excellent **Teatr Ósmego Dnia** ("Theatre of the Eighth Day") from Poznań, who also moved to Italy subsequently, carried the torch through the trials of martial law in the early 1980s, developing a probing, politically engaged theatre that closely reflected the struggles of the period. Till his death in 1992 **Tadeusz Kantor**, an experimental director of international stature and long based in Kraków, was another figure at the creative forefront of contemporary Polish theatre. Among a handful of companies currently in demand internationally is **Gardziennice**, a consistently innovative experimental group based in a village near Lublin of the same name who specialise in field trips to villages throughout eastern Europe where oral cultural traditions are kept alive. The resulting productions, led by the company's founder and director Włodzimierz Staniewski, a close collaborator with Grotowski in the 1970s, are inspirational part-improvised, part-scripted happenings drawing on a wealth of dramatic resources.

GAYS AND LESBIANS

Although there are few telltale signs of a dynamic sub-culture emerging in post-communist Poland, life for **Polish gays and lesbians** is not as bleak as the featureless gay landscape might suggest. Unlike the grim juridical situation prevailing in much of the former Soviet Union, homosexuality is not proscribed under the provisions of Poland's 1963 criminal code. The statutory age of consent is 15, irrespective of the sexual orientation of the partners. Indeed, in this regard Polish **laws** governing sexual behaviour actually are relatively more liberal than those in Britain, where the age of consent for male homosexuals stands at 21, not to mention those in nearly half of the states in the USA whose sodomy statutes continue to outlaw gay sexual relations altogether. Polish gays and lesbians also are legally free to establish clubs and newspapers and all of the other paraphernalia sexual minorities seeking a voice in, say, New York or London employ.

For the gay and especially the lesbian visitor accustomed to the energetic lavender sub-cultures flourishing in cities in the United States, Britain and other western European countries, the **Polish gay scene** may seem a bit of a disappointment. A few soft-porn magazines (catering mostly to men) and other gay-oriented publications have begun to appear for sale in some shops and kiosks in recent years, but there are otherwise few visible traces of an active gay urban insurgency. The "scene" as such still remains largely subterranean (in some cases quite literally), and tends to be limited to clandestine cruising activities in such traditional locales as railway stations, parks and public toilets. **Visitors** to the major Polish cities should not expect to find a thriving gay nightlife oriented around discos and watering holes; one way into making contact with local gays and lesbians,

though, is to head for bars and cafés with reputations for attracting a mixed clientele or in a very few instances, with an explicitly gay profile (see "Listings" in the relevant city sections), though even here you should bear in mind that tracking down gay haunts in Poland is still most reliably accomplished on a word-of-mouth basis. Perhaps it's not surprising that there's a worryingly low prevailing level of "safe sex" and AIDS awareness in Polish society. (See also "Contraceptives" in "Directory" p.44). As in other homophobically inclined cultures, too, caution is generally the watchword – **gay-bashings** do occur outside places known to be frequented by homosexuals.

GAY ORGANISATIONS

Two organisations worth contacting before or during a visit to Poland are the Warsaw-based **Pink Service**, the country's only established agency for gays and lesbians, at ul. Mickiewicza 60 (☎334-672; office open Mon–Fri, 10am–4pm), which also welcomes foreign visitors. The Pink Service's activities include acting as an information resource for and about the Polish lesbian and gay scene, running an annual Gay Pride Day, publishing their own magazines – *Men* (for gays), *Arabella* (for lesbians) and an occasional English-language gay newsletter – as well as distributing international gay publications. The Poznań-based **Inaczej** Agency (PO Box 84, 61-255 Poznań 59) publish an annual *Gay Guide to Eastern Europe*: though the listings can be a bit hard to decode it's nevertheless a useful source of gay contacts and addresses in Poland and other countries in the region. For an inside perspective on the Polish **gay and lesbian scene** see *Contexts*, p. 542. For more on the **Polish Women's Movement**, see "Directory" overleaf.

POLICE AND TROUBLE

Nothing epitomises recent political change in Poland better than what's happened to the police. Gone now is the secret police structure and the *ZOMO*, the hated riot squads responsible for quelling the big demonstrations from martial law onwards. What's left is the *milicja*, or, as they've been diplomatically renamed now, the *policja*, who are responsible for everyday law enforcement.

Transforming the ethos of a force accustomed to operating outside the bounds of public control is a difficult task, and all in all the *policja* seem to be in a pretty demoralised state, with the entire force supposedly being put through retraining programmes. In common with other east European countries Poland has experienced a huge increase in crime over the last year, the police seemingly unable or unwilling to do much about it. Sales of alarms, small firearms and other security paraphernalia are on the increase, and residents of Warsaw's high-rise blocks have resorted to organising their own night watches to stem the flood of car break-ins.

TROUBLE

For Westerners, the biggest potential hassles are **hotel room thefts**, **pickpocketing** in the markets and **car break-ins**, though there has also been a recent spate of thefts on international trains, especially at night. Sensible precautions should include avoiding leaving cars unattended overnight anywhere in the city centres (larger hotels have guarded parking lots: *parking strzeżony*); keeping valuables on you at all times; and trying not to look conspicuously affluent. Your best and only protection ultimately is to take out travel insurance before you go, as the chances of getting your gear back are virtually zero.

On a bureaucratic level, Poles are still supposed to carry some form of **ID** with them: you should always keep your passport with you, even though you're unlikely to get stopped unless you're in a car; Western number plates provide the excuse for occasional unprovoked spot checks – particularly late at night, when the police tend to think you'll turn out to be a Pole travelling in a stolen vehicle.

SEXUAL HARASSMENT

Sexual harassment is less obviously present than in the West, but lack of familiarity with the cultural norms means it's easier to misinterpret situations, and rural Poland is still extremely conservative culturally: the further out you go, the more likely it is that women travelling alone will attract bemused stares.

Polish women tend to claim that men leave off as soon as you tell them to leave you alone, but this isn't always the case, particularly with anyone who's had a few drinks.

However, if you do encounter problems, you'll invariably find other Poles stepping in to help – the Polish people are renowned for their hospitality to strangers and will do much to make you feel welcome. The only particular places to avoid are the drinking haunts and hotel nightclubs, where plenty of men will assume you're a prostitute.

DIRECTORY

ADDRESSES The street name is always written before the number. The word for street (*ulica*, abbreviated to *ul.*) or avenue (*aleja*, abbreviated *al.*) is often missed out – for example ulica Senatorska is simply known as Senatorska. The other frequent abbreviation is *pl.*, short for *plac* (square). In towns and villages across the country, **street names** taking the stars and dates of Polish and international communism are slowly being replaced. Where a prewar name existed, that name is being reinstated, but with new streets there's much controversy over whether to use prewar names or to adopt new heroes (the pope – Jan Paweł II – being a chief contender). Figures on the way out include General Swierczewski, Nowotko, Marchlewski, Dzierżyński and the once-ubiquitous Lenin. See *Contexts* for details on the most common street names.

AIDS Though the exact figures are not known, Poland has the highest incidence of AIDS in eastern Europe. The Church's influence is something of a hindrance in combating the disease, but AIDS helplines are becoming established in the major cities.

BOTTLES All nationally produced drinks come in bottles which have a deposit on them. Shops will accept bottles from other outfits providing they stock the type you're trying to fob off on them.

CIGARETTES Most Polish brands are pretty bad. *Extra Mocne* are the cheapest – bonfire-smokey, highly damaging and popular; *Klubowe, Giewont*

and *Popularne* are similar; *Carmen* and *Caro* are more upmarket. Among imported brands, *Marlboro* and *Camel* lead the way. Matches are *zapałki*. Smoking is banned in all public buildings and on most public transport within towns.

CINEMA Western movies are released in Poland very soon after their UK or US release, and are usually dubbed, but sometimes subtitled.

CONTRACEPTIVES Polish-produced condoms (*prezerwatywa*) of uncertain quality are available from most kiosks and some chemists, though with Catholic mores in operation, many pharmacies are reticent to stock them. *Pewex* shops (see opposite) are a rather better bet, selling imported condoms, but it's wiser to bring your own.

DISABLED TRAVELLERS At the moment there is very little provision for disabled travellers in Poland, though lifts and escalators are becoming more common in public places.

ELECTRICITY is the standard continental 220 volts. Round two-pin plugs are used so you'll need to bring an adaptor.

EMBASSIES AND CONSULATES All foreign embassies are in Warsaw, though a number of countries maintain consulates in Gdańsk and Kraków. See respective listings for addresses.

EMERGENCIES Police ☎997; fire ☎998; ambulance ☎999.

FILM Domestic colour films are poor quality (and you may have problems getting them developed at home), but imported ones are widely available at the Western-style rapid-developing shops you can now find in many towns.

FOOTBALL Franz Beckenbauer described the Polish national side as "the best team in the world" in 1974, and in that year's World Cup – and the following two tournaments – Polish players such as Lato, Denya and Boniek became household names. Polish football is currently in the doldrums, though and they have no club sides to rank with Europe's best. Nonetheless, the top teams are still worth a look, producing football that is up to the standard of middle-order Premier Division stuff. The top team is Górnik Zabrze (14-times league champions), followed by GKS Katowice, Legia Warszawa, Ruch Chorzów and the two Łódź sides. The season lasts from August to November, then resumes in March until June.

"HARD CURRENCY" SHOPS A leftover from the bad old days before the złoty became convertible, *Pewex* shops are found in all major towns and in *Orbis* hotels; their big sellers are alcohol, tobacco, confectionery and perfumes – larger *Pewex* places may also sell electrical goods. Western goods are often cheaper here than back home, and they can be exported duty-free, provided all receipts are kept for customs. *Baltona* shops are less numerous and sell Western goods only. All shops take złotys and often other major currencies.

JAYWALKING is illegal and if caught you'll be fined on the spot.

LANGUAGE COURSES Summer Polish language schools are run by the universities of Kraków, Poznań, Lublin (KUL) and Łódź. Courses last from two to six weeks, covering all levels from beginners to advanced; a six-week course with full board and lodging will cost in the region of £350. Information on these courses can be obtained from the Polish Cultural Institute, 34 Portland Place, London W1N 4HQ (☎071/636 6032). One of the better private schools is in Sopot: *Sopocka Szkoła Języka Polskiego*, ul. Tatrzańska 4/56, 81-814 Sopot, Poland (☎058/510700). A four-week course costs around $US340, and the school arranges cheap accommodation.

LAUNDRY Launderettes (*pralnia*) exist in the major cities, but are very scarce, and will do service washes only. Elsewhere you can get things service washed in the more upmarket hotels. Dry cleaners – also *pralnia* – are far more numerous.

STUDENT CARDS Carrying an ISIC card (available from your student union or Campus Travel offices – see p.3) brings a host of reductions, most notably on train fares. It will also save you a few pence in admission fees to museums.

TAMPONS Sanitary towels (*podpaski higieniczne*) are cheap and available from some chemists; tampons (*tampony*) similarly suffer from supply problems and, though improving, are mostly poor quality – it's best to bring your own.

TIME Poland is generally one hour ahead of GMT and BST, and six hours ahead of EST. The clocks go forward as late as May and back again sometime during September – the exact date changes from year to year.

TOILETS Public toilets (*toalety*, *ubikacja* or *WC*) are few and far between (except in the biggest cities) and would win few design awards; restaurants or hotels are a better bet. Once in, you can buy toilet paper (by the sheet) and ask for use of the (yes, *the*) towel from the attendant, whom you also have to tip (signs usually indicate the amount). Only in the top-class hotels does toilet paper come free. Gents are marked ▼, ladies ●.

WOMEN'S MOVEMENT Following the demise of communism and concurrent with the growing ascendancy of Catholic mores in the country's social and political life, the status of **women** is on the political agenda – in particular, what many see as their treatment as second-class citizens. The biggest single cause of this is the heated debate about **abortion** sparked by government moves to criminalise abortion in all but the most exceptional circumstances, moves that have put Poland on a par with Eire in the regressive abortion legislation league. A feminist **women's movement** is weak at the popular level, ironically part of the reason being a widespread adverse reaction to campaigns for sexual equality as a relic of communist-era sloganeering. Women's groups currently campaigning on issues such as reproductive rights and abortion include the *Polish Feminist Association*, which has active chapters in Warsaw, Kraków, Poznań and Łódź, and the Polish Women's League (*Liga Kobiet Polskich*). The latter's contact address is: ul. Karowa 31, Warsaw 00 324 (☎48 22/26 88 25). For a perspective on women's situation in post-communist Poland see the piece by Małgorzata Tarasiewicz in *Contexts*, p. 539.

PART TWO

THE

GUIDE

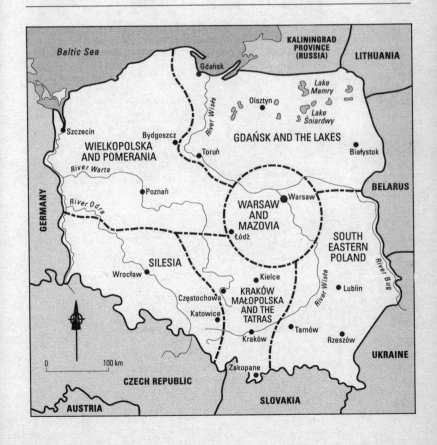

Baltic Sea

KALININGRAD
PROVINCE
(RUSSIA)

LITHUANIA

Gdańsk

Lake
Mamry

Olsztyn

Lake
Śniardwy

Szczecin

Bydgoszcz

River Wisła

GDAŃSK AND THE LAKES

Białystok

Toruń

WIELKOPOLSKA
AND POMERANIA

River Warta

BELARUS

Poznań

River Odra

WARSAW
AND
MAZOVIA

Warsaw

GERMANY

Łódź

SOUTH
EASTERN
POLAND

SILESIA

Kielce

Wrocław

River Wisła

River Bug

Lublin

Częstochowa

KRAKÓW
MAŁOPOLSKA
AND THE
TATRAS

Katowice

Tarnów

Kraków

Rzeszów

N

UKRAINE

0   100 km

Zakopane

CZECH REPUBLIC

AUSTRIA

SLOVAKIA

CHAPTER ONE

WARSAW AND MAZOVIA

Warsaw has two enduring points of definition: the Wisła River, running south to north across the Mazovian plains, and the Moscow–Berlin road, stretching across this terrain – and through the city – east to west. Such a location, and four hundred years of capital status, have ensured a history writ large with occupations and uprisings, intrigues and heroism. Warsaw's sufferings, its near-total obliteration in World War II and subsequent resurrection from the ashes, has lodged the city in the national consciousness and explains why an often ugly city is held in such affection. In the latest era of political struggle – the fall of communism, the emergence of Solidarity and the current democratic experiment – Warsaw has at times seemed overshadowed by events in Gdańsk and the industrial centres of the south, but its role has been a key one nonetheless, as a focus of popular and intellectual opposition to communism and the site of past and future power.

Likely to be most visitors' first experience of Poland, Warsaw makes an initial impression which is all too often negative. The years of communist rule have left no great aesthetic glories, and there's sometimes a hollowness to the faithful reconstructions of earlier eras. However, as throughout Poland, the pace of social change is tangible and fascinating, as the openings provided by the post-communist order turn the streets into a continuous marketplace. The once grey and tawdry state shopfronts of the city centre are giving way to colourful new private initiatives – the Benetton effect, as journalists would have it – while the postwar dearth of nightlife and entertainments is gradually becoming a complaint of the past, as a plethora of new bars, restaurants and clubs establish themselves.

Though the villages of **Mazovia** – *Mazowsze* in Polish – are the favoured summer abodes of wealthier Varsovians, these surrounding plains are historically one of the poorer regions of Poland, their peasant population eking a precarious existence from the notoriously infertile sandy soil. It is not the most arresting of landscapes, but contains a half-dozen rewarding day trips to ease your passage into the rural Polish experience. The **Kampinoski National Park** – spreading northwest of Warsaw – is the remnant of the primaeval forests that once covered this region, with tranquil villages dotted along its southern rim. A little further west is **Żelazowa Wola**, the much-visited birthplace of Chopin, and on the opposite side of the river, the historic church complex at Czerwińsk nad Wisła. **Łowicz** is well known as a centre of Mazovian folk culture, while the Radziwiłł palace at **Nieborów** is one of the finest and best-preserved aristocratic mansions in the country. Southwest of the capital lies industrial **Łódź**, the country's second city and an important cultural centre, while to the north there are historic old Mazovian centres, notably the market town of **Pułtusk**. Finally, fans of Secessionist art won't want to miss **Płock**, west along the river.

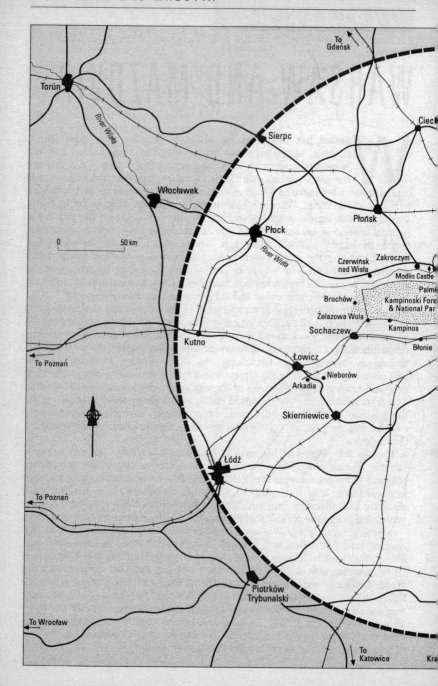

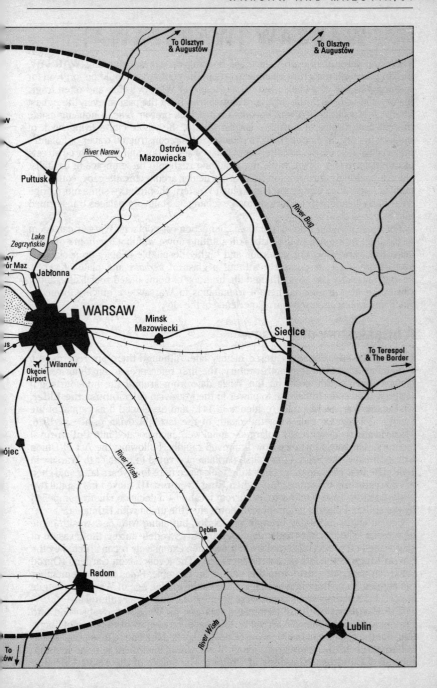

WARSAW (WARSZAWA)

Travelling through the grey, faceless housing estates surrounding **WARSAW**, walking through the grimy Stalinist tracts in the centre, you could be forgiven for wishing yourself elsewhere. But a knowledge of Warsaw's rich and often tragic history can transform the city, revealing voices from the past in even the ugliest quarters: a pockmarked wall becomes a precious prewar relic, a housing estate the one-time centre of Europe's largest ghetto, the whole city a living book of modern history. In among the concrete there are reconstructed traces of Poland's imperial past – a castle, a scattering of palaces and parks, and the restored streets of the historic Old Town, while the headlong rush into the embrace of capitalist culture is already throwing up its own particular architectural legacy, some of it familiar – towering skyscrapers and plush Western shopfronts – some more original – Party headquarters turned stock exchanges, Stalin-era palaces transformed into business centres.

For those arriving without personal connections or contacts, Warsaw can seem forbidding, with much of the place still shutting down within a few hours of darkness. But Varsovians are generous and highly hospitable people: no social call, even to an office, is complete without a glass of *herbata* and plate of cakes. Postwar austerity has strengthened the tradition of home-based socialising, and if you strike up a friendship here – friendships in Warsaw are quickly formed – you'll find much to enrich your experience of the city.

A brief history of Warsaw

For a capital city, Warsaw entered history late. Although there are records of a settlement here from the tenth century, the first references to anything resembling a town at this point on the Wisła date from around the mid-fourteenth century. It owes its initial rise to power to the Mazovian ruler **Janusz the Elder**, who made Warsaw his main residence in 1413 and developed it as capital of the Duchy of Mazovia. Following the death of the last Mazovian prince in 1526, Mazovia and its now greatly enlarged capital were incorporated into **Polish** royal territory. The city's fortunes now improved rapidly. Following the Act of Union with Lithuania, the Sejm – the Polish parliament – voted to transfer to Warsaw in 1569. The first election of a Polish king took place here four years later, and then in 1596 came the crowning glory, when **King Zygmunt III** moved his capital two hundred miles from Kraków to its current location – a decision chiefly compelled by the shift in Poland's geographical centre after the union with Lithuania.

Capital status inevitably brought prosperity, but along with new wealth came new perils. The city was badly damaged by the **Swedes** during the invasion of 1655 – the first of several assaults – and was then extensively reconstructed by the **Saxon kings** in the late seventeenth century. The lovely Saxon Gardens (Ogród Saski), in the centre, date from this period, for example. Poles tend to remember the eighteenth century in a nostalgic haze as the golden age of Warsaw, when its concert halls, theatres and salons were prominent in European cultural life.

The **Partitions** abruptly terminated this era, as Warsaw was absorbed into Prussia in 1795. Napoleon's arrival in 1806 gave Varsovians brief hopes of liberation, but the collapse of his Moscow campaign spelled the end of those hopes, and following the 1815 Congress of Vienna, Warsaw was integrated into the Russian-controlled **Congress Kingdom of Poland**. The failure of the **1830 Uprising**

INTERNATIONAL CONNECTIONS

Trains
The central train station serves all international routes and the major national ones – Poznań, Kraków, Gdańsk, Lublin etc. Northbound trains also stop at Warszawa Gdańska (ul. Buczka 4), west- and southbound at Dworzec Zachodni (ul. Towarowa 1), eastbound at Dworzec Wschodnia (ul. Lubelska 1). Śródmiescie station, just east of the central station, handles local traffic – Łowicz, Pruszkow, Skierniewice etc.

Tickets
For **international tickets**, booking at least 24 hours in advance is highly advisable, not least because of the long queues you're likely to have to deal with. An alternative to long queues at the station's *kasa mijdzynarodowa* (international counters), which are upstairs on the second floor, is to book at Orbis offices, and the same goes for domestic tickets; the offices at ul. Bracka 16, pl. Konstytucji 4, ul. Swiitojańska 23/25 and upstairs in the *Metropol* hotel on Marszałkowska all sell international and domestic tickets. The *Wagon Lits Tourisme* office, Nowy Qwiat, sells tickets for western European destinations.

Bus departures and tickets
The main **bus station**, Dworzec Centralny Warszawa Zachodni, out west on al. Jerozolimskie, is for all international departures and for major national destinations south and west. Dworzec Stadion, next to the Praga train station on the line from Dw. Sródmiescie, is for northern and eastern destinations. International and advance **bus tickets** to all destinations are available from the main station, from the Orbis office at ul. Puławska 43 (Mon–Fri 9am–4pm) and from the PKS bureau at ul. Yurawia 26. National bus tickets are available at the appropriate station or from the Syrena office at ul. Krucza 16/22.

brought severe reprisals: Warsaw was relegated to the status of "provincial town" and all Polish institutes and places of learning were closed. It was only with the outbreak of **World War I** that Russian control began to crumble, and late in 1914 the **Germans** occupied the city, remaining to the end of the war.

Following the return of Polish independence, Warsaw reverted to its position as capital; but then, with the outbreak of **World War II**, came the progressive annihilation of the city. The Nazi assault in September 1939 was followed by round-ups, executions and deportations – savagery directed above all at the Jewish community, who were crammed into a tiny ghetto area and forced to live on a near-starvation diet. It was the Jews who instigated the first open revolt, the **Ghetto Uprising** of April 1943, which resulted in the wholesale destruction of the ancient Warsaw Jewry.

As the war progressed and the wave of German defeats on the eastern front provoked a tightening of the Nazi grip on Warsaw, **resistance** stiffened in the city. In August 1944 virtually the whole civilian population participated in the **Warsaw Uprising**, an attempt both to liberate the city and ensure the emergence of an independent Poland. It failed on both counts. Hitler, infuriated by the resistance, ordered the total elimination of Warsaw and, with the surviving populace driven out of the city, the SS systematically destroyed the remaining buildings. In one of his final speeches to the Reichstag, Hitler was able to claim with

WARSAW

0   500m   1 km

Powązki Cemetery

MARIANA BUCZKA

To Żoliborz and Gdańsk

Citadel

NOWE MIASTO

OLD TOWN (STARE MIASTO)

Umschlagplatz Monument

Żob Bunker Site

UL. MIŁA

UL. ZAMENHOFA

AL. GEN. W. ANDERSA

Ghetto Monument

UL. ANIELEWICZA

St John's Cathedra

OKOPOWA

AL. JANA PAWŁA II

Jewish Cemetery

MURANOW

GHETTO AREA

AL. SOLIDARNOŚCI

AL. SOLIDARNOŚCI

See City Centre Map

Saxon Garden

Orbis

Hala Mirowska

Lutheran Church

MARSZAŁKOWSKA

Nożyk Synagogue

MIRÓW

UL. GRZYBOWSKA

Post Office

Jewish Theatre

ŚWIĘTOKRZYSKA

Filharmoni

TOWAROWA

PL. DEFILAD

EMILII PLATER

Palace of Culture

Central Station

LOT Building

To Bus Station & West Station

AL. JEROZOLIMSKIE

UL. NOWOGRODZKA

CHAŁUPIN

Marriott Hotel

Operetta

To Kraków

UL. KOSZYKOWA

OCHOTA

Polytechnic

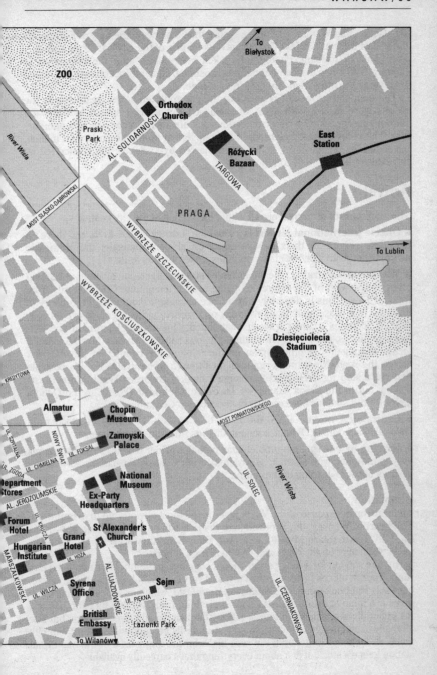

ZOO

Orthodox
Church

Praski
Park

AL. SOLIDARNOŚCI

River Wisła

MOST ŚLĄSKO-DĄBROWSKI

To
Białystok

Różycki
Bazaar

TARGOWA

East
Station

PRAGA

WYBRZEŻE SZCZECIŃSKIE

To Lublin

WYBRZEŻE KOŚCIUSZKOWSKIE

Dziesięciolecia
Stadium

KREDYTOWA

Almatur

Chopin
Museum

Zamoyski
Palace

UL. SPITALNA

NOWY ŚWIAT

UL. FOKSAL

MOST PONIATOWSKIEGO

UL. ZGODA

UL. CHMIELNA

National
Museum

Department
Stores

AL. JEROZOLIMSKIE

Ex-Party
Headquarters

UL. SOLEC

River Wisła

Forum
Hotel

UL. KRUCZA

St Alexander's
Church

Grand
Hotel

Hungarian
Institute

MARSZAŁKOWSKA

UL. HOŻA

AL. UJAZDOWSKIE

UL. CZERNIAKOWSKA

Syrena
Office

Sejm

UL. WILCZA

UL. PIĘKNA

British
Embassy

Łazienki Park

To Wilanów

satisfaction that Warsaw was now no more than a name on the map of Europe. By the end of the war 850,000 Varsovians – two-thirds of the city's 1939 population – were dead or missing. Photographs taken immediately after the **liberation** in January 1945 show a scene not unlike Hiroshima: General Eisenhower described Warsaw as the most tragic thing he'd ever seen.

The momentous task of **rebuilding** the city took ten years. Aesthetically the results were mixed, with acres of socialist functionalism spread between the Baroque palaces, but it was a tremendous feat of national reconstruction nonetheless. The recovery that has brought the population up to one and a half million, exceeding its prewar level, is, however, marred by a silence: the silence left by the exterminated Jewish community.

Arrival

The main **points of arrival** are all within easy reach of the city centre.

● **Okęcie international airport** is a half-hour journey by bus #175, and there's a *LOT* bus service to their new terminal on al. Jerozolimskie; the **domestic airport** (Lotnisko Krajowe) is ten minutes closer, on bus route #114.

● **Warszawa Centralna**, the main **train station**, hang-out of dubious-looking touts, is just west of the central shopping area, a ten-minute #175 bus ride from the Old Town. This is definitely **not** a place to hang around at night: robbery of unsuspecting passengers is an everyday occurrence, so keep a close eye on your gear at all times – never leave it unattended. Queues are lengthy at the **left-luggage** offices, particularly in summer; if you're lucky you may be able to get a locker downstairs. Another option is the left-luggage counter in the *Marriott* across the road. Most trains run straight through to Centralna but it's possible that you'll stop (or even need to change trains) at **Dworzec Wschodnia** (East) station, out in the Praga suburb, or **Dworzec Zachodni** (West), in the Ochota district. Both stations have regular connections to Centralna.

● **Centralny Dworzec PKS**, the main **bus station**, is across the road from Dworzec Zachodni in Ochota, a ten-minute bus ride into the city centre.

● **Arriving by car** isn't too problematic: potholes aside, Warsaw's road system is easy to navigate, with all the major routes – from Gdańsk, Poznań, Kraków or the Belarus border – leading to the centre.

Orientation

The wide open expanse of the Wisła River is the most obvious aid to **orientation**. The heart of Warsaw, the **Śródmieście** district, sits on the left bank; above it is the **Old Town** (Stare Miasto) area, with **plac Zamkowy** a useful central reference, while over on the east bank lies the **Praga** suburb.

Anyone staying for a long period should consider getting hold of a detailed **city map**. Tourist offices hand out town plans of varying quality, but the thing to look out for is the book-format *Warszawa – plan miasta*, which as well as having clear maps is a mine of useful addresses for everything from restaurants to embassies. It's generally available from tourist offices, bookshops and street sellers, but like all really useful things in Poland could just as easily be impossible to find. For city maps, as for maps in general, the *ruch* kiosk on the lower level of the main train station keeps a stock of just about everything that's currently available.

GETTING INTO TOWN FROM THE AIRPORT

The brand new, hi-tech international terminal (*lotnisko mijdzynarodowe*) at **Okęcie airport** is a half-hour journey (buses #175, #188 and #488) from the city centre. From the old **domestic airport** (*lotnisko krajowe*) just up the road, take bus #114 into town. In addition, **LOT** run a bus service (cost currently around £1) to their new terminal on al. Jerozolimskie, which also drops people off at the major centre-town hotels. The city's notorious **taxi drivers** are at their worst at the airport – even the officially registered ones may well try to sting you for upwards of £10 for the ride into town. Settle the price (which shouldn't be more than around £5 at current rates) *before* setting off. The cheapest way of getting a taxi into town is to order one from **Radio Taxi** (☎919) – they usually turn up within ten minutes, and also currently charge a fare multiple below the usual rate (see overleaf).

Information

For general practical **information** the place to head for is the *Informator Turystyczny* (IT) office on plac Zamkowy (8am–6pm; ☎635-1881). Service is gradually improving, though you can't always count on staff being multilingual. There are rudimentary information desks in the airport arrivals lounge and the central station. The Orbis office at the corner of Królewska and Marszałkowska has an information desk (that's often crowded), and most of the big hotels have IT points too.

The growing influx of Western tourists has resulted in a couple of English-language **publications** directly aimed at visitors: *Welcome to Warsaw* and *Warsaw: What Where When?* (the latter also in German) are both glossy, advertising-based magazines with a useful set of current listings and general information. You can pick them up (free) at the airport and in the lobbies of the more upmarket hotels. Equally informative and less obviously commercially biased is the weekly English-language newspaper *Warsaw Voice* (see *Basics*), which you can buy at hotels and many kiosks around town. For really comprehensive listings, you can't beat the local weekend editions of *Gazeta Wyborcza* and *Zycie Warszawy*, particularly useful for a stop-press on films and concerts around town.

Getting around

Bus and **tram** are the main forms of city transport, and even after the big price rises of the early 1990s, both are still very cheap for foreigners. They get very crowded at peak hours but services are remarkably punctual. Trams are best for short hops around the centre. Regular bus and tram routes close down about midnight; from 11pm to 5am **night buses** leave from behind the Palace of Culture on ul. Emilii Plater at 17 and 47 minutes past the hour; tickets can be bought from the driver.

Tickets

Tickets (*bilety*) for both trams and buses are bought from *ruch* counters (not from drivers) displaying the MZK logo, or from street sellers, normally in batches of ten or twenty, and currently cost 4000zł. each – but prices will certainly go up. For buses or trams numbered #1–199 you need one ticket, for #400–599 and *pospieszne* (speed) buses marked A–U you need two, and for night buses (#600 and up) three.

Punch your tickets in the machines on board – pleas of ignorance don't cut much ice with inspectors, who'll fine you at least 150,000zł. on the spot if they catch you without a validated ticket.

Taxis

For Poles, recurrent price increases have made **taxis** a luxury, though for Westerners they're still reasonable – and easy to get. In a reversal of twenty years' established practice, taxis now queue for customers at the main taxi stops, not vice versa. That said, you need to be aware that an alarming proportion of the post-communist brand of Warsaw cab driver are little more than licensed bandits, who'll take every opportunity to rip off anyone they sense doesn't know the ropes – and even many that do.

Make sure the **meter** has been turned on when you set off: the fare is currently the price displayed multiplied by (at last count) 500; there should be a little sign giving the present multiple. Some taxis operate a different **multiple system** – 10 on the meter equals 10,000 zloty is a common one now – often deliberately calculated, you suspect, to confuse people, making a rip-off that much easier to carry off. Especially at night, or from hotels, the airport and the train station you should be prepared to deal with the drivers who will try to get away with charging you well above the going rate: knowing what you ought to be paying – hotel reception desks, IT points or friendly locals can usually help out – is always a good starter, but in the worst cases you may have to resign to paying up.

Radio taxis (☎919), now joined by the privately run *Supertaxi* (☎9622), are pretty reliable, though sometimes hard to get hold of at night. The former has the advantage of the cheapest fares on offer. If you really need to be sure of getting a taxi you can usually order cabs a day in advance.

The Metro

At the time of writing, a north–south Warsaw **metro** is under construction. The government's current austerity programme, however, means there's little chance of it being finished before the mid-1990s, if at all.

The Warsaw telephone code is ☎022 for six-digit numbers, ☎02 for seven digits.

Accommodation

The sunsequent listings give a pretty comprehensive rundown of the accommodation available in the city area: hotels, hostels, private rooms and even a couple of campsites. The lack of cheap, decent-quality hotel accommodation makes renting a private room a particularly attractive option.

As mentioned earlier, finding an office or information point in town to help you make a **reservation** is hard work – the queues, at the airport and train station information desks especially, can be forbidding. The best bets for hotel bookings are the reception of the *Grand* hotel, ul. Krucza 28 (☎294-051), which can help with Orbis places, and the Syrena office, ul. Krucza 16/22 (☎217-864 or ☎628-7540), which handles Syrena-run hotels, as well as private room bookings (see overleaf). Otherwise it's a case of phoning or calling in person – staff in larger hotels usually speak English or German.

Hotels

The only way to ensure a hotel room in season is to book before coming: in summer even the biggest hotels can be booked out solidly for weeks in a row. Rooms in the moderate-to-expensive categories will have a bathroom, and normally include breakfast in the price. Prices have stabilised recently, but inflation means they're still rising noticeably each year.

CHEAPER HOTELS AND PENSIONS

Places at the bottom end of the scale vary a lot in quality and accessibility. At around £10–20 a night, though, these are about the only places, apart from hostels, that most Poles can afford. Consequently, getting a bed can be tricky, especially in summer – and be aware that the three sports-stadium hotels listed at the end of this section are a long way out of town.

ZNP ("Teacher's Hotel"), Wybrzeże Kościuszki 33 (☎262-600). Near the waterfront, a short walk down from Nowy Świat; takes non-teachers when rooms are free – more likely in term time than not. A good budget option.

PTTK Dom Turysty, Krakowskie Przedmieście 4/6 (☎263-011/260-071). Located just below the university campus. A step down in quality, offering doubles but messy communal bathrooms and toilets.

Druh, ul. Niemcewicza 17 (☎6590-011). West of the main station off Puławska. Dingy hotel, popular with students – a marginally more attractive option than the *Dom Turysty*; tram #7, #8, #9 or #25.

Pensjonat Stegny, ul. Inspektowa 4 (☎422-768). A sports-stadium hotel, on the way to Wilanów. Three-bedded rooms, camping nearby. Bus #116, #195.

Skra, ul. Wawelska 5 (☎255-100). Sited next to the Skra stadium in Ochota; bus #167, #187 or #188.

Orzel, ul. Podskarbińska 11/15 (☎105-060). By another stadium in southern Praga; bus #102 or #115.

Additionally, a number of former workers' hotels and other previously state-run ventures are starting to open up to tourists – check with the main IT for the latest details.

Garnizonowy, ul. Mazowiecka 10 (☎309-3565). Centrally located former soldier's overnighter.

Gwardia, ul. Racławicka 132 (☎446-274). Another cheap sports hotel, in the southern Rakowiec district.

Ikar, Nowoursynowska 161 (☎472-903). Cheapish, comfortable student hotel well south of the centre in Wilanów – Wilanów buses pass close by.

ZNP ul. Targowiecka 55 (☎6102-535). Another cheap teachers' hostel, this time well out in the eastern Praga district.

Riviera-Remont, ul. Waryńskiego 12 (☎257-497). Cheap student hotel off the southern end of Marszałkowska. Triple rooms only.

MODERATE

In contrast to the posher hotels, of which a whole host have sprung up in recent years, smaller, moderately priced hotels in the £20–40 range remain an underdeveloped category of accommodation in the capital – a pity, since the city could use a few more smaller, decent-quality places of this type.

Maria, al. Jana Pawła II 71 (☎383-840). Small, privately (and well) run hotel on northern side of the city. Deservedly popular in summer, so booking ahead may be a good idea.

Boss, ul. Żwanowiecka 20 (☎129-953). Cosy, quietly situated hotel on the rural southeastern outskirts of the city. Bus #C passes close by. Nice restaurant too.

Na Wodzie, ul. Zamoyskiego 2 (☎194-012 ext. 59). Converted river boat moored on the Wisła near the East station (Dworzec Wschodnią). Doubles and triples, plus a small breakfast restaurant.

Dom Chłopa, pl. Powstanców Warszawy 2 (☎279-251). Used by a wider clientele than its name (Farmers' House) suggests.

Nowa Praga, ul. Brechta 7 (☎195-051). Humdrum place at the cheaper end of the scale – and way out to the east in Praga; any bus going over the Śląsko-Dąbrowski bridge takes you nearby.

Syrena, ul. Syreny 23 (☎328-297). This time well out to the west of town; still, there's generally a good chance of a room here if all else fails.

Saski, pl. Bankowy 1 (☎201-115). The cheapest and nicest of the bunch, well located just off Saski Park, with decent rooms and plenty of character. Only drawback is the occasional legions of Russian mafia types.

Warszawa, pl. Powstańców Warszawy 9 (☎269-421). Just off Świętokrzyska; popular with East European tourist groups.

Polonia, al. Jerozolimskie 45 (☎628-7241). Just round the corner from the similar *Metropol* (see below), but noisier. Top end of the scale.

Metropol, Marszałkowska 99a (☎294-001). Sited within easy walking distance of the Central station, which means this is often full. Book ahead if possible.

MDM, pl. Konstytucji 1 (☎216-211). Rooms here are quieter and pleasanter (though also pricier) than its location and external appearance might suggest.

UPMARKET

Upmarket hotels are quite a growth sector in Warsaw, a by-product of the government's drive to attract Western capital. Prices of £100 and upwards for double rooms are now standard for the top-bracket international hotels (the last four in this list); for the rest (again in ascending order of price), count on around £50–70.

Novotel, ul. 1 Sierpnia 1 (☎464-051). Motel with swimming pool, close to the airport.

Grand, ul. Krucza 28 (☎294-051). One of a string of drab Orbis places – the advantage of this one being its relatively central location. Lively bar and billiards room upstairs.

Solec, ul. Zagórna 1 (☎259-241). Another unexciting Orbis hotel, located south of the centre, near the river.

Vera, Boh. Bitwy Warszawskiej 1920r 16 (☎227-421). Ditto, this time just down from the bus station.

Zajazd Napoleoński, ul. Plowiecka 83 (☎153-068). Small luxury inn reputedly frequented by Napoleon, well out of the centre in the Praga district.

Europejski, Krakowskie Przedmieście 13 (☎265-051). Across from the *Victoria*. The shabbiness of this nineteenth-century building makes it one of the more appealing upper-bracket hotels.

Victoria, ul. Królewska 11 (☎279-271). Traditional favourite with businesspeople, journalists and upmarket tourist groups; overlooking plac Piłsudskiego.

Forum, ul. Nowogrodzka 24/26 (☎210-271). Skyscraper haunt of Orbis package tours, on the corner of busy Marszałkowska and al. Jerozolimskie. Good views over the city.

Bristol, Krakowskie Przedmieście 42/44 (☎625-2525). Legendary prewar hotel recently reopened under Trust House Forte auspices after complete overhaul. As swish – and expensive – as they come.

Jan Sobieski, pl. Artura Zawiszy (☎221-265/658-444). Glamorous new Austrian-backed hotel in Ochota, west of the Central station – the wacky exterior colour remains a local source of contention.

Holiday Inn, ul. Złota 2 (☎220-341). Similar ethos, also within striking distance of the Central station.

Marriot, al. Jerozolimskie 65/79 (☎630-6306). Top of the pile, in terms of price; and a casino for the jet set too.

Hostels and student hotels

Warsaw has two **IYHF hostels**. At either, you have to be out of the building from 10am to 5pm and reception is from 5 to 9pm. The one at **ul. Smolna 30** (☎278-952) is on the fourth floor of a grey concrete building just a five-minute bus ride along al. Jerozolimskie from the main station – any bus heading towards Nowy Świat will drop you at the corner of the street. Predictably, the central location means it gets very crowded in summer. The other one, at **ul. Karolkowa 53a** (☎328-829), is further out in the western Wola district – take tram #1, 13, 20, or #24 north from the main station towards the Mirów district and get off on al. Solidarności, near the *Wola* department store. It's less likely to be full, but don't bank on it. Additionally, there's a smallish summer-only (April 15–Sept 30) hostel at ul. Miedzyparkowa 46 (☎236-242) not far from the Gdańsk railway station, on the edge of the northern Żoliborz district. Check in is between 5pm and 10pm.

During July and August the Almatur-run **international student hotels** are another inexpensive possibility. The Almatur office at ul. Kopernika 15 (☎262-356) has current location details and the required vouchers for those who haven't bought them beforehand (see *Basics*). Reservations for the 2–4-person rooms aren't needed as long as you get there before 2pm.

Private rooms

The main source of information for **private rooms** is Syrena's often grumpy *biuro kwatery prywatnych* office, ul. Krucza 16/22 (☎628-7450/217-864), a fifteen-minute walk east from the train station, just down from the *Grand* hotel. It's open Monday to Saturday from 8am to 7.30pm, but get there as early as possible – finding anything after 4pm is pushing your luck. Check locations carefully, as you may well be offered something on the far edge of the city: showers are included in each room.

Until recently the only alternative to the Syrena office was to trust one of the eager individuals touting rooms at the train station and other tourist haunts. All this has changed now and a number of privately run bureaux are now functioning, the most reliable of which is the *Romeo and Juliet*, on the third floor at Emilii Plater 30, across al. Jerozolimskie from the main station (Mon–Sat 9am–7pm; ☎292-993). The English-speaking proprietor guarantees to find you a decent-quality room inside central Warsaw, with a telephone; prices – dollars only – work out similar to those at the Syrena office, at about £10–15 for a double.

Campsites

Even in Warsaw camping is extremely cheap and popular, with Poles and foreigners alike. On the whole, site facilities are reasonable too.

Camping Gromada, ul. Zwirki i Wigury 32 (☎254-391). Best and most popular of the Warsaw campsites, on the way out to the airport – bus #128, #136 or #175 will get you there. As well as tent space the site has a number of cheap bungalows – though these are often all spoken for.

Wisła, Boh. Bitwy Warszawskiej 1920r. 15/17 (☎233-748). Just south of the bus station – take bus #154. Less crowded than the *Gromada* site. Some bungalows too.

PTTK Camping, ul. Połczyńska 6a. (☎366-716). Out in the Wola district.

Turysta, ul. Grochowska 1. (☎6106-364). Quite a distance out of town on the road to Terespol, useful if you're making an early morning start for the border.

Stegny, Next to the *Pensjonat* Stegny; see p.59 for details.

The City

Wending its way north towards Gdańsk and the Baltic Sea, the **Wisła** River divides Warsaw neatly in half: the main sights are located on the western bank, the eastern consisting predominantly of residential and business districts. Somewhat to the north of the centre, the busy **Old Town (Stare Miasto)** provides the historic focal point. Rebuilt from scratch after the war, like most of Warsaw, the magnificent **Royal Castle**, ancient **St John's Cathedral** and the **Old Town Square** are the most striking examples of the capital's reconstruction. Baroque churches and the former palaces of the aristocracy line the streets west of the ring of defensive walls and to the north in the quietly atmospheric **New Town (Nowe Miasto)**.

West of the Old Town, in the **Muranów** and **Mirów** districts, is the former **Ghetto** area, where the Nożyck Synagogue and the ul. Okopowa cemetery bear poignant testimony to the lost Jewish population. South from the Old Town lies **Śródmieście**, the city's commercial centre, its skyline dominated by the Palace of Culture, Stalin's permanent legacy to the citizens of Warsaw. Linking the Old Town and Sródmiescie, **Krakowskie Przedmieście** is dotted with palaces and Baroque spires, and forms the first leg of the **Royal Way**, a procession of open boulevards stretching all the way from plac Zamkowy to the stately king's residence at **Wilanów** on the southern outskirts of the city. Along the way is **Łazienki Park**, one of Warsaw's many delightful green spaces and the setting for the charming **Łazienki Palace**, the so-called "palace on the water".

Further out, the city becomes a welter of high-rise developments, but among them historic suburbs like **Żoliborz** and **Praga** – on the east side of the river – give a flavour of the authentic life of contemporary Warsaw.

The Old Town (Stare Miasto)

The title "Old Town" – Stare Miasto – is in some respects a misnomer for the historic nucleus of Warsaw. Forty-five years ago this compact network of streets and alleyways lay in rubble: even the cobblestones are meticulously assembled replacements. Yet surveying the tiered houses of the main square, for example, it's hard to believe they've been here only decades. Some older residents even claim that the restored version is in some respects an improvement.

Plac Zamkowy (Castle Square), on the south side of the Old Town, is the obvious place to start a tour. Here the first thing to catch your eye is the bronze **statue** of Zygmunt III Waza, the king who made Warsaw the capital. Installed on his column in 1640, Zygmunt suffered a direct hit from a tank in September 1944, but has now been replaced on his lookout; the base, these days, is a popular and convenient rendezvous point.

The Royal Castle

On the east side of the square is the former **Royal Castle** (Zamek Królewski), once home of the royal family and seat of the Polish parliament, now the **Castle Museum** (guided tours Tues–Sun 10am–4pm; last admission 3pm). Dynamited by German troops in the aftermath of the Warsaw Uprising, the seventeenth-century castle was rebuilt as recently as the 1970s. In July 1974 a huge crowd gathered to witness the clock of the domed Zygmunt tower starting

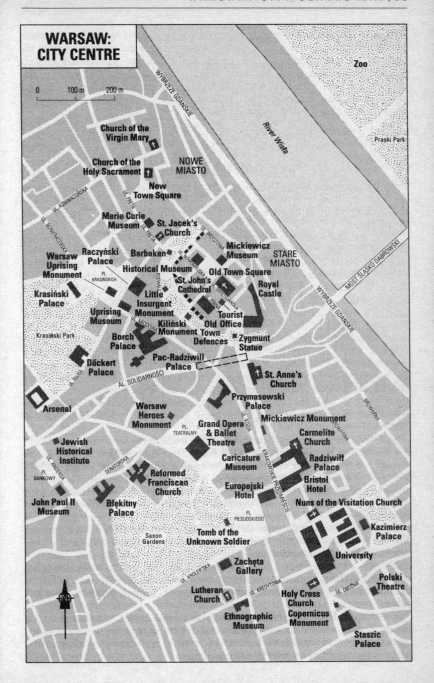

WARSAW: CITY CENTRE

0 100 m 200 m

Zoo

Praski Park

River Wista

WYBRZEŻE GDAŃSKIE

Church of the Virgin Mary

Church of the Holy Sacrament

NOWE MIASTO

New Town Square

UL. KONWIKTORSKA

UL. BONIFRATERSKA

UL. FRETA

Marie Curie Museum

St. Jacek's Church

UL. FRETA

Mickiewicz Museum

STARE MIASTO

Warsaw Uprising Monument

Raczyński Palace

Barbakan

Historical Museum

PL. KRASIŃSKICH

Old Town Square

Krasiński Palace

Little Insurgent Monument

St. John's Cathedral

Royal Castle

Uprising Museum

Kiliński Monument

Tourist Old Office

Krasiński Park

Borch Palace

Town Defences

Zygmunt Statue

Dückert Palace

Pac-Radziwill Palace

AL. SOLIDARNOŚCI

St. Anne's Church

Arsenal

Warsaw Heroes Monument

Przymasowski Palace

Mickiewicz Monument

PL. TEATRALNY

Grand Opera & Ballet Theatre

Carmelite Church

Jewish Historical Institute

Caricature Museum

Radziwiłł Palace

UL. ANDERSA

SENATORSKA

Reformed Franciscan Church

Bristol Hotel

PL. BANKOWY

Europejski Hotel

Nuns of the Visitation Church

John Paul II Museum

Błękitny Palace

KRAKOWSKIE PRZEDMIEŚCIE

PL. PIŁSUDSKIEGO

Saxon Gardens

Tomb of the Unknown Soldier

Kazimierz Palace

University

Zachęta Gallery

Polski Theatre

UL. KRÓLEWSKA

Lutheran Church

UL. KREDYTOWA

Holy Cross Church

UL. OBOŹNA

Ethnographic Museum

Copernicus Monument

Staszic Palace

MOST ŚLĄSKO DĄBROWSKI

WYBRZEŻE GDAŃSKIE

BROWARNA

UL. MIODOWA

UL. DŁUGA

UL. KOZIA

up again – the hands set exactly where they were stopped by the first Luftwaffe attack. Attachment to a crucial symbol of independent nationhood explains the resurrected magnificence of the castle: the rebuilding was almost entirely financed by private donations from Poles – from all over the world – and hundreds of volunteers helped with the labour. Though the structure is a replica, many of its furnishings are the originals, scooted into hiding by percipient employees during the first bombing raids.

Entry is through the Senatorial Gate and a vaulted hallway that's always bustling with tourist groups. During the summer months, the obligatory guided tours are often heavily booked up, so buy your tickets in advance if possible; failing that, get here well before opening time and join the queue. The first part of the set tour takes you through the **Jagiellonian Rooms**, overlooking the river from the northeast wing. Originally part of the residence of Zygmunt August, they are adorned with portraits of the Jagiellonian royal families and some outstanding Flemish tapestries, including the ominously titled *Tragedy of the Jewish People*.

Next are the chambers where the Sejm – the parliament – used to meet. Beyond the chancellery, which features more tapestries and portraits of the last dukes of Mazovia, comes the **Chamber of Deputies**, formerly the debating chamber. During parliamentary sessions, the deputies sat on benches on the left side of the chamber, with the Speaker in the centre of the room, while members of the public could stand and listen on the right-hand side. Democracy as practised here was something of a mixed blessing. On the one hand, the founding decree of the Polish Commonwealth, hammered out here in 1573, demonstrated an exceptionally tolerant attitude to religious differences; on the other, it was also here that the principle of *liberum veto* – unanimity as a prerequisite for the passing of new laws – was established in 1652, often seen as the beginning of the end of effective government in Poland. Arguably the Sejm's finest hour, however, came precisely at the moment when political developments threatened it and the country's very existence: the famous **Third May Constitution,** passed here in 1791, being one of the radical highpoints of European constitutional history.

The seventeenth-century **Grand Staircase** leads to the most lavish section of the castle, the **Royal Apartments of King Stanisław August**. Through two smaller rooms you come eventually to the magnificent **Canaletto Room**, with its views of Warsaw by Bernardo Bellotto, a nephew of the famous Canaletto – whose name he appropriated to make his pictures sell better. Marvellous in their detail, these cityscapes provided important information for the architects involved in rebuilding the city after the war. Next door is the richly decorated **Royal Chapel**, where an urn contains the heart – sacred to many Poles – of Tadeusz Kościuszko, swashbuckling leader of the 1794 insurrection and hero of the American War of Independence. Like many other rooms on this floor, the **Audience Chamber** has a beautiful parquet floor as well as several original furnishings. The four pictures on display here are by Bacciarelli, court painter to Stanisław August, symbolise the cardinal virtues of Courage, Wisdom, Piety and Justice.

The **King's Bedroom**, another lavishly decorated set-up, is followed by the **Study Room**, where Napoleon is supposed to have slept during his short stay – apparently he had Stanisław's bed moved in here, not wishing to sleep in the bedroom occupied so recently by a deposed ruler.

From here you proceed through to the reception rooms, where the **Marble Room** is dominated by portraits of the twenty-two Polish monarchs, including a much-reproduced portrait of Stanisław August in his coronation robes. Highlight of the parade of royal splendour is the **Ball Room**, the largest room in the castle, with its aptly titled ceiling allegory by Bacciarelli, *The Dissolution of Chaos*. Napoleon met the elite of Warsaw society here in 1806, the occasion on which he made his comments (legendary in Poland) about the beauty of Polish women – his mistress-to-be Countess Maria Walewska included, presumably.

The final leg of the tour – which for the less than obsessionally interested can, by this stage, feel something of an endurance test – is a climb to the upper part of the **north wing**, where paintings by Matejko invest key moments of Polish history with romantic fervour. *Rejtan* shows a deputy blocking the path of a group of deputies preparing to accept the First Partition, imploring them to kill him rather than Poland, while *The Third of May Constitution* celebrates an enlightened moment – the declaration of one of the first democratic constitutions in Europe – in a similarly intense vein.

North of the castle

Shops, bars, restaurants and impromptu pavement stalls line **Piwna** and **Swiętojańska**, the two narrow cobbled streets leading northwards from plac Zamkowy. There's a lot of junk about, but occasional nuggets too, especially in the record and book shops. Each street has a church worth a stop-off as well. On Piwna there's **St Martin's**, a fourteenth-century structure whose Baroque interior was carefully restored after the war; amongst those buried here is Adam Jarzębski, king's musician and author of the first guide to Warsaw – written in verse.

On Swiętojańska is the entrance to **St John's Cathedral** (*Archikatedra św. Jana*), the main city church, an early fourteenth-century structure built on the site of an earlier wooden shrine and subsequently remodeled in the local Mazovian Gothic style. Some of the bitterest fighting of the 1944 Warsaw Uprising took place around here – German tanks entered the church after destroying its southern side, and you can still see sections of their caterpillar tracks built into the wall along ul. Dziekania – and after the war a lot of money was invested in rebuilding the cathedral in its original brick Gothic style.

For all the hard work, though, the cathedral's a bare, rather cold sort of place, interest mainly provided by the tombstones of the Dukes of Mazovia and a number of famous Poles lodged in the crypt, notably Nobel-prize winning writer **Henryk Sienkiewicz**, former Primate of Poland **Cardinal Wyszyński** and, the most recent addition, former pianist and prime minister **Ignacy Paderewski** whose remains were installed here amidst much ceremony in July 1992 in the presence of presidents Lech Wałesa and George Bush during the ex-US leader's last visit to the country – a fulfilment of the exile Paderewski's last wish that his body only be returned to a free Poland. The Catholic-dominated governments of the post-communist era have seen to it that the church's old official functions are revived, so especially at weekends there's a fair chance of your visit being cut short by the arrival of a visiting foreign dignitary.

Next to the cathedral is the **Sanctuary of Our Lady of Charity**, a Jesuit-run shrine to the city's patron saint, its high belfry – the tallest in the Old Town area – standing out for miles around.

The Old Town Square

The compact Old Town Square – **Rynek Starego Miasto** – is one of the most remarkable bits of postwar reconstruction anywhere in Europe. Flattened during the Warsaw Uprising, the three-storey merchants' houses surrounding the square have been scrupulously rebuilt to their seventeenth- and eighteenth-century designs, multicoloured facades included. By day the buzzing Rynek teems with visitors, who are catered for by buskers, artists, cafés, moneychangers and *doroski*, the traditional horse-drawn carts that clatter tourists round the Old Town for a sizeable fee.

The **Warsaw Historical Museum** (Tues–Sun 10am–4pm) takes up a large part of Strona Dekerta, the north side of the square: entrance is through a house known as the Pod Murzynkiem, where a sculpted black head on the facade symbolises the first owner's overseas trading concerns. Exhibitions here cover every aspect of Warsaw's life from its beginnings to the present day, with a particularly moving chronicle of everyday resistance to the Nazis – an uplifting complement to the wartime horrors documented in the film shown every hour from 9.30am to 3.30pm.

ADAM MICKIEWICZ (1798–1855)

If one person can be said to personify the Polish literary Romantic tradition it is **Adam Mickiewicz**. A passionate, mystically inclined writer, Mickiewicz's unabashedly patriotic writings have long served as a central literary (and sometimes, in times of crisis, political) reference point for generations of Poles. Quotations from and references to Mickiewicz's considerable volume of writings litter subsequent Polish literature and politics – even the avowedly unacademic Lech Wałesa has been known to cite a line or two from the hugely popular epic poem, *Pan Tadeusz* – and performances of his plays are still numbered among the most popular in the country. More controversially, there's an increasing (though muted) discussion of the man's "ethnic" origins, with several scholars now claiming that at least one of Mickiewicz's parents was **Jewish**, a view that might go some way, it is argued, to accounting for the sympathetic portrayal of Jews – notably the musical inn-keeper, Jankiel – in a work like *Pan Tadeusz*: rest assured, though, that aired publicly to the average Pole, this view provokes plenty of controversy. Despite the fact that the best of Mickiewicz's writings rank among the finest outpourings of nineteenth-century Romanticism, he's still relatively unknown in the West, a situation not helped by the general lack of decent translations of his works.

Born in Lithuania of an impoverished Polish *szlachta* family, Mickiewicz studied at **Vilnius University** where he, like many of his generation, was rapidly drawn into conspiratorial anti-Russian plotting.

Already a budding writer – *Poezye*, his first collection of ballads and romances based on Lithuanian folklore, appeared in 1822 – Mickiewicz was arrested along with fellow members of a secret student organisation on suspicion of "spreading Polish nationalism" and was deported to Russia in 1823, where he remained, mostly in **Moscow**, for the rest of the decade, befriending a number of Russian writers, Pushkin included, in the process. Notable literary products of this period include *Dziady* ("Forefather's Eve"), the innovative patriotic drama whose Warsaw performance in spring 1968 sparked subsequent student protests, and *Konrad Wallenrod*, a popular epic poem depicting the medieval struggle between Teutonic Knights and Lithuanians, in reality a thinly disguised allegory of the age-old Polish–German conflict.

On the square's east side – Strona Barssa – the **Mickiewicz Museum** (Mon, Tues, Fri 10am–3pm, Wed & Thurs 11am–6pm, Sun 11am–5pm) is a temple to the Romantic national poet. Amongst a stack of first editions, contemporary newspapers and family memorabilia there's actually a shrine room, with portrait and crucifix enveloped in church-like gloom.

If the crowds in the open-air cafés are too much for you, the *Manekin*, in the southeast corner, is a nice little coffee dive with a bar at the back. The south side – Strona·Zakrzewskiego – is also mainly about eating and drinking, the exclusive *Bazyliszek* restaurant being the most famous attraction. If you're happy with something a little less grand, the Hortex *Jezuicka* café is an acceptable alternative, and there are a couple of popular café-restaurants and wine cellars on the west side too (see "Eating and drinking") – plus a good poster shop at no. 23.

Inevitably, Western-style cafés are asserting themselves over the traditional Polish squareside haunts: on the brighter side though, as in Kraków the whole area is beginning to show the benefits of the comprehensive **clean-up programme** of the buildings undertaken in the last few years, adding a touch of sparkle to the immaculately reconstructed houses on and around the Rynek.

Following the failure of the **November 1830 Uprising**, like many Polish intellectuals Mickiewicz moved to exile in **Paris**, and quickly immersed himself in émigré politics. It was here too that Mickiewicz wrote *Pan Tadeusz* (1834), his greatest epic poem; modelled on the novels of Walter Scott, it is a masterful, richly lyrical depiction of traditional gentry life in his native Polish–Lithuanian homeland, a region dear to many Polish writers – Miłosz and Konwicki are two contemporary examples – both for its outstanding natural beauty and powerful historical Polish associations.

The remaining years of Mickiewicz's life read like a litany of personal and political disappointments. Appointed to a professorship in Lausanne in 1839, Mickiewicz resigned in the following year to teach Slavonic literature at the Collège de France. Increasingly drawn to mystical and theosophical doctrines, the uncompromising Mickiewicz was suspended from his post in 1844. With the outbreak of the **1848 revolutions** in central Europe, the "Springtime of the Nations" that briefly appeared to herald a new dawn for the oppressed nations of the region, Mickiewicz travelled to Rome to try and persuade the new Pope Pius IX to come out in support of the cause of Polish independence. Later the impassioned Mickiewicz also organised a small Polish military unit to fight with Garibaldi's forces – the nucleus, he hoped, of a future Polish national liberation army – and assumed editorship of the radical agitprop newspaper *Tribune des Peuples* ("Tribune of the Peoples"), a move which led to dismissal from his tenure at the Collège de France by Napoleon III.

The writer's life came abruptly to an end in 1855 when Prince Adam Czartoryski, a leader of the Paris exile community, sent Mickiewicz on a mission to Turkey to try and resolve the factional quarrels bedevilling the Polish military forces that had volunteered to fight against Russia in the approaching Crimean War: after contracting typhus soon after his arrival, Mickiewicz died in November 1855 in **Istanbul**, a fact commemorated in the museum to him set up in the Turkish capital that remains there to this day. He was already a national hero of almost mythic proportions, and his remains were eventually brought back to Poland and placed, along with other Polish "greats", in the crypt of Kraków's Wawel Cathedral.

The west side of the Rynek, Strona Hugo-Kołłątaja, named after the co-author of the famous 1791 Constitution, features a number of fine reconstructed residences, notably the **Fukier House** (no. 27), longtime home of one of the city's best-known *winiarnia* and still going strong, and the **Klucznikowska mansion** (no. 21), which includes a carefully reconstructed Gothic doorway among its features.

The Old Town may be liveliest by day, but night-time is when it's at its most atmospheric. Backstreets like ul. Brzozowa, between the Rynek and the river, are particularly handsome, the slanting tiled roofs, silent courtyards and tight passageways seemingly untouched by time.

West of the Rynek, the narrow cobbled streets and alleyways bring you out to a long section the old **city walls**, split-level fortifications with ramparts, rebuilt watchtowers and apple trees lining their grassy approaches. Along Podwale, the open path surrounding the walls – a favourite with evening strollers – an array of plaques commemorates foreigners who supported the Polish cause, notably the French poet Alfred de la Vigne. Here, as in many places around the city, the fresh flowers laid on the ground mark places where the Nazis carried out wartime executions.

The most poignant of the memorials, however, is the recently raised **Monument to the Little Insurgent**, a bronze figure of a small boy with an oversized helmet carrying an automatic rifle – a solitary figure commemorating the children and young people killed fighting in the Warsaw Uprising, personifying all that was heroic, yet so singularly tragic, in the city's resistance to the Nazis.

North of the Rynek ... and over the water

From the Rynek, ul. Nowomiejska runs north to the edge of the Old Town, passing the city archives (no. 12; entrance by appointment) and an excellent postcard shop (no. 19). The street ends at the sixteenth-century **Barbakan**, which formerly guarded the Nowomiejska Gate, the northern entrance to the city. The fortress is part of the old town defences, running all the way round from plac Zamkowy to the northeastern edge of the district. In summer the Barbakan attracts street artists, buskers and hawkers of kitsch souvenir jewellery – credit cards accepted.

Walk east along the walls to the Marshal's Tower, and you have a good view over the river to the Praga district. Conversely, some of the best views of the Old Town itself are from the **Praga waterfront**: take any tram over the bridge immediately south of the Old Town (Most Śląsko-Dąbrowski), get off at the first stop and cross into **Praski Park** then down to the river bank. Walk further north through the park and you'll find yourself amid the questionable pleasures of the Warsaw Zoo.

The New Town (Nowe Miasto)

Cross the ramparts from the Barbakan and you're into the **New Town** district, which despite its name dates from the early fifteenth century, but was formally joined to Warsaw only at the end of the eighteenth. At that time the wooden buildings of the artisan settlement were replaced by brick houses, and it's in this style that the area has been rebuilt.

Up to the Market Square

The eighteenth-century **Raczyński Palace**, a little way down ul. Długa (the first street to the left over the rampart bridge), was one of several field hospitals in the city centre during the Warsaw Uprising: a tablet on the corner with ul. Kilińskiego commemorates over 400 wounded insurrectionists murdered in their beds when the Nazis marched into the Old Town. It's now an archive.

Back up to the bridge, **ul. Freta** – the continuation of Nowomiejska – runs north through the heart of the New Town. On the right, **St Jacek's Church**, a Dominican foundation, is an effective blend of Gothic and early Baroque. The adjoining monastery, the largest in Warsaw, was another field hospital and was heavily bombed as a consequence; hundreds died here when the Nazis regained control in October 1944. The *Pod Samsonen* gallery at ul. Freta 3 holds occasional exhibitions of Asian and Pacific art, shown alongside a small permanent collection (Tues–Sun noon–6pm). For a time the German Romantic writer E.T.A. Hoffmann lived at ul. Freta no. 5, and no. 16 was the birthplace of one of Poland's most famous women: **Marie Skłodowska-Curie**, the double Nobel Prize-winning discoverer of radium. Inside there's a small **museum** dedicated to her life and work (Tues–Sat 10am–4.30pm, Sun 10am–2pm).

Ul. Freta leads to the New Town Market Square – **Rynek Nowego Miasta** – once the commercial hub of the district. Surrounded by elegantly reconstructed eighteenth-century facades, this pleasant square makes a soothing change from the bustle of the Old Town. Tucked into the eastern corner is the **Church of the Holy Sacrament**, commissioned by Queen Maria Sobieska in memory of her husband Jan's victory over the Turks at Vienna in 1683 (see *Contexts*); as you might expect, highlight of the remarkably sober interior is the Sobieski funeral chapel. The architect, Tylman of Gameren, was the most important figure in the rebuilding of Warsaw after the destruction of the Swedish wars in the 1660s. Invited to Poland from Utrecht by Count Jerzy Lubomirski, he went on to redesign what seems like half the city in his distinctive, rather austere Palladian style.

Just off the northern edge of the square, the early fifteenth-century **Church of the Virgin Mary** – once the New Town parish church and one of the oldest churches in Warsaw – has retained something of its Gothic character despite later remodellings; the adjoining belfry is a New Town landmark, easily identifiable from the other side of the river.

The Uprising Monument and Krasiński Palace

The streets northwest of the square lead across ul. Bonifraterska to ul. Gen. W. Andersa, a main thoroughfare which marks the boundaries of Muranów (see p.72). Southwards, ul. Bonifraterska leads to the large plac Krasińkich, now augmented by the **Warsaw Uprising Monument**, a controversial piece commissioned by the communist authorities and consequently disliked by many Varsovians. Built on the spot where Home Army (AK) battalions launched their assault on the Nazis on August 1, 1944, it's a memorably dramatic piece nonetheless, the large metal sculpture depicting AK insurgents surfacing from streetside manholes to begin their attack on the Germans. Just beyond the monument on the corner of ul. Miodowa is the recently-opened **Museum of the Warsaw Uprising** (10am–6pm, July 1–September 30 only): organised by the Union of Warsaw Insurgents – surviving combatants from the Uprising – the small exhibition details the course of the 63-day long Uprising in different parts of the city, showing, among other things, how the AK used old aerial maps of the city to plan their initial assaults on German positions. There's an English-language brochure you can borrow to take round the displays and fill you in on the details. Additionally there's a short but sobering film chronicling the events of the Uprising, shown downstairs regularly throughout the day.

MARIE CURIE (1867–1934)

Nobel Prize-winning scientist **Marie Curie** is a good instance of the "famous person/anonymous Pole" syndrome – Joseph Conrad is the other obvious example. To anyone brought up on a conventional diet of school science it comes as something a surprise to discover that unlike her French husband Pierre and despite her adoptive country, France, Curie (née **Manya Skłodowska**) was a Pole – and a strongly patriotic one at that – through and through. Born into a scientifically oriented Warsaw family – her father was a physics teacher – the young Manya showed academic promise from the start. After completing her secondary education at the city's Russian lyceum – also engaging in the clandestine "free university" organised by fellow Polish patriots – Curie travelled to Paris in early 1890 to follow the lectures of the prominent French physicists of the day at the Sorbonne.

The intellectually voracious Curie threw herself into the Parisian scientific *milieu*, landing a job in the laboratory of the noted physicist Gabriel Lipmann and meeting fellow-researcher Pierre Curie, whom she married in 1895. Thus began a partnership that was to result in a number of spectacular scientific achievements, most famously the discovery of **polonium** – so named in honour of her native country – in summer 1898, and soon afterwards, **radium**. Following her colleague Henri Becquerel's discovery of the phenomenon she eventually dubbed "radioactivity", Curie set to work on systematic research into the revolutionary new wonder, work which eventually gained worldwide recognition in the **Nobel Prize for Physics** which she, Pierre Curie and Becquerel were awarded jointly in 1903. Pierre's sudden death in 1906 was a heavy emotional blow, but one which led to Curie's appointment to the professorship her husband vacated, making her the first woman ever to teach at the Sorbonne. A second **Nobel Prize**, this time in chemistry, came in 1911 for the isolation of pure radium.

Despite the upheavals of World War I, with the assistance of one of her two daughters Curie worked on developing the use of **X-rays** and was a prime mover in the founding in 1918 of the famous **Institut de Radium**, which rapidly developed into a worldwide centre for chemistry and nuclear physics. By now a figure of world renown, and deeply committed to developing the medical applications of the new radiological science, in 1921 Curie and her daughters visited the US, receiving a symbolic gram of prized radium from the president, Warren G. Harding, in the course of the visit. During the rest of the 1920s Curie travelled and lectured widely, founding her own **Curie Foundation** in Paris and eventually realising a long-standing ambition, the setting up of a Radium Institute in her native Warsaw in 1932, of which her sister Bronia was appointed director. The constant exposure to radiation was beginning to have its effect, however, and in early 1934 it was discovered that Curie had **leukaemia**, of which she died only a few months later, in July 1934. The scientific community in particular mourned the loss of one of its outstanding figures, a woman whose research into the effects of radioactivity pioneered both its medical and research-oriented application, simultaneously paving the way for the major subsequent developments in nuclear physics.

Overlooking the west side is the huge and majestic **Krasiński Palace**, built for regional governor Jan Krasiński by the tireless Tylman of Gameren, its facade bearing fine sculptures by Andreas Schlüter. Most of the palace's collection of documents – 40,000 items in all – was destroyed in the war, so today's collection comes from a whole host of sources. Theoretically the building is only open to official visitors but enquiries at the door should get you in to see at least some of the library: the inside of the palace is splendid, the Neoclassical decorations being restored versions of the designs executed by Merlini in the 1780s.

Behind the palace are the **gardens**, now a public park, and beyond that the Ghetto area (see overleaf). If you've got the stomach for it, the **Pawiak Prison Museum**, over to the west at ul. Dzielna 24/26 (Tues–Sat 9am–4pm, Sun 9am–3pm), tells the grim story of Warsaw's most notorious prison from czarist times to the Nazi occupation.

On and around ulica Długa

Further down ul. Bonifraterska, at the corner of ul. Długa and ul. Miodowa, is a small streetside **plaque**, one of the least conspicuous yet most poignant memorials in the city. It commemorates the Warsaw Uprising, and in particular the thousands of half-starved Varsovians who attempted to escape from the besieged Old Town through the sewer network. Many drowned in the filthy passageways, or were killed by grenades lobbed into the tunnels, or were shot upon emerging, but a hundred or so did make it to freedom. The bitter saga was the subject of Andrzej Wajda's film *Kanal*, the second in his brilliant war trilogy.

A number of old patrician residences are to be seen west along ul. Długa, which leads to the **Warsaw Archaeological Museum** (Tues–Fri 9am–4pm, Sat & Sun 10am–5pm), housed in the seventeenth-century arsenal. Starting with Neolithic, Palaeolithic and Bronze Age sites, the museum continues through to early medieval Polish settlements, the highlight being a reconstruction of the early Slav settlements in Wielkopolska and records of forty other excavations from around the country, notably the Jacwingian burial site at Jegleniec near Suwałki (see p.207).

Palaces on Miodowa

Back up to plac Krasińskich and turning south along ul. Miodowa, you find yourself in the heart of aristocratic old Warsaw. The palaces lining Miodowa mainly date from the prosperous pre-Partition era, when this section of the city hummed with the life of European high society. Next door to the **Przymasowski Palace** – now the residence of the Catholic Primate, Cardinal Glemp – stands the **Radziwiłł Palace**, designed by Tylman of Gameren and adjoined by the later Pac Palace, with its distinctive frieze-topped entrance, while across the street is the Basilan Church and Monastery, the city's only Greek Catholic (Uniate) church, designed with an octagonal interior by Merlini in the 1780s.

Close by is the late seventeenth-century **Capuchin Church**, repository of the heart of Jan Sobieski, while off to the left, on ul. Podwale, the **Jan Kiliński monument** commemorates another stirring figure in the country's history. During the 1794 Insurrection it was the shoemaker Kiliński who led the citizens of Warsaw in their assault on the czarist ambassador's residence on this street. His special place in local consciousness was amply demonstrated during World War II after the Nazi governor took down the uncomfortably defiant-looking monument and locked it up in the National Museum: the next day this message was scrawled on the museum wall: "People of Warsaw, here I am! Jan Kiliński."

Muranów and Mirów: Jewish Warsaw

Like Łódź, Białystok and Kraków, Warsaw was for centuries one of the great Jewish centres of Poland. In 1939 there were an estimated 380,000 Jews living in and around the city – one-third of the total population. By May 1945, around 300 were left. Most of Jewish Warsaw was destroyed after the Ghetto Uprising (see box opposite), to be replaced by the sprawling housing estates and tree-lined thoroughfares of the **Muranów** and **Mirów** districts, a little to the west of the city centre. However, a few traces of the Jewish presence in Warsaw do remain, and there's a small but increasingly visible Jewish community here – well supported by its exiled diaspora.

Nożyk Synagogue

First stop on any itinerary of Jewish Warsaw is the **Nożyk Synagogue** on ul. Twarda, the only one of the Ghetto's three synagogues still standing. The majestic Great Synagogue on ul. Tłomackie – which held up to three thousand people – was blown up by the Nazis; in a gesture of crass insensitivity, the Polish authorities decided to build a skyscraper on the site.

The Nożyk, a more modest affair, was built in the early 1900s, gutted during the war, and reopened in 1983 after a complete restoration. The refined interior is theoretically open to tourists only from 10am to 3pm on Thursdays, but in practice it's possible to get in at other times with a little diplomacy. The **Jewish Theatre**, rehoused just south of the synagogue on plac Grzybowski, continues the theatrical traditions of the Ghetto.

The Ghetto Heroes Monument and Jewish Cemetery

Marooned in the middle of a drab square to the north of the Ghetto area, the imposing **Ghetto Heroes Monument** – unveiled in 1948 on the fifth anniversary of the Uprising – stresses both the courage of the Jewish resistance and the helplessness of the deportees. It is made from materials ordered by Hitler in 1942 to construct a monument to the Third Reich's anticipated victory.

North along ul. Zamenhofa brings you to ul. Miła and the memorial mound covering the **ŻOB bunker** at no. 18, its height representing the level of rubble left after the destruction of the Ghetto area. In several of the surrounding streets you'll find houses starting from a similar level – the postwar communist authorities simply built the new housing blocks on top of the remains of the Ghetto. Continue north along ul. Karmelicka to the corner of ul. Stawki, and there on the edge of a housing estate is the **Umschlagplatz**, where Jews were loaded onto cattle wagons bound for Treblinka and the other death camps.

The simple white marble **monument** standing here, raised in the late 1980s and designed to resemble the cattle trucks used in the transportations, is covered inside with a list of four hundred Jewish first names, the chosen way of symbolising the estimated 300,000 Jews deported from here to the death camps. A stone stands at the exact point from which the trains departed, while across the road one of the few surviving prewar buildings (no. 5/7) was the house of the SS commander supervising operations at the Umschlagplatz.

Walk west along ul. Stawki and down ul. Okopowa for the **Jewish Cemetery** (10am–3pm, closed Fri & Sat), where the tombs range from colossal Gothic follies to simple engraved stones, rather like a Jewish Highgate. Unlike most

Jewish cemeteries in Poland, this site was left almost untouched during the war, the reason being that, unlike in smaller Polish towns, the Nazis didn't need the materials for building new roads here.

Scattered amongst the plots are the graves of eminent Polish Jews like Ludwig Zamenhof, the inventor of Esperanto (see p.221), early socialist activist Stanisław Mendelson and writer D.H. Nomberg. The caretaker at the entrance lodge has detailed guides to the tombstones for anyone wanting to know more.

The Jewish Historical Institute

A final stop should be the **Jewish Historical Institute**, next to the site of the Great Synagogue at ul. Tłomackie 3/5. Itself standing on the site of the prewar Judaic Library, the Institute is part museum (Mon–Fri 9am–3pm), part library and research archive (Mon–Fri 8am–4pm). The museum details life in the wartime Ghetto, a fascinating and moving corrective to the familiar images of passive victims. The international section of the library includes English-language books and journals about Polish Jewry and related issues. To meet an increasing demand, the Institute has now published an indispensible *Guide to Jewish Warsaw*, also on sale at the cemetery.

Śródmieście

The large area which stretches from the Old Town down towards Łazienki Park – **Śródmieście** – is the increasingly fast-paced heart of Warsaw, but in keeping with the Polish spirit of reverence for the past, the sector immediately below the Old Town contains an impressive number of reconstructed palaces, parks, churches and museums, all contributing to a distinctive atmosphere of slightly grubby grandeur.

Further south, below ul. Swiętokrzyska and east of the Palace of Culture, the brash shopfronts, tower blocks and fast-food stands of the main commercial zone epitomise the changing face of Warsaw city life.

THE WARSAW GHETTO

From the middle of 1940 the Jews of Warsaw were sealed behind the walls of the Nazi-designated Ghetto area, and by the next year nearly one and a half million Jews from all over Poland had been crammed into this insanitary zone, with starvation and epidemics the predictable and intended consequence.

Deportations to the death camps began in summer 1942 – 300,000 to Treblinka in that summer alone. After further mass round-ups, the Nazis moved in to "clean out" the Ghetto in January 1943, by which time there were only 60,000 people left. Sporadic resistance forced them to retreat, but only until April, when a full-scale Nazi assault provoked the **Ghetto Uprising** under the leadership of the Jewish Combat Organisation (ŻOB). For nearly a month Jewish partisans battled against overwhelming Nazi firepower, before ŻOB's bunker headquarters on the corner of ul. Miła and Zamenhofa were finally breached on May 9, following the suicide of the legendary Mordechai Anieliewicz and his entire staff. A very few combatants survived and escaped to join up with the Polish resistance in the "Aryan" sector of the city. Of those remaining in the Ghetto, 7000 were shot immediately, the rest despatched to the camps.

From plac Zamkowy to Aleje Ujazdowskie

Running west from plac Zamkowy is ul. Senatorska, once one of Warsaw's smartest shopping streets, now studded with wall plaques recording the civilian victims of Nazi street executions. As the name suggests, the pseudo-classical giant dominating the nearby plac Teatralny is the **Grand Opera and Ballet Theatre**, a monster playhouse designed by Corazzi in the 1820s, with a fine classicist facade decorated with Greek sculptures. Rebuilt and enlarged after wartime destruction, the main theatre now holds almost 2000 people, though even then it regularly sells out in summer. Inside, the elegant entrance hall has a sumptuous rotunda overhead and an intricate parquet floor, and overall the building's worth a look-in even if you're not planning to attend one of the lavish operas, theatre or ballet productions which are staged here throughout the year, with an emphasis on the classics (see "Nightlife"). The redoubtable sword-waving figure rising from the stone plinth on the other side of the square is the **Warsaw Heroes Monument**, the state's tribute to the war dead; like most Warsaw monuments, it could do with a cleaner environment. Continuing west along Senatorska, the Baroque **Reformed Franciscan Church** – a quiet place with restful cloisters – is followed by the **Mniszech Palace** and the **Błękitny Palace**, where Chopin gave one of his earliest concerts at the age of six. Tragically, the palace's destruction in 1944 engulfed the fabulous Zamoyski library of over 250,000 books and manuscripts. Senatorska ends at plac Bankowy, formerly plac Dzierżyńskiego: the giant statue of the unloved Russian revolutionary who was formerly its namesake was removed in 1990 to public rejoicing.

ROUND PLAC BANKOWY

On the northeast corner of the square is a tall, silver-looking skyscraper that's long been a city talking point: built on the former site of the Great Synagogue (see p.72) – and cursed, according to local legend, as a consequence – it's taken over twenty years to complete this lumbering Yugoslav-financed giant of a project. The west edge of the increasingly smart-looking square is taken up by a palatial-looking early nineteenth-century complex designed by Antoni Corazzi, and originally housing Congress Kingdom-era government offices: these days it's occupied by the Warsaw city authorities. On the southwest corner of the square is the old **National Bank** building – hence the square's new (i.e. old) name – until recently the official Museum of the Workers' Movement but now taken over by the rather different type of collection of the John Paul II Museum (see opposite).

PLAC PIŁSUDSKIEGO

Returning to plac Teatralny, the way from the south side of the theatre leads onto an even larger square, **plac Piłsudskiego**, where a huge flower cross lay for some time after martial law was imposed. After the authorities had cleared the cross away, the whole area was closed off for public works for years, presumably to prevent embarrassing demonstrations happening in full view of the tourists staying in the *Victoria* and *Europejski* hotels. These days the military guard in front of the **Tomb of the Unknown Soldier** is the only permanent security presence.

AROUND THE SAXON GARDENS (OGRÓD SASKI)

Behind it stretch the handsome and well-used promenades of the **Saxon Gardens** (Ogród Saski), laid out for August II by Tylman of Gameren in the early 1700s and landscaped as a public garden in the following century. What's missing here now is the **royal palace** built in the gardens by August II: blown up by the Nazis in

1944 and never rebuilt, the Tomb of the Unknown Soldier is the only surviving bit of the building. Other bits of the park were luckier, notably the scattering of Baroque sculptures, symbolising the Virtues, Sciences and Elements, an elegant nineteenth-century fountain pool above the main pathway, the old **water tower** (Warsaw's first) built by Marconi in the 1850s and the park's fine crop of **trees** – over a hundred species in all.

THE ZACHĘTA GALLERY
Immediately south of the gardens on plac Małachowskiego, to the west of the plush *Victoria*, is the **Zachęta Gallery** (Tues–Sun 10am–6pm), built at the turn of the century as the headquarters of the Warsaw Fine Arts Society and one of the few buildings in central Warsaw left standing at the end of World War II – the stucco decoration in the entrance giving a taste of the building's original qualities. The gallery's considerable original art collection (Matejko's *Battle of Grunwald* included) was packed off into hiding in the National Museum at the start of the war, subsequently forming part of the museum's permanent collection. Its place has been taken by a contemporary art gallery operating under the patronage of the recently reformed Fine Arts Society, one of the city's most thriving organisations, which stages a wealth of generally high-quality exhibitions (see "Listings").

The John Paul II Museum
Established on the basis of the large art collection (some 400 paintings in all) assembled by the wealthy émigré Carroll-Portczński family in the early 1980s and donated to the Polish Catholic church a few years later, the **John Paul II collection** (Tues–Thurs, Sat & Sun 10am–5pm, Fri 9.30am–5pm) has given Warsaw a significant new museum, with art ranging from the fourteenth to the twentieth centuries, though with a heavy emphasis on religious works. Already, the museum has been controversial: sections of the academic art world are proving reticent about the value of the collection, and the Portczyńskis recently went to great – and ultimately unsuccessful – lengths to try to block the publication of an article by a leading Polish art expert claiming that several of the more famous paintings, in particular the early Italian works, are actually fakes. Alongside the museum's unquestionably high artistic aspirations there's an unabashedly catachestic tone to the place, the portraits of the Pope and current Catholic Primate Cardinal Glemp placed at the entrance reminding you who the collection is supposed to be in honour of. Most of the collections, too, are arranged according to themes drawn from the Catholic theological canon – the Bible and Saints, the Life of Mary, Myth and Allegory, Motherhood and the like – the rest being set up on the basis of national "schools" of art.

ITALIAN AND GERMAN WORKS
Once into the museum, tour groups make straight for the main ground-floor room, a large domed auditorium once occupied by the Warsaw Bourse that now doubles as a concert recital hall – hence the chairs filling the body of the building. The large collection of portraits lining the walls is divided into national "schools", as are most of the ground-floor collections. The **Italian school** features a fine *Death of Lucretia* from the Titian school, as well as a notable *Sacrifice of the Dead Abraham* from the Caravaggio workshop, probably a replica of a smaller painting of the same title housed in the Ufizi in Florence. Highlights of the **German** collection include portraits of Luther and his wife Catherine by Cranach the elder, and one of the oldest known versions of the lost *St Anne* by Albrecht Dürer, dated 1523.

FLEMISH AND DUTCH WORKS

The big guns of **Flemish and Dutch** Baroque provide some of the museum's leading works, with self-portraits of Rubens and Rembrandt, the latter placed alongside the thoughtful *Portrait of a Nobleman* by van Dyck beneath the impassive bust of patron John Paul peering out over the auditorium. Additionally there are a couple of works by Jordaens, while *Farm in Hoogeveen*, a typically brooding early Van Gogh, is one of several works in the "Still Lifes and Landscapes" section housed in an adjoining room, which also features a Constable still life and an evocative pair of landscapes by the French-born English painter Alfred Sisley: here as elsewhere in the collection, enjoyment is somewhat marred by the neck-wrenching height at which the pictures have been hung.

FRENCH, ENGLISH AND SPANISH WORKS

The **French** collection is particularly strong on portraiture, featuring a wealth of courtly eighteenth-century aristocracy, a fine portrait of Henry IV, a Renoir picture of his son, Pierre, and a plaster mould head of John the Baptist by Rodin. The same goes for the **English** section, notable works here including Sir Joshua Reynolds' penetrating *Portrait of Miss Nelly O'Brien* – one of three he painted of the Irish woman – and a noble-looking self-portrait by him. **Spanish** artists provide some of the most powerful works in the auditorium, notably the self-portraits by Murillo and Veląsquez, Ribera's hauntingly intense *Portrait of a Philosopher,* and *Woman Carrying Water*, a powerful later Goya work.

THE UPPER FLOORS

The upper floors of the building house the theologically orientated "theme" rooms, including the art-crammed "mother and child" section populated by the inevitable welter of fleshy-looking Baroque cherubs. The upper sections contain plenty of notable works too, though, **Italian** artists providing the earliest (and most controversial) works, notably a fine *Jesus' Offertory in the Temple* from the circle of Jacopo Bellini, a mid-fourteenth-century *Virgin and Child* from the Marches school (the oldest painting in the collection), a *Madonna and Child* by Carucci, Titian's *Child from the Medici Family*, and a *Last Supper* by Tintoretto. Works from other countries include another *Last Supper* by Brueghel the Younger, a dreamy *Ecstasy of St Francis* by David Teniers, and an outstanding Mannerist *Crucifixion* by Cornelis van Haarlem housed in the crucifixion room whose centrepiece is a huge, dramatic depiction of Calvary by the Polish nineteenth-century artist Wojciech Gerson.

Along Krakowskie Przedśiescie

Of all the long thoroughfares bisecting central Warsaw from north to south, the most important is the one often known as the Royal Way, which runs almost uninterrupted from plac Zamkowy to the palace of Wilanów. **Krakowskie Przedmieście**, the first part of the Royal Way, is lined with historic buildings. **St Anne's**, directly below plac Zamkowy, is where Polish princes used to swear homage to the king; founded in 1454, the church was destroyed in 1656 by the besieging Swedes, then rebuilt in Baroque style in the following century. There's a fine view over the Wisła from the courtyard next to the church, though your enjoyment of it is somewhat marred by the traffic thundering through the tunnel below. By the second year of martial law resourceful oppositionists had moved their flower cross to this courtyard after the authorities removed the huge one from plac Piłsudskiego, previously Zwycięstwa. For an even better view, for a small fee you can climb the belfry tower on the northern side of the courtyard.

South of St Anne's the bus-congested street broadens to incorporate a small green. The **Mickiewicz Statue** stuck in the middle of it is the first of many you'll see if you travel round the country – he's a hero with whom everyone seems comfortable, communist governments included (see p.66). Unveiled on the centenary of the poet's birth, before a 12,000-strong crowd (the Russians were enforcing a ban on rallies and speeches at the time), it's one of the monuments the cleaners clearly haven't got round to brushing up yet.

Just south of the statue stands the seventeenth-century **Carmelite church** whose finely wrought facade, complete with a distinctive globe of the world, is one of the first examples of genuine classicism in Poland. Next door in the **Radziwiłł Palace** is where the Warsaw Pact was formally created in 1955, at the height of the Cold War. Thirty-four years later it hosted another equally momentous event in the spring 1989 "Round Table" talks between the country's communist authorities and the Solidarity-led opposition. In front of the palace's large courtyard is a statue of another national favourite, Józef Poniatowski, nephew of the last king of Poland and a die-hard patriot who fought in the 1794 Insurrection.

Just west of the main street on ul. Kozia, a quiet, atmospheric cobbled backstreet, is the **Museum of Caricatures** (Tues–Sun 11am–5pm), a quirky but enjoyable set-up featuring exhibitions of work by Polish cartoonists. The main feature for some time to come is likely to continue to be a large display of work by the late Eryk Lipiński, a veteran cartoonist whose satirical portraits seem to cover just about every famous Pole you're likely to have heard of, and many more besides. The overall tone of his pictures is hearteningly irreverent – no one is sacrosanct, not even the Pope nor other national icons past and present – leaving you wondering whether the current crop of politicians aren't quietly grateful to have lost such a waspish commentator.

Back onto Krakowskie Przedmieście, two grand old hotels face each other a little further down the street: the *Europejski*, Warsaw's oldest hotel, and the *Bristol*. Begun in the 1850s, the **Europejski**, was badly hit in World War II, but it's been restored well enough to preserve at least a hint of *fin-de-siècle* grandeur. After years out of action the *Bristol*, a neo-Renaissance completed in 1899, is finally back in business. Once owned by musician–premier Ignacy Paderewski and a legendary prewar journalist's hang-out, it's been transformed into a super-luxury hotel by the English Trust House Forte group, its new owners.

Even in a city not lacking in Baroque churches, the triple-naved **Church of the Nuns of the Visitation** stands out, with its columned, statue-topped facade; it's also one of the very few buildings in central Warsaw to have come through World War II unscathed. Its main claim to fame in Polish eyes is that Chopin used to play the church organ here, mainly during services for schoolchildren.

THE UNIVERSITY

Most of the rest of Krakowskie Przedmieście is taken up by **Warsaw University**. Established in 1818, it was closed by the Czar in 1832 as part of the punishment for the 1831 Insurrection, and remained closed till 1915. During the Nazi occupation educational activity of any sort was made a capital offence, and thousands of academics and students were murdered, and yet clandestine university courses continued throughout the war – a tradition revived in the

1970s with the "Flying University", which involved opposition figures moving around the city giving open lectures on politically controversial issues. Today the university's reputation remains as much political as academic, and even the new political order doesn't seem to have extinguished the traditional radicalism. During term time you'll find groups hustling books and leaflets on the streets outside the main entrance; if they can speak English, a political discussion won't be hard to initiate either – like many Poles, the students love a good argument. The cafés, restaurants and milk bars just down the street and round the corner on ul. Oboźna are established student hang-outs.

On the main campus courtyard, the **Library** stands in front of the seventeenth-century **Kazimierz Palace**, once a royal summer residence, while across the street from the gates is the former **Czapski Palace**, now home of the Academy of Fine Arts. Just south is the twin-towered Baroque **Holy Cross Church** (Kosciól Świętego Krzyża), which was ruined by a two-week battle inside the building during the Warsaw Uprising; photographs of the distinctive figure of Christ left standing among the ruins became poignant emblems of Warsaw's suffering. Another factor increases local affection for this church: on a pillar on the left side of the nave there's an urn containing Chopin's heart.

Biggest among Warsaw's consistently big palaces is the early nineteenth-century **Staszic Palace**, which virtually blocks the end of Krakowskie Przedmieście; once a Russian boys' grammar school, it's now the headquarters of the Polish Academy of Sciences. In front of the palace is the august **Copernicus monument**, designed by the Danish sculptor Bertel Thorvaldsen in the 1830s and showing the great astronomer holding one of his revolutionary heliocentric models. Past the monument down the narrow ul. Oboźna is the Polish Theatre (*Teatr Polski*) building.

The Nowy Świat district

South from the Staszic, the main street becomes **Nowy Świat (New World)**, an area first settled in the mid-seventeenth century. As you move down this wide boulevard, the palaces of the aristocracy give way to shops, offices and cafés: the *Nowy Świat* café, on the corner with Świętokrzyska, is a popular coffee shop, while the *Blikle* further down still produces the cakes for which it's been famed since 1869.

Numerous cultural luminaries have inhabited this street at one time or another, the most famous being Joseph Conrad, who lived at no. 45. A left turn down ul. Ordynacka brings you to the **Chopin Museum** (Mon–Wed, Fri & Sat 10am–2pm, Thurs noon–6pm), housed in the late seventeenth-century Ostrogski Palace on ul. Okólnik, which also forms the headquarters of the Chopin Society. Memorabilia on display includes the last piano played by him, now used for occasional concerts.

The neo-Renaissance **Zamoyski Palace**, off to the left of Nowy Świat at the end of ul. Foksal, is one of the few Warsaw palaces you can actually see inside. In 1863 an abortive attempt to assassinate the czarist governor was made here; as a consequence the palace was confiscated and ransacked by Cossacks, who hurled a grand piano used by Chopin out of the window of his sister's flat in the palace. These days it's a suitably elegant setting for an architectural institute, with a restaurant and a nice quiet café open to the public.

Further down Nowy Świat, the concrete monster on the southern side of the junction with al. Jerozolimskie was for decades the headquarters of the now defunct **Polish Communist Party**. After protracted wrangling over who should take it over, it was finally decided (with pleasing irony) to turn the building into the new Warsaw Stock Exchange; hence the parade of chauffeur-driven top-range BMWs and Mercedes outside.

THE NATIONAL MUSEUM

Immediately west along al. Jerozolimskie is the **National Museum** (Tues & Sun 10am–5pm, Wed, Fri & Sat 10am–4pm, Thurs noon–6pm), an equally ugly and daunting building. Its collections are an impressive compendium of art and archaeology, but be warned that lack of staff means that at least a handful of galleries are always shut.

The displays begin to the right of the entrance with the department of **ancient art** – assorted Egyptian, Greek, Roman and Etruscan finds. These, however, are completely overshadowed by the stunning array in the corresponding wing to the left of **art from Faras**, a town in Nubia (the present-day Sudan) excavated by Polish archaeologists in the early 1960s. There are capitals, friezes, columns and other architectural fragments, together with 69 murals dating from between the eighth and thirteenth centuries. The earliest paintings – notably *St Anne, The Archangels Michael and Gabriel* and *SS Peter and John Enthroned* – are direct and powerful images comparable in quality with the much later productions of the European Romanesque, and prove the vibrancy of African culture at this period. No less striking are the later, and presumably true-to-life, portraits such as the tenth-century *Bishop Petros with St Peter* and the eleventh-century *Bishop Marianos*.

In the rooms off the central hall, in which stand notable sculptures by Adrian de Vries, Bernini and Canova, is the museum's other star collection, that of **medieval art**, which is dominated by a kaleidoscopic array of carved and painted altarpieces. Although all the objects come from within the modern borders of Poland, the predominance of works from Silesia and the Gdańsk area suggests that most were created by German or Bohemian craftsmen, whose style was closely imitated elsewhere. Highlights include a lovely late fourteenth-century "Soft Style" polyptych from the castle chapel in Grudziądz; the monumental fifteenth-century canopied altar from St Mary in Gdańsk; and the altar from Pławno depicting the life of Saint Stanisław, painted by Hans Süss von Kulmbach, a pupil of Dürer who spent part of his career in Poland.

Much of the first floor is given over to **Polish painting**, beginning with a number of examples of what is a quintessential national art form, the coffin portrait. There's a comprehensive collection of works by nineteenth-century and modern artists, many of them relatively little known; an important section is the group of works from the turn-of-the century *Młoda Polska* school (see *Kraków* in Chapter Four). Stanisław Wyspiański's intense self-portraits stand out, as do Jacek Malczewski's haunting images of Death disguised as an angel. Matejko is represented by some of his most heroic efforts, notably the huge *Battle of Grunwald*, which depicts one of the most momentous clashes of the Middle Ages, the defeat of the Teutonic Knights by combined Polish–Lithuanian forces.

The left wing of the first floor, plus all of the second floor, are given over to the extensive but patchy department of **foreign paintings**. In the Italian section, look out for some notable Renaissance panels, such as the tondo of *The Madonna and Child with St John* from the workshop of Botticelli, *Portrait of a Venetian Admiral* by Tintoretto, and *Christ among the Doctors* by Cima da Conegliano. Among the

French paintings in the following rooms are a badly damaged little canvas called *The Polish Woman* attributed to Watteau, Ingres' sensual *Academic Study*, and one of the great masterpieces of Neoclassical portraiture, *Stanisław Kostka Potocki on Horseback* by Jacques-Louis David. Upstairs, the German Renaissance is represented by a fine group of works – including *Adam and Eve*, *The Massacre of the Innocents* and *Portrait of a Princess* – by Cranach, and *Hercules and Anteus* by Baldung. From the same period in the Low Countries are an impressive *Ecce Homo* triptych by van Heemskerk and the satirical *Money Changers* by van Reymerswaele. Later Dutch works include *Queen Sylvia*, a brilliant Mannerist composition by Goltizius and a couple of striking examples of Tenebrism: *King David Playing the Harp* by Terbrugghen and *Boy Blowing Charcoal* by Rembrandt's collaborator, Jan Lievens.

The **Army Museum** next door (same times) stirs pride in many Poles, but few foreigners get further than the World War II heavy armour outside.

THE PARLIAMENT AND SENATE
South of the museum, plac Trzech Krzyzy (Three Crosses), with the Pantheon-style **St Alexander's** church in the centre, leads to the tree-lined pavements and magisterial embassy buildings of al. Ujazdowskie. Past the unattractive US embassy and off to the left down ul. Jana Matejki is the squat 1920s **Parliament** (Sejm) and **Senate** building. Hardly worth a mention a few years ago, these days it's where veteran Solidarity oppositionists rub shoulders with, and occasionally dismiss, their former jailers, though the perennial national tendency towards factional political intriguing on show in the first few years of post-communist rule is doing little to endear the new breed of politicians to the wider public.

Downtown Warsaw
The area below the Saxon Gardens and west of Krakowskie Przedmieście is the busiest commercial zone. **Marszałkowska**, the main road running south from the western tip of the park, is lined with department stores and privately run clothes shops and workshops selling everything from jewellery to car spares. South of ul. Swiętokrzyska, in the long narrow streets surrounding Chmielna and Zgoda, it's worth scouting around for good-quality items like heavy winter coats and hand-crafted leather goods.

North of ul. Swiętokrzyska, on ul. Kreditowa, the eighteenth-century **Lutheran Church** is topped with Warsaw's largest dome. The building's excellent acoustics have long made it popular with musicians – Chopin played a concert here when aged 14, and the church still holds regular choral and chamber concerts (see "Nightlife"). Opposite stands the **Ethnographic Museum** (Tues, Thurs & Fri 9am–4pm, Wed 11am–6pm, Sat & Sun 10am–5pm), whose collection of over 30,000 items was virtually destroyed in the war. They've done pretty well to revive the place since then, restocking with African tribal artefacts, Latin American outfits and local folk items. Polish objects take up much of the second floor, a highlight being an absorbing collection of traditional costumes from all over the country. Folklore enthusiasts will enjoy the section devoted to straw men, winter processions and a host of other arcane rural customs.

Towering over everything in this part of the city is the **Palace of Culture**, a gift from Stalin to the Polish people, and not one that could be refused. Popularly known as "the Russian cake", this neo-Byzantine leviathan provokes both intense revulsion and admiration for its sheer audacity. These days slogans about

"Kapitalizm" and "biznes" have replaced Marx and Lenin on the banners over the giant entrance up the steps from the expansive plac Defilad – recently the subject of an international design competition. The winning proposal – to fill the area with medium-sized buildings and a pedestrian boulevard, but leave the palace essentially untouched – has angered many Varsovians, a good few of whom support the idea of demolishing the whole thing. The debate still rages, and it's unlikely that work of any sort will begin before the mid-1990s. Apart from a vast conference hall, the cavernous interior contains offices, cinemas, swimming pools, some good foreign-language bookshops, and – the ultimate capitalistic revenge – a casino. The locals say that the best view of Warsaw is from the top floor – the only viewpoint from which one can't see the palace. A lift whisks visitors up to the 30th-floor platform from where, on a good day, you can see out into the plains of Mazovia.

While the planners debate the future, the area immediately in front of the palace is now filled with a series of huge makeshift covered **markets**. The piped Muzak, sense of institutionalisation and well-organised stalls are a definite step further along the capitalist path from the scramble of open-air vendors that previously occupied the area.

Al. Jerozolimskie, the major highway south of the palace, is dominated by the gleaming chrome and marble of the new *LOT* building and Warsaw's latest Western marvel, the luxury **Marriot Hotel**. (The opening of the *Holiday Inn* just north of the station has confirmed this region as Warsaw's top-bracket tourist quarter.) The department stores continue southwards down tramlined Marszałkowska towards plac Konstytucji, interspersed with tourist offices, glitzy shops and cultural institutes of other erstwhile communist countries. Cross-streets such as Hoża and Wilcza comprise a residental area whose discreetly well-heeled inhabitants are served by increasing numbers of chic little stores.

West of plac Konstytucji, on Nowowiejska, is the turn-of-the-century **Warsaw Polytechnic** building, where the political groups often hold meetings. If you happen to be there at the right time, there's nothing to stop you sitting in on these impassioned mini-parliaments, which are sometimes attended by government ministers and other political luminaries.

Łazienki Park and Palace

Parks are one of Warsaw's distinctive and most attractive features. South of the commercial district, on the east side of al. Ujazdowskie, is one of the best, the **Łazienki Park**. Once a hunting ground on the periphery of town, the area was bought by King Stanisław August in the 1760s and turned into an English-style park with formal gardens. A few years later the slender Neoclassical **Łazienki Palace** was built across the park lake; designed for the king by the Italian architect Domenico Merlini, in collaboration with teams of sculptors and other architects, it's the best memorial to the country's last and most cultured monarch. Before this summer residence was commissioned, a bathhouse built by Tylman of Gameren for Prince Stanisław Lubomirski stood here – hence the name "Łazienki", meaning simply "baths".

The oak-lined promenades and pathways leading from the park entrance to the palace are a favourite with both Varsovians and tourists. On summer Sunday lunchtimes, concerts and other events take place under the watchful eye of the ponderous **Chopin Monument**, just beyond the entrance; they are an enjoyable introduction to Polish culture in populist form – stirring performances of Chopin études or mazurkas, declamatory readings from Mickiewicz and other Romantics, and so on. On the way down to the lake you'll pass a couple of the many buildings designed for King Stanisław by Merlini: the **New Guardhouse**, just before the palace, is now a pleasant terrace café.

The Palace

The only way to see the **palace interior** (Tues–Sun 9.30am–3pm; last entrance 2.20pm; park open to sunset) is on a group tour, and these get booked early in the day – so get there by 9.30am in summer or be prepared for a long wait. Nazi damage to the rooms themselves was not irreparable, and most of the lavish furnishings, paintings and sculptures survived the war intact, having been hidden during the occupation.

First on the ground floor are rooms incorporated from the earlier bathhouse; the baths themselves are long gone, but the bas reliefs decorating the walls serve as a reminder of the original waterbound function. Moving into the main section of the palace, the stuccoed **ballroom**, the biggest ground-floor room, is a fine example of Stanisław's classicist predilections, lined with a tasteful collection of busts and classical sculptures. As the adjoining **picture galleries** demonstrate, Stanisław was a discerning art collector. The Nazis got hold of some of the best pieces – three Rembrandts included – but a large collection drawn from all over Europe remains, with an accent on Dutch and Flemish artists.

Upstairs are the **king's private apartments**, most of them entirely reconstructed since the war. Again, period art and furniture dominate these handsome chambers: a stately and uncomfortable-looking four-poster bed fills the royal bedroom, while in the study a Bellotto canvas accurately depicts the original Łazienki bathhouse. An exhibition devoted to the history of Łazienki completes the tour.

The Park

The buildings scattered round the park are all in some way connected with King Stanisław. Across the lake and north along the water's edge is the **Old Guardhouse,** built in the 1780s in a style matching the north facade of the main palace, which features regular exhibitions of contemporary art. Immediately next to it is the so-called **Great Outbuilding** (*Wielka Oficyna*), another Merlini construction, the former officer's training school where young cadets hatched the anti-Czarist conspiracy that resulted in the November 1830 Uprising. The building now houses the **Paderewski Museum** (Tues–Sun 10am–5pm) inaugurated during the summer 1992 celebrations surrounding the return of the composer's body to Warsaw from the US. Much of the museum's collection consists of items bequeathed to the country by the exile Paderewski in his will. Pride of place goes to the grand piano Paderewski used at his longtime home on the shores of Lake Geneva. Standing on it, as during the man's lifetime, are the improbably paired autographed photos of fellow composer Saint-Saëns and Queen Victoria, while the walls are decorated with Paderewski's personal art collection. Adjoining rooms contain the dazzling array of prizes, medals and other honours awarded Paderewski during his distinguished musical and political career, as well as his fine personal collection of assorted Chinese porcelain and enamel ware. To finish off there's a section devoted to mementoes of the Polish *emigracjay*.

Immediately next to the museum is the **Myślewicki Palace**, a present from the king to his nephew Prince Józef Poniatowski, which imitates the studied decorum of the main palace. In summer the Greek-inspired **Amphitheatre**, constructed for the king on an islet just along from the palace, still stages the occasional open-air performance; rustling trees and the background duck chorus are a bit of an intrusion.

Back up towards the park entrance, past the guardhouse, is the **White House** (*Biały Dom*), the residence built in the 1770s by Merlini for King Stanisław August to live in while the main Łazienki palace was being finished, and which retains the majority of its original eighteenth-century interiors, including a **dining room** decorated with a wealth of grotesque animal frescoes, and an octagonal-shaped **study** which features enjoyable trompe l'oeil floral decoration.

Just beyond it the main **Orangery** houses a well-preserved wooden theatre (one of the few in Europe to retain its original eighteenth-century decor), with room for over two hundred people, royal boxes not included; to complete the classical pose, pieces from King Stanisław's extensive sculpture collection fill the long galleries behind the auditorium.

Back out on al. Ujazdowskie, south from the Chopin monument, stands the **Belvedere Palace**, another eighteenth-century royal residence redesigned in the 1820s for the governor of Warsaw, the czar's brother Konstantine. Official residence of Polish heads of state since the end of World War I (with a brief interlude as home of the Nazi governor Hans Frank), for ten years it was used by General Jaruzelski, now supplanted by Lech Wałęsa, the country's first freely elected president in over fifty years.

The Royal Way from here slopes gently down towards the Mokotów district, passing the huge **Russian embassy** building – its security looking a lot more relaxed these days – and the *Universus*, Warsaw's largest bookshop, at the bottom of the hill. The Royal Way then continues a few kilometres south to Wilanów, its ultimate destination.

Wilanów

The grandest of Warsaw's palaces, **Wilanów** is tucked away in almost rural surroundings on the outskirts of Warsaw, and makes an easy excursion from the city centre: buses #B, # 122, #130, #180, #193 and #422 run to the station just over the road from the palace entrance. Sometimes called the Polish Versailles, it was originally the brainchild of King Jan Sobieski, who purchased the existing manor house and estate in 1677; he spent nearly twenty years turning it into his ideal country residence, which was later extended by a succession of monarchs and aristocratic families. Predictably, it was badly damaged during World War II, when the Nazis stole the cream of the Wilanów art collection and tore up the park and surrounding buildings. In 1945 the palace became state property, and for eleven years was extensively renovated and its art collection refurbished. It's now a tourist favourite, and at the height of summer the welter of coach parties can make it almost impossible for individual visitors to get in . Your best bets for ensuring easy entry are either to get there early (as always), to go on a Sunday (theoretically the non-group visitors' day), or to swallow your pride and sign up for an Orbis tour.

The approach to the palace takes you past former outhouses, including the smithy, the butcher's and an **inn**, now an exclusive restaurant (see "Eating and drinking"). Also close at hand are some decent **cafés**, welcome refuges after the palace tour. The domed eighteenth-century **St Anne's Church** and ornate neo-Gothic Potocki mausoleum across the road lead to the gates, where you buy your tickets – if the crowds are big you'll be given a wooden token telling you what time your designated group is going to be let in.

The Palace

Among the sixty-odd rooms of Wilanów's **interior** (Wed–Mon 9.30am–2.30pm; park open till sunset) you'll find styles ranging from the lavish early Baroque of the apartments of Jan Sobieski and John III to the classical grace of the nineteenth-century Potocki museum rooms. Some might find the cumulative effect of all this pomp and glory rather deadening – even the official guides seem to recognise this, easing off with the facts and figures in the last part of the guided tour.

The first rooms after the entrance, amongst the oldest in the palace, contain a number of casket images, intended to be interred with the subject but sometimes removed from the coffin before burial. They are part of a total collection of over 250 portraits, most of which are hung in long corridor galleries – an intriguing introduction to the development of Polish fashion, with its peculiar synthesis of Western *haute couture* and Eastern influences such as shaved heads and wide sashes. If you've already visited other museums, the portrait of Jan Sobieski in the **Sobieski Family Room** will probably look familiar – the portly military hero most often crops up charging Lone Ranger-like towards a smouldering Vienna, trampling a few Turks on the way.

After Sobieski's **Library**, with its beautiful marble-tiled floor and allegorical ceiling paintings, you come to the plushest rooms of the lot – the **Queen's Apartments**, where velvet-covered walls surround a rich collection of seventeenth-century cabinets. In frigid contrast, the **Faience Room** is clad in blue and white tiles and topped by a high cupola. Restoration work in the next-door **Quiet Room** has uncovered seventeenth-century frescoes of preening Greek goddesses. Of the eighteenth-century rooms the most impressive is King August III's **Great Dining Hall**, complete with galleries for the royal music ensemble. The north wing of the palace mostly consists of nineteenth-century apartments, of which the grandest are the **Crimson Room**, the **Great Crimson Room** and sections of the **Potocki Art Museum** – dominated by statuary.

The Grounds

If your interest hasn't flagged after the palace tour, there are a couple of other places of interest within the grounds. The gate on the left side beyond the main entrance opens onto the stately **palace gardens** (10am till sunset). The ornate statue-topped facade overlooking the gardens contains a golden sundial that tells not just the time but also – thanks to an innovation from the Gdańsk astronomer Hevelius – the astrological sign.

The gardens reach down to the waterside, continuing rather less tidily along the lakeside to the north and south; in autumn this is a fine place for a Sunday afternoon scuffle through the falling oak leaves. Beyond the Orangery is the so-called **English Park**, whose main feature is a Chinese pavilion. Just down from the main gates is the **Poster Museum** (10am–4pm), a mish-mash of the inspired and the bizarre from an art form which has long had major currency in Poland.

The Suburbs

For most visitors anything outside the central town and Royal Way remains an unknown quantity. Visually engaging they may not be, yet some of the Warsaw **suburbs** are worth visiting both for their atmosphere and for their historic resonance, while at its furthest limits the city merges into the villages of the Mazovian countryside, with head-scarved peasants and horse-drawn carriages replacing the bustle of city life.

Żoliborz

Until the last century the **Żoliborz** district (whose name comes from a corruption of the French "joli bord"), due north of the centre, was an extension of the Kampinoski forest (the Bielany reserve in the northern reaches is a remnant), but then evolved into a working-class stronghold. The district's heart is the large square at the top of **ul. Mickiewicza** – the northwards extension of Marszałkowska and Gen. Andersa. Officially restored to its prewar name, **plac Wilsona** has a gritty, down-to-earth feeling that contrasts strongly with the gentrified airs of the city centre. Politics are gritty here too: the tough campaign fought by local resident and veteran oppositionist turned government minister Jacek Kuroń in the 1989 elections led to a sizzling confrontation with his Christian Democrat opponent before a packed audience at the old *Wisła* cinema on the square.

St Stanisław Kostka's Church, off to the west side of plac Wilsona, was Solidarity priest Jerzy Popiełuszko's parish church until he was murdered by security police in 1985 – whereupon his church became a Solidarity sanctuary and a focus for popular opposition. Although Western politicians no longer troop here, the custom of newlyweds dropping by to pay their respects at Father Jerzy's shrine continues. In the grounds there's a Via Dolorosa – a path marking the Stations of the Cross – taking you through the major landmarks of modern Polish history.

South of plac Wilsona, bordering on the New Town, is an altogether more sinister place, the **Citadel** (Cytadela). These decaying fortifications are the remains of the massive fortress built here by Czar Nicholas I in the wake of the 1831 Uprising. Houses were demolished to make way for it, and Varsovians even had to pay the costs of the intended instrument of their punishment. For the next eighty years or so suspected activists were brought here for interrogation and eventual imprisonment, execution or exile.

The large steps up the hill lead to the grim **Gate of Executions**, where partisans were shot and hanged, with particular regularity after the 1863 Uprising. Uneasy with so obvious a symbol of Russian oppression and Polish nationalist aspirations, the postwar communist party attempted to present the Citadel as a "mausoleum of the Polish revolutionary, socialist and workers' movement": thus alongside the plaque commemorating the leaders of 1863, there are memorials to the czarist-era Socialist Party, the Polish Communist Party and "the proletariat". Part of the prison is now a **historical museum** (Tues–Sun 9am–4pm), with a few preserved cells and some harrowing pictures by former inmates depicting the agonies of Siberia. The wagon in the courtyard is a reconstruction of the vehicles used to transport the condemned to that bleak exile.

West of the Citadel across plac Inwalidów is the grim **Museum of Struggle and Martyrdom**, al. Wojska Polskiego 25 (Wed–Sun 9am–4pm); housed in the former Gestapo headquarters, it focuses on the World War II bloodshed.

Praga

Across the river from the Old Town, the large **Praga** suburb was the main residential area for the legions of czarist bureaucrats throughout the nineteenth century – particularly the Saska Kempa district, south of al. Waszyngtona. The neo-Byzantine **Russian Orthodox Church** just beyond Praski Park is one remaining sign of their presence. But Praga's most notorious connection with Russians stems from a later date. At the beginning of September 1944, Soviet forces reached the outer reaches of Praga. Insurrectionists from the besieged town centre were dispatched to plead with them to intervene against the Nazis – to no avail. All through the Warsaw Uprising, Soviet tanks sat and waited on the edges, moving in to flush out the Nazis only when the city had been virtually eradicated. For the next forty years, the official account gave "insufficient Soviet forces" as the reason for the non-intervention; as with the Katyn massacre, every Pole knew otherwise.

On a lighter note, Warsaw's best-known and shadiest **flea market** – the Różyckiego Bazar – is five minutes' walk south from the Orthodox church on ul. Ząbkowska. The claim that you can buy almost anything here if the price is right still holds, though with perhaps less drama than in the mid-1980s, when you could reputedly pick up the odd contraband Kalashnikov from Afghanistan. If you do go, keep all valuables well in hand – pickpockets are numerous and skilful. Further south along the river, close to the Poniatowski bridge, is the **Dziesięciolecia stadium**, the city's largest sports stadium, now invaded by a sprawling outdoor market. When the traders aren't occupying the place it's also Warsaw's premier rock concert venue.

For motorists, the other main pull of Praga may turn out to be the garages and spare-parts shops scattered round its eastern stretches: the high incidence of break-ins on unattended cars nowadays makes a hunt for side-windows a common exercise for foreigners and Varsovians alike.

Eating and drinking

It doesn't seem that long ago since Warsaw had a reputation as a gastronome's nightmare, the majority of eating places marred by dingy surroundings, unimaginative menus and a lack of interest in the concept of service. One of the definite plusses of the post-communist era, therefore, has been a gradual but marked turnaround in the city's **restaurant** culture. Though the emphasis often tends to be on imitating Western habits – fast food included – the main thrust of change is towards diversity rather than uniformity. Alongside a good smattering of places specialising in traditional Polish cuisine, there's a welcome trend towards culinary variety– a collection of **ethnic restaurants** being the most obvious expression of this fact – giving Varsovians the chance to savour genuine Indian, Japanese and other ethnic cuisines on their home patch for the first time. Sadly, **prices** – increasingly comparable to Western ones – by and large ensure it's only the more wealthy city inhabitants who get to savour the best of the city's new food culture.

Similar types of comment apply to **cafés**; here too a wealth of new or renovated places have sprung up in the past few years, with everything from the most calorific haunts to down-to-earth student meeting points. Cakes and pastries worthy of the best of central Europe are no longer hard to come by, and if you follow the traditional local example you'll doubtless find yourself passing many hours musing over the edge of a cup of coffee, or Russian-style, a glass of tea.

Bars, traditionally something of a low spot of Warsaw nightlife, are improving in leaps and bounds. Alongside the ubiquitous traditional "drink-bars" serving hard spirits to hard-drinking locals, there's now a wide choice of newer, Western-influenced places, many of them only serving big-name German and other European brands, aimed partly at the tourists, partly at the city's young and upwardly mobile.

Meals and snacks

Though many **restaurants**, especially cheaper places, still follow the traditional communist-era practice of shutting up shop relatively early (9–10pm), a positive result of the current transformation of the city's eating culture is the increasing number of place that stay open late: and if you can't find a place to eat late, you'll always get something in the Central station. Foreign-language menus are available in the hotels and pricier restaurants, but don't count on it; if you're stuck, refer to the food section in *Basics* for help with the vocabulary. Remember the basic rule that only things with prices next to them are likely to be available – even then, *niema* (there is none) is a word you'll soon get used to. Unless you're really pushing the boat out, nowhere in Warsaw apart from the really top-category places is going to make a serious dent in your finances; our two categories take in "Moderate" (around £5–7 a head) and "First-class" (£7–12). Of the restaurants listed under the **"ethnic"** category – mostly newer places – the majority fall in the first-class category when it comes to prices, though several offer cheaper set-menu lunches. The rapid demise of the **milk bar** means there's precious few of these traditional low-cost haunts left in the city.

Moderate restaurants

Bistro Corner, ul. Marszałkowska 82. Reasonably priced restaurant close to the *Forum* hotel. A centre-of-town shopper's lunchtime favourite.

Bong Sen, ul. Poznańska 12. Goodish Vietnamese restaurant on a quiet central backstreet. Open 11am–10pm. Booking recommended (☎212-713).

Capri, ul. Smolna 14. Straightforward pizzeria opposite the National Museum, useful for museum-goers.

Da Elio, ul. Żurawia 20a. Popular new pizzeria with excellent adjacent salad bar – stack your plate for a quid. Open til midnight.

Don Giovanni, Krakowskie Przedmieście 37. Serviceable pizzeria, popular with Westerners – take-away and local deliveries too (☎262-788). Open till 11pm.

Galleria, Marszałkowska 34. Reasonably priced and good-quality joint upstairs in a shopping centre, popular with Warsaw intellectuals and dedicated card-players.

Habana, ul. Piękna 28. Supposedly Cuban restaurant with very little identifiably Hispanic about it. Passable pork dishes are the mainstay, but beware the occasional evening cabaret/ strip shows. Open noon–11pm.

Insam, ul. Senatorska 27. A passable if characterless Korean restaurant, a short walk west from the Old Town. It tends to get packed quickly, so turn up early, or better still book (☎279-707).

Kamienne Schodki, Rynek Starego Miasta 6. Duck with apples is the house speciality in this simple but popular Old Town hang-out.

Kuchcik, Nowy Świat 64. Respectable Polish nosh in comfortable surroundings.

Kuźnia, Wiertnicza 24. Wilanów's second-string restaurant. Pork dishes are a good bet, as are the peach and pear desserts. Open 10am–11pm.

Le Petit Trianon, ul. Piwna 40/42 (☎317-313). Good traditional Polish cuisine in small Old Town tourist trap that's beginning to nudge up into the expensive bracket. Tiny, so reservations are recommended in season. Open till midnight.

London Steak House, al. Jerozolimskie 42. The name says it all – roast beef and Yorkshire pud, across from the main station. Open till midnight.

Mekong, ul. Wspólna 35. Excellent small restaurant, owned by a Vietnamese student who stayed on. The fish dishes are definitely worth the extra twenty-minute wait. Open 10am–10pm. Booking recommended (☎211-881).

Nowe Miasto, corner of New Town square. Trendy, self-styled "ecological" restaurant (ignore the rainforest furniture) with good, mostly vegetarian menu. Highly popular.

Pod Krokodylem, Rynek Starego Miasta 19. Low ceilings and decent Polish cuisine in an Old Town basement venue that's a favourite with provincial Poles bingeing it for a weekend in the capital. Open 1pm–3am.

Pod Retmanem, ul. Bednarska 9. Gdańsk is the theme of the decor in this popular fish-orientated restaurant. Try the house drink, *napój rajeów Gdański*, for a pleasant surprise. Open Mon–Sat 11am–10pm.

Rycerska, ul. Szeroki Dunaj 9/11. Popular Old Town venue swamped in boar's heads and suits of armour. If they're available, the lamb dishes are worth a try. Reservations are a good idea (☎313-688). Open 10am–11pm.

Sinfonia, ul. Jasna 5. The concert hall restaurant. Advantages of this relatively unknown hangout are the grand decor, the occasional supplies of excellent Russian champagne and opening hours till midnight.

Sofia, pl. Powstanców Warszawy 315. Bulgarian joint in the town centre. The food is reasonable, the wines excellent. Open 11am–3pm.

Staropolska, ul. Krakowskie Przedmieście 8. Gloomy decor and erratic service is offset by a good, inevitably pork-based menu. A handy place if you're in the university area. Open late.

Szanghaj, ul. Marszałkowska 55/57. An ugly building houses Warsaw's best-known but hardly its best Chinese restaurant. The humdrum menu is backed by dubious music most evenings. Open 11am–11pm.

First-class restaurants

Ambassador, al. Ujazdowskie 8 (☎259-961). Luxurious establishment over the road from the US embassy. Good *zurek*, pork dishes and Georgian mineral water – reputedly Stalin's favourite. Open 11am–11pm.

Bazyliszek, Rynek Starego Miasta (☎311-841). Traditional Polish cuisine, with an emphasis on fish (eels and carp) and game (boar and wild pig) in glamorous old-world surroundings. Open weekdays 10am–midnight, weekends 10am–1am; reservations essential.

Belvedere, in Łazienki Park. Classy new restaurant inside the elegant park orangerie. Ideal for a (pricey) summer evening binge – it's worth going for the traditional Polish menu instead of the more touted (and expensive) French one. Reservations advisable in summer and at weekends (☎414-806). Open till midnight.

Cristal Budapeszt, ul. Marszałkowska 21 (☎253-433). Decent Hungarian nosh and wine with a sprinkling of Polish dishes; has a folk band and dancing in the evenings. Open 11am–1am – later at weekends.

Europeijski Hotel, ul. Krakowskie Przedmieście 13 (☎265-051). The smaller hotel restaurant is open 11am–9pm, the main restaurant 1pm–midnight, with dancing show and hence obligatory ticket purchase after 7pm. Dependable if unexceptional Orbis fare.

Foksal, ul. Foksal 3/5. One of the best of the top-bracket restaurants, premium French-based cuisine that'll leave a sizeable hole in your wallet. Reservations ☎277-225. Open till 3am.

Forum Hotel, ul. Nowogrodzka 24/26 (☎210-271). Has two decent restaurants mainly for tourists, both open 7am–11am & 1pm–midnight – very useful if you arrive in town late and famished, though they like to keep you waiting however empty they are. Reservations are a good idea for larger groups.

Gessler, ul. Senatorska 37 (☎270-633). A newish restaurant that's fast become one of Warsaw's smartest and trendiest. Gourmet European cuisine in demure surroundings. Prices are among the highest in town. Open 10am till late. Reservations definitely advisable.

Lers, Długa 29 (☎635-3888). Within walking distance of the Old Town and much frequented by wealthier tourist groups – which is why a reservation is essential in summer.

Montmartre, Nowy Świat 7. Spacious, chic new centre-of -town French restaurant – bring the credit card along for this one. Open midnight (☎6286-315).

Sobieski, pl. A. Zawiszy. Three restaurants – all pricey – of which the excellent Polish one (traditional dishes) stands out.

Świętoszek, ul. Jezuicka 2. High-class Old Town haunt – strictly suit and tie – with a notable line in Polish specialities. Reservations almost essential (☎315-634).

Victoria Hotel, ul. Królewska (☎278-011). Contains two well-established luxury eateries, the *Canaletto* and the *Hetmańska*, both open 1pm–midnight. The former is one of the best Orbis places in town, with a good line in traditional fowl and game dishes. Reservations essential at weekends.

Wilanów, Wiertnicza 27 (☎421-363). Right outside Wilanów Palace. Exclusive and expensive joint frequented by diplomats – many of whom live nearby – and visiting dignitaries. The "old Polish" spread is good, the waiters amongst the most obsequious you'll ever encounter. Reservations essential.

Zajazd Napoleoński, ul. Płowiecka 83 (☎153-068). Small, exclusive Praga restaurant, housed in an inn where Napoleon is supposed to have stayed en route for Moscow. Popular with the smart set. Reservations essential. Open late.

Ethnic restaurants

Tokio, ul. Dobra 17. Japanese eaterie with a high-quality *sushi* bar. Open till 10pm (bar 8pm).

Tsumbame, ul. Folksal 16. Excellent Japanese restaurant and accompanying *sushi* bar off Nowy Świat. Cheap lunchtime menus. Open till midnight.

Maharaja, ul. Ostrzycka 2/4. Commendable new Indian venture with a Nepalese chef – curries as hot as you want them. In the Praga district. Reservations advisable at weekends (☎134-874). Open till midnight.

Menora, pl. Grzybowski 2. Genuine new kosher restaurant across from the synagogue – the gefilte fish is worth a tryout.

Parnas, ul. Krakowskie Przedmieście 4/6 (☎260-071). Posh town-centre Greek restaurant and coffee house: cheaper eaterie upstairs.

Szecherezada, ul. Zajązkowska 11(☎410-269). Syrian-run place, giving Warsaw its first taste of Middle Eastern cuisine: kitsch Arabian nights decor, good *szaslik* dishes.

Valencia, ul. Smocza 27. Pricey, disappointingly *ersatz* Spanish joint partially redeemed by the live flamenco guitar.

Milk bars, snack bars and other cheap eateries

Arrosto, ul. Poznańska 4. Small and cheap with good, fast lunchtime service.

Bambino, ul. Krucza 21. Budget eaterie near the *Grand* hotel – good range of Polish dishes.

Bambola, ul. Wspólna 27. Nice pizzeria, with seventeen kinds of pizza to eat in or take away. Other branches on Puławska and Al. Terozolimskie. All open till 10pm.

Café Pinguin, al. Jerozolimskie 42. Quick-service restaurant offering regular meat-and-potatoes-type lunches.

Delhi Dabar, Nowogrodzka 22. Tiny Indian takeaway (standing table only) opposite the Forum. Biryanis are worth a try.

Dziekanka, Krakowskie Przedmieście 56. Popular student hang-out with an emphasis on fast food – though it's possible to sit down. Open till midnight.

Economistów, Nowy Świat 49. Basic student cafeteria that's as economical as its name suggests. The *barszcz* and chicken dishes are both recommended.

Expres, ul. Bracka 20. A tiny, private operation offering efficient lunch service, but it gets very full around midday.

Expresso, ul. Bracka 18. Cheap, central joint offering Polish-style basics. Open for breakfast.

Familijny, Nowy Świat 30. Solid traditional-style milk bar, mostly vegetarian dishes.

Giros, ul. Różana 1. Succulent filled pitta take aways – cheap too.

Grill Bar, ul. Zgoda 4. Ex-milk bar turned budget diner. Good for late breakfasts.

Krokiecik, ul. Zgody 1. Good fast service, in useful downtown shoppers' location.

Kubuś, ul. Ordynacka. Good soups and other filling, low-cost meals.

Max, ul. Poznańska 38. Small private bar serving good Arab nosh, particularly kebabs and shashlik; close to the Central station.

Mesa, pl. Zbawiciela. Small downtown restaurant with a special line in Polish-style fish dishes.

Murżynem, ul. Nowomeijska 13. A good basic spaghetti and pizza house just north of the Old Town square.

Pod Barbakanem, ul. Mostowa 27/29. Deservedly popular milk bar-turned-restaurant near the Barbakan where you can sit outside and watch the crowds.

Pod Gołebami, ul. Piwna. Slightly upmarket Old Town bistro, popular with tourists.

Pod Samsonem, ul. Freta 3/5. Popular New Town restaurant offering cheap, good-quality Polish menu.

Salad Bar, ul. Tamka 17. Cheapish good-quality salad bar so tiny you're best eating away.

Stylandia, ul. Marszałkowska 18. Cheap central eaterie with good line in Chinese snacks.

Uniwersytecki, Krakowskie Przedmieście 20. Milk bar much frequented by students; just up from the university gates.

Victor, ul. Kostancińska 3. Privately run milk bar with a good selection of trad Polish nosh.

Wygodna, ul. Chmielna 23. Another unpretentious lunchtime restaurant in a useful central shopping location.

Zapiecek, ul. Piwna 34/36. Old Town student haunt, good for a breakfast fill-up: opens 9am.

Zodiak, ul. Widok 26. Basic town-centre cafeteria to fill yourself up at lunchtime. Just across from the *Forum* hotel.

Fast food

Western-style **fast food** has finally hit the streets of the capital in a big way. Alongside the real thing – *McDonalds* and *Burger King* are among the big names that have recently got in on the act – you'll find plenty of Polish imitations. In addition to the hamburger joints and hot-dog stalls springing up on every street corner, **pizza** in various shapes and sizes is a well-established favourite, either in Italian form or in the tasty traditional Polish variant of the *zapiekanki*, a half baguette type morsel with liberal sprinklings of cheese on top. The **Central station** has now been invaded by a variety of fast-food stands ranging in quality from bog-standard to fairly classy; several are open round the clock, meaning you're guaranteed a burger at almost any time of day – providing you're prepared to brave the generally dubious late-night company.

Cafés and bars

Cafés are usually enjoyable in Warsaw, though, as stressed earlier, interest is as much social as gastronomic. In the better-stocked places, the things to ask for are *ciastka* (cakes) and *cukiernia* (sweets); when available, they tend to be excellent. The *Hortex* cocktail bars (nothing to do with alcohol) are known for some of the best ice creams in town – besides the *Jezuicka* (see opposite), there's also one at ul. Świętokrzyska 35 and on plac Konstytucji.

Most of the **bars** are of the archetypal Polish "drink bar" variety. If you don't fancy their atmosphere, hotel bars are always an option; for a good general choice try the places along Krakowskie Przedmieście, the main street south from the Old Town. And if seedy drink bars really do appeal, you'll find a number of them at the top end of ul. Freta, in the New Town.

Cafés

Amatorska, Nowy Świat. 21. Trendy, popular and in a classic location.

Blikle's, Nowy Świat 25. The oldest cake shop in the city: you won't get coffee here, just some of the most mouth-watering pastries anywhere.

Bowta, ul. Freta. A very pleasant café with outside seating on the New Town square.

Café Columbia, al. Jerozolimskie 42. A centre-of-town joint serving respectable coffee and *ciastka* in rather funereal surroundings.

Danusia, al. Jerozolimskie 57. A cosy little morning coffee shop, next door to the British Institute, close to the main station.

Eljat, al. Ujazdowskie 47. Coffee house run by the Polish–Israeli Friendship Society.

Europejski, corner of Krakowskie Przedmieście. Deliciously calorific pastries and ices, in hotel coffee shop.

Harenda, ul. Oboźna 4. Student hang-out.

Jezuicka, Rynek Starego Miasto 15, below the *Bazyliszek* restaurant. A busy Old Town rendezvous. The creamy *ciastka* desserts and ice creams are good, the service unpredictable.

Manekin, Rynek Starego Miasto 27. An enjoyable basement coffee dive on the Old Town square, with a bar at the back.

Nowa Oranżeria, ul. Freta. Enjoyable indoor café in grounds of Łazienki Park. Next to smart *Belvedere* restaurant. The *Amfiteatr* café by the lake is equally good – and pricey.

Pasieka, ul. Freta. Small intimate pizzeria more noted for the delicious house drink – hot honey with cinnamon or crunched cardamom.

Pod Krokodyl, Rynek Starego Miasto 19. Popular Old Town café-cum-restaurant.

Polonia, al. Jerozolimskie 45. The hotel's *cukiernia* is a congenial central stop-off with a good selection of cakes, ice creams and desserts.

U Pana Michała, ul. Freta. Small, rather sedate coffee shop in the New Town.

U Szczepka i Tońka, ul. Jan Pawła 36. Café-bar run by local Lwów (L'viv) Friendship Foundation, re-creating prewar atmosphere of the former eastern Polish "capital".

Wedel's, Corner of ul. Szpitalna. Next to *Wedel* shop. Excellent rich hot chocolate and chocolate waffles.

Bars

Drinking out has become a lot easier than it used to be. In the city centre especially you can find numerous Western-style watering holes, many of them open into the early hours of the morning. **Pubs** (both English and Irish) have quickly established themselves as a trendy city favourite, though with the price of a pint matching (and in some cases exceeding) that back home it's a mystery how anyone but foreigners and the most wealthy Poles can afford them. Watch spirit prices – anything beyond a Polish-produced vodka or *winiak* tends to make a noticeable dent in the wallet.

Der Elefant, ul. Mickiewicza 20. Popular bar near the *Sobieski* hotel.

Europejski, Krakowskie Przedmieście 13. In summer the hotel's terrace café is one of the nicest places in town to sit out and enjoy an early evening drink.

Fugazi, ul. Leszno 5. Determinedly alternative hang-out that's popular with the city's punks and other black-clad types. Enjoy your beer sitting in half a bus – live gigs too.

Hacienda, ul. Freta 18. Near the Barbakan. Student pizza joint doubling as a bar.

Harenda, ul. Obozna 4. Hip student café-bar in the university area serving draught Guinness.

Irish Pub, ul. Miodowa 3. Deservedly popular Irish joint with plenty of atmosphere; despite stiffish prices, the place regularly can't fit everyone who wants to be there. Live music (cajun, c&w and Polish–Irish mix) every night of the week. The Guinness is pricey – you're better off with the cheaper draught *Żywiec* instead. Get there early, at least for a seat. Also see "Clubs and gigs" below.

John Bull Pub, ul. Jezuicka 4. Old Town attempt at the genuine British article – polished wooden bar, back copies of *The Times* and draught keg bitter at over two quid a pint is the result. Live jazz Thursday evenings. Open till 11pm.

Lapidarium, ul. Nowomiejska 4. Upmarket bar-restaurant inside scenic ivy-decked Old Town courtyard. Entrance fee includes a drink. Live music most evenings in in summer.

Maria, Podwale 19. Cheap studenty hang-out in the Old Town area.

Marywil, ul. Senatorska 27. Old-style *winiarnia* near the opera – as you'd expect, a wide selection of wines on offer.

Na Barce, near the Śląsko-Dąbrowski bridge. Waterside barge turned into a imaginatively done-up bar/club in summer. Entrance fee includes a drink. Alternative-oriented music, occasional raves and acid house. Excellent fun.

Na Trakcie, Krakowskie Przedmieście 47. Popular bar with ritzy background Muzak, open late. Serves food, too.

Okrąglak, Emilii Plater. On the square below the Palace of Culture. Popular local drinking spot housed in a ex-public loo: a local vodka-swillers favourite.

Pod Herbami, ul. Piwna 21/23. An archetypal "drink bar" – but one that hip young Varsovians now like to be seen in.

Studio M, Krakowskie Przedmieście 27. Trendy, expensive designer bar frequented by arty types – there's even a small gallery. Open till 1am.

That's it Pub, Marszałkowska 55. Anodyne town-centre pub run by *Quick* burgers downstairs, the ambience rescued by some solid occasional live blues and rock performances.

U Hopfera, Krakowskie Przedmieście 55. Wine-bar and restaurant that's a favourite with students, but closes at 10pm.

U Fukiera, Rynek Starego Miasta 27. Smoky traditional wine bar on the square, complete with gypsy band.

Nightlife

If Chopin concerts and intense avant-garde dramas are your idea of a good night out, you're unlikely to be disappointed by Warsaw **nightlife**: in summer especially, high-quality theatre productions, operas and recitals abound, many of them as popular with tourists as with Varsovians themselves. At the other end of the scale there's the schmaltzy nightclub/cabaret scene centred on the big hotels, a bigger pull for businesstypes and prostitutes than for your average punter.

Finding something in between – in other words, the sort of places that would appeal to the average fun-loving visitor's idea of a club – still isn't as easy as many would like. The centre-of-town student clubs are still the most reliable places for a good bop – don't let the name put non-students off though – and it's always worth checking out what's going on in and around the university area. Additionally there's also a (slowly) growing selection of bars and cafés that regularly feature live music, usually free, for the customer's benefit.

For up-to-date **information** about what's on, check the current listings sections to be found in the Warsaw *Voice*, *Welcome to Warsaw* or *Warsaw: What Where*

When (see "Information" on p.57) For really comprehensive listings, you can't beat the local weekend editions of *Gazeta Wyborcza* and *Zycie Warszawy*, particularly useful for a stop-press on films and concerts around town.

Regular Warsaw **festivals** include the excellent annual **Jazz Jamboree** in October (Miles Davis, Michael Brecker, John McLaughlin are among recent headline artists), the biannual **Warsaw Film Festival**, the **Festival of Contemporary Music** held every September, and the five-yearly **Chopin Piano Competition** – always a launch-pad for a major international career. The **October Film Week**, organised by the *Hybrydy* club, is a vaguely alternative arts event.

Clubs and gigs

Warsaw's few decent clubs have been feeling the economic pinch in recent years, and the same goes for the night scene generally: appearances by major Western bands are still a rarity. When artists with the pulling power of Stevie Wonder do turn up, they generally play outdoors at the large **Dziesięciolecia** stadium in Praga, near the river.

Except for the big names, the touring circuit for **Polish bands** is confined to student clubs and the occasional one-off festival. **Jazz clubs** are scarce, a pity in view of the number of excellent local jazz musicians, some of them international figures – such as Zbigniew Namysłowski (tenor sax) and Tomas Stanko (trumpet). As a rule, **discos** are tacky, Europop affairs, frequented by a combination of young reticents and inveterate drunkards. Most of the clubs listed below are known as student venues, though students aren't the only customers. With nearly all of them, it's worth calling in advance – or checking listings – for the current programme.

Akwarium, ul. Emilii Plater 49 (☎205-072). Just behind the Palace of Culture. The only genuine jazz club in town, it has at least one good Polish or foreign act a week. The MTV screen in the café downstairs attracts the Warsaw trendies. Unfortunately it's still plagued by early closing restrictions.

Centrum, Marszałkowska. Upstairs in the shopping centre immediately north of the *Forum* hotel. A taste of the archetypal Polish-style disco – if you can get past the bouncer.

Fugazi, ul. Leszno 5. Premier alternative live venue, and always worth checking for current action. Also see "Bars", p.91.

Fiolka, ul. Puławska 257. Lively café cum disco (normally runs late) with regular hip-hop/rap dance sessions and a weekly gay disco. Also does food. Call for current details (☎439-822).

Hybrydy, ul. Złota 7/9 (☎273-763). Behind the *Centrum* department store on Marszałkowska. Weekend discos with a decent beat, a "Rap-Club" and occasional live gigs. Photo exhibitions too.

Irish Pub, ul. Miodowa 3. Live music every night of the week: unpredictable mix of traditional Irish, cajun and c&w. Get there early, at least for a seat. (See "Bars", p.91).

Na Barce, near the Sląsko-Dąbrowski bridge. Alternative-oriented DJs, occasional raves and acid house events. (See "Bars", p.91).

Ochota, Cultural Centre ul. Grójecka 75. Regular live gigs, especially reggae.

Park, al. Niepodległości 196 (☎257-199). In the Piłsudski Park, southwest of the town centre. Regular late-night dancing; some live bands, too.

Remont, ul. Waryńskiego 12 (☎257-497). Best of the student clubs, with regular rock, folk and jazz concerts, discos – and weekly Hare Krishna meditation sessions.

Stodoła, ul. Batorego 10 (☎256-031). Ten minutes' walk from the *Park*. Lively spot at weekends, with a late disco. Large dance floor.

Opera and concerts

Opera is a big favourite in Warsaw, and classical concerts – especially anything with a piano in it (preferably Chopin) – tend to attract big audiences, so it's always advisable to book. Tickets for many concerts are available from the theatre ticket office (Kasa Teatralny) at al. Jerozolimskie 25, a little along from the *Forum* hotel (Mon–Fri 10.30am–6.30pm; ☎219-454/383).

Filharmonia, ul. Jasna 5 (☎267-281). Regular performances by the excellent National Philharmonic Orchestra and visiting ensembles. Tickets from the box office at ul. Sienkiewicza 12.

Akademia Muzyczna, ul. Okólnik 2. Regular concerts by talented students. Free entry.

Chopin Museum, ul. Okólnik 1. Piano recitals and other occasional performances.

Evangelical Church, pl. Małachowskiego. Focus on organ and choral music, often with visiting choirs. Excellent acoustics.

Łazienki Park, al. Ujazdowskie. Varied summer programme of orchestral, choral and chamber concerts, often held in the Orangery.

Opera Kameralna, al. Solidarności 76b (☎312-240). Chamber opera performances in a magnificent white and gold stucco auditorium.

Operetka Warszawska, ul Nowogrodzka 49 (☎628-0360). Operetta and occasional chamber music performances.

Teatr Wielki Operyi Balet, pl. Teatralny (☎263-001). The big opera performances – everything from Mozart to contemporary Polish composers such as Moniuszko and Penderecki, in suitably grandiose surroundings. Tickets bookable by phone up to 14 days in advance.

Theatre and cinema

Theatre is one of the most popular and artistically strong forms of entertainment in Warsaw. Not speaking Polish is, of course, an obstacle, but for the acting style alone it's worth considering a performance at one of the major theatres such as the *Atenaeum*, ul. Jaracza 2, the venerable old *Polski*, ul. Karasia 2, the *Studio* (inside the Palace of Culture), or the *Powszechny*, ul. Zamoyskiego 20. There is usually quite a range of productions on offer – translations of Shakespeare, adaptations of classical European drama, Polish musicals and some remarkable home-grown avant-garde. For tickets, both advance and on the day, as well as a lowdown on current productions, check at the Kasa Teatralny (see above).

The traditional mixture in Warsaw's **cinemas** of "safe" Western pictures, eastern European art movies and home-grown hits is gradually broadening towards a more varied Western selection, including soft porn – much to the Church's horror. As on television, subtitling rather than dubbing is the rule. Places with regular showings of **foreign films** include the *Atlantic* and *Non-Stop*, both at ul. Chmielna 33, the *Relax*, ul. Złota 8, the *Polonia* at Marszałkowska 56 and the *Iluzjon*, ul. Wspólna 5, which has a regular schedule of classics and art films. The *Kultura*, Krakowskie Przedmieście 21/23, close to the Old Town, is one of the few cinemas in the country equipped with a fully up-to-date Dolby sound system, though others are supposed to be following suit in the near future.

Gay Warsaw

Despite the difficulties of operating in the current Catholic-dominated political climate, the city has now developed an (admittedly small) network of **gay nightlife**. The organisational lynchpin of Warsaw's gay community is the **Pink Service**, the country's only agency for gays and lesbians – their office is at ul. Mickiewicza 60 (☎334-672) in the Żoliborz district. (Mon–Fri 10am–4pm). The Pink Service's principal activities include acting as an information resource for and about the Polish lesbian and gay scene, running an annual Gay Pride Day, publishing their own magazines – *Men* (for gays), *Arabella* (for lesbians) and an occasional English-language gay newsletter – as well as distributing international gay publications. Their office, which welcomes foreign visitors, is without doubt your best source of information for local gay events and happenings, new bars and clubs included. Listed below are a couple of the most popular current gay haunts.

Café Fiolka, ul. Puławska 257 (☎439-822). Gay and lesbian discos on Fridays (10pm–5am) run by the Pink Service. Membership cards from the office.

Café Rudawka, ul. Elbląska. North town café with gay and lesbian disco on Friday nights.

Polonia, al. Jerozolimskie 25. Small central bar near Nowy Świat favoured by city gays.

Corner, ul. Żurawia. Gay café haunt near the *Grand* hotel.

The gay **student group**, *Słowarzyszenie Grup Lambda*, also welcomes contact and runs a semi-underground club; their address is Uniwersytet Warszawski, ul. Krakowskie Przedmieście 24, 00325 Warszawa.

Shopping

For anyone who knew the place a few years ago, **shopping** in Warsaw these days can be a bewildering experience. The old state-owned shops were one of the first things to go with the end of the communist era, replaced in the majority of cases by the wide array of privately owned concerns, both Polish and Western-owned corner shops that now the adorn the streets of the capital. While it's not exactly Paris or Frankfurt, yet there are enough chic boutiques and other upmarket-looking places around the commercially bustling central areas of Warsaw to have you thinking twice about where you've landed. There's no shortage of goods either, specialist shops catering to most conceivable consumerist whims alongside the regular diet of general stores: bananas and exotic fruits, for instance, virtually unobtainable only a few years back, can now be picked up almost anywhere – at Western prices – as can similarly priced regular items. A specific touch of Polishness is provided by the welter of markets, bazaars and street traders – a traditional Polish speciality – you'll find around the capital, these increasingly organised gatherings adding a characteristic element of energy – and occasionally, uneasy hustle – to the commercial proceedings.

Clothes, crafts and hard-currency shops

The shops at the northern end of Marszałkowska and the streets east of the Palace of Culture are the places to hunt for **clothes**, shoes and general finery. It's also worth looking in at the big department stores of Marszałkowska for clothes, and women might turn up something at the *Moda Polska* department store on ul. Swiętokrzyska – particularly items like winter coats and hats. Another bargain are handmade shoes, made to high quality by cobblers like the one just below pl. Trzech Krzyzy on al. Ujazdowskie.

Quality and taste is variable at the *Cepelia* **handicraft shops** scattered around town. The biggest is at Marszałkowska 99/101, where you can find wooden boxes and the occasional bit of attractive jewellery. *Polski Len* shops, like the one on ul. Targowa, are worth checking for linen (always 100 percent pure).

The old **hard-currency** *Baltona* and *Pewex* shops aren't quite as important as they used to be, given the increased availability of Western goods, but they're still useful for alcohol, tobacco, confectionery and luxury goods as well as basic items like toothpaste and toothbrushes. You'll find them in the big hotels and at other locations all over town, such as in the *LOT/Marriot* building on al. Jerozolimskie (Mon–Fri 8am–8pm, Sat 8am–4pm).

Books, cards and records

For **books**, the *antykwariaty* scattered around the Old Town and central shopping area sometimes produce gems, especially in the art field. Several contemporary bookshops, like the huge *Universus* store at ul. Belwederska 20/22 or the ones in the Palace of Culture, are also worth checking out. Other bookshops to look out for include *Omega*, ul. Piekna 8, and *Lexicon*, Nowy Świat 9. *Im. B. Prusa*, the large main university bookshop also on Nowy Świat, is one also of the best around. If you're desperate for an English-language paperback the *Penguin* bookshop on al. Jerozolimskie, close to the British Institute, has all the latest Penguin titles, often cheaper than in Britain. The best selection of art **postcards**, old and new, is in the shop at ul. Nowomiejska 17, near the Barbakan.

Records and **cassettes** are more unpredictable. Really good buys like Chopin boxed sets on the state labels are hard to get hold of, precisely because they are so good. Selections in the bigger stores, like those on Nowy Świat, still tend to be a bit limited, though for rock music they're rivalled by the ranks of street entrepreneurs trading in the latest Western sounds, particularly pirated cassettes of varying quality. About the best selection of **CDs** around is at the *Salon Muzyczny*, ul. Mazowiecka 9 (near the *Warszawa* hotel), particularly worth checking for Polish-label classical selections. For everything but Polish-produced releases, **prices** for records, tapes and CDs aren't much different from what you'd pay at home. The pirate cassettes – normally no more than a couple of quid each – are a different matter, though the virtual boycott of live gigs by major rock and pop bands they have caused might make you want to think twice about buying them.

Galleries and antiques

The commercial **galleries** scattered around the city centre range from the arty to the downright tacky, with the biggest concentrations on Marszałkowska and Krakowskie Przedmieście. *Piotr Nowicki's*, on Nowy Świat, has a good range of modern jewellery, but ignore the paintings. The art at *Zapiecek* in the Old Town on ul. Zapiecek is worth checking out, and *Dziekanka* and *Kordegarda* galleries on Krakowskie Przedmieście often have interesting exhibitions, as does the *Folksal* gallery in the regal-looking building on the corner of ul. Folksal and Nowy Świat. Another particularly well-known gallery is the *Zachęta* at pl. Malachowskiego 3, just below the Saxon Gardens (see p.52), while the *ZPAF* gallery, pl. Zamkowy 8, run by the city photographer's club, has regular exhibitions by both Polish and foreign photographers. *Gallery SPAM*, the artists and musicians union centre at ul. Krucza 14, is a trendy hang-out with the art crowd – as well as exhibitions they also have occasional live music performances.

Antiques enthusiasts interested in hunting down bargains should seek out the Sunday **Koło bazaar** (see "Markets" opposite). Of the established antique dealers the formerly state-owned *Desa* chain of shops are worth checking out: they have four city-centre outlets, at al. Andersa 20, Marszałkowska 34, Nowy Świat 48 and pl. Zamkowy 4/6. Other dealers include *Rempex*, Krakowskie Przedmieście 4/6, *Optimus* (graphics, coins), Mokotowska 45, and *Kolekcjoner* (maps, graphics), ul. Targowa 19. For old cameras and lenses, especially Soviet models, there's a special market every Sunday at the *Stodoła* student club on ul. Batorego (see "Clubs and gigs", p.93).

Supermarkets and food stalls

With queues, low-quality products and scarce supplies now a thing of the past, picking up mealtime supplies from **supermarkets** is a more feasible prospect than anyone could have dreamt of a few years ago, especially if you're on a tight budget. Though many places stock a reasonably comprehensive range of Western products it pays to look out for the generally cheaper Polish version, particularly if you're after meats, cheeses and other dairy products. For alcohol to wash down an *al fresco* meal, you'll save money buying a Polish beer (bottled or canned) or Hungarian and Bulgarian wine, widely available, as opposed to the pricier German or Dutch lagers that status-conscious Poles seem to be going for these days. Fresh fruit and vegetables are generally better bought from **street stalls and vendors** than the supermarkets – the quality and range available tends to be better.

One modern supermarket chain with a number of stores round the central city area is **W W**, ul. Przechodnia 2, ul. Złota 9 and Lazurowa 8. The stock a full range of Polish and imported products. Open Mon–Sat 7am–10pm, Sun 9am–3pm.

Markets and bazaars

At weekends, traditional market areas like the **Hala Mirowska** are now packed with stalls and worth visiting for the atmosphere alone. There are also a few established specialist **markets** worth exploring:

Centrum, in front of the Palace of Culture. Large array of stalls, mostly clothes, hi-fi and bric-a-brac. Now joined by two large covered market areas for the more established shops.

Dziesięciolecia stadium, Praga district, near Poniatowski bridge. Biggest of the outdoor city markets held around outside tiers of a sports stadium – where many street vendors moved when the city authorities cleared them out of the city centre. Everything you could imagine anyone thinking of selling – Soviet bric-a-brac, cars, rifles, fur coats and all things in between.

Różycki market, Praga (see the "Praga" section). The ranks of Polish and gypsy traders here are swelled these days by increasing numbers of Romanians and Russians – a Warsaw experience not to be missed. All day, every day.

Koło bazaar, ul. Obozowa, in the Wola district (near the end of tram lines #1, #13 and #24, or bus #159, #167). The main antiques and bric-a-brac market, with everything from sofas and old Russian samovars to a genuine Iron Cross on offer. Recommended. Sundays.

Ciuchy bazaar, Rembertów, in the south of the Praga district. Look for clothes bargains.

Food market, ul. Polna. If you want your avocados or papayas and still can't find them on street stalls, this is where the affluent stock up, diplomats included.

Night shopping

For anyone caught short of a bottle of vodka for an impromptu party, or just desperate for a late-night snack, the following shops will be useful.

Michel Badre, Puławska 53, in Mokotów. A newly opened French establishment open round the clock, selling *baguettes*, beer, champagne, Western newspapers and so on at French prices.

German shop, corner of al. Niepodległości and Wawelska. Similar style to the above – substituting Deutsch for Français.

Sklepy Nocne (Night Shops) are at: Grójecka 86 (8am–1pm); ul. Puławska at the corner of ul. Dolna (*Max*; 8pm–2am); al. Soldiarności 72 and ul. Targowa 26/30 (*Hala Człuchowska*; 8pm–2am); Przy Agorze 22 (8pm–3am); ul. Targowa (*Kijowanka;* 8pm–6am).

Listings

Airlines The *LOT* building at al. Jerozolimskie 65/79 (☎305-678) makes bookings for domestic and foreign flights, as do all the major Orbis offices. All the big international airlines have offices in the city, mainly on ul. Krucza, ul. Szpitalna and ul. Marszałkowska, as well as booking desks at Okęcie airport.

Airport information Domestic airport ☎469-750/70; Okęcie international airport ☎469-624.

American Express Krakowskie Przedmieście 11 (☎635 2002). Open Mon–Fri 9am–5pm.

Banks *Narodowy Bank Polski:* ul. Świętokrzyska 11/12 & pl. Pow. Warszawy 4; *PKO*, ul. Trauguta 7/9. Open 8am–4pm.

Billiards Join the latest national craze at one of the number of newly established pool halls such as *Valdi*, ul. Piźkna 7/9, *Bilard Amerykanski* (in the *Metropol* hotel), *U Docenta*, ul. Banacha 2.

Boat trips Along the Wisła to the Zegrze Bay and back. Food on board. Daily (May–Oct) from Most Poniatowskiego. Depart 9am, return 5pm (☎628-0526/194-011 ext. 50).

British Institute Al. Jerozolimskie 59 (Mon–Fri 8.30am–5.30pm; ☎6287-401); the library has English newspapers.

Car hire *Orbis* rental service, ul. Nowogrodzka 27 (Mon–Sat 8am–8pm; ☎211-360); *Budget*: Okęcie airport (☎467-310 – 8am–8pm)) and the *Marriot* hotel (☎630-7280 – 7am–10pm); *Avis*: Airport (☎469-872 – 7am–10pm) and the *Marriot* (☎630-7316 – 8am–6pm).

Chemists All-night *apteka* at ul. Zielna 45, ul. Freta 13, ul. Leszno 38, ul. Żeromskiego 13 and ul. Puławska 39. For homeopathic treatments try ul. Miła 33 and Marszałkowska 11a.

Embassies *Australia*, ul. Estońska 3/5 (☎176-081/6); *Austria*, ul. Gagarina 34 (☎410-081/5); *Belgium*, ul. Senatorska 34 (☎270-233/5); *Bulgaria*, al. Ujazdowskie 33/35 (☎294-071); *Canada*, ul. J. Matejki 1/5 (☎298-051); *Czech*, ul. Koszykowa 18 (☎6287-221); *Denmark*, ul. Starościńska 5 (☎490-056/79); *Finland*, ul. Chopina 4/8 (☎294-091); *France*, ul. Piękna 1 (☎6288-401); *Germany*, ul. Dąbrowiecka 30 (☎173-011); *Israel*, ul. Krzywickiego 24 (☎250-023/8); *Italy*, pl. Dąbrowskiego 6 (☎263-471); *Netherlands*, ul. Rakowiecka 19 (☎492-351); *Norway*, ul. Chopina 2a (☎214-231); *Romania*, ul. Chopina 10 (☎6283-156); *Russia*, ul. Belwederska 49 (☎213-453/75); *Sweden*, ul. Bagatela 3 (☎493-351); *UK*, al. Roż 1 (☎6281-001/5); *USA*, al. Ujazdowskie 29 (☎6283-041/9).

Emergencies Police ☎997; fire ☎998; ambulance ☎999 or ☎6282-424.

Fax *Komertel* communications centre, ul. Nowogrodzka 45. Fax and satellite telecommunications service 24hr a day.

Ferries Polish Baltic Steamship Company, ul. Chałubińskiego 8. (Ferry information, ☎302-963, ☎300-930.)

Football The stadium of *Legia Warszawa*, the city team, is at Lazienkowska to the southeast of the city centre.

Foreign cultural institutes *Goethe Institute* (German), ul. Świętokrzyska 18; *France*, ul. Świętokrzyska 36; *Italy*, ul. Foksal 11; *Russia*, ul. Foksal 10.

Health food shops *Bios*, ul. Folksal 8, *Corcot*, Marszałkowska 56, *Kabanos*, ul. Puławska 52, *U Stańczyków*, ul. Wilcza 23.

Hitchhiking The *Biuro Autostop*, ul. Narbutta 27a (Mon–Fri 9am–4pm), has English-language information about the ins and outs of hitching in Poland, and sells maps and autostop coupons.

Horse-racing In a country famous for producing Arabian thoroughbreds it's not surprising to discover that a day out at the races is a popular pastime among Varsovians. The main race track is in the southern **Służewiec** district of town, ul. Wyścigowa 1 (trams #14, #19, #33, or #36 from the centre), the big annual events (e.g. the Warsaw Derby, held on the first Sunday of July, and the Great Warsaw races) drawing crowds of 40,000 and up. The season runs from April to November. Races are on Wed, Sat & Sun. Check local listings for the current details.

International operator ☎900.

Launderette Ul. Mordechaja Anielewicza, on corner of the Ghetto monument square; bus #180 passes right by (Mon–Fri 9am–7pm, Sat 9am–4pm).

Local tours Apart from the obvious Orbis choice there are a wealth of small private agencies around town now. A couple worth knowing are *Mazurka* (☎291-249), based inside the *Forum* and *Novotel* and offering tours round the city and coach excursions to Żelazowa Wola; and *Trakt*, the Warsaw Guides Association, ul. Kredytowa 6 (☎278-068/69), offering individual guides, bus tours and a ticket-booking service.

Lost property On city transport, ul. Słowackiego 45. Otherwise the offices at ul. Floriańska 10 and ul. Wery Kostrzewy 11.

Maps The IT on plac Zamkowy and the *Atlas* bookshop at al. Jan Pawłka II have some of the best selection of Polish maps.

Medical attention *Central Medical Centre*, ul. Hoża 56.

Money Any of the *kantors*, tourist offices or hotels can change money. Orbis accept travellers' cheques, but they may try to extract a 10 percent commission, so a hotel (or American Express) can be a better bet. The *National Bank* at ul. Świętokrzyska 11/21 can help with transferring money from abroad, though this (like all other transactions) can take a long time.

Motorists The main office of *PZMot*, the Polish motorists' association, is at al. Jerozolimskie 63. Twenty-four-hour breakdown service, run by *PZMot*, is at ul. Kaszubska 2b (☎981 or ☎416-621/410-423). The *Polmozbyt* breakdown service at ul. Omulewska 27 in southern Praga is open 6am–10pm (☎954). Both should be able to track down mechanics for most Western makes of car. For spare parts, the *Baltona* shop at ul. Radzymińska 78 in Praga is a good starting point (Mon–Sat 10am–6pm; ☎195-554).

Newspapers You can now find yesterday's and occasionally the same day's editions of Western newspapers like *The Herald Tribune*, *Le Monde*, *The Financial Times* and *The European*, as well as mainstream magazines like *Time* and *Newsweek*, in major hotel lobbies plus the *Kodak* "Fast Film" photo shops in the *Centrum Shopping Centre* on Marszałkowska and in the Old Town, and the *Fuji* shops on ul. Bagatela and in the Old Town. For Polish news, the English-language weekly *The Warsaw Voice* is indispensable.

Opticians Contact lens specialists include: ul. Bełwederska 4, ul. Bracka 22, ul. Złota 11 and Nowy Świat 50.

Parking Hotel car parks aside, the multi-storey car park on the appropriately named ul. Parkingowa, behind the *Forum* hotel, is the safest place in the centre. Other guarded parking lots in the centre are on ul. Sentorska, ul. Boleść, ul. Ossolińskich, ul. Górskiego, ul. Ludna and ul. Żelazna.

Post offices Main offices are at ul. Świętokrzyska 31/33 and in the main train station; both open 24hr for telephones, 8am–8pm for post. Both provide *poste restante*: Warsaw 1 is the code number for the former, Warsaw 120 for the latter.

Robberies A depressingly common experience. Report to police office at ul. Wilcza 21, including full list of stolen items and value in sterling.

Skating Ice rink in winter at *Torwar*, ul. Łazienkowska 6 and in Stegny, the open-air rink at ul. Idzikowskiego 4.

Student office Almatur, ul. Kopernika 23 (☎263-512). Open 9am–3pm.

Swimming pools In summer a number of crowded and over-chlorinated open-air pools are open: at ul. Gorczewska 69/73, Namysłowska 8, ul. Puławska 101, ul. Racłaicka 132, ul. Wawelska 5 and at the Gwardia stadium. Indoor pools at the *Victoria*, *Holiday Inn*, *Novotel* and *Solec* hotels charge a fee to non-guests, but you might be able to bluff your way in.

Taxis ☎919: or *Supertaxi* (☎9622).

Tennis courts Legia, ul. Łazienkowska 96a, *Syrena*, ul. Batory 16, *Gwardia*, ul. Racławicka 132, *Solec*, ul. Solec 71. The courts are open 7am to dusk in the summer.

Travel information Bus schedules ☎236-304, train schedules: ☎200-361.

Youth hostels The central office of *PTSM*, the Polish youth hostel federation, is at ul. Chocimska 28, fourth floor, room 423 (Mon–Fri 8am–3pm); they produce a book listing hostels all over Poland.

MAZOVIA

The attractions of **Mazovia** – the plain surrounding Warsaw – are outlined briefly in the introduction to this chapter. If time is limited, then at least take a break outside the city in the beautiful forest of the **Kampinoski National Park**, or to Chopin's birthplace at **Żelazowa Wola**. Southwest of the capital, the great manufacturing city of **Łódź** offers a major dose of culture. Other towns south of Warsaw are less inviting, and industrial centres such as **Skierniewice** and **Radom** are likely to be low on most people's priorities. **Płock**, under two hours by train west of the city, is altogether more enticing, with an historic old town complex and a couple of notable museums. The northern stretches of Mazovia offer some promising day excursions, chiefly the palace at **Jabłonna** and the market town of **Pułtusk**.

Just about everywhere covered in the following section can be reached from Warsaw on **local buses and trains**, though prospective day-trippers to the forest will need to watch out for erratic evening bus services back to the city. Łódź is particularly well served by regular express trains, making a day's outing from Warsaw an easy option.

The Kampinoski National Park

With its boundaries touching the edge of Warsaw's Żoliborz suburb, the Puszcza Kampinoska – or **Kampinoski National Park** – stretches some 30km kilometres west of the capital, a rare example of an extensive forest area coexisting with a major urban complex (in Europe, at least). An ideal retreat, this open forest harbours the summer houses of numerous Varsovians, and in autumn is a favoured weekend haunt for legions of mushroom-pickers. As with all national parks, the forest's nature reserves are carefully controlled to help preserve the rich plant and animal life – elks, wild boars and beavers (recently reintroduced here from the northeast of the country) are sighted from time to time – but access for walkers (and cross-country skiers) is pretty much unrestricted. Beware that it's all too easy to get lost in the woods, so unless your scouting is Brownie-plus standard stick to marked routes: signposts at the edge of the forest show clearly the main paths.

Originally submerged under the waters of the Wisła, which now flows north of the forest, the picturesque park landscape intersperses dense tracts of woodland – pines, hornbeams, birch and oaks are the most common trees – with a patchwork terrain of swamp-like marshes and belts of sand dune. Though most of the forest is now under local forestry commission management, a few parts of the area still retain the wildness that long made them a favourite hunting spot with the Polish monarchy.

Truskaw and Palmiry

Bus #708 from the Marymont bus station in northern Żoliborz takes you out to **TRUSKAW**, a small village about 10km from town on the eastern edge of the forest: a rapidly developing place, the village houses the headquarters of the park authorities, where there's a small museum detailing the often bloody history of the forest as well as a section devoted to the local flora and fauna. From here it's a pleasant five-kilometre walk to the hamlet of **PALMIRY**, along sandy paths that seem a world removed from the bustle of the city – as do the villages, where children stare at passers-by as much as in the remoter parts of the country. People in the scattered older houses will give you well-water if you ask, and may even part with a jar of the excellent local honey for a price.

The forest's proximity to town made it a centre of resistance activity – notably during the 1863 Uprising and World War II – and also made it an obvious killing ground for the Nazis. The war cemetery that you pass on this walk contains the bodies of about 2000 prisoners and civilians, herded out to the forest, shot, and hurled into pits. To get back into Warsaw, walk the one-kilometre track north from Palmiry to the main road bus stop and take any bus to Marymont station.

If you're not in a hurry to get back it's worth crossing the main road and continuing on a couple of kilometres east to the village of **Dziekanów Polski** on the banks of the Wisła. The area round the village is one of several noted birdwatcher's haunts in and around the national park, a fact explained by the forest's location along one of the country's main bird migration routes. Among the birds regularly sited here is the ubiquitous **white stork**, whose nests are a common sight in and around the village, some of the telegraph poles sporting special platforms to which the storks return each year to raise their young. Into the fields and dense undergrowth that develops closer to the river you may be able to catch the call of the **lapwing**, while nearer to the water you can spot brilliantly coloured **kingfishers** and **bluethroats** as well as a variety of gulls, terns and ducks.

Zaborów, Leszno and Kampinos

If you're feeling more adventurous, you can head further into the forest from the villages of **ZABORÓW**, **LESZNO** or **KAMPINOS**, all of which are sited along the main road that skirts the southern edge of the forest on its way to Żelazowa Wola (see below). To get to them, take a blue regional bus from the Dworzec Zachodnia bus station.

A number of walking options suggest themselves. An obvious one is to get off at Leszno and take the marked forest path to Kampinos, a good twelve-kilometre walk in all (17km from Zaborów), or do the same route in the opposite direction. An advantage of the latter course is that the PTTK hostel and the GS hotel in Kampinos both have basic **restaurants** in which to fortify yourself before heading off. Walk north through the village on the marked path and you're soon in the swampy edges of the forest; in summer you'll need to watch out for the particularly bloodthirsty mosquitoes, but the forest itself is a treat, with acres of undisturbed woodland and only very occasional human company. Unless you plan to stay overnight in Kampinos, start out early from Warsaw, as return buses stop at about 6pm, after which the only option is a taxi, charging double for journeys outside the city.

Żelazowa Wola

Fifty kilometres west of Warsaw, just beyond the western edge of the Kampinoski National Park, is the little village of **ŻELAZOWA WOLA**, the birthplace of composer and national hero **Frédéric Chopin**. The journey through the rolling Mazovian countryside makes an enjoyable day out from the city: unless you've got a car, you should either book up with an Orbis excursion or make the hour-long bus journey from the main bus station (direction Sochaczew).

The house where Chopin was born is now a **museum** (May–Sept Tues–Fri & Sun 10am–5.30pm, Sat 10am–2.30pm; Oct–April Tues–Fri & Sun 10am–4pm, Sat 10am–2.30pm) surrounded by a large garden. The Chopin family lived here for only a year after their son's birth in 1810, but young Frédéric returned frequently to what was long his favourite place, and one which provided him with contact with the Polish countryside and, most importantly, the folk musical traditions of Mazovia that formed the inspirational basis of much of his later work. Bought by public subscription in 1929, the Chopin family residence was subsequently restored and turned into a museum to the composer run by the Warsaw-based Chopin Society. The piano recitals held here every Sunday at 11am and 3pm from the beginning of May to the end of September – check Warsaw listings sources for the current programme details – are a popular tourist attraction, and are included in the Orbis and other organised tours.

The house itself is a typical *dwór*, the traditional country residence of the *szlacter* (gentlefolk) class, numerous examples of which can be found all over

FRÉDÉRIC CHOPIN (1810–49)

Of all the major Polish artists, **Frédéric Chopin** – Fryderyk Szopen as he was baptised in Polish – is the one whose work has achieved the greatest international recognition. He is to all intents and purposes *the* national composer, a fact attested to in the wealth of festivals, concerts and most importantly the famous international piano competition held in his name. Like other Polish creative spirits of the nineteenth century, the life of this brilliantly talented composer and performer reflects the political upheavals of Partitition-era Poland. Born of mixed Polish–French parentage in the Mazovian village of Żelazowa Wola, where his father was a tutor to a local aristocratic family, Frédéric spent his early years in and around Warsaw, holidays in the surrounding countryside giving him an early introduction to the Mazovian folk tunes that permeate his compositions. Musical talent began to show through from an early age: at six Chopin was already making up tunes, a year later he started to play the piano, and his first concert performance came at the age of eight. After a couple of years' schooling at the Warsaw lyceum, the budding composer – his first polonaises and mazurkas had already been written and performed – was enrolled at the newly created Warsaw Music Conservatory.

Chopin's first journey abroad was in August 1829, to Vienna, where he gave a couple of concert performances to finance the publication of some recent compositions, a set of Mozart variations. Returning to Warsaw soon afterwards, Chopin made his official **public debut**, performing the virtuoso Second Piano Concerto (F Minor), its melancholic slow movement inspired, as he himself admitted, by an (unrequited) love affair with a fellow Conservatory student and aspiring opera singer. In the autumn of 1830 he travelled to Vienna, only to hear news of the **November Uprising** against the Russians at home. Already set upon moving to Paris, the heartbroken Chopin was inspired by the stirring yet tragic events in Poland to write the famous *Revolutionary Étude*, among a string of other works. As it turned out, he was never to return to Poland, a fate shared by many of the fellow exiles whose Parisian enclave he entered in 1831. He rapidly befriended them and the host of young composers (including Berlioz, Bellini, Liszt and Mendelssohn) who lived in the city. The elegantly dressed, artistically sensitive Chopin soon became a Parisian high society favourite, earning his living teaching and giving the occasional recital. Some relatively problem-free years followed, during which he

rural Poland – Mazovia and Małopolska in particular. All the rooms have been restored to period perfection and contain a collection of family portraits and other Chopin memorabilia. Through the main entrance way the old kitchen, the first room on your right, has an attractively painted characteristic nineteenth-century Mazovian ceiling.

Next along is the **music room**, the exhibits here including a caseful of manuscripts of early Chopin piano works as well as a plaster cast of the virtuoso pianist's left hand. If you've come for the popular Sunday **piano recitals** – often by noted international performers who consider it an honour to play at the house – this is where they're held, performed on a luxury Steinway grand donated by wealthy Polish-Americans. On fine days the audience sits outside, the music wafting through the open windows – an eminently uplifting and pleasurable experience.

The **dining room** walls sport some original Canaletto copper-worked views of Warsaw, while upstairs is the bedroom where the infant Frédéric was born, now

---

produced a welter of new compositions, notably the rhapsodic *Fantaisie-Impromptu*, a book of études and a stream of nationalistically inspired polonaises and mazurkas.

Chopin's life changed dramatically in 1836 following his encounter with the radical novelist **George Sand**, who promptly fell in love with him and suggested she become his mistress. After over a year spent hesitating over the proposal in the winter of 1838, Chopin – by now ill – travelled with her and her two children to Majorca. Though musically productive – the B Flat Minor Sonata and its famous funeral march date from this period – the stay was not a success, Chopin's rapidly deteriorating health forcing a return to France to seek the help of a doctor in Marseilles. Thereafter Chopin was forced to give up composing for a while, earning his living giving piano lessons to rich Parisians and spending the summers with an increasingly maternal Sand at her country house at **Nohant** south of Paris. The rural environment temporarily did wonders for Chopin's health, and it was in Nohant that he produced some of his most powerful music, including the sublime *Polonaise Fantasie*, the third sonata and several of the major ballades. Increasingly strained relations with Sand, however, finally snapped when she finally broke with him in 1847: miserable and almost penniless, Chopin accepted an invitation from an admiring Scottish pupil Jane Stirling to visit **Britain**. Despite mounting illness, Chopin gave numerous concerts and recitals in London, also making friends with Carlyle, Dickens and other luminaries of English artistic life. Increasingly weak, and unable either to compose or return Stirling's devoted affections, a depressed Chopin returned to Paris in November 1848.

The illness-induced end came a year later at his apartment on place de Vendôme in central Paris: in accordance with his deathbed wish Mozart's *Requiem* was sung at Chopin's funeral, and his body was buried in the **Père-Lachaise cemetery**, the grave topped, a year later, with a monument of a weeping muse sprinkled with earth from his native Mazovia. Admired by his friends yet also criticised by many of his peers, the music Chopin created during his short life achieved a synthesis only few fellow Polish artists have matched: a distinctive Polishness combined with a universality of emotional and aesthetic appeal. For fellow Poles, as well as for many foreigners, the emotive Polish content is particularly significant: many, indeed, feel his music expresses the essence of the national psyche, alternating wistful romanticism with storms of turbulent, restless protest – "guns hidden in flowerbeds", in fellow composer Schumann's memorable description.

transformed into something of a Chopin shrine. Back outside it's worth taking a leisurely stroll through the house grounds, turned into a sort of botanical **park** following the place's conversion into a museum. In spring or autumn you'll catch the scented blossoms of the rich variety of trees and bushes assembled around the grounds on the basis of an impressive set of donations from botanical gardens around the world. Nearby there's a tourist-orientated restaurant for a quick bite before the return journey.

If you're travelling by car (many of the coach tours stop off here too), you could consider making a brief detour 11km north to the village of **Brochów**. The brick **parish church**, an unusual fortified sixteenth-century structure, became the Chopin family place of Sunday worship following the parent's marriage here in the early 1800s. The original of young Frédéric's birth certificate is proudly displayed in the sacristy, along with assorted other Chopin family records.

Łowicz and around

At first sight **ŁOWICZ**, thirty-odd kilometres southwest of Żelazowa Wola, looks like just any other small, concrete-ridden central Polish town, but this apparently drab place is in fact a well-established centre of folk art and craft. Locally produced handicrafts, handwoven materials, carved wood ornaments and *wycinanki* – coloured paper cutouts – in particular are popular throughout the country, the brilliantly coloured local Mazowsze costumes (*pasiaki*) being the town's best-known artistic product. Historically Łowicz has not been without importance, for several centuries providing the main residence of the archbishops of Gniezno, normally the Catholic primates of all Poland, who endowed Łowicz with its scattering of historic building – chiefly churches.

The ideal time to come here is at **Corpus Christi** (late May/early June) – or, failing that, one of the other major **church festivals** – when many of the women turn out in beautiful handmade traditional costumes for the procession to the Collegiate church. Wearing full skirts, embroidered cotton blouses and colourful headscarves, they are followed by neat lines of young girls preparing for their first Communion. The crowds gathered in the main square might well contain a sizeable contingent of camera-clicking foreigners, but they are never numerous enough to ruin the event's character and sense of tradition.

Łowicz is a ninety-minute train journey from Warsaw: there's a regular local service from Śródmiescie station. The old **Rynek**, ten minutes from the station, is the pivot of the town, along with the vast **Collegiate Church**, a brick fifteenth-century construction, remodelled to its present form in the mid-seventeenth century. Size apart, its most striking features are the richly decorated tombstones of the archbishops of Gniezno and the ornate series of Baroque chapels.

The other attraction is the **local museum** across the square (Tues–Sun 10am–3.30pm), housed in a missionary college designed by Tylman of Gameren. It contains an extensive and carefully presented collection of regional folk artefacts, including furniture, pottery, tools and costumes whose basic styles are the same as those still worn on feast days. Many houses contain examples of the distinctive coloured cut-out decorations on display in the museum too. The back of the museum is a kind of mini-*skansen*, containing two old cottages complete with their original furnishings.

For an overnight stay, the only real options are the down-at-heel *Turystyczny* **hotel** at ul. Sienkiewicza 1 (☎6960), south of the main square, the reasonable *Łowicki*, ul. Blich 36 (☎4164) on the Poznan road on the western side of town, and the **youth hostel** at ul. Poznańska 30 (June–July). The hotel has a passable restaurant; otherwise try the *Polonia* in the main square – but don't expect too much.

Arkadia and Nieborów

A short distance east of Łowicz are a couple of sights – a park and a palace – redolent of the bygone Polish aristocracy. They combine for an easy and enjoyable day trip, or, for those into a village stay, a night's stopover.

Arkadia Park

The eighteenth-century **Arkadia Park** is as wistfully romantic a spot as you could wish for an afternoon stroll. Conceived by Princess Helen Radziwiłł as an "ancient monument to beautiful Greece", the classical park is dotted with lakes and walkways, a jumble of reproduction classical temples and pavilions, a sphinx and a mock-Gothic house that wouldn't look out of place in a Hammer Films production. Its air of decay adds to the evocation of an age, only fifty years past, consigned firmly to history.

The park lies about 4km from Łowicz down the Skierniewice road – reached by local bus from the station in the north of town.

Nieborów

The Arkadia bus continues on for 6km to the village of **NIEBORÓW**, whose country **palace** was designed by the ever-present Tylman of Gameren and owned for most of its history, like the park, by the powerful Radziwiłł clan – just one of dozens this family possessed right up until World War II. Now part of the National Museum, the Nieborów palace is one of the handsomest and best-maintained in the country, surrounded by outbuildings and a manicured **park and gardens**.

The palace **interior** (Tues–Sun 10am–3.30pm), restored after the war, is furnished on the basis of the original eighteenth- and nineteenth-century contents of the main rooms – a lavish restoration that makes you wonder whether Polish communists suffered from a kind of ideological schizophrenia. Roman tombstones and sculptural fragments fill a lot of space downstairs, gathered about the palace's prize exhibit, the **Nieborów Apollo**; the grandest apartments (including a library with a fine collection of globes) are on the first floor, reached by a staircase clad in nicely decorated Delft tiles. It all has an air, these days, of studied aristocratic respectability, somewhat belying Radziwiłł history. Karol Radziwiłł, for example, head of the dynasty in the late eighteenth century, used to hold vast banquets in the course of which he'd drink himself into a stupor, and, as often as not, kill someone in a brawl. He would then, as Adam Zamoyski puts it, "stumble into his private chapel and bawl himself back to sobriety by singing hymns". A far cry from today's genteel environment, which in the spring is host to a much publicised series of **classical concerts** by international artists.

For overnighters Nieborów village offers a small regional-style *Jagusia* **restaurant**, a seasonal **youth hostel** (May–Sept) and a PTTK **campsite**. There are springwaters, too, and a sanatorium for those who come to imbibe.

North of Warsaw

North of Warsaw the main routes whisk you through the suburbs and out into the flat Mazovian countryside, its scattered farmland bisected by the Wisła from the west and by the smaller (and less polluted) River Narew to the east. Close to Warsaw – des res territory for the increasing number of city commuters – the towns and villages are beginning to show signs of benefiting from the country's current economic transformation. Slightly further afield but still in striking distance of Warsaw are a number of older centres, notably **Pułtusk** and **Ciechanów,** which retain the rustic feel of a traditional Mazovian market town. Other attractions include the palace at **Jabłonna,** close enough to the city for a leisurely afternoon outing. **Transport links** are pretty straightforward this close to the capital, a well-serviced network of **local buses** providing the most convenient form of transport.

Jabłonna

North of the city the built-up suburban sprawl stretches out across the flat landscape, finally petering into the fields of rural Mazovia. Sixteen kilometres north of the city – a half-hour bus journey (#133, #723 or #801 from Dworzec Marymont) – is **JABŁONNA,** a small commuter-belt town that's clearly benefiting from its location close to the main roads into Warsaw. The town itself is nondescript, the main attraction being the fine Neoclassical **palace** built on the edge of town in the 1770s by architect Domenico Merlini (of Warsaw's Łazienki Park fame) for Prince Józef Poniatowski. In easy reach of the city centre, the palace makes for an enjoyable afternoon excursion from Warsaw. At the moment, there are no official **opening hours** since the palace is undergoing restoration: during working hours, though, you stand a good chance of seeing at least the ground floor and gardens.

The Palace

As you enter the palace gates from the edge of the main through road from Warsaw (the bus stop is just across the road), the elegant bestatued facade of the main **palace building** stands some way back from the entrance, in the middle of a large park. A one-time Potocki family possession, since World War II the palace has been used by the Polish Academy of Sciences – a suitably grand location for august academic meetings, conferences and the like. Badly damaged during the war, the palace was, at time of writing, undergoing a complete overhaul, but for the moment you can simply turn up and ask to look round. Inside the building the ground floor follows a conventional pattern with ornate reception rooms, a glamorous **ballroom** complete with graceful high cupola – it's still used for the occasional concerts – the Rococo room, with a portrait of a victorious Prince Poniatowski after the battle of Raszyn, and an elaborate Moorish room. Some of the palace's original eighteenth-century frescoes were uncovered during postwar reconstruction work downstairs in the basement: it's all a bit gloomy down there at the moment, but you'll soon be able to enjoy the frescoes while relaxing in the upmarket palace restaurant that's supposed to be starting up sóon.

Back out of the main entrance, the **hotel** currently under construction in the palace building to the left looks set to prove an attractive proposition. The ramshackle palace **park** – all 75 acres of it – was clearly once a grand affair. It's ideal for a Sunday walk, with broody, overgrown woods stretching all the way down to the nearby banks of the Wisła. Several of the old palace outbuildings survive: an orangery, a pagoda, and most impressively a classical triumphal arch erected to commemorate the death of the dashing Prince Poniatowski – one of the real national heroes – at the battle of Leipzig in 1813.

An additional curio is the **tunnel** that runs underneath part of the palace grounds, formerly used by members of the diplomat's club that used to function here to get members from the river bank – the Wisła used to run much closer to the palace – to the palace in secret. Later used as a World War II hideout by Polish resistance fighters, the tunnel is now unusable, though you can still see the ruins of the small fortified stronghold where the boats of publicity-shunning diplomats used to alight.

Lake Zegrzyński

North from Jabłonna the main E61 road heads across **Lake Zegrzyński** (*Zalew Zegrzyński*), a wide lagoon-like expanse of water fed by the River Narew that's a popular sailing venue and weekend outing spot for Varsovians. Beyond the lake the main road continues along the banks of the River Narew, through a pleasant stretch of open Mazovia countryside to **Pułtusk**.

Pułtusk

Sixty kilometres north of Warsaw along the west bank of the River Narew stands **PUŁTUSK**, a lively provincial Mazovian market town that's a popular day-tripper's outing from Warsaw. One of the earliest towns founded in the region, and established on the site of an earlier trading settlement, for many years Pułtusk was a leading grain-trading centre on the river route to Gdańsk, the town's political influence stemming from the presence of the powerful bishops of Płock, whose seat the town was for several centuries. Moving forward in time, the town twice hit the headlines in the nineteenth century, first in 1806 when Napoleonic and Russian forces fought a major battle here – a French victory recorded alongside Bonaparte's other notable triumphs on the walls of the Arc de Triomphe – and later, in 1868, when a huge meteorite – known, unsurprisingly, as the Pułtusk meteorite – fell near the town. Badly clobbered, like much of northern Mazovia, during the Soviet advance of winter 1944–45 – 80 percent of the buildings were destroyed – the town has nevertheless managed to retain its oldtime market town atmosphere, thanks, in part, to a major postwar reconstruction programme focussing on the town centre.

The Town

As often the **market square** provides the main focus of the town. In the large cobbled area – at nearly 400m long, the square is claimed to be one of the biggest in Europe – a number of the original eighteenth- and nineteenth-century burghers' houses are still in evidence, several of them showing the benefits of a recent local clean-up effort. These apart, the square is mostly surpassingly tasteful postwar reconstruction, the main excitement currently being provided by the Russian number-plated cars lined up in the centre, their owners enthusiastically peddling their wares to the slightly cautious-looking locals.

The imposing high Gothic **brick tower** tacked on to the town hall bang in the middle of the square houses the enjoyable **regional museum** (Tues–Sat 10am–4pm, Sun 10–2pm). Erected in the 1400s, the tower was originally part of the town's defences, subsequently serving as a craftsman's storehouse, Jesuit boarding-school house and local prison. Inside the first-floor exhibitions cover the wealth of archaeological finds uncovered when the square and surroundings were systematically excavated in the 1970s.

The array of mostly medieval objects on display includes reconstructed early wooden sailing vessels, military paraphernalia, silver and metal work, and some fine decorated tiles from the castle area. The collection of folk art and craft on other floors comes mostly from the forested **Kurpie region** to the east of the town, an area noted for its strong folk artistic traditions. It's worth climbing the full six floors of the tower for the panoramic view over the town and surroundings from the top of the building– especially good on a fine day; you can borrow binoculars from the woman at the entrance.

THE TOWN CASTLE/DOM POLONII

Walk south off the end of the square and you come to the **town castle,** one-time residence of the bishops of Płock, an oft-rebuilt semi-circular brick structure straddled across an artificial raised mound overlooking the banks of the Narew. A wooden fortification was in place here by the early 1300s, destroyed soon after (along with the rest of the town) by marauding Lithuanians. Rebuilt from scratch in the 1520s, the arcaded bridge leading up to the brick castle was added a century later, only to be pummelled by the Swedes in the 1650s. The castle's claim to historical fame is as the site of the first public theatre in Poland, opened here by the Jesuits in 1565.

As with many towns in Mazovia there's a Napoleonic connection too: Bonaparte stayed here with his brother Jerome in 1806, prior to the nearby battle against Russian forces, and again in 1812 during the disastrous retreat from Moscow; it's also one of several places where he is supposed to have first met his lover-to-be, Maria Walewska.

The tourist potential of the place having been recognised, in the 1970s the castle was taken over by *Polonia*, the state-sponsored organisation dedicated to maintaining links between émigré Poles and their home country. As a result the **Dom Polonii,** as it's known, has now been converted into a luxury hotel and holiday/conference centre for the huge Polish diaspora, with émigré Poles young and old from all over the world – the USA and Germany in particular – taking part in events here throughout the year.

You don't have to be a third-generation Chicago Pole to stay here (though it probably helps): the swish **hotel** (☎2031/4081) isn't cheap though, but for anyone tempted by a stay out in the country the castle can't be bettered for its quiet location close to Warsaw. The castle restaurant, housed in a magisterial-looking dining room, is also reasonably pricey, but again worth trying, especially for the traditionally prepared duck dishes.

The **gardens**, laid out when the moat was drained and covered in the sixteenth century, lead down to the water's edge – a pleasant, tranquil place for a stroll, with sailing and other aquatic activities much in evidence during the summer season. In summer there's also a café operating by the water. Back out towards the main square is the old castle **chapel**, a Renaissance structure largely rebuilt after wartime destruction.

THE COLLEGIATE CHURCH ANDNOSKOWSKI CHAPEL

The monumental **Collegiate Church** at the north end of the square is a Gothic brick basilica, remodeled in the sixteenth century by the Venetian architect Giovanni Battista. A striking feature is the arched vault of·the nave, the design motif of circles connected by belts being a characteristic ornamental element of Renaissance-era churches in the Mazovia and Podlasie regions. The Renaissance **Noskowski Chapel,** modeled on the Wawel Sigismund Chapel, is a beauty, featuring a Renaissance copy of Michelangelo's famous *Pietà*, and some delicate original polychromy. More eccentric is the main rear chapel stuffed with local Catholic standards for use on Holy Day processions and lined from floor to ceiling with blue Dordrecht tiles.

Practicalities

The **train station** is some way to the west of the town centre; the **bus station**, on the Nowy Rynek, is closer – a ten-minute walk to the Rynek. For **information** you can try the PTTK office, Rynek 5, on the main square, or the reception desk at the **Dom Polonii** (see opposite). For a bite to eat the castle restaurant is streets ahead the best – though also the most expensive – bet. Alternatives are the *Arkadia* on the Rynek or the *Słoneczna* on the Nowy Rynek, while the *Magdalenka* is a down-to-earth café at the castle end of the main square.

Ciechanów

Continuing northwest some 40km brings you to **CIECHANÓW**, a largish, dowdy-looking Mazovian town where life passes slowly – someone forgot to give the place a centre too. There's nothing here to get the crowds stampeding in, but if you happen to be passing through it's worth stopping off to see the remains of the imposing fourteenth-century **Mazovian Dukes' Castle** stuck out on a limb on the eastern edge of town, one of the scattering of fortifications around the region originally occupied by the medieval rulers of Mazovia. A redoubtably solid-looking brick structure – the walls are over 55m high – the interior houses a minor **museum** (Tues–Sun 10–4pm), the main point of going in being for the chance to look around the castle itself. Totally unlike the Teutonic castles of the Gdańsk region in look or feel – an ancestral Highlands pile would be a more appropriate comparison – the castle has only two towers of the original building still standing. Back into town over a river and past the solemn Neogothic Town Hall, the local **museum**, on central ul. Sienkiewicza (Tues–Sun 10am–4pm), is a rather unimaginatively presented display of nevertheless colourful local crafts and folk items.

The parish **church of St Joseph,** off what passes for the main town square, is a good example of Mazovian Gothic, a high brick structure with a tiered facade arranged in thin pointed layers. The vaulted interior boasts some solid chunky-looking Gothic pillars: locally it's known as the church that writer **Ignacy Krasiński** attended regularly. Next door to the church you'll find something of a Polish rarity: a local Catholic teetotallers' club. Immediately north of town the countryside is scattered with **military cemeteries**, a reminder of the major battle fought here in September 1939, where German forces attempting to push straight to Warsaw encountered some stiff resistance from the retreating Polish Army.

If you need **accommodation**, the options, both hotels, are *Zacisze*, ul. Nowozagumienna (☎2046) or *Polonia*, ul. Warszawska 40 (☎3459). For restaurants, try the *Zacisze*, the *Jagienka*, ul. Strazacka 5, or *U Bony*, ul. Sienkiewicza 81.

West along the Wisła

West of Warsaw the Mazovian countryside is dominated by the meandering expanse of the Wisła as it continues its trek towards the Baltic Sea, many of the towns ranged along its banks still bearing the imprint of the river-bound trade they once thrived on. Of these the most important is **Płock**, one-time capital of Mazovia and a thriving industrial centre that's recently been attracting some of the biggest new Western investments in Poland to date. With a major museum and an enjoyable historic complex it makes an eminently worthwhile outing from Warsaw. Closer to the capital and equally worthwhile is the ancient church complex at **Czerwińsk nad Wisłą,** serviced by occasional **boat trips** along the Wisła.

Modlin castle

Some 36km northwest of Warsaw, at the intersection of the Wisła and the Narew rivers, stand the eerie ruins of **Modlin castle** – you can see them from north-bound E77 road to Gdańsk. A huge earth and brick fortress raised in the early nineteenth century on Napoleon's orders, the already large complex was restored and extended by Russian forces in the 1830s and 1840s: at its height the huge complex accommodated a garrison of some 26,000 people. It was devastated during the early part of World War II, but you can still wander through the eerily atmospheric ruins of the castle, which offer a pleasant view over the river below.

Czerwińsk nad Wisłą

CZERWIŃSK NAD WISŁĄ, around 70km from Warsaw along the main Płock turnoff just beyond Modlin, presents another worthwhile day trip from the capital: a placid riverside village overlooking the banks of the Wisła. What pulls the crowds (and there can be plenty of them in summer) to this idyllic, out of the way setting is the Romanesque **church and monastery complex**, one of the oldest – and finest – historic ensembles in the Mazovia region.

THE CHURCH AND MONASTERY COMPLEX

Sitting atop the hill above the village, the ancient **church complex**, founded by the monks who were brought here in the early twelfth century by the dukes of Mazovia to hasten along the conversion of the region, retains much of its original Romanesque structure, still visible amid the later Gothic and Baroque additions. The entrance, flanked by high twin towers, is through a delicately carved, brick Romanesque **portal** inside the brick facade added onto the building in the seventeenth century, its original ceiling decorated with some delightful geometrically patterned frescoes featuring plant motifs and representations of the Virgin Mary. Inside the building a couple of fine Romanesque stone columns have survived, as has a remarkable selection of early polychromy, notably in the **chapel** off the east aisle, whose luminous Romanesque frescoes were uncovered in the 1950s during renovation work on the building. The late Gothic **belltower** near the church, whose powerful bells are among the oldest in the country, was once the gateway to the town. If you're there during the summer season, you should be able to climb this or one of the church towers for the panoramic view they provide over the flat pastoral surroundings. Round the back of the church is the **monastery complex**, now occupied by a Salesian Fathers seminary, some of whose members act as guides in summer – if you ask, you should be able to get hold of someone who speaks English to take you round. If you're there during normal daytime hours it's also worth asking to see round the **cloisters**, which contain a fine Gothic refectory and a small **museum** of local ethnography and church art, the quiet toing and froing of the seminarists blending in with the restful, contemplative feel of the whole place.

THE VILLAGE
If you haven't climbed one of the towers there's a nice view over the river from the terrace in front of the church. With time to spare it's also worth taking a stroll down the hill into the tumbledown **village**, which has a notable predominance of wooden houses, and on down to the river bank, as peaceful a rural setting as you could wish for. In summer the village is a stopoff point for weekly **boat trips** down the Wisła – the tourist information office in Warsaw will have the current details. Despite the summer tourist crowds, curiously no one in the village has thought to start up a restaurant or snack bar yet, so unless the seminary invites you in for a meal the village shop is the only place you'll find anything to eat.

If you're not travelling by boat or on a coach tour, local buses (blue line) to Czerwińsk from Warsaw run via Nowy Dwór (8 daily) to Warsaw, a journey of an hour and a half approximately each way.

Płock

Initial impressions of **PŁOCK**, the major town of western Mazovia located some 115km west of Warsaw, suggest there aren't going to be many reasons to hang around here for very long. First appearances can be deceiving, though, for in the midst of the sprawling industrial-looking connurbation spread along the banks of Wisła is actually the oldest urban settlement in Mazovia, founded some time before the first kings of Poland took up residence here in the eleventh century, where they remained for nearly a century. An important bishopric and one of the number of strategically located riverside towns that grew fat on the medieval Wisła-bound commercial boom, like other Polish trading centres Płock felt the full weight of mid-seventeenth-century Swedish invasions of the country, whose Scandinavian perpetrators purloined the Płock bishopric's valuable library and took it to Uppsala, where it still remains. A modern industrial centre, whose huge petro-chemical works and oil refinery located just north of the town centre add a definite tang to the local air, Płock's strategic location and large workforce have made both the town and surrounding region a prime target for foreign investment, multinational jeans giants Levis amongst those who've recently established major new plants in the area. Close enough to Warsaw to make a day trip from the capital a feasible proposition, the city's historic centre and notable pair of museums provide the makings of an enjoyable day's outing.

Practicalities
The **bus and train stations**, a little way apart, are both on the northern side of town some 15 minutes' walk from the old town centre. For **information** the most useful of the various tourist bureaux is the PTTK office, at ul. Tumska 4 (☎29497) (Mon–Sat 7.30am–3.30pm) close to the old town complex. There's nothing very exciting on offer as far as **accommodation** goes, the main options being the humdrum *Wisla*, al. S. Janowicza 38 (☎23456) in a noisy but central location, and

the *Petropol*, just down the road at al. S. Janowicza 49 (☎24451), a faded-looking Orbis joint with a passable restaurant. If you don't mind the marked step-down in quality, the PTTK hostel, Piekarska 1, close to the cathedral (see below), makes up for lack of comfort in its excellent scenic location. For **restaurants**, *Mr. Smarty's*, ul. Tumska 14, Płock's own McDonald's lookalike, is now the town's most popular venue, part of the chain of hamburger joints set up around the country run by a Swedish-Polish joint venture. Alongside the *Petropol*, the only other option of any note is the nearby *Stylowa*, al. S. Janowicza 44.

Round the old town

Nestled on a clifftop overlooking the wide expanses of the Wisła, the **old town area**, a small central part of modern-day Płock, provides the town's focal point of interest. Known locally as "little Kraków" – as in its southern successor as capital, the important buildings are grouped together at the top of a hill – the old town area has undergone recent excavations which have unearthed an ancient (c. 400 BC) stone altar and pillar, indicating the early presence of pagan cults here. Walking down to the old town from either the bus or train station takes you along **ul. Tumska**, a busy pedestrianised thoroughfare and the town's main shopping area. Crossing ul. Kollegialna, Tumska leads directly into the ancient core of the town.

THE CATHEDRAL

Past the tourist office, first stop is the medieval **Cathedral**, a magnificent Romanesque building begun after the installation of the Płock bishopric in 1075 and completed in the following century. A monumental basilical structure with an imposing cupola almost worthy of St Paul's in London, the cathedral was clearly intended to dominate the surroundings, an effect it definitely achieves. Successive rebuildings, the most significant of them being the classicist remodeling undertaken by Italian architect Merlini in the mid-eighteenth century, mean there are few traces left of the building's original Romanesque character. The sumptuous interior decoration, however, including some ornate choir stalls and a magnificently carved pulpit, all indicate that the oldtime bishops of Płock were a pretty well-heeled bunch.

Other notable features of the building are the **royal chapel** containing the Romanesque sarcophagi of Polish princes **Władysław Herman** (1040–1102) and his son, **Bolesław the Wrymouth** (Krzywousty; 1086–1138) and the Secessionist frescoes decorating parts of the building. Last but not least is the sculptured **bronze door**, probably the cathedral's most famous feature and the subject of a major piece of architectural detective work. The Romanesque originals commissioned by the bishop of Płock from the Magdeburg artist Riquin in the mid-twelfth century have been missing for over six centuries, ever since Władysław King Jagiełło gave them to his Russian counterpart as a present around the time his own brother became Prince of Novgorod. Subsequently hung in the entrance to the Orthodox church of Saint Sophia in Novgorod and adorned with fake Cyrillic inscriptions identifying them as booty from a twelfth-century Russian expedition to Sweden, the doors, by now presumed lost, were located in 1970 by a Polish academic, who noticed the Latin inscriptions mentioning Płock on a late nineteenth-century gypsum copy of the doors hanging in the Historical Museum in Moscow. A further bronze copy of the original (still in Novgorod) was made for the cathedral after the discovery, and it's these you see today, two dozen **panels** filled with a magnificent series of **reliefs** depicting scenes from the Old

Testament, the Gospels as well as a number of allegorical pieces. Back from the building, the skyline is dominated by the twin brick Gothic **Zegarowa** and **Szlachecka towers** beside the cathedral – the former the cathedral belfry – the best-preserved fragments of the fourteenth century castle that once stood here.

THE REGIONAL AND DIOCESAN MUSEUMS
Back up from the cathedral is the other major monument, the Gothic former **Mazovian dukes' castle**, home of the **Regional Museum** (Fri 10am–5pm, Sun 10am–3pm, Tues–Thurs & Sat 9am–3pm), one of the oldest such exhibitions in Europe, established here by the local Historical Society in 1820. The main reason for traipsing round this museum is the superb selection of turn-of-the-century **Secessionist** work. Art Nouveau in all its various artistic forms is represented here, with a wide array of paintings, ceramics, sculpture, glass and metalware both from the Polish "Młoda Polska" movement and from other countries – Austria and Germany included – where the style gained a strong following. Anyone drawn to the sensuous curves, intricate colouring and flowing figures of *fin-de-siècle* central European art will have a field day wandering around the rich collection of objects assembled here. The really outstanding feature, however, is the **re-creation** of several rooms – dining, living and sleeping rooms – furnished, decorated and accessoried as they would have been when Art Deco was in vogue. For anyone whose principal acquaintance with the style is via the *Jugendstil* architecture of Vienna and other central European cities, it will come as a revelation to see how the style was applied to the ordinary everyday business of living.

Directly across from the castle entrance is the **Diocesan Museum** (Wed–Sat 10am–3pm, Sun 11am–4pm), very much the old town's "other" collection but housing a worthy exhibition of sacral art both Polish and foreign, nonetheless. Back up along ul. Tumska and west past the former bishop's palace, halfway down ul. Małachowskiego is the **Płock lyceum**, founded in the 1180s and still going strong 800 years later – the oldest school in the country. Next to it is a gallery sitting on the foundations of two recently uncovered Romanesque pillars located in the west wing of the school.

ALONG THE WATERFRONT
As you turn back towards the cathedral the eye is drawn naturally to the high **platform** to the left of the building, overlooking the Wisła waterfront. An open, blustery spot on a fine day, it offers huge panoramas over the wide expanse of the river below – at its widest around Płock – and the boats moored along the shore. If you're up for a gentle walk you could do worse than take a stroll along the wooded path leading off in both directions along the clifftop, the Wisła spread below you along with the sandy promontories running out into the main stream of the river. Walking north there's the possibility of a refreshment stop at the run-down PTTK **café/restaurant**, the dramatic views from the terrace just about making up for poor food quality; directly below the terrace close to the river bank is an open-air amphitheatre much in use in the summer for folk dance festivals and other musical spectaculars. South from the cathedral terrace and down through a park brings you to the **Dominican church and monastery,** a thirteenth-century edifice originally built for Duke Konrad of Mazovia, later given a predictably ornate classicist treatment. A Protestant church up until 1945, it sits isolated from the town in the middle of a park, part of the rolling woodland that covers much of the waterfront below the old town.

Łódź

Mention **ŁÓDŹ** (pronounced "Woodge") to many Poles and all you'll get is a grimace. Poland's second city is certainly no beauty, but it does have an important place in the country's development – and a unique atmosphere that grows on you the longer you stay. Essentially a creation of the Industrial Revolution and appropriately nicknamed the "Polish Manchester", Łódź is still an important manufacturing centre. Much of it survives unchanged – the tall, smoking chimneys of the castellated redbrick factories; the grand historicist and Secessionist villas of the industrialists; the theatres, art galleries and philanthropic societies… and the slum quarters. It served as the ready-made location for Andrzej Wajda's film *The Promised Land*, based on the novel by Nobel Prize-winning author Władysław Reymont.

International business and trade fairs account for most of Łódź's visitors, but its cultural scene is pretty lively as well. The orchestra is one of the best in the country, and there's an impressive array of theatres, museums and opera houses here. The Łódź **film school** is also internationally renowned, attracting aspiring movie-makers aiming to follow in the footsteps of alumni such as Wajda, Polański, Kieślowski and Zanussi.

A brief history

Missionaries came to the site of Łódź in the twelfth century, but the first permanent settlement does not seem to have taken root until a couple of hundred years later, and at the end of the 1700s it was still an obscure village of fewer than two hundred inhabitants. Impulse towards its development, strangely enough, only came during the Partition period, with the **1820 edict** of the Russian-ruled Congress Kingdom of Poland, which officially designated Łódź as a new industrial centre and encouraged foreign weavers and manufacturers to come and settle.

People poured in by the thousand each year, and within twenty years Łódź had become the nation's second largest city, a position it has maintained ever since. Despite being the imperial rulers, the Russians played little more than an administrative role, though they adopted a higher profile following the failed nationalist insurrection of 1863. The true political elite consisted in the main of **German entrepreneurs**, most of them Protestant, who founded large textile factories which made vast fortunes within a very short period of time. These were operated principally by **Polish peasants** enticed by the prospect of a better standard of living than they could claw from their meagre patches of land. By the end of the century, the urban proletariat had swelled to over 300,000. Industrialisation brought politicisation, and Łódź, like other new cities such as Białystok, had become a centre for working-class and anti-czarist agitation.

The **Jews** were another highly significant community; when they first arrived, they functioned mainly as artisans and traders, but a number managed to rise to the status of great industrial magnates, notably the Poznańskis, whose luxurious homes now house many of the city's institutions. The Jewish contribution to the cultural life of Łódź was immense, two of the city's most famous sons being the pianist Artur Rubinstein and the poet Julian Tùwim.

Łódź's reputation as a melting-pot of four great peoples and religions was only marginally affected by the fall of the czarist empire, but was dealt a terminal blow by World War II. At first, the Nazis aimed to make it the capital of the rump Polish protectorate, the so-called General Government, but, incensed by the

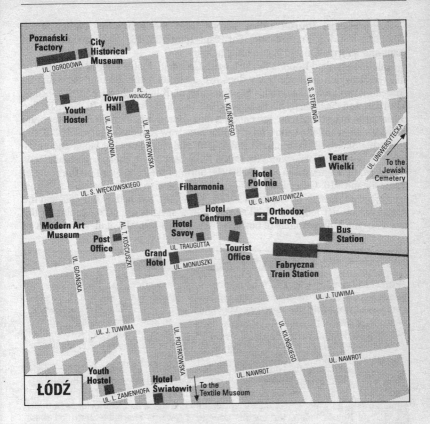

ŁÓDŹ

largely hostile stance adopted by the powerful local German community, incorporated it into the Reich. In the process, they renamed it "Litzmannstadt" in honour of a somewhat obscure general who had made a breakthrough against the nearby Russian line in 1914, and established the first and longest-lasting of their notorious urban ghettos (see overleaf).

For all the visual similarities, postwar Łódź has been, in an important sense, a spectre of its former self: nearly all the Jews were wiped out, while most of the German expatriates fled westwards, leaving only a tiny minority behind.

Arriving and finding a place to stay

The main **train station**, Łódź Fabryczna, and the **bus station** are right next to each other in the heart of the city. Note that the former is a dead-end terminus of the line from Warsaw; through trains (especially from the west and north) tend not to make the long detour necessary to reach it, stopping instead at the Kaliska station, a couple of kilometres to the west of the city centre and connected to it by tram #12. It's also possible you could arrive at the Chojny station, which is even further out in the southern suburbs: from there, take tram #5 from the left of the entrance, or tram #7 from the right.

The municipal **tourist office** across from the Fabryczna station at ul. Traugutta 18 (Mon–Fri 9am–5pm, Sat 10am–1pm; ☎337-169) has a good supply of maps and information and is generally helpful.

Łódź's top-ranked **hotel** is the Orbis-run *Grand*, ul. Piotrowska 72 (☎339-920 or ☎321-995), which for once really does live up to its name. Its four-star rating is shared by two modern alternatives – *Centrum*, ul. Kilińskiego 59/63 (☎328-640 or 339-195), and *Światowit*, al. Kościuszki 68 (☎363-044 or 363-817). Next in line come three two-star places: the concrete box *Mazowiecki* is midway between the Kaliska station and the centre on ul. Pułku Strzelców Kaniowskich (☎374-333), the venerable *Savoy*, ul. Traugutta 6 (☎329-360), and the somewhat faded and good-value *Polonia*, ul. Narutowicza 38 (☎328-773). Best of the cheaper possibilities is *Uni-Hotel*, ul. Łagiewnicka 54 (☎553-494), north of the centre and on the route of trams #8 and #16. Other low-cost alternatives, likewise in the northern suburbs, are *Zajazd na Rogach*, ul. Łupkowa 10/16 (☎574-616), reached by bus #60, and the *Arturówek* tourist lodge at ul. Skrzydlata 75, a spartan set of log cabins in the woods beyond the terminus of bus #56. Both **youth hostels**, at ul. Zamenhofa 13

THE ŁÓDŹ GHETTO

The fate of the **Jews** of Łódź, who numbered over a quarter of a million in 1939, is undoubtedly one of the most poignant and tragic episodes of World War II, particularly as a pivotal role was played by one of their own number, **Chaim Rumkowski**. He has become the most controversial figure in modern Jewish history, widely denounced as the worst sort of collaborator yet seen by others as a man who worked heroically to save at least some vestiges of the doomed community to which he belonged.

Within two days of the Nazi occupation of the city on September 8, the first definite anti-semitic measures were taken, with Jews hauled at random off the streets and forced to undertake seemingly pointless manual tasks. The following month, Rumkowski, a former velvet manufacturer who had made and lost fortunes in both Łódź and Russia before turning his attentions towards charitable activities, was selected by the Nazis as the "elder" of the Jews, giving him absolute power over the internal affairs of his community and the sole right to be their spokesman and negotiator. Plans were made to turn the entire Jewish community into a vast pool of slave labour for the Nazi war machine, and the run-down suburb of **Baluty** to the north of the centre was earmarked for this ghetto, partly because this was where the bulk of the Jews lived. Those who resided elsewhere were rounded up into barracks or else chosen for the first transportations to the death camps. By the following spring, the area of the ghetto had been sealed off from the rest of the city, and anyone who dared come near either side of its perimeter fences was shot dead.

Rumkowski soon made the ghetto a self-sufficient and highly profitable enterprise, which pleased his Nazi masters no end, even though this conclusively disproved a key tenet of their racist ideology, namely that Jews were inherently lazy and parasitical. He ruled his domain as a ruthless **petty despot**, attended by a court of sycophants and protected by his own police force and network of informers; his vanity extended to the minting of coins and manufacturing of stamps bearing his own image. Anyone who crossed him did so at their peril, as his omnipotent powers extended to the distribution of the meagre food supplies and to selecting those who had to make up the regular quotas demanded by the Nazis for deportation to the concentration camps. He cultivated a variation on the oratorical style of Hitler for

(☎366-599) and ul. Obrońców Stalingradu 27 (☎330-365), are on the fringes of the central area and open all year. The **campsite** is at ul. Rzgowska 247 (☎812-551), south of the Chojny station and a few minutes' walk beyond the terminus of trams #2, #4 and #18. If, as is probable, the tourist office can't help with **private rooms**, try the *Centrum Usług Turystycznych*, pl. Wolności 10 (☎361-046). Other travel bureaux worth knowing about are **Almatur**, ul. Piotrkowska 59 (☎336-112), **Orbis**, ul. Piotrkowska 68 (☎369-798) and **LOT**, ul. Piotrkowska 122 (☎334-859).

The City

The first sight for visitors arriving at Łódź Fabryczna – the central train station – is the **Orthodox church** across the road. Once used by the city's Russian rulers, it's a good example of nineteenth-century Orthodox architecture, which is something of a rarity in central Poland; unfortunately, it's generally kept locked. A couple of blocks west of here is **ul. Piotrkowska**, which bisects the city from north to south. Most of Łódź's sights are located on or around this avenue.

---

his frequent addresses to the community. The most notorious and shocking of these was his "Give me your children" speech of 1942, in which he made an emotional appeal to his subjects to send their children off to the camps, in order that able-bodied adults could be spared.

Whether or not Rumkowski knew that he was sending people to their deaths is unclear. There is no doubt that he saw the ghetto as at least the **embryonic fulfilment of the Zionist ideal** and believed that, after the Nazis had won the war, they would establish a Jewish protectorate in central Europe, with himself as its head. He also seems to have had few qualms about his role, insisting he would be prepared to submit himself for trial to a Jewish court of law once the war was over. It seems that his repeated claims to have cut the numbers demanded for each quota were true, and it's also the case that the ghetto was far from being a place with no hope. On the contrary, there was a rich communal life of schooling, concerts and theatre, and many inhabitants were inspired to make detailed diaries recording its history.

The Łódź ghetto was **liquidated** in the autumn of 1944, following a virulent dispute at the top of the Nazi hierarchy between Speer, who was keen to preserve it as a valuable contributor to the war effort, and Himmler, who was determined to enforce the "Final Solution". Some 1000 Jews were allowed to remain in Łódź to dismantle the valuable plants and machinery; Rumkowski voluntarily chose to go with the others to Auschwitz, albeit armed with an official letter confirming his special status. He died there soon afterwards, though there are three versions of how he met his end: that he was lynched by his incensed fellow Jews; that he was immediately selected for the gas chambers on account of his age; and that he was taken on a tour of the camp as a supposedly honoured guest, and thrown into the ovens without being gassed first. Had he remained in Łódź, he would have been among those who were **liberated** by the Red Army soon afterwards. Perhaps not surprisingly, the staunchest apologists for Rumkowski's policies have come from this group of survivors.

A large and fascinating collection of extracts from diaries kept by members of the ghetto, along with transcriptions of Rumkowski's speeches and many photographs, including some in colour, can be found in *The Łódź Ghetto*, edited by Alan Adelson and Robert Lapides.

The northern area

Plac Koscielny, the old market square beyond the north end of ul. Piotrkowska, is dominated by the twin brick towers of the neo-Gothic **Church of the Ascension**; on the other side is the rather forlorn Stary Rynek, which soon lost its original function as the hub of everyday life as the city rapidly expanded southwards.

From here, walk one block south and another west to the junction of ul. Zachodnia and ul. Ogrodowa, where stands one of the most complete complexes to have survived from the Industrial Revolution anywhere in Europe. On the corner itself is the haughty stone bulk of the **Poznański Palace**, formerly the main residence of the celebrated Jewish manufacturing family. Right alongside is their still-functioning **factory**, behind whose monumental mock-Gothic brickwork facade are weaving and spinning mills plus a number of warehouses, while across the street are the tenement flats of the workforce.

The palace, now designated the **City Historical Museum** (Tues & Thurs–Sat 10am–2pm, Wed 2–6pm), is an excellent example of the way Łódź's nouveau riche aped the tastes of the aristocracy, transferring, both inside and out, the chief elements of a Baroque stately home to an urban setting. Downstairs are temporary exhibitions of modern art and photography, while up the heavily grand staircase are the showpiece chambers, the dining room and the ballroom, along with others of more modest size which are now devoted to displays on different aspects of the city's history. Archive photographs show the appearance of prewar Łódź, including the now-demolished synagogues, while there's an extensive collection of memorabilia of **Artur Rubinstein**, one of the greatest pianists of this century. He was particularly celebrated for his performances of Chopin, and his recordings remain the interpretative touchstone for this composer. A quintessential hedonist, he was reputed to have played more music, loved more women and drunk more champagne than any other man – yet he was able to keep up the itinerant lifestyle of the modern concert virtuoso almost to the end of his ninety years.

Walking a block to the south then one to the west brings you to the circular pl. Wolności, with the Neoclassical Town Hall, regulation Kościuszko statue, and the domed Greek cross-plan Uniate church. At no. 14 on this square is the **Archaeology and Ethnography Museum** (Tues & Fri 11am–6pm, Wed & Thurs 10am–5pm, Sat 9am–3pm, Sun 10am–3pm), which has a wide-ranging collection of local artefacts, costumes and archaeological finds.

The Modern Art Gallery

A couple of blocks further south, then off to the right at ul. Więckowskiego 36, is the **Modern Art Gallery** or Galeria Sztuki (Tues 10am–5pm, Wed & Fri 11am–5pm, Thurs noon–7pm, Sat & Sun 10am–4pm), installed in a mock-Renaissance palace – complete with stained glass windows – which once belonged to the Poznański clan. Founded in 1925, when it was one of the world's first museums devoted to the avant-garde, it is the finest modern art collection in the country (though it also contains some earlier pieces). Major artists represented include Chagall, Picasso, Paul Klee, Max Ernst and Ferdinand Léger, but there's also an excellent selection of work by modern Polish painters such as Strzeminski (quite a revelation if you've not come upon his work before), Wojciechowski, Witkowski, Witkiewicz and the Jewish artist Jakiel Adler. From a memorable collection of Stalinist-era socialist realism, the lower-floor displays move on to the 1960s and 1970s, where for some reason British artists are strongly represented. The ground floor includes an assortment of "events" by contemporary artists – colour effects, bricks, rotating boxes and other everyday objects – guaranteed to raise a laugh and infuriate traditionalists. Be warned, however, that there are occasions when the permanent collection is packed away completely and replaced by a temporary loan exhibition.

Down ul. Piotrkowska

From the Modern Art Gallery, return to ul. Piotrkowska, which is worth following all the way south. At the back of the *Grand* hotel, take a detour along **ul. Moniuszki**, an uninterrupted row of plush neo-Renaissance family houses. More fine mansions can be seen three blocks further south, on the west side of ul. Piotrkowska. Another three blocks on, this time on the opposite side of the street, and you come to the large *Olympia* factory, followed by several more villas of the old industrial tycoons, often set in spacious grounds and showing an eclectic mix of architectural styles.

Across from them are two of the city's most important churches. The neo-Gothic **Cathedral**, dedicated to St Stanisław Kosta, looks rather unprepossessing from the outside, mainly because of the cheapskate yellow bricks used in its construction; the interior, with its spacious feel and bright stained glass windows, is altogether more impressive.

A little further on is the Lutheran church of **St Matthew**, a ponderous mid-nineteenth-century temple which is used by the descendants of the old German oligarchy. Frequent recitals are given on its Romantic-style organ, the finest instrument of its kind in Poland.

Towards the end of ul. Piotrkowska, at no. 280, is the huge **White Factory**, the oldest mechanically operated mill in the city. Part of it is now given over to the **Textile Museum** (Tues & Sat 10am–4pm, Wed & Fri 9am–5pm, Thurs 10am–5pm, Sun 10am–3pm), which features a large number of historic looms, documentary material on the history of the industry in Łódź, and an impressive exhibition of contemporary examples of the weaver's art.

The eastern area

Łódź's newest museum, the **Herbst Palace** or Księży Młyn (Tues 10am–5pm, Wed & Fri noon–5pm, Thurs noon–7pm, Sat & Sun 11am–4pm), is situated in the eastern part of the city at ul. Prędzalniana 72: to get there from the White Factory, it's a fifteen-minute walk along ul. Przybyszewskiego, followed by a left turn once you reach its junction with ul. Prędzalniana; from the centre, take tram #9 and alight when you reach the palace's lakeside park. The building, which belonged to one of the leading German families, outwardly resembles the Renaissance villas built by Palladio in northern Italy. Its interiors – with the grand public rooms downstairs, the intimate family ones above – are evidence of decidedly catholic tastes, with influences ranging from ancient Rome via the Orient to Art Nouveau. The ballroom, which was added as an afterthought, is an effective pastiche of the English Tudor style.

A few minutes' walk west of here on ul. Tylna, and likewise at the corner of a park, is the **Grohmann Villa**, which is also due to be opened as a museum in due course. From here, continue due north to the vast pl. Zwycięstwa, which spans both sides of the busy al. Piłsudskiego. Its southern side is almost entirely occupied by the fortress-like **Scheibler Palace**, the former home of the most powerful of the German textile families. Part of it now houses the **Cinematography Museum** (Wed–Fri 10am–2pm, Sat & Sun 11am–5pm, but seemingly subject to random closure), which celebrates Łódź's status as one of Europe's major training grounds for film makers.

The Cemeteries

Perhaps appropriately, the most potent reminders of the cultural diversity of Łódź's past come in the form of its **cemeteries**. The two most worthwhile are some way from the centre of town, but they reward the effort of getting there. Of these, the Christian **necropolis** is the more accessible in every sense: it's kept open throughout the day, and can be reached by means of a ten-minute walk west from the Poznański factory along ul. Ogrodowa. It's divided into three interconnected plots, by far the largest being the Catholic cemetery, whose monuments, with rare exceptions, are fairly simple. Even less ostentatious is its Orthodox counterpart, containing the graves of civil servants, soldiers and policemen from the czarist period. In contrast, the Protestant cemetery is full of appropriately grandiose memorials to deceased captains of industry. Towering over all the other graves, though now crumbling and boarded up, is the **Scheibler family mausoleum**, a miniaturised Gothic cathedral with a soaring Germanic openwork spire.

The **Jewish cemetery**, the largest in Europe with some 180,000 tombstones, including many of great beauty, is situated on ul. Bracka, right beside the terminus of trams #1, #15 and #19. Unfortunately, it's nearly always kept locked, though it would be easy enough to enter over the low wall beside the main gate. If you've a serious interest, it's best to ask for the key at the city centre synagogue and prayer house at ul. Zachodnia 78 before setting out.

Eating and entertainment

Restaurants are not Łódź's most exciting feature. Besides those in the hotels – the *Grand* has the best (and most expensive) – a sparse list of recommendations would include *Europa*, al. Kościuszki 116/118, *Halka*, ul. Moniuszki 1, *Smakosz*, ul. 6 Serpnia 2, and a decent Chinese restaurant, *Złota Kaczka*, on ul. Piotrkowska, across from and just south of the *Grand*. There's a string of old and new style snack bars all along the top end of ul. Piotrkowska.

As for the **cultural scene**, the *Teatr Wielki* on pl. Dąbrowskiego (☎339-960) presents both drama and opera; visiting foreign companies regularly perform both there and at the *Teatr Nowy*, ul. Więckowskiego 15 (☎334-494). For kids, there are the puppet shows at *Arlekin*, ul. Wólczańska 5 (☎325-899), and *Pinokio*, ul. Kopernika 16 (☎365-988). The concert programmes of the *Państwowa Filharmonia*, ul. Narutowicza 20 (☎372-653), feature soloists of international renown, while the *Teatr Muzyczny*, ul. Połnocna 47/51 (☎783-511), is the main venue for operetta and musicals. Among regular special events are the **opera festival** (March), a **ballet festival** (May–June every other year), and a **student theatre festival** (March). Check at the box office at ul. Moniuszki 5 for current details of what's happening in town, or pick up the monthly *Kalejdoskop* from the tourist office. Of the two **football** teams, *Widzew Łódź* play at the stadium at al. Piłsudskiego 138, just before the eastern terminus of trams #10 and #25, while *ŁKS'* ground is at ul. Unii 2, north of the Kaliska station, on the route of tram #17.

travel details

Trains from Warsaw

Domestic services: to Białystok (14 daily; 3–4hr); Bydgoszcz (6 daily; 3hr 30min–5hr); Częstochowa (13 daily; 3–5hr); Gdańsk/Gdynia (19 daily; 3hr 30min–5hr; expresses at 6am & 5pm); Jelenia Góra (4 daily; 10hr; couchettes); Katowice (17 daily; 3–5hr); Kielce (12 daily; 3–4hr); Kraków (18 daily; 3–6hr; expresses at 6am, 9am, 4.25pm & 5.45pm); Krynica (2 daily; 10–13hr; couchettes); Lublin (11 daily; 2hr 30min–3hr); Łódź (7 daily; 2–2hr 30min); Olsztyn (8 daily; 3–5hr); Poznań (19 daily; 4hr); Przemyśl (4 daily; 6–8hr); Rzeszów (4 daily; 5–6hr); Suwałki (6 daily; 4–6hr); Świnoujście (3 daily; 10 hr; couchettes); Szczecin (5 daily; 6–8hr); Toruń (6 daily; 3–4hr); Wrocław (16 daily; 5–6hr; couchettes); Zagórz, for Sanok (2 daily; 11hr); Zakopane (6 daily; 6–10hr; expresses at 6.15 & 6.35am; couchettes).

International services: to Aachen (3 daily); Belgrade (1 daily); Berlin (12 daily); Brest (13 daily); Bucharest (1 daily); Budapest (3 daily); Frankfurt (1 daily); Grodno (5 daily); Hook of Holland (3 daily); Istanbul (1 daily); Cologne (4 daily); Kiev (3 daily); Leipzig (2 daily); Moscow (7 daily); Munich (1 daily); Odessa (1 daily); Ostend (2 daily); Paris (3 daily); Prague (1 daily); Riga (2 daily); Rome (1 daily); St Petersburg (2 daily); Sofia (1 daily); Vilnius (4 daily); Vienna (2 daily).

Trains from Łódź

Domestic services: to Bydgoszcz (10 daily; 3–4hr); Częstochowa (9 daily; 2hr 30min–3hr 30min); Gdańsk (6 daily; 6hr); Katowice (7 daily; 4hr); Kraków (6 daily; 5–6hr); Lublin (5 daily; 5–6hr); Poznań (7 daily; 4–5hr); Warsaw (20 daily; 2–3hr); Wrocław (15 daily; 4–5hr).

Buses from Warsaw

Domestic services: from Dworzec Zachodni to Koszalin (1 daily), Krosno (1 daily), Mikołajki (1 daily), Olsztyn (3 daily), Rzeszów (1 daily), Toruń (1 daily), Zakopane (1 daily); from Dworzec Stadion to Lublin (2 daily), Przemyśl (1 daily), Zamość (3 daily).

International services.

There are plenty of newly established private bus companies now advertising in Warsaw, particularly in the *Zycie Warszawy* newspaper, but they're not as reliable as the following state-run services:

Orbis: to Hamburg (2 per month); Nuremberg–Munich–Stuttgart (1 weekly); Brunswick–Hanover–Dortmund–Cologne (2 per month); Hanover–London (3 per month).

Pekaes: to Oslo (1 per month); Venice–Bologna–Florence–Rome (2 per month); Hamburg–London–Nottingham–Manchester (1–2 per month); Cologne–Liège–Brussels–Ostend–London (3–4 per month); Frankfurt–Paris (4–5 per month).

Flights from Warsaw

Domestic flights: to Gdańsk (2–6 daily); Katowice (1 daily, May–Oct only); Koszalin (1–3 daily); Kraków (2–6 daily); Szczecin (1–2 daily); Wrocław (2–6 daily).

International flights: to Amsterdam (7 weekly); Athens (4 weekly); Barcelona (1 weekly); Belgrade (4 weekly); Berlin (12 weekly); Bratislava (2 weekly); Brussels (5 weekly); Bucharest (3 weekly); Budapest (15 weekly); Copenhagen (10 weekly); Düsseldorf (1 weekly); Frankfurt (13 weekly); Geneva (2–3 weekly); Hamburg (2–3 weekly); Helsinki (3–5 weekly); Istanbul (2 weekly); Cologne (3 weekly); Kiev (2 weekly); London (12–14 weekly); Los Angles (2 weekly); L'viv (1 weekly); Lyon (1–3 weekly); Madrid (2–3 weekly); Miami (2 weekly); Milan (3 weekly); Minsk (2 weekly); Montreal (2 weekly); Moscow (14–17 weekly); New York (4–6 weekly); Paris (7–11 weekly); Perth (2 weekly); Prague (12–13 weekly); Rio (1 weekly); Rome (6 weekly); St Petersburg (5–6 weekly); San Francisco (2 weekly); Seattle (3–4 weekly); Singapore (1 weekly); Sofia (10–14 weekly); Stockholm (2–3 weekly); Tel Aviv (1–2 weekly); Tokyo (1 weekly); Vienna (12 weekly); Washington (2 weekly); Zurich (9 weekly).

CHAPTER TWO

GDAŃSK AND THE LAKES

E ven in a country accustomed to shifts in its borders, northeastern Poland presents an unusually tortuous historical puzzle. Successively the domain of a Germanic crusading order, of the Hansa merchants and of the Prussians, it's only in the last forty years that the region has really become Polish. Right up to the end of World War II large parts of the area belonged to the territories of East Prussia, and although you won't see the old place names displayed any more, even the most patriotic Pole would have to acknowledge that Gdańsk, Olsztyn and Toruń have made their mark on history under the German names of Danzig, Allenstein and Thorn. Twentieth-century Germany has left terrible scars: it was here that the first shots of World War II were fired, and the bitter fighting during the Nazi retreat in 1945 left many historic towns as sad shadows of their former selves.

Gdańsk, **Sopot** and **Gdynia** – the **Tri-City** as they are collectively known – dominate the area from their coastal vantage point. Like Warsaw, historic Gdańsk was obliterated in World War II but now offers some reconstructed quarters, in addition to its contemporary political interest as the birthplace of Solidarity. It makes an enjoyable base for exploring neighbouring **Kashubia**, to the west, with its rolling hills, lakeside forests and distinctive communities of Prussianised Slavs. While waters round the Tri-City are a dubious proposition, the **Hel Peninsula** and the coast further west make a pleasant seaside option. On the other side of the Tri-City, **Frombork**, chief of many towns in the region associated with the astronomer Nicolaus Copernicus, is an attractive and historic lagoon-side town across the water from the **Wiślana Peninsula**, a beachside holidaymakers' favourite.

South from Gdańsk, a collection of **Teutonic castles** and Hanseatic centres dot the banks of the Wisła and its tributaries. Highlights include the huge medieval fortress at **Malbork**, long the headquarters of the Teutonic Knights, and **Toruń**, with its spectacular medieval ensemble. Eastwards stretches **Mazury**, Poland's biggest lakeland district, long popular with Polish holidaymakers and, increasingly, with the Germans. Canoe and yacht hire are the main attractions of its resorts, but for anyone wanting to get away from the crowds there are much less frequented patches of water and nature to explore, both in Mazury and, above all, in the neighbouring **Suwalszczyna** and **Augustów** region.

Southwards again, lakes give way to the forests, open plains and Orthodox villages of **Podlasie**, the border region with the Soviet Union, centred on the city of **Białystok**. Both city and region maintain one of Poland's most fascinating ethnic mixes, with a significant **Belarussian** population and smaller communities of **Tartars**. The Nazis wiped out the **Jewish** population, but their history is important in these parts too, with one of Poland's finest synagogues well restored at **Tykocin**.

GDAŃSK AND AROUND

With a population of around 750,000, the conurbation comprising **Gdańsk**, **Gdynia** and **Sopot** – the so-called **Tri-City** (Trojmiasto) – ranks as one of the largest in the country. It's an enjoyable area to move about, with ferries tripping between the three centres and up to the **Hel Peninsula**, and you get a good mix of Poland's northern attractions: politics and monuments in Gdańsk, seaside chic in Sopot, gritty port life in Gdynia, and sandy beaches and clean water up at the Hel Peninsula. The lakes and forests of **Kashubia** are just an hour or two from Gdańsk by bus, and **Frombork**, too, makes an easy day trip, as do Elbląg and the Wiślana Peninsula. As you'd expect, Gdańsk also has excellent **transport connections** with the rest of Poland, with a host of buses, trains and flights.

Gdańsk

For outsiders, **GDAŃSK** is perhaps the most familiar city in Poland. The home of Lech Wałęsa, Solidarity and the former Lenin Shipyards, its images have flashed across a decade of news bulletins. Expectations formed from the newsreels are fulfilled by the industrial landscape, and suggestions of latent discontent, radicalism and future strikes are all tangible. What is more surprising, at least for those with no great knowledge of Polish history, is the cultural complexity of the place. Prewar Gdańsk – or **Danzig** as it then was – was forged by years of Prussian and Hanseatic domination, and the reconstructed city centre looks not unlike Amsterdam, making an elegant and bourgeois backdrop. What has changed entirely, however, is the city's demography. At the outbreak of the last war nearly all of the 400,000 citizens were German-speaking, with fewer than 16,000 Poles. The postwar years marked a radical shift from all that went before, as the ethnic Germans were expelled and Gdańsk became Polish for the first time since 1308.

Some history

The city's position at the meeting point of the Wisła and the Baltic has long made Danzig/Gdańsk an immense strategic asset: in the words of Frederick the Great, whoever controlled it could be considered "more master of Poland than any king ruling there". First settled in the tenth century, the city assumed prominence when the **Teutonic Knights** arrived in 1308, at the invitation of a population constantly threatened from the west by the Margraves of Brandenburg. The Knights established themselves in their accustomed style, massacring the locals and installing a colony of German settlers in their place.

The city's economy flourished, however, and with the ending of the Knights' rule in 1454, Danzig became to all intents and purposes an independent city-state, with its own legislature, judiciary and monopolies on the Wisła trade routes, restricted only by the necessity of paying homage and an annual tax to the Polish monarch. The key elements of Danzig/Gdańsk history were thus emerging: autonomy, economic power, cultural cosmopolitanism and German-Polish rivalry for control of the city.

The city's main period of development occurred between the sixteenth century and the Partitions of the late eighteenth century. An indication of the scale of the city's **trading empire** is given by statistics showing that the Danzig Eastland Company had a bigger turnover than even London's mighty East India Company.

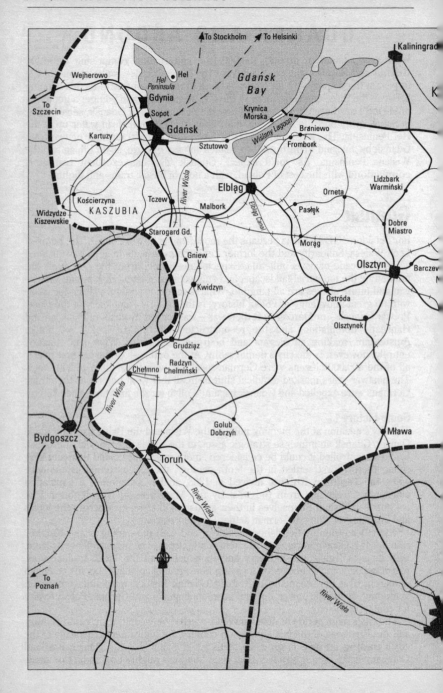

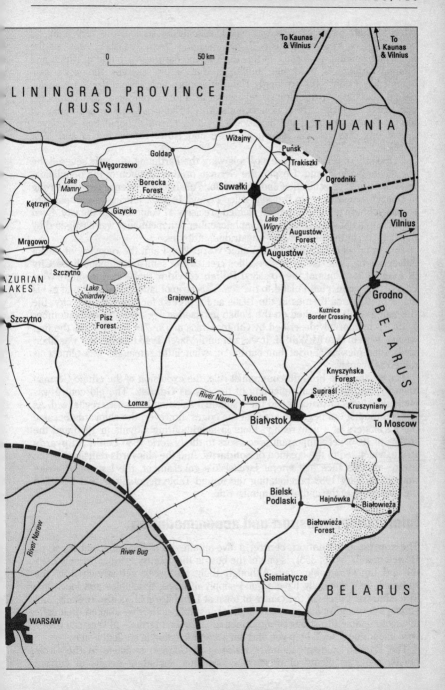

(One of their major exports was wood, specifically spruce, the very name of which derives from the Polish *Z Prus*, meaning "from Prussia".) Most of the important building took place at this time, as the burghers brought in Dutch and Flemish architects to design buildings that would express the city's self-confidence – hence the strikingly Hanseatic appearance. From the Renaissance period also dates a tradition of religious toleration, a pluralism that combined with trade to forge strong connections with Britain: a sizeable contingent of foreign Protestant merchants included a significant Scottish population, who lived in the city districts still known as Stare and Nowe Szkoty – Old and New Scotland.

Prussian annexation of the city, following the Partitions, abruptly severed the connection with Poland. Despite the German origins of much of the population, resistance to Prussianisation and support for Polish independence were as strong in Danzig as elsewhere in Prussian-ruled Poland. In 1807, a Prussian campaign to recruit soldiers to fight Napoleon yielded precisely 47 volunteers in the city. Even as German a native of Danzig as the philosopher Schopenhauer was castigated by the Prussian authorities for his "unpatriotic" attitudes.

Territorial status changed again after World War I and the recovery of Polish independence. The Treaty of Versailles created the semi-autonomous **Free City of Danzig**, terminus of the so-called **Polish corridor** that sliced through West Prussia and connected Poland to the sea. This strip of land gave Hitler one of his major propaganda themes in the 1930s and a pretext for attacking the city: the German assault unleashed on the Polish garrison at Westerplatte on September 1, 1939 – memorably described by Günter Grass in *The Tin Drum* – was the first engagement of **World War II**. It was not until March 1945 that the city was liberated, after massive Soviet bombardment; what little remained was almost as ruined as Warsaw.

The postwar era brought communist rule, the expulsion of the ethnic German majority, and the formal renaming of the city as **Gdańsk**. The old centre was meticulously reconstructed and the traditional shipping industries revitalised. As the communist era began to crack at the edges, however, the shipyards became the harbingers of a new reality. Riots in neighbouring Gdynia in 1970 and the strikes of 1976 were important precursors to the historic 1980 **Lenin Shipyards** strike, which led to the creation of **Solidarity**. And the shipyards remained at the centre of resistance to General Jaruzelski's government, the last major strike wave in January 1989 precipitating the Round Table negotiations that heralded the beginning of the end of communist rule.

Information, transport and accommodation

The **tourist information centre**, a five-minute walk from the station at ul. Heweliusza 27 (☎314-355), is one of the best in the country, with extremely helpful and knowledgeable staff. Although their resources get stretched in the summer, they generally have a good supply of maps, timetables and local tips. The **Almatur office**, in the centre of town at Długi Targ 11, is also friendly, and employs several English-speakers; unlike most offices they've adapted their style to accommodate the strange requirements – in Polish terms – of Western travellers. In summer they'll help you sort out accommodation in student hotels.

The English-language monthly *Welcome to Gdańsk*, available in the Orbis hotels, provides plenty of practical information, including details of current events. More comprehensively – but only in Polish – *Tydzień w Trojmieście*, the local listings magazine, can be bought in kiosks and certain bookshops.

Orientation is fairly straightforward, the main sites of interest being located in three historic districts: Główne Miasto, Stare Miasto and Stare Przedmieście. **Główne Miasto** (Main Town), the central area, is in easy walking distance of the main station – if you value your life don't be tempted to try jaywalking across Podwale Grodzkie but take the underground passageway like everyone else. The main pedestrianised avenues, ul. Długa and its continuation Długi Targ, form the heart of the district, which backs east onto the attractive waterfront of the Motława Canal and the island of Spichlerze. To the north is the **Stare Miasto** (Old Town), bounded by the towering cranes of the shipyards, beyond which the suburbs of Wrzeszcz, Zaspa and Oliwa sprawl towards Sopot. South of the centre stands the quieter **Stare Przedmieście** (Old Suburb).

Getting around

Travelling within the city area is pretty straightforward. A regular **train** service between the main station, Sopot and Gdynia, with plenty of stops in between, carries on well into the evening; tickets can be bought in the passage beneath the main station or at any local station (some have ticket machines). Interail cards are valid for all local trains too.

Trams run within each part of the Tri-City, but not between them. **Buses**, however, operate right across the conurbation. The large-scale **map** of Gdańsk available from kiosks and some bookshops gives all bus and tram routes. Tickets for both trams and buses can be bought from any kiosk or street-side vendor (locals generally buy them in multiples of ten): one ticket punched both ends is enough for short hops; you'll need two for night buses and *pospieszne* (speed bus) routes, more for longer journeys.

> The telephone code for the Tri-City is ☎ 058.

Finding a place to stay

As in the other big tourist cities, accommodation in Gdańsk ranges from the ultra-plush to the ultra-basic – and rooms in the centre are at a premium in summer. At the top end of the scale, Orbis run a string of **hotels** aimed very firmly at Western tourists and businesspeople. Lower down the price scale, hotels are still surprisingly thin in the ground, but **private rooms** are a good option, while **youth hostels** provide the usual not very central fall-backs.

HOTELS

As before, hotels are listed in ascending order of price; the last four are all Orbis-run, with doubles priced from £30 to £50; the first four are in the £15–25 range.

Dom Nauczyciela, ul. Upenhaga 28 (☎419-916). Nice location out in Wrzeszcz – five minutes' walk north of Gdańsk-Politechnika station – in a quiet side street. Single to four-person rooms, some with loo and shower. Has restaurant.

Jantar, Długi Targ 19 (☎316-241). Excellent location in the heart of the Old Town makes it very difficult to get into this one. The view from the top-floor rooms is magnificent. Avoid first-floor rooms – live music right below.

Zabianka, ul. Dickmana 15 (☎521-201). Smallish, decent quality place, the disadvantage being the off-centre location – halfway between Oliwa and Zabianka streets.

Wydmy, ul. Wydmy 1 (☎385-633). Seaside pension in the Stogi resort east of the city. Good if you want the beach.

Poseidon, ul. Kapliczna 30 (☎530-803). Sited halfway between Gdańsk and Sopot, this is arguably the nicest Orbis hotel in town. Balconied rooms, some with a sea view, others looking onto the woods. Has a popular nightclub.

Marina, ul. Jetlikowska 30 (☎532-079). A "luxury" Orbis hotel on the seafront, complete with a tennis court. No balconies and lots of concrete.

Novotel, ul. Pszenna (☎315-611). A typical and quite friendly motel.

Hewelius, ul. Heweliusza 22 (☎315-631). The big Orbis showpiece – pretentious and a bit too overt a contrast with regular Gdańsk life.

PRIVATE ROOMS

Private rooms can be arranged either with the efficient **Biuro Zakwaterowań** at ul. Elzbietańska 10 (daily 7am–7pm in summer; closes 5pm in winter; ☎319-371), or with the locals who hang about outside here and at the main train station.

HOSTELS

There are four **youth hostels** open year-round, each of them often full in season; the student hotel is worth trying for its functional rooms.

Ul. Wałowa 21 (☎312-313). The most central hostel – a sizeable redbrick building ten minutes' walk from the main station.

Ul. Grunwaldzka 238/40 (☎411-660). Near Oliwa in the northern Wrzeszcz suburb. A decent-quality hostel inside a sports centre; to get there take a local train to Gdańsk-Zaspa or tram #8, #12 or #15.

Ul. Smoluchowskiego 11 (☎323-820). Also in Wrzeszcz; take tram #2, #6, #8, #12, #13 or #14.

Ul. Legionów 11 (☎414-108). A lower quality hostel, once again in Wrzeszcz. Take trams #2, #4, #7, #8 or #14 or walk from the Gdańsk-Wrzeszcz station.

Ul. Morska 108c (☎270-055). Summer-only hostel near the seaside. Close to the *Poseidon* up in Jetlikowo.

Student hotel, ul. Wyspańskiego 7 (☎414-414). Cheap rooms in student lodgings.

CAMPSITES

All the campsites below are open from June to September.

Ul. Jetlikowska 23 (☎532-731). Near the beach at Jetlikowo. Regular camping facilities plus bungalows – at around £5 a bed, a bargain if you can get one. It's a short walk from the terminus of trams #2, #4 and #15.

Al. Hallera 234 (☎566-531). In the suburb of Brzeźno, due north of the town centre; trams #7, #13 and #15, and buses #124 and #148 pass nearby.

Ul. Lazurowa 6 (☎380-796). Even further out in Orle, east of the city along the Martwa Wisła; bus #112 passes it.

The City

The **Główne Miasto**, the largest of the historic quarters, is the obvious starting point for an exploration of the city; the **Stare Miasto**, across the thin ribbon of the Raduna Canal, is the natural progression. The third, southern quarter, **Stare Przedmieście**, cut off by the Podwale Przedmieskie, has its main focus for visitors in the National Museum. Moving north, out towards Sopot, is the **Oliwa** suburb with its cathedral – one of the city's most distinctive landmarks – and park.

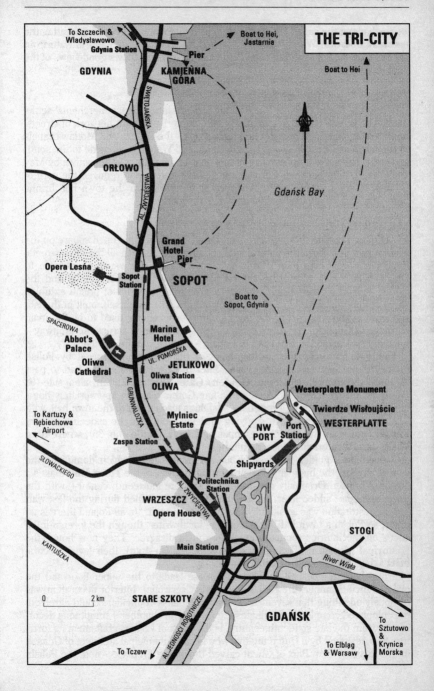

THE TRI-CITY

To Szczecin &
Władysławowo
Gdynia Station

Boat to Hel,
Jastarnia

Pier

Boat to Hel

GDYNIA

KAMIENNA
GÓRA

ŚWIĘTOJAŃSKA

ORŁOWO

AL. ZWYCIĘSTWA

Gdańsk Bay

Grand
Hotel
Pier

Opera Leśna

Sopot
Station

SOPOT

Boat to
Sopot, Gdynia

SPACEROWA

Marina
Hotel

Abbot's
Palace

UL. POMORSKA

JETLIKOWO

Oliwa
Cathedral

AL. GRUNWALDZKA

Oliwa Station

OLIWA

Westerplatte Monument

Twierdze Wisłoujście

To Kartuzy &
Rębiechowa
Airport

Mylniec
Estate

NW
PORT

Port
Station

WESTERPLATTE

Zaspa Station

SŁOWACKIEGO

Shipyards

Politechnika
Station

WRZESZCZ

AL. ZWYCIĘSTWA

Opera House

STOGI

KARTUSZKA

Main Station

River Wisła

0   2 km

STARE SZKOTY

AL. JEDNOŚCI ROBOTNICZEJ

GDAŃSK

To Sztutowo
& Krynica
Morska

To Tczew

To Elbląg
& Warsaw

North along the canal, **Westerplatte** – with its monument commemorating the outbreak of World War II – can be reached by **boat** from the central waterfront (as can Gdynia, Sopot and the Hel Peninsula), a trip that allows good views of the famous **shipyards**.

The Main Town (Główne Miasto)

Entering the **Main Town** is like walking straight into a Hansa merchants' settlement. The layout, typical of a medieval port, comprises a tight network of streets, bounded on four sides by water and main roads – the Raduna and Motława canals to the north and east, Podwale Przedmieskie and Wały Jagiellońskie to the south and west. The ancient appearance of this quarter's buildings is deceptive: by May 1945 the fighting between German and Russian forces had reduced the core of Gdańsk to smouldering ruins. A glance at the photos in the town hall brings home the scale of the destruction and of its reversal.

ULICA DŁUGA, THE TOWN HALL AND DŁUGI TARG

Ul. **Długa**, the main thoroughfare, and **Długi Targ**, the wide open square on the eastern part of it, form the natural focus of attention. As with all the main streets, huge stone gateways guard both entrances. Before the western entrance to Długa, take a look round the outer **Upland Gate** (Brama Wyżynna) and the Gothic **Prison Tower** which contains a gruesome museum of prison exhibits, some of them displayed in the torture chambers. The gate itself, built in the late sixteenth century as part of the town's outer fortifications, used to be the main entrance to Gdańsk. The three coats of arms emblazoned across the archway – Poland, Prussia and the free town of Danzig – encapsulate the city's history.

This gate was also the starting point of the "royal route" used by Polish monarchs on their annual state visits. After the Upland Gate they had to pass through the richly decorated **Golden Gate** (Brama Złota), alongside **St George's Court** (Dwór św. Jerzego), a fine Gothic mansion appropriately housing the architects' society. From here, ul. Długa leads down to the town hall, with several gabled facades worth studying in detail – such as the sixteenth-century **Ferber mansion** (no. 28) or the imposing **Lion's Castle** (no. 35), where King Władysław IV entertained local dignitaries.

Topped by a golden statue of King Zygmunt August which dominates the central skyline, the huge and well-proportioned tower of the **Town Hall** makes a powerful impact. Originally constructed in the late fourteenth century, with the tower and spire added later, the building was totally ruined during the last war, but the restoration was so skilful you'd hardly believe it. "In all Poland there is no other, so Polish a town hall" observed one local writer, though the foreign influences on the interior rooms might lead you to disagree. They now house the **Historical Museum** (Tues–Thurs, Sat & Sun 10am–4pm), their lavish decorations almost upstaging the exhibits on display.

From the entrance hall an ornate staircase leads to the upper floor and the main council chamber, the **Red Room** (Sala Czerwona). Interior decoration was obviously one thing that seventeenth-century Gdańsk councillors could agree on: the colour red completely dominates the room. The chamber's sumptuous decor, mostly from the late sixteenth century, is the work of various craftsmen: its furniture was designed by a Dutch fugitive who became municipal architect of Gdańsk in the 1590s; Willem Bart of Ghent carved the ornate fireplace – note the Polish-looking Neptunes in the supports; while most of the ceiling and wall paintings were produced by another Dutchman, Johan Verberman de Vries. The central oval ceiling painting, by another Dutchman, Isaac van den Block, is titled *The Glorification of the Unity of Gdańsk with Poland*, a period panorama of the city, stressing its Polish ties. The council used this chamber only in summer; in winter they moved into the adjoining smaller room, entered through the wooden door to the right of the fireplace.

As well as another reconstructed seventeenth-century fireplace, the next room, the **court room**, contains a haunting photomontage of the ruins of Gdańsk in 1945. One floor up, the **archive rooms** now house permanent exhibitions including a display of prewar Gdańsk photographs, plus temporary shows like a recent one of engravings by the city's best known writer, Günter Grass. The old municipal finance office contains a pair of paintings by van den Block, one a forbidding representation of the Flood, and a statue of King Jagiełło taken from the neighbouring Artus Court.

Past the town hall the street opens onto the wide expanses of **Długi Targ**, where the **Artus Court** (Dwór Artusa) stands out in a square filled with many fine mansions. Reconstruction work should be completed by the beginning of 1994, and if it's closed when you visit you'll have to content yourself with admiring the Renaissance frontages of this and the nearby **Golden House** (Złota Kamienczka; no. 41). The square itself has many moods: in summer, with tourists and pigeons gathered round the fountain statue of Neptune, the light, open atmosphere recalls an Italian piazza; but on a misty autumn evening, as the streets resound with the chimes of the town hall clock, you could almost imagine yourself in an old Norman cathedral city.

THE WATERFRONT AND MARITIME MUSEUM

The archways of the **Green Gate** (Most Zielona), a former royal residence for the annual visit, open directly onto the **waterfront**. From the bridge over the Motława Canal you get a good view of the old granaries on **Spichlerze** Island to the right (there used to be over 300 of them), and to the left of the old harbour quay, now a tourist hang-out and local promenade.

Halfway down is the massive and largely original fifteenth-century **Gdańsk Crane** (Żuraw Gdański), the biggest in medieval Europe; it and a number of buildings make up the **Maritime Museum** (Tues–Fri 9.30am–4pm, Sat–Sun 10am–4pm, extended opening hours in summer, last tickets 1hr before closing), one of the best-organised and most interesting in the country. Only the ticket system remains a bit of a trial: there are different stubs for each part of the museum, so you end up carrying round what seem like bundles of the things. All, though, can be bought at the *kasa* inside the Crane: they're cheap, so the easiest thing is probably just to pick up the lot.

The **Crane** itself houses a colourful and, for once, well laid-out collection of marine-life specimens from around the world, a selection of sea birds, swordfish, dried star-fish, delicate coral sea shells and some huge lobsters greeting you from the corners. Like their countryman Joseph Conrad, Poles have long been avid seafarers and explorers: mementoes of some of their travels around the world have been gathered together, the exhibition animated by some rollicking recordings of Polish sea shanties playing in the background, the occasional Liverpool melody included. An additional bonus is the bird's-eye view of the inner workings of the massive crane from the museum rooms sitting above its enormous wheels.

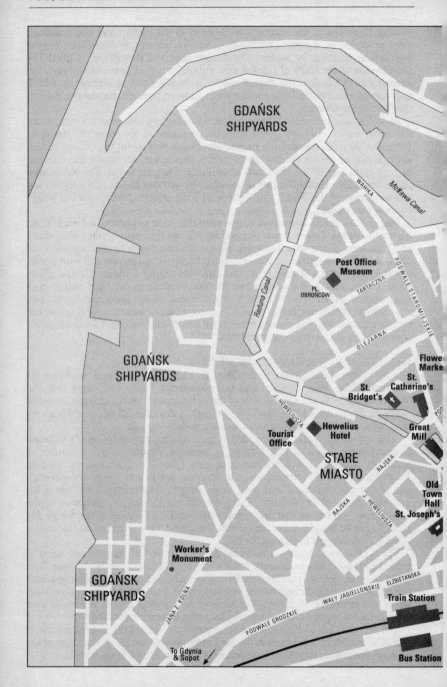

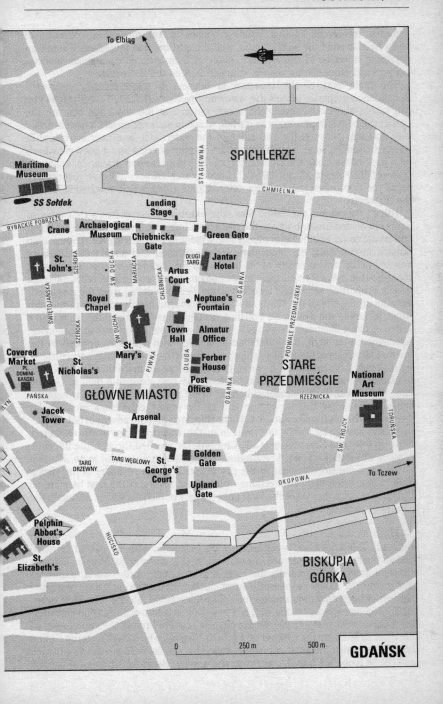

To Elbląg

SPICHLERZE

STAGIEWNA

CHMIELNA

Maritime Museum

SS Sołdek

Landing Stage

RYBACKIE POBRZEŻE

Crane

Archaelogical Museum

Chiebnicka Gate

Green Gate

DŁUGI TARG

Jantar Hotel

St. John's

SZEROKA

SW DUCHA

MARIACKA

CHLEBNICKA

Artus Court

OGARNA

Royal Chapel

Neptune's Fountain

SWIĘTOJAŃSKA

SW DUCHA

SZEROKA

St. Mary's

Town Hall

Almatur Office

PODWALE PRZEDMIEJSKIE

PIWNA

DLUGA

Ferber House

Covered Market

PL DOMINI-KAŃSKI

St. Nicholas's

Post Office

STARE PRZEDMIEŚCIE

National Art Museum

TORUŃSKA

PAŃSKA

GŁÓWNE MIASTO

OGARNA

RZEZNICKA

Jacek Tower

Arsenal

SW. TROJCY

TARG DRZEWNY

TARG WĘGLOWY

St. George's Court

Golden Gate

To Tczew

OKOPOWA

Upland Gate

Pelphin Abbot's House

HUGISKO

BISKUPIA GÓRKA

St. Elizabeth's

0   250 m   500 m

GDAŃSK

Across the street, another building houses an anthropological collection of boats from around the world: again, well thought out and presented. There's an enjoyable selection of vessels here, many of them painted canoes, catamarans, barques and other fishing vessels from Africa, Asia and Polynesia.

The main part of the museum is housed in three recently renovated Renaissance granaries across the water on Spichlerze Island. To get across you can take a short boat trip in the vessel moored at the waterside beneath the Crane: the boat leaves as soon as it's full, which in summer means it travels pretty well non-stop between the two sides of the water: last boat over is at 4pm in winter (extended service in summer), the journey offering you a good view back onto the houses along the city waterfront. The stout-looking granaries, known as *"Panna"* (The Virgin Mary), *"Miedz"* (Copper) and *"Oliwski"* (Oliwa), respectively recall the days when the bustling, international Gdańsk port reached right into the city centre.

Titled "Poland and the Baltic Sea", the **exhibition** comprises a rich array of items connected in some way to the city's maritime past. Everything the maritime enthusiast could want is here: model ships, paintings on stirring sea themes, ship fittings, instruments, old binoculars and compasses, and an extensive display devoted to the various stages of the traditional ship-building process. The biggest room houses a fearsome display of cannons mounted on their wooden rollers, a goodly proportion seemingly Swedish-origin weapons dating from the mammoth assaults on the city of the 1650s and 1660s. Colourful mastheads recovered from ships, including the decorative Polish *Artus* figurehead, decorate the walls, and a series of maps illustrate the struggle for control of the Baltic over the centuries. Appropriately enough, the exhibition concludes with a display devoted to the modern struggles of the Gdańsk shipyards, the birth of Solidarity in particular.

Back out of the granaries, if you've got an appetite for more there's the chance to clamber around the solid-looking *Sołdek*, the first steamship built in Gdańsk after World War II, that's moored in front of the granaries. The trek through the ship's holds, crew cabins, engine and boiler rooms culminates in a display devoted to the 1980 strikes in the Gdańsk shipyards and the advent of Solidarity.

All the streets back into the town from the waterfront are worth exploring. Next up from the Green Gate is **ul. Chlebnicka**, reached through the fifteenth-century **Chlebnicka Gate**. The **English House** (Dom Angielski) at no. 16, built in 1569 and the largest house in the city at the time, is a reminder of the strong Reformation-era trading connections with Britain. Several of the best bars are on Chlebnicka, as is the HQ of the local police – they're the lads sitting around in the carelessly parked cars.

ST MARY'S

Both ul. Chlebnicka and neighbouring ul. Mariacka, with its gabled terraced houses and expensive clothes shops, end at the gigantic **St Mary's Church** (Kościół Mariacka), reputedly the biggest brick church in the world. Estimates that it could fit 20,000 people were substantiated during the early days of martial law, when huge crowds crammed the cold whitewashed interior. The **high altar**, totally reconstructed after the war, is a powerful sixteenth-century triptych featuring a *Coronation of the Virgin*. Of the chapels scattered round the church, two of the most striking are the **Chapel of 11,000 Virgins**, which has a tortured Gothic crucifix for which the artist apparently nailed his son-in-law to a cross as a model, and the **St Anne's Chapel**, containing the wooden *Beautiful Madonna of Gdańsk* from around 1415. A curiosity is the fifteenth-century **astronomical clock,** which tells not only the day, month and year but the whole saints' calendar and the phases of the moon; when completed in 1470 it was the world's tallest clock.

If you're feeling fit, make sure you climb up St Mary's **tower** – on a good day the view over Gdańsk and the plains is excellent; for a few złotys the old man who sits up there all day will let you look around with his binoculars. After the bareness of the church, the Baroque exuberance of the **Royal Chapel,** directly opposite on ul. św. Ducha, makes a refreshing change. The **Archaeological Museum** (Tues–Sun 10am–5pm), at the east end of ul. Mariacka, is a bit of a disappointment, perhaps unavoidably after the maritime museum: the exhibitions are dry and lifeless, with only the Peruvian finds lightening the tone.

FROM THE ARSENAL TO THE FLOWER MARKET

Ul. Piwna, another street of high terraced houses west of the church entrance, ends at the monumental **Great Arsenal** (Wielka Zbrojowna), an early seventeenth-century armoury facing the **Coal Market** (Targ Węglowy). Now a busy shopping centre, the coal market leads north to the **Wood Market** (Targ Drzewny), and on to the Old Town over the other side of the canal. Ul. Szeroka, first off to the right, is another charming old street with a nice view of St Mary's from the corner with ul. Furty Groba.

The Dominican-run **St Nicholas' Church** (św. Mikołaja) on ul. Świętojańska is another fourteenth-century brick structure with relatively tasteful Baroque additions, while **St John's** (św. Jana), further down the same street, is a reputedly beautiful church currently closed for restoration. Continuing north towards the canal, at the edge of pl. Obrónczów stands the old **Danzig Post Office** building immortalised by Günter Grass in *The Tin Drum.* Rebuilt after the war, it's here that a small contingent of employees of the Free City's *Poczta Polska* (Polish Post Office) battled it out with German forces in September 1939. As at Westerplatte the Germans clearly weren't anticipating such spirited resistance; despite the overwhelmingly superior firepower ranged against them the Poles held out for nine hours, finally surrendering when the Nazis sent in flamethrowers. Official postwar accounts maintained that the survivors were taken to the nearby Zaspa cemetery and summarily shot. At least two appear to have survived, in fact, surfacing in recent years to tell their own story.

The spiky-looking monument on the square in front of the building commemorates an event that played an important role in the city's postwar communist mythology, the Poles' heroic resistance presented as a further vindication of the claimed "Polishness" of the city. Inside the post office there's a small **museum** (Tues–Sat 10am–4pm) mainly devoted to the events of 1939, including copies of Nazi photos of the attack on the building. Additionally there's an exhibition of local postal history underscoring the importance of postal communications to the city ever since its early trading days.

The terraced houses and shops tail off as you approach the outer limits of the main town, marked by several towers and other remnants of the **town wall**. **Baszta Jacek,** the tower nearest the canal, stands guard over the Pod Myślinksa, the main route over the canal into the Old Town. The **flower market** opposite is a fine example of the Polish attachment to the finer things of life – even when there was nothing in the food shops, you still found roses or carnations in one of the stalls here. Ceremonious trimming and wrapping make you feel special in a way nothing else quite can.

The Old Town (Stare Miasto) and the shipyards

Crossing the canal bridge brings you into the **Old Town** (Stare Miasto). Dominating the waterside is the seven-storey **Great Mill** (Wielki Mlyn), built in the mid-fourteenth century by the Teutonic Knights and another Gdańsk "largest" – in this case the biggest mill in medieval Europe. Its eighteen races milled corn for 600 years; even in the 1930s it was still grinding out 200 tons of flour a day, and local enthusiasts see no reason why it couldn't be doing the same again. At present it's used as an office block, with a large murky Pewex in the basement to give it that sensitive historical touch.

St Catherine's Church (Katarzynka), the former parish church of the Old Town, to the right of the crossway, is one of the nicest in the city. Fourteenth century – and built in brick like almost all churches in the region – it has a well-preserved and luminous interior. If you're keen to catch a glimpse of **Lech Wałęsa**, there's a good chance of seeing him at his local church, **St Bridget's** (św. Brigida), next to St Catherine's, on Sundays. Under the charismatic guidance of Father Jankowski, still a close confidant of Wałęsa, the church became a local Solidarity stronghold in the 1980s. The oil painting of the Black Madonna in a T-shirt sporting the *Solidarność* logo says it all. Although the political importance of the church is diminishing now that Solidarity holds the reins of power, it's still worth visiting places like this – ideally on a Sunday – to experience the specifically Polish mixture of religion and politics that is personified in the man whose statue watches over the church, Karol Wojtyła, aka John Paul II.

Moving further into the Old Town, the merchants' mansions give way to postwar housing, the tattier bits looking like something off the set of *1984*. The most interesting part of the district is just west along the canal from the mill, centred on the **Old Town Hall** (Ratusz Staromiejski), on the corner of ul. Bielanska and Korzenna. Built by the architect of the main town hall, this delicate Renaissance construction is still occupied by local government offices, but you can wander in to look at the Baroque paintings and sculptures in the main hall. The bronze figure in the entrance hall is of Jan Hevelius, the Polish astronomer after whom Orbis have named their nearby skyscraper hotel. Like the better-known Mr Fahrenheit, he was a Gdańsk boy.

Continuing west from the town hall, Gothic **St Joseph's** (św. Jożefa) and **St Elizabeth's** (św. Elżbiety) – facing each other across ul. Elzbietańska – and the Renaissance **House of the Abbots of Pelplin** (Dom Opatów Pelplińskich) make a fine historic entourage. From here you're only a short walk through the tunnels under the main road (Podwale Grodzkie) from the station.

THE (EX-)LENIN SHIPYARDS

Looming large in the distance are the cranes of the famous **Gdańsk Shipyards** (Stocznia Gdańska) – Lenin's name was dropped in the late 1980s. With the Nowa Huta steelworks outside Kraków, this was the crucible of the political struggles of the 1980s.

Ten minutes' walk or one tram stop north along the main road brings you to the shipyard gates on plac Solidarnośći Robotniczej. In front of them stands an ugly set of steel crosses, a **monument** to workers killed during the **1970 shipyard riots**; it was inaugurated in 1980 in the presence of Party, Church and opposition leaders. A precursor to the organised strikes of the 1980s, the 1970 riots erupted when workers took to the streets in protest at price rises, setting fire to the Party headquarters after police opened fire. Riots erupted again in 1976, once more in protest at price rises on basic foodstuffs, and then in **August 1980** Gdańsk came to the forefront of world attention when a protest at the sacking of workers rapidly developed into a national strike.

The formation of **Solidarity**, the first independent trade union in the Soviet bloc, was a direct result of the Gdańsk strike, instigated by the Lenin Shipyards workers and their charismatic leader **Lech Wałęsa**. Throughout the 1980s the Gdańsk workers remained in the vanguard of political protest. Strikes here in 1988 and 1989 led to the **Round Table Talks** which forced the Communist Party into power-sharing and, ultimately, democratic elections.

Standing at the gates today, you may find it hard to experience this as the place where, in a sense, contemporary Poland began to take shape. Yet ironically the shipyards remain at the leading edge of political developments: the government is attempting (unsuccessfully so far) to sell them off to Western investors.

The Old Suburb (Stare Przedmieście)

Stare Przedmieście – the lower part of old Gdańsk – was the limit of the original town, as testified by the ring of seventeenth-century bastions running east from plac Wałowy over the Motława.

The main attraction today is the **National Art Museum** (Tues–Thurs, Sat & Sun 10am–3pm), housed in a former Franciscan monastery at ul. Toruńska 1. There's enough local Gothic art and sculpture here to keep enthusiasts going all day, as well as a varied collection of fabrics, chests, gold and silverware – all redolent of the town's former wealth. The range of Dutch and Flemish art in the "foreign galleries" – Memling, the younger Brueghel, Cuyp and van Dyck are the best-known names – attests to the city's strong links with the Netherlands.

The museum's most famous work is Hans Memling's colossal *Last Judgement* (1473), the painter's earliest known work – though he was already in his thirties and a mature artist. The painting has had a more than usually chequered past, having been commissioned by the Medici in Florence, then diverted to Gdańsk, looted by Napoleon, moved to Berlin, returned to Gdańsk, stolen by the Nazis and finally, after being discovered by the Red Army, hidden in the Thuringian hills, to be returned to Gdańsk by the Russians in 1956.

Twierdze Wisłoujście

A half hour bus journey from the city centre out along the Westerplate peninsula is the old **Gdańsk Fortress** (*Twierdze Wisłoujście*), from which the local *kaper* defence force (see below) use to guard the city port. Long neglected, it's now been substantially renovated and turned into a section of the city **Historical Museum** (May–Sept, Tues–Sun, 10am–3pm, otherwise by appointment – the tourist office has the current details).

Designed by Dutch architects using the octagonal zigzag defence plan popular at the time, the first fortifications for the two-storey fortress were put up in the 1480s, with additions built on throughout the following century. Doubling as the main port lighthouse, the whole construction was enlarged to its current size in the mid-eighteenth century, and reinforced by Napoleon's forces – Napoleon himself visited the place on his way to Moscow – in the early nineteenth. The city's Partition-era Prussian masters used the fortress as a jail, notably for Polish political prisoners, which probably explains why they didn't dismantle it along with all the other port fortifications in the 1870s.

Despite years of modern neglect the fortress still looks formidable: through the heavily fortified entrance you enter the main courtyard, with the high former lighthouse tower – as featured on the local *Kaper* beer label – in the centre. Clamber up to the top of the tower, the walls of which are lined with prints of the old Prussian plans of the fortress, for an excellent view out over the city, with the shipyards to the south and Westerplatte and beyond it the Hel Peninsula out to the north.

Back down to ground level you can wander around the ramparts, stopping now and then to peer out through the menacing-looking cannon holes looking out onto the waters of the harbour approach – not a pretty sight for a passing assailant.

If you're with the guide he'll show you the dank, old, sixteenth-century kitchens as well as the former Commandant's room, currently *remont* (like much of the building), and due to be converted into a tourist café/restaurant. Finally you can wander through the cavernous fortress cellars reaching down to, and in some places below the water's edge. Big enough to hold supplies to keep the *kaper* going for a whole year, these days the smoke-blackened cellars are piled high with barrels of strawberries for jam-making, a commercial revival, apparently, of an old mercenary pastime.

THE *KAPER* OF GDAŃSK

In a city with a tradition of cosmopolitan and independent-minded attitudes the story of Gdańsk's one-time mercenary naval defence force is instructive. Right from the city's early days the citizen merchants of Gdańsk appreciated the need for some form of sea-based protection to keep potential invaders out. The first Polish king to try and establish a proper navy was Kazimierz Jagiellończyk (1444–92), during his thirteen-year long war with the Teutonic Knights. A significant portion of his navy actually consisted of local mercenaries – **kaper** as they came to be known, after *kaap*, the Old Dutch for "ship" – who agreed to work on contract for the king but not officially as his representatives.

The crews on the *kaper* vessels were a mixed bunch, the contingent of locals from the Gdańsk and Elbląg regions supplemented by an assortment of Swedish, Flemish, Scottish and Kashubian adventurers. Skilled sailors keen on risk, ostensibly the *kaper* had as their main mission to guard the Gdańsk merchant fleet, which by the late fifteenth century was already nearly 100 vessels strong. In 1482 the newly constructed fortress at Wisłoujście became the base of their operations. Protecting the harbour aside, the *kaper* clearly weren't averse to a bit of adventuring-cum-piracy. Under the designation "the king's maritime military", King Zygmunt Stary employed a *kaper* force for his assault on Moscow in 1517; their main interest, however, was actually in the Baltic port of Memling, which the *kaper* captured single-handedly under the leadership of one Adrian Flint, an English adventurer.

With their own base, ships and uniforms, by the mid-sixteenth century the increasingly ill-disciplined *kaper* appear to have developed into a fully fledged paramilitary naval outfit capturing 20 vessels in one year (1568) alone. Recognising that the Gdańsk *kaper* were flourishing in the vacuum left by the absence of a proper navy, King Zygmunt Wasa set about creating a standing force and in 1600 asked *kaper* to work for him. It was left to King Jan Sobieski, however, to reign the *kaper* in fully, and finally to integrate them into a fully fledged Polish navy.

There are a number of ways of getting to the fortress: after passing the huge local sulphur factory, bus #106 from outside the main station stops close by, continuing on to Westerplatte; a more attractive alternative is to take a tram or bus to Nowy Port, then a ferry (depart every half-hour in summer) across to the fortress.

Westerplatte

It was at **Westerplatte**, the promontory guarding the harbour entrance, that the German battleship *Schleswig-Holstein* fired the first salvo of World War II. For a full week the garrison of 170 badly equipped Poles held off the combined assault of aircraft, heavy guns and over 3000 German troops, setting the tone for the Poles' response to the subsequent Nazi–Soviet invasion. The ruined army guard-house and barracks are still there, one of the surviving buildings housing a small **Museum** (Tues–Sun 10am–4pm) chronicling the momentous events of September 1939. Beyond the museum it's a fifteen-minute walk to the main **Westerplatte monument,** a grim, ugly-looking 1960s slab in the best socialist-realist traditions, whose symbolism conveys a tangible sense of history. The green surroundings of the exposed peninsula make a nice, if generally blustery, walk to the coast, with good views out on to the Baltic from along the coast.

You can get to Westerplatte by a #106 or #158 bus from the centre, but a much better way is to take one of the tourist **boats** from the main city waterfront, just north of the Brama Zielona. (There are boats to several destinations – Gdynia, Sopot and Hel included – so make sure you're on the right one.) Taking about thirty minutes each way, the trip provides an excellent view of the **shipyards**, along with the array of international vessels anchored there.

Wrzeszcz

Moving north from the centre, the **Wrzeszcz** district is a leafy, quietly affluent suburb that's popular among the city's better-off. Wrzeszcz, or Langfuhr as it was known in the days of the Free City, also happens to have been Günter Grass' childhood stamping ground in the years immediately before and during World War II: it's in the streets round the family flat near Wrzeszcz station, for example, that the central action of *The Tin Drum* takes place. Though much of Wrzeszcz was destroyed in 1945, one building Grass would certainly still recognise is the old **Gdańsk Brewery** on ul. Wajdeloty, just behind the railway station.

Oliwa

The modern Oliwa suburb, the northernmost area of Gdańsk, has one of the best-known buildings in the city, **Oliwa Cathedral**. To get there, take the local train to Gdańsk-Oliwa station, and walk across the park west of the main Sopot road.

Originally part of the monastery founded by the Danish Cistercians who settled here in the mid twelfth century at the invitation of a local Pomeranian prince, the cathedral has seen its fair share of action over the years. First in a long line of plunderers were the Teutonic Knights, who repeatedly ransacked the place in the 1240s and 1250s. A fire in the 1350s led to a major Gothic-style overhaul, the structural essence of which remains to this day. The wars of the seventeenth century had a marked impact on Oliwa, the Swedish army carrying off much of the cathedral's by then sumptuous collection of furnishings as booty in 1626, the church bells and main altarpiece included. The second major Swedish assault of 1655–60

THE GDAŃSK BREWERY

Built in the 1870s, the Gdańsk Brewery – *Kleinhammer Brauerei* as it was originally called – is currently undergoing something of a revival following its purchase by an Australian company. For the first time in many decades decent, locally brewed beer is now plentifully available in bars, restaurants and shops around the Tri-City, though it's having to put up with some stiff competition from the (often inferior) Western (particularly German) brews that have flooded the Polish market. Five beers, mostly bottled but some on draught, are currently produced by the brewery:

Gdańskie. A light, full-flavoured lunchtime beer. May have to change soon due to extortionate rates demanded by the local authorities for use of the city name.

Remus. Named after local Kashubian hero, another lighter beer aimed at the (large) Kashubian market .

Artus. Popular prewar brand revived 10 years ago. A stronger, full-bodied lager beer.

Hewelius. Named after the seventeenth-century Gdańsk-born astronomer who also kept his own private brewery. An excellent, hoppy pilsner worthy of the great astronomer-brewer's name.

Kaper. "Pirate's brew" would be a loose translation. Strong, dark and heavy porter-type ale popular among the heavy drinkers.

If you've the time and interest, the **brewery** itself makes an enjoyable visit: you need to book in advance (☎415-215) for the guided tours – with the chance to do a bit of beer-tasting at the end of the visit. To get to the brewery take the local train to Wrzeszcz station, and from there it's two minutes' walk to the brewery gates. Much of the building (and brewing equipment) is pretty old-fashioned, not to say clapped-out, but things are changing fast as a result of the new owner's ambitious modernisation plans. In among the mixture of 1950s equipment and 1990s hi-tech apparatus you can still see several bits of the original brewery, including the attractive stained glass windows, carthorses' entrance and solid *Danziger* walls.

eventually led to the Oliwa peace treaty (1660), signed in the abbey hall: the following century brought lavish refurbishment of the building, (notably the organ, begun in 1755), most of which you can still see today. The Prussian Partition-era takeover of Gdańsk spelled the end of the by then fabulously wealthy abbey's glory days, the monastery finally being officially abolished in 1831. Unlike most of its surroundings, the cathedral miraculously came through the end of World War II largely unscathed, though the retreating Nazis torched the abbey complex: long held with special affection by Polish Catholics, since 1945, both the cathedral and the abbey have been thoroughly renovated and restored to the elegant complex you encounter today.

THE CATHEDRAL COMPLEX

Approached from the square in front of the building, the towering main **facade** combines twin Gothic brick towers peaked with Renaissance spires and dazzling white Rococo stuccowork to unusually striking effect. Through the fine, late seventeenth-century portal brings you into the lofty central **nave**, a dazzlingly exuberant structure topped by a star-spangled vaulted ceiling supported on arched pillars. Past the side chapels filling the two side aisles the eye is immediately drawn to the **high altar**, a sumptuous Baroque piece from the 1680s containing several pictures from the Gdańsk workshops of the period, including one ascribed to Andreas Schlüter the Younger. Above the altar rises a deliciously over-the-top decorative ensemble, a swirling mass of beatific-looking cherubs being sucked into a heavenly whirlpool, surrounded by angels and with gilded sun rays breaking out in all directions, the whole thing leading towards a central stained glass window.

Apart from some fine Baroque choir stalls and the old Renaissance high altarpiece, now in the northern transept, the building's finest – and most famous – feature is the exuberantly decorated eighteenth-century **organ** which completely fills the back of the nave. In its day the largest instrument in Europe – seven men were needed to operate the bellows – the dark heavy oak of the organ is ornamented with a mass of sumptuous Rococo wood carving, the whole instrument framing a stained glass window of Mary and Child, a mass of supporting angels and cherubs again filling out the picture. It's a beautiful instrument with a rich, sonorous tone and a wealth of moving parts, trumpet-blowing angels included, and in summer you can hear organ recitals daily at noon and 1pm, on Sundays at 3pm and 4pm.

Passing through the gateway round the edge of the cathedral will bring you into the old **bishop's palace complex,** originally the abbey buildings. The stately main palace building now houses a **modern art museum** (Tués–Sat 9am–3pm, Sun 9.30am–3pm). Past the upmarket shop at the entrance flogging "modern art" to the tourists, the ground-floor rooms are mostly changing graphic exhibitions by local artists: upstairs is an enjoyable gallery of twentieth-century Polish art, the centrepiece being a large selection of 1960s pop art, Tate-style "events" and other weird and wonderful sculpted constructions. Several better-known modern artists are represented, most notably Jan Łodiński, as well as a whole room of works by Henryk Staszewski (1894–1988). The palace rooms themselves are pretty grand too, notably the old bishop's dining room, now also used for concerts.

Across the courtyard from the palace the old bishop's granary contains an **ethnographic museum** (same opening times), a smallish collection of local exhibits taking you through the distict's complicated historical heritage. Surrounding the complex is the old **Palace Park,** a pleasant, shaded spot verging on a botanical gardens with an enjoyable collection of exotic trees, hanging willows and a stream meandering through the middle – a pleasant place for an afternoon stroll. Unfortunately the one tree you won't find here is the olive whose branches the Cistercians adopted as their symbol and after which they named the monetary they founded here. Olive motifs do crop up in the cathedral decorations around, however, most notably on the back of the high south window. If you happen to be here on **All Souls' Day** (November 1), the large **cemetery** over the road is an amazing sight, illuminated by thousands of candles placed on the gravestones. Whole families come to visit the individual graves and communal memorials to the unknown dead, in a powerful display of remembrance which says much about the intertwining of Catholicism and the collective memory of national sufferings.

AROUND THE CATHEDRAL

Another national monument lives just down the road. **Lech Wałęsa**, having vacated the people's paradise of the Młyniec housing estate, is now in residence in the wealthier zone west of the railway track, though his elevation to president means he's hardly here these days.

Like several Polish cities, Gdańsk has a small, low-profile **Tartar** community (see also "Białystock", p.216). They're currently putting the finishing touches to a new **mosque** not far from Wałęsa's house; already in use by local Muslims, including the Arab student population, the mosque is at the south end of ul. Polanki, on the corner with ul. Abrahama (nearest station Gdańsk-Zaspa; trams #6, #12 and #15 also run nearby). Further up the same road, the attractive, late eighteenth-century mansion at number 122 is where **Schopenhauer**, the Danzig-born philosopher, grew up.

Eating and drinking

In a city accustomed to tourism, finding a place to eat is relatively straightforward: there's a good range of cafés and snack bars, with an increasing emphasis on Western fast-food lookalikes, as well as some genuinely recommendable restaurants. On the down side, heavy demand in summer makes queueing a frequent ordeal, and with the best places it's quite common to turn up only to find them reserved for tourist groups. As for local specialities, fish dishes are generally worth sampling, as long as you're unworried by a dose of Baltic pollution.

Drinking in the city centres on a number of bars and cafés on ul. Długa and parallel streets to the north. In summer the attractive terrace cafés of ul. Chlebnicka and Mariacka make the ideal place to sit out and enjoy the sun – and more often than not a decent *espresso*.

Restaurants

As throughout Poland, keep in mind that it can be difficult to find a restaurant open after 9pm, except in Orbis hotels, which are more adapted to tourist habits.

Milano, ul. Chlebnicka 50. Quiet, good-quality pizzeria in the town centre with a nice line in lasagna. Open till midnight.

Pod Żurawiem, ul. Warzywnicza 10. On the waterfront, one of the few places where you can eat outside. Solid Polish food.

Kubicki, ul. Wartka 5. Good local food in slightly murky maritime-influenced surroundings. Popular with foreign sailors, hence the multilingual menus.

Żolty Kur, ul. Długa 4. A decent cheap eatery in a central location, with Delft tiles for decoration. Chicken specialities.

Karczma Michał, ul. Jana Z. Kolna 8. Cosy little place close to the shipyards, where the world's media used to hang out during the strikes. Good solid local food from the owner's farm outside town.

Tawerna, ul. Powrźnicza 19–20. Decent nosh, especially the steak and duck – but only till 8.30pm; drinks till about 10pm.

Athena, ul. Długa. Regular-quality Greek restaurant. Good value.

Retman, ul. Stągiewna 1. Situated by the waterfront, serving good fish dishes with salmon a speciality. Increasingly orientated towards German tourists, with prices to match. Open till around midnight.

Pod Wieżą, ul. Piwna 51. A favourite stopoff with tourists trekking round the Old Town, though rather lacking in atmosphere.

Pod Łososiem, ul. Szeroka 54 (☎317-652). The most luxurious and expensive in town. Specialises in seafood; also known locally as originator of *Goldwasser* liqueur, a thick yellow concoction with flakes of real gold that's as Prussian as its name suggests.

Marina, ul. Jetlikowska 30. Good Orbis hotel restaurant; try the duck and poultry.

Hewelius, ul. Heweliusza 22 (☎315-631). If you don't mind paying for it, this Orbis hotel restaurant offers dishes you won't find in many other places. The smooth-talking waiters are a bit of a trial, though.

Birland, ul. Chlebnicka 26. Beery former ZOMO (security police) hang-out: basic Polish cuisine – and casino.

Czardasz, ul. Śląska 66. Wholesome Hungarian nosh in Oliwa, but watch out for unpredictable early closing times.

La Famiglia, ul. Szeroka 31/32. Solid, Italian-owned and run eaterie in the Old Town. Good no-nonsense pasta and pizza, also takeaways.

Monika, ul. Piwna 52/53. Presentable if unexciting pizzeria, ideally located for lunchtime stopoff.

Pizza Bella, ul. Pilotów 9a. One of the best of the new pizza joints in town. Open till 10pm.

Pod Zieloną Bramą, Długi Targ 17/18. Good fish dishes, friendly service. Open till 10pm.

Stara Karczma Gdańska, ul. Sienna 9. Off the beaten track east of the centre, surprisingly good Lithuanian-influenced cuisine. Closes early.

Tan-Viet, ul. Podmłyńska 1/5. Presentable new Vietnamese joint close to the town centre. Open till 10pm. Also takeaway.

Trakia, Gospody 3. Well north of centre, excellent value, good-quality Polish food in pleasant surroundings. Open late.

Wielki Shanghai, al. Grunwaldzka 82. Passable new Asian restaurant in Wrzeszcz with Chinese-based menu. Open till 11pm.

Fast food

Baryłka, Długie Pobrzeże 24. Bistro-type hang-out on the main waterfront. Open till 10pm.

Neptuny, ul. Długa 32. One of the city's classic milk bars – try the specialities of the day.

Itaka, ul. Długa 18. One of the first genuine Polish fast-food joints, with hamburgers, fries and all the rest. Poles love it, as much for the novelty of fast (ie normal) service as anything else.

Mleczny, ul. Długa 33/34. Business as usual in one of a couple of old-style milk bars in town to survive privatisation.

Gyros, Pańska 9/11. Vaguely Greek-style fast food – kebabs and the like.

Uniwersalny, Korzenna 1. Another traditional milk bar: offers basic Polish nosh at ultra-low prices.

Cafés

LOT, Wały Jagiellońskie 2/4. Airline café that serves a decent cup of coffee in upmarket surroundings, adorned with paintings by art students.

Palowa, ul. Długa 47, underneath the Town Hall. An ideal rendezvous point, and often has a good selection of cakes too. Service is what Poles would call "relaxed".

Artus, Długi Targ 1/7. Centrally located, this a prime tourist spot. Open late in summer.

Café de Columbia, ul. Długa 77/78. Passable centre of town café-bar (bar closes earlier).

C14, Barbary 3. Avant-garde artists haunt in dynamic new gallery.

Istra, ul. Piwna 64/65. Pleasant, French-style café in useful location, disadvantage being early closing hours.

Marysieńka, ul. Szeroka 37/39. Enjoyable Old Town café.

Nad Motławą, Długie Pobrzeże 5. Waterfront café, good place to sit out in summer.

Pod Holendrem, ul. Mariacka 37/39. Terrace café with good local cakes and pastries.

Café Lord, ul. Gen. Hallera 241. Café-bar, the Tri-City's most popular local gay and lesbian haunt. Discos (gay and lesbian) Wed, Fri and Sat.

Pod Zagłobą, Pod Staromiejskie 62. Popular Old Town bar, stays open a bit later than many.

Rudy Kot, ul. Gamcarska 18/20. Out-of-centre haunt popular with local student crowd.

Trops, ul. Czyżewskiego 29. Café with live music, with lots going on, especially at weekends.

Bars and clubs

U Szkota, ul. Chlebnicka. Popular, enjoyable Scottish-theme bar, small and often difficult to get a table in – but you can normally sit at the bar downstairs.

GTPS Artists' Bar, ul. Piwna. Open till late; helps if you look the part.

Architects' Club, just off Targ Węglowy. A great spot. Talk your way in with a Polish friend and have a great time with the architecture students.

Vinifera, Wodopój 7. A nice canal-side bar-cum-café in a doll-size house, with seats outside. A good place to relax in the city; open till midnight.

Klub Aktora, ul. Mariacka 1/3. Quiet, relaxed Western-style bar – too expensive for the vodka-swillers, so no hassle from local drunks. Also serves food.

Coton Club, Złotników 25/29. Fashionable bar/nightclub frequented by local Solidarity politicians and Gdańsk yuppies. Irish music a couple of nights a week.

Flisak, ul. Chlebnicka 9/10. Smoky dive for serious drinkers only. Open till 2am.

Żak, ul. Wały Jagiellońskie. Best of a lively bunch of student clubs, just down from the main station. Live bands (rock and jazz), art film club, and plenty more going on.

Pierot, Węglarska 5. Basic beer-swillers haunt in the town centre. Closes early.

Punkt, ul. Chlebnicka 2. Pub-type joint aimed at locals as much as tourists. Open till 1pm.

Staromiejska, Korzenna 33/35. Cellar wine bar with a good line in beef *stroganoff*. Open till 10pm.

Alex, ul. Grunwaldzka 87/91. Trendy night-club/restaurant in the Wrzeszcz district.

Yellow Jazz Club. A boat moored off Targ Rybny in summer months, with live jazz and a good bar.

The **unnamed club** on Wały Piastowskie, open every evening, has some live bands (rock, jazz) and a rousing disco at weekends.

Entertainments

The *National Philharmonic and Opera House*, al. Zwycięstwa 15 (nearest station Gdańsk Politechnika) is one of the best **classical venues** in the country, with a varied programme of classical performances, occasional ballet productions included. Information and ticket reservations from the box office (410-563). The *Wybrzeże* theatre, ul. św. Ducha 2, just behind the Armoury, is the main city centre **theatre**. In a recessionary economic climate, the *Żak* club (see "Bars and clubs", above) is about the only place seriously geared towards **youth culture**. *Café C14* (see "Cafés", p.143) has evening musical and literary events once or twice a week. Check listings section at the front of *Tydzien W Trójmieście* for a comprehensive guide to what's going on each week.

Listings

Airport At **Rębiechowa**, half-an-hour's bus journey from Targ Węglowy, in the centre. International departures to Athens, Moscow, St Petersburg, Hamburg and Heathrow with *LOT* or *Aeroflot*. Domestic connections to Warsaw, Kraków, Katowice, Poznań, Rzeszów, Wrocław and Szczecin. Information ☎415-110/415-162/415-131.

Air tickets From Orbis, pl. Gorkiego 1 (☎314-045/314-944), or the *LOT* building, ul. Wały Jagiellońskie 2/4 (☎312-821/311-161), or the airport (reservations ☎415-251/412-335).

Banks *Narodowy Bank Polski*, Okopowa 1, *Bank Gdański*, Targ Drzewny 1 and Długi Targ 14/16 for international transactions. *Kantor* shops are fine for regular foreign exchange.

Billiards In Gdańsk as elsewhere the latest craze to hit the country. If you fancy a frame or two of *bilardy* the *Klub Bilardy*, ul. Wajdeloty 12/13 in the town centre, is currently the most popular haunt. Open till midnight.

Chemists In Main Town: Długa 54/56, Chmielna 47/52 and Grobla III 1/6. There are always a few all-night chemists on duty on a rotating basis; check local papers for details.

Children There are a number of worthwhile diversions and entertainments for kids in town. The open-air *Cricoland* amusement park just north of the main railway station has all the usual fairground attractions: stalls, roller-coasters, ghost trains, and a hall of mirrors. You pay for the rides with tokens. Open all year. The *Lazurkowa* centre in Gdynia has a children's paddling pool, with open-air terraces surrounding it for parents to keep an eye on things from. The *Miniatura* puppet theatre, ul. Grunwaldzka 16 (☎412-386), is excellent: performances every Saturday and Sunday with weekday morning performances for schools. Buy tickets one hour in advance. Nice theatre interior, and children love the performances. Cinemas often have matinees. Check the local paper and *Tydzien W Trójmieście* listings for details of performances. Finally there's the zoo in Oliwa (Karwińska 3).

Cinemas The latest Western – in particular US – movies make their way to Gdańsk pretty speedily these days. The main centre-of-town cinema complex is at ul. Długa 57. The *Żak* cinema club is art-orientated.

Consulates *Germany*, al Zwycistwa 23 (☎414-366); *France*, Waty Piastowskiel 1 (☎314-444); *Sweden, Norway & Denmark*, ul. Jana z Kolna 25 (☎216-216); *Belgium*, ul. Świętojańska 32; *Holland*, Waty Jagiellońskie 36 (311-601); *Italy*, ul. Świętojańska 32; *Finland*, Grunwaldzka 132a (☎415-222). No US or British consulates – the embassies in Warsaw are the nearest.

Emergency Ambulance 999, Fire 998, Police 997.

Ferries Local ferries between Gdańsk (waterfront), Sopot (the pier) and Gdynia as well as boats to Hel and Jastarnia, also from the landing stage on the waterfront by the Green Gate Current timetables (adjusted seasonally) posted at all landing stages.

Ferry office ul. Wartka 4: ☎314-926. Information: ☎317-231; advance booking: ☎311-975; in Sopot, ☎511-293, in Gdynia, ☎202-642.

Festivals The Tri-City boasts a variety of festivals and other major cultural get-togethers. The Dominican Fair (*Jarmark Dominikański*) held annually in the first three weeks of August is an important local event, with artistes and craftspeople setting up shop in the centre of town, accompanied by street theatre and a wealth of other cultural events. St Nicola's Fair (*Jarmark Mikołaja*) in the first three weeks of December is a pre-Christmas variation on the same theme. Musically there's the annual international *Chamber Music Festival* timed to coincide with the Dominican Fair, an *International Choral Festival*, held in the Town Hall (☎June–Aug) and the *Festival of Organ Music* in Oliwa Cathedral during July and August. For film buffs there's the *Gdańsk Film Festival* in late September.

Football The aptly named *Lechia Gdańsk* are a solid First Division side – despite a purple and white strip that makes *Aston Villa*'s outfit look like an Armani job. They play at the BKS Lechia stadium on ul. Traugutta; nearest station is Gdańsk-Politechnika.

Galleries Of the wealth of galleries in the city many are fairly upmarket places with Western tourists very much in mind. The local art scene is pretty lively too – alongside Kraków the Tri-City is one of the main student art centres. A couple of the more interesting galleries in town are *Malarze Kobiet*, ul. św. Barbary 3/4, a women's art centre with regular artistic happenings; *Gdańska Galeria Fotografii*, ul. Grobla 11; *ZPAP*, Długi Targ 35/38; and *FOS*, ul. Długie Pobrzeże 29.

Gays and lesbians Local contact: *Lambda Gdańsk*, PO Box 265, 81-806 Sopot 6. Also *Café Lord* (see "Cafés", p.143).

Hospitals Wrzeszcz, al. Zwycięstwa 49 (☎411-000/322-929); Zaspa, al. Jan Pawła 11 50 (☎478-251).

International ferries From Nowy Port, opposite Westerplatte. Take a train to Nowy Port station, or the much slower tram #10. Ferries depart for Travemunde (Germany), Ystad and Oxelösund (Sweden) and Helsinki. *PolFerries* tickets can be booked through Orbis or the ferry office at ul. Świętojańska 132 (☎431-887).

Music and theatre The *National Opera and Philharmonia House*, al. Zwycięstwa 15, has world-class opera and orchestral concerts. The *Gdańsk City Theatre*, in the centre of town at ul. św. Ducha 2, is worth checking out, particularly for classical Polish theatre pieces.

Newspapers Dailies *Głos Wybrzeze* and *Gazeta Gdańska* both give detailed listings for local events and a host of other useful local information, as does the Friday edition of *Dziennik Bałtycki*.

Parking (guarded). Jaśkowa Dolina 101, Pilotów 18, pl. Gorkiego 1 and Startowa 23 plus all the Orbis hotels.

Petrol stations The following are open 24hr a day: in Gdańsk, ul. Dąbrowskiego 4 & ul. Elbląska; in Oliwa, ul. Grunwaldzka & ul. Dąbrowszczaków; in Sopot, ul. 3 Maja 51; in Gdynia, ul. Śląską and ul. Chylońska.

Police City headquarters, ul. Okopowa 15, (☎316-221).

Post office Main office (for *poste restante* etc) is at ul. Długa 22; open 24hr for telephones, 8am–8pm for postal business.

Radio The local *Radio Gdańsk* (67.85FM) is a decent-quality FM station with an emphasis on rock music and phone-ins.

Radio taxi ☎9192/314-949, ☎315-517 or *Tele-Taxi*, ☎202-500: Sopot, ☎511-213, Gdynia, ☎205-072.

Rail tickets International rail tickets from Orbis, pl. Gorkiego 1, and from main stations in Gdańsk and Gdynia.

Rent-a-car At the *Hevelius* hotel (☎314-045).

Service stations Repairs: ul. Dąbrowszczaków 14 (☎531-652), al. Grunwaldzka 339 (☎522-812). Breakdown service: in Gdańsk, Kartuska 187 (☎323-555) & al. Hallera (☎411-693); in Sopot, ul. 3 Maja 51 (☎518-030); in Gdynia, ul. Olsztyńska 35 (☎202-541) & ul. 3 Maja 20 (☎210-522).

Shopping The *Hala Targowa* on ul. Pańska has vegetables and fresh chickens outside, loads of small stalls inside, selling anything from caviar to condoms – price often negotiable. There's a good **bookshop** in the shopping arcade on ul. Heveliusza opposite the *Hewelius*. The *Pewex* in the Old Mill by the canal stocks the usual range of luxury Western goods. **Ul. Mariacka**, east from Saint Mary's, is a lovely shopping street that somehow retains its peaceful atmosphere even at the height of the summer tourist onslaught. The street-level shops sell jewellery, amber products and quality leather at Western prices.

Solarium/Gym. *Studio* club ul. Osiek 19/20 (☎313-774).

Sports equipment (sailing, canoeing etc). On hire from *MOSiR*, ul. Ogarna 29.

Swimming pools Indoor pools at the *Marina* and *Poseidon* hotels; in Sopot, ul. Haffnera 55; and in the *Gydnia Hotel* in Gdynia.

Tennis courts At the Hotel *Marina*, ul. Wiejska 1 and ul. Ks. Sychty 23. In Sopot, *Sopocki Klub Tenisowy*, ul. Ceynowy 5/7; in Gdynia, *Klub Arka*, ul. Ejsmonda 1.

Yacht rental *Polski Klub Morski*, Targ Rybny 6A (☎318-272).

Zoo Karwińska 3, in Oliwa.

Sopot

One-time stamping ground for the rich and famous, who came from all over the world to sample the casinos and the high life in the 1920s and 1930s, **SOPOT** is still a popular beach resort with landlocked Poles, and is increasingly attractive to Westerners – Germans and Swedes in particular. It has an altogether different atmosphere from its neighbour: the fashionable clothes shops and bars scattered round ul. Bohaterów Monte Cassino – the main avenue down to the pier – seem light years away from both historic central Gdańsk and the industrial grimness of the shipyards. If you're tired of tramping the streets of Gdańsk, Sopot's an excellent place for a seaside change of air.

The **pier**, constructed in 1928 but later rebuilt, is the longest in the whole Baltic area. Long sandy beaches stretch away on both sides; on the northern section you'll find ranks of bathing huts, some with marvellous 1920s wicker beach chairs for hire. Be warned, though, that the untreated filth pouring from the Wisła means that the whole Gdańsk bay is heavily **polluted**: some locals even consider lying on the sand a bit risky. The city authorities are finally beginning to tackle the pollution, but despite publicity stunts from the mayor of Sopot – a dip by the beach to prove he's not afraid – you'd be well advised to keep well out of the water for the forseeable future. Further north from the pier there's a beach restaurant, a sauna and, right at the end, some very cheap tennis courts.

Upper Sopot, as the western part of town is known, is a wealthy suburb of entrepreneurs, architects and artists – a sort of Polish Hampstead. Here and in other residential areas of Sopot, many of the houses have a touch of Art Nouveau style to them – look out for the turrets built for sunrise viewing. The **park** in upper Sopot offers lovely walks in the wooded hills around Łysa Góra, where there's a ski track in winter.

Accommodation

Sopot's holiday popularity means that rooms can be scarce. As well as the places given below, there are several seasonal hostels and hotels, details of which are given out by the PTTK office at ul. Bohaterów Monte Cassino 31 on the square opposite the train station. Private rooms are a plausible alternative: if the PTTK can't help you, you're more than likely to be offered something if you stand around outside long enough.

Best of the **hotels** is the *Grand Hotel*, near the sea on ul. Powstańców Warszawy (☎510-041), which for once more than lives up to its name. Built in the 1920s in regal period style, the *Grand* was a favourite with President de Gaulle, Giscard d'Estaing and the Shah of Iran, and after a long interval it has recently reopened its casino. Though shabbier than it used to be, it retains some of its former magnificence; huge old rooms at £30–50 a night for doubles, £25–40 for singles, make this an enjoyable indulgence for the Westerner, if prohibitive for Poles. Of the other options, the *Miramar*, ul. Zamkowa Góra 21/25 (☎518-011), well north of the town centre near Kamieny Potok station, is cheaper but full in summer; unfortunately the same generally goes for the *Pensjonat Maryła*, ul. Sepia 22 (☎510-034), and the better quality *Hotel Sopot*, ul. Haffnera 81 (☎515-171). Another cheap option is the *Jeżdziecki*, ul. Polna 1 (☎512-011), a basic, old state holiday hotel. A number of other former state workers' holiday hotels are in line for privatisation – ask at the tourist office for details, as they're bound to be inexpensive.

Finally, **campers** have two options, both reasonable: the PTTK site at Kamienica Potok (train to Kamienny Potok) next to the *Miramar*; and *Sopot Camping*, close to the beach at Bitwy Pod Plowcami 79, about a kilometre south from the pier (June–Aug).

Restaurants, bars and cafés

The *Grand Hotel* **restaurant** is a treat, with excellent salmon, trout and smoked eel; the hotel café is great for afternoon coffee – and men shouldn't miss the luxurious old *pissoirs*. The *Pod Strecha*, further up the promenade at ul. Bohaterów Monte Cassino 42, is a trendy eating place, while the *Albatros*, opposite the station at pl. Konstytutcji 3 Maja 2, is more down to earth. Further up ul. Monte Cassino the trendy haunts continue, notably *Złoty Ul* at no. 37, with some nice, recently rediscovered Art Deco interior decoration; the *Teatralna*, at no. 50; and, chicest of the lot, *Bazaar* at no. 5, at the far end of the street, a designer café-restaurant favoured by youthful arty types – occasional live bands too. The *Saj-Gon*, Grunwaldzka 8, is a popular Vietnamese eatery, while the self-consciously old-fashioned *Staropolska*, ul. 3 Maja 7, emphasises traditional Polish cuisine. If you're up in the hills of west Sopot, the old *Parkowy* motel restaurant (the motel part has now disappeared) is a quiet, relaxing spot. Also more out of the way but worthwhile are the *Belfer*, ul. Kościuszki 64, a popular bar serving down-to-earth traditional fare.

In summer especially, the **pier area** is full of bars, coffee shops and pleasant old milk bars, with Western-style fast-food joints making noticeable inroads of late. The *Fantom* near the pier entrance is the **café** from which to watch the promenaders and skateborders. On ul. Haffnera, just off the promenade, the *Miramar* has lousy service but great cakes, which you may be forced to buy in absurdly large portions. *Spatif*, the artists' club upstairs at no. 54 on the promenade, has an eccentrically decadent cabaret tradition – look artistic to get in.

The lower part of the promenade is the place to be seen in Sopot: the *Niki* and *Alga* **clubs**, near the pier, are popular evening hang-outs, especially with Arab students and Syrians from Berlin. Billiards fans head for the *Snooker Pub* ul. Wejherowska 35 – open till 3am.

Entertainments

The open-air **Opera Leśna**, in the peaceful hilly park in the west of Sopot, hosts big-scale productions including an **International Song Festival** in August which includes big names from the Western rock scene alongside homegrown performers; local hotels are filled to bursting point during the days it's on. The "Friends of Sopot" hold **chamber music** concerts every Thursday at ul. Czyzewskiego 12 (off al. Bohaterów), in a room where Chopin is said to have played.

The *Sopot* hotel has a **swimming pool** and good **tennis courts** – Davis Cup matches are sometimes played here. In upper Sopot there's a racecourse that puts on showjumping and horse races every June.

Gdynia

Half an hour's train journey from central Gdańsk (trains every 5–10min), **GDYNIA** is the northernmost section of the Tri-City. Originally a small Kashubian village, from the fourteenth to the eighteenth centuries it was the property of the Cistercian monks of Oliwa. Boom time came after World War I, when Gdynia, unlike Gdańsk, returned to Polish jurisdiction. The limited coastline ceded to the new Poland – a thirty-two-kilometre strip of land stretching northwards from Gdynia – left the country strapped for coastal outlets, so the Polish authorities embarked on a massive port-building programme, which by the mid-1930s had transformed Gdynia from a small village into a bustling harbour. Following its capture in 1939, the Germans deported most of the Polish population, established a naval base, and to add insult to injury renamed the town Gotenhafen. Their retreat in 1945 was accompanied by wholesale destruction of the harbour installations, which were subsequently rebuilt by the communist authorities. The endearingly run-down, almost seedy atmosphere of today's port makes an interesting contrast to the more cultured Gdańsk. Of late the centre of Gdynia has undergone something of a transformation too: rapid privatisation of state-owned shops – thanks to Gdynia's historical position within Polish territory a much easier business than in the old Free City, where establishing retroactive property rights is proving a tricky business – has given centre-of-town shopping streets like ul. Starowiejska a brash facelift.

Unless you like faceless 1950s city centres, the place to head for is the **port area**, directly east across town from the main station. From the station walk down bustling ul. Starowiejska past the *Lark* hotel, and after the bizarre concrete "Monument of Thankfulness" to the Soviets you'll find yourself at the foot of the large southernmost **pier**. Moored on its northern side is the *Błyskawica*, a World War II destroyer now housing a miniature **maritime museum** (May–Sept Tues–Sun 10am–4pm); for British visitors the sailors manning the ship are quick to point out the decktop plaque commemorating the vessel's year-long wartime sojourn in Cowes on the Isle of Wight, where it helped to defend the port against a major German attack in May 1942. Often anchored in the yacht basin beyond the ferry embarkation point is another proudly Polish vessel, the three-masted frigate *Dar Pomorza*, built in Hamburg in 1909 and now a training ship; guided tours are given when it's in dock (Tues–Sun 10am–4pm). At the very end of the pier, a hamfisted monument to Polish seafarer and novelist Joseph Conrad stands near the **aquarium**, where the fish are presumably healthier than the ones being caught by the fishermen ranged along the pier head.

If you want more local maritime history, the **Naval Museum** on Bulwar Nadmorski, south of the pier (Tues–Sun 10am–4pm), fills in the details of Polish seafaring from early Slav times to World War II. To complete the tour there's a nice view over the harbour from the hilltop of Kamienna Góra, a shortish walk south of the town centre.

Accommodation

The *Gdynia*, ul. Armii Krajowej 22 (☎206-661), is a flashy modern Orbis joint for the rich sailing contingent who hang out here in the summer; the rooms are nothing much to talk about, and prices are the same as Orbis hotels in Gdańsk. The *Lark* (☎218-046), on ul. Starowiejska in the town centre, is a sensibly priced alternative. Other options are the reasonably upmarket *Bałtyk*, ul. Kielecka 2a (☎210-649), the cheaper *Antracyt*, ul. Korzenowskiego 190 (☎206-811); *Nadmorski*, ul. Ejsmonda 2, the *Olimpijski* (☎223-215) and the *Garnizonowy*, ul. Jana Z Kolna 25.

Private rooms are organised by the *biuro zakwaterowań* at ul. Dworcowa 7 (daily 8am–5pm; ☎218-265). The main **youth hostel**, open all year, is at ul. Morska 108C (☎204-423); take the local train to Gdynia-Grabowek, or bus #109, #125, #141, or tram #22, #25, #26 or #30. There's also a summer **hostel** at ul. Wiczlińska 93. There are two **campsites** in south Gdynia: at ul. Świętopełka 19/23 right by the sea, and at Spacerowa 7; for both, take the train to Gdynia-Orłowo station.

Restaurants, bars and cafés

The *Gdynia* has a restaurant which is considered by some to be one of the best in the region; fine if you like an expensive Westernised menu and can put up with the jet set. The *George* at ul. 3 Maja 21, *Ermitage* at Świętojańska 39, *Mysliwśka* at ul. Abrahama 18, and *Róza Wiatrow,* ul. Zjednoczenia 2 on the pier, are all better priced and more Polish alternatives. The *Lark* has a restaurant and adjoining beer bar serving the enjoyable *Elbląg* special brew that's a popular spot with the locals.

There's also a host of assorted milk bars and greasy spoons dotted around the town centre. For a coffee break, the *Ambrozja*, at ul. Starowiejska 14, has a good selection of *sernik* and other home-baked cakes, while the *Checz Kaszubska* further down at no. 32 offers local Kashubian specialities.

Entertainments

The **Musical Theatre** (*Teatr Muszyczny*), pl. Grunwaldzki 1, near the Gdynia hotel, is a favourite venue with Poles and tourists alike, featuring quality Polish musicals, as well as all-too-frequent productions of the Andrew Lloyd Webber oeuvre. Tickets (hard to find in the summer season) from the box office or the Orbis bureau in the *Gdynia*. Emphasising the naval connection there's also an annual Sea Shanty festival held here in August. The new money coming into town has brought a splash of **nightclubs** in its wake: obvious places like the *Gdynia* aside, enthusiasts of ritzy Polish nightlife can check out the *Bodega*, Chylońska 341, the *Ermitage*, Swiętojańska 39 or *Vega*, Sędzkiego 19, all open to the small hours at weekends.

The Hel Peninsula

For the bucket-and-spade brigade, relief from the pollution of the Gdańsk bay is at hand in the shape of the **Hel Peninsula**, a long thin strip of land sticking out into the Baltic Sea 20km above Gdańsk. The sandy beaches dotted along the north side of the peninsula are well away from the poisonous Wisła outlet, making the water around here as clean as you'll get on the Baltic coast; what's more, they are easily accessible and almost never overcrowded.

Hel...

HEL, the small fishing port at the tip of the peninsula, is the main destination. It's an enjoyable two-and-a-half-hour trip from Gdańsk in an open boat from the Motława waterfront (first departure 9am in summer), giving you the chance to see the shipyard complex on the way out to sea.

Despite heavy fighting – a German army of 100,000 men was rounded up on the peninsula in 1945 – the main street retains some nineteenth-century wooden fishermen's cottages. For the locals the main attraction seems to be the bar/restaurant on this main drag, which unlike virtually any known bar in Gdańsk serves strong "Gdańsk Export" draught beer in apparently limitless quantities.

Hel's **Maritime Museum** (Tues–Sun 10am–4pm), housed in the village's Gothic former church, has plenty of model ships and fishing tackle as well as some local folk art. As on the adjoining mainland, the people of the peninsula are predominantly Kashubian (see "Kashubia", opposite), as evidenced in the local dialect and the distinctive embroidery styles on show in the museum.

...and beyond

If you're not in a hurry to get back to town, you could take one of the regular trains along the wooded, sandy shoreline for an afternoon swim; the really energetic could do the thirty-odd kilometres of the peninsula in a solid day's walking, beach stops included. Whichever way you do it, two worthwhile stopping-off places are the small harbour at **JASTARNIA**, a few kilometres to the west of Hel with a large lighthouse nearby, and **KUŹNICA**, a short way further still.

Jastarnia has two *pensjonat* – the *Albin*, ul. Mickiewicza 54, and *U Franka*, ul. Stelmaszczyka 6 – a **PTTK hostel** at ul. Baltycka 5, a campsite and one or two basic eating places; Kuźnica, like nearby CHAŁUPY, is basically a good beach with camping space nearby.

You touch down on the mainland at WŁADYSŁAWOWO, a small but busy fishing port. The old fish hall, the **Dom Rybacka**, has a restaurant on the second floor – the local fish dishes are excellent, but some customers might be deterred by the pollution hazards. For local **information** try the tourist office at Gen. Hallera, just up from the hall; accommodation options include two decent *pensjonat*: the summer-only *Altona*, ul. Młyńska 36 (☎740–321), and the *Perełka*, al. Zeromskiego 1 (☎740-791), open all year, as well as the basic hotel on the upper floor of the Dom Rybacka (☎740-211). There's a summer campsite on ul. Helska. Regular local trains run from here to Gdynia and Gdańsk, taking between an hour and ninety minutes.

A ten-kilometre bus journey further along the coast is JASTRZĘBIA GÓRA, a popular holiday resort perched on a cliff overlooking the sea with a quaint 1930s Margate air to it and some good nearby beaches. Wholesale privatisation in what used to be one of the main worker's holiday resorts on the Polish Baltic coast has left the place with a fair selection of nicely situated seaside accommodation: the local tourist industry knows it's onto a good thing, and you're already as likely to find yourself rubbing shoulders on the beach with British tour groups as Polish holidaymakers, many of whom can no longer afford the costs of coming here, even though they're modest by Western standards.

The **tourist office** at ul. Królewska 5, the western part of the main drag through town, has all the local details. Of a wealth of accommodation options the *Europa* hotel, ul. Topolowa 9 (☎749-552; all mod cons included), is the swankiest. The *Pod Zaglem,* on ul. Rozewska in the resort centre, is a passable enough motel. *Pensjonat* include the *Leśna Perła*, ul. Leśna 2 (☎749-718), the *Atlantyda*, ul. Zygmunt 111 Waza 9 (☎749-629), the *Astore*, ul. Wesoła 10 (☎749-092), the *Gwarek*, ul. Jantarowa 3 – one of the few open all year round – and the *Barbara*, ul. Topolowa 22 (☎749-045). The nearest campsite is at LISI JAR, just east of the main resort. Hotels and boarding houses aside, the *Faleza*, ul. Klifowa 5, in Lisi Jar is about the best restaurant around.

Kashubia

The large area of lakes and hills to the west of Gdańsk – **Kashubia** – is the homeland of one of Poland's lesser-known ethnic minorities, the **Kashubians**. "Not German enough for the Germans, nor Polish enough for the Poles" – Grandma Koljiaczek's wry observation in *The Tin Drum* – sums up the historic predicament of this group.

Originally a western Slav people linked ethnically to Poles, they were subjected to a German cultural onslaught during the Partition period, when the area was incorporated into Prussia. The process was resisted fiercely: in the 1910 regional census, only 6 out of the 455 inhabitants of one typical village gave their nationality as German.

But the Kashubians' treatment by the Poles has not always been better, and it's often argued that Gdańsk's domination of the region has kept the development of a Kashubian national identity in check. Certainly the local museums are sometimes guilty of consigning the Kashubians to the realm of quaint historical phenomena, denying the reality of what is still a living culture. You can hear the distinctive Kashubian language spoken all over the region, particularly by older people, and many villages still produce such Kashubian handicrafts as embroidered cloths and tapestries.

Zukowo and Kartuzy

The old capital of the region, Kartuzy, is tucked away among the lakes and woods 30km west of Gdańsk. From the main Gdańsk station a bus climbs up through **ZUKOWO**, the first Kashubian village. The fourteenth-century **Norbertine church and convent** here has a rich Baroque interior and organ, resembling a country version of St Nicholas in Gdańsk. The arrangement of buildings – church, convent, vicarage and adjoining barns – has a distinctly feudal feel. Leaving Zukowo, on the Kartuzy road, gourmets should keep an eye out for the Swiss restaurant signposted off to the right – it's rated among the best in the region.

Though it can be reached in just an hour, the dusty, rather run-down market town of **KARTUZY** feels a long way from Gdańsk. The **Kashubian Regional Museum** at ul. Ludowa Polskiego 1 (March–Oct Tues–Sat 9am–4pm, Sun 9am–3pm; Nov–April closed Sun) will introduce you to some of the intricacies of Kashubian domestic, cultural and religious traditions. Highlight of the curator's guided tour is his performance of a Kashubian folk song complete with dramatic accompaniment – introducing the musical and theatrical delights of such instruments as the *bazuna*, *burchybas* and *skrzypce diabelskie*. The Gothic **church**, part of a group of buildings erected in 1380 on the northern edge of town by Carthusian monks from Bohemia, is a sombre sort of place: the building itself is coffin-shaped – the original monks actually used to sleep in coffins – while the pendulum of the church clock hanging below the organ sports a skull-like angel swinging the Grim Reaper's scythe and bears the cheery inscription "Each passing second brings you closer to death". Apart from the church, nothing much remains of the original monastery. More appealing are the paths leading through the beech groves which surround nearby **Lake Klasztorne**, a nice place to cool off on a hot summer's day.

If you decide to make a night of it, you can try either the *Rugan* **hostel**, ul. 39 (☎15-83), or find out about **private rooms** by asking at the **tourist office** at ul. Dworcowa 4/8 (☎18-19). Otherwise, there's the summer **youth hostel** at ul. Ks Sciegiennego 3. With the exception of a few *kawiarnia*, the only restaurant in Kartuzy worth mentioning is the *Kashubska* at ul. Szymbaka 6, but you shouldn't expect too much however, alternatives are a couple of snack bars around the station area.

The strawberry festival

In the postwar years, Kashubia has gathered some wealth through the development of strawberry production: if you want to sample the crop, the June **strawberry festival** held on a hill 2km out of Kartuzy (anyone will direct you) provides an ideal opportunity. The occasion is part market, part fair – a little like a German *Jahrmarkt* – with the local farmers bringing baskets of strawberries to the church at nearby WYGODA.

Around Kashubia

Behind Kartuzy the heartland of Kashubia opens out into a high plateau of **lakes**, low hills and tranquil woodland dotted with villages and the occasional small town. Running round the whole area is the **Ostrzydkie Circle**, an Ice Age hill formation that has a winter ski slope at **Wieżyca**, some 10km south of Kartuzy on the road to Kościerzyna. Being an intensely religious region, Kashubia is especially worth visiting during any of the major **Catholic festivals** – Corpus Christi for example, or Marian festivals such as the Dormition of the Virgin on August 15.

Buses and a couple of local **train lines** service the region, but a car is a definite bonus. In summer, bus excursions are usually on offer from Gdańsk to Wdzydze Kiszewski and elsewhere; ask at Orbis or the Gdańsk tourist offices for details of current offers.

Round the Ostrzydkie Circle

With its rolling hills and quiet backwater villages the **Ostrzydkie Circle** – known locally as "Kashubian Switzerland" – makes a good introduction to the region. Alpine hyperbole aside, there's undeniably a special charm to the area, the tranquil lakes, green meadows and thickly wooded slopes providing an ideal holiday spot, a fact evidenced in the welter of old workers' resorts scattered around the bigger lakes within the Circle. If you've got your own transport it's worth considering doing the round trip. Travelling from Kartuzy you approach the Circle from Brodnica Górna, from where the road begins the climb upwards. Instead of heading directly west, however, it's better to take the longer route south via **Wieżyca**, where you can find a 320-metre high winter ski slope (the uppermost point in the region) complete with ski-lift. Predictably the ski slope has generated something of a mini winter tourist centre: a good place to stay is the nearby *Jezorianka* (☎59-83) at the edge of Lake Patulskie; for a good view, though, you can't beat the *Hubertówka* (☎55-96), a holiday hotel signposted off the road high up overlooking the lake. New places are springing up all the time round here, so watch roadside signs for details. Continuing south from Wieżyca there's a beautiful drive round the lake through some wonderful hilly countryside, a sort of mini Polish version of the Lake District without the in-season crowds.

Chmielno and Sierakowice

Of several holiday centres around the area, **CHMIELNO**, at the western edge of the **Ostrzydkie Circle**, is the most idyllic. Set in tranquil, beautiful surroundings overlooking the shores of Lake Kłodno, the waterside nearest the village is dotted with workers' rest centres, many of them looking a little derelict these days. Despite the village's holidaytime popularity if you decide to stay – which you may well want to – you shouldn't have any trouble finding a hut or bungalow to rent. A centre of traditional Kashubian ceramics, the village has a pottery run by the Nelc family, with an attractive range of pots and plates on sale – visitors are invited into the pottery to have a look round. South of the village lies **Lake Radunia**, a long, thin fjord-like strip of water firmly established as one of the region's most popular sailing and canoeing spots. Ask around at the holiday centres in and around Chmielno and you may be able to secure yourself a canoe or yacht for the day. For a lakeside stay the *Wodnik*, a *pensjonat* 2km out of the village on the road south, is the obvious venue.

Moving west, the town of **SIERAKOWICE**, 15km further on, borders on a large expanse of rolling forestland, some of the prettiest in the region, and deservedly popular hiking country. **MIRACHOWO**, a ten-kilometre bus journey northeast across the forest, is a good base for walkers. The village has several traditional half-timbered Kashubian houses – and one old manor house in the same style – similar in style to some of those featured at the *skansen* at Wdzydze Kiszewskie (see below), the difference being that here you can actually see them *in situ*. The same holds for **Łebno**, some 15km north, and many of the surrounding villages, a firm indication that you're in the heart of traditional Kashubian territory.

Wdzydze Kiszewskie

Continuing south through the region, **KOŚCIERZYNA**, the other main regional centre some 40km south of Kartuzy, is an undistinguished market town – bus change or a bite to eat on the way to Wdzydze aside, there's no reason for stopping over here. A look at the tarted-up shops on the main town square suggests money is starting to come in. Local lines of commerce stretch far: down below the Baroque parish church a smattering of Russian "trade tourists" have now set up an impromptu bazaar in the car park. The *Miejski*, ul. Gdańska 15 (☎438), and the *Bazuny*, ul. Kościuszki 17, are the only places to stay in town, while the newish-looking *Pizza Mamorosa* on the main square provides a decent bite to eat.

Sixteen kilometres on through the sandy forests south of Kościerzyna brings you to **WDZYDZE KISZEWSKIE**: if your tongue has trouble getting round this tongue-twister of a name, simple *"skansen"* will probably do the trick when asking for the right bus. Feasible as a day trip from Gdańsk (72km) – in summer buses travel direct, at other times you have to change in Kościerzyna – the *skansen* here (Tues–Sun 9am–4pm, last tickets 3.30pm) is one of the best of its kind, bringing together a large and carefully preserved set of **traditional Kashubian wooden buildings** collected from around the region. Spread out in a field overlooking the nearby Lake Goluń, the *skansen*'s location couldn't be more peaceful. After the real towns and villages of the region there's a slightly artificial "reservation" feel to the place however – buildings without the people: that said the *skansen* is clearly a labour of love, an expression of local determination to preserve and popularise traditional Kashubian folk culture. Out through the opening exhibition outlining the history of the *skansen*, most people join the hourly **guided tours** round the site (English- and German-speaking guides are available in summer): while you can strike out on your own it's probably best to join or at least follow one of the groups, since most of the buildings are kept locked when a guide's not present.

The panoply of buildings, most culled from local farms, ranges from old windmills and peasant cottages to barns, wells, furnaces, a pigsty and a small sawmill with a frame saw so big that it was originally driven by a steam engine. The early eighteenth-century **wooden church** from the village of Swornegacie in the south of the region, renovated on the *skansen* grounds, is a treat: topped by a traditional wood-shingled roof, the interior is covered with regional folk-baroque designs and biblical motifs, with the patron Saint Barbara and a ubiquitous all-seeing eye of God peering down from the centre of the ceiling. The thatched cottage interiors are immaculately restored with original beds and furniture to reflect the typical domestic set-up of the mostly extremely poor Kashubian peasantry of a century ago. Even the old-style front gardens have been laid out exactly as they used to be. Finances permitting, there are plans to expand the collection of buildings to reflect a broader selection of regional architectural styles.

Skansen aside, the lakeside village is another popular local holiday spot. In summer private rooms are on offer in the houses by the lake: in addition there's a seasonal youth hostel and a number of camping sites. The rather run-down *Pod Niedzwiadkiem* hotel 1.5km down the road from the *skansen* is the only place open all year. If you feel like joining the welter of watersports enthusiasts you can hire canoes, small boats and the like from the hotel.

ALONG THE WISŁA

Following the **Wisła** south from Gdańsk takes you into the heart of the territory once ruled by the **Teutonic Knights**. From a string of fortresses overlooking the river this religio-militaristic order controlled the lucrative medieval grain trade, and it was under their protection that merchant colonists from the northern Hanseatic League cities established themselves down the Wisła as far south as Toruń. The Knights' architectural legacies are distinctive redbrick constructions: tower-churches, sturdy granaries, solid burghers' mansions surrounded by rings of defensive walls and protected by castles. **Malbork**, the Knights' headquarters, is the prime example – a town settled within and below one of the largest fortresses of medieval Europe. Continuing downriver a string of lesser fortified towns – **Kwidzyn, Gniew, Grudziądz** and **Chełmno** – lead to the ancient city of **Toruń**.

During the Partitions era – from the late eighteenth century up until World War I – this upper stretch of the Wisła was **Prussian** territory, an ownership that has left its own mark on the neat towns and cities. After 1918, part of the territory returned to Poland, part remained in East Prussia; in World War II, as throughout this region, much was destroyed during the German retreat.

Physically, the **river delta** is a flat plain of isolated villages, narrow roads and drained farmland, with the towns an occasional and imposing presence. The river itself is wide, slow-moving and dirty, the landscape all open vistas under frequently sullen skies. **Travel connections** aren't too bad, with buses and trains between the main towns (and cross-river ferries at several points along the Wisła), all of which are within reasonable striking distance of Gdańsk.

Malbork

For Poles brought up on the novels of Henryk Sienkiewicz, the massive riverside fortress of **MALBORK** conjures up the epic medieval struggles between Poles and Germans that he so vividly described in *The Teutonic Knights*. Approached from any angle, the intimidating stronghold dominates the town, imparting the threatening atmosphere of an ancient military headquarters to an otherwise quiet, undistinguished and, following war damage, predominantly modern town.

The history of the town and castle is intimately connected with that of the **Teutonic Knights** (see box overleaf), who established themselves here in the late thirteenth century and proceeded to turn a modest fortress into the labyrinthine monster whose remains you can see today. After two centuries of Teutonic domination, the town returned to Polish control in 1457, and for the next three hundred years the castle was a royal residence, used by Polish monarchs as a stopover en route between Warsaw and Gdańsk.

Following the Partitions, the **Prussians** turned the castle into a barracks and set about dismantling large sections of the masonry – a process halted only by public outcry in Berlin. The eastern wings aside, the castle came through World War II largely unharmed.

The Castle

You approach the main fortress (May–Sept Tues–Sun 9am–4.30pm; Oct–April 9am–3pm) through the old outer castle, a zone of utility buildings which was never rebuilt after the war. The fortress itself was restored from 1817, work seen as a glorious reminder of Prussia's medieval past, and which has been continued by the Poles – with rather less of an eye to ideology – since the 1950s.

Passing over the moat and through the daunting main gate, you come to the **Middle Castle**, built following the Knights' decision to move their headquarters to Malbork in 1309. Spread out around an open courtyard, this part of the complex contains the Grand Master's palace, of which the **Main Refectory** is the highlight. Begun in 1330, this huge vaulted chamber is one of the few rooms still preserved in pretty much its original condition; the elegant palm vaulting, supported on slender granite pillars, shows the growing influence of the Gothic cathedral architecture developed elsewhere in Europe. Displays of weaponry are arranged round the refectory, but more interesting is the painting that fills one of the walls: *The Battle of Grunwald* is archetypal Matejko romanticism, an heroic, action-packed interpretation of a key moment in Polish history.

Leading off from the **courtyard** are a host of dark, cavernous chambers. The largest ones contain collections of ceramics, glass, sculpture, paintings and, most importantly, a large display of Baltic **amber**, the trade which formed the backbone of the order's fabulous wealth. Innumerable amber pieces of all shapes and sizes are on show here – everything from beautiful miniature altars and exotic jewellery pieces to an assembly of plants and million-year-old-flies encased in the precious resin. If you're visiting in summer, the main courtyard provides the spectacular backdrop for the castle's *son et lumière* shows.

From the Middle Castle a passage rises to the smaller courtyard of the **High Castle**, the oldest section of the fortress, which dates from the late thirteenth century. Climbing up from the courtyard you enter a maze of passages leading to turrets whose slit windows scan the approaches to Malbork. The religious focus of the Knights' austere monasticism was the vast **Castle Church**, complete with seven-pillared refectory and cloisters; features from the church's delicately sculptured **Golden Gate** are mirrored in the portals of the **Chapel of St Anne**, a later extension of the main structure. The Knights' spartan sleeping quarters are nearby, down the passageway running to the Gdanisko Tower – the castle loo.

When you've finished looking round inside, head **over the bridge** to the other side of the river (technically the Nogat – a tributary of the Wisła), where the view of the castle allows you to appreciate what a Babylonian project it must have seemed to medieval visitors and the people of the surrounding country. The hot-dog stall stationed on hand might help fuel the imagination.

Practicalities

The castle aside, there is little to say about Malbork, whose Old Town was virtually razed in World War II. Evidence of the intense fighting which took place in these parts is to be seen in the **Commonwealth War Graves** on the edge of the town.

THE TEUTONIC KNIGHTS

The Templars, the Hospitallers and the **Teutonic Knights** were the three major military-religious orders to emerge from the Crusades. Founded in 1190 as a fraternity serving the sick, the order combined the ascetic ideals of monasticism with the military training of a knight. Eclipsed by their rivals in the Holy Land, the Knights – the Teutonic Order of the Hospital of Saint Mary, to give them their full title – established their first base in Poland at Chełmno in 1225, following an appeal from Duke Konrad of Mazovia for protection against the pagan Lithuanians, Jacwingians and Prussians. The Knights proceeded to annihilate the Prussian population, establishing German colonies in their place. It's ironic that the people known as Prussians in modern European history are not descendants of these original Slavic populations, but the Germanic settlers who annihilated them.

With the loss of their last base in Palestine in 1271, the Teutonic Knights started looking around for a European site for their headquarters. Three years later they began the construction of Malbork Castle – **Marienburg**, "the fortress of Mary", as they named it – and in 1309 the Grand Master transferred here from Venice.

Economically the Knights' chief targets were control of the **Hanseatic cities** and the trade in Baltic amber, over which they gained a virtual monopoly. Politically their main aim was territorial conquest, especially to the east – which, with their religious zealotry established in Palestine, they saw as a crusade to set up a theocratic political order. Although the Polish kings soon began to realise the mistake of inviting the Knights in, until the start of the fifteenth century most European monarchs were still convinced by the order's religious ideology; their cause was aided by the fact that the Lithuanians, Europe's last pagan population, remained unconverted until well into the fourteenth century.

The showdown with Poland came in 1410 at the **Battle of Grunwald**, one of the most momentous clashes of medieval Europe. Recognising a common enemy, an allied force of Poles and Lithuanians inflicted the first really decisive defeat on the Knights, yet failed to follow up the victory, and allowed them to retreat to Malbork unchallenged. It wasn't until 1457 that they were driven out of their Malbork stronghold by King Kazimierz Jagiełło. The Grand Master of the Order fled eastward to Königsberg.

In 1525, the Grand Master, Albrecht von Hohenzollern, having converted to Lutheranism, decided to dissolve the order and transform its holdings into a secular duchy, with himself as its head. Initially, political considerations meant he was obliged to accept the Polish king as his overlord, and thus he paid homage before King Zygmunt in the marketplace at Kraków in 1525. But the duchy had full jurisdiction over its internal affairs, which allowed for the adoption of Protestantism as its religion. This turned out to be a crucially important step in the history of Europe, as it gave the ambitious Hohenzollern family a power base outside the structures of the Holy Roman Empire, an autonomy that was later to be of vital importance to them in their ultimately successful drive to weld the German nation into a united state.

The **train station** and **bus station** are sited next to each other about ten minutes' walk south of the castle; Malbork is on the main Warsaw line, so there are plenty of trains from Gdańsk – a one-hour journey – as well as a regular bus service. Tourist **information** is available from the **PTTK office** located inside the castle area at ul. Hibnera 4, or from the *Hotel Zbyszko*, between the stations and castle.

There are three **hotels**. The run-down *Zbyszko*, ul. Kościuszki 43 (☎3394), is marginally preferable to the dingy *Sportowy* (☎2413) east of the castle at ul. Portowa 3, or the *Dom Wycieczkowy* (☎3311) at ul. Mickiewicza 26. If you'd rather stay in someone's home, **private rooms** should be available through the reception at the *Zbyszko*. The youth **hostel** is at ul. Żeromskiego 45 (July & Aug), about 2km south of the station along al. W. Polskiego. There's a decent **campsite** at ul. Portowa 1 (June–Sept). For a **meal** try either the *Zbyszko* restaurant or *Nad Nogatem* on pl. Słowianski, just west of the castle complex; neither is anything out of the ordinary.

Kwidzyn

Set in the loop of a tributary a few kilometres east of the Wisła, **KWIDZYN** is a smallish fortified town amid a sprawling, dirty industrial belt. The first stronghold established by the Teutonic Knights – in the 1230s, some forty years before the move to Malbork – its original fortress was rapidly joined by a bishop's residence and cathedral.

Three hundred years on, the castle was pulled down and rebuilt, but the cathedral and bishop's chapter house were left untouched: unlike the rest of the Old Town area, the entire complex survived the fierce fighting in 1945 unscathed.

The castle complex

Most of the **Castle** is poised on a hilltop over the River Liwa, but the most immediately striking feature is the tower stranded out in what used to be the river bed; connected to the main building by means of a precarious roofed walkway, it looks more like the remains of a bridge-builder's folly than a solid defensive structure.

Ranged around a large open courtyard, the castle houses a rather run-down local **Museum** (Tues–Sun 10am–4pm; last tickets 3.30pm), charting the early development of human settlements along the length of the Wisła basin, with additional sections on folklore, natural history and the tangled ethnography of the region.

Despite later reconstructions the large, moody **Cathedral**, adjoining the castle, retains several original Gothic features, the most noteworthy being a beautiful late fourteenth-century mosaic in the southern vestibule.

Practicalities

There's no particularly good reason to stop over in what – cathedral and castle apart – is a pretty undistinguished sort of place. However, **accommodation** is provided by the **hotels** *Saga*, ul. Chopina 42 (☎3731), the *Miejski*, ul. Braterstwa Narodów 42 (☎3732), the *Pensjonat Miłosna* on ul. Miłosna (☎4052), and the **youth hostel** (June & July) on ul. Braterstwa Narodów 58 (☎3876). There's also a **campsite** on ul. Sportowa, on the edge of town.

For **eating**, the *Piastowska* and the *Kaskada* on ul. Chopina are the main options; other than this, the hotels are the best options. Tourist **information** is handled by the *Saga*.

The town has regular **bus** services to Tczew, Malbork and Grudziądz. Trains run to Gdańsk twice daily (1hr 30min).

Across the river

If you're travelling by car, from Kwidzyn it's worth continuing west some 20km through the lush farmland of the Wisła delta to the river banks just beyond the village of Janowo and the **ferry crossing** over to Gniew (see below). "Ferry" *(rzeka)* in this case means an amazingly dilapidated old contraption operated by an extraordinary Heath Robinson-like mechanical chain system. It's one of three similarly archaic-looking vessels in operation along the northern stretches of the Wisła. All run from early morning till around sunset (seasonally adjusted). The trip costs nothing, since by law the local authorities are obliged to provide free transportation wherever a river "breaks" a road. The boats aren't large – the maximum car load at Janowo is four at a time – so especially in summer car passengers may face a bit of a wait for the blustery ten-minute boat trip. It's an experience not to be missed though, giving you probably your only chance to see the river – and the sadly polluted state of it – from close up.

The other two ferry crossing points are at **Korzeniewo**, west of Kwidzyn, and **Swibno** right up by the coast. Further east on the River Nogat, two crossing points operate northwest of Elbląg (**Kępiny** and **Kępki**), with a further one on the River Elbląg at **Nowakowo**, close to the coast just north of the city.

Gniew

Sixty-five kilometres south of Gdańsk, the little town of **GNIEW** is one of the most attractive and least known of the former Teutonic strongholds studding the northern shores of the Wisła, an out-of-the-way place that's worth a stopover. Clearly visible from the ferry, thanks to the Wisła's changing course the town has been left stranded on the top of a hill a kilometre back from the river. Gniew's original strategic location overlooking the river led the Teutonic Knights to set themselves up here in the 1280s, taking the place over from the Cistercian Order and completing the requisite castle within a few years. Untouched by wars, it's a quiet and, by Polish standards, remarkably well-preserved country town, one of those places modern history seems simply to have passed by. It's also a curiously unknown spot – the standard tourist literature barely mentions the town – so you're unlikely to encounter many other visitors, the odd German tour group excepted.

At the centre of the old town the solid-looking brick **Town Hall** provides the focus of such action as the deserted surrounding square sees – mostly kids kicking their footballs against the building. The atmosphere is enhanced, however, by the many original sixteenth- and eighteenth-century dwellings lining the square. West of the square the Gothic **Parish Church** is a typically dark, moody building filled, as often, with wizened old characters reciting their rosaries. A short walk east of the square brings you to the battered remains of the **Castle**, a huge deserted ruin of a place that would make an ideal Gothic horror movie set, its cavernous heights dimly hinting at the past glories of the place. Ask at the **tourist office** – more accurately, makeshift shed (10am–4pm) – in front of the castle for details of a guided tour round what was clearly once an impressive fortress. A little way behind the castle perched on the spur overlooking the river, the **Marysienki Palace,** added on by King Jan Sobieski in the late seventeenth century for his wife, is a real find: a cheap and scenically situated **hotel** (☎25-37), an excellent restaurant, and view over the Wisła from the hotel balcony that's one of the best in the region.

Reasonably regular **buses** to and from Gdańsk (1hr 20mins), Tczew and Grudziądz stop off at Gniew from the shelter on western edge of the town centre.

Grudziądz

The garrison town of **GRUDZIĄDZ**, 35km downriver of Kwidzyn, was another early Teutonic stronghold and is again flanked by unprepossessing industrial development, a huge power station dominating the town centre. Bus and train terminals are right in the centre: a short walk west towards the river and you're inside the more attractive confines of the **Old Town**, overlooking the river.

The Old Town

Grudziądz has changed hands several times. The Teutonic Knights took control of an early Polish settlement on this site, then were forced to hand it back in 1454. Included in territory annexed by Prussia during the Partitions period, it became part of the inter-war Polish corridor, was nabbed by the Germans in 1939 and finally returned to Poland in 1945. Those years of Prussian control explain the Germanic feel of the town, which despite the damage of the war retains several old buildings.

For all the faded shopfronts and crumbling houses, the orderly arrangement of the charming **Rynek** bespeaks Prussian orderliness and sense of proportion. As the cars and coaches parked below the Old Town indicate, slowly but surely Germans are coming back to old haunts like these, to visit the homes of their ancestors or the scenes of their own childhoods. Most of the sights are a few minutes' walk from the Rynek. The Gothic **Parish Church**, to the north, is a typically Teutonic high brick construction, with an equally typical Baroque overlay applied to the interior. To the south, the **Benedictine Monastery** houses a museum (Tues–Sun 10am–4pm, Wed 10am–3pm) that's as interesting for the exhibitions by local artists as for the established displays recounting the town's history.

Above the river, the **granaries** built into the hillside fortifications are a reminder of the importance once attached to the grain trade. Together with the **mansions** topping the walls they form the centrepoint of the famous view of the town from the other side of the river; one of the best vantage points is from the train to or from Bydgoszcz and Gdańsk. The hill north from the Rynek – **Góra Zamkowa** – is the former castle site, now scattered with just a few foundations and an obelisk modelled on an ancient pagan statue of Światowid, a Slav deity.

As with Malbork, the area surrounding Grudziądz is peppered with **war memorials**. A particularly moving one, in the forest near the village of GRUPA, 3km out of town on the west bank of the river, commemorates more than 10,000 local Poles, most of them civilians, who were murdered here by the Nazis between 1939 and 1945.

Practicalities

For an overnight stay in the town, the *Nadwiślanin*, a short walk south of the Old Town at ul. Toruńska 28 (☎260-30), is definitely the **hotel** to go for; as well as an IT point selling local maps, it's got the best **restaurant** in town. Other options are the *Pomorzanin*, ul. Kwiatowa 28 (☎261-41), the *Garnizonowy*, ul.

Świerczewskiego 53 (☎264-46), and the all-year **youth hostel** at ul. Obr. Piłsudskiego 102 (☎231-18), a bus ride south from the centre.

Trains run frequently to Bydgoszcz and Toruń (both 1hr) and twice daily to Gdańsk (2hr). There are **bus** connections with Kwidzyn, Chełmno and Toruń.

Radzyn Chełmiński

For every well-known Teutonic castle in the region there's at least one other one that's a neglected ruin. The fortress at **RADZYN CHEŁMIŃSKI** 20 km south of Grudziądz is a particularly memorable example of the phenomenon. Stuck out at the edge of a nondescript little town, in its time the castle here was the largest Teutonic stronghold after Malbork. Surrounded by a large dry moat, the walls of the ruins, which you can wander around the edge of, have a lost but rather epic feel to them. The "keep out" sign stuck up on the gateway claiming that the castle will open as soon as reconstruction is completed has obviously been there for years.

Chełmno

The hilltop town of **CHEŁMNO**, another important old Prussian centre, escaped from World War II undamaged and has remained untouched by postwar industrial development. Perhaps the most memorable thing about the place is its atmosphere – the archetypal quiet rural town, steeped in the powerful mixture of the Polish and Prussian that characterises the region as a whole.

Although a Polish stronghold is known to have existed here as early as the eleventh century, Chełmno really came to life in 1225 with the arrival of the Teutonic Knights. They made the town their first political and administrative centre, which led to rapid and impressive development. An academy was founded in 1386 on the model of the famed University of Bologna, and despite the damage inflicted by the Swedes in the 1650s, the town continued to thrive right up to the time of the Partitions, when it lapsed into provincial Prussian obscurity.

The Old Town

To enter the Old Town area pedestrians pass through the **Grudziądz Gate**, a well-proportioned fourteenth-century Gothic construction topped by fine Renaissance gables; cars have to park outside the gate. Continue along ul. Grudziądzka and you're soon amid the Prussian ensemble of the **Rynek**, a grand open space at the heart of the grid-like network of streets. Gracing the centre of the square is the brilliant white **Town Hall**, its facade exuding a real hat-in-the-air exuberance. Rebuilt in the 1560s on the basis of an earlier Gothic hall, its elegant facade, decorated attic and soaring tower are one of the great examples of Polish Renaissance architecture. It houses a rather inconsequential **Museum** (Tues–Sun 10am–4pm), whose main attraction is the chance to look around the building.

Most of Chełmno's seven churches are Gothic, their redbrick towers and facades punctuating the streets of the Old Town at regular intervals. Best of the lot is the **Parish Church** standing just off the Rynek to the west, an imposing thirteenth-century building with a fine carved doorway. The interior retains sculpted pillars, a Romanesque stone font and fragmentary frescoes. Further west, past St James' church, is an early fourteenth-century **Monastery**, former

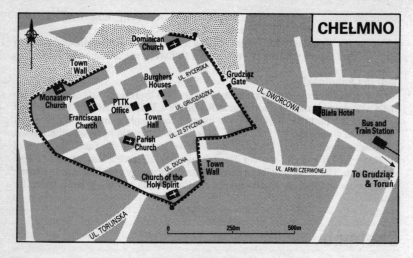

home to a succession of Cistercian and Benedictine orders, and now to Catholic sisters who run a handicapped children's hostel here. Its church, whose Baroque altar is reputed to be the tallest in the country, features some original Gothic painting and a curious twin-level nave. The church backs onto the western corner of the town walls, crumbling but complete and walkable for excellent views over the Wisła and low-lying plains.

Practicalities

For a town with some potential commercial pull, there are precious few tourist facilities here. The **bus station** is on ul. Dworcowa, a fifteen-minute walk to the west of the Old Town.

There's no real information office to speak of, but it might be worth trying the PTTK on the main square at no. 12. The *Centralna*, ul. Dworcowa 23 (☎86-02-12), just up from the station, is the only decent **hotel** and the only **restaurant** worthy of the name. Enter the *Pod Kogutem* at Rynek 5 at your peril – it's a serious dive. A **youth hostel** (June & July) operates at ul. Klasztorna 12 (☎86-24-70), on the western edge of the Old Town, or there's a Sports Hotel, just south of the station at Hacierska (☎86-27-50).

Toruń

Poles are apt to wax lyrical on the glories of their ancient cities, and with **TORUŃ** – the biggest and most important of the Hanseatic trading centres along the Wisła – it is more than justified. Miraculously surviving the recurrent wars afflicting the region, the historic centre remains one of the country's most evocative, bringing together a rich assembly of architectural styles. The city's main claim to fame is as the birthplace of Nicolaus Copernicus (see p.176), whose house still stands. Today, it is a university city: large, reasonably prosperous and – once you're through the standard postwar suburbs – with a definitely cultured air.

Some history

The pattern of Toruń's early history is similar to that of other towns along the northern Wisła. Starting out as a Polish settlement, it was overrun by Prussian tribes from the east towards the end of the twelfth century, and soon afterwards the Teutonic Knights moved in. The Knights rapidly developed the town, thanks to its access to the burgeoning river-borne grain trade, a position further consolidated with its entry to the Hanseatic League. As in rival Gdańsk, economic prosperity was expressed in a mass of building projects through the following century; together these make up the majority of the historic sites in the city.

Growing disenchantment with the Teutonic Knights' rule and heavy taxation, especially among the merchants, led to the formation of the Prussian Union in 1440, based in Toruń . In 1454, as war broke out between the Knights and Poland, the townspeople destroyed the castle in Toruń and chased the Order out of town. The 1466 Treaty of Toruń finally terminated the Knights' control of the area.

The next two centuries brought even greater wealth as the town thrived on extensive royal privileges and increased access to goods from all over Poland. The Swedish invasion of the 1650s was the first significant setback, but the really decisive blow to the city's fortunes came a century later with the Partitions, when Toruń was annexed to Prussia and thus severed from its hinterlands, which by now were Russian. Like much of the region, Toruń was subjected to systematic Germanisation, but as in many other cities a strongly Polish identity remained, clearly manifested in the cultural associations that flourished in the latter part of the nineteenth century. Toruń returned to Poland under the terms of the 1919 Versailles treaty as part of the "Polish corridor" that was to enrage Hitler; it was liberated from the Nazis in 1945.

The Toruń area telephone code is ☎056.

Arriving and finding a place to stay

The main **stations** are on opposite sides of the Old Town. Toruń Główny, the main **train station**, is south of the river: leave the station by the subway on the north (left) of the entrance, emerging a short way from the bus stop for the centre; buses #12 and #22 run over the bridge to pl. Rapackiego, on the west of the Old Town. From the **bus station** on ul. Dąbrowskiego it is a short walk north to the centre.

The well-organised main **tourist office**, in the Town Hall, (Mon & Sat 9am–4pm, Tues–Fri 9am–6pm; April–Sept also Sun 9am–1pm; ☎237–46), doles out free brochures and maps and is a useful source of info for the whole region. **Orbis**, on the corner of the Rynek at ul. Żeglarska 31, issues travel tickets, while **Almatur**, near the university at ul. Gagarina 21, sorts out beds in student hotels.

There's a reasonable choice of **accommodation** on offer. Orbis have two hotels aimed at foreign tourist groups: the *Kosmos*, ul. Portowa 2 (☎289-00), west near the river, and the inferior *Helios*, ul. Kraszewskiego 1/3 (☎250-3318), northwest of the centre. Slightly cheaper and a lot more attractive is the *Zajazd Staropolski*, ul. Żeglarska 10/14 (☎260-61/260-63), well situated just down from the Rynek; it's very popular in summer though, so you'll be lucky to get a room on spec. A step down in quality are the *Polonia*, pl. Teatralny 5 (☎230-28), and the *Zajazd Wileski*, ul. Mostowa 7 (☎250-24), though both are in easy walking distance of the Rynek.

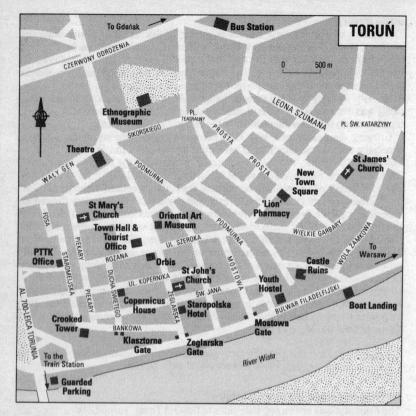

The recently renovated *Pod Trzema Koronami*, Rynek Staromiejski 21 (☎260-31), has a good location on the edge of the main square, overlooking the town hall. Other options include the *Wodnik*, ul. Bulwar Filadelfijski 12 (☎260-49), overlooking the waterfront; the *Garnizonowy*, ul. Wola Zamkowa 16 (☎162-883), an old army hotel in the New Town area; and the extremely basic *Statek Kilinski*, ul. Turystyczia 135 (☎486-927), well east of the centre in the Klaszczorek district. Consider the PTTK *hostel*, well north of the centre at ul. Legionów 24, only as a last resort.

Of the two all-year **youth hostels**, the one at ul. Podmurna 4 (☎235-53) is excellently located in a Gothic tower overlooking the river. If you can't get in – a distinct possibility in summer – you'll have to settle for the one over the river some way to the east of the train station at ul. Rudacka 15 (☎272-42); bus #13 runs nearby.

The *Tramp* **campsite** at ul. Kujawska 14, a short walk west of the train station, has some bungalows for hire as well as tent space – and it's not a bad setting. As a final option, during the summer months the university runs **international student hotels** – details of which are available from the Almatur office (see p.163).

The City

The historic core of Toruń is divided into Old Town and New Town areas, both established in the early years of Teutonic rule. Traditional economic divisions are apparent here, the Old Town quarter being home for the merchants, the other for the artisans; each had its own square, market area and town hall.

Overlooking the river from a gentle rise, the medieval centre constitutes a relatively small section of the modern city and is clearly separated from it by a ring of signs pointing to the centre: ask for the way to the Stare Miasto. For motorists, the Old Town centre's impenetrable one-way system is pretty much a case of "abandon hope all ye who enter here" – you're better off walking.

The Old Town (Stare Miasto)

The Old Town area is the obvious place to start looking around – and as usual it's the **Rynek**, in particular the **Town Hall**, that provides the focal point. Town halls don't come much bigger or more striking than this: raised in the late fourteenth century on the site of earlier cloth halls and trading stalls, this elegant work is one of the finest Gothic buildings in northern Europe. A three-storey brick structure topped by a sturdy tower, its outer walls are punctuated by indented windows, framed by a rhythmic succession of high arches peaking just beneath the roof, and complemented by graceful Renaissance turrets and high gables.

The south side entrance leads to an inner courtyard surrounded by fine brick doorways, the main one leading to the **Town Museum** (Tues–Sat 10am–4pm), which now occupies much of the building. Over the centuries Toruń's wealth attracted artists and craftsmen of every type, and it's their work that features strongest here. Most of the ground floor – once the wine cellar – is devoted to medieval artefacts, with a gorgeous collection of the **stained glass** for which the city was famed and some fine **sculptures** – especially the celebrated "Beautiful Madonnas". Also housed on this floor is an extensive archaeological section, bringing together highlights of a vast array of Neolithic and early Bronze Age relics uncovered in this region. On the first floor, painting takes over, with rooms covered in portraits of Polish kings and wealthy Toruń citizens. A small portrait of the most famous city burgher, Copernicus, basks in the limelight of a Baroque gallery. Before leaving it's worth climbing the **tower** for the view of the city and the course of the Wisła, stretching into the plain on the southern horizon.

Lining the square itself are the stately mansions of the Hansa merchants, many of whose high parapets and decorated facades are preserved intact. The finest houses flank the east side of the square. Number 35, next to one of the Copernicus family houses, is the fifteenth-century **Pod Gwiazdą**, with a finely modelled late Baroque facade; inside, a superbly carved wooden staircase ends with a statue of Minerva, spear in hand. The house is now a small **Oriental Museum** (Tues–Sun 10am–4pm), based on a private collection of art from China, India and other Far Eastern countries.

Off to the west of the square stands **St Mary's Church**, a large fourteenth-century building with elements of its early decoration retained in the sombre interior. There's no tower to the building, supposedly because the church's Franciscan founders didn't permit such things; monastic modesty may also help to explain the high wall separating the church from the street. Back across the square, on the other side of the town hall, a blackened but noble **statue of Copernicus** watches over the crowds scurrying round the building.

South of the square, on the dusty, narrow and atmospheric ul. Żeglarska, is **St John's Church**, another large, magnificent Gothic structure, whose clockface served as a reference point for loggers piloting their way downstream. The presbytery, the oldest part of the building, dates from the 1260s, but the main nave and aisles were not completed till the mid-fifteenth century. Entering from the heat of the summer sun, you're immediately enveloped in an ancient calm, heightened by the damp, chilly air rising from the flagstones and by the imposing rose window. The tower, completed late in the church's life, houses a magnificent fifteenth-century bell, the *Tuba Dei*, which can be heard all over town.

West from St John's runs ul. Kopernika, halfway down which you'll find the **Copernicus Museum** (Tues–Sat 10am–4pm), installed in the high brick house where the great man was born. Restored in recent decades to something resembling its original layout, this Gothic mansion contains a studiously assembled collection of Copernicus artefacts: priceless first editions of the momentous *De Revolutionibus*, models of gyroscopes and other astronomical instruments, original household furniture, early portraits. Authenticity is abandoned on the upper floors, which are given over to products of the modern Copernicus industry: Copernicus coins, badges, stamps, even honey pots and tea labels.

Ul. Kopernika and its dingy side streets, lined with crumbling Gothic mansions and granaries, blend past glory and shabbier contemporary reality. Further down towards the river, the high, narrow streets meet the old defensive **walls**, now separating the Old Town from the main road. These fortifications survived virtually intact right up to the late nineteenth century, but then some enterprising Prussian town planners decided to knock them down, sparing only a small section near the river's edge which didn't obstruct their plans. This short fragment remains today, the walls interspersed by the old gates and towers at the ends of the streets.

To the west, at the bottom of ul. Pod Krzywa Wieża, stands the mid-fourteenth-century **Crooked Tower** (Krzywa Wieża), followed in quick succession by the **Monastery Gate** (Brama Klasztorna) and **Sailors' Gate** (Brama Żeglarska), all from the same period, the last originally leading to the main harbour.

Heading east, past the large **Bridge Gate** (Brama Mostowa), brings you to the ruins of the **Teutonic Knights' Castle**, sandwiched between the two halves of the medieval city. While not in the same league as the later Malbork fortress, the scale of the ruins here is enough to leave you impressed by the Toruń citizenry's efforts in laying it waste. In the vaults, a small **Museum** (summer Tues–Sun 10am–4pm) recounts the history of this redoubtable building.

A little further east along the river bank is a **landing stage**, from which in summer you can take a ninety-minute **boat trip** downriver and back. One glance at the state of the water will be enough to wipe out any thoughts of a quick dip.

The New Town (Nowe Miasto)

Following ul. Przedzamcze north from the castle brings you onto ul. Szeroka, the main thoroughfare linking the Old and New Town districts. Less grand than its mercantile neighbour, the **New Town** still boasts a number of illustrious commercial residences, most of them grouped around the **Rynek Nowomiejski**. On the west side of this square, the fifteenth-century **Pod Modrym Faruchem** inn (no. 8) and the Gothic **pharmacy** at no. 13 are particularly striking, while the old **Murarska** inn at no. 17, on the east side, currently houses an art gallery displaying children's work from all over the country.

The fourteenth-century **St James' Church**, south of the market area of the Rynek, completes the city's collection of Gothic churches. Unusual features of this brick basilica are its flying buttresses – a common enough sight in western Europe but extremely rare in Poland. Inside, mainly Baroque decoration is relieved by occasional Gothic frescoes, panel paintings and sculpture – most notably a large fourteenth-century crucifix.

North of the square, ul. Prosta leads onto Wały Sikorskego, a ring road which more or less marks the line of the old fortifications. Across it there's a small park, in the middle of which stands the former arsenal, now an **Ethnographic Museum** (Tues–Sat 10am–4pm) dealing with the customs and crafts of northern Poland. The displays covering historical traditions are enhanced by imaginative attention to contemporary folk artists, musicians and writers, whose work is actively collected and promoted by the museum.

The Park

If you're feeling the need for a bit of tranquillity, there's a pleasant park along the water's edge west of the city centre, reached by tram #3 or #4 from pl. Rapackiego. On weekends you'll be joined at the waterside by picknickers and the odd group of horse-riders.

Eating, drinking and entertainment

The hotels provide some of the better places to **eat**. Gothic brickwork, stone floors and high wooden ceilings are the decor in *Zajazd Staropolski* restaurant, which offers a considerably better than average menu. The *Helios* and *Kosmos* have the usual uninspiring Orbis decor but decent, if predictable, Orbis food. The noisier *Polonia* is okay; *Pod Trzema Koronami*'s restaurant is probably best avoided, as food poisoning and drunken brawlers are not unknown.

A number of places have opened recently, the best noticeable for the high amount of foreigners using them – most Poles can't afford the prices. The renovated *Staromiejska*, ul. Szcztyna 2/4 is now a fairly good Western-style restaurant with an emphasis on traditional Polish specialities – and the Gothic brick decor is a treat too. *Zamek*, ul. Przedzamcze 5, is a respectable Chinese joint, open late; the *Palomino*, ul. Wielkie Garbary 18, offers standard Western fare, and the *Bella Italia* on the main square serves straightforward pizza.

Additional, if undistinguished, eateries and milk bars include the *Pomorzanka*, ul. Szeroka 22, *Hungaria*, ul. Prosta 19, and *Pod Arkadami*, ul. Rózana 1 – there's really not much between them. Western-style fast food has moved in in a big way too, with the (Swedish) *Mr Smarty's* hamburger chain leading the way. Finally, *Kombinat*, ul. Reya 25, is a cheap no-nonsense eatery popular with students.

Cafés are in good supply, with terrace places on streets such as ul. Szeroka providing an opportunity to enjoy the atmosphere of the Old Town. The regal *Pod Atlantem* in ul. św. Ducha stays open late, while at the nearby *Flisaka*, an old loggers' haunt, you can sit outside and enjoy the view over the river. The *Pod Kryża Wieża* on the same street is an enjoyable haunt, while the terrace at the *Pod Gotembia*, ul. Szerska, provides a good vantage point over the main square. Bar life is picking up too: the *Czarna Obraza* on the eastern edge of the Rynek serves draught Guinness and DAB; the *Piwarnia* on the northeast corner of the square is more basic, but ultimately more enjoyable. The "pub" on ul. Browarna in the New Town has live music, mostly blues and country, several times a week. The curiously named *Political Club* on ul. Bankowa is a tiny trendy bar, crammed inside an old-style Toruń burgher's house. Ul. Kopernika and the surrounding streets are developing their own slightly ritzy tourist-oriented bar and nightclub culture. Try places like the *Kaitachino* or the *Azyl*, a bar and billiards haunt, if you're feeling like joining in.

Don't leave town without trying some **gingerbread**, a local delicacy already popular here by the fourteenth century – as attested by the moulds in the town museum. It comes in ornate shapes: stagecoaches, eighteenth-century figures and Copernicus are among the most popular. Numerous shops round the Old Town sell the stuff; eat it on the spot, as it goes rock hard pretty quickly.

Finally, if you're up for a bit of local culture, see what's playing at the grand old **Toruń Theatre** on pl. Teatralny, home of one of the country's most highly regarded repertory companies – and check the listings in the local newspaper for occasional classical **concerts** in the town hall. In term time, the university area can be worth a scout around, too, for the occasional **gig** or **disco**.

Golub-Dobrzyń

About 30km east of Toruń, the elegant facades of the castle at **GOLUB-DOBRZYŃ** are a traditional Orbis poster favourite. While the town itself is nothing to write home about, the Renaissance castle, located high up on a hill overlooking the town, is an impressive sight. Coming in on the long, straight approach road from Toruń, the castle is signposted off to right just before you enter the town – if you're coming by bus ask the driver to drop you off near the castle (*zamek*).

Some history
A Teutonic stronghold raised in the early 1300s on the site of an early Slav settlement, the original castle was built on the square ground plan with arcaded central courtyard that survives today. Following the conclusion of the Treaty of Toruń (1460) the place fell into Polish hands; the real changes to the building came in the early 1600s, when Anna Waza, sister of King Sigismund III, acquired the castle. The redoubtable king's sister had the whole place remodeled in Polish Renaissance style, adding the elegantly sculptured facades and Italianate courtyard you see today. After taking a severe battering during the Swedish wars of the 1650s the abandoned castle was left to crumble away, restoration work beginning following the town's final return to Polish territory in the postwar era.

The castle buildings
Past the large cannons greeting you at the entrance the **Castle Museum** (Tues–Sun, 9am–3pm, hourly guided tours only) begins unpromisingly, with a small regional museum housed in one of the ground-floor rooms containing a routine collection of straw shoes, local costumes and assorted wooden objects, many of them related to the river economy.

Up the stairs to the second floor things get more interesting. The classy main **banqueting hall** sports the coats of arms of all the major old Polish aristocratic families – the Jaruzelski clan included – as well as the emblem of the castle's last eighteenth-century owners, the Dutch Van Doren family. In recent years the castle has begun hosting annual New Year medieval banquets – as you'd expect, by invitation only – with everyone turning up dressed in period costume. There are even plans now to set up a "period" medieval restaurant here on a commercial basis.

The former castle **Chapel** next door is anything but religious in atmosphere, being filled to the brim with replicas of Polish battle standards from the battle of Grunwald as well as an amazing array of old cannon, including tiny fourteenth-century pieces to monster seventeenth-century contraptions – and just about everything in between. The original Gothic structure built by the Teutonic Knights underwent substantial alterations in Anna Waza's time, her strict Protestant convictions possibly accounting for the severe feel of the place. The rest of the rooms on this floor once comprised the Knights' living quarters: apparently everyone used to ride their horses straight up the stairs to their rooms, the resulting local legend holding that anyone who merely walks up the stairs is liable to break out in unexpected public fits of neighing – you have been warned.

The upper rooms of the castle are now a fairly basic **hotel** (☎24-55). Irritatingly there's no restaurant, just a daytime café, the *Rycerska* on the ground floor. Out of the castle it's worth strolling out to the viewpoint at the edge of the field next to the building for the view over the surroundings. Every July (15–18) the field here is the scene of a major international **chivalry tournament**, with national teams of jousters battling it out on horseback: a spectacular event by all accounts, it's worth trying to catch the event if you're in the area at the time.

East of Gdańsk

East from Gdańsk takes you onto the short stretch of Baltic coastline leading up the Russian border and, beyond, to **Kaliningrad**: an attractive and largely unspoilt region, the beaches of the **Wiślana Peninsula** and its approaches are deservedly popular seaside holiday country with Poles and, increasingly, returnee Germans. Inland the lush rural terrain, well watered by countless little tributaries of the Wisła, boasts a host of quiet, sturdy-looking old Prussian villages, and more ominously, the Nazi concentration camp at **Stutthof**. This is the region most closely associated with astronomer Nicholas Copernicus, and several towns, notably the medieval coastal centre of **Frombork**, bear his imprint. Of the other urban sites, **Elbląg** is a major old Prussian centre now finally regaining something of its old character. As for **transport**, cross-country **bus links** are generally good in this part of the country, with the additional option of a scenic coastal **train** route along the southern shore of the **Wiślany Lagoon** and short-hop **ferry services** in several places.

The Wiślany Lagoon and around

Through the flatlands of the former Wisła basin, the coast road eastwards passes the popular local seaside resort of **STOGI**, the only place in the city's immediate vicinity where the water is definitely clean enough to swim in: additionally there's a nudist beach 2km east of the main resort. Continuing east, at ŚWIBNO, the ferry takes you across one of the small Wisła tributaries. Over the other side, if you've a car, it's worth making a short detour 6km south to **Drewnica**, where there's a fine example of the old wooden windmills that used to cover the area. If you happen to be heading south along the main Elbląg–Warsaw road instead, the *Złota Podkowa* restaurant in the village of **Przejazdowo**, 8km out of town, is well worth a stopoff; house speciality is excellently prepared local duck dishes.

Back on the main coastal road 15km further east you come to **STEGNA,** an attractive spot with a charming, half-timbered brick church that wouldn't look out of place in a Bavarian village, the ornate Baroque frescoes decorating the interior enhancing the feel of an archetypal German country church. Elsewhere in the village the smattering of "zimmer frei" signs in the windows tell you you've hit what's now become a popular German holiday centre.

Stutthof (Sztutowo) concentration camp

May our fate be a warning to you – not a legend. Should man grow silent, the very stones will scream.

Franciszek Fenikowski, Requiem Mass, quoted in camp guidebook.

Two kilometres further east on the main coastal road the sense of rural idyll is rudely shattered by the signs pointing north to gates of the Nazi **concentration camp site** at **Stutthof (Sztutowo)**. The first camp to be built inside what is now Poland (construction began in August 1939, before the German invasion), it started as an internment camp for local Poles but eventually became a Nazi extermination centre for the whole of northern Europe. The first Polish prisoners arrived at Stutthof early in September 1939, their numbers rapidly swelled by legions of other locals deemed "undesirables" by the Nazis. The decision to transform Stutthof into an international camp came in 1942, and eventually, in June 1944, the camp was incorporated into the Nazi scheme for the "Final Solution", the whole place being considerably enlarged and the gas ovens installed. Although not on the same scale as other death camps, the toll in human lives speaks for itself: by the time the Red Army liberated the camp under a year later, in May 1945, an estimated 65,000 to 85,000 people had disappeared into the ovens .

The Camp

Out in a large forest clearing surrounded by a wire fence and watchtowers, at first the camp's peaceful, completely isolated setting makes the whole idea seem unreal. In through the entrance gate, though, like all the Nazi concentration camps it's a depressing and shocking place to visit (open May–Sept 8am–6pm, Oct–April 8am–3pm, children under 13 not allowed). Rows of stark wooden barrack blocks are interspersed with empty sites with nothing but the bare foundations left. Much of the camp was torn down in 1945 and used as firewood; the narrow gauge railway still criss-crossing the site reminds you of the methodical planning that went into the policy of mass murder carried out here.

A **museum** housed in the barracks details life and death in the camp, the crude wooden bunks and threadbare mats indicating the "living" conditions the inmates had to endure. A harrowing gallery of photographs of gaunt-looking inmates brings home the human reality of what happened here: name, date of birth, country of origin and "offence" are listed below each of the faces staring down from the walls, the 25 nationalities present including a significant contingent of political prisoners, communists and gays included. Over in the far corner of the camp stand the gas ovens and crematoria, flowers at the foot of the ovens, as well a large monument to the murdered close by. "Offer them a rose from the warmth of your heart and leave – here lies infamy": the words from Polish poet Jan Górec-Rosiński's elegy on visiting the camp, quoted in the official guidebook, seem an appropriate response.

By bus the Stutthof camp is a 75-minute journey from Gdańsk (buses travel here from Elbląg too): get off at the Sztutowo-Museum stop, and walk up from the main road.

The Wiślana Peninsula

East from Stutthof the coast road leads onto the **Wiślana Peninsula** (*Mierzeja Wiślana*), a long, thin promontory dividing the sea from the **Wiślana Lagoon** (*Zalew Wiślany*), a land-locked tract of water known as the "Frische Haff" in Prussian times that continues some 60km up towards Kaliningrad. On the northern side of the peninsula a dense covering of mixed beech and birch forest suddenly gives way to the sea, while to the south, the marshy shore beyond the road looks out over the tranquil lagoon – 15km across at its widest – and beyond that **Frombork** and the mainland. A naturalist's paradise, the peninsula forest is idyllic walking country, while the northern coastline offers some of the best and most unspoilt beaches on the Baltic coast. A couple of resorts aside, the camping sites dotted along the peninsula provide the main source of local accommodation.

Four kilometres along the peninsula is **KĄTY RYBACKIE**, an attractive little resort town and fishing port with long sandy beaches stretching out as far as the eye can see along the coast up by the harbour. Several houses in the village offer rooms in season, so you shouldn't have trouble finding a place to stay, though the place does get pretty crowded in high season: for many, the scenically situated camping site is the obvious alternative.

Just east of the village off the main road is another natural wonder, Europe's largest **cormorant sanctuary**. Beautifully situated in the middle of some thick forestland, the sanctuary is a bird-watchers' delight, with every chance of spotting the large flocks of cormorants, providing you don't make too much of a racket. Twenty-five kilometres on, the road brings you to **Krynica Morska**, a few kilometres short of the Russian border and the main holiday resort on the peninsula. For **campers** the site at ul. Marynarzy 1 (☎126) near the beach is an attractive option, otherwise the best thing to do is check at the *biuro zakwaterowania* on ul Gdańska (☎155) for private rooms. The wonderful beaches actually continue further up at **PIASKI**, 2km from the border. In summer a **ferry** crosses the lagoon from Krynica Morska to Elbląg and, less frequently, Frombork.

Elbląg

After Gdańsk the region's most important town, the ancient settlement of **ELBLĄG** was severely hammered at the end of World War II: its old town centre, reputed to have been Gdańsk's equal in beauty, was totally flattened in the bitter fighting that followed the Nazi retreat in 1945. After languishing for decades in a postwar architectural limbo, Elbląg is now finally getting the regenerative pick-me-up it badly needs. The old town area is being totally rebuilt, the deal being that investors – of whom there are apparently plenty – copy the feel of the city's prewar architecture. Since its inception in 1991 the project has already proved a real success: several half-timbered brick houses have already gone up – hard not to believe there's some German capital coming in here – with more clearly in the pipeline. If things carry on the way they've started, by the end of the decade Elbląg should once again have the handsome town centre it deserves.

KALININGRAD

The longtime capital of East Prussia annexed by the Soviet Union at the end of World War II, **Kaliningrad** – formerly Königsberg – was left by the collapse of the Soviet Union geographically stranded outside the Russian Federation, of which it is still technically a part. How long this situation will continue remains unclear, and for a variety of reasons a number of countries are taking a keen interest in discussions of the region's future, Poland and Lithuania, its immediate neighbours, included.

A heavily militarised area often referred to as Russia's "western aircraft-carrier", Kaliningrad occupied an important place in Soviet strategic military thinking. A key air defence centre, the region also houses the main base of the former Soviet, now Russian Baltic Fleet at Baltysk, as well as a number of infantry divisions. A drive through the Kaliningrad *oblast* confirms the weight of local military presence: in between the crumbling Prussian villages you can easily spot a welter of air defence installations, some camouflaged, some not. Estimates of current force levels vary widely, but it's likely that at least 150,000 troops remain in the region. The picture's still pretty tangled: while the units being transferred from Germany continue to trundle in, the Russian military are also pulling out some others; additionally, they're now being physically prevented from bringing new conscripts into the area by the determined blocking of entry points now being carried out by the Baltic states.

The former threat of military confrontation may have subsided, but while agreeing that troop levels should be reduced to "reasonable" levels, so far the Russian authorities have stopped short of accepting Polish and Lithuanian calls to demilitarise the region completely. As with earlier negotiations on troop withdrawals in eastern Europe, behind this stance lurks the genuine and difficult issue of what to do with returning soldiers in a country already deep in the throes of a serious economic crisis, not least suffering from a chronic lack of employment and housing opportunities.

Predictably enough, a key player in the Kaliningrad saga is **Germany**. As with all of former East Prussia there still remain strong emotional bonds linking many older-generation Germans to their former *Heimat*. Since the border of this formerly closed area reopened in 1989 it's they – 60,000 in summer 1992 alone, with numbers expected to increase in future – who have been pouring over to visit the city. Informal opinion surveys carried out among Kaliningrad residents suggest they welcome reviving German interest – and in particular German investment – in the region. In deference, perhaps, to the historical sensitivities of neighbouring countries, to date German officials have been taking a cautious line on Kaliningrad, with both the former foreign minister Hans-Dietrich Genscher and his successor Klaus Kinkel consistently rejecting the notion of any German claim on the city.

Though clearly nervous about anything that smacks of a German reoccupation of its former eastern possessions, the main current **Polish** interest in Kaliningrad (Króliewiec) nevertheless seems to be developing business links and rebuilding the local cross-border infrastructure as part of an overall strategy of economic regeneration for the northern Baltic region.

In this sense the Polish authorities appear to have no objection to German involvement in the Kaliningrad region – especially if it means financial investment – and have reacted to various proposals for a definite German stake in the region with a noticeable lack of alarm. With Russia, Polish officials have already had a number of direct talks with their Moscow counterparts over Kaliningrad, most significantly during Lech Wałęsa's visit to Moscow in May 1992, when the Polish president signed an agreement with Russian officials concerning the development of cross-border cooperation in the region. Commercial interest already seems to be bearing fruit: the Olsztyn region has signed a reciprocal trade agreement with Kaliningrad, and 80 percent of the joint ventures already established in the region involve Polish trading concerns.

To date the **Lithuanian** position on Kaliningrad has been a bit more obscure. Citing the region's medieval positioning within Lithuanian territory, of late at least one senior official has suggested that Kaliningrad – *Karaliaucius* as it's called in Lithuanian – ought really to be "returned" to their control. Quite how seriously such statements are supposed to be taken is unclear: what is evident, however, is Lithuanian concern over the Russian military presence in the region, in particular the vexed issue of troop transits.

The country's infrastructure has already been badly damaged by recent troop withdrawals – ploughed-up roads, damaged rail track and so on – and the prospect of more of the same following a Russian pull-out from Kaliningrad is viewed with understandable alarm. Whichever way things go, however, Lithuania will certainly press for recognition of its interests in what was at one time known as "lesser Lithuania".

So what will happen in the future? One serious proposal recently floated is to turn the region into a (joint) **Russian-German-Polish condominium**. A new fourth independent Baltic state has also been suggested, though the experience of becoming a **special economic zone**, as the region has officially been designated since January 1992, suggests that Kaliningrad would have a tough time going it alone economically.

Visiting Kaliningrad

For all the recent tourist influx there's actually not a great deal worth seeing in Kaliningrad, since most of the city was first flattened by Allied bombing raids, then by the fighting around the city in 1945, and afterwards rebuilt in what seems like the crassest and ugliest way the Soviets could come up with. In the old city only the ruins of the medieval **cathedral** survive, with a special stone marking the **grave of Immanuel Kant**, the city's most famous philosopher and about the only one deemed acceptable by the postwar Soviet authorities. Moving out into the suburbs, however, the uniform concrete blocks begin to give way to sections of the characteristic old Prussian houses which can be found throughout former East Prussia.

How to get there

Special **buses** now run from Warsaw to Kaliningrad crossing the border at Bezledy–Bagrationovsk, about 40km north of Lidzbark Warmiński. Only open at daytime, at the time of writing the crossing's still theoretically closed to non-Poles or Russians, though bus passengers seem to get through OK providing they have a visa, of course. **By train**, there are now some direct connections from Berlin that cross the border at Gronowo–Mamonowo just north of Braniewo. From Poland the best way of getting to Kaliningrad is by **boat**: in summer day trips run across the bay from Gdańsk. leaving early-ish in the morning and returning in the evening – a two-hour trip each way. Visas are sorted out on the boat. There are also rumours of a similar ferry service starting up from Elbląg – check with the Gdańsk or Elbląg tourist offices for the latest details.

Practicalities

The **bus** and **train stations** are close to each other, a 15-minute walk east of the old town centre. For **information**, try the tourist office at ul. 1 Maja 30 or the Orbis bureau, ul. Hetmanska 24. For **accommodation**, if you're feeling like splashing out the swish *Elzam*, an old Party hotel close to the cathedral done up super-posh and clearly aimed at German tourists, will set you back a few złotys. Alternatives are the *Żuławy*, ul. Królewicka 126 (☎457-11), a cheaper decent-quality place with a good restaurant, the basic *Dworczowy*, ul. Grunwaldzka 49 (☎270-11), across the road from the stations, and the centrally located PTTK, ul. Krótka 5 (☎248-08). The main **camping site** is at ul. Panieńska 14, on the river close to the old town. While you're here it's worth seeking out the local Elbląg Special, a decent brew produced in the recently revived town brewery (there's also a branch in Braniewo): you'll find it on tap at the *Aliva* bar, on the square just down from the cathedral.

Round the old town

Surrounded by an undistinguished postwar urban sprawl, the **old town** is a small section at the heart of modern Elbląg. Some parts of the old city walls are still there, mostly notably around the old **Brama Targowa** (Market Gate) at the northern entrance to the area. Elbląg played an important role in Hitler's wartime plans, specifically as a centre of U-boat production – the city's easy access to the sea, via the Wiślana Lagoon, made it a perfect spot. The empty area between here and the cathedral hides the ruins of the dry docks where scores of newly produced submarines, completed at the U-boat factory in town (now taken over by Swedish-Swiss multinational ABB), were launched into wartime action – no wonder the Soviets hammered the place.

Standing out like a bit of a sore thumb, the **Cathedral**, rebuilt after the war, is another massive brick Gothic structure, its huge tower the biggest in the region. Despite the restorers' efforts to give the building back some of its former character, the job was clearly a bit of an uphill struggle. A couple of fine original Gothic triptychs and statues, and some traces of the original ornamentation aside, the interior is mostly rather vapid postwar decoration, leaving the place with a sad, rather empty feel to it. The area immediately surrounding the cathedral is where the main reconstruction work on the old town is going on: a few restaurants, bars and cafés have already sprung up, with more in the pipeline, mostly catering for the coachloads of (principally German) day-trippers piling in throughout the summer season.

Not far from the cathedral is the Gothic **St Mary's Church**: no longer consecrated, the building houses a small rather downbeat **modern art gallery** (Mon–Fri 10am–5pm, Sat–Sun 10am–4pm) in the cloisters. More interesting than the pictures on display are old gravestones and tablets lining the walls, notably that of Englishman Samuel Butler, a onetime city inhabitant.

East of Elbląg

Continuing east towards the Russian border, the high morainic inclines of the Elbląg plateau (*Wzniesienie Elbląskie*) stretch east along the high ridge overlooking the coast. A stirring piece of Cheddar Gorge-like terrain scarred by deep ravines and craggy rock, beyond it lies the cathedral town of **Frombork**, below it

Kaiser Wilhelm's old stables at **Kadyny,** and a little further east the Russian border. The closer you get to the Russian frontier the more deserted things become, with few cars in evidence near the border crossing just north of Braniewo. The **main road** east of Elbląg, the old **prewar motorway** from Berlin to Königsberg via Elbląg (Elbling), will be familiar to anyone who has driven on the autobahn of the former GDR, a Hitler-era construction that doesn't look – or drive – as if it's been touched since. Just short of the border the road ends abruptly at an enormous wartime crater left slap bang in the middle – the map simply indicates that beyond this it's "forbidden to cars". Plans are now afoot to turn this road into the major transit route for returning Russian troops in 1993, in which case expect to encounter avalanches of heavy army trucks.

Kadyny

Twenty kilometres east along the coastal road, through some stunningly beautiful scenery, the village of **KADYNY** (Cadinen) conceals one of the region's real surprises: German Kaiser Wilhelm II's personal **stables and stud farm**. Established in 1898 as part of the Kaiser's summer residence here, the stables are still going strong, with 170 high-quality horses kept in trim for use by a predominantly German tourist clientele. Along with the stables the half-timbered buildings of the Kaiser's **palace** have recently been bought up by a US company, restored to their former Prussian opulence and converted into a luxury **hotel** (☎16120/174, £40 single, £60 double). The rooms are small, though equipped with all the usual Western accessories. The excellent but pricey hotel **restaurant**, housed inside the old stable brewery, still has its old cast-iron staircases and large windows. The hotel's already proving very popular, with plenty of group bookings in summer, so if you want to stay you'd be well advised to reserve well in advance. Up behind the palace it's worth wandering up to see the Kaiser's private chapel: it's kept locked, but ask at reception and they'll organise entry.

The magnificent **stables** are mostly for use by hotel guests, but turn up early enough and you could probably negotiate for a day's riding, with or without escort – you have the option of bare-back or saddle. The main riding routes are along the coast and up along the plateau: reports from riding enthusiasts indicate that the plateau routes in particular make for some exhilarating riding.

To **get to Kadyny**, take the **bus** from Elbląg (25 minutes) or the local **train** on the coastal line between Elbląg and Braniewo, via Frombork.

Frombork

A little seaside town 90km east along the Baltic coast from Gdańsk, **FROMBORK** was the home of **Nicolaus Copernicus**, the Renaissance astronomer whose ideas overturned Church-approved scientific notions, specifically the earth-centred model of the universe. Most of the research for his famous *De Revolutionibus* (see below) was carried out around this town, and it was here that he died and was buried in 1543. Just over a century later, Frombork was badly mauled by marauding Swedes, who carted off most of Copernicus' belongings, including his library. The town was wrecked in World War II, after which virtually none of the old town was left standing. Today it's an out-of-the-way place, as peaceful as it probably was in Copernicus' time, though of late the town has been rocked over land ownership

---

NICOLAUS COPERNICUS

Nicolaus Copernicus – Mikołaj Kopernik as he's known to Poles — was born in Toruń in 1473. The son of a wealthy merchant family with strong church connections, he entered Kraków's Jagiellonian University and subsequently joined the priesthood. Like most educated Poles of his time, he travelled abroad to continue his studies, spending time at the famous Renaissance universities of Bologna and Padua.

On his return home in 1497 he became administrator for the northern bishopric of Warmia, developing a wide field of interests, working as a doctor, lawyer, architect and soldier (he supervised the defence of nearby Olsztyn against the Teutonic Knights) – the archetypal Renaissance man. He lived for some fifteen years as canon of the Frombork chapter house and here constructed an observatory, where he undertook the research that provided the empirical substance for the *De Revolutionibus Orbium Caelestium*, whose revolutionary contention was that the sun, not the earth, was at the centre of the planetary system. The work was published by the Church authorities in Nuremberg in the year of Copernicus' death in 1543; it was later banned by the papacy.

– the Church, which owned much of the town centre before World War II, is now claiming the whole place back.

Around the cathedral

The only part of Frombork to escape unscathed from the last war was the **Cathedral Hill**, up from the old market square in the centre of town. A compact unit surrounded by high defensive walls, its main element is the dramatic fourteenth-century Gothic **cathedral**, with its huge red-tiled and turreted roof. Inside, the lofty expanses of brick rise above a series of lavish Baroque altars –the High Altar is a copy of the Wawel altarpiece in Kraków. The wealth of tombstones, many lavishly decorated, provide a snapshot of Warmian life in past centuries; Copernicus himself is also buried here. The seventeenth-century **organ** towering over the nave is one of the best in the country, and the Sunday afternoon recitals in summer are an established feature: check the concert programme at the tourist office in Gdańsk. If you like organ music but can't make it to a concert, Frombork organ records are available from the unofficial guide who hangs around outside the cathedral; he is also an authority on the intricacies of local ethnic history.

To the west of the cathedral, the **Copernicus Tower** is supposed to have been the great man's workshop and observatory. Doubting that the local authorities would have let him make use of a part of the town defences, some maintain that he's more likely to have studied at his home, just north of the cathedral complex. The **Radziejowski Tower**, in the southwest corner of the walls, houses an assortment of Copernicus-related astronomical instruments and has an excellent view of the Wiślana Lagoon stretching 70km north towards Kaliningrad. Further equipment and memorabilia of the astronomer are to be found in the **Copernicus Museum** in the Warmia Bishops' Palace, across the tree-lined cathedral courtyard (Tues–Sun 9am–3pm).

Among the exhibits are early editions of Copernicus' astronomical treatises, along with a number of his lesser-known works on medical, political and economic questions, a collection of astrolabes, sextants and other instruments, plus pictures and portraits.

Practicalities

For an overnight stay the best of a limited choice of rooms is a decent-quality **PTTK hostel** at ul. Krasickiego 3 (☎72-51). The other options are the *Słoneczny*, a basic hotel near the cathedral at ul. Koscielna 2 (☎72-85), or the summer youth hostel at ul. Elblągska 11. The **PTTK camping** on ul. Braniewska (May 15–Sept 15) is some way from the centre. Apart from some summer takeaway bars, the only places to **eat** are the *Pod Wzgorzem* on ul. Rynek and the restaurant in the PTTK hostel.

Frombork's **bus and train stations** are located next to each other not far from the seafront; you're likely to use the PKP only if you're making your way towards Elbląg. The bus journey from Gdańsk central station takes between two and three hours – for a day trip take the earlier of the two morning buses, returning late afternoon: if there's no direct bus back, take one to Elbląg and change there.

Braniewo

Another old Copernicus hang-out, and onetime Hansa League member, the little Prussian town of **BRANIEWO** really got it in the neck in 1945, when some 85 percent of the buildings were destroyed: German resistance was stiff, as evidenced by more than 30,000 Soviet soldiers buried in the local cemetery. As the last stop before the border – hence, so the local quip goes now, the returnees from Russia kissing the ground on arrival – the town is assuming greater prominence: if the plethora of satellite dishes dotted around the roofs in town are anything to go by, too, Braniewo is already doing very nicely out of the growing cross-border traffic. An additional source of income is the large army barracks on the edge of town, hence the droves of (Polish) soldiers milling around the centre. That said there's not much see here, though the place does have a curiously genteel atmosphere to it, Prussian returnees aside the journey on to the border being most visitors' reason for coming here.

The Centre

As usual the few sites in town are grouped round the old **town centre**. The ruins of the town fortifications are clearly visible around **Holy Cross (Sw. Krzyża) church**. Another fine Gothic brick structure badly mauled in the war, reconstruction was only finished in 1980s, but they've done a good job of it – so good in fact it's hard to believe the photos from 1945 of a desolate wreck of a building stuck up in the porch. Inside the bareness of the high brick nave is offset at points by traces of the original structure and accompanying decoration. Round the back of the cathedral the park gives onto a brick tower that formed part of fortifications: the tower now houses an enjoyable new bar, the *Pod Baszta*, serving cocktails and respectable cappucino with a nice view over the surroundings from the top floor.

The main **stations**, right by each other, are both near the town centre. The hotel *Warmia*, ul. Kościuszki 70 (☎20-29), which has a decent restaurant, and the *Kopernik* (☎7285), are the main **accommodation** options. As in Elbląg, a pint of the locally-brewed Special is firmly recommended – if you can find it.

Buses run here from Elbląg (1hr), Frombork, and Gdańsk via Elbląg (2hrs 30mins), trains on the scenic coastal line to Frombork, Kadyny and Elbląg. Additionally there's a daily **train** to Kaliningrad.

South from Elbląg

Travelling south from Elbląg, the main approach route to the Mazurian Lakes runs through some characteristic and attractive rural terrain, the historic towns of **Pasłęk** and **Morąg** providing the main points of architectural interest. If you're travelling by car, it's worth driving off the main road to check out some of the backwoods villages of the area, many of them hiding atmospheric and sometimes beautifully decorated old Prussian country churches.

Pasłęk

Twenty-five kilometres south of Elbląg just off the main road into Mazury, lies the charming old town of **PASŁĘK** – Preussich Holland (Holąd Pruski), as it used to be known, a name commemorating the Dutch Mennonites who settled here in the seventeenth century to escape persecution at home, their descendants helping to build the Elbląg canal (see p.180) two centuries later. An early Baltic Prussian settlement seized and colonised by the Teutonic Knights in the late thirteenth century, Pasłęk had a pretty quiet time of it until 1945, when much of the town was suddenly reduced to ruins. Still a peaceful out-of-the-way spot, the town's tranquil provinciality encapsulates the combination of bygone rural Prussia and contemporary Polishness that characterises the surrounding region.

Round the Old Town

From the bus and train station a ten-minute walk north through the New Town area – undistinguished blocks in the main – brings you to plac Tysiąclecia, the town hub, and beyond it the walls of the Old Town. Up through the renovated Gothic **Wysoka Brama** (High Gate), you enter the Old Town area, a characteristic mix of old Prussian dwellings interspersed with the unimaginative slabs of concrete that passed for modern flats in Polish postwar architecture. Predictably, the **parish church of St Bartholomew** is brick Gothic: unusually, though, the interior – generally locked, but you can ask for the key from the priest's house just north of the main entrance – has classical arched pillars rather than the usual brick supports, a result of nineteenth-century Protestant renovation of the building, making the whole building lighter than usual. With the exception of some luminous early Gothic polychromy in the presbytery, it's pretty much all basic Baroque otherwise.

The **modern history** of this church says a lot about the region's tortuous ethnic and religious development. As a result of the church being taken over by the town's minority Protestant population in the early 1800s, Pasłęk's Catholic majority was forced to build itself a small **chapel** east of the Old Town, which remained their main place of worship until the end of World War II. With the tables turned after 1945, the Catholics reoccupied St Bartholomew's: in a laudably conciliatory gesture, however, the Catholic authorities have now given the town's dwindling Protestant population – a few of the older ones are Autochtones (see the box on East Prussia, p.182) – use of the selfsame chapel: they share it with another minority, the local Ukrainian-origin **Uniate population**, on alternating weeks – hence the icons inside and Cyrillic-language signs you'll see posted on the noticeboard in the porch. To get to the chapel go through the Gothic **Brama Młynska** just east of the church and walk up the hill through the main cemetery.

At the northern edge of the area overlooking the approach to the town the former **Teutonic Knights' Castle**, rebuilt after wartime destruction, is now nothing more threatening than local government offices and the public library. A scattering of Partitions-era burghers' houses apart, the only other significant survivor of the prewar ensemble is the **Town Hall**, a typical Gothic-Renaissance arcaded brick structure close by the church.

Practicalities

For an overnight stopover the run-down looking *Kormoran*, ul. Bohaterów Westerplatte 8, on the way up from the station, is about your only option. It also claims to double as the main tourist information point. The hotel restaurant aside, the *Ratuszowa* up by the town hall is the only presentable culinary refuge.

Pasłęk is on the main Gdańsk–Elbląg **train** line, so services in both directions are reasonably frequent. **Bus** services run to Elbląg (30 min), Morąg (40min) Gdańsk (2hr 30min) and Olsztyn (1hr 30min).

Morąg

Twenty-five kilometres further south, **MORĄG** is another notable old Prussian settlement: travelling by car you can either take the main route via Małdyty or the charming cross-country backroad signposted as you leave Pasłęk: on this route you pass through KWITAJNY, where there's a large World War I monument to the German soldiers of *Kwittin* – its Prussian name – killed in Flanders. Historically Morąg's chief claim to fame is as birthplace of the German Enlightenment poet and philosopher **Johan Gottfried Herder** (1744–1803), a thinker known for his generally pro-Slav sympathies, a fact which explains German President Richard von Weizsäcker's decision to stop off at the town during his first state visit to Poland, specifically to inspect the great man's birthplace.

As usual the **old town centre**, in slightly better shape than many neighbouring places, provides the focus of interest of an otherwise unmemorable postwar sprawl: the entrance to the empty-looking Gothic **Town Hall** in the middle of the main square sports a pair of French cannon captured by German forces during the 1870 Franco-Prussian War. The brick-vaulted Gothic **Parish Church** nearby received the usual heavy-duty Rococo-Baroque treatment, though overall there's a distinctly Protestant feel to the building – which is what it was until 1945. Later additions aside, some sections of Renaissance polychromy are still visible in the presbytery, and there's a memorial tablet to Herder at the back. Behind the church the ruins of the **Teutonic Knights' Castle**, embedded in the old town walls, afford a fine view over the surrounding countryside, nearby Lake Skiertąg included. Close by a newish-looking **statue** of Herder – it hasn't always been exactly kosher to commemorate famous Germans born inside the borders of modern Poland – stands opposite the house where he was born.

The Dohnów palace and museum

Continuing the Herder theme, the elegant seventeenth-century **Dohnów Palace** off the other side of the square, destroyed during the war and rebuilt to the original design, is now a branch of the Warmia and Mazury **Regional Museum** (Tues–Sun 9am–5pm).

The first room contains an exhibition of the **life of Herder**: first editions of his work, manuscripts, paintings, busts and other contemporary memorabilia place the man firmly in his historical context, emphasising Herder's extensive network of contacts with other Enlightenment thinkers around Europe – a testament to the eminent sanity and level-headedness of an internationalist-minded philosopher. A large chunk of the rest of the museum is devoted to some impressive and well-displayed collections of art, furniture and handicrafts including porcelain, glass and metal work culled from four artistic schools – Baroque, Beidermeier, Secessionist and Second Empire style. If you like lamps, tea-sets and other period household paraphernalia you're in for a treat. Last but by no means least comes the museum's artistic showpiece, a large collection of Dutch seventeenth-century portraits and landscapes by, among others, the Honthorst brothers, Pieter Nason and Caspar Netscher. The historical connection with Warmia is underlined by the portraits of the Dohna family, a branch of which moved to Warmia in the seventeenth century and built the palace here. The current exhibition, it turns out, substantially reassembles the palace's own prewar family portrait collection, carefully restored in the 1970s and 1980s at the castle museum in Olsztyn.

There's little in the way of **accommodation** or **restaurants** in the town, the *Dom Wycieczkowy*, ul. Żeromskiego 36, being the only obvious choice. The town has regular **bus** connections to Pasłęk, Gdańsk and Olsztyn, while by train it's on the main Malbork–Olsztyn line.

The Elbląg Canal

Part of the network of canals stretching east to Augustow and over the Belarus border, the 81-kilometre long **Elbląg Canal** was constructed in the mid-nineteenth century as part of the Prussian scheme to improve the region's economic infrastructure. Building the canal presented significant technical difficulties (it took over 30 years to complete the project), in particular the large difference in water level (over 100m) between the beginning and end points. To deal with this problem Prussian engineers devised an intricate and often ingenious system of locks, choke-points and slipways: the slipways, the canal's best-known feature, are serviced by large rail-bound carriages that haul the boats overland along the sections of rail tracks that cover the sections of the route where there's no water. Five of these amazing Fitzcarraldo-like constructions operate over a 10km stretch of the northern section of the canal, located roughly halfway between Elbląg and the village of **MAŁDYTY**.

If you feel like travelling on the canal, for the real enthusiasts day trips along the whole stretch of the route operate daily from mid-May to the end of September, though these are sometimes canceled if too few people turn up: in high summer you should have no problem, but it's probably still best to check with the Elbląg PTTK (☎248-08) or main Olsztyn tourist office before setting out. **Boats** start at 8am from Elbląg, arriving in **OSTRÓDA**, at the southern tip of the canal, in the early evening – a total journey time of 11–12 hours: alternatively you can travel in the other direction on the boat leaving Ostróda at the same time and finishing up in Elbląg in the evening. If you don't feel like trekking the whole distance, you can at least follow a section of the canal from Małdyty, an attractive village just east of the main Elbląg–Ostróda road some 40km south of Elbląg. If you're travelling by car and want to glance at those **slipways**, turn west off the main road at **Marzewo**, a few kilometres north of Małdyty, and you'll meet the canal 5km down the road.

THE LAKES

The woodlands that open up to the east of Morąg signal the advent of **Mazury or Mazuria**, the "land of a thousand lakes" that occupies the northeast corner of the country, stretching for some 300km towards the Lithuanian border. Geologically, the region's current form was determined by the last Ice Age, the myriad lakes a product of the retreat of the last great Scandinavian glacier. A sparsely populated area of thick forests and innumerable lakes and rivers, Mazury is one of the country's main holiday districts – and rightfully so. It's a wonderful haunt for walkers, campers, watersports enthusiasts or just for taking it easy.

Coming from Gdańsk, **Olsztyn** is the first major town and provides a good base for exploring the lesser-known western parts of Mazury, a landscape of rolling woodland interspersed with farming villages. Enjoyable as this area is, though, most holidaymakers head east to the area around lakes **Mamry** and **Śniardwy** – the two largest of the region – and to more developed tourist towns like **Giżycko**, **Mrągowo** and **Mikołajki**. Further east still, up beyond **Ełk**, is the **Suwalszczyna**, tucked away by the border, in many ways the most enchanting part of the region. As with other border areas there is a minority population, in this case Lithuanians.

Transport links within the region are reasonably well developed if slow. Local trains and/or buses run between all the main destinations: further afield, notably in the Suwalszczyna, the bus service becomes more unpredictable, so you may have to rely on hitching – which is not too much of a problem in the holiday season. Approaching Mazury from the south can be tricky, however, as the lakelands were in a different country until 45 years ago. Olsztyn and Augustów are on main rail lines from Warsaw; anything in between may involve a couple of changes, so the bus from Warsaw to Mikołajki may be a better idea if you're heading direct to the central lakes.

For **trekking** or **canoeing**, a tent, a sleeping roll, food supplies and the right clothing are essential – don't count on being able to buy equipment in Poland. Canoe hire can usually be organised by Almatur or PTTK, and sometimes by Orbis, though all three should be contacted well in advance (see *Basics* for addresses). As tourism develops, however, there's a fair chance that you may find facilities on offer from new local operators, or established workers' holiday homes which are now having to make their own way.

Olsztyn

Of several possible stepping-off points for the lakes, **OLSZTYN** is the biggest and the easiest to reach, and owing to the summertime tourist influx it's well kitted-out to deal with visitors. The town itself is located in pleasant woodland, but owing to wartime destruction – Russian troops burnt the place down in 1945 after the fighting had ceased – much of the old centre is the usual residential postwar greyness. Nestled among the concrete blocks and dusty main thoroughfares, though, quiet streets of the neat brick houses built by the city's former German inhabitants remain, their durability and calm orderliness forming a strong contrast with the often shabby modern constructions.

Olsztyn was something of a latecomer, gaining municipal status in 1353, twenty years after its castle was begun. Following the 1466 Toruń Treaty, the town was reintegrated into Polish territory, finally escaping the clutches of the Teutonic

EAST PRUSSIA

Present-day Warmia and Mazuria make up the heartlands of what until forty years ago was called **East Prussia** (Ostpreussen). Essentially the domains ruled by the Teutonic Knights at the height of their power, the whole area was originally populated by pagan Baltic and Borussian (later known as Prussian) tribes, most of whom were wiped out by the Teutonic colonisers. **Warmia** (Royal Prussia), the main part of the territory, whose name derives from the Prussian tribe of the Warms that once lived there, passed into Polish control following the Treaty of Toruń (1466), after which Polish settlers began moving into the area in numbers. It remained part of Poland until the First Partition (1772) when it was annexed by Prussia.

Mazuria proper, the eastern part of the territory – Ducal Prussia as it eventually became known – has been **German ruled** for most of its modern history. Following the secularisation of the Teutonic Knights' lands in 1525, the Brandenberg Hohenzollern family acquired the region as a hereditary duchy, though they were still obliged to pay homage to the Polish king.

This was not the end of the original **"German question"**, however, for in 1657, under the pressure of the Swedish wars, King Jan Kazimierz released the branch of the powerful Hohenzollern family ruling Ducal Prussia from any form of Polish jurisdiction, allowing them to merge the province with their own German territories. By 1701 Elector Frederick III was able to proclaim himself king of an independent Ducal Prussia, and impose limits on Polish settlement in the region: the way was now cleared for – from the Polish point of view – the disastrous slide to Frederick the Great and Partition-era Prussia.

From the German point of view Prussia's first real setback in centuries came at the end of **World War I**, when the region was reduced to the status of a *Land* within the Weimar Republic and subjected to a series of plebiscites to determine whether Germany or Poland should have control of several parts of the territory. As it turned out, both the Warmian and Mazurian provinces voted to remain in Germany, with the easternmost area around Suwałki going to Poland. Heavily militarised during the course of **World War II**, in 1945 East Prussia was sliced across the middle, the northern half, including the capital Königsberg, designated a new province of the Russian Federation (though separated from it by Lithuania), the southern half becoming part of Poland.

Prusso-German culture had a strong impact on the character of the area, as evidenced by the many Protestant churches and German-looking towns dotted around – Olsztyn was once known as Allenstein, Elbląg as Elbling, Ełk as Lyck. Today the most obvious sign of Prussian influence is the influx of Germans who flock to the major lakeside holiday resorts in the summer. The Mercedes and BMW bikes look out of place in tatty Polish tourist towns, but many of the older visitors had family roots here until 1945, when – as in other areas of newly liberated Poland – everybody of German origin was ordered to leave. Most fled to West Germany, joining the millions of other displaced or uprooted peoples moving across Europe in the immediate postwar period.

A particularly sad example of the Polish government's rigid displacement policy occurred with the **Autochtones**, a peasant minority from the villages around Olsztyn. Like the other historic peoples of Warmia, the Autochtones were of Baltic origin, but unlike the original Baltic Prussians they survived the onslaughts of the Teutonic Knights, only to be strongly Germanised then Polonised during the Polish rule of Ducal Prussia. Yet after centuries of tending the forests, they were pressurised into leaving the Olsztyn area for good on account of the German taint in their history – and they're probably not the ones coming back in the BMWs now either.

Knights. Half a century later Nicolaus Copernicus took up residence as an administrator of the province of Warmia, and in 1521 helped organise the defence of the town against the Knights.

Coming under Prussian control after the First Partition, it remained part of East Prussia until 1945. Resistance to Germanisation during this period was symbolised by the establishment here, in 1921, of the Association of Poles in Germany, an organisation dedicated to keeping Polish culture alive within the Reich. With Hitler's accession, the Association became a target for Nazi terror, and most of its members perished in the concentration camps. The town also suffered, roughly forty percent being demolished by 1945.

Nonetheless, postwar development has established Olsztyn as the region's major industrial centre, with a population of nearly 100,000. Ethnically they are quite a mixed bunch: the majority of the German-speaking population, expelled from the town after World War II, was replaced by settlers from all over Poland, particularly the eastern provinces annexed by the Soviet Union, and from even further afield – such as a small community of Latvians.

The Town

The main places to see are concentrated in the **Old Town**, fifteen minutes' walk to the west of the **bus and train stations**. As an alternative to walking, just about any bus heading down al. Partyzantów will drop you at **plac Wolnośći**, the town's main square, with the Gothic **High Gate** (Brama Wysoka) – the entrance to the Old Town – a short walk away at the end of ul. 22 Lipca.

Once through the gate, ul. Staromiejska brings you to the **Rynek**, which retains a few of its old buildings, most notably the Prussian-looking town hall, appearing rather stranded in its centre.

Over to the west is the **Castle**, fourteenth century but extensively rebuilt, surveying the steep little valley of the River Lyna. Its **museum** (Tues–Sun 10am–4pm) is an institution with an ideological mission: defining the region's historical record from an unashamedly Polish perspective. The ethnography section contains a good selection of folk costumes, art and furniture, while the historical section stresses the Warmians' general resistance to all things German. There's also a large archaeological collection, including objects from ancient burial grounds – look out for the mysterious granite figure in the castle courtyard, a relic of the original Slavic Prussians. **Copernicus' living quarters**, on the first floor of the southwest wing, are the castle's other main feature: along with a wistful portrait by Matejko and several of the astronomer's instruments, the rooms contain a sundial supposed to have been designed by Copernicus himself. It's also worth making the climb up the **castle tower** (same times) for the view over the town and surroundings. Directly below the castle is a large open-air **amphitheatre**, much in use for theatre and concert performances in summertime, nestled on the leafy banks of the River Łyna. Coming out of the back of the castle you can stroll across the bridge over the gently coursing river to the park on the other side – an atmospheric spot, particularly at sunset.

Back towards the centre, up from the castle entrance there's a stern neo-Gothic **Protestant church**, formerly used by the predominantly non-Catholic German population. To get to the early fifteenth-century – and Catholic – **Cathedral**, whose high brick tower dominates the surroundings, walk back across the Rynek. Originally a grand parish church, including an intricately patterned brick ceiling that's among the most beautiful in the region and a powerful crucifixion triptych hanging over the high altar, this retains some of its original Gothic features: despite extensive renovations it's still a moodily atmospheric place.

Practicalities

The well-organised **COIT office**, part of a tourist office complex just down from the High Gate on pl. Jedności Słowianskiej (☎272-738), will give you all the information you need, probably in English, both for the town itself and journeys on into the lakes – several of the staff speak English too. The **PTTK shop** next door is the place to stock up on outdoor equipment – tents, waterproofs, gas stores and the like. They also have a good store of regional maps. A good **place to stay** right in the centre is the **PTTK hostel** (☎273-675); housed in the gate itself, it is a nice, unpretentious overnighter, if you can get a room. **Hotels** include the exclusive *Kormoran*, near the station at pl. Konstytucji 3 Maya 4 (☎335-864) and popular with German tourists, the *Relax*, ul. Zołnierska 13a (☎375-864), the central *Nad Łyną*, ul. Wojska Polskiego 14 (☎267-166), and the *Garnizonowy*, Gietkowska 1. The upmarket *Warmiński*, ul. Głowackiego 8 (☎246-64), recently renovated, has one of the best restaurants in town. The Orbis *Novotel* motel is out on the western edge of town, at ul. Sielska 4a (☎274-571). Finally the *Park*, ul. Warszawska 119 (☎236-604), 2km south of town on the Warsaw road and part of the international "Park" chain, is the classiest – and most expensive – addition to the town's accommodation stock.

For **private rooms**, ask at the COIT office. The main **youth hostel** is at ul. Kopernika 45 (☎276-650; open all year). In summer, cheap beds are also available in the **student hotels** at the Agricultural College in the southern suburb of Kortowo; ask at the COIT office or go straight to the **Almatur** office on the site (☎278-653). Finally, there's a good, large PTTK **campsite** (June–Sept) by Lake Krzywe, near the *Novotel* (May–Sept).

Restaurants in Olsztyn seem to be on the up. Aside from the *Warmiński*, there is a good French place, the *Francuska* at ul. Dąbrowszczakow 39, and a heartily recommended Syrian restaurant, the *Eridu* at ul. Prosta 3–4 in the Old Town. Other options include the *Kasztelanka*, ul. Mieszka 1 in the old town centre with a nice bar, the *Andromeda*, ul. Piłsudskiego, and the *Kolorowa*, al. Wojska Polskiego 74. The *Staromiejska*, on the main square, is a lively bar-café with live music a couple of nights a week. The *ZPAF* gallery, inside the castle grounds, has a popular bar that fills with tourists in summer.

North of Olsztyn

If you're not eager to press straight on to the lakes, it's worth considering a day trip – feasible by bus – through the attractive countryside north of Olsztyn to the town of **Lidzbark Warmiński**.

The forty-kilometre journey takes you through the open woodlands and undulating farmland characteristic of western Mazury, and if you've caught an early bus there's enough time for a stopoff en route at **DOBRE MIASTO**, a small town with a vast Gothic church, rising majestically from the edge of the main road. Baroque ornamentation overlays much of the interior, and there's a florid late-Gothic replica of Kraków's Mariacki altar; the collegiate buildings round the back house a minor local museum.

Lidzbark Warmiński

Set amid open pastureland watered by the River Łyna, **LIDZBARK WARMIŃSKI** started out as one of the numerous outposts of the Teutonic Knights. When they'd finished conquering the region, they handed the town over to the bishops of Warmia, who used it as their main residence from 1350 until the late eighteenth century. Following the Toruń Treaty, Lidzbark came under Polish rule, becoming an important centre of culture and learning – Copernicus lived here (of course), just one member of a community of artists and scientists. A later luminary of the intellectual scene in Lidzbark was **Ignacy Krasicki** (1735–1801), a staunch defender of all things Polish; after Prussian rule had done him out of his job as archbishop, he turned his attention to writing, producing a string of translations, social satires and one of the first Polish novels.

The Castle

Sadly, much of the old town centre was wiped out in 1945, only the parish church, town gate and a few sections of the fortifications managing to survive the fighting. Lidzbark's impressive Teutonic **Castle**, however, came through unscathed, a stylish, well-preserved, riverside fortress which ranks as one of the architectural gems of the region. Used as a fortified residence for the Warmian bishops, it has the familiar regional period look to it: the square brick structure echoes Frombork cathedral in its tiled roof, Malbork in the turreted towers rising from the corners.

Moving through the main gate you find yourself in a courtyard, with arcaded galleries rising dreamily above, while at ground level there are Gothic cellars with delicate ribbed vaulting. Inside the main structure, fragments of fifteenth-century frescoes are visible in places, and the **chapel** retains its sumptuous Rococo decorations. But the chief interest comes from the exhibits in the **regional museum** (Tues–Sun 10am–4pm) that now occupies much of the building. The displays begin with excellent Gothic sculpture in the **Great Refectory**, featuring the tombstones of several Warmian bishops, whose heraldic devices still cover the walls. On the second floor are a collection of modern Polish art, not very riveting, and an exquisite exhibition of **icons**. These come from the convent at Wojnowo (see p.201), where the nuns are members of the strongly traditionalist Starowiercy (Old Believers) sect, a grouping which broke away from official Orthodoxy in protest at the religious reforms instigated by Peter the Great.

The east wing of the castle was demolished in the mid-eighteenth century to make way for a bishop's palace and gardens. The **winter garden** opposite the approach to the castle is the most attractive bit left, with a Neoclassical orangery that wouldn't be out of place in a royal residence. Into the town centre the tall **Parish Church** is another Gothic brick hall structure, similar in style to Dobre Miasto: the aisles off the vaulted nave reveal some fine Renaissance side altars and old tombstones. The old **Protestant Church** in town is now an Orthodox *cerkiew* used by the Eastern settlers who moved here following the postwar border shifts.

Practicalities

The High Gate, now the local **PTTK hostel** (☎521), is a good place for an overnight stay, closely followed by the *Pod Kłobukiem*, ul. Olsztyńska (☎32-91). The other options are the **youth hostel** at ul. Piłsudskiej 3 (July & Aug; ☎31-47), not far from the station, and the summer **campsite** next to the *Pod Kłobukiem*.

Orneta

Just under 50km northwest of Olsztyn lies **ORNETA**, a small market town that boasts one of the finest of the many Gothic brick churches scattered around Warmia. Arriving in town by bus brings you almost immediately into the attractive old market square, at one end of which stands the Gothic brick **Town Hall**, with a snazzy new *kawiarnia* and billiard hall tucked away in its dimly lit medieval cellars.

Off the other end of the square stands the magnificent, robust-looking Gothic **St John's Church** (Kosciol św. Jana). Here for once the austere brick facade customary in the Gothic churches of northern Poland is transformed by some imaginative and exuberant decoration. A welter of tall slender parapets rise up on all sides of the building, while close inspection of the carved walls reveals sequences of grotesquely contorted faces leering out at the world – the masons obviously retained their sense of humour. Above them a set of five menacing-looking dragon heads jut out from the roof edge, jaws agape and spitting fire down on the onlooker. Surmounting the church is a characteristic high brick tower, thicker and stockier than usual, lending solidity to the ensemble.

After the fabulous exterior the interior lives up to expectations, the highlight being the complex geometrically patterned decorations on the brick vault soaring above the high nave. An even more than usually ornate high altarpiece and pulpit are matched by the large, solid-looking Baroque organ astride the entrance portal. A fine Gothic triptych stands in the right-hand aisle and Gothic and Renaissance murals decorate several of the side chapels, one sporting a colourful portrait of Renaissance-era Warmian cardinal Stanislaus Hosius. One of the most satisfying Gothic buildings in the region, it's well worth the detour needed to get here.

By **bus** the town's a one-and-a-half-hour journey from Olsztyn, making it another feasible day trip. Like Dobre Miasto, it's also on the main Olsztyn–Braniewo **rail** line, with services running a couple of times a day in each direction.

South from Olsztyn

South of Olsztyn takes you into more of the attractive rolling countryside for which the approaches to Mazuria are known. For most people, however, the main reason for heading this way is the battlefield at **Grunwald**, the well-kept *skansen* at **Olsztynek** providing an additional worthwhile stopoff.

The Olsztynek skansen

OLSZTYNEK, 26km south of Olsztyn, is home to an excellent *skansen* (Tues–Sun 10am–4pm). Located on the northern edge of the small town, the park is devoted to eighteenth- and nineteenth-century folk architecture from Warmia, Mazuria and, surprisingly, Lithuania as well. Many fine examples of sturdy regional architecture have been gathered here: take a close look at the joints on some of the half-timbered cottages and you'll appreciate the superb workmanship that went into these buildings. Alongside a welter of assorted farm buildings, barns, workshops, and a watermill, there's a fine, early eighteenth-century wooden Protestant church with a thatched roof: the highlight of the lot, though, is undoubtedly the group of old windmills, two of them over two hundred years old. With its huge coloured blades and sturdy plank frame, the Lithuanian mill at the edge of the park, known as "Paltrak", is a picture-postcard favourite.

For an **overnight stay** in Olsztynek – the town makes a good base if you're going onto Grunwald – the *Mazurski*, ul. Gdańska 15 (☎485), is the obvious venue: there's also a good **restaurant** here, with the excellent local fish dishes a house speciality.

The Hindenburg Mausoleum

About a kilometre west of the *skansen* close to the village of Sudwa lie the ruins of the notorious **Hindenburg Mausoleum**. The original monument was built here by the German army after World War I to commemorate victory under the command of Field Marshal Paul von Hindenburg over Russian forces at the battle of Tannenberg in August 1914. Following Hindenburg's death in 1934, Hitler ordered a huge mausoleum to be built for one of his favourite Prussian military figures. With defeat in sight the retreating Nazis moved his remains to Worms Cathedral in Germany in 1945. The mausoleum was obliterated by Soviet forces soon afterwards, the stones eventually being used for a Soviet war monument near Olsztyn. The site isn't marked on the road, but you'll find it in the forest behind the village, a large enclosure marking the site of what was by all accounts a massive structure.

Grunwald

If there's one historical event every Polish school child can give you a date for it's the battle of **Grunwald** (1410), the local equivalent of England's 1066 in the national consciousness, the difference being that the Poles actually won this one. One of the most important European battles of the medieval era, in Polish mythology the victory at Grunwald came to assume the status of an eternal symbol of the nation's resistance to – and on this occasion triumph over – German militarism. Predictably, the reality of the battle was rather more complicated. Commanded by King Władysław Jagiełło, the combined Polish-Lithuanian army opposing Grand Master Ulrich von Jungingen and his Knights included plenty of other nationalities among its ranks, including Czechs, Hungarians, Ruthenians, Russians and Tartars. In an era when the modern concept of the nation-state was far from established the straight Polish-German struggle proposed in latterday nationalist interpretations of the event seems something of an oversimplfication. What *is* certain is the fact that Grunwald was one of the biggest – over 30,000 men on each side – and bloodiest of medieval battles. The eventual rout of the Knights left the Grand Master and 11,000 of his men dead, with another 14,000 taken prisoner. The defeat at Grunwald finally broke the back of the Knights' hitherto boundless expansionist ambitions and paved the way for the first of a succession of peace treaties (1411) with Poland-Lithuania that decisively weakened their control over the northern and eastern territories.

The Battlefield

The battle site lies 20km southwest of Olsztynek. It's not easy to get there without your own vehicle – by public transport local buses run from Olsztynek and, less frequently, Olsztyn. Stuck out in the middle of the pleasant, tranquil Warmian countryside, it's hard to square the surroundings with your idea of a major battle site. The odd modern farmhouse apart, though, the battlefield probably doesn't look that different today from the site that greeted the opposing armies 580-odd years ago. Walking up from the bus stop past the souvenir kiosk brings you to the centrepiece of the site, an imposing thirty-metre high steel monument set on a hilltop overlooking the battlefield that looks uncannily like the Gdańsk shipyard memorial. To help you visualise the whole thing in context, just beyond the monument there's a large stone diagram set out on the gound illustrating the battle positions of the two armies and their movements throughout the fighting. Back behind the monument the Grunwald **museum** (May–Sept Mon–Sun 9am–6pm Oct–April 10am–4pm) contains a heavyweight display of armour, weapons, standards and other military paraphernalia from the battle, some original, most later copies. The shield inscribed "Grunwald 1410, Berlin 1945" says much about the postwar Polish state's appropriation of Grunwald for its own specific ideological ends.

Barczewo

Seventeen kilometres east of Olsztyn, set back from the main E16 road into Mazuria, is **BARCZEWO**, another dusty old provincial town where nothing much seems to be changing: the main reason most Poles have heard of the place is the fact that the notorious former Nazi Gauleiter of Mazuria, **Jozef Koch**, was imprisoned here until his death, aged 92, in the early 1980s.

Surprisingly for a town of this size, Barczewo boasts two attractive Gothic churches: altar triptych apart, the austere interior of the **Parish Church of St Anne's,** a chunky brick edifice overlooking the river, looks as though it was given a thorough Prussian Protestant reworking. By contrast **St Andrew's Church**, a fourteenth-century Franciscan foundation off the square, is basic Gothic with a strongly Baroque overlay, the main feature being a delicately sculptured marble Renaissance memorial to Warmian bishop Andreas Batory and his brother Balthazar, designed by Dutch architect Wilhelm van den Blocke of Gdańsk fame. Batory's actual remains aren't here, however, but lost in the Moldavian countryside, where he died in the early 1600s fighting for the independence of his Transylvanian homeland.

Mazuria's not a region usually associated with **Jewish culture**, though until the Nazi era there were in fact plenty of Jews living in the region. South of the square on ul. Kościuszki stands the mid-nineteenth-century former **synagogue**, one of the very few in the region to survive the war. A wartime Nazi ammunition dump, the synagogue was converted into a *Dom Kultury* after 1945.

In 1980 it also became the workshop of local textile artist Barbara Hulanicka, who lives next door at no. 13 – call at her place to get into the synagogue. A skilled weaver with an impressive track record of international exhibitions, Hulanicka has devoted herself to reviving and promoting the folk weaving traditions of Warmia and Mazuria. Using some wonderful old nineteenth-century looms she's rescued from surrounding villages, Hulanicka produces unusual tapestries, often with themes drawn from different world religions, and several of which you'll find adorning the walls of the building. A mine of information about the region, she's always pleased to show visitors round the workshop, fellow artists in particular.

If you decide to **stay over**, about your only option is the old workers' hotel just down from the square at ul. Wojska Polskiego 48.

The Mazurian Lakes

East of Olsztyn, the central Mazury lakeland opens out amidst thickening forests. In summer the biggest lakes – **Mamry** and **Śniardwy** – are real crowd-pullers, with all the advantages and disadvantages that brings. On the plus side, tourist facilities are well developed in many places, and you can hire sailing and canoeing equipment in all the major resorts. On the other hand, the crush can be intolerable, and the primitive sewage facilities of the bigger towns has led to severe pollution. If solitude and clean water are what you're after, the best advice is to get a detailed map and head for the smaller lakes: as a general principle, tranquillity increases as you travel east.

Among highlights, **Mrągowo**, the most westerly of the major holiday resorts, is now at least as well known for its country and western festival. Perched on the southern edge of Lake Mamry, **Giżycko** attracts yachters and canoeists and would be a useful base for exploring the lakes, while **Mikołajki** to the east is arguably the most pleasant and most attractively located of the major-league lakeside resorts. And in a region of summer cottages and wooded lakes it's quite a shock to come upon Hitler's wartime base at **Gierłoz** – one of the strangest and most chilling of all World War II relics. Alongside the holiday centres Mazury also boasts a wealth of historic churches and castles, some like the monastery complex at **Święta Lipka** famous, others, such as the Gothic ensembles at **Reszel**, less well known but noteworthy nonetheless. A detour into the region's tangled ethnic history comes in the shape of the Orthodox nunnery at **Wojnowo**.

On the whole, **transport** around the lakes isn't too problematic. While a car is a definite advantage for venturing into the further-flung reaches, bus and train connections between the main centres are more than adequate.

Mrągowo

MRĄGOWO, situated on the main Olsztyn–Augustów road, is one of the principal centres of the district, and if you're anywhere near in July it would be folly to miss its acclaimed **Country Picnic Festival**, held in an amphitheatre adjoining the Orbis *Hotel Mrągowia*. In Poland, as elsewhere in eastern Europe, C&W is big news, and the festival is an opportunity for aspiring Slav Hank Williamses, and Dolly Partons to croon their hearts out in front of large, appreciative audiences; American stars add a bit of muscle.

Festival aside, Mrągowo is a pleasant enough resort town, with a decidedly German feel to its architecture – hardly surprising when you consider it was a Prussian possession for almost seven centuries. Focus of the town is the central square, just up from the edge of Lake Czos, a small expanse of water that sees plenty of activity in season. The **local museum** (Tues–Sun 10am–3pm), housed

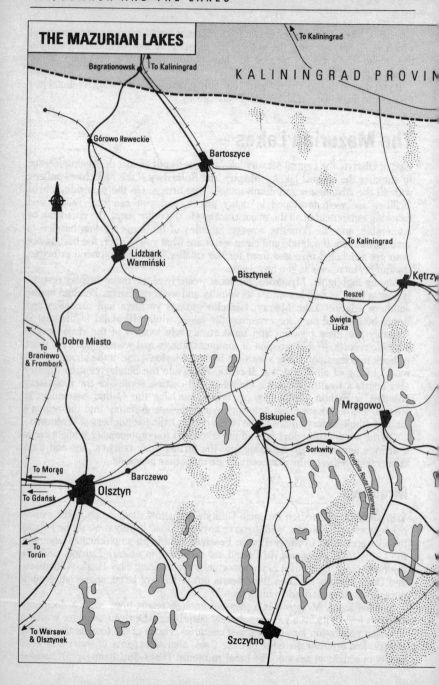

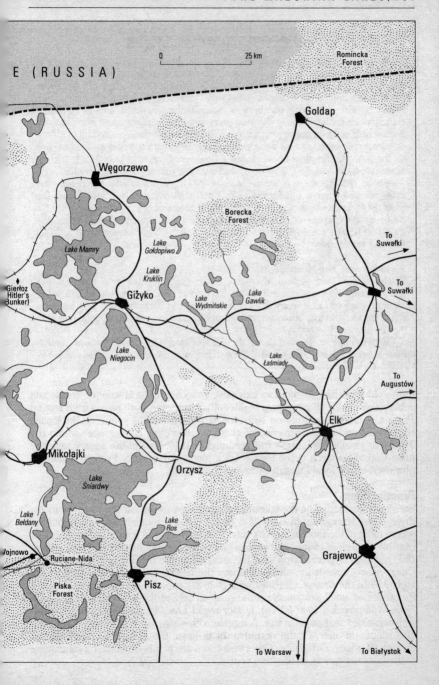

CANOEING IN THE LAKES

If you like messing about in **boats**, one of the best and most exciting ways of exploring the region is from the water. The vast complex of lakes, rivers and waterways means there are literally thousands of options to choose from. For those who haven't lugged their canoes, kayaks and yachts on trailers all the way across Poland – and increasing numbers of Scandinavians, French and in particular Germans are joining Poles in doing so every summer – the key issue is going to be getting hold of the necessary equipment. With the tourist trade opened up to private operators it's becoming easier and easier simply to turn up and hire yourself a canoe on the spot. On the more popular routes, however, demand is increasingly high in season, so it would definitely pay to try and organise yourself a boat in advance.

A good resource here is the network of **PTTK offices** around the region, the main office in Olsztyn (ul. Staromiejska 1 ☎275158/5015, fax ☎273442) being the most useful point of contact. Plenty of detailed **maps** of the region appropriate for canoeists have come on the market, the most useful general one being the 1:120,000 *Wielkie Jezioro Mazurskie* and a new Polish/English language 1: 300, 000 *Warmia and Masuria*.

Sorkwity And The Krutynia Route

SORKWITY, 12km west of Mrągowo, is the starting point for a beautiful and popular canoeing run which ends 90km downstream at Lake Bełdany, adjoining the western edge of Lake Sniardwy. The Orbis hotel in Mrągowo can help sort out canoe hire for the trip, but in summer advance notice is virtually essential (see also the Almatur entry in *Basics*).

Canoeists generally start from the PTTK waterside hostel (*stanica wodna*; May–Sept) at the edge of Sorkwity village. Known as the **Krutynia route**, after the

in the old town hall, features an extensive collection of local wooden chests and cabinets alongside some elegant eighteenth-century furniture pieces from around Prussia. A display centring on **Krzystof Mrongoviusz** fills you in on the locally born priest and nineteenth-century champion of Polish culture after whom the town – originally Sensburg – was renamed in 1945. East of the square near the main Catholic church is the town's brick nineteenth-century Protestant temple, now used by the local Russian Orthodox community.

Practicalities

Scenically positioned on the lakeside facing the town – by car it's a two-kilometre drive – the *Mrongovia*, ul Giżycka 6 (☎32-21/22), a much-hyped Orbis joint, is where most of the foreign tourists stay. It's also your best source of tourist **information**. As well as canoes and kayaks on the lake in summer the hotel also offers (fairly pricey) **byplane trips** over the area; ask at the hotel reception for details. Cheaper accommodation alternatives are the central *Polonia* at ul. Warszawska 10 (☎35-72), the *Krajan*, ul. Kolejowa 9 (☎26-21) opposite the railway station, and the welter of small *pensjonaty* on the road up behind the *Mrongovia*. The *Camp Park*, Wilamówek 1 (☎87-50/70), in **Borowski Las**, 9km southwest of town is a well-organised and popular site, complete with shop and restaurant – there are also rooms on offer. Of the **restaurants** in town, the *Mrongovia* offers decent enough, if pricey, Orbis fare. Otherwise there are plenty of smaller joints, many of the fast-food variety, in the town centre.

narrow, winding river that makes up the last part of the journey, the route takes you through a succession of eighteen lakes, connected by narrow stretches of river, the banks often covered with dense forest. The journey usually takes anything from nine days upwards, with Ruciane-Nida or Mikołajki the final destination. Overnight stops are generally in the following places (in *stanice wodne* unless specified):

- **day one** at BIEŃKI (15km),
- **day two**, BABIITA (12km) (there's also a youth hostel (July-Aug) here),
- **day three** in SPYCHOWO (12.5km),
- **day four** ZGONIE (10.5km),
- **day five** at KRUTYŃ(14km),
- **day six** in UTKA (18.5km), the first stop on the Krutynia river itself,
- **day seven** at NOWY MOST (6.5km),
- **day eight** KAMIEŃ (10.5km) on the beautiful **Lake Bełdany**, the final
- **day nine** ending up at RUCIANE-NIDA (13.5km) (See p.200) – a total 113km trip. The Krutynia route is very popular in high summer, so the local wisdom is that the best time to make the trip is either in spring (April–May) or late summer (late August–September).

If this ambitious excursion sounds appealing, the **Olsztyn PTTK** offer ten-day kayak trips along the route outlined above, with overnight stops at waterside hostels (*stanice wodne*) included, for under £100. You will need to provide your own gear for the trip though, sleeping bag included. For **advance booking** (strongly recommended in summer) write or even call – if you do there's usually someone there who speaks English and/or German. Alternatively, for shorter excursions the *Hotel Mrongowia* in Mrągowo may be able to sort you out with a canoe, though here again, in summer advance notice is virtually essential.

North from Mrągowo

The fields and woods stretching to the north of Mrągowo conceal a couple of contrasting historical curiosities: the well-known pilgrimage centre of **Święta Lipka** and, somewhat more chillingly, Hitler's wartime headquarters at **Gierłoz**, near the old Teutonic centre of **Kętrzyn**. Further historic interest comes in the shape of **Reszel**, another onetime Teutonic haunt with a fine Gothic church and castle.

Święta Lipka

Twenty kilometres north and a forty-minute bus ride from Mrągowo is the church at **Święta Lipka**, probably the country's most famous Baroque shrine. Lodged on a thin strip of land in between two lakes, the magnificent church is stuck out in the middle of nowhere. As an approach area stuffed with souvenir stalls and locals peddling "folk art" at inflated prices suggests, the out-of-the-way location doesn't stop the tourists turning up in droves. As often in Poland, the draw of the church isn't purely for its architectural qualities; Święta Lipka is also an important centre of pilgrimage and Marian devotion, as it has been for centuries, and during religious festivals the church is absolutely jammed with pilgrims, creating an intense atmosphere of fervent Catholic devotion.

Some history

The name Święta Lipka – literally "holy linden tree" – derives from a local medieval legend according to which a Prussian tribal leader, released from imprisonment by the Teutonic Knights – it didn't happen to many of them – is supposed to have placed a statue of the Virgin in a linden tree as a token of thanks. Within a few years healing miracles were being reported at the place, and a chapel was eventually built on the site by the Knights in 1320. The fame and supposed curative powers of the shrine increased by leaps and bounds, to such an extent that by the end of the fifteenth century it had become an important centre of pilgrimage. Following their conversion to Lutheranism the Teutonic Knights destroyed the chapel in 1526, in characteristically brutal fashion placing gallows in front of the site in a bid to deter pilgrims. In 1620 Poles managed to purchase the ruins, and another chapel was constructed under the direction of Stefan Sadorski, King Sigismund II's private secretary, and handed over to Jesuits from the Lithuanian section of the Order in the 1630s. With pilgrims turning up in ever-increasing numbers the Jesuits decided to build a new and more ambitious sanctuary. Work on the Baroque edifice you see today was begun in 1687 under the direction of Jerzy Ertly, an architect from Vilnius, so to anyone familiar with the churches of the Lithuanian capital and its surroundings the "eastern" Baroque of Święta Lipka will come as no surprise.

The Church

In a country with a major predilection for Baroque richness the Święta Lipka complex is unquestionably one of the most exuberant of them all. Approached from a country road, the low cloisters, tapering twin towers of the church facade and plain yellow and white stucco covering the exterior are quintessential eastern Polish Baroque. Entrance to the complex (Mon–Sat 8am–6pm, Sundays in between masses) is through a magnificent early eighteenth-century wrought-iron gate designed by Johann Schwartz, a local from Reszel, the surrounding cloisters topped by 44 stone statues representing the genealogy of Christ.

Through the main door you enter the body of the building, a rectangular structure with a long central nave, side aisles divided from the nave on each side by four sets of pillars supporting overhanging galleries and a presbytery. First thing to catch the eye is the superb **fresco work** covering every inch of the ceiling, the work of one Maciej Meyer from nearby Lidzbark Warmiński, which draws on a wide range of themes ranging from the lives of Christ and Mary and Old Testament stories, to depictions of Jesuit missions and the Marian cult of Święta Lipka itself. A young Meyer was sent off to Rome in the early 1700s to improve his craft, in particular the execution of three-dimensional and *trompe l'oeil* effects. He clearly learned a thing or two: particularly in the central nave's vaulted ceiling the polychromy is a triumph, several of the frescoes employing the newly acquired *trompe l'oeil* techniques to powerful effect.

Towering above the nave the lofty main **altarpiece**, an imposing wooden structure completed in 1714, has three levels; the upper two contain pictures on biblical themes, the lowest a seventeenth century icon of the Madonna and Child – the holy Mother of God of Święta Lipka as it's known locally – based on an original kept at Santa Maria Maggiore's in Rome: much revered by Polish pilgrims, the Madonna figure was adorned with its crown in the 1960s by then Polish Catholic Primate Cardinal Wyszyński, with a certain Karol Wojtyła in attendance. Imitating the original medieval shrine, to the left of the altar stands a rather grubby-looking eighteenth-century **linden tree**, topped by a silver statue of the Virgin and Child, the base smothered in pennants pinned there by virtuous pilgrims. It's about the only thing in the church that does look like it needs a clean: by the beginning of this century, years of accumulated smoke from pilgrims' candles had reduced the fresco work to a sorry state. A major cleanup operation took place in the 1920s, with crusts of old bread apparently proving the most effective way of touching up the plaster-based polychromy.

Filling virtually the entire west end of the building is the church's famous Baroque **organ**. Built in 1720 by Johann Mozengel, a Jew from Königsberg – many of the church artists and sculptors came from the old East Prussian capital – it's a huge, fantastically ornate creation, decked with two layers of blue gilded turrets topped by figures of the saints. Renovated by one of the Jesuit brothers during the 1960s, the instrument is in fine shape, producing a marvellously rich sound.

When enough people are around short concerts are given by one of the brothers, the real show-stopper being the exhibition pieces when the instrument's celestial assortment of moving parts are brought into action: the whole organ appears to come alive, gyrating angels blowing their horns, cherubs waving, stars jingling and cymbals crashing – Bach fugues with a heavenly back-up group in accompaniment.

It's certainly an extraordinary sight and sound, worth capturing on one of the tapes or CDs you can pick up from the kiosk outside the church. Additionally there are special evening organ concerts every second and fourth Friday of the month from June to August, the second Friday of the month only in September.

Back out of the main building, the **cloisters** are a nice calm spot to recuperate in after the exertions of the church, the ceilings featuring more sumptuous polychromy by Meyer, most notably in the domed cupolas ornamenting the four corners of the structure.

If material refreshment's more what you need after a stint in the church the basic *Zalesie* restaurant on the road facing the cloisters will do the honours.

As well as the regular local services to Mrągowo and Kętrzyn, buses run to Olsztyn (via Reszel), Gdańsk and Suwałki.

Reszel

Four kilometres west of Święta Lipka is the historic Warmian centre of **RESZEL**. Seat of the bishops of Warmia for over five centuries, from the establishment of Christianity in the region (1254) until the First Partition (1772), Reszel is also one of Copernicus's many old regional haunts. These days the town is another quiet end-of-the-world provincial hang-out, the main attraction being the old town area that sits atop a plateau overlooking the surroundings.

Of the many Gothic country churches in Warmia, Reszel's **Church of St Peter and Paul** is one of the most immediately striking. Hardly the most elegant of buildings from the exterior, what the church lacks in delicacy it certainly makes up for in sheer size – perhaps that's how those bishops preferred things on their home patch. The monster **Church Tower** is visible for miles around, and from close up you feel almost as dwarfed as in St Mary's in Gdańsk. The altarpiece is a fine piece of Neoclassical elegance, the nave vaulting displaying some of the intricate geometric brick patternwork common throughout the region. On a more delicate note, early Renaissance polychromy using enjoyable plant and animal motifs is still in evidence on the pillars and arches of the nave.

Bulk is also the name of the game in the fourteenth-century **Bishop's Castle**, just up from the church, an impressive hulk surrounded by the ruins of the old town walls. The castle now houses a rather superior **art gallery** (Tues–Sun 10am–4pm) featuring regular exhibitions – generally of the "disturbed and alienated" variety – by well-known contemporary artists, both Polish and foreign. In fact painters and sculptors are regularly invited to live and work in the castle for a few months, so in summer particularly the place is a mine of creative activity. For those mere mortals who aren't offered a castle bedroom of their own there's the possibility of climbing up the castle tower (same hours as gallery) for the view over the surroundings. The chic café inside the castle courtyard is exactly what you'd expect of an artists' centre – more *Quartier Latin* than back-of-the-woods Warmia.

THE JULY BOMB PLOT

In the summer of 1944, the Wolf's Lair was the scene of the assassination attempt on Adolf Hitler that came closest to success – the **July Bomb Plot**. Its leader, **Count Claus Schenk von Stauffenberg**, an aristocratic officer and member of the General Staff, had gained the support of several high-ranking members of the German army. Sickened by atrocities on the eastern front, and rapidly realising that the Wehrmacht was fighting a war that could not possibly be won, von Stauffenberg and his fellow conspirators decided to kill the Führer, seize control of army head-quarters in Berlin and sue for peace with the Allies. Germany was on the precipice of total destruction by the Allies and the Soviet Army: only such a desperate act, reasoned the plotters, could save the Fatherland.

On July 20, Stauffenberg was summoned to the Wolf's Lair to brief Hitler on troop movements on the eastern front. In his briefcase was a small bomb, packed with high explosive: once triggered, it would explode in under ten minutes. As Stauffenberg approached the specially built conference hut, he triggered the device. Taking his place a few feet from Hitler, Stauffenberg positioned the briefcase under the table, leaning it against one of the table's stout legs no more than six feet away from the Führer. Five minutes before the bomb exploded, Stauffenberg quietly slipped from the room unnoticed by the generals and advisers, who were listening to a report on the central Russian front. One of the officers moved closer to the table to get a better look at the campaign maps and, finding the briefcase in the way of his feet under the table, picked it up and moved it to the other side of the table leg. Now, the very solid support of the table leg lay between the briefcase and Hitler.

At 12.42 the bomb went off. Stauffenberg, watching the hut from a few hundred yards away, was shocked by the force of the explosion. It was, he said, as if the hut had been hit by a 155mm shell; there was no doubt that the Führer, along with every-one else in the room, was dead.

Stauffenberg hurried off to a waiting plane and made his way to Berlin to join the other conspirators. Meanwhile, back in the wreckage of the hut, Hitler and the survi-vors staggered out into the daylight: four people had been killed or were dying of their wounds, including Colonel Brandt, who had moved Stauffenberg's briefcase and thus unwittingly saved the Führer's life. Hitler himself, despite being badly shaken, suffered no more than a perforated eardrum and minor injuries. After being attended to, he prepared himself for a meeting with Mussolini later that afternoon.

It was quickly realised what had happened, and the hunt for Stauffenberg was on. Hitler issued orders to the SS in Berlin to summarily execute anyone who was

Kętrzyn and the Wolf's Lair

Known as Rastenburg until its return to Polish rule in 1945, **KĘTRZYN**, 15km east of Święta Lipka, is a quiet, unexceptional town whose main interest lies in its proximity to Gierłoz – Hitler's "Wolf's Lair" (see below).

If you've time to spare, a short walk up the hill from the railway station stands the old Teutonic town complex, itself built on the site of an earlier Prussian settlement. Badly destroyed in 1945, the well-restored Gothic **Teutonic Knights' Castle** houses a **regional museum** (Tues–Thurs, Sat–Sun 10am–4pm, Fri 10am–5pm) housing an exhibition combining local archaeology and wildlife. If you never get to see boars, beavers or badgers in the Mazurian wild you'll find plenty of stuffed ones here, alongside a selection of similarly preserved birds, eagles, owls

slightly suspect, and dispatched Himmler to the city to quell the rebellion. Back in the military Supreme Command headquarters in Berlin, the conspiracy was in chaos. Word reached Stauffenberg and the two main army conspirators, generals Beck and Witzleben, that the Führer was still alive: they had already lost hours of essential time by failing to issue the carefully planned order to mobilise their sympathisers in the city and elsewhere, and had even failed to carry out the obvious precaution of severing all communications out of the city. After a few hours of tragi-comic scenes as the conspirators tried to persuade high-ranking officials to join them, the Supreme Command HQ was surrounded by SS troops, and it was announced that the Führer would broadcast to the nation later that evening. The coup was over.

The conspirators were gathered together, given paper to write farewell messages to their wives, taken to the courtyard of the HQ and, under the orders of one General Fromm, shot by firing squad. Stauffenberg's last words were "Long live our sacred Germany!"

Fromm had known about the plot almost from the beginning, but had refused to join it. By executing the leaders he hoped to save his own skin – and, it must be added, knowingly saved them from the torturers of the SS.

Hitler's ruthless revenge on the conspirators was without parallel even in the bloody annals of the Third Reich. All the colleagues, friends and immediate relatives of Stauffenberg and the other conspirators were rounded up, tortured and taken before the "People's Court", where they were humiliated and given more-or-less automatic death sentences. Many of those executed knew nothing of the plot and were found guilty merely by association. As the blood lust grew, the Nazi party used the plot as a pretext for settling old scores, and eradicated anyone who had the slightest hint of anything less than total dedication to the Führer. General Fromm, who had ordered the execution of the conspirators, was among those tried, found guilty of cowardice and shot by firing squad. Those whose names were blurted under torture were quickly arrested, the most notable being Field Marshal Rommel, who, because of his popularity, was given the choice of a trial in the People's Court – or suicide and a state funeral.

The July Bomb Plot caused the deaths of at least 5000 people, including some of Germany's most brilliant military thinkers and almost all of those who would have been best qualified to run the postwar German government. Within six months the country lay in ruins as the Allies and Soviet Army advanced; had events at Rastenburg been only a little different, the entire course of the war – and European history – would have been altered incalculably.

and cormorants. If the bolshy attendants let you get that far, the second floor is largely devoted to **Wojtech Ketrzyn**, a postwar nineteenth century local historian and patriot, the epitome of the sort of characters after whom the postwar Polish authorities renamed the Mazurian towns .

Across from the castle the Gothic **St George's Church**, also rebuilt after 1945, is a rather barren, sorry-looking place, a couple of old Prussian memorial tablets all that's left of the original interior decoration. The small fourteenth-century chapel next door, rebuilt in the seventeenth century, and a small house down the hill are both Protestant chapels, while on the other side of town, on ul. Mickiewicza, there's an early nineteenth-century freemasons' lodge, now a *Dom Kultury*.

If you're planning on **staying over**, the *Agros*, ul. Kasztanowa 1 (52-40), a *pensjonat* on the western side of town, is your best bet – the hotel also organises rooms in private houses.

Gierłoz

GIERŁOZ lies 8km east of Kętrzyn and can be reached by local bus or the steam train from Węgorzewo, which stops at Parcz a kilometre from the site (be careful to check return times). If you're driving here from Kętrzyn, watch carefully for signposts – the route is badly marked.

Here, deep in the Mazurian forests, Hitler established his military headquarters in the so-called **Wolf's Lair** (Wilczy Szaniec; Tues–Sun 8am–6pm), a huge underground complex from which the Germans' eastward advance was conducted. Other satellite bunker complexes were built for the army and Luftwaffe and are spread out in a forty-kilometre radius round the site, mostly now overgrown ruins.

Encased in several metres of concrete were private bunkers for Göring, Bormann, Himmler and Hitler himself, alongside offices, SS quarters and operations rooms. The 27-acre complex was camouflaged by a suspended screen of vegetation that was altered to match the changing seasons, and was permanently mined "in case of necessity". In 1945 the retreating army fired the detonator, but it merely cracked the bunkers, throwing out flailing tentacles of metal reinforcements. Most of today's visitors come in tourist groups – an English-speaking guide is generally on hand to take you round.

Peering into these cavernous monsters today is an eerie experience. You can see the place, for example, where the assassination attempt on Hitler failed in July 1944,* the SS living quarters, the staff cinema, and other ancillaries of domestic Nazi life. Gruesome photographs and films remind visitors of the scale of German atrocities, but as so often with official anti-fascist material, there's a tendency to resort to horrifying images at the expense of information and critical understanding.

For anybody up to staying, there's a basic **hostel**, **campsite** and **restaurant** at the bunker site. If you're interested in the nuts and bolts of the site there's a special edition of the UK magazine *After the Battle* available from one of the guides, devoted to a meticulously researched account of a postwar attempt to identify every building on the site.

---

*The **airstrip** from which Stauffenberg departed after his abortive assassination attempt is a couple of kilometres east from the main site, a lone runway in the middle of some heathland – you'll need a guide to show you the way.

Mikólajki

Hyped in the brochures as the "Mazurian Venice", **MIKOŁAJKI** is unquestionably the most attractive of the top Mazurian resorts. Straddled across the meeting point of two attractive small lakes – the Tałty and Mikołajskie – the small town has long provided a base for yachters on popular nearby Lake Śniardwy. Legend associates the town's name with a monster creature, known as the King of the Whitefish, that terrorises the local fisherman and destroyed their nets. The beast finally met its match in a young local called Mikołajek who caught the huge fish in a steel fishing net. Cobbled streets, half timbered houdes and the old fishing boats lined up on the lake shore give the town a pleasing feeling of authenticity – something that is lacking in the other big lakeside tourist centres. Judging by the rows of foreign number plates parked on the main square, the word about Mikołajki is out too: despite a relative abundance of decent accommadation it can still be hard work finding a place to stay in high summer.

The Town

If you walk around the town centre you'll see a couple of buildings to remind you of the town's historic Protestant roots. Unusually for modern Poland, the main church in town is the Protestant **Church of the Holy Trinity,** overlooking the shores of Lake Tałty. Designed by German architect Franz Schinki, this solid-looking early nineteenth-century structure is the centre of worship for the region's Protestant community. Portraits of two early pastors apart it's a fairly spartan place, light years away in feel from the usual Catholic churches. Talk to the minister, a jovial character and mine of local information who lives just across from the church, and he'll probably offer to show you the newly completed parish building, a posh German-financed setup used for international conferences.

For more insights into the Protestant life of the country check out the **Museum of the Polish Reformation** (Tues–Sun, 10am–4pm) in the large *Dom Kultury* just up the road. Set up by the retired former town pastor, it features an collection of old Protestant hymnals, Bibles and prayerbooks from around the country: as well as describing each object in minute detail, the pastor's likely to try and collar you for a sizeable donation towards the museum.

Practicalities

The **train station**, on the main Olsztyn–Ełk line, is some way out northeast of the town centre. The **bus station** is closer in, over the road from the Protestant church. The *Wigry* tourist office, ul. Kolejowa 9 near the bus station, is the best source of **tourist information**. For **accommodation** there's a fair range of places to choose from: at the top end of the scale the hotels are the luxury *Golębski*, ul. Mrągowska 34 (☎16-517), on the northern edge of town, and the *Król Sielaw*, ul. Kajki 9 (☎18-323), a new and already highly rated place aimed at Westerners and bang in the centre. Other cheaper options are the *Złoty Widok* guest house, ul. Leśna 7 (☎16-164), and the *pensjonat Mikołajki*, ul. Kajki 18 (☎16-437), another new, good-quality place close to the centre. Moving further out of centre, the *Na Skarpie*, ul. Kajki 130 (☎16-418), and *Wodnik* (☎16-141), 2km east of town, are both good bets; the latter in particular has a beautiful quiet waterside location, canoeing equipment to hand and is run by a helpful and extremely accommodating couple. Other *pensjonaty* out of town are the *Złote Wrota*, Stare Sady 3 (☎16-520), at the edge of Lake Tałty 3km north of town, and the *Tałty*

(☎16-398), 2km further out on the other side of the same lake. Finally there's a good **camping site**, *Camping Wagabunda* at ul. Leśna 2 (☎16-018) 2km west of town, with four-person bungalows also on the site, and a (summer only) youth hostel in town (☎18-293). With the exception of the *Golębski* most places are only open from June to mid-October, so it's probably best to phone ahead if you're planning to come at any other time of year.

Most of the lakeside places have their own stock of canoes and water equipment for use by guests, some also extending to bicycles, handy if you want to visit the nature reserve round **Lake Łukajno**, 4km east of town, the home of one of Europe's largest remaining colonies of wild swans. Many of the hotels and *pensjonaty* also have decent restaurants, which you'll probably want to use if you're staying. Predictably, fish – eel in particular – is the local speciality, most of it fresh out of the surrounding lakes. If you want to fry your own the *Centralna Rybna* fish market just off the square at 3 ul.1-go Maja has a good selection of the day's catch on offer.

For **yachting and watersports** there are several centres dotted around the lakeside in and around town. Consult the tourist office or the centres themselves for details of what's on offer currently. The embarkation point and ticket office for passenger boat trips on the lakes (*przystań żeglugi pasażerski*) is just down from market square. Again, check there for details of the available options.

South from Mikołajki

Travelling south from Mikołajki you're soon into the depths of the Puszcza Piska, a characteristic Mazurian mix of woodlands and water. A huge tangle of crystal-clear lakes, lazy winding rivers and dense forest thickets, it's the largest *puszcza* in the region, one of the surviving remnants of the primaeval forest that once covered much of northeastern Europe. The forest is mainly pine, many of the trees reaching 30 to 40 metres in height, with some magnificent pockets of mixed oak, beech and spruce in between. A favourite with both canoers – the Krutynia River (see p.192) runs south through the middle of the forest – and walkers, who use the area's developed network of hiking trails, the Puscza Piska is a delightful area well worth exploring, with the forest lakeside resort of **Ruciane-Nida** providing the obvious base for doing so.

Ruciane-Nida

Twenty-five kilometres south of Mikołajki along a scenic forest road brings you to the lakeside resort of **Ruciane-Nida**. Actually two towns connected by a short stretch of road, it's an understandably popular holiday centre, the combination of forest and lakeland offering options for both the active and not-so-active.

Arriving by train or bus **RUCIANE** is the first stop-off point. Walk just south of the mainline station and you're at the water's edge, in this case the narrow canal connecting the two lakes nearest the town: the jetty with the sign marked *Żegluga Mazurska* is the boarding point for excursion boats on the Giżyck-Mikołajki-Ruciane line, the boats travelling through the connecting series of lakes culminating in Lake Nidzkie running south from the town.

A kilometre further down the lakeside road, **NIDA** is the main centre of activity, with plenty of canoeists and other sporty-looking types in evidence in season. The town's beautiful location makes a mockery of the unimaginative grey blocks of much of the centre, though it gets better the nearer the waterside you go. Ul. Gałczynskiego, the main drag, is showing signs of picking up Western habits, as evidenced by the slick-looking *Cafe Rebecca* and the *Dab Pub*. If you're planning on staying, the lakeside *Perła Jezior* camping/holiday bungalow site, off the road halfway between the two towns, is an ideal location, the other obvious option being the PTTK *Dom Wycieczkowy*, ul. Mazurska 16, north of the railway station in Ruciane.

Despite its forest location the town is actually fairly accessible, with regular trains west to Olsztyn, east on to Ełk and, less frequently, buses (45mins) to Mikołajki.

The Wojnowo nunnery

For much of the last two centuries the area round Ruciane-Nida has been populated by communities of Orthodox **Old Believers** – *Starowiercy* as they're called in Polish. The quiet seclusion of the forests and the proximity to water made the area an obvious choice for a habitually shy and retiring people. Slowly but surely the local Old Believers are dwindling in numbers, but you'll still find some of them living in the villages north of the town.

Some 6km west of Ruciane, however, is the best-known monument to their presence in the region, the **nunnery** at **WOJNOWO**. Established in the mid-nineteenth century as a centre for promoting and preserving the old-style Orthodox faith in Mazuria, today this once-thriving community is down to two nuns, both well over 80, who are cared for by a local fellow-believer. Coming up the track leading off from the Ruciane–Babięta road the first impression is that you must have entered a local farm by mistake. Through the gateway it turns out to be the nunnery after all, the main building set between farmyard barns and stables on one side and a plain white church on the other.

At their age, the nuns are past showing anyone round, but knock at the main door and you should find the caretaker who'll be able to take you up to the church. If you have to wait while she finishes off in the kitchens, you could take a short stroll up to the community's **cemetery**, a small rather melancholy enclosure of Cyrillic-enscribed gravestones which overlook the banks of the **Krutynia**. The setting is a wonder though, the swaying trees, tall waterside rushes and graceful contours of the river making this a peaceful and memorable spot.

The church **interior** is laid out on the conventional Orthodox pattern, with a notable iconostasis and accompanying collection of old icons. It's actually only a small part of the community's icon collection, the rest having been moved some years ago to the castle museum at Lidzbark Warmiński (see p.185) once the dwindling community of nuns no longer felt able to look after them. You're not allowed to take pictures, but if you ask, the caretaker will sell you a postcard.

Giżycko and around

Squeezed between Lake Niegocin and the marshy backwaters of Lake Mamry, **GIŻYCKO** is one of the main lakeland centres. It was flattened in 1945, however, and the rebuilding didn't create a lot of character: if greyish holiday resort architecture lowers your spirits, don't plan to stay for long before heading out for the lakes. Wilkasy (see below) is a much more pleasant base.

Incongruously, the **Orbis** office at ul. Dąbrowskiego has glossy brochures and ticket-booking facilities for anywhere on the other side of the globe, but absolutely nothing about Giżycko or its surroundings. As indicated by the ranks of German vehicles parked outside, the central *Wodnik* **hotel**, ul. 3 Maja 2 (☎38-72), is the hub of foreign tourist activity; it's expensive and difficult to get into. More likely to have space is the *Zamek*, a large motel in the ruins of the Teutonic castle at ul. Moniuszki 1 (☎24-19), which also has a **campsite** close by (☎34-10). With privatisation opening up an increasing number of former workers' holiday homes to tourists, there are also the *Dom Wycieczkowy*, ul. Nadbrzeżebna 11, right in the centre by the side of the lake, and the nearby *Garnizonowy*, ul. Olsztynska 10a. Within walking distance of the train station there are also two **youth hostels**, at ul. Mickiewicza 27 (☎29-87) and ul. Wiejska 50 (☎21-35); both of these are open from July to September only.

Lakes near Giżycko

East of Giżycko, the tourists thin out and the lakes get quieter and cleaner. There's little accommodation, though, so you'll need to come equipped with a tent or a car, allowing you to venture out for day trips along the picturesque country roads.

Ten kilometres northeast from Giżycko are the adjoining **Gołdopiwo** and **Kruklin lakes**, located a couple of kilometres from the edge of the **Borecka forest**. A bus from Giżycko will take you to the village of KRUKLANKI on the southern edge of Lake Gołdopiwo, and from there you're pretty much on your own. Twenty kilometres to the southeast of Giżycko there's another enchanting string of lakes – **Wydmińskie**, **Jedzelewo** and **Lasmiady** – linked by the River Gawlik: they're all easily reached, being close to stations on the Giżycko–Ełk rail line.

Wilkasy

WILKASY is a five-kilometre bus ride southwest of Giżycko; the train from Kętrzyn stops here too, at the Niegocin station. If you want to experience how Poles take their Mazurian holidays, this is the place to head for, with its assortment of lakeside rest homes, holiday cabins and hostels. Apart from some nice enclosed swimming areas by the lake, the other attraction of Wilkasy is that it's much easier to **hire canoes or kayaks** here. Before they are allowed to set oar to water, Poles have to produce an official card proving they can swim, but you should be able to persuade the attendants to let you aboard. It makes for a pleasant day, paddling round the lake, hiving off into reed beds or canals as the fancy takes you – even though the pollution becomes more obvious the nearer you get to Giżycko.

A good place to stay is the **PTTK hostel** (May–Sept; ☎30-78) situated near the bus stop just up from the water; the hostel or one of the neighbouring houses will also allow camping in the garden for a small fee. There's also the *Vaga*, ul. Szkolna 25 (28-79), a decent *pensjonat* close to the lake's edge. The **restaurant** over the road is mainly patronised by groups of holidaymakers eating their set meals in rotas; it isn't exactly a gastronomic paradise but is, without doubt, very Polish, and as in all major tourist resorts you won't have any trouble getting a beer or ten – if you want to follow local male holidaying habits.

BOAT TRIPS ON THE MAIN LAKES

Throughout the summer – in most cases this means from May to September – regular tourist **boat services** run on the main lakes on the following routes:

Giżycko–Mikołajki (4hr)

Mikołajki–Ruciane–Nida (3hr)

Giżycko–Węgorzewo (25km; June–Aug only)

At peak season (June–July) boats depart daily; otherwise, depending on demand, it's likely to be weekends and national holidays only. Often packed, the boats are mostly large, open-deck steamers with a basic snack bar on board for refreshments. **Timetables** (*rozkłady*) for departures are posted by the main jetties at all the major lakeside stop-off points. For enquiries contact the *Mazur Tourist* offices in Olsztyn, ul. Staromiejksa 6 (☎274-125), Giżycko, ul. 3-go Maja 2 (☎38-72) or the harbour office in Mikołajki (☎16-102).

Węgorzewo

Twenty-five kilometres north of Giżycko on the furthest edge of Lake Mamry is **WĘGORZEWO**, another former Teutonic stronghold established on the site of an earlier Prussian settlement and one of the major holiday centres, for the central Mazurian lakelands: despite the enjoyable rural setting, however, like its bigger cousin Giżycko, the town itself is a formless, unprepossessing sort of place, the only real reason to come here being the access it offers to Lake Mamry, the second largest in the region. The ruins of the Teutonic Knights castle, destroyed in 1945, and the old Protestant, now Catholic church apart, there's nothing to detain you.

For **tourist information** the Orbis office (Mon–Fri 8am–4pm) on pl. Wolności, the main town square, is the place to head for. For **accommodation** there's the *pensjonat* at ul. Sienkiewicza 13 (tel 20-49), a *Dom Wycieczkowy*, ul Turystyczna 13 (28-42) and a basic PTTK hostel, ul. Nabrzeżna 10 (24-43). For campers there's the *Rusałka*, a good site with restaurant nicely situated on the shores of Lake Święcajty south of the town. Best of a basically undistinguished selection of restaurants are the *DAAB*, on ul. Jasna, and the *Szkwał*, pl. Wolności 13.

Ełk

EŁK, the easternmost main town of Mazury, is the area's major bus and train interchange. Established by the Teutonic Knights as a base from which to "protect" the locals and keep an eye on the heathen Lithuanian hordes, the town was colonised by Poles in the sixteenth century, before becoming an East Prussian border post during the Partitions.

It remained an important East Prussian centre until 1945, and suffered comprehensive damage during the war; the ruins of the Teutonic castle apart, it's got little to show for its past now.

Most visitors don't get much further than the shabby square below the train station; there really isn't much to detain you in the sprawling, tatty town centre. If you're forced to spend the night here, head for the **hotel** *Mazurski*, at ul. Słowackiego 28 (☎41-15), or failing that the *Dom Turystyczny* at ul. Armii Krajowej 32 (☎24-19), where there's also a basic **restaurant**. For local information, the

Orbis office at ul. Mickiewicza 15 is not far from the train and bus stations, both of which are close to the centre.

Augustów and the Suwalszczyna

The region around the towns of **Augustów** and **Suwałki** is one of the least visited areas of Poland: even for Poles, anything beyond Mazury is still pretty much terra incognita. As with most parts of eastern Poland, the region north of Suwałki – the **Suwalszczyna** – is little developed economically: a region of peasant farmers and tortuous ethnic and religious loyalties. And like the Bieszczady mountains (see Chapter Three), its counterpart in obscurity, the Suwalszczyna is one of the most beautiful, unspoilt territories in Europe. Once a part of the Czarist empire, much of the region's older architecture – most notably in the regional capital, **Suwałki** – has a decidely Russian feel to it. **Jews** were long a major element of the region's fluid ethnic mix, almost the only surviving sign of this being the **cemeteries** you find rotting away at the edge of numerous towns and villages throughout the area. The region's proximity to Lithuania is reflected too in the sizeable **Lithuanian minority** concentrated in the northeast corner of the region.

Visually the striking feature of the northern part of the Suwalszczyna is a pleasing landscape of rolling hills and fields interspersed with crystal-clear lakes – often small, but extremely deep – the end product of the final retreat of the Scandinavian glacier that once covered the area. Much of the southern stretch of this region is covered by the **Puszcza Augustówska**, the remains of the vast forest that once extended well into Lithuania. In the north, by contrast, wonderfully open countryside is interspersed with villages and lakes – some reasonably well known, like **Lake Hańcza** (the deepest in Poland), others, often the most beautiful, rarely visited. Wandering through the fields and woodland thickets you'll find storks, swallows, brilliantly coloured butterflies and wild flowers in abundance, while in the villages the twentieth century often seems to have made only modest incursions, leaving plenty of time to sit on the porch and talk.

Getting around isn't exactly straightforward: buses operate in most of the region, but frequency declines the closer you get to the Lithuanian border. Suwałki and Augustów both have mainline train connections to Warsaw, and, slowly but surely, a fledgling network of rail, bus and air connections on into Lithuania is developing.

Augustów and around

The region around **AUGUSTÓW** was settled at some indistinct time in the early Middle Ages by Jacwingians, a pagan Baltic Slav tribe. By the end of the thirteenth century, however, they had been wiped out, leaving as testimony only a few sites such as the burial mound near Suwałki (see p.207) and a scattering of place names. The area remained almost deserted for the next two centuries or so, until the town's establishment in 1557 by King Zygmunt August (hence the name) as a supply stopoff on the eastern trade routes from Gdańsk. It only really developed after the construction of the **Augustów canal** in the nineteenth century. A hundred-kilometre network of rivers, lakes and artificial channels, this waterway was cut to connect the town to the River Niemen in the east, providing a transport route for the region's most important natural commodity, wood. Still in use today, the canal offers the most convenient approach to the heart of the forest (see below).

Thanks to its location on the edge of the *puszcza* and the surrounding abundance of water, Augustów has carved out a growing niche for itself as a holiday centre. As a town, though, it's no great shakes. Caught on the frontline of the Soviet assault in late 1944, it has few prewar buildings, save a handful of nineteenth-century tenements, an old sawmill, and the 1920s PTTK hostel on the edge of Lake Necko. Its appeal is as a base for countryside exploration.

Practicalities

The **bus station** is right in the middle of town on plac Zymunta Augusta; the nearest **train** stop – Augustów Port – a couple of kilometres' bus ride from the centre. The **tourist information centre** on pl. Augusta is reasonably sussed and helpful, though they may not be able to offer much on **accommodation** in high season, when the hotels are generally pretty full. The first-choice places are the *Dom Nauczyciela* at ul. 29 Listopada 9 (☎20-21), the **PTTK hostel** (☎34-55/56) and **campsite** at ul. Sportowa 1 in Augustów Port, or – most expensively – the *Polmozbytu* motel at ul. Mazurska 4 (☎28-67) on the southern edge of town. From July to September there's a **youth hostel** at ul. Konopnickiej 9; if there are any **private rooms** going, the information office will know about them. They can also point you in the direction of a number of old workers' holiday homes by the lake, now open for private business. It's just possible that you'll arrive to find everything fully booked, in which case, if you have a sleeping bag, make for the Almatur *baza studentowa* (student base) by the lakeside at STUDZIENICZNA, a six-kilometre bus journey east; there's no food, so bring your own.

In town, the only **restaurants** worth mentioning are the *Albatros* at ul. Mostowa 5, in the centre, and the motel. Cafés and bars are the big current growth area – worth trying are the *Marco* and the *Delikatesy*, both on the main square, as well as the *Żagielek*, ul. 29 Listopada 7, a ritzier nighttime haunt for local smoothies down by the boat embarkation point on the canal.

The Forest

The combination of wild forest, lakes, and narrow winding rivers has made the *puszcza* a favourite with canoeists, walkers and naturalists alike. Following in the footsteps of their partisan ancestors, whose anti-czarist forces found shelter here, adventurous Poles spend days and sometimes weeks paddling or trekking through the forest. Such expeditions require preparation, so for most people the practical way to sample the mysteries of the forest is to take a **day trip** from Augustów along the canal system. Boats leave from the embarkation point at ul. 29 Listopada 7, fifteen minutes' walk from the town centre – *żegług* (boat) is the key word when asking the way. First departure is at 8.30am, and you should get there early to queue for tickets. It's also a good idea to take some food: most boats don't have any, and restaurant stops on the way are unpredictable.

The shortest trips – a couple of hours – go east through the **Necko**, **Białe** and **Studzieniczne** lakes to SWOBODA or SUCHA RZECZKA, giving at least a taste of the beauty of the forest. Other boats go onward to PLASKA and the lock at PERKUC, returning in the evening; beyond this point, the canal is for canoeists only, and even they can only go another twenty-odd kilometres to the Soviet border.

The **forest** is mainly coniferous, but with impressive sections of elm, larch, hornbeam and ancient oak creating a slightly sombre atmosphere, particularly along the alley-like section of the canal between Swoboda and Sucha Rzeczka – the tallest trees blot out the sun, billowing reeds brush the boat, and the silence is suddenly broken by echoing bird calls. Amongst the varied wildlife of the forest, cranes, grey herons and even the occasional beaver can be spotted on the banks of the canal, while deeper into the *puszcza* you might glimpse wild boars or elks.

Gabowe Grądy

Six kilometres south of Augustów down a track through the woods (the nearest bus stop is about a kilometre east), the village of **GABOWE GRĄDY** is populated by a sizeable number of Russian Orthodox "Old Believers" (*Starowierców*) families. The wizened old characters with flowing white beards sitting by their front gates indicate you've arrived in the right place. People apart, the main interest here is the church, or *molenna* as the Old Believers commonly call it, at the north end of the village, one of three remaining such places of Orthodox worship in the region. The Gabowe Grądy *molenna* boasts a superb all-women **choir**, the only such group in the country: you can usually hear them at the Sunday morning service, the only time you're guaranteed to be able to get into the place anyway. For anyone interested in Orthodox music this is a must, the sonorous harmonies of the old liturgical chants intermeshing with the joyous, full-throated exuberance of the women's melodising. They've not been recorded on disc yet – it's about time someone did – but for a sample of Old Believer music you can check out the recent WOMAD/Real World Release by the *Dmitri Potrovsky Ensemble*, which includes a couple of Old Believer songs originating from Russia.

Suwałki and around

Founded as late as the 1720s, **SUWAŁKI** is another slow-paced provincial town with a decidedly eastern ambience. Perhaps feeling the need to keep the intellectuals in touch with life out in the sticks (or vice versa), Solidarity nominated the medieval historian Bronisław Geremek and the film director Andrzej Wajda as candidates for the Suwałki region in the 1989 elections: accounts of their campaign encounters with local farmers suggest it wasn't all plain sailing, scepticism about the men from Warsaw's capacity to represent regional concerns being a key issue. Thanks in part to the increasing cross-border traffic with Lithuania – Lithuanian number plates are an everyday sight here – Suwałki has been picking up recently, the town centre acquiring the typical trappings of the new consumer's Poland – smart clothes shops, hi-fi shops and the like.

A rambling, unfocused sort of place, Suwałki presents a mix of fine Neoclassical architecture and Russian-looking nineteenth-century buildings, with the usual postwar blocks around the outskirts. Religion is a mixed business here as well: the majority Catholic population uses the stately Neoclassical parish church of St Alexandra on pl. Wolnosci, but there's also an Evangelical church, further down on the main ul. Kosciuszki, and the **Molenna**, a small wooden building serving the town's Old Believer population and retaining some fine original icons. It is tucked away on a side street off al. Sejneńska close to the station; the only reliable time to gain entry is during the Sunday morning service.

Practicalities

The **train station**, terminus of the line from Warsaw, lies east of the centre – take bus #1, #8 or #12 into town. The **bus station**, on ul. Brzostowskiego, at the edge of the large pl. Piłsudskiego, is more central. Information is available from the regional **tourist office** at ul. Wojska Polskiego, next to the *Hańcza* hotel.

Suwałki doesn't go overboard on **hotels**. The *Hańcza* at ul. Wojska Polskiego 2 (☎32-81), near the river in the south of town, is reasonably comfortable, reasonably priced and also has a restaurant. The revamped *Dom Nouczyciela*, ul. Kościuszki 120 (☎629-00), is better and more expensive – the restaurant is pretty good too. That's it, apart from **private rooms**, available from the tourist office, and a summer **youth hostel** at ul. Klonowa 51 (☎51-40). The only real **restaurants**, apart from the hotels, are the *Jacwieska*, 1 Maja 14, and the *Pod Temidą*, ul, Kościuszki 82, both in the central area and both distinctly ordinary.

The Jacwingian burial site

The ancient Jacwingian burial ground, 4km north of Suwałki, is one of the few sites left by these ancient people, and a must for lovers of mystic sites. To reach it take a #7 bus to SZWACJARIA, or the Jeleniewo road by car: in both cases you'll see a sign at the roadside pointing you to the **Cementarzysko Jacwingów**. A short walk through the fields and over an overgrown ridge brings you to the burial mounds, discernible through a tangled mass of trees and undergrowth, just beyond the large war cemetery on the right-hand side of the road – more than 40,000 Soviets troops died in Nazi POW camps around here. Excavations around the sites have revealed a little about the Jacwingians – burying horses with their masters seems to have been a common practice. In general, though, little is known of this pagan people, but stay long enough in this beautiful and peaceful spot and you conjure up your own images of how they might once have lived.

Lake Wigry and the National Park

Lake Wigry, the district's largest lake, is just 11km southeast of Suwałki. The lake and a large part of the surrounding area were designated a **national park** in 1989, an unspoilt area of nearly 15,000 hectares comprising a mixture of lake, river, forest land and agricultural territory. The lake in particular is a stunningly beautiful spot, a peaceful haven of creeks, marshes and lakeside woods with the occasional village in between. A wealth of wildlife shelters largely undisturbed in and around its waters: the lake itself harbours over twenty species of fish, lavaret, whitefish, smelt and river trout included, while in the shoreland woods you can find stag, wild boar, elk, martens and badgers. Wigry's most characteristic animal, however, is the **beaver**, and particularly round the lake's southern and western shores you'll find plenty of evidence of their presence in the reservations set aside for colonies of the creatures. For access to the park from Suwałki, take a local bus to the holiday centre of STARY FOLWARK, where there's a **PTTK hostel** (☎12-23) and **campsite** near the water. You may be able to **hire canoes** or other boats here with which to explore the lake.

If you do get hold of a boat, head across the lake from Stary Folwark and you come to **Wigry church**, part of a monastery founded here by King Władysław IV Waza in the 1660s. A typical piece of Polish Baroque, it has exuberant frescoes in the main church and monks' skeletons in the catacombs. The **monastery** itself has been turned into a conference-centre-cum-hotel (☎12-28), with a goodish restaurant; it's worth considering for a comfortable stop in peaceful surroundings.

The Suwalszczyna

North of Suwałki the forests give way to the lush, rolling hills of the **Suwalszczyna**. Two roads take you through the heart of the region, towards the Lithuanian border: the first heads due north then veers westward through sporadic villages to **Wiżajny**; the other – along with a highly recommended steam railway – runs some way to the east, covering the 30km to **Puńsk**.

Suwałki to Wiżajny

The great appeal of this route lies in getting right off the beaten track – and tracks don't get much less beaten than that to **WODZIŁKI**, tucked away in a quiet wooded valley, around 10km north of Suwałki. The hamlet is home to a small community of Orthodox Old Believers, whose original wooden *cerkiew* is still in use, along with a nearby *bania* (sauna).

Life in this rural settlement seems to have changed little since the first settlers moved here in the 1750s: the houses are simple, earth-floored buildings with few concessions to modernity, the old men grow long white beards, the women don't

---

CANOEING DOWN THE CZARNA HANCZA RIVER

Along with the Krutynia (see p.192) the **Czarna Hańcza River** is one of the most beautiful – and popular – canoeing routes in the northeast Polish lakelands, and part of the five percent of Polish rivers still designated as grade 1 (i.e. "clean") water. If you've ever had a hankering for a backwater canoeing expedition this is as good a chance as any to satisfy it.

Starting from over the border in Belarus the 140-kilometre long river, a tributary of the Niemen, flows into the Puszcza Augustowska, winding its way through the Wigry National Park up to **Lake Hańcza**, 15km northwest of Suwałki. On the usual canoe route, the first leg of the journey starts from **Augustów**, following the Augustów canal (see p.204) east to the point where it meeets the Czarna Hańcza a few kilometres short of the Belarussian border: from there the route continues on up the river to **Suwałki** and, stamina allowing, beyond to Lake Hańcza. The local **PTTK offices** in both Suwałki and Augustów offer organised trips following this route, with the option of a detour into Lake Wigry and the surrounding national park another equally enticing alternative.

In this instance, starting from Augustów the canoes again head east along the canal, turning northwards at **Swoboda,** (12km) into **Lake Serwy**, an attractive forest-bound tributary. From there the canoes are transported across land to the village of **Bryzgiel,** on the southern shores of Lake Wigry.

Three days are given over to exploring the peaceful and unspoilt lake and its protected surroundings. Overnight camps are on the island of **Kamien**, one of several on the lake, and by the lakeside at **Stary Folwark** (see p.193) with a trip up to the monastery included. Leaving Wigry near the **Klasztorny peninsula**, the canoes re-enter the Czarna Hańcza, heading southwards through a spectacular forest-bound section of the river before rejoining the Augustów canal and making their way back to Augustów. Both the PTTK canoe trips take 10–11 days, with accommodation – mostly in *stanice wodne* (waterside hostels) – and meals provided throughout: you'll need to provide your own sleeping bag, wellies (ideally) and appropriate clothing. Current cost for both trips is £70 – a real bargain. The PTTK offices to contact are: **Suwałki**; ul. Koqciuszki 37 (☎59-81), **Augustów**, ul. Sportowa 1 (☎34-55/56).

appear to cut their hair, the children run barefoot. If you're lucky enough to get invited into one of their homes, you'll see amazing collections of icons, rosaries, Bibles and other precious relics. The easiest way to get to the hamlet is to take the bus through JELENIEWO. If possible take one that's turning off to TURTUL RUTKA, from where it's thirty minutes' walk north to Wodziłki; otherwise get off at Sidorówka, the next stop after Jeleniewo, which leaves five kilometres' walk

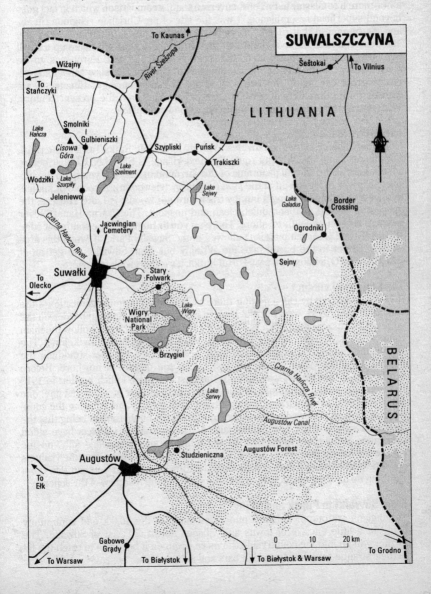

west, skirting **Lake Szurpiły**. The lake itself is great for swimming, and an ideal camping spot, provided the mosquitoes aren't out in force.

CISOWA GÓRA

The next bus stop after Sidorówka is **GULBIENISKI**, the point of access for the hill called **Cisowa Góra**. Though known as "The Polish Fujiyama", at 258m it looks more like Glastonbury Tor than a mountain, a comparison which in fact goes beyond superficial resemblance: it was the site of pre-Christian religious rituals, and it's rumoured that rites connected with Perkun, the Lithuanian firegod, are still observed here. Bear in mind that the Lithuanians, who still make up a small percentage of the population of this region, were the last Europeans to be converted to Christianity, in the late fourteenth century. Czesław Miłosz's semi-autobiographical novel *The Issa Valley*, set in neighbouring Lithuania, bears witness to the durability of pre-Christian beliefs right into the present century. Whatever the historical reality of the hill, it's a powerful place.

LAKE HAŃCZA

North of Gulbieniski the road divides: Wiżajny to the left, Rutka Tarta to the right. Continuing along the Wiżajny route the next village is **SMOLNIKI**, just before which there's a wonderful panorama of the surrounding lakes: if you're on the bus ask the driver to let you off at the *punkt wyściowy* (viewpoint). A couple of kilometres west of Smolniki, along a bumpy track through woods, is **Lake Hańcza**, the deepest in Poland at 108m, quiet, clean and unspoilt. The Czarna Hańcza River joins the lake on its southern shore. There's a **youth hostel** on the southeast edge at BŁASKOWIZNA; camping isn't allowed in the Suwałki Park, of which this area is part. To get to the hostel take the Wiżajny bus from Suwałki and get off at BACHANOWO, a kilometre past Turtul Rutka; it's a short walk from here.

The Stańczyki viaduct

If you're travelling by car – getting there by bus would require dedication – the viaduct at **Stańczyki,** west of Lake Hańcza close up by the Russian border on the edge of the Puszcza Romincka, is a must for lovers of the bizarre. (Follow the main route west of Wiżajny, turning left off the road about 4km past Zytkejmy.) The reason for coming is to admire the huge deserted twin **viaduct** straddling the Błędzianka River valley, seemingly lost out in the middle of nowhere. Before World War II this hamlet was right on the East Prussian/Polish border: in 1910 the Germans built a mammoth double viaduct here as part of a new rail line, one side scheduled to carry trains leaving Prussia, the other trains entering the country from Poland. The viaduct was duly completed, the only problem being that the promised railway track never materialised. The crumbling viaducts have stood ever since, a towering monument to an architects' and engineers' folly, no-one apparently having the heart – or cash – to pull them down. These days the viaducts are a favourite Sunday outing with locals. With a bit of effort you can join them climbing up onto the viaducts to savour the view and the madness of the scheme.

From Suwałki to Puńsk and Sejny

Lithuanians are one of Poland's minorities, most of the 40,000-odd community living in a little enclave of towns and villages north and east of Suwałki. The further you go into the countryside the more common it becomes to catch the lilt of their strange-sounding tongue in bars and at bus stops.

The village of **Puńsk**, close to the border, has the highest proportion of Lithuanians in the area and is surrounded by some of the loveliest countryside. There are two ways of covering the 30km from Suwałki. The first is to take the twice-daily **train** to TRAKISZKI (departs at 4.30am and 4.30pm) and walk the last two kilometres. The attraction of this is that the line is still run almost exclusively by old **steam trains**, which enhance the time-slip quality of a journey that takes you through ancient meadows – their hedgerows a brilliant mass of flora – and fields tilled by horse-drawn ploughs. Keep your passport handy as the border police are sometimes in Trakiszki to check what you're up to. If you feel like a swim first, **Lake Sejwy**, 3km down the road, is an excellent spot. To get there, follow the path parallel to the railway, turn right where the path forks and left by the first field. The other option is to travel by **bus**, changing at SZYPLISZKI. The bar opposite Szypliszki's bus stop serves a decent local beer, or if you fancy a more salubrious pastime you could walk the couple of kilometres west through the fields to **Lake Szelment**, another untouched corner of the region.

PUŃSK

Tucked away a few kilometres from the Lithuanian border, **PUŃSK** used to be sunk in complete obscurity, but since 1989 has been the object of unprecedented attention. The reason is the village's **Lithuanians** – some seventy percent of the population – who, despite their small numbers, maintain a Lithuanian cultural centre, choir and weekly newspaper, giving the place a decidedly un-Polish feel. In the summer of 1989 Lithuanian flags and the symbol of Sajudis (the Lithuanian Popular Front) became common sights here, and when the Soviet blockade of Lithuania began in March 1990, the response in Puńsk was immediate: it became the collection point for supplies to Lithuania from all over Poland, and demonstrations in support of Lithuanian independence were held after mass every Sunday. Now that independence has been achieved, things have quietened down, though locals still gripe at the logistical restraints on crossing the border to visit relatives.

The neo-Gothic **Parish Church** might look nothing special as a building, but turn up on a Sunday at 11am and you'll find the place packed for mass in Lithuanian. If it's a major feast day, you may also see a procession afterwards, for which the women, especially, don the curiously Inca-looking national costume. Enquiries in the bar or shops should track down the old man who set up the local **Lithuanian Museum**, on the edge of the village; it's not yet officially open but if you've got a car, offers of transport will help persuade him to show you round. Inside there's an interesting collection of local ethnography, including some wonderful decorative fabrics and crafts, bizarre-looking farm implements, and prewar Lithuanian books and magazines, as well as maps that illuminate the tangled question of the Polish-Lithuanian border. There's also recent Sajudis material, a section that will doubtless grow over the next few years.

Although there is no regular **accommodation** in the village, Lithuanians are immensely hospitable people, so it's worthwhile asking at the *Rutka* restaurant/bar about the possibility of a bed for the night. The *Rutka* isn't the best you'll ever visit, but a couple of beers into a chat with locals and you'll probably get some insights into local Polish-Lithuanian relations. Despite their support for Lithuanian independence and general lack of enthusiasm for things Polish, most Lithuanians seem content to stay in Poland, at least for the moment. As with other Polish minorities, however, there's a strong desire for more

POLES AND LITHUANIANS

At the moment there's no question that Poland's relations with Lithuania are worse than with any of the other neighbouring countries. Historically speaking on both sides the picture is dominated by the experience of the **Polish-Lithuanian Commonwealth**, where for almost four centuries the two countries were formally united into what was the largest European empire of the time. Here already though, differences began to surface: while Poles tend to view the Commonwealth as the "golden age" of the nation's history, an era characterised by tolerance, cooperation and benign political influence and power, in Lithuania the picture is a little different. As with Poland's other eastern neighbours, the image of Poles as a dominant, imperial big sibling whose ruling aristocratic class built its wealth on harsh exploitation of its vast eastern estates – in Lithuania included – runs deep in the national psyche.

Tensions between the two countries surfaced clearly during the **interwar period**, following Piłsudski's eastern military campaign of 1919-20 against Trotsky's Red Army and the subsequent **annexation of Vilnius** and its surroundings, a region which, despite its predominantly Polish-speaking population, was earmarked for the newly independent Lithuanian state. Antagonism over Vilnius was never really settled, and diplomatic relations – and the border – between the two countries remained severed for most of the 1920s and 1930s. The outbreak of World War II and the wartime traumas suffered by both countries put a lid on mutual Polish-Lithuanian recriminations, though even here Poles have tended to see the Lithuanians as willing collaborators with the Nazis. Lithuania's forced incorporation into the Soviet Union in 1940 and the postwar imposition of communism in Poland enforced a new type of isolation between the two countries, with official Party-based relations about the only sanctioned source of contact right up into the mid-1980s.

The *glasnost* era, the collapse of communist power in Poland and the Lithuanian achievement of independence in 1991 opened the way for a new, and many hoped better, era in relations between the countries. To date, however, the record has not been good. The key source of conflict remains the **national minorities** residing in both countries.

Mostly located in the border area between Sejny and Puńsk, Poland's 40,000-strong **Lithuanian minority** continues to demand better educational and cultural resources for the community, in particular increased provision for native-tongue teachers, books and classes in primary and secondary schools in the region. With the notable exception of the 1989-91 struggle for Lithuanian independence, when local demonstrations in Puńsk were a regular news-feature on Polish TV, the Lithuanian community tends to be a quiet, rather introverted bunch, happy to remain in Poland as long as there's no problem with visiting relatives and maintaining contacts across the border.

Lithuania's **Polish minority** is altogether a different story. Numbering around a quarter of a million, the Poles are a significant national force – some seven percent of the total population, the largest minority grouping after Russians. The majority of them live in the eastern part of the country, in particular in the Vilnius and

cultural rights, including more provision for Lithuanian language-teaching in local schools. It remains to be seen how far overwhelmingly Polish post-communist governments are prepared to go on this issue.

As well as Lithuanians, Puńsk was for centuries home to another minority – Jews. Almost every Jew from this region was either slaughtered or uprooted, but

Salcininkai districts, where they comprise sixty and eighty percent of the populations, respectively. The biggest recent source of controversy has been the Lithuanian authorities' decision to suspend and subsequently dissolve local Polish-controlled government authorities in the Vilnius and Salcininkai districts and to transfer them to Lithuanian administrative control. Prompted by evidence that local Polish officials had actively collaborated with the organisers of the August 1991 Moscow coup attempt led by Gennady Yanayev, the Lithuanian move, officially announced in September 1991, unleashed a torrent of mutual recrimination and caused a significant setback in the (until then) steady development of diplomatic and political relations between the two countries.

Poles both inside and outside Lithuania argue that the main issue is democracy and the defence of minority rights: furious at the local Polish officials' support for their former Soviet oppressors, Lithuanian officials have described external Polish pressure on the issue as direct interference in the country's internal affairs, a throwback to the arrogant imperial habits of the past. At the popular level the row has reinforced the Lithuanian tendency to view Poles as "Fifth Columnists", whose primary loyalty is to the Polish state.

Despite Polish pressure, and only two months after the countries' foreign ministers signed an official friendship declaration, in March 1992 the Lithuanian Supreme Council postponed discussions of new local government elections until the autumn – though by early 1993 these still hadn't happened. New laws making it harder for non-Lithuanian speakers to qualify automatically for Lithuanian citizenship haven't improved the political atmosphere either – many ethnic Poles remain legal "non-citizens", having elected not to apply for Lithuanian nationality under the new rules.

For all the unpleasantness of the current standoff, the situation may not be quite as bad as the details at first suggest: viewed from a broader East European perspective it may be that resurfacing of long-buried ethnic tensions and rivalries is an almost unavoidable element of the transition to democratic rule, a transition in which minorities become a symbolic focal-point for other anxieties and tensions. Faced with the reality of Lithuanian independence the country's Polish population, like its Russian counterpart, is fearful for its own identity: the often hysterical reaction of organisations such as the Lithuanian Union of Poles, the main community body, suggests it isn't finding this easy.

Worrying though the situation still is, compared to other current regional ethnic tensions and conflicts – the Balts' "Russian question" included – ultimately the current Polish-Lithuanian impasse still seems a fairly tame affair: on both sides, too, there's a significant body of opinion, politicians included, that genuinely wants to solve the problem on a mutually agreed basis and build better relations rather than simply fan the flames of nationalist recrimination. As so often, the success or failure of the enterprise depends on the ability to overcome, or at least sidestep, historical prejudices and suspicions and get down to the business of developing sane, tolerant relations with each other. On the practical level, an agreement on finally opening a couple more border crossings – a victim of the current difficulties – wouldn't be a bad first step.

a few signs of the past – predictably ignored in the official Polish guides and maps – are still left. The *Dom Handlowy* on the main street in Puńsk used to be the rabbi's house, and the older locals can point you in the direction of the abandoned **Jewish cemetery**, on the northern edge of the village, where a few Hebrew inscriptions are still visible among the grass and trees.

SEJNY

Instead of returning directly to Suwałki, you might try the bus trip via the market town of **SEJNY**, 25km south of Puńsk, a cross-country journey that's a treat in itself. Sejny is dominated by a Dominican **monastery complex** at the top of the town, which contains a grandiose late-Renaissance church refurbished in Rococo style in the mid-eighteenth century. The surrounding monastic buildings are currently under restoration, and likely to remain so for some time.

The main square just down the main street now hosts a regular **bazaar**, with Lithuanian traders from across the border much in evidence – the locals don't like it much, and the atmosphere can get a little tense for comfort. At the other end of town is the former **synagogue**, its size indicating that the Jewish population here used to be quite large. Carefully restored, it's now a **museum** and cultural centre (Mon–Fri 10.30am–4.30pm). If your Polish is up to it, the curator can fill you in on local history, particularly the Lithuanian, Jewish and Old Believer minorities.

ON TO LITHUANIA

With cross-border **travel between Poland and Lithuania** easier than at any time in the postwar period – though still complicated by continuing tensions between the two countries – a trip over the border to the Lithuanian capital, Vilnius, is now a genuinely feasible option.

Situated around 160km east of Suwałki, along with Ukrainian L'viv **VILNIUS** (in Polish, Wilno) is *the* great former Polish city of the east – not a point to emphasise when you're there, incidentally – with a large old town complex that despite post-war neglect still ranks among the finest in Europe. Anyone expecting an orderly Protestant Hansa-town on the lines of Baltic neighbours Riga, Tallinn or even Helsinki, though, will be disappointed. Vilnius is unmistakably Catholic – and Polish – in feel and atmosphere, a jumbled mix of cobbled alleyways, high spires, Catholic shrines, *cerkwi* and old Jewish monuments. Largely unscarred by the Second World War, Vilnius's best-known monuments include the **Ostra Brama gate**, a street gallery shrine housing Eastern Catholicism's most venerated icon of the Madonna, and the fabulous **St Anne's church**, an extraordinarily exuberant Gothic masterpiece which Napoleon is supposed to have contemplated dismantling and moving to Paris.

The city's **tourist infrastructure** still has some way to go: decent restaurants are thin on the ground and accommodation is an unpredictable business. *Vilnius in Your Pocket*, available from hotels, kiosks and bookshops, provides you with all the basic tourist information. Lithuanians are a friendly and hospitable lot on the whole, and anyone tempted by the prospect of making the journey east will find it's well worth the effort.

PRACTICALITIES

British, Irish and Danish citizens excepted, foreign nationals need a **visa** to enter the country: technically valid for all three Baltic republics, in theory at least visas are obtainable at the Lithuanian border, though it's probably better to secure your visa in advance, either at Lithuanian (as well as Latvian and Estonian) embassies and consulates established in several countries, including the USA, Britain, Germany, France, Belgium, Sweden, Canada, Australia and Norway, or at the Lithuanian embassy in Warsaw, al. Ujazdowskie 13-12 (☎694-2487).

Every April the synagogue plays host to an **international culture festival**, organised by the local *Funacja Podgranicze* ("The Borderland Foundation") and dedicated to promoting the culture, music and art between what it calls "the borderland nations". Now in its third year, the festival attracts an increasing range of theatre groups, artists and musicians from all over Europe, though the emphasis remains on "local" cross-border groups – Lithuanians, BelArussians, Ukranians and Russians. For details of the festival and the foundation's other activities, contact the office at ul. J. Piłsudskiego 37, 16500 Sejny (☎189/200).

Despite signs in the town centre, the information office does not exist any more, while the only chance of a room is at the **restaurant** *Na Skarpie* at ul. 1 Maja 15 (☎65), the main street, or at the summer **youth hostel** on the outskirts at ul. Łąkowa. Don't be surprised, incidentally, to see Russian and Lithuanian registration cars and trucks rumbling through Sejny. OGRODNIKI, the only border crossing into Lithuania, is just 20km to the east.

There are several options for **travel** to Vilnius. *Car* is definitely the slowest: at the time of writing there's still only one official border-crossing point, at **Ogrodniki-Lazdijai**, east of Sejny. Stuck out in the middle of nowhere with no facilities to speak of, the tiny crossing point is completely inadequate to the task, and the tailbacks on both sides of the frontier mean you can expect a long wait, particularly in summer when a couple of days' queuing is not unknown. On the Lithuanian side at least, dollar bribes are reported to be common. There's now a daily early-morning *train* (6.50am) from Suwałki to Sestokai, just over the border, with a connecting service on to Vilnius. Since tickets are still handwritten at the station on the Lithuanian side you'll probably have to buy one from the conductor, who'll charge you £2 for the privilege.

As well as the local service, a daily train runs from Warsaw to Vilnius travelling via Belarus, with transit visas (£10) supposedly now available on the spot. Especially at weekends these trains are often full to the brim with local day-trippers plus the usual consignment of "trade tourists", so be prepared to share your corridor space with the odd TV or computer.

As with other cross-border journeys east, going by *bus* is currently the best option: the special priority accorded **PKS buses** at the border means you're through the queues and document formalities fairly speedily. Journey time from Suwałki to Vilnius is around three hours: in addition buses run from Gdańsk (8hrs), Olsztyn (6hrs) and Warsaw (9hrs). Again the demand, particularly in summer, is high, so advance purchase of tickets from the Suwałki bus station is strongly advisable. If you're returning to Poland by bus, the journey back is with one of the privately run **minibus services** operating from the Vilnius bus station. The drivers *only* accept payment in US dollars – for once even Deutschmarks won't do the trick – so make sure you bring some with you; otherwise you'll be forced into last-minute street trading. At around £5 to Suwałki, the current price, for Westerners at least, is pretty reasonable.

The final option is by *plane*. A local company now operates daily flights from Suwałki to Vilnius: departure is at around 8am, with a return plane in the evening, making the notion of a day trip to Vilnius a feasible, if expensive, theoretical option. Cost for the return trip is currently around £60. For details ask at the Suwałki tourist office or phone the airport, actually the local aviation club south-west of town, *Aeroklub Suwalski*, at ul. Wojczyńskiego (☎52-79).

BIAŁYSTOK AND THE BELARUSSIAN BORDERLANDS

As you head south from the lakes or east from Warsaw, you find yourself in a region of complex ethnicity, situated right up against the borders of Belarus. The Poles call the area **Podlasie** – literally "Under the Trees" – which gives little hint of its landscape of wide, open plains, tracts of primaeval forest, and dark skies. Even without the increasing presence of onion-domed Orthodox churches, it would feel eastern, more like Russia than Poland. The whole area also feels extremely poor, and is one of the most neglected regions of the country, with an overwhelmingly peasant population. On the long potholed country roads you see as many horsecarts as cars, in the fields as many horse-drawn ploughs as tractors. In the **Białowieża Forest** the isolation has ensured the survival of continental Europe's last belt of virgin forest – the haunt of bison, elk and hundreds of varieties of flora and fauna, and home, too, of the wondrous *Zybrówka* "bison grass" vodka.

Belarussians are the principal ethnic minority, numbering some 200,000 in all. Before the war, Polish territory stretched far across the current Belarussian border, and today communities on either side are scarcely distinguishable, save that those on the eastern side are, if anything, poorer still. Another historic, but declining, minority are the **Tartars**, who settled here centuries ago and whose wooden mosques at **Bohoniki** and **Kruszyniamy** are one of the sights of the Polish east. (There are several more over the border.) Long a melting-pot of cultures, Białystok and the surrounding region were also one of the main areas of **Jewish settlement** in Poland. Before the war almost every town in the region boasted at least one synagogue, often more: many of these were wooden structures, whose exuberant design clearly reflected the influence of the indigenous folk architecture. Sadly almost all the wooden synagogues – pictures suggest many of them were spectacular – were burned down by the Nazis. A wealth of brick and stone **Jewish monuments** survive, though, and on any journey through the outlying towns and villages, you'll encounter former synagogue buildings and crumbling Jewish cemeteries. Of these the restored synagogue complex at **Tykocin** is one of the most evocative Jewish monuments in the country – as in the rest of the region, the community itself was wiped out by the Nazis.

Once again, local **transport** consists mainly of buses, with services diminishing the nearer the border you get.

Białystok

Even the habitually enthusiastic official Polish guidebooks are mute on the glories of **BIAŁYSTOK**, industrial centre of northeast Poland; it's not a beautiful place and its main development occurred during the industrialisation of the nineteenth century. Unique among major Polish cities today, however, it has kept the healthy ethnic and religious mix – Poles, Belarussians and Ukrainians, Catholic and Orthodox – characteristic of the country before the war, though the Jews, of course, are absent. And for all the industry, it's one of the country's least polluted cities.

Some history

According to legend, Białystok was founded in 1320 by Gedymin, the Grand Duke of Lithuania, but its emergence really began in the 1740s when local aristocrat Jan Branicki built a palace in the town centre. Partitioned off to Prussia and then to Russia, Białystok rapidly developed as a textile city, in competition with Prussian-dominated Łódź. In both cities industrialisation fostered the growth of a sizeable urban proletariat and a large and influential Jewish community. Factory strikes in the 1880s demonstrated the potency of working-class protest, as did the anti-czarist demonstrations which broke out here in 1905. Echoing protests in other parts of the Russian empire, they elicited a similar response – an officially instigated pogrom, during which many Białystok Jews lost their lives. Fifteen years later, anticipating a victory that never came against Piłsudski's apparently demoralised forces, Lenin's troops installed a provisional government in Białystok led by Felix Dzierżyński, the notorious Polish commander of the secret police.

World War II brought destruction and slaughter to Białystok. Hitler seized the town in 1939, then handed it over to Stalin before reoccupying it in 1941 – which is when the Jewish population was herded into a ghetto area and deported to the death camps. The heroic Białystok **ghetto uprising** of August 1943 – the first within the Reich – presaged the extinction of the city's Jewry. Nor was the killing confined to Jews. By 1945, over half the city's population were dead, with three-quarters of the town centre destroyed.

Following the end of the war, the authorities set about rebuilding the town and its industrial base. From a strictly utilitarian point of view they succeeded: Białystok is a developed economic centre for textiles, metals and timber, with a population of over 250,000. The aesthetic cost has been high, though – the usual billowing smokestacks, ugly tower blocks and faceless open streets of postwar development. But Białystok has its share of historic sights – mostly associated with its Orthodox Belarussian community – and it makes an ideal base for exploring the border region to the east.

The Town

Białystok's historic centrepoint is the **Rynek**, an unusual triangular-shaped space with a large Baroque town hall in the middle. The main sights are situated on and around ul. Lipowa, the main thoroughfare cutting from east to west across the city centre. The church of **St Nicholas** here was built in the 1840s to serve the swelling ranks of Russian settlers. A typically dark, icon-filled place of Orthodox devotion, its ornate frescoes are careful copies of those in the Orthodox cathedral in Kiev. It is filled to capacity for the Sunday services – worth coinciding with to hear the choir. Further down ul. Lipowa the **Orthodox cemetery** contains another enchanting *cerkiew* – though your only chance of getting in to look around is during the Sunday morning service.

Catholic competition comes from the huge **Parish Church** nearby and the imposing 1920s **St Roch**, at the western end of the street. With its high space-ship-like towers, the parish church is something of a historical curio: next to it is a small seventeenth-century parish church built by the Branicki family, while the main structure is a vast 1900 neo-Gothic building, almost twenty times the size and only permitted by the czarist authorities because its official request billed it as an "addition". The streets south of ul. Lipowa comprise part of the old **ghetto area**. A tablet in Polish and Hebrew on the side of a building opposite the local court house on ul. Suraska commemorates the 1000 Jews burned to death in June

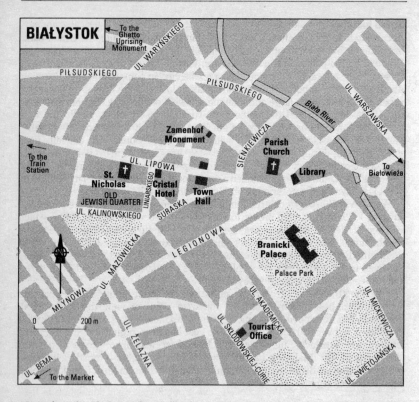

1941 when the Nazis set fire to the **Great Synagogue**, reputedly one of the finest in Poland, which used to stand on this site.

For a town whose population was roughly 70 percent Jewish at the turn of the century there are precious few other Jewish monuments left. Though you'd hardly guess so from today's uniform blocks, the streets leading north of ul. Lipowa were all mainly Jewish-inhabited before the war. Across the road from the town hall in the leafy little park on the edge of ul. Malmeda a **statue** commemorates the town's most famous Jewish citizen, **Ludwik Zamenhof,** the founder of Esperanto (see p.221). Continuing northwest over busy ul. Piłsudskiego and through streets of high concrete blocks brings you to another park, off ul. Zabia. Seemingly in the middle of nowhere, a **monument to the Białystok Ghetto Uprising** (August 16, 1943) recalls an important moment in the wartime history of the town. As with many Jewish war monuments in Poland, it's easy to miss – there's no sign and the place isn't even named on the city map – but the older local inhabitants usually know where to point you if you ask.

The most striking building in the town centre is the **Branicki Palace**, destroyed by the Nazis in 1944 but rebuilt on the lines of the eighteenth-century building commissioned by Jan Branicki – itself a reconstruction of an earlier palace. It's difficult to get inside, as the main building is now a medical academy, but you can stroll unhindered through the park and admire its classical grandeur from a distance. Look out, too, for the main front balcony, the so-called **Dzierżyński Balcony**, from which Felix Dzierzyński and associates proclaimed the creation of the Polish Soviet Socialist Republic in 1920.

Despite the heavy wartime destruction a number of characteristic examples of the regional **wooden architecture** have survived in parts of the city, most notably in the houses along streets like ul. Grunwaldzka, Żelazna and Mazowiecka down from the railway station in the southern section of the centre.

Stranded on a small island at the eastern end of ul. Lipowa the **Town Hall**, a small, squat eighteenth-century building, was reconstructed from scratch after the war: these days it houses a local **art museum** (Tues–Sun 10am–5pm). A good selection of works by some of the better-known nineteenth- and twentieth-century artists – Malczewski, Witkiewicz, Krzyzanowski and the like – is complemented by an enjoyable collection of local art, the portraits and landscapes displaying a strong feeling for the distinctive character of the region. In addition, the museum has regular temporary thematic exhibitions of works culled from other national museums, the imagination with which they're presented suggesting a serious attempt to get on the national art map.

Białystok's proximity to the Belarussian border ensures it a key place among the growing number of Polish towns heavily involved in "trade tourism". On Sunday mornings the open-air **market** – strategically located by the police station on ul. Bem – is thronged with Belarussians, Ukrainians and others from across the border plying a strange assortment of consumer goods: gold, clothes, hi-fis, antiques, cosmetics, anything that Poles are prepared to buy. If you want **caviar**, this is the place to buy it, as the nearer the border you get, the lower the price: Gdańsk is fifty percent higher, Warsaw seventy-five. Pay in dollars only if you have to, be prepared to haggle, buy glass containers (not metal), and bear in mind that taking caviar out of Poland is illegal. Keep in mind, too, that the crowds are a haven for pickpockets.

Perhaps the saddest reminder of the city's onetime Jewish population is the **Jewish cemetery**, off ul. Wschodnia on the northeast edge of the city. Starting from Rynek Kościuszki in the centre of town bus #3 drops you close by just west of the cemetery – get off at the junction of ul. Władysława Wysockiego and ul. Władysława Raginisa, a 10–15-minute journey. With Catholic cemeteries on both sides, an Orthodox church under construction at the back, and children playing along the walls, the large and badly neglected cemetery looks and feels a beleaguered place. The few surviving gravestones are scattered around in the undergrowth, some of them still legible, but if things carry on this way there may not be any left in the not-too-distant future.

Practicalities

The main **train station**, a dingy pink building that wouldn't look out of place in Moscow, is a five-minute bus ride (#2, #4 or #21) west of the city centre – supposedly it was built outside the centre as a punishment for anti-czarist protests in the city. Close by, on ul. Bohaterów Monte Cassino, is the **bus station**. Irritatingly, the **tourist information office** (8am–5pm) is well south of the town centre at the bottom of an apartment block at ul. Skłtodowskiej 13: if you get there, it has a plentiful supply of maps and brochures and can make useful suggestions about places to stay. **Almatur**, at ul. Zwierzyniecka 12 (☎220-41 ext. 153) on the southern side of the centre (bus #10 from the rail station), runs a lot of youth and student camps in the area, as well as arranging boat and canoe hire. They may also be able to tell you the current whereabouts of **student hotels** (open June–Aug), whose venues change year by year.

Of the **hotels**, most handy is the *Cristal*, ul. Lipowa 3/5 (☎250-61), a serviceable place popular with visiting Russians that's bang in the town centre. Other options are the *Turkus*, ul. Zwycięstwa 54 (☎511-211), west of the train station, the *Leśny*, ul. Zwycięstwa 77 (☎511-641), considerably further west along the same road, the main route to Warsaw, and the *Zwierzyniec*, ul. 11 Listopada 28 (☎226-29), a cheaper, lower-quality alternative. The **youth hostel**, al. Piłsudskiego 7b (☎524-250), is not far east of the rail station, while campers should head for the *Gromada* site next to the *Leśny* hotel.

All the main hotels have **restaurants**, of which the *Cristal* and *Leśny* are the more enticing. The *Grodno* at ul. Sienkiewicza 28 offers its version of Belarussian cuisine, while the *Kaunas*, ul. Wesola 18, has Lithuanian specialities like *chłodnik*. Other reasonable options are the *Karczma Słupska* on ul. św. Rocha 29, *Hubertówka* at ul. Broniewskiego 28, the *Astoria*, ul. Sienkiewicza 4 and the *Avanti* next door, a self-styled Italian joint. A number of new bars are scattered along ul. Lipowa, each serving bottled German beers. For local **nightlife** try *Casablanca*, Św. Rocha 15, a popular music club that's open late and features local blues bands.

Around Białystok

With time on your hands a handful of trips in the city's immediate surroundings are worth considering, notably the fine icon museum in **Supraśl**, north of the city, the Branicki palace at **Choroszcz** and the synagogue of **Tykocin**. The city surroundings offer some decent walking country too, chiefly the tranquil **Puszcza Knyszyńska** stretching east of the town, a popular weekend haunt with city folk. All of these are accessible using local bus connections.

Supraśl

A sixteen-kilometre bus journey northeast of Białystok is **SUPRAŚL**, a sleepy provincial eastern hang-out on the edge of the Puszcza Knyszyńska. The chief attraction here is the **Bishop's Palace**, a grand, crumbling seventeenth-century structure now used as a school. Slap in the middle of the palace courtyard is a large early sixteenth-century brick Orthodox *cerkiew*, built by Grand Hetman of Lithuania Aleksander Chodkiewicz for the Orthodox order of St Basil, which became one of the spiritual centres of Orthodoxy in the Polish-Lithuanian Commonwealth. Said to have boasted a fine interior combining Gothic and Byzantine styles – the Nazis mauled the place during the war – the whole building is currently being completely renovated.

Improbably for such an out-of-the-way place, the former palace chapel contains a small but stunning **Orthodox museum** (theoretically, Tues–Sun 10am–4pm though the lone caretaker has a habit of taking off an hour or so earlier), housing some of the original frescoes and icons taken from the main *cerkiew*.

The works gathered here encompass a range of themes and images: scenes from the lives of Mary and Jesus, benign-looking early church fathers and saints, ethereal archangels and cherubim, a wonderful panorama of Orthodox art and

LUDWIK ZAMENHOF AND THE ESPERANTO MOVEMENT

Białystok's most famous son is probably **Ludwik Zamenhof** (1859–1917), the creator of Esperanto, the artificial language invented as an instrument of international communication. Born in what was then a colonial outpost of the czarist empire, Zamenhof grew up in an environment coloured by the continuing struggle between the indigenous Polish population and its Russian rulers – both of whom were apt to turn on the Jews as and when the occasion suited them.

Perhaps because of this experience, from an early stage Zamenhof, an eye doctor by training, dedicated himself to the cause of racial tolerance and understanding. Zamenhof's attention focused on the fruits of the mythical Tower of Babel, the profusion of human languages: if a new, easily learnable international language could be devised it would, he believed, remove a key obstacle not only to people's ability to communicate directly with each other, but also to their ability to live together peacably. On the basis of extensive studies of the major Western classical and modern languages, Zamenhof – Doktoro Esperanto or "Doctor Hopeful" as he came to be known – set himself the task of inventing just such a language, the key source being root words common to European, and in particular Romance, languages.

The first primer, *Dr. Esperanto's International Language,* was published in 1887, but Zamenhof continued to develop his language by translating a whole range of major literary works, *Hamlet,* Goethe and Molière's plays and the entire Old Testament included. The new language rapidly gained international attention, and the first world Esperanto congress was held in France in 1905. In the same year Zamenhof completed *Fundamento de Esperanto* (1905), his main work, which soon became the basic Esperanto textbook and the one still most commonly in use today.

Even if it has never quite realised Zamenhof's dreams of universal acceptance, Esperanto – *Lingvo Internacia* as it calls itself – has proved considerably more successful than any other "invented" language. With a worldwide membership of over 100,000 and national associations in around 50 countries, the *Universala Esperanto Associo* represents a significant international movement of people attracted to the universalist ideals as much as the linguistic practice of Esperanto. In Białystok itself there's a thriving Esperanto-speaking community that welcomes visitors at its main office at ul. Lipowa 14 (regular office hours).

spirituality and one in which, particularly in the frescoes, the art historians detect a strong Serbian Orthodox influence.

The Puszcza Knyszyńska

If you've come by bus from Białystok you could consider hiking back through the **Puszcza Knyszyńska,** a popular walking area with Białystok residents. The sandy local terrain is pretty easy-going underfoot, but the lack of signs once you get into the forest makes a local map, e.g. *Okolice Białegostoku* 1: 150,000, readily available in Białystok, essential.

On a good day it's attractive and enjoyable walking country, the silence of the forest broken at intervals by cackling crows overhead or startled deer breaking for cover. Starting from the southern edge of Supraśl, a marked path takes you south through the lofty expanses of forest to the village of CIASNE, ending up by the bus stop near GRABÓWKA at the edge of the main road back in to Białystok – a twelve-kilometre hike in total.

Choroszcz

The highways and byways of eastern Poland hide a wealth of neglected old aristocratic piles, most of them relics of a not-so-distant period when a small group of fabulously wealthy families owned most of the eastern part of the country.

The eighteenth-century **Branicki summer palace** at **CHOROSZCZ,** located 10km west of Białystok off the main Warsaw road, is a fine example of this phenomenon, the key difference being that the palace here has been completely renovated and converted into a **museum** (Tues–Sun 10am–3pm). To **get here,** catch a local bus from Białystok; the palace is just a short walk from the main stop.

The Palace

From Białystok, you'll find that the elegant statue-topped palace facade makes quite a contrast from the architectural rigours of the city, with the tranquil country location on the edge of the grounds of the local hospital another agreeable feature. Few of the building's original furnishings remain, most of them having been replaced by period replicas of the kind of things the Branickis are supposed to have liked. The main ground-floor room is the **salon**, its sedate parquet floor complemented by a choice collection of period furniture. Along with a number of family portraits, one of the original master of the house, Jan Branicki, hangs in the hallway, the finely wrought iron balustrades of the staircase illuminated by a lamp held aloft by a rather tortured-looking classical figure. The **second floor** is equally ornate, featuring a number of meticulously decorated apartment rooms, a dining room with a fine set of mid-eighteenth-century Meissen porcelain and a **Chippendale room**. Back out of the building it's worth taking a stroll along the canal running from beneath the salon windows at the back of the palace, the overgrown palace grounds stretching out in all directions. From the bridge over the canal you have a good view of the whole feudal-like palace ensemble, the old lodge house and manor farm included.

Tykocin

Forty kilometres west of Białystok, north of the main Warsaw road (E18), is the quaint, sleepy little town of **TYKOCIN**, set in the open vistas of the Podlasie countryside. Tykocin's size belies its historical significance. As well as the former site of the national arsenal, it also has one of the best-restored **synagogues** in Poland today, a reminder that this was once home to an important Jewish community. It's a one-hour journey from the main bus station in Białystok; buses leave regularly throughout the day.

The Town

The bus deposits you in the enchanting **town square**, bordered on several of its sides by well-preserved nineteenth-century wooden houses. The **statue** of Stefan Czarnecki in the centre of the square was put up by his grandson Jan Branicki in 1770, while Branicki was busy rebuilding this town and his adopted home of Białystok.

The Baroque **Parish Church**, commissioned by the energetic Branicki in 1741 and recently restored, has a beautiful polychrome ceiling, a finely ornamented side chapel of the Virgin and a functioning Baroque organ. The portraits of Branicki and his wife Izabella Poniatowska are by Silvester de Mirys, a Scot who became the resident artist at the Branicki palace in Białystok. Also founded by Branicki was the nearby **Bernardine Convent**, now a Catholic seminary. Next to the church looking on to the river bridge is the **Alumnat**, a hospice for war veterans founded in 1633 – a world first. Continue out of town over the River Narew and you'll come to the ruins of the sixteenth-century **Radziwiłł Palace**, where the national arsenal was once kept; it was destroyed by the Swedes in 1657.

POLES AND BELARUSSIANS

Poles and Belarussians have a long history of living together but also one of long-suppressed cultural and political antagonisms, which have recently begun to surface. In the communist era, minorities were actively recruited into the party and state security apparatus, and their religion given active state backing – so long as the community kept its separatist or nationalist impulses in check. Use of the Belarussian language was forbidden in public, and there were no concessions to the culture in schools or cultural institutions. Despite this, a handful of Belarussian *samizdat* publications circulated during the communist years.

The result of these years of active state co-option, inevitably, was to reinforce Catholic Polish suspicion of their neighbours, which, with the state controls off, is surfacing in occasional bouts of openly expressed hostility. Meanwhile, for Belarussians, the new Polish political climate and freedoms, the disintegration of the Soviet empire and ever-burgeoning Polish nationalism have reawakened their own search for a meaningful national identity. In Białystok, nationalist Belarussian candidates ran against Solidarity in the 1989 elections, and the community is taking steps to re-establish its language and culture.

The radical changes of the early 1990s – most importantly, of course, the emergence of Belarus as an independent state – added a whole new dimension to the situation faced by the Polish Belarussian community. The cautious line previously adopted by many community leaders has given way to a much more self-confident, assertive attitude. Cultural, political and religious associations are flourishing, Belarussian newspapers, magazines and books are published in abundance, while the local radio station recently established in central Białystok with Orthodox church backing has finally given Belarussians their own independent access to the media. Belarussians are also part of the joint working group established in 1992 under the auspices of the Polish Helsinki Committee by representatives of the various ethnic minority groups to defend and extend the rights of all minorities in the country. Inevitably, a key concern for the Belarussians is the question of cross-border ties with the Belarus "homeland" itself.

Occasional difficulties over Belarussian claims that Białystok and its surroundings should really belong to them aside, official relations between Poland and Belarus seem to have been progressing reasonably smoothly since the signing of an economic and trade agreement in October 1991, with additional wide-ranging trade agreements and a number of new border- crossing points reportedly in the pipeline.

As in other borderlands, domestically the underlying issue here is whether the post-communist government policy on minorities will go further than declarations and lead to active support for their development.

Jews first came to Tykocin in 1522, and by the early nineteenth century seventy percent of the population was Jewish, the figure declining to around fifty percent by 1900. The original wooden **synagogue** in the town centre was replaced in 1642 by the Baroque building still standing today. Carefully restored in the 1970s, it now houses an excellent **Jewish museum** (Tues–Sun 10am–5pm), where background recordings of Jewish music and prayers add to a mournfully evocative atmosphere.

Information sheets in English and German give detailed background on both the building and the history of Tykocin Jewry. Beautifully illustrated Hebrew inscriptions adorn parts of the interior walls, but most striking of all is the Baroque bima, the four-pillared central podium from which the cantor led the services. Valuable religious artefacts are on display, as well as historical documents relating to the now-lost community. Over the square in the old **Talmud house** there's a well-kept **local history museum**, featuring an intact apothecary's shop.

Practicalities

The only **restaurant** in town, the *Narnianka*, just off the square on ul. Bernardyńska, is pretty squalid: wait to get back to Białystok before eating unless you're starving. The **PTTK hostel** is closed at the moment, so the only official accommodation is a **youth hostel** on ul. Kochanowskiego (June & July; ☎136-85).

Kruszyniamy and Bohoniki

Hard up near the Belarussian frontier, the old Tartar villages of **Kruszyniamy** and **Bohoniki** are an intriguing ethnic component of Poland's eastern borderlands, with their wooden mosques and Muslim graveyards. The story of how these people came to be here is fascinating in itself (see box opposite), and a visit to the villages is an instructive and impressive experience.

Getting to them is no mean feat. Direct **buses to Kruszyniamy** from Białystok are scarce: the alternative is to take the bus to KRYNKI (about 40km) and wait for a connection to Kruszyniamy. If there aren't any of these, the only thing left to do is hitch. The only **buses to Bohoniki** are from SOKOŁKA, an hour's train journey north of Białystok. If you're trying to visit both villages in the same day, the best advice is to go to Kruszyniamy first, return to Krynki (probably by hitching) then take a bus towards Sokołka. Ask the driver to let you off at STARA KAMIONKA, and walk the remaining 4km eastwards along the final stretch of the "Tartar Way" (*Szlak Tartarski Duży*), which runs between the two villages. To get back to Białystok, take the late afternoon bus to Sokołka, then a train back to the city.

The Villages

Walking through **KRUSZYNIAMY** is like moving back a century or two: the painted wooden houses, cobbled road and wizened old peasants staring at you from their front porches are like something out of Tolstoy. Surrounded by trees and set back from the road is the eighteenth-century **mosque**, recognisable by the Islamic crescent hanging over the entrance gate. Despite initial protests and

THE TARTARS

Early in the thirteenth century, the nomadic Mongol people of central Asia were welded into a confederation of tribes under the rule of Genghis Khan. In 1241 the most ferocious of these tribes, the **Tartars**, came charging out of the steppes and divided into two armies, one of which swept towards Poland, the other through Hungary. Lightly armoured, these natural horsemen moved with a speed that no European soldiery could match, and fought in a fashion as savage as the diet that sustained them – raw meat and horse's milk mixed with blood. On Easter Day they destroyed Kraków, and in April came up against the forces of the Silesian ruler Duke Henryk the Pious at Legnica. Henryk's troops were annihilated, and a contemporary journal records that "terror and doubt took hold of every mind" throughout the Christian west. Before the eventual withdrawal of the Tartar hordes, all of southern Poland was ravaged repeatedly – Kraków, for example, was devastated in 1259 and again in 1287.

By the fourteenth century, however, the greatest threat to Poland was presented by the Teutonic Knights (see "Malbork", p.155), and the participation of a contingent of Tartars in the Polish defeat of the Knights at Grunwald in 1410 signalled a new kind of connection. Communities of Tartars were now living close to the borders of the country (the Cossacks, for instance, were an offshoot of a Tartar tribe) and were steadily encroaching westward. It was in the late seventeenth century that Poland received its first peaceable Tartar settlers, when King Jan Sobieski granted land in eastern Poland to those who had taken part in his military campaigns.

Today some 6000 descendants of these first Muslim citizens of Poland are spread all over the country, particularly the Szczecin, Gdańsk and Białystok areas. Though thoroughly integrated into Polish society, they are distinctive both for their Asiatic appearance and their faith – the Tartars of Gdańsk, for example, have just completed a mosque. Apart from the mosques and graveyards at Bohoniki and Kruszyniamy, little is left of the old settlements in the region east of Białystok, but there are a number of mosques still standing over the border in Belarus.

general grumpiness, the caretaker will let you in if you're properly dressed, which means no bare legs or revealing tops. Though the Tartar population is dwindling, the mosque's predominantly wooden interior is well maintained – a glance at the list of Arab diplomats in the visitor's book explains where the money comes from, and the imam won't refuse a donation from you either.

The mosque in remoter **BOHONIKI** is a similar building, looked after by a woman who is a direct descendant of the settlers who established themselves here in 1697. She lives at no. 26 (there's only one road), and she or one of her family will open up the mosque, and the village *ruch* if you want postcards.

In the **Tartar cemetery**, hidden in a copse half a kilometre south of the village, gravestones are inscribed in both Polish and Arabic with characteristic Tartar names like Ibrahimowicz and Bohdanowicz – in other words, Muslim names with a Polish ending tacked on. Search through the undergrowth right at the back of the cemetery and you'll find older, tumbled-down gravestones inscribed in Russian, from the days when Bohoniki was an outpost of the czarist empire. Tartars from all over Poland are still buried here, as they have been since Sobieski's time.

South from Białystok

Moving south of Białystok you're soon into the villages and fields of **Podlasie**, the heartland of the country's Belarussian population – you'll see the Cyrillic figures of their language on posters (though not as yet on street signs) throughout the area.

It is a poor, predominantly rural region that retains a distinctively Eastern feel, and for visitors the best-known attraction is the ancient **Białowieża Forest** straddling the border with neighbouring Belarus. **Bielsk Podlaski**, the regional capital, and **Siemiatycze** are both worth investigating, the latter being near the extraordinary convent at **Grabarka**, focal point of Orthodox pilgrimage in Poland.

The Białowieża Forest

For a country with a reputation as an environmental disaster zone, Poland has an amazing number of beauty spots. One hundred kilometres southeast of Białystok is one of the best-known of these, the **Białowieża Forest** (Puszcza Białowieska). Covering 312,000 acres and spreading way over the border into Belarus, Białowieża is the last primaeval forest in Europe, but its fame and popularity rest as much on the forest's large population of **European bison** as on its antiquity and beauty.

For centuries Białowieża was a private hunting ground for a succession of Lithuanian and Belarussian princes, Polish kings, Russian czars and other potentates – patronage which ensured the forest survived largely intact. Recognising its environmental importance, the Polish government turned large sections of the *puszcza* into a national park in the 1920s, not least to protect its bison herds, which had been eaten almost to extinction by famished soldiers during World War I. Like most *puszcza*, Białowieża has hidden its fair share of partisan armies, most notably during the 1863 Uprising and World War II: monuments scatter the area, as no doubt do the bones of countless unknown dead.

A large section of forest on the Polish side of the border is now a strictly controlled reserve, but the rest is open for **guided visits**. The unique atmosphere of the place makes even a day trip an experience not to be missed.

Getting there

Białowieża is a bus journey of a couple of hours from Białystok; for a day trip there and back, take the 6.30am bus – and in summer, get there early, as tickets sell out quickly. (There are trains too, but they involve changes at BIELSK PODLASKI and HAJNÓWKA and take much longer.) On the way through the flat, wooded greenery of the Podlasie countryside you'll probably see more Orthodox onion domes than Catholic spires; the spanking new *cerkiew* in Hajnówka, the last town before the forest area, is a spiritual centre of the Belarussian revival; there's also a small museum devoted to local Belarussian culture in the village.

Białowieża village and the forest

From Hajnówka the forest road runs straight for 20km through the forest to the village of **BIAŁOWIEŻA**, a mere 2km from the border. The bus stops at the gates of the **Palace Park**, opposite a typical late nineteenth-century *cerkiew*, with a unique tiled iconostasis. Inside the park, the Białowieża **museum** (Tues–Sun

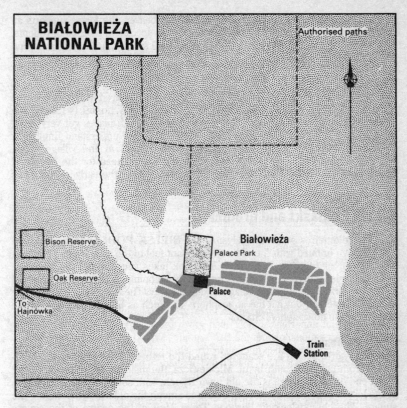

8am–4pm) provides a detailed introduction to the natural history of the forest, including examples of the amazingly diverse flora and fauna.

Access to the forest itself is controlled: unless you want to negotiate for a private guide to take you into the forest reserve, the only way in is to charter a horse-drawn cart from the nearby tourist office. Prices are reasonable, but you may have to wait some time if there are a lot of people around – a good argument for getting there early. The two- to three-hour cart tour takes you along the forest paths to the **bison reserve** (open all year), a few kilometres from the village, where some of the forest's 250 specimens can be seen lounging around – the rest are out in the wilds. The horses also kept in the reserve area are wild **tarpans**, relations of the original steppe horses which are gradually being bred back to their original genetic stock after centuries of interbreeding.

Interesting though these animals are, the main impressions of the forest stem from the ancient *puszcza* itself. At times the serenity of the forest's seemingly endless depths is exhilarating, then suddenly the trunks of oak, spruce and hornbeam swell threateningly to a dense canopy, momentarily pierced by shafts of sunlight that sparkle briefly before subsiding into gloom. One memorable thicket, which the guide will take you to, consists of a group of forty-metre-high oaks, each named after a Polish monarch.

Apart from the rarer animals such as elk and beaver, the forest supports an astounding profusion of **flora and fauna**: over 20 species of tree, 20 of rodents, 13 varieties of bat, 228 of birds – all told over 3000 species, not counting around 8000 different insect species.

Staying

The *Iwa* **hotel** in the park grounds (☎122-60/123-84) is geared to Western tourist requirements, and priced accordingly. The nearby **PTTK hostel** (☎125-05) is a perfectly comfortable, cheaper alternative. In season both places get very busy, so reserving in advance is a good idea – they'll probably understand English or German at reception. The decent-sized **youth hostel** in the village at ul. Waszkiewicza 4 (☎125-60) is open all year. For meals, head for the *Iwa* hotel **restaurant**, especially if you need a good breakfast after the early-morning bus journey.

Bielsk Podlaski and around

Fifty-five kilometres south of Białystok lies **BIELSK PODLASKI**, a dusty old market town imbued with the old-world peasant feel of the surrounding countryside. By car or train the route from Białystok takes you through the attractive open Podlasie landscape, with opportunities for stopping off at the often beautiful Orthodox *cerkwi* you'll find in villages along the way. The town itself has a couple of sites of interest, but it's the atmosphere, as much as buildings, that lend the place a certain down-at-heel charm.

Bielsk Podlaski

The sites worth seeing are scattered round the rather diffuse town centre intersected from north to south by ul. Mickiewicza, the main shopping street. At the north end of Mickiewicza is the old town **Rynek**, with some attractive examples of the local wooden architecture in evidence among the older houses ringing the square. The chunky-looking Baroque **Town Hall** at the centre of the square houses a small **museum** (Tues–Sun 10am–5pm) featuring local craft work and occasional art exhibitions. Just west of the square stands the Neoclassical **Catholic Parish Church**, built in the 1780s at Izabella Branicki's orders; north of the *rynek* is good example of that local speciality, the impromptu **open air market**: this one's a muddy patch generally swarming with Belarussians and other "trade tourists" from across the border camped around their cars, flogging motley assortments of clothes, jewellery, hi-fis and other knick-knacks to the locals. Local traders prefer the traditional horse-and-cart method of travel – hence the "no horses" signs dotted along the approaches to the town centre. Just beyond the market is the seventeenth-century **Carmelite Church and Monastery**: a characteristic Polish Baroque structure, the interior's being totally redone, leaving you to wander through the hollow shell of the building and wooden scaffolding surrounding it.

South along ul. Mickiewicza brings you to the ornate **Church of St Michael**, a large, bulbous blue *cerkiew* and the main centre of Orthodox worship in town. As often, except during services the building's nearly always closed, so you'll have to ask next door at the parish house to get in and see the fine iconstasis. When he's not dealing with parishioners the local priest, a beatific-looking character with a beard worthy of Mount Athos, will open up the building and take you through the details of Orthodox church architecture. If you want to pursue the subject further, there are a couple more Orthodox churches in town, most notably the small yellow wooden *cerkiew* on ul. Jagiellońska east of ul. Mickiewicza.

Practicalities

The **bus and train station** is ten minutes' walk south of the town centre. For local **information** try the Orbis office, ul. Mickiewicza 62, in the centre. There's not much in the way of decent accommodation, the best bet being the hotel *Unibud*, ul. Widowska 4 (☎28-41) on the northeast edge of town, with the *Dworek Smólskich*, ul. Hołowieska 7 (☎36-10) a lesser alternative. For a meal the *Podlasianka*, ul. Mickiewicza 37, complete with regular evening dance-band, is about the best on offer: for an afternoon coffee the *Hajduczek*, ul. Mickieicza 25, is a presentable enough *kawiarnia*.

Siemiatycze

Fifty kilometres south on through the quiet Podlasie countryside brings you to **SIEMIATYCZE**, a scruffy-looking place with all the hallmarks of a town suffering from the severe depression currently afflicting the rural Polish economy. As usual the main square forms the focal point of the town. The **Catholic Parish Church** is ornate early Baroque with a triumphal-looking altarpiece and the characteristic yellow and white stucco decoration. Following the Soviet invasion of eastern Poland at the outbreak of World War II, the people of Siemiatycze found themselves inside Soviet territory, a fact recalled in the recently erected plaque inside the church commemorating the many local people deported to Siberia, most of them never to return. Just down the hill is the main local **Orthodox church**, currently undergoing a complete overhaul.

Orthodox aside, the other main religious community here used to be **Jews**: typically for the region, before the war Jews comprised some forty percent of the town's population. South of the square off ul. Pałacowa is the former town **synagogue**, an eighteenth-century brick building that somehow survived the depredations of the Nazis. Following wartime use as an arsenal, the synagogue was restored in the 1960s and turned into the local *Dom Kultury*. If you ask, the staff can point out surviving features of the building's original architecture. As often, the **Jewish Cemetery**, east past the bus station on ul. Polna, is run down and wildly overgrown. Back in town the **Local Museum** (Tues–Sun 10am–4pm) on ul. 11 Listopada south of the centre has a presentable collection of local exhibits enhanced by some displays devoted to local Jewish themes.

For a place to stay, the *U Kmicica* (☎24-32), well south of the centre at the end of ul. Waska, is about the only option, with the *Ratuszowa* and *Oleńka*, both on the main square, the available restaurants.

The Grabarka Convent

Hidden away in the woods round Siemiatycze, the **Convent** near the village of Grabarka, 10km east of town, is the spiritual centre of contemporary Polish Orthodoxy: primarily a place of pilgrimage, it occupies a place in Polish Orthodox devotions similar to that of Częstochowa for Catholics. The contrast between the two religious centres couldn't be more striking, however: where the Jasna Góra monastery is all urban pomp and majesty, the Grabarka site is steeped in a powerful aura of time-honoured rural mystery. If you've become accustomed to processions of Catholic sisters on the streets of Polish cities, the sight of the twenty or so Orthodox-robed nuns making their way to the church in Grabarka comes as quite a surprise.

Approached by a sandy forest track, the hill up to the small convent leads to the community buildings next to the main **Church**: whether by accident or design – local opinion is divided on the issue – the church was burnt to the ground in 1991, a cause of great sadness among the Belarussian and Orthodox communities for whom it's long been a treasured shrine. Workmen are now hard at it rebuilding it – judging by the brass plating being used on the onion-domed roof, no expense is being spared either – and the church will probably soon be functional again. The place's best-known and certainly most striking feature, however, is the thicket of **wooden crosses** packing the slopes below the church. A traditional gesture of piety carried by pilgrims and placed here on completing their journey, the literally thousands of characteristic Orthodox crucifixes clustered together in all shapes and sizes are an extraordinarily powerful sight: with all this wood around, the no lighting-up signs sprinkled among the crosses come as no surprise.

Despite the convent's backwoods location, groups of devotees can be found visiting the place at most times of the year. The biggest pilgrimages, however, centre round major Orthodox feast and holy days, notably September 19, the **Przemienienia Panskiego (Spasa)** – "Feast of the Transfiguration of the Host" would be an approximate translation – when thousands of Orthodox faithful from around the country flock to Grabarka, many by foot, for several days of celebrations. As much celebrations of cultural identity as their Catholic counterparts are for Poles, the festivals at Grabarka offer a powerful insight into the roots of traditional, predominantly peasant Orthodox devotion.

If you don't have your own transport, **buses** run to the Grabarka village – roughly half a kilometre from the convent – two or three times a day from Siemiatycze, more often in summer.

travel details

Trains

Gdańsk to Białystok (2 daily; 8–9hr); Bydgoszcz (hourly; 2–3hr); Częstochowa (5 daily; 7–8hr); Elbląg (11 daily; 1–2hr); Hel (6–9 daily; 2–2hr 30min); Katowice (8 daily; 7–8hr; couchettes); Kołobrzeg (4 daily; 4–5hr); Koszalin (13 daily; 3–4hr); Kraków (6 daily; 6–10hr); Lublin (2 daily; 7hr 30min); Łódź (6 daily; 5hr 30min–7hr); Olsztyn (6 daily; 3hr 30min); Poznań (7 daily; 4hr); Przemyśl (1 daily; 13hr); Rzeszów (1–2 daily; 11–14hr; couchettes); Szczecin (8 daily; 4hr 30min–6hr); Toruń (5 daily; 3–4hr); Warsaw (19 daily; 3hr 30min–5hr); Wrocław (7 daily; 7–8hr; couchettes); Zakopane (1 daily; 13hr; couchettes).

Toruń to Bydgoszcz (30min–1hr); Gdańsk (5 daily; 3–4hr); Kraków (3 daily; 7–8hr); Łódź (11–14 daily; 2–4hr); Olsztyn (7–9 daily; 2–3hr); Poznań (5 daily; 2–3hr); Rzeszów & Przemyśl; (1 daily June–Sept; 10hr 30min; couchettes); Warsaw (6 daily; 3–5hr); Wrocław (2 daily; 5–6hr).

Olsztyn to Białystok (4 daily; 5–7 hr); Elbląg (10 daily; 1hr 30min–2hr); Gdańsk (6 daily; 3–4hr); Kraków (2 daily; 7–12hr); Poznań (4 daily; 5–7hr); Suwałki (2 daily; 5–6hr); Szczecin (5 daily; 8–10hr); Toruń (8 daily; 3–4hr); Warsaw (8 daily; 3hr

30min–6hr); Wrocław (2 daily; 7–8hr); Zakopane (1 daily; 16hr).

Suwałki to Białystok (4 daily; 2hr 30min–3hr 30min); Kraków (1 daily June–Sept; 12hr); Olsztyn (2 daily; 6–8hr); Warsaw (4–6 daily; 4–8hr; couchettes June–Sept).

Białystok to Gdańsk (2 daily; 9hr; couchettes); Kraków (1 daily; 9hr; couchettes); Lublin (1 daily; 9hr); Olsztyn (5–6 daily; 6hr); Poznań (1 daily; 10hr; couchettes); Suwałki via Augustów (4–5 daily; 2hr 30min–3hr),

Useful bus routes

Gdańsk to Kartuzy; Kwidzyn; Grudziądz; Chełmno; Toruń.

Toruń to Bydgoszcz; Gdańsk; Olsztyn; Warsaw.

Chełmno to Toruń; Bydgoszcz; Grudządz.

Olsztyn to Lidzbark Warmiński; Mrągowo; Białystok; Ełk; Augustów.

Augustów to Olsztyn; Suwałki; Warsaw; Białystok; Ełk; Giżycko; Sejny.

Białystok to Lublin; Olsztyn; Augustów.

Suwałki to Gdańsk; Warsaw; Grudziądz; Bydgoszcz; Olsztyn; Kwidzyn.

CHAPTER THREE

SOUTHEASTERN POLAND

The southeast is the least populated and least known part of Poland: a great swathe of border country, its agricultural plains punctuated by remote, backwoods villages and a few market towns. It is peasant land, the remnants of the great European *latifundia* – the feudal grain estates – whose legacy was massive emigration from the late 1800s until World War II to France, Germany and, above all, the USA.

Borders have played an equally disruptive role in recent history. Today's **eastern Polish frontier**, established after the last war, sliced through the middle of what was long the heartland of the Polish **Ukraine**, leaving towns like Lublin (and L'viv, inside the Ukraine) deprived of their historic links. As border restrictions ease, the prewar links are reasserting themselves in the flood of ex-Soviet "trade tourists" – essentially car boot sale merchants – who give an international touch to the street markets of towns like Przemyśl and Rzeszów. On the Polish side potatoes are now a major peasant crop of the southeast, for private sale to Ukrainians. In the genuine wilderness of the **highland areas** you come upon a more extreme political repercussion of the war, with the minority **Lemks** and **Boyks** just beginning to re-establish themselves, having been expelled in the wake of the civil war that raged here from 1945 to 1947. And this area's ethnic diversity is further complicated by divisions between Catholic, Uniate and Orthodox communities.

None of this may inspire a visit, yet aspects of the east can be among the highlights of any Polish trip. The **mountains**, though not as high nor as dramatic as the Tatras to the west, are totally unexploited. A week or so hiking in the **Bieszczady** is time well spent, the pleasures of the landscapes reinforced by easy contact with the locals – a welcoming bunch, and drinkers to match any in the country. The **Beskid Niski**, to the west, has some great rewards too: in particular its amazing **wooden churches** or *cerkwi*, whose pagoda-like domes and canopies are among the most spectacular folk architecture of central-eastern Europe.

The undeniable historic appeal of **Lublin**, the region's major city and for centuries the home of a famous Jewish community, is overshadowed in part by the sombre sight of the Majdanek death camp on its outskirts. However, the smaller towns, like the old trading centres of **Kazimierz Dolny** and **Sandomierz** along the Wisła River, are among the country's most beautiful, long favoured by artists and retaining majestic historic centres – though again the absence of the Jews casts a pall. Over to the east, **Zamość** has a superb Renaissance centre, miraculously preserved from the war and well worth a detour, while in the south there's the stately **Łancut Castle**, an extraordinary reminder of prewar, aristocratic Poland. Each summer the castle hosts a chamber music festival, one of the most prestigious Polish music events. The most intriguing festival, however, takes place at nearby **Rzeszów** in June and July every third year, when folklore groups from *emigracja* communities get together for a riot of singing, dancing and nostalgia.

Other towns of note in the region include **Tarnów**, much of its medieval centre intact, **Jarostów**, another of the procession of formerly Jewish-dominated towns situated along the old East–West trading routes. Beer-lovers will probably want to make a bee-line for **Leżajsk**, whose honeyed local brew is at least as popular with visitors as the annual pilgrimages to its renowned church.

Lublin

In the shops, oil lamps and candles were lit. Bearded Jews dressed in long cloaks and wearing wide boots moved through the streets on the way to evening prayers. The world beyond was in turmoil. Jews everywhere were being driven from their villages. But here in Lublin one felt only the stability of a long established community.

Isaac Bashevis Singer, *The Magician of Lublin*.

The city of **LUBLIN**, the largest in eastern Poland, presents an all too familiar ambivalence, with sprawling high-rise blocks and Stalinist smokestacks surrounding an historic centre. Once you're in the heart of the place, however, it's all cobbled streets and dilapidated mansions – a wistful reminder of the city's past glories. The fabric of this old quarter came through World War II relatively undamaged, and although years of postwar neglect left it in a pretty shambolic state, a slow-moving reconstruction programme is now under way.

In amongst the numerous churches you'll find reminders that for centuries Lublin was home to a large and vibrant **Jewish community**, a population exterminated in the Nazi concentration camp at **Majdanek**, just 3km from the city centre.

Some history

Like many eastern towns, Lublin started as a medieval trade settlement and guard post, in this case on the trade route linking the Baltic ports with Kiev and the Black Sea. Somehow managing to survive numerous depredations and invasions – the fearsome Tartar onslaughts in particular – Lublin by the sixteenth century was well established as a commercial and cultural centre.

As every Polish schoolchild knows, the city's finest hour came in 1569 when the Polish and Lithuanian kings met here to unite the two countries – the so-called **Lublin Union** – thereby creating the largest mainland empire in Europe, stretching from the Baltic to the Black Sea. Over a century of prosperity followed, during which the arts flourished and many fine buildings were added to the city. The Partitions rudely interrupted this process, leaving Lublin to languish on the edge of the Russian-ruled Duchy of Warsaw for the next hundred years or so.

Following World War I and the regaining of national independence in 1918, a Catholic university – the only one in eastern Europe – was established, which is now a cradle of the Polish Catholic intelligentsia. It was to Lublin, too, that a group of Polish communists known as the Lublin Committee returned in 1944 from their wartime refuge in the Soviet Union to set up a new communist government. Since the end of the war, the town's industrial and commercial importance has grown considerably, with a belt of factories mushrooming around the town centre.

Lublin may also one day come to be seen as one of the birthplaces of Solidarity. Some Poles claim that it was a strike in Lublin in May 1980 – four months before the Gdańsk shipyard sit-ins – that decisively demonstrated the power of workers' self-organisation to the country.

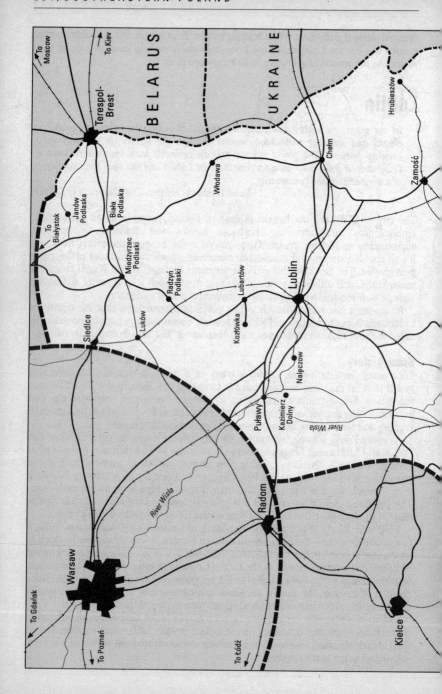

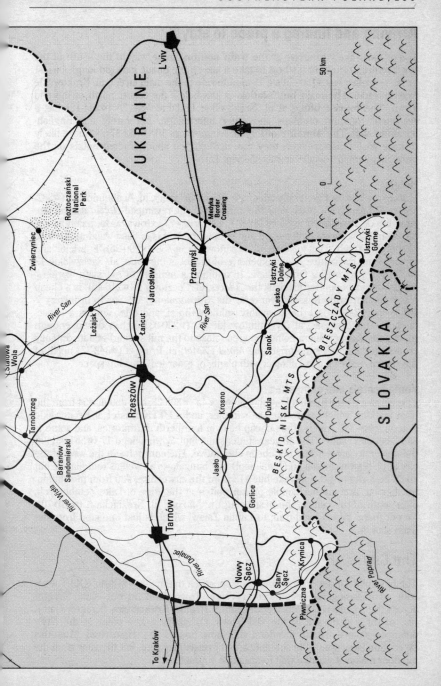

Arriving and finding a place to stay

You're most likely to arrive at the **train station**, some way to the south of the town centre; from here it's best to take a taxi (if the queue isn't too long), bus #1 or #3, or trolley bus #150 – it's a 15-minute ride to the main street, ul. Krakowskie Przedmieście. The main **bus station** is just below the castle, north of the Old Town. The **tourist office** at ul. Krakowskie Przedmieście 78 (☎244-12) has a reasonable amount of maps and other information, but rarely has English-speaking staff. The **Almatur office**, ul. Langiewicza 10 (☎332-37), is more likely to have an English-speaker; they can also tell you about student hotels on the university campus (available July 15–Sept 15).

Hotels

Hotels are few, but generally adequate. *Dom Noclegowy*, ul. Academicka 4 (☎382-35), is a cheap, basic place near the university. The revamped *Hotel Lublinianka*, Krakowskie Przedmieście 56 (☎242-61), a Czarist-era extravaganza, has reasonable rooms, a separate coffee shop and restaurant, and is in easy walking distance of the Old Town. The *Victoria*, ul. Narutowicza 56/58 (☎290-26), is pricier and further from the centre. Most expensive of the lot is the *Unia*, al. Raclawickie 12 (☎320-61), part of the Orbis chain. In addition a number of old state workers' hotels are now open for tourists: the *Adaces*, ul. Pocztowa 2 (☎216-46), is a cheap place popular with Russian workers; the *Garnozonowy*, ul. Spadachroniarzy 7 (☎305-36/723-070) is a better-quality soldiers' hotel, and often full as a consequence. The *Bystrzyce*, al. Zygmuntowskie 40 (☎230-0315), has decent-enough rooms, the main problem being the area (close to the rail station) and its dubious crime reputation. For motorists the *Motel PZMot*, ul. Prusa 8 (☎342-32) north of the centre, makes a good choice, with plenty of (guarded) parking space.

Youth hostels and campsites

There's also a **youth hostel**, at ul. Długosza 4a (☎306-28; bus #50 or #54 from the train station), which is crowded in summer, and a **PTTK hostel** at Krakowskie Przedmieście 29, which offers cheap beds in four-berth dormitories, and some 1- and 2-bedded rooms. The all-year student hotel, ul. Sowinskiego 17 (☎551-081) in the university area, is another cheap alternative. The **campsite** in the west of the city at ul. Sławinkowska 46 (June–Sept) has bungalows as well as tent places, but you'll be lucky to get one; take bus #18 from the city centre, #20 from the station. Further out are another couple of **campsites** at the edge of Lake Zemborzyck, 3km south of the centre, the best being the *Marina*, ul. Krężnicka 6 (☎410-70). To get there, take a local train to Lublin Zalew, which is just one stop from the main station.

The City

The busy plac Łokietka forms the main approach to the Stare Miasto (Old Town), with an imposing nineteenth-century **New Town Hall** on one side. Straight across the square is the fourteenth-century **Brama Krakowska** (Kraków Gate), one of three gateways to the Old Town. Originally a key point in the city's defences against Tartar invaders, this now houses the **Historical Museum** (Wed–Sun 9am–4pm); the contents aren't greatly inspiring, but the view from the top floor makes it worth a visit to orientate yourself.

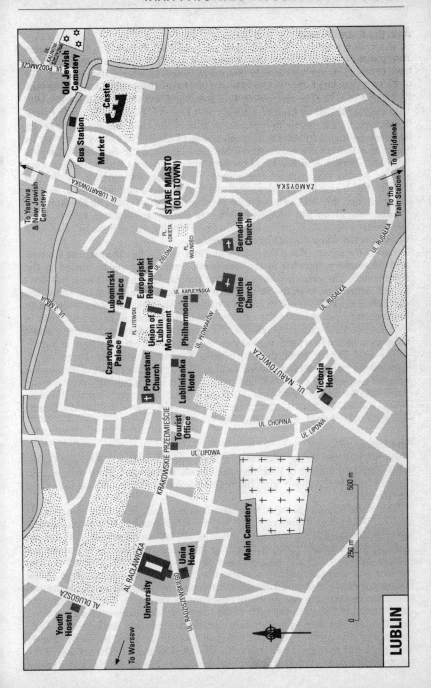

LUBLIN

Old Jewish Cemetery

UL. KALINOWSZCZYZNA

UL. PODZAMCZE

Castle

Bus Station

Market

To Yeshiva & New Jewish Cemetery

UL. LUBARTOWSKA

STARE MIASTO (OLD TOWN)

ZAMOYSKA

To the Train Station

To Majdanek

PL. ŁOKIETKA

Bernadine Church

PL. WOLNOŚCI

UL. ZIELONA

Lubomirski Palace

Europejski Restaurant

UL. KAPUCYŃSKA

Brigittine Church

UL. 3 MAJA

Czartoryski Palace

PL. LITEWSKI

Union of Lublin Monument

Philharmonia

UL. PEOWIAKÓW

UL. RUSAŁKA

UL. RUSAŁKA

Protestant Church

Lublinianka Hotel

UL. NARUTOWICZA

Victoria Hotel

Tourist Office

KRAKOWSKIE PRZEDMIEŚCIE

UL. CHOPINA

UL. LIPOWA

UL. LIPOWA

Main Cemetery

AL. RACŁAWICKA

Unia Hotel

UL. RADZISZEWSKIEGO

AL. DŁUGOSZA

University

Youth Hostel

To Warsaw

0   250 m   500 m

Into the Stare Miasto

A short walk round to the right along ul. Królewska brings you to the **Brama Trinitarska** (Trinity Gate), and opposite it the **Cathedral**, a large sixteenth-century basilica with an entrance framed by ornate classical-looking pillars. The gate itself opens onto the Rynek, dominated by the outsize **Old Town Hall**; built in 1389, it later became the seat of a royal tribunal, and was given a Neoclassical remodelling in 1781 by Merlini, the man who designed Warsaw's Łazienki Palace. Getting round the square is tortuous, as a lot of the buildings are under reconstruction – judging by recent progress, a state of affairs that's likely to remain for years to come. Of the surrounding burghers' houses, the **Sobieski Mansion** (no. 12) – where Charles XII of Sweden and Peter the Great were both once guests – has Renaissance sculptures decorating its exterior, while the Lubomelski house (no. 8) hides some racy fourteenth-century frescoes in its wine cellars, which the workmen might be persuaded to show you. The **Konopniców House** (no. 9) on the southeast corner of the square features further lively Renaissance decoration on the facade, a fierce looking pair of lions included – it'll be even better when the builders have finished.

East of the square, down the narrow ul. Złota, lies the fine **Dominican Church and Monastery**, founded in the fourteenth century and reconstructed in the seventeenth. The church suffers from the familiar Baroque additions, but don't let that deflect you from the Renaissance **Firlej family chapel** at the end of the southern aisle, built for one of Lublin's leading aristocratic families, nor the eighteenth-century panorama of the city just inside the entrance. Round the back of the monastery is a popular playhouse, the **Teatr im. Andersen**, one of the oldest theatres in the country, with a good view over the town from the square in front.

The Old Town's other theatre, **Studio Teatralne**, near the centre at ul. Grodzka 32, has a gallery featuring local artists. Grodzka was part of the **Jewish quarter** and several of the buildings on the street bear memorials in Polish and Yiddish to the former inhabitants. Lublin was one of the main centres of Hassidic Jewry and its **Yeshiva** – now a medical academy – was the world's largest Talmudic school right up to the war (see box p.242).

The castle complex

On a hill just east of the Old Town is the **Castle**, an offbeat 1820s neo-Gothic edifice built on the site of Kazimierz the Great's fourteenth-century fortress, and linked by a raised pathway from the Brama Zamkowa (Castle Gate) at the end of ul. Grodzka.

The castle houses a sizeable **museum** (summer daily 9am–4pm; winter Wed–Sun only), the high points of which are the **ethnography** section, including a good selection of local costumes, religious art and woodcarving, and the **art gallery**, where moody nineteenth-century landscapes and scenes of peasant life mingle with portraits and historical pieces. Among the latter, look out for two famous and characteristically operatic works by Matejko: the massive *Lublin Union* portrays Polish and Lithuanian noblemen debating the union of the two countries in 1569; the equally huge *Admission of the Jews to Poland* depicts the Jews' arrival in Poland in the early Middle Ages, the two sides eyeing each other suspiciously. Another upstairs room contains an excellent collection of eighteenth- and nineteenth-century **Orthodox icons** from the Brest (formerly Brześć) area, now just over the other side of the Belarussian border. The section of the museum devoted to World War II recalls the castle's use by the Nazis as a prison and interrogation centre. Polish civilian prisoners were shot in the courtyard and over 400,000 Jews were detained here before being sent to Majdanek or other concentration camps.

The **Church of the Holy Trinity**, behind one of the two remaining towers in the corner of the courtyard, is closed for restoration: officially the building is currently open on the last Sunday of the month only, from 10am to 3pm, though with a bit of cajoling you may be able to persuade the main castle office to let you in. Behind rickety scaffolding are a glorious set of Byzantine-looking frescoes, unlike anything you'll find in your average Roman Catholic church. Uncovered in the last century, they were painted by a group of Ruthenian artists from the Ukraine – exceptionally for the time, the main artist, Master Andrew, signed his name and the date, 1418.

On the way back to the Old Town, check out the **market** just below the castle: you may find something interesting among the mixture of junk and contraband. As in many eastern towns, the squat peasants with stand-out accents selling caviar, gold and radios for dollars are from just over the border. They're what are euphemistically known as "trade tourists", an enduring eastern European practice whereby itinerant traders buy and sell products unobtainable in neighbouring countries.

West of the Old Town

West of pl. Łokietka stretches **Krakowskie Przedmieście**, a busy shop-lined thoroughfare with a number of sites worth taking in on and around its vicinity. Immediately west of the New Town Hall is **Holy Ghost Church** (Św. Ducha), a small, early fifteenth-century structure with the familiar Baroque overlay and a quiet, restful feel to it.

Immediately opposite the church a turn southwards takes you onto pl. Wolności, a car-jammed square surrounded by building activity. The fifteenth-century **Bernardine Church** on the south side of the square is a large Gothic construction with a sumptuously ornate Baroque interior: there's a good view over the southern rim of the city from the platform at the back of the building. On the western edge of the square the **Brigittine Church**, raised in the 1420s by King Władisław Jagiełło as a gesture of thanks for victory at the battle of Grunwald, is another Gothic structure with the customary high brick period facade. Opposite the church stands the **Juliusz Osterwa Theatre** (see 'Nightlife'), an enjoyable *fin-de-siècle* playhouse with an august old stage.

Back onto Krakowskie Przedmieście, north of the main street on ul. Zielona, a narrow side passage contains the tiny **St Joseph's Church**, founded by Greek Catholic merchants in the 1790s and used by the local Uniates into this century, though there's nothing now there to inform you of the fact. Just beyond on the corner of ul. St Staszica is the crumbling eighteenth-century **Potocki Palace**, one of a several patrician mansions in this part of the city.

Krakowskie Przedmieście soon brings you to **plac Litweski**, a large open square that's a lively hub of activity, with lots of people milling about and, in summer, a host of chess games in progress. The monuments ranged along the edge of the square include the cast-iron **Union of Lublin monument**, marking the Polish-Lithuanian concordat established here in 1569, the **Unknown Soldier memorial** and the **Third of May Constitution (1791) monument**, marking another significant event in the country's history. The north side of the square features two of the city's old aristocratic palaces, both currently used by the university: first is the former **Czartoryski Palace**, in the northeast corner, a smallish building occupied by the Lublin Scholarly Society. Next on is the fading seventeenth-century **Lubomirski Palace,** with a Neoclassicist facade designed by Marconi in the 1830s. The imperial-looking building to its left is just that, the old czarist-era city governor's residence built in the 1850s.

If it's open, the eighteenth-century **Protestant Church** on ul. Ewangelicka, further along to the north of Krakowskie Przedmieście, is worth a brief look in: an austere, Huguenot-style temple with classicist stylings, it has memorial tablets ranged around the walls, mostly to the church's former German-speaking congregation.

Continuing west along Krakowskie Przedmieście turn south on ul. Lipowa, by the tourist information office, and a five-minute walk brings you to the gates of the **main cemetery**. A stroll round this peaceful, wooded graveyard provides an absorbing insight into local history.

The cemetery is separated into confessional sections; to the north the predictably large **Catholic** section, with a large group of "unknown soldier" graves from both world wars, is flanked by the **Protestant** and **Orthodox** cemeteries. The Orthodox section, with its own mock-Byzantine chapel, contains more wartime graves – Russian soldiers this time – as well as a sprinkling of older, Czarist-era Cyrillic tablets, including many of the city's one-time imperial administrators and rulers. The graves in the **Protestant** section reveal many German-sounding names, and many of the stones date from before and during World War I, when the city was occupied for several years by the Kaiser's forces. Finally, inspection of the group of plain tombstones without crucifixes in the western section of the graveyard reveals them to belong to those local Party members committed enough to the atheist cause to refuse Catholic burial.

Around Jewish Lublin

For anyone interested in **Lublin's Jewish history**, a scattering of monuments around the city's former Jewish quarters are worth visiting, most of them marked by (hard-to-spot) tablets in Hebrew and Polish.

The Old Town

Starting in the **Old Town** – much of it long Jewish-inhabited – are a couple of buildings with wartime Jewish connections: on the corner of ul. Noworybna, east of the square, is the small house where the first **Committee of Jewish war survivors** was set up in November 1944. Continuing on down to ul. Grodzka, at no. 11 is another plaque commemorating the **Jewish orphanage** in operation here from 1862 up to March 1942, when the Nazis removed all 108 children and shot them in the fields behind the Majdanek camp.

Continuing along Grodzka and down to pl. Zamkowy, at the foot of the stairs up to the castle a plaque on a raised pedestal shows a detailed **plan** of the surrounding **Podzamcze district**, the main Jewish quarter destroyed by the Nazis in 1942 (see box overleaf). The Nazi devastation was so thorough that it's hard to visualise the densely packed network of houses, shops and synagogues that used to exist in the streets around what's now a noisy main road (al. Tysiąlecia), a tatty square, the adjoining main bus station and an **Orthodox Church** – the only one remaining in town, originally a Uniate building – immediately east of it.

THE OLD JEWISH CEMETERY

Continue east along al. Tysiąlecia and opposite the bus station, on the approaches to the castle, you'll find another plaque marking the prewar site of the main **Maharszal and Maharam synagogue**, originally constructed in the 1530s and razed, along with all the surrounding buildings, in 1942.

Cross the main road and walk along cobbled ul. Kalinowszczyzna, take the first right off ul. Lwowska and you find yourself at the **old Jewish cemetery**, a large walled area which covers a ramshackle, overgrown hill, set in almost rural surroundings.

Unless a group happens to be there at the time, to get in you'll have to contact the caretaker, Mr Józef Honig, at ul. Dembowskiego 4, apt. #17 (☎778-676), across from the main cemetery entrance. Despite the Nazis' best efforts to destroy the oldest-known Jewish cemetery in the country – literally thousands of the gravestones were used for wartime building purposes – the surviving tombstones display the full stylistic variety of Jewish monumental art.

Alongside the oldest, dating from 1541, is a fine range of Renaissance, Baroque and Neoclassicial ornamental tombstones. The oldest section of the cemetery houses the graves of many famous Jews, among them the legendary Hassidic

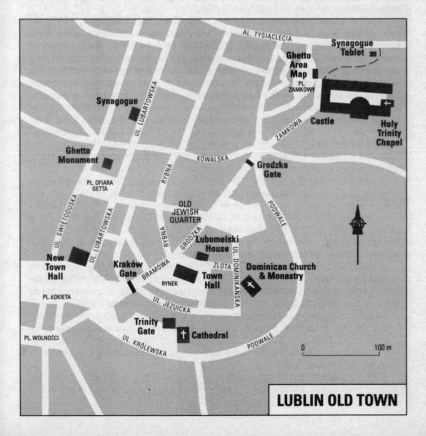

LUBLIN OLD TOWN

leader **Jaskow Itzak Hurwicz** (see box below), one of several here regularly covered with pilgrims' candles, and **Shalom Schachna ben Josef**, the renowned sixteenth-century master of the Lublin *yeshiva*. Climbing to the top of the cemetery hill will give you a fine view back over the Old Town and the old Jewish quarter.

THE NEW CEMETERY AND MAUSOLEUM

Leaving the cemetery and heading north along ul. Lwowska and into ul. Walecznych brings you to the entrance of the **new cemetery.** Established in 1829 in what was then the outskirts of town, the cemetery was predictably plundered and destroyed by the Nazis, who also used it for mass executions. The cemetery you see today covers a fragment of the original plot, the northern

---

THE JEWS OF LUBLIN

Along with Kraków and L'viv, for centuries Lublin ranked as one of the major – if not the most important – of the Jewish centres in Poland: at its peak the **Lublin Jewry** exerted a Europe-wide influence, dispatching locally trained rabbis to serve communities as far away as Spain and Portugal.

The **first recorded account** of Jews in Lublin dates from 1316, though it's quite possible that merchants had established themselves here considerably earlier. King Kazimierz's extension of the **statute of privilege** for Jews to the whole territory of Poland in the mid-fourteenth century paved the way for the development of the first major Jewish settlement in the **Podzamcze** district, located below the castle walls: originally a marshy river delta, the area was bought up by Jewish merchants, who drained the waters and established a community there. The first brick **synagogue** and *yeshiva* (Talmudic school) were built in the mid-sixteenth century: from then on synagogues and other religious buildings proliferated – by the 1930s there were more than 100 synagogues in operation inside the city area. Lublin's increasingly important position on trade routes resulted in its choice as one of two locations (Jarosław was the other) for meetings of the **Council of the Four Lands**, traditionally the main consultative body of Polish Jewry, a position it retained up to the 1760s.

Occasional outbreaks of Church-inspired **"ritual murder" accusations** apart, local Jewish-Christian relations seem to have been fairly tolerant at this stage, the main blows coming in the form of outside assaults, notably the **Chmielnicki Insurrection** (1648), when Cossacks slaughtered thousands of Jews throughout eastern Poland, and the Russian siege of the city in 1655, when much of the Podzamcze district was razed. The whole area was subsequently rebuilt, this time with an emphasis on solid, brick buildings.

In the 1790s Lublin emerged as an important centre of **Hassidism**, the ecstatic revivalist movement that swept through eastern Jewry in the latter part of the eighteenth century. The charismatic Hassidic leader **Jaskow Itzak Hurwicz** settled in town in the 1790s, drawing crowds of followers from all over Poland – by all accounts, the Hassids were no respecters of Poland's Partitions-era borders – to his "court" in the Podzamcze district. Always a controversial figure – contemporary opponents, for example, claimed that Hurwicz died of "excessive alcohol consumption" – Jews from all over the world continue to make the pilgrimage to his grave in the old Jewish cemetery.

With the town's Jewish population increasing rapidly, in the mid-nineteenth century Jews began moving into the Old Town area, also occupying much of the

section having been cleared and levelled in the 1960s to make way for a trunk road (ul. Somorawińskiego).

There are precious few graves left inside, most of them dating from the late nineteenth century and the postwar years, as well as a number of collective graves for Nazi wartime victims. The whole cemetery has been renovated in the past few years with financial support from the Frenkel family, whose families died in Majdanek.

The domed **mausoleum** (10am–4pm), recently erected behind the cemetery entrance, houses a small exhibition detailing the history of the Lublin Jewry. To get in you'll have to negotiate your way past the menacing-looking guard dog protecting the premises: in daylight hours a ring of the bell will do the trick – wandering in is not recommended.

---

new district that developed around ul. Lubartowska, to the north of the Old Town. At the close of the century Jews numbered around 24,000 – a little over 50 percent of the town's mushrooming population.

Following the trials of **World War I,** during which many Lublin Jews died fighting in both the Russian and Austro-Hungarian armies, Lublin Jewry flourished in the **inter-war years**, developing an active web of religious and cultural associations, publishing houses, newspapers (notably the daily *Lubliner Sztyme* – "Lublin Voice"), trade unions and political organisations.

Following their capture of the town in September 1939 the **Nazis** quickly set about the business of confining and eventually murdering the nearly 40,000-strong Lublin Jewry. By December 1939 transports of Jews were being brought into the city from other parts of Europe, and in early 1940 Lublin was chosen as the co-ordinating centre for the Nazis' efforts to liquidate the Jewish population of the *Général Gouvernement*. With the Old Town area already filled to bursting with destitute Jews, an official **ghetto area** was established in March 1941 by Governor Hans Frank.

Work on constructing the **Majdanek death camp** in a southern suburb of the city began in July 1941, and in February 1942 the hideous business of **liquidating the ghetto population** began in earnest. After initial expulsions at the end of March 1942, Jews were driven to the ghetto square (next to the modern main bus station): the old and sick were shot on the spot, the rest taken to waiting railway wagons and transported to the death camps, mostly **Treblinka** and **Bełzec**. Over the next few months, the remaining population was either taken and shot in the **Krkpiecki Forest** on the outskirts of the city or moved to a new ghetto area established close to Majdanek. The effective end of over 600 years of traditional Jewish life in Lublin came on November 3, 1943, when the remaining 18,000 ghetto inhabitants were shot at Majdanek in an extermination *Aktion* codenamed *Erntfest* – "Harvest Home". Following the *Aktion*'s "successful" conclusion the Nazis systematically demolished the buildings of Wieniawa, an outlying Jewish settlement, and the Podzamcze district.

The city was liberated by Soviet troops in July 1944, after which **Jewish partisan groups** began using Lublin as their operational base. At the end of the war several thousand Jewish refugees resettled in Lublin: as a result of **anti-Semitic outbreaks** around Poland in 1945-46, however, many of them emigrated, others following in the wake of the anti-Semitic purges of 1968, as in Kraków and Warsaw. The tiny remaining Jewish population keeps a low profile, many now too old to take an active role in the revival of local Jewish life encouraged by the increasing number of Western Jews visiting the city.

THE YESHIVA AND JEWISH HOSPITAL
Out of the cemetery and west along ul. Unicka brings you to the corner of ul. Lubartowska, a long, straight thoroughfare running through the heart of the prewar Jewish quarter. The large classical-looking yellow building at the top corner of Lubartowska is the site of the prewar **yeshiva** – "The School of the Sages of Lublin" as it was known – a palatial structure now occupied by the local Medical Academy. Built in the late 1920s using funds collected from Jewish communities around the world specifically for the purpose, the Lublin *yeshiva* was set up as an international Talmudic school to train rabbis and other senior community functionaries. It functioned for just over nine years until 1939, when the Nazis closed it down and eventually plundered or destroyed the huge library.

To any but the trained eye there's precious little evidence of the building's former use, a simple plaque on the outside wall briefly stating the historical facts.

Next building down on the same side of Lubartowska (no. 81) is another fine palatial-looking building, erected in 1886 – the former **Jewish hospital**, still an obstetric clinic: a plaque outside commemorates the hospital staff and patients murdered in March 1942 in the course of a Nazi liquidation *Aktion*.

The old ghetto district

Continuing south along Lubartowska takes you through the heart of the old **ghetto district**; a grubby, lively area of shops and tenement houses. While there are no Jews left to speak of, wandering through the arched entrance ways into the back courtyards or scanning the small shops you can imagine what it must have been like here half a century ago. Right up towards the top of the street – a 1.5-kilometre walk – a backroom at no. 10 (the entrance through the gateway round the side of no. 8, and up the stairs) houses the city's only functioning **synagogue**. (Officially open Sun 1–3pm: the moody old caretaker pops in and out, so the rest of the time it's a question of either trying your luck or calling him – same number as for the old cemetery).

Established in 1920 by the local undertakers' guild, after World War II it became the principal synagogue for the city's surviving Jews. It is still in use today; visiting Jewish tourist groups regularly hold services here. An informative collection of photos and other archival materials relating to the Lublin Jewry lines the walls, along with a small collection of ritual religious objects and some plaques dedicated to local Poles who protected Jews during the wars.

Finally, at the top of Lubartowska on the approach to the old city is pl. Bohaterów Getta ("Ghetto Heroes"), a bustling square that used to be one of the main Jewish marketplaces. A simple **monument to the ghetto victims** stands in the square centre, engraved with the legend "Honour to the Polish citizens of Jewish nationality from the Lublin region, whose lives were bestially cut short by the Nazi fascists during World War II. The people of Lublin."

Majdanek

The proximity of **Majdanek concentration camp** is a shock in itself. Established on Himmler's orders in October 1941, this was no semi-hidden location that local people could claim or strive to remain in ignorance of – a plea that is more debatable at Auschwitz and Treblinka. Inside the camp, the shock intensifies. Wandering among the barbed wire and watchtowers, staring at crematoria and rows of shabby wooden barracks, it's hard to take in the brutal fact that over 200,000 people of more than twenty nations were murdered here, a significant number of them Jews. In one week in October 1943, 45,000 survivors of the Warsaw ghetto were murdered here, shot by machine gun fire; 18,000 were killed in a single day. The **camp museum** (summer Tues–Sun 8am–6pm; closes 3pm in winter) in a former barracks tells the terrible story in detail. **Buses** #14, #23, #28 and #153 run to Majdanek from pl. Wolności. For further details on the camps and Polish-Jewish relations, see the Auschwitz section in Chapter Four.

Eating, drinking and entertainment

For a city of its size, Lublin offers remarkably little in the way of diversion. Decent **restaurants** in particular are thin on the ground, with the trend towards private ownership taking its time to penetrate east. The *Unia* hotel, an old Party dignitaries' haunt, has the best and most expensive food in town – fine if you're prepared for obsequious waiters and the inevitable "dancing" band blasting away in the corner. The restaurant of the *Lublinianka* hotel stays open later than most, does a good *żurek* soup, and attracts a contingent of hardened local boozers. The gloomy *Europa* at Krakowskie Przedmieście 29 has revamped itself up to "credit card" status; the *Karczma Lubelska* at pl. Litewski 2 is ok but nothing more; and the same goes for the *Karczma Słupska*, al. Racławickie 22, and the *Powszechna*, Krakowskie Przedmieście 56, while the nearby *Wisła* (no. 59) represents a step up in quality. *Jazz Pizza*, opposite the tourist office, offers just what its name suggests: live jazz with pizza.

As in other eastern towns, **milk bars** are still hanging in here: the local options include the *Staromiejski*, just inside the Old Town at ul. Trybunalska 1, and the *Turystyczny* on Krakowskie Przedmieście. For breakfast, the *kawiarnia* in the *Lublinianka* does scrambled eggs and coffee till quite late. Of the Old Town **cafés**, the *Czarcia Łapa* on ul. Bramowa has a good cheesecake, the *Mieszczka*, ul. Grodzka 7, a decent café-au-lait, while the upbeat *Przy Bramie*, next to the Brama Krakowska, is a good place to sit outside and enjoy an ice cream in summer.

Nightlife
Despite its student population, the city doesn't exactly bristle with **nightlife**, though **bar life** is showing tentative signs of picking up: the *Pod Papugami*, Krakowskie Przedmieście 30, is a trendy new student haunt; *Chmielewski*, further down the street at no. 8, is a popular bar and local cultural centre that includes live gigs among its activities: you can also catch the occasional band at nearby *Chata Zaka* as well. In the Old Town *U Bisów*, Rynek 18, is a nice enough beer-drinker's haunt. Typically the locals are proudest of the *Old Pub*, at ul. Grodzka 8 just east of the Old Town square, where you can pick up draught German lager or a pint of Guinness – anything as long as it isn't Polish, in fact.

The *Hades*, ul. Peowiaków 12, a *Dom Kultury* just round the corner from the *Philharmonia*, has a restaurant, bar, pool hall and also hosts regular gigs with an emphasis on experimental rock and Polish rap bands – recommended. During term time the *Chata Zaka* club, behind the Catholic University (KUL) on ul. Radziszewskiego, is a popular student dive where you can also catch the occasional live band. There are a number of other **student clubs** dotted around the university campuses and halls of residence. The best bet is to wander into either KUL or the nearby state university area and ask what's going on; many students speak English, and there's an even chance of getting invited to some or other event, usually of a heavy drinking nature.

On a more cultural front, the *Philharmonia*, ul. Osterwy 7, has a regular programme of high-quality classical **concerts**, and the *Teatr im. J. Osterwy*, ul. Narutowicza 17, offers an imaginative and varied programme of modern and classical Polish **drama** – worth seeing even if you don't speak the language.

North from Lublin

North of the city takes you into the **Biała Podlaska** region, a pleasant agricultural farming area of ramshackle old market towns and sparsely populated villages that still retains a markedly old-world eastern feel. Like most of eastern Poland this region has its share of grand old **palaces**, many of them showing the effects of decades of neglect. The palaces at **Lubartów,** nearby **Kozłówka, Radzyń Podlaski** and **Biała Podlaska**, the regional capital, all offer striking examples of the phenomenon, well worth checking out if you like rural aristocratic piles. A range of Catholic, Orthodox, Jewish and occasional Tartar monuments provide the region's mixed ethnic and religious profile. In a country of traditional horse-lovers the breeding stables at **Janów Podlaski**, hard up by the Belarus border, are perhaps the area's best-known attraction.

As in many of the country's further-flung regions, local **buses** are the main form of transport. For motorists heading east the main route from Warsaw to Moscow runs across the region, reaching the border at **Terespol**, east of Biała Podlaska.

Lubartów

Twenty kilometres from Lublin – a half-hour bus journey along the main road north of the city – the market town of **LUBARTÓW** is a historical curio worth a brief stopoff on your way elsewhere. A small, undistinguished market centre facing the banks of the Wieprz River to the east, Lubartów is a good example of an eastern town effectively created by a big-league local magnate, in this case the Firlej family who moved here in the 1540s.

The fine sixteenth-century **Firlej Palace** in the town centre is the most tangible reminder of the local grandees. A large white-stuccoed building currently occupied by local government offices, the fading facade boasts four elegant sets of double pillars surmounted by a large classical frieze. The palace **park** behind the building is a pleasant spot with some traces of its former grandeur, the orangerie included, in evidence. The **Parish Church** next to the palace is classic Polish Baroque (a Renaissance doorway excepted), with numerous funeral tablets – in this case, mainly of the Sanguszko family, who took over the palace in the eighteenth century – covering the interior. If you've time the **Local Museum** (Tues–Sun 10am–3pm) down to the right of the church on ul. Kościuszki is worth a brief look, the locally based exhibits changing on a regular basis. As in all the Lublin region **Jews** were long a feature of the town: first mentioned in 1567, at the start of World War II they comprised some 45 percent of the local population. The entire **Jewish population** was deported to the death camps at Bełzec and Sobibór in October 1942, and most of the community buildings, including two synagogues on ul. Lubelska, were destroyed. A memorial built out of tombstone fragments and thirty or so extant tombstones are all that remains of the **Jewish cemetery** at the corner of ul. Cicha and ul. 1 Maja, on the southern side of town.

For an **overnight stay**, the *Unitra*, ul. Lubelska 104a (36-10) on the main through-town drag, is the only real option, with the *Ariańska*, further down the same road at ul. Lubelska 52, a solid if basic restaurant.

Kozłówka palace

Nine kilometres west of Lubartów – 35km if you're coming direct by bus from Lublin – the **Zamoyski Palace** at **KOZŁÓWKA** is among the grandest in the region. With recent restoration work on the building virtually complete, the palace is getting a fair amount of tourist hype – hence the processions of day-tripper coaches already lining up outside the entrance gates. All in all it's a good example of the nostalgia for the "good old days" of the prewar era that's in vogue in Poland now. With admiration of and aesthetic preference for all things grand and aristocratic back at the forefront of officially sanctioned culture, it's hardly surprising to find emphasis being placed on places like this: whether you're taken with this kind of opulent aristocratic overload is very much a question of personal taste.

Some history

Built in the 1740s by the Bieliński family, after they inherited the local estate, the original two-storey Baroque palace complex, surrounded by a courtyard to the front and gardens at the back, was reconstructed and expanded in the early 1900s by its longtime owner, Count Konstanty Zamoyski, whose family took over the property in 1799 and kept it up to the beginning of World War II. Zamoyski's remodelling retained the essentials of the original Baroque design, adding a number of fine outbuildings, the iron gateway, chapel and elegant porticoed terrace leading up to the entrance to the building that you'll find today.

Tickets

Getting into the palace can actually be a bit of a performance. The opening times (Tues, Thurs–Fri 10am–4pm, Wed 10am–5pm, Sat–Sun 9am–5pm; open March 1–Nov 30; guided tours only, last tickets 1 hr before closing) are subject to variations, so you'd be well advised to check at the Lublin tourist office before setting out; theoretically at least, on weekdays you can only tour the palace if you're part of a prebooked party, though in practice you'll be fine tagging along with any group that happens to be there, which can mean anything from German tourist buses to school kids or the local works outing.

The Interior

Safely **inside the palace** you're immediately enveloped in a riot of artistic elegance. The whole place is positively dripping in pictures, mostly family portraits and copies of Rubens, Canaletto and the like, along with a profusion of sculptures and period furniture, every corner of the richly decorated building crammed with something decorative. First port of call is the **hallway**, the gloom partially lightened by sumptuous lamps and the delicate stucco work of the ceiling. Past the huge Meissner stoves and up the portrait-lined **marble staircase** brings you to the main palace rooms. On through **Count Konstanty's private rooms** the procession of family portraits and superior repro art continues relentlessly, the elaborate Czech porcelain toilet set in the bedroom suggesting a man of fastidious personal hygiene. After the countess' bedroom and its handsome selection of Empire furniture, the tour takes you into the voluminous **Red Salon** an impressive ensemble with embroidered canopies enveloping the doors and a mass of heavy red velvet curtains. The portraits are at their thickest here, the emphasis being on kings, hetmans and other national figures collected by Count Konstanty during the Partition years as a personal gesture of patriotic remembrance.

The rest of the palace is pretty much more of the same; the **exotic room** houses a fine selection of chinoiserie, while the **dining room** is sumptuous, heavy Baroque with a mixture of Gdańsk and Venetian furniture and enough period trinkets to keep a hoard of collectors happy. As you'd expect, the **library** contains endless shelves full of books ranged around a classic old billiard table lit by a kerosene lamp in the middle. The **chapel**, out round the side of the palace, is a fine though rather cold place partly modelled on the royal chapel in Versailles and built in the early 1900s.

The Museum

After overdosing on opulence, the **museum** (same opening hours) housed in the one-time palace theatre makes for a real surprise. Entitled "Art and Struggle in Socialism", the exhibition brings together a large collection of postwar Polish socialist realist art and sculpture, most of it culled from museums around the region and kept here out of harm's way once its subjects had become politically unacceptable. The whole pantheon of international Stalinist iconography is here: Bolesław Bierut, Mao, Ho Chi Minh, Kim Il Sung and a beaming Stalin himself. Alongside the leaders there's a gallery of sturdy proletarian and peasant types building factories, heroically swathing corn, implementing the Five Year Plan, joining the Party and other everyday communist activities. Standout among the statues is black American singer Paul Robeson declaiming in full voice, a particularly effective piece of agitprop sculpture. If you need a walk after all the viewing, the elegantly contoured **palace gardens** stretching out behind the back of the building provide the necessary space. Material refreshment comes from the palace **café** back out near the entrance gate.

Radzyń Podlaski

Forty kilometres north of Lubartów on the main Lublin–Białystok road is **RADZYŃ PODLASKI**, another sleepy provincial market town marked by its historic association with Polish aristocracy, in this case the powerful Potocki family, who descended on the town in the early eighteenth century and built one of their many eastern palaces here on the site of an earlier castle belonging to the Mniszchów family. Badly damaged in 1944, in its heyday the **Potocki Palace** was said to be one of the finest Rococo residences of the east. Despite the fact that it was never fully repaired after the war – much of the palace is local administrative offices now – walking round the large inner courtyard you can still sense something of the building's former grandeur. Although pretty overgrown the **palace gardens**, now the town park, are similarly enjoyable, a soothing spot to cool off in on a summer's day. These days the orangerie is a *Dom Kultury* and Video Club, which probably accounts for the graffiti scrawled all over its walls. Across the road from the palace the eighteenth-century **Parish Church** is a fine Mannerist building whose architecture echoes the Collegiate churches in Zamość and Kazimierz Dolny.

If you are stopping off for a **meal,** the *Polonia* on ul. Ostrowiecka east of the bus station, will do the honours. **Buses** continue on to Białystok (3hr 30mins), Biała Podlaska (1hr), and south to Lublin (1hr 30 mins).

Biała Podlaska

The provincial capital **BIAŁA PODLASKA** offers a curious mixture of both the old and the new Poland. Weighing heavily on the town today is its strategic position along the main high road from Warsaw to the eastern border (the railway station is similarly placed on the main Warsaw–Moscow line). Day and night, transit lorries thunder along the road to and from the border crossing at Terespol forty-odd kilometres east, and local rumour has it that the Russian mafia has already gained a firm foothold in the town.

Judging by some of the menacing-looking characters to be seen hanging round the town square at night it's not a proposition the visitor should discount, either, especially when it comes to parking cars in the centre. That said, there are a number of things worth seeing, many of them associated with the powerful Radziwiłł family, the town's fifteenth-century founders and longtime aristocratic benefactors.

Practicalities

The **train station** is on the southern side of the town, a five-minute bus ride from the centre, the **bus station** on pl. Wojska Polskiego a little to the east of the main square along ul. Brzeska. For **tourist information** the Orbis office located on pl. Wolności, the central square, is your best bet. **Accommodation** options are pretty limited. The PTTK hotel, ul. Pokoju 14 (☎43-56-46), is really very basic, and some way to the west of the centre – although bus #17, #18 or #19 will drop you reasonably close by. The sports hotel, at ul. Piłsudskiego 38 (☎43-45-50) next to the local stadium, is similarly basic but closer to the centre.

The *U Radziwiłła*, ul. Powstancόw 4 (☎43-53-40), is the best-quality place around, though the hotel's location 2km west of town means you'll have to take a taxi if you don't have your own transport. As the hotel is popular both with local lads and cross-border travellers of the shadier variety, anyone with a room on the first floor may find themselves having to contend with riotous all-night Russian parties being held just along the corridor – one option, of course, being simply to join in.

Finally there's a (summer only) **youth hostel** at ul. Sidorska 30, not far from the rail station. Of the **restaurants** the dining room in the *U Radziwiłła* is serviceable enough, though you'll probably have to put up with a "dance" (read "Muzak") band. In the town centre the *Stylowa*, ul. Brezska 16, and the *Adria*, on pl. Wolności, are the main options.

Round the town

Inevitably for a town established by aristocracy, the former **Radziwiłł Castle Complex** west of the main square provides the town's main focus of historic interest. Left, like most other such complexes, to go to seed in the postwar era, much of the damage was actually done earlier, the main palace section of the original seventeenth-century complex having been destroyed by the czarist authorities in the 1870s.

Castle grounds apart, of what remains today the main building, currently being renovated, is a combined school and music academy, while the old **Tower House** contains a well-organised **regional museum** (Tues–Sun 10am–5pm June–Aug, 9am–4pm Sept–May). Judging by the illustrations displayed here the original castle complex was a very grand affair. The exhibitions on the upper floor feature an interesting display of local ethnography, including textiles, folk tapestries and examples of the pagan-influenced "sun" crucifixes typical of the Lithuanian part of the old Commonwealth. The artwork housed in the next room reflects traditional regional themes – hunting, horses, soldiers and the old Jewish marketplace. Of a number of churches in town the basilica-shaped **St Anne's Parish Church**, just up from the palace, is the most striking, an exuberant late sixteenth-century structure with twin cupolas and a richly decorated side chapel devoted to the Radziwiłłs as well as one curiously Celtic-looking tombstone in the graveyard outside, a contrast to the kitschy electric Marian shrine standing nearby.

The statue back across the road standing on the corner of ul. Brzeska is of the popular writer **Józef Ignacy Kraszewski** (1821–87), who attended the 350-year old local school: the old *Akademii Bialskiej* (Biała Academy), which was originally affiliated with the Kraków Academy and later with the Academy in Wilno (Vilnius).

Janów Podlaski

Twenty kilometres north of Biała Podlaska close up by the Belarus border, the town of **JANÓW PODLASKI** has the country's most famous **stud farm**, specialising in the rearing of thoroughbred Arab horses. Luminaries of the world

---

CROSSING THE EASTERN BORDER

Despite the rapidly increasing volume of traffic, travel across Poland's **eastern borders** in any form – car especially – is still liable to be a major performance. Behind the socialist unity rhetoric of the postwar era, up until very recently the reality was a strictly controlled border at least as strongly policed at major crossing points as the former East–West Germany border. The political climate may have changed radically, but in practical terms getting into (or out of) Belarus and Ukraine from Poland remains fraught with practical complications, and is likely to remain so for the foreseeable future.

Crossing points
For motorists the key problem is the lack of **crossing points**, a problem compounded by the ponderous Soviet-style customs setup on the eastern side of the border and the sheer volume of traffic attempting to get across. Two major border crossings – **Terespol** near Biała Podlaska and **Medyka** near Przemyśl – were adequate as long as few people were able to travel: with the recent explosion of travel facilitated by the new political situation it's an absurd situation, as everyone recognises. Amazing stories of border incidents abound: one recently doing the rounds in Poland is of a car stopped at customs on account of the peculiar smell emanating from the vehicle. Close examination of a back-seat passenger revealed that he had died (from a stroke) during the long wait: not wanting to lose their precious place in the queue, the other passengers had decided to keep the body in the car until they crossed the border.

horse scene are regular visitors – it would have to be something special to drag people out to the wilds of the borders – principally during the annual international **auctions** of the stud farm's magnificent Arabian horses, which are held every September.

Established by Czar Alexander 1 in 1817, the stud was intended to produce top-quality horses for his personal use. The farm has gone through its ups and downs: the stock was badly decimated by German soldiers in the latter stages of World War I, and again taken over by the Nazis during World War II, when the horses were transported to Germany, many dying in the notorious Allied bombing of Dresden in February 1944. The elegant stable complex you see today is essentially that designed by the Warsaw architect Marconi in the 1830s and 1840s. Janów horses are highly prized in the equestrian world, and with price tags often in the hundreds of thousands it's very much a rich person's pursuit. For the less affluent however, there's always the option of having a look around the stables: turning up without an appointment (preferably made in the Orbis office in Biała Podlaska) is not wildly popular, though generally the staff will let you in if you are persuasive.

From its founding in the 1420s the **town** (the main stud farm is 2km east of the centre) became an important stopoff point on the main Kraków to Vilnius road. The solid, imposing Baroque collegiate church with adjoining belltower stands as a reminder of better days. For a bite to eat there's the *Janowianka* on pl. Partyzantów, the main square, while for accommodation the *Dom Wycieczkowy*, (☎225) at ul. 1 Maja 1, is the only presentable option. Janów is a half-hour bus ride from Biała Podlaska, with the possibility of connecting buses on to Białystok (2hr), Lublin and Terespol (border).

By car

Motorists can expect waits of anything from two to four days at either of the major crossings in the several-kilometre-long queues backed up round the clock on both sides of the border. In summer particularly conditions at Terespol verge on the nightmarish – there are no roadside toilet or washing facilities to speak of, with food and other supplies coming from the vendors in vans parked up on the side of the road. Thousands of stationary cars – especially those with Western number-plates – are a sitting target for robbers, so you're well advised to keep a close watch on your vehicle at all times.

By bus

Crossing the border **by bus** is a different story: all PKS buses get special treatment, so unless there's trouble with customs as a result of some of the passengers' "baggage" – a not infrequent occurrence – you should be through the border in a matter of hours as opposed to days. For any cross-border bus journey it's a good idea to buy your ticket in advance though.

By train

By train you probably won't face such a long wait – though even here a caveat is needed since if you've arrived without one purchasing a visa from the conductor can be a long and drawn-out affair. To date, Ukrainian officials are proving better in this respect than the Belarussians, though it's important to stress that everything is in a state of flux at the moment. In the final analysis, apart from a few sensible precautions, it's very much a case of turning up and seeing what happens.

West to Kazimierz

The Lublin–Warsaw route has a major attraction in the town of **Kazimierz**, an ancient and highly picturesque grain town set above the Wisła. To reach it on public transport, the easiest approach from Warsaw is to go by train to **Puławy** and catch a connecting bus from there; from Lublin there are direct buses via the old spa town of **Nałęczów**.

Nałęczów

Twenty-five kilometres west of Lublin (regular buses: destination Puławy and/or Kazimierz Dolny), **NAŁĘCZÓW** saw its heyday at the end of the last century, when Polish writers and artists, including the popular novelists Bolesław Prus and Stefan Żeromski and pianist-prime minister Ignacy Paderewski hung out here.

Even today the spa is still renowned for its therapeutic waters, heart specialists and generally medicinal climate, and the town retains much of its old-time appearance and atmosphere. A leisurely stroll through the town park brings you to the Neoclassical **Małachowski Palace**, which is part health centre and part **museum** (Tues–Sun 10am–3pm), devoted to Prus and the "positivist" literary movement he promoted in reaction to traditional insurrectionary romanticism. Nearby is the **Sanatorium**, fronted by a monument to **Żeromski**, and, over the road, up ul. Żeromskiego, the writer's Podhale-style cottage – now a small museum. For an instant iron-deficiency remedy, you can taste the local **waters** in the park.

There is just one **hotel** in town, the *Dom Wycieczkowy* at ul. 1 Maja 6 (☎129), which provides the bare essentials, restaurant included; it might also be able to arrange **private rooms**.

Puławy

Sprawling over the eastern banks of the Wisła, **PUŁAWY** is a grubby, medium-sized industrial town whose only real attraction is the seventeenth-century **Czartoryski Palace** and its landscaped gardens. A mock-Gothic Temple of Sibyl and an orangery, both built in the second half of the eighteenth century by Adam Czartoryski and his wife Izabella, give the park a slightly decadent air, reminiscent of the royal residence at Wilanów. During the Partitions period the palace – now an agricultural research institute – became an important intellectual centre, amassing a huge library and art collection in the process. The Russians confiscated the whole estate following the failure of the 1831 Insurrection, in which the Czartoryskis were deeply implicated, even going so far as to change the town's name to "New Alexandria". The main palace collection was moved to Kraków, where it makes up the core of the Czartoryski Museum (see Chapter Four).

If you're stranded, there are various accommodation options: the central *Hotel Izabella*, ul. Lubelska 1 (☎3041), aimed at foreign tourists and with a reasonable if expensive restaurant; the ZNP teachers' hotel, ul. Kołłątaja 7 (☎30-48); a **PTTK hostel** at ul. Rybacka 7 (☎30-48), cheaper and more basic; and an all-year **youth hostel** at ul. Włostowicka 27 (☎33-67). The main **tourist information point** is in the *Izabella* hotel. *Dom Chemika*, ul. Wojska Polskiego 4, is a nice *kawiarnia* with live jazz several weekends a month. The town is on a major train line from Warsaw (2hr) and has regular bus connections with Lublin (1hr).

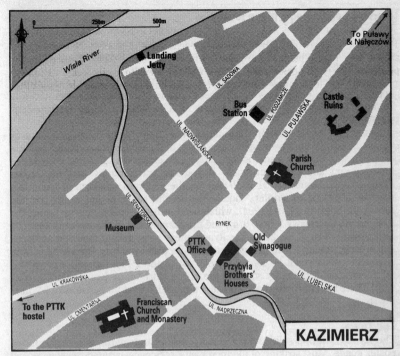

Kazimierz Dolny

Don't be surprised if your first impression of **KAZIMIERZ DOLNY** is one of *déjà vu*: recognising celluloid potential when they see it, numerous film directors – and not just Polish ones – have used the scenic backdrop of this well-preserved town for historical thrillers and tragic romances. Artists, too, have long been drawn to Kazimierz's effervescent light and ancient buildings.

Historically, the place is closely associated with its royal namesake, Kazimierz the Great (1333–70), who rescued Poland from dynastic and economic chaos and transformed the country's landscape in the process. It is said of him that he "found a wooden Poland and left a Poland of stone", and Kazimierz Dolny (Lower Kazimierz) is perhaps the best remaining example of his ambitious town-building programme. Thanks to the king's promotion of the Wisła grain and timber trade, a minor village was transformed into a prosperous mercantile town by the end of the fourteenth century, gaining the nickname "little Danzig" in the process on account of the goods' ultimate destination. Much of the money that poured in was used to build the ornate burghers' houses that are today's prime tourist attraction.

It was during this period, too, that Jews began to settle in Kazimierz and other neighbouring towns, grateful for the legal protection proclaimed for them throughout Poland by King Kazimierz. Dynamic Jewish communities of traders and shopkeepers were integral to the character of towns like Kazimierz for over five hundred years: at one time eighty percent of the inhabitants of Kazimierz were Jewish. The soul of the town, you feel, died in the death camps.

Arriving and finding a place to stay

Unless you have access to a car, the only way to get to Kazimierz Dolny is by **bus** from Puławy, 15km to the north. From Puławy's bus and train stations bus #12 takes you to Kazimierz. The Kazimierz bus station – really just a drop-off point – is on ul. Podzamcze, within spitting distance of the Rynek.

There's a helpful **PTTK office** at no. 27 on the Rynek; for **accommodation**, a good bet is one of the **private rooms**, available at reasonable prices (even in summer) from the *Biuro Zakwaterowania* at ul. Lubelska 7 (Mon–Sat 9am–3pm; ☎10-101).

As a prime tourist location, Kazimierz is one of the towns whose accommodation situation has improved rapidly as a result of the new private-oriented political order. Best of the new places is the *Łaznia*, ul. Senatorska 21 (☎10-298) between the museum and the river bank. If you are travelling by car, the *Zajazd Piastowski*, ul. Słoneczna 31 (☎10-351) on the southern outskirts of town, is a reasonably priced ex-workers' hotel. Also to the south of the centre are the *Karlik*, ul. Filtrowa 11 (☎10-294), which used to be a miners' holiday home; the *Arkadia*, ul. Czerniawy 1 (☎10-074); and the *Rzemieślnik*, ul. Nadrzeczna 48c. The *Dom Architectowy* at no. 20 on the Rynek offers beds, decent food and an excellent setting, though it's not a regular tourist place and you may need to be persuasive. Otherwise, you'll be forced further out to the **PTTK hostel**, a converted fourteenth-century granary south of the town centre on ul. Krakowska 59 (☎10-036). There's a **campsite** here, too, and a noisier one at ul. Senatorska 24, near the river.

The Town

The **Rynek**, with its solid-looking wooden well at the centre, is a classic Orbis poster image. Most striking of the merchants' residences around the square – all of which were restored after the war – are the **Przybyła Brothers' Houses**, both on the southern edge. Built in 1615, they bear some striking Renaissance sculpture; the guidebooks will tell you that the largest one shows Saint Christopher, but his tree trunk of a staff and zodiacal entourage suggest something more like a Polish version of the Green Giant. Next door is the former **Lustig House** – once home to a notable local Jewish mercantile dynasty, its beams displaying the only surviving original Hebrew inscription in town, a quotation from the Psalms.

Other houses still carrying their Renaissance decorations can be seen on ul. Senatorka, which runs alongside the stream south of the square. One of these, no. 17, houses the **town museum** (Tues–Sun 10am–3pm); along with paintings of Kazimierz and its surroundings, the museum documents – albeit sketchily – the history of the town's Jewish community.

The nineteenth-century paintings focus largely on the Jews – a kind of Orientalist fascination seems to have gripped the predominantly gentile Polish artists – and evoke an almost palpable atmosphere. On the streets it's not hard to conjure up this atmosphere, either, though specifically Jewish buildings are scarce. The old **Synagogue** is sited off ul. Lubelska, to the east of the Rynek; constructed in King Kazimierz's reign, it was once a fine building. Following wartime destruction by the Nazis it was rebuilt in the 1950s and converted into a cinema. Of the decoration only the octagonal wooden dome characteristic of many Polish synagogues has been reconstructed.

Crossing the stream and following ul. Cmentarna up the hill brings you to the late sixteenth-century **Franciscan Church and Monastery**, from where there's a nice view back down over the winding streets and tiled rooftops. Up the hill on the other side of the square is the **Parish Church**, remodelled impressively in the early seventeenth century.

Further up, there's an excellent view from the ruins of the fourteenth-century **Castle**, built by King Kazimierz and destroyed by the Russians in 1792, in the run-up to the Second Partition. The panorama from the top of the **watchtower** above the castle is even better, taking in the Wisła and the sweep of the countryside.

On the southern side of town, a two-kilometre walk brings you to the **Czerniawa Gorge**, the site of the main **Jewish cemetery**. First mentioned in 1568, the cemetery was destroyed by the Nazis, who ripped up the tombstones and used them to pave the courtyard of their headquarters in town. In the 1980s the tombstones scattered around the area were collected here and assembled into a wall-like monument – six hundred fragments in all – to moving and dramatic effect.

Into the countryside

There's some good **walking** territory around Kazimierz. If you really want to get the feel of the town's gentle surroundings, follow one of the marked paths from the town centre: either the five-kilometre green path which takes you southwest past the PTTK hostel and along the **river cliff** to MECMIERZ; or the four-kilometre red path that heads northeast to the ruined **castle** of BOCHOTNICA. King Kazimierz is said to have built the castle here for one of his favourite mistresses, a Jewess called Esterka, with a secret tunnel connecting the two fortresses under the river.

Another option is to take the **ferry** (summer only) to the ruins of the sixteenth-century **Firlej family castle** at JANOWIEC, also situated in attractive countryside. There's an equally improbable tunnel story connected with this castle as well, namely that the well doubled as the entrance to a passage joining this fortress to that of Kazimierz.

Eating and entertainment

The town's **food** situation has also improved of late. All the hotels and former workers' holiday homes now have decent restaurants, notably the *Zajazd Piastowski* – well worth the journey if you've got transport available – and the *Dom Prasy*.

Other options include the upmarket *Staropolska*, ul. Nadrzeczna 14, which has a good line in traditional Polish cuisine, the *Club XI*, ul. Krakowska 11, and the teetotal *Amfibar*, ul. Sadowa 18, down by the waterfront. Otherwise, the *kawiarnia* and fast-food joints on the square offer snacks, and you can get chips and (sporadically) fish or chicken at a makeshift takeaway stand just off the south end of the square.

For sampling the joys of Polish folk music, Kazimierz is the place to be in summer: a week-long **Folk Groups and Singers Festival** takes place here in late June or early July. Unless you have a tent, expect to rough it if you're in town then, as the meagre accommodation is snapped up instantly.

Sandomierz

SANDOMIERZ, 80km south of Kazimierz along the Wisła, is another of those small towns described as "quaint" or "picturesque" in the brochures. Its hilltop location certainly fits the bill, though the charm is dented by the evil stench rising from the polluted Wisła. However, a visit is definitely worthwhile, and access is straightforward, with regular train services from Warsaw and buses from Lublin. The one problem is accommodation: the town gets a lot of summer tourists and rooms in season can be very tricky to find; if you're energetic, it's a conceivable day trip from Lublin.

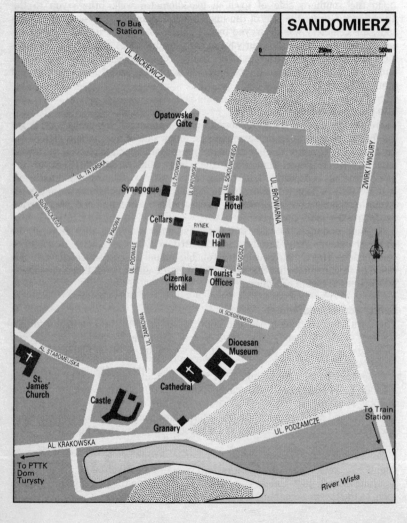

Like other towns in the southeast, Sandomierz rose to prominence through its position on the **medieval trade route** running from the Middle East, through southern Russia and the Ukraine, into central Europe. The town was sacked by the Tartars (twice) and the Lithuanians, in the thirteenth and fourteenth centuries respectively, then completely rebuilt by **Kazimierz the Great**, who gave it a castle, defensive walls, cathedral and town plan – still visible in the Old Town. Subsequently Sandomierz flourished on the timber and corn trade, with its links along the Wisła to the Baltic ports. It was also the scene of one of the key religious events in Polish history. In 1570, while Catholics and Protestants were slitting each others' throats in the rest of Europe, members of Poland's non-Catholic churches met here to formulate the so-called **Sandomierz Agreement**, basis for the legally enshrined freedom of conscience later established throughout the country.

Physically, Sandomierz suffered badly at the hands of the Swedes, who blew up the town castle in 1656, and it was only thanks to a minor miracle that it survived World War II intact. In August 1944, as the **Red Army** pushed the Germans back across Poland, the front line moved closer and closer to Sandomierz. A popular story in the town relates how one Colonel Skopenko, an admirer of Sandomierz, managed to steer the fighting away from the town. He was later killed further west: his last wish, duly honoured, was to be buried in the cemetery at Sandomierz.

The Town

The **train and bus stations** are on opposite sides of town, a bus ride from the centre. Coming in through the nondescript slabs of modern Sandomierz, get off at the fourteenth-century **Brama Opatowska**, part of King Kazimierz's fortifications and the entrance to the Old Town.

From here on it's alleyways and cobblestones, as ul. Skopenki leads to the delightful **Rynek**, an atmospheric square with plenty of places for a leisurely coffee. At its heart is the fourteenth-century **Town Hall**, a Gothic building which had its decorative attic, hexagonal tower and belfry added in the seventeenth and eighteenth centuries. Many of the well-preserved **burghers' houses** around positively shout their prosperity: nos. 5 and 10 are particularly fine Renaissance examples. There's a Tuesday market on the square, which on the first Tuesday of the month regularly becomes a major rural event, with livestock and produce driven in from the countryside.

A hidden aspect of old Sandomierz is revealed by a PTTK guided tour (Tues–Sun 10am–5pm) of the wine and grain **cellars** under the Rynek; entered from ul. Olesnickich, just off the square, the cellars extend under the town hall, reaching a depth of twelve metres at one point. The registrar's office on nearby ul. Basztowa was an eighteenth-century **synagogue**, though there is – as so often – little to indicate its origins.

A stroll down either of the streets leading off the southern edge of the square will bring you to the murky **Cathedral**, constructed around 1360 on the site of an earlier Romanesque church, though now with substantial Baroque additions. It is worth a look within for the Byzantine-looking **murals** in the presbytery and a gruesome series of paintings in the nave, showing the Tartars enjoying a massacre of the populace in 1259 and the Swedes blowing up the castle four centuries later.

Set back from the cathedral, the **Diocesan Museum** (summer Tues–Sun 10am–5pm; winter closes 3pm) was the home of Jan Długosz (1415–80), author of one of the first histories of Poland. The building is filled to bursting with religious art, ceramics, glass and other curios, including a collection of Renaissance locks and keys, and a wonderful old pipe supposed to have belonged to Mickiewicz. Among the best works are a twelfth-century stone *Madonna and Child*, a *John the Baptist* by Caravaggio, and a fifteenth-century *Three Saints* triptych from Kraków.

Downhill from the cathedral is the **Castle**, currently being restored; it is used occasionally for concerts and plays but otherwise has little going for it. Towards the river stands a medieval **Granary**; others are to be found north along the river. Aleja Staromeijska runs from in front of the castle to the **Church of St James** (Kościół św. Jakuba), a lime-shaded late-Romanesque building that's thought to be the first brick basilica in Poland; its restored entrance portal is particularly striking. The area around the church was the site of the original town, destroyed by the Tartars; recent archaeological digs in the area uncovered a twelfth-century chess set, the oldest in Europe. This whole southern district has had to be shored up, owing to subsidence caused by the network of tunnels and cellars dug for grain storage and running for hundreds of metres through the soft undersoil.

Head back down the path in front of St James and you re-enter the town walls through the **Ucho Igielne**, a small entrance shaped like the eye of a needle.

Practicalities

The town has two **tourist offices**, sited next door to each other in a corner of the Rynek; Orbis (at no. 24) deals with ticket bookings, PTTK (no. 25/26) with maps and other local information, including accommodation.

Accommodation is in extremely short supply. The *Hotel Ciżemką*, Rynek 27 (☎225-49), is ideally situated but has just fifteen rooms. The *Flisak*, off the square at ul. Gen. Sokolnickiego 3 (☎236-68), is also small and thus generally full. The only other options are the very basic PTTK *Dom Wycieczkowy* at ul. Stefana Zeromskiego 10 (☎30-88), on the way into town from the bus station; the more pleasant *Dom Turysty* PTTK, ul. Krakowska 34 (☎222-84), which has a restaurant but is further out of town; and the **youth hostel**, ul. Flisaków 26 (☎25-63). There is also a **campsite** on ul. Podzamcze, right by the river.

The best **restaurants** are in the hotels. The *Cizenka* does an excellent *krupnik* soup but otherwise predictable food; its basement bar is popular with tourists and the local drinking crowd. The only serious alternative in the town centre, the *Ludowa* at ul. Mariacka 5, is drab; while the restaurant in the *Dom Turysty*, though better, is only worth visiting if you're staying there. The *Flisak* doesn't do meals, but has a friendly **bar**. As Sandomierz is a day-trippers' favourite, ice cream and coffee bars are open all over the town centre in summer.

South from Sandomierz

South of Sandomierz along the Wisła basin you soon find yourself heading into the gritty landscape of **TARNOBRZEG**, a major industrial centre with similarly dim surroundings. Although it was previously a poor and neglected rural backwater, since World War II the region has been transformed by the growth of the mining industry built up as a result of the large sulphur deposits discovered around the town.

The sulphur may have done wonders for the local economy, but its exploitation has had serious effects on the environment; travelling through you can see and smell the stuff everywhere. Similar comments apply to **STALOWA WOLA**, 30km east of Tarnobrzeg, another major industrial city created round a burgeoning steel and metal industry in the late 1930s. The castle at **Baranów Sandomierski**, significantly affected by the pollution, will be most people's main reason for visiting the area.

Baranów Sandomierski

Fifteen kilometres south of Tarnobrzeg on the eastern bank of the Wisła, **BARANÓW SANDOMIERSKI**'s chief claim to fame is the spectacular **castle** located at the edge of the town.

Erected on the site of a fortified medieval structure owned by the Baranów family, the exquisitely formed and well-preserved Renaissance castle is as fine a period piece as you'll come across anywhere, well worth the out-of-the way trek needed to get here. The epithet "castle" is actually a bit of a misnomer – behind an elegant Italianate facade the rectangular building is really a glorified palace with some fortifications added on to the front for appearance's sake. The place's sumptuously palatial feel is confirmed, too, by a wander through the carefully manicured gardens on the south side of the building. Built in the 1590s for the wealthy Leszczyyński family, the **Castle** (Tues–Sat 9am–2.30pm, Sun 9am–3pm) is constructed on a rectangular plan with an inner courtyard, corner towners and a gateway. The facade is crowned by an attic with a cheerful frieze decoration. In through the gateway you find yourself in a delicately cool, animated Italianate courtyard surrounded on three sides by two tiers of sinuously arcaded passageway, their ceilings decorated with a wealth of family emblems. To reach the upper level you climb the sweeping outer staircase – a later addition – on the southern side of the courtyard. Before doing that it's worth studying the entertaining collection of face-pulling grotesques, many of them animal figures, that decorate the base of the rosette-topped pillars ranged around the courtyard.

Inside the building the ground floor houses a **museum** displaying exhibits relating to the local sulphur industry – hardly surprising, since the castle is owned by one of the major Tarnobrzeg industrial sulphur concerns. The lavishly decorated rooms of the upper floors of the castle (and the modern building next door) are occupied by a luxury hotel (☎55 48 76/77) with a high-quality **restaurant** used for luxury banquets. Though moderately highly priced, the place is understandably popular, so particularly in summer you'd be well advised to book ahead.

Unless you've your own transport the only way to **get to the castle** is by bus: local services run fairly regularly from Tarnobrzeg (30 min) or Sandomierz (1hr 30min, change at Tarnobrzeg) to the bus stop beyond the castle entrance gates.

Zamość

The old towns and palaces of southeast Poland often have a Latin feel to them, and none more so than **ZAMOŚĆ**, 96km from Lublin. The brainchild of the dynamic sixteenth-century chancellor Jan Zamoyski (he of the vodka), the town is a remarkable demonstration of the way the Polish intelligentsia and ruling class looked towards Italy for ideas, despite the proximity of Russia. Zamoyski, in many ways the archetypal Polish Renaissance man, built this model town to his own ideological specifications close to his childhood village, commissioning the design from Bernardo Morando of Padua – the city where he had earlier studied. Morando produced a beautiful Italianate period piece, with a wide piazza, grid-plan streets, an academy, and defensive bastions. These fortifications were obviously well thought out, as Zamość was one of the few places to withstand the seventeenth-century "Swedish Deluge" that flattened so many other Polish towns.

War returned to Zamość early this century, when the area was the scene of an important battle during the Polish-Russian war of 1919–20. The Red Army, which only weeks before had looked set to take Warsaw, was beaten decisively near the town, forcing Lenin to sue for peace with his newly independent neighbours. Somehow, Zamość managed also to get through World War II unscathed, so what you see today is one of Europe's best-preserved Renaissance town centres, classified by UNESCO as an outstanding historical monument.

The Old Town

Regulation-issue urban development surrounds Zamość's historic core, and both **bus** and **train stations** are sited some way from the centre. It's worth taking a bus or taxi to the edge of **plac Wolności**, bordering the Rynek. Once there, you should have no problem finding your way around the Renaissance grid.

The Rynek

The **Rynek**, also known as plac Mickiewicza, is a couple of blocks in from plac Wolności and the partly preserved circuit of walls. Ringed by a low arcade and the decorative former homes of the Zamość mercantile bourgeoisie, the geometrically designed **square** – exactly 100 metres in both width and length – is a superb example of Renaissance town architecture, a wide-open space whose columned arcades, decorated **facades** and breezy **walkways** exude an upliftingly light, airy warmth. Dominating the ensemble from the north side of the square is the **Town Hall**, a soaring showstopper that's among the most photographed buildings in the country. A solid, three-storey structure topped by a tall clock tower and spire, the original, lower construction designed by Morando acquired its present Mannerist modelling in the 1640s, the sweeping, fan-shaped double stairway jutting out from the entrance being added in the following century. Successive renovations have kept the building in pretty good shape, though the peeling plasterwork on the staircase could do with some attention: the floodlighting used at night in summer heightens the power of the building, combining with the visual backdrop of the square to undeniably impressive effect. Occupied by local government offices, the town hall doesn't offer much to see inside; even the room commemorating the pivotal socialist-feminist theorist Rosa Luxemburg, born east of the square at ul. Staszica 37, is now apparently under threat of removal.

The Wilczek house and town museum

From the town hall the vaulted arcade stretching east along ul. Ormiańska features several of the finest houses on the square. Once inhabited by the Armenian merchants who moved here under special privilege in 1585, the houses are fronted by facades that are a whirl of rich, decorative ornamentation, with a noticeable intermesh of oriental motifs. First along is the splendid **Wilczek**

House, built by an early professor at the Zamość academy, with some fine decorated bas-reliefs of Christ, Mary and the Apostles gracing the upper story of the
facade. Number 26 sports similarly exuberant decoration, this time using animal
themes, lions and dragons included. It and the adjoining mansions house the
Town Museum (Tues–Sun 10am–3pm): inevitably, the exhibitions focus on the
Zamoyskis, with plenty of portraits of the town's founder and other assorted
family memorabilia. An additional plus is the interior, with much of the original
decoration, wooden ceilings, carved portals and fresco decoration well restored
and preserved. Back out of the museum the sumptuous facades continue, no. 24
(part of the museum) featuring a prim-looking Renaissance couple peering down
from between the windows and no. 22 next door a relief of a beatific Mary trampling a fierce-looking dragon underfoot.

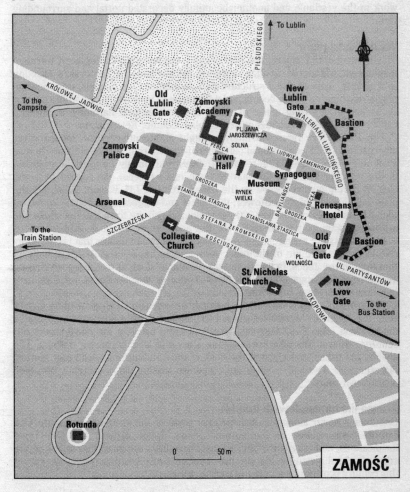

The Morando Tenement House

The **east side** of the square, once another haunt of Armenian merchants and teachers at the Academy, is similarly enjoyable: here as all around the square it's well worth wandering along the vaulted passageways and in through the doorways, many now shops and several of them beautifully decorated, notably at no. 6, a bookshop, and no. 2, a 350-year-old apothecary. The **southern side** of the square contains some of the oldest and most obviously Italian-influenced mansions, two-storey buildings with regularly proportioned facades, several designed by Morando himself.

The **Morando Tenement House** at no. 25, where the great architect himself used to live, boasts an impressive facade with exuberant Mannerist friezes, while the PTTK office at no. 31, in the corner of the square, features some fine stucco work in the vestibule and another beautifully decorated portal and surrounding vault.

West of the square

Moving west of the square, first port of call is the towering **Collegiate Church**, a magnificent Mannerist basilica designed by Morando to Zamoyski's exacting instructions. A three-aisled structure with numerous side chapels, thin, delicate pillars reaching up to the ceiling and a fine vaulted presbytery, the whole interior is marked by a strong sense of visual and architectural harmony, a powerful expression of the self-confidence of the Polish Counter-Reformation.

The **Presbytery** houses a finely wrought eighteenth-century Rococo silver tabernacle, as well as a series of paintings of scenes from the life of Saint Thomas attributed to Domenico Tintoretto. The **Zamoyski family chapel**, the grandest in the building, contains the marble tomb of Chancellor Jan topped by some elegant Baroque stucco work by the Italian architect J.B. Falconi. Adjoining the main building is a high **belltower**, the oldest and biggest of its bells – known as Jan after its benefactor – over 300 years old. As with the town hall the whole site is floodlit (again, only in summer), creating another impressive ensemble.

West across the main road, ul. Academicka, are two buildings that played a key role in the historic life of the town. As its name implies the **Arsenal**, built by Morando in the 1580s, is where the town's ample stock of weaponry used to be kept alongside Zamoyski spoils of war. These days it houses a small military museum (10am–4pm Tues–Sun).

The massive **Zamoyski Palace** beyond the arsenal is a shadow of its former self, the original Morando-designed building having undergone substantial modification after the Zamoyskis abandoned the place in the early nineteenth century, when it was taken over by the army and later became a hospital. The shabby old palace courtyard at the back of the building hints at former glories, but otherwise it's a rather mournful, run-down looking place, currently occupied by the town court.

Around the former Jewish Quarter

Continuing north along ul. Academicka, west of the main street is the **Old Lublin Gate**, oldest of the entrance ways dotted around the Old Town fortifications, and long since bricked up. These days the gate is stranded on the edge of school playing fields, the bas relief uncovered during renovation earlier this century providing a glimpse of earlier glories.

The impressive-looking former **Zamoyski Academy** across the street, built in the 1630s and an important Polish centre of learning until its enforced closure at the start of the Partitions era, is now a school, albeit on a humbler scale than originally. Beyond it, much of the northern section of the Old Town belongs to the former **Jewish quarter**, centred around ul. Zamenhofa and Rynek Solny. As in so many other eastern towns, Jews made up a significant portion of the population of Zamość – some 45 percent on the eve of World War II: the first Sephardic Jews from L'viv arrived here in the 1580s, their numbers subsequently swelled by kindred settlers from Turkey, Italy and Holland, to be displaced subsequently by the powerful local Askenazi community. With much of eastern Polish Jewry in the grip of the mystical Hassidic revival, uniquely in the Lublin region Zamość developed as a centre for the progressive *Haskalah*, an Enlightenment-inspired movement originating in Germany that advocated social emancipation, the acceptance of "European" culture, and scientific and educational progress within the Jewish community. Amongst its products were **Itzak Peretz**, a notable nineteenth-century Yiddish novelist born here, and **Rosa Luxemburg**, though it's as a radical communist theorist and activist rather than Jewish progressive that she's primarily known.

Most of the buildings in the old Jewish quarter are currently being renovated – another *remont* that looks set to run and run – but from the edge of the building site you can still peer through at some of the old Jewish merchants' houses ranged around the small square. The most impressive Jewish monument, however, is the former **Synagogue**, now a public library, a fine early seventeenth-century structure built as part of Zamoyski's original town scheme. Following wartime devastation by the Nazis, who used the building as a carpentry shop, the synagogue was carefully renovated in the 1960s, and its exterior elevations reconstructed. Traces of the dazzling original decoration have survived too, notably the rich polychromy that once filled the interior, sections of which are still visible behind the stacks of library books filling the main body of the building.

The Fortifications

East across ul. Łukasińskiego takes you over onto the former town **fortifications**. Designed by Morando, the original Italian-inspired fortifications consisted of a set of seven bastions interspersed with three main gates with wide moats and artificial lakes blocking the approaches to the town on every side. After holding out so impressively against the Cossacks and the Swedes, the whole defensive system went under in 1866, when the Russians ordered the upper set of battlements to be blown up and the town fortress liquidated. A park area covers much of the battlements now, leaving you free to wander along the tops and see for yourself why the marauding Swedes drew a blank at Zamość. The ornamental **Old Lvov Gate**, another Morando construction, bricked up in the 1820s, and the **New Lvov Gate**, added at the same time, complete the surviving elements of the fortifications.

Across pl. Wolności the former **Franciscan Church**, part of an old monastic complex and now an art school, is only half the building it used to be, having lost its Baroque towers in the 1870s. Into the southern section of the Old Town the former Orthodox **Church of St Nicholas** at the bottom of ul. Bazylianska, a small domed building originally used by the town's many eastern merchants, still has some of its fine original Renaissance stucco, uncovered during recent renovations of the interior.

The Rotunda

The Nazis spared the buildings of Zamość, but not its people. In the **Rotunda**, a nineteenth-century arsenal south of the Old Town on ul. Wyspiańskiego, over 8000 local people were executed by the Germans; a simple museum there tells the story of the town's wartime trauma. In fact, Zamość (preposterously renamed "Himmlerstadt") and the surrounding area were the target of a brutal "relocation" scheme of the kind already carried out by the Nazis in Western Prussia. From 1942 to 1943 nearly 300 villages were cleared of their Polish inhabitants and their houses taken by German settlers – all part of Hitler's plan to create an Aryan eastern bulwark of the Third Reich. The remaining villages were apparently left alone only because the SS didn't have enough forces to clear them out.

Practicalities and entertainment

Zamość is easiest approached by bus from Lublin; trains take a very roundabout route. The main **bus station** is over to the east of the town centre; for details of departures, check at the **tourist office** at Rynek 13, underneath the town hall (Mon–Fri 8am–5pm, Sat & Sun 9am–noon). The nearby Orbis office at ul. Grodzka 13 deals with advance bus and train tickets. The best **hotel** option is the ugly *Renesans*, behind the tourist office on ul. Grecka 6 (☎20-01); it's moderately priced and conveniently close to the Old Town, but very full in summer. A cheap, central alternative is the basic *Dom PTTK*, ul. Zamenhofa (☎26-39), though it is again extremely busy in season. The *Hotel Jubilat* on ul. Kardynota Wyszńskiego (☎64-00) is noisy, more expensive and a fair walk from the Old Town. The **youth hostel**, ul. Młodziezowa 6 (June–Aug), is better placed, between the bus station and Old Town. And, as ever, it's always worth asking at the tourist office about **private rooms**, especially in summer; taxi drivers or people hanging around at the stations are other sources of information. The PTTK **campsite** on ul. Krolowej Jadwigi is some way to the west of the town centre.

Food and drink

Under the influences of privatisation and a growing tourist trade **restaurant** and **bar** life in the Old Town is gradually picking up. Outside the summer season, though, most places shut early in the evening, and anytime after about 8pm you may be hard-pressed to get a meal. In the Old Town the *Royal Kadex*, ul. Żeromskiego 22, is a passable new restaurant, as are the established *Staromiejska*, ul. Pereca 12, and *Centralka*, ul. Żeromskiego 3, which provides the usual soup-and-pork-chop menu. The *bar mleczny* at ul. Staszica 10 is exacly what you'd expect of an old-time milk bar, good for a cheap, straightforward daytime fill-up. Of the hotels, when not being repaired (which seems to be quite often), with a little cajoling the café in the *Renesans* serves up standard breakfasts of eggs, cheese and coffee, as well as basic daytime fare. Like the hotel itself, the restaurant in the *Jubilat* hotel is a touch more upmarket, though the menu is fairly limited.

In summer the square is lined with **outdoor cafés** and ice cream stalls. The appropriately named *Café Padua*, Rynek 23, with a wonderful original ceiling, does a respectable coffee. The slick *Ratuszowa*, strategically placed under the town hall, is top of the new-look Zamość cafes: as well as decent cappuccinos and cakes they do meals during the daytime. For **drinking** the *Piwnica Pod Arkadami*, Rynek 25, is a basement beer dive, another beery option being the bar round the back of the *Renesans* hotel.

Cultural events

If you happen to be in town at the right time there are several annual cultural happenings worth checking out. The Zamość **Jazz Festival**, usually held in the last week of May, is popular with Polish and other Slav jazzers, as is the **International Meeting of Jazz Vocalists** in the last week of September. **Theatrical Summer**, a drama festival held in the latter part of June and early July, features some excellent theatre groups from all over the country, many of whom perform on the stairway in front of the town hall.

The Roztoczański National Park

Twenty kilometres southwest of Zamość the wild expanses of the **Roztoczański National Park** are a must for both walkers and naturalists. Part of the huge former Zamoyski family estates that used to cover much of the Zamość region, the park, created in 1974, occupies a central section of the Roztocze district, a picturesque region of undulating, forest-covered hills, rising to 350 metres at their highest point, with a varied and colourful flora and fauna, including over 160 different species of birds.

Cutting across the heart of the park is the beautiful and largely uncontaminated River Wieprz, which has its source just east of the park. Most of the park consists of forest and woodland, with pine, fir and pockets of towering beeches (up to 50 metres) the commonest trees. Grey stalks, cranes, lizards, wild horses, a wealth of butterflies and, along the banks of the Wieprz, beavers are among the creatures populating the area.

Frequent local bus and train connections to **ZWIERZYNIEC**, at the western edge of the park, make a day trip from the town a feasible prospect. One popular trail is the marked path running south from Zwierzyniec to the edge of the forest in the direction of the village of Sochy, with fine scenic views along the way. Maps and further detailed information about hiking routes in the park are available from the director's office, ul. Plażowa 2, Zwierzyniec (☎108-126).

Rzeszów

RZESZÓW was essentially a postwar attempt to revive the southeast, providing industry and an administrative centre for an area that had seen the previous half-dozen decades' heaviest emigration. The city's population of over 100,000 is evidence of some sort of success, even if this rapid expansion has produced a soulless urban sprawl. Yet the hinterland still consists of the small villages characteristic of this corner of Poland for centuries, which explains why in 1980 Rzeszów became a nucleus of Rural Solidarity, the independent farmers' and peasants' union formed in the wake of its better-known urban counterpart. If the above suggests you might not want to spend Christmas in Rzeszów, there's little that a visit will do to persuade you otherwise: essentially this is a city to see in transit.

Coming in, the **bus and train stations** are adjacent to each other, a short walk north from the centre. The city also has an **airport** (11km out), which could provide a useful route into the region from Warsaw, Gdańsk or Szczecin; there is a LOT office at pl. Zwycięstwa 6 (☎332-34 or ☎335-50). **Tourist information** is available from the main tourist office at ul. Żeromskiego 2 (☎382-64), between the stations and the Old Town (all Mon–Fri 9am–4pm).

The Old Town

Everything worth seeing is located within the compact confines of the Old Town area south of the main stations across al. Piłsudskiego. First stop are the two former **synagogues** facing each other along ul. Bónicza at the edge of pl. Ofiara Getta, the heart of the old ghetto area and all that remains of the town's formerly sizeable Jewish population. First comes the **New Synagogue**, a large seventeenth-century brick building designed by Italian architect Giovanni Bellotti that is now an artists' centre: wander up to the *kawiarnia* on the first floor and you'll probably find someone able to point out the surviving features of the original synagogue. The **Old Synagogue**, over a century older and gutted by the Nazis, houses the town archives as well as a recently formed research institute devoted to the history of the Rzeszów Jewry. A short walk south brings you to the Rynek, a bustling, chaotic place still in the throes of major restoration: if work ever finally finishes it will be a fine location. Plumped in the square centre, as ever, is the **Town Hall**, a squat sixteenth-century edifice remodelled in the nineteenth with a fine Renaissance facade. The **Ethnographic Museum** (Tues–Thurs 9am–2pm, Fri 9am–5pm) in one of the older burghers' houses on the south side of the square contains a small but well-presented collection of local ethnography: exhibits include a fine set of the colourful eastern-influenced traditional local costumes and some good examples of the naive folk art of the region, as well as a couple of complete wayside shrines of the kind you find dotting local highways and byways. The statue of Kosciuśzko on the square, removed by the Germans in 1940, was finally replaced in 1980, thanks to the efforts of the local Solidarity committee.

Directly west of the Rynek is the main **Parish Church**, a Gothic structure which was given its current Baroque overlay in the eighteenth century, notable exceptions being the fine Renaissance decoration in the vaulted nave ceiling and a number of early tombstone tablets up by the altar. On south down ul. 3 Maja, the main shopping thoroughfare, brings you to a former Piarist monastery complex, home of the well-stocked **Town Museum** (Tues & Fri 10am–5pm, Wed–Thurs 10am–3pm, Sat & Sun 9am–2pm) ranged around the monastery courtyard. As well as Polish and European painting, the collection includes the frescoes that once decorated the former cloister arcade and a revealing set of exhibits detailing the mass emigrations from the region in the late nineteenth century. Inevitably, the exhibition finishes with details of both local resistance and Nazi atrocities against the town's Jewish population during World War II. The **Monastery Church** next door has a typically elegant Baroque facade fashioned by Tylman of Gameren in the early 1700s, and a small but well-proportioned interior.

On to the bottom of ul. 3 Maja past the post office takes you past the **Lubomirski Palace**, another early eighteenth-century Tylman of Gameren creation set in a small, quiet park away from the town bustle. An elegant-looking palace originally owned by one of the country's most powerful aristocratic clans, it's now occupied by the local music academy. From here it's a short way further south to the walls of the **Old Town Castle** (currently *remont*), a huge seventeenth-century edifice also once owned by the Lubomirskis. The castle was converted into a prison by the Austrian rulers of Galicia – of which Rzeszów was a part – at the turn of the century and is now the law courts.

Finally, back up in the northwest corner of the Old Town is the **Bernardine Church**, another sumptuous early seventeenth-century structure considerably more attractive than the nearby Monument to the Revolutionary Movement, a typically ugly, grey communist-era offering that has thankfully now finally been removed from the front of local tourist brochures.

Practicalities

All the **hotels** are reasonably close to the stations. The *Rzeszów*, al. Cieplińskiego 2 (☎374-41), is reasonable in the drab, unexciting way of modern Polish hotels. The *Polonia*, ul. Grottgera 16 (☎320-61), is cheaper and dirtier, but very close to the stations. The *Sportowy*, ul. Jatowego 23a (☎340-77), is low-grade and slightly further out. Right by the station at plac Kilińskiego 6 is the *Dom Wycieczkowy* (☎356-76), a typical PTTK place – cheap, basic, but all right. The all-year **youth hostel** (☎344-30) is well situated bang in the square at Rynek 25. An additional option is the *Budynek*, a luxury 4-star joint under construction south of the river.

Among **restaurants**, the *Rzeszów* hotel is the business types' hang-out, offering local specialities including duck, goose and wonderful *Lezajsk* beer from the nearby town of the same name. Ethnic variety is provided by the *Hungaria* at ul. Dąbrowskiego 33, a good Hungarian restaurant south of the Old Town centre, and the *Ha-Long* off the Rynek at ul. Matejki 2, an upmarket Chinese place aimed at businesspeople and tourists. The *Alko*, on the north side of the Rynek, is a pizza place with accompanying disco. Alternatives are the *Rarytas* at ul. Marszałkowska 15 and the *Rzeszówska* at ul. Kościuszki 9, both within walking distance of the centre. If you prefer **milk bars**, there's the *Centralny* at ul. 3 Maja 8, or the downstairs bar of the PTTK hostel. **Cafés** are one of the city's growth industries, with both the Rynek and bustling ul. 3 Maja, the main shopping street, already boasting a number of bright new Western-style hang-outs. *Club No. 1*, ul. Hetmańska 20 south of the Old Town, is a modernist café-restaurant popular with the local trendies.

Appropriately enough for a town with such a long history of emigration, the **Festival of Polonia Music and Dance Ensembles** takes place in Rzeszów in June and July every third year (next one is in 1995). It's a riotous assembly of groups from *emigracja* communities all over the world, including Britain, France, USA, Argentina and Australia.

West from Rzeszów: Tarnów

First impressions of **TARNÓW** are less than promising. A major regional centre with a population close on 100,000, much of the city is decidedly lacking in character. At the heart of Tarnów, though, is a medieval Old Town area that more than makes up for the rest in interest. As you'd expect, the background story here is essentially commercial. Founded in the 1330s, like several towns in the southeast of the country Tarnów rapidly grew fat on the back of the lucrative trade routes running east from Kraków down into Hungary and east on into the Ukraine. Long the seat of the wealthy local Tarnowski family – it remained a privately owned town right up to the end of the eighteenth century – under their patronage it grew to become an important Renaissance-era centre of learning within the Polish Commonwealth, a branch of the Jagiellonian University in Kraków being set up here in the mid-1500s.

Later centuries of wars and partition brought the inevitable decline: in this century Tarnów's significant and long-standing Jewish population was a particular target for the Nazis, but the city's notable scattering of surviving Jewish monuments combine with the historic Old Town centre to provide the makings of an enjoyable short visit, with enough here to detain you for a good day's sightseeing.

The old town

The central Old Town area, only a small part of modern Tarnów, retains the essentials of its original medieval layout. A chequerboard network of angular streets, cobbled alleyways and open squares, the oval-shaped Old Town is ringed by the roads built over the ruins of the sturdy defensive walls, pulled down by the Austrians in the late nineteenth century. Within the area the compact medieval ensemble retains its original two-tier layout, stone stairways connecting the lower and upper sections of the area.

The Rynek

Approached from the south side of town the steps up from the lower level lead on to the **Rynek**. Overall there's an enjoyably relaxed feel to the place, with arcaded Renaissance burghers' mansions occupying sections of the square, notably the trio of parapeted houses on the **north** side, the facades adorned with their colourful original freizes. The central building of the three (no. 21) is the entrance to an extension of the **town museum** (same opening times as below) displaying varying exhibitions of works by contemporary local and national artists: an additional plus here are the number of wood-beamed rooms retaining their Renaissance fresco decoration. Centrepiece of the square, though, is the fifteenth-century **Town Hall**, a chunky, single-storey building with a roofed circular tower and an arched Renaissance brick parapet topped by a series of sculpted animal figures, a device reminiscent of the Sukiennice in the town's former trading rival, Kraków. Through the attractive Renaissance portal on the south side of the building takes you into the main **Town Museum** (Tues & Wed 10am–5pm, Thurs 9am–3pm, Sat & Sun 10am–2pm) housed in the building. Several rooms here also have their original polychrome decoration, notably the long central room which displays a typical set of Polish seventeenth- and eighteenth-century portraits, members of the wealthy local Rzewuski and Sanguszko families sporting eastern-influenced period Sarmatian dress being well to the fore. In addition there's a wealth of exhibits relating to local hero Józef Bem (see opposite) and his military wanderings, other rooms containing a largish assortment of European furniture, porcelain, art and sculpture of the same era.

The Cathedral and diocesan museum

West of the Rynek on pl. Katedralny stands the Gothic **Cathedral**, a cheerful-looking statue of the Pope greeting you near the entrance. Though much rebuilt in subsequent centuries, the rather gloomy interior still has a fair bit of its early Gothic and Renaissance decoration. As well as the early sixteenth-century entrance portal (feauring some fine stone polychromy topped by a figure Christ and Madonna), the cathedral boasts a fine collection of Renaissance tombstones. Particularly impressive are the grand sixteeenth-century memorial to **Jan Tarnowski**, designed by Giovanni Maria Mosca and surrounded with friezes representing his military triumphs, and the Mannerist Ostrogski family monument, a sumptuous marble ensemble with sculpted representations of family members kneeling beneath a crucifix at the centre. Back out on the square, the

JÓZEF BEM

Born in Tarnów in the early Partition years, General **Józef Bem** (1794–1850) was a leading figure in the failed 1830–31 Uprising against Poland's Czarist rulers, a role for which he soon became widely celebrated. A prototype of the dashing military figures beloved of the Polish Romantic tradition, the swashbuckling general is almost equally renowned in Hungary for his heroic part in the 1848 rising in Vienna, immediately after which he joined the leadership of the anti-Hapsburg forces in Hungary. Heroic adventurer to the core, following the failure of the Hungarian revolt Bem travelled east to join Turkish forces in their struggle with Russia, assuming the name Murat following a rapid (and doubtless tactically appropriate) conversion to Islam: before having the chance to do much militarily for the Turks he died, however, in Aleppo, Syria, his cult status among resistance-minded Poles already safely assured. One of many "oppositional" figures from Polish history the country's former communist rulers were anxious to play down, in recent years Bem has been the subject of a welter of monuments that have gone up around his home town, the most recent addition being a statue of the man on the eastern edge of the Old Town raised by the Polish-Hungarian Friendship Society, a move illustrative of the historic sense of communality between the two countries.

former collegiate buildings round the back of the cathedral house the **Diocesan Museum** (Tues–Sat 10am–3pm, Sun 9am–2pm), the oldest and one of the biggest such collections in the country; notable exhibits here include a couple of roomfuls of Gothic religious art, sculpture and other artefacts chiefly from the local Kraków-Sącz artistic school, the highlight being a graceful set of fourteenth- and fifteenth-century wooden *piéta*. Out behind the museum, here as at several points around the Old Town area, you can see surviving sections of the Old Town walls.

South of the Old Town and across ul. Bernardyńska, on the bustling market square below the main road is the birthplace of **Józef Bem**, after whom the square is named, a plaque on a house on the north side of the square commemorating the fact. East along ul. Bernardyńska stands the **Bernardine Church**, part of the fortified monastery complex established here in the late fifteenth century: clearly a grandish place in its heyday, the surviving remants of the original building decoration include some attractive and richly sculpted Renaissance wooden choir stalls.

Jewish Tarnów

East of the Rynek takes you into what used to be the **Jewish-inhabited section** of the town, a fact recalled in the names of streets such as ul. Żydowska and Wekslarska ("money-lenders"). Jews have a long history in Tarnów: the first settlers arrived here in the mid-fifteenth century, and right into the pre-World War II era Jews constituted roughly 40 percent of the town's population. Following their capture of the town in 1939 the Nazis rapidly established a ghetto area to the east of the Old Town, filling it with all local Jews as well as many transported in from other parts of the country. At its height the population of the massively overcrowded ghetto area rose to 40,000, with all the usual attendant consequences in disease and hunger. Between June 1942 and September 1943 virtually the entire ghetto population was either shot or deported to the death camps, principally Auschwitz, and most of the area itself was destroyed. A few Jewish monuments, however, remain in and around the Old Town area.

Architecturally the moody, narrow streets around ul. Żydowska, all of which escaped wartime destruction, are essentially as they were before the war, with traces of the characteristic *mezuza* boxes visible in a couple of doorways. The battered *bimah* covered by a four brick pillared ceiling that stands forlornly in the middle of a small empty square north of ul. Żydowska is what remains of the magnificent sixteenth-century **Synagogue** that stood here until the Nazis gutted it in November 1939. Over ul. Wałowa into ul. Goldhammer, named after a prominent local politician from the turn of the century, no. 1 houses the town's only remaining **functioning synagogue** (Sun 1–3pm), while no. 5, a classicist building from the 1890s, is the former home of the local Jewish Credit Company. Turning east into ul. Waryńskiego, past the corner with ul. Kupiecka, where the gate to the Nazi ghetto area stood, the corner of ul. Nowa is the former site of the **New Synagogue**, the biggest and most ornate in the town. Also known as the "Jubilee of Franz Joseph synagogue" (it was consecrated on the emperor's birthday in 1908), the place burned for three days in 1939 before the Nazis finally resorted to blowing up the remains. The bottom of ul. Nowa leads onto pl. Bohaterów Getta. Across the square is the battered-looking old **ritual bathhouse**: it was from here that a group of 728 local Jews were transported to Auschwitz in June 1940, the first inmates of the camp, a fact commemorated by the monument off the square on ul. Dębowa. Final stop is the **Jewish cemetery**, a fifteen-minute walk north along ul. Nowodąbrowska. One of the largest and oldest Jewish graveyards in Poland, the cemetery was established as early as the 1580s, though the oldest surviving gravestone dates from considerably later. Surprisingly untouched by the Nazis, the overgrown cemetery contains a large number of tombstones, the emphasis being on the traditional type of tablet in which biblical and other illustrative reliefs are used only sparingly: next to the entrance way on ul. Słoneczna – the cemetery's original gates are now in the Holocaust Museum in New York – stands a monument to the Jews of Tarnów incorporating a column from the devastated New Synagogue.

Practicalities

The main **bus and railway stations** are situated next to each other on the southwest side of town, a twenty-minute walk from the Old Town centre – a number of buses (e.g. #41) drop you on the edge of pl. Katedralna at the southern side of the Old Town. Theoretically there should be **tourist information** at the PTTK office at ul. Żydowska 20, but the office in the *Hotel Tarnovia* (see below) is currently a more reliable source.

Accommodation

For a **place to stay**, the top hotel in town is the *Tarnovia*, ul. Kościuszki 10 (☎212-671) near the railway station, a pricey, reasonably upmarket setup. Other alternatives are the serviceable *Polonia*, ul. Wałowa 21 (☎220-842), strategically located on the northern rim of the Old Town, the small and lower-grade PTTK-run *Pod Murami*, ul. Żydowska 16 (☎216-229), the only advantage here being the central location, and the better-quality *Pod Dębem*, ul. Heleny Marusarz 9 (☎210-020), well east of town to the north of the main Rzeszów road. The all-year **youth hostel** at ul. Konarskiego 17 (☎216-916) is a short walk south of the Old Town area and has its own restaurant. **Camping** is at the site on ul. Piłsudskiego 28 on the northern side of town – bus #30 from the railway staion will take you there.

Food

Tarnów doesn't exactly bristle with good **restaurants**, a notable exception being the *Kemora*, ul. Żydowska 13, which boasts of being the only Roma-run restaurant in the country, and worth trying for that reason alone. Unless you want snack food – plentifully available at the fast-food joints springing up all over the town – the hotels, notably the *Tarnovia* and *Pod Dębem*, are the best alternatives.

East from Rzeszów

From Rzeszów the main road and railway head towards the Ukrainian borderlands. A characteristic eastern mix of villages, farmsteads and wayside shrines is the region's main feature, along with a smattering of historic towns and aristocratic palaces, notably **Łańcut**, **Leżajsk** and **Jarosław**. All are within an easy travelling distance of Rzeszów, a mix of local bus and train providing the main means of **transport** around the area.

Łańcut

First impressions of the **fortress** that dominates the centre of **ŁAŃCUT** (pronounced "Winesoot"), 17km east of Rzeszów, suggest that it must have seen rather more high-society engagements than military ones. There has been some serious action around here, though. The first building on the site, constructed by the Pilecki family in the second half of the fourteenth century, was burnt down in 1608 when royal troops ambushed its robber-baron owner Stanisław Stadnicki, known by his contemporaries as "The Devil of Łańcut". The estate was then bought by Stanisław Lubomirski, who set about building the sturdier construction that forms the basis of today's castle. Following contemporary military theory, the four-sided castle was surrounded by a pentagonal outer defence of moat and ramparts, the outlines of which remain.

The fortifications were dismantled in 1760 by Izabella Czartoryska (see "Puławy"), wife of the last Lubomirski owner, who turned Łańcut into one of her artistic salons, laid out the surrounding park and built a theatre in the castle. Louis XIII of France was among those entertained at Łańcut during this period, and the next owners, the Potocki family, carried on in pretty much the same style, Kaiser Franz Josef being one of their guests. Count Alfred Potocki, the last private owner, abandoned the place in the summer of 1944 as Soviet troops advanced across Poland. Having dispatched 600 crates of the castle's most precious objects to liberated Vienna, Potocki himself then departed, ordering a Russian sign reading "Polish National Museum" to be posted on the gates. The Soviets left the castle untouched, and it was opened as a museum later the same year.

The Castle

Forty or so of the castle's hundreds of rooms are open to the public (Tues–Sat 9am–4pm, Sun 9am–3.30pm, opens Sun 10am in winter; closed Mon & Dec 15–Jan 15; last entry 1hr before closing), and in summer they are crammed with organised tour groups. Ask at the ticket office if one of the two English-speaking guides can take you round – they're worth it for the anecdotes. If you're really lucky your guide might be the highly knowledgeable museum curator.

Most of the interesting rooms are on the **first floor**, reached by a staircase close to the entrance hall, which is large enough to allow horse-drawn carriages to drop off their passengers. The **corridors** are an art show in themselves: family portraits and busts, paintings by seventeenth-century Italian, Dutch and Flemish artists, and eighteenth-century classical copies commissioned by Izabella. Some of the nearby bedrooms have beautiful inlaid wooden floors, while the bathrooms have giant old-fashioned bathtubs and enormous taps.

Moving through the **Chinese apartments**, remodelled by Izabella at the height of the vogue for chinoiserie, the **ballroom** and **dining room**, you reach the **old study**, decorated in frilliest Rococo style – all mirrors and gilding – and with a fine set of eighteenth-century French furniture. In the west corner of this floor, the domed ceiling of the **Zodiac Room** still has its Italian seventeenth-century stucco decorations. Beyond is the old **library**, where among the leather tomes you'll find bound sets of English magazines like *Country Life* and *Punch* from the 1870s – which only goes to show how the old European aristocracy stuck together.

On the **ground floor**, the **Turkish apartments** contain a turbaned portrait of Izabella and a suite of English eighteenth-century furniture. Don't miss the extraordinary eighty-seater **Łańcut theatre** commissioned by Izabella: as well as the ornate gallery and stalls, the romantic scenic backdrops are still there, as is the stage machinery to crank them up and down.

The **Carriage Museum** (same hours) in the old coach house is a treat, including horse-drawn vehicles for every conceivable purpose, from state ceremonies to delivering the mail. Next door, the **old stables** house a beautiful collection of Ruthenian **icons**, so numerous that they are hung from the walls in huge racks.

The Town

Łańcut town has one other main point of interest, the old **Synagogue**, just off the main square on ul. Zamkowa. It's currently closed for renovation and reconstruction of its museum, but if you ask at the castle office you should be able to find someone to let you in. Built in 1751 on the site of an old wooden synagogue, it has somehow retained some of its original ceiling decorations.

The **Jewish cemetery**, ten minutes' walk south of the town centre, off ul. Bohaterow Westerplatte, contains the Ohel, grave of the famous nineteenth-century Hassidic rabbi Hurwitz.

Practicalities

Łańcut's **train station** is a taxi ride north from the centre; the **bus station**, however, is only five minutes' walk from the castle. If you're planning to stay overnight, first choice is the wonderful *Zamkowy* hotel (☎2671 or ☎2672), a period piece occupying the south wing of the castle, with a good **restaurant** just opposite. This small hotel is predictably popular, and in the summer you won't get in unless you've booked three months in advance. The only other option is the **PTTK hostel** at ul. Dominikańska 1 (☎2512), just north of the Rynek: it too has a restaurant, as well as housing a PTTK tourist office. As an alternative, the *Zamkowy* hotel staff can sometimes help with fixing **private rooms** in town.

Every May, Łańcut castle hosts a series of **international chamber music** concerts, and in the summer there are international master classes for aspiring young instrumentalists.

Leżajsk

Thirty kilometres north of Rzeszów on the verges of the River San, at first sight **LEŻAJSK** is a typical bustling market town with a main square, a church and precious little else to show for itself. For many, though, the town's name at least will be familiar thanks to the local brewery, long-established producer of one of the country's leading – and best – range of beers. For Catholic pilgrims – and lovers of organ music – the monastery church in the north of town makes the place the subject of a special journey.

The Bernardine church and monastery

Leżajsk's main attraction is some way north of the town centre: arriving by bus or train at the combined central station it's about a two-kilometres walk or bus ride north to the vast **Bernardine Church and Monastery**. Built in the late 1670s inside a fortress-like defensive structure, the vast Baroque basilica is an established and important centre of pilgrimage thanks to an icon of the Madonna and Child placed here, venerated for centuries by Catholics as a miracle-worker. On religious holidays, notably the **Feast of the Assumption** (August), the church draws huge crowds, and at just about any time of year you're likely to find buses full of school children or OAPs doing the rounds of the church and stations of the cross situated in the woods behind the building. The cavernous church interior is a mass of Baroque decoration, with numerous side altars, religious paintings, some finely-carved wooden choir stalls and a huge guilded main altarpiece.

Pride of place, however, goes to the monster Baroque **organ** filling the back of the nave, one of the finest – and certainly one of the most famous – in Poland. With nearly 6000 pipes, 4 manuals and over 70 different registers the exquisitely decorated instrument produces a stunning sound more than capable of filling the building.

Services apart, you can also get to hear the organ at the concerts held regularly in summer – check with the tourist offices in Rzeszów for details. The **international organ festival** held here every May is a mecca for fellow players and a major musical event well worth coinciding with.

Elsewhere in town

Just south of the monastery gates over ul. Klasztorna is the **Leżajsk Brewery**: you can try the draught version of the tasty local brew at the roadside bar along with the hardened local consumers; if the prospect intimidates, however, you can stock up on cans of the stuff at the shop next door.

Back into the town centre, the late Renaissance **Parish Church**, east of the square, is worth a quick look, featuring some fine early fresco-work in the nave. For **accommodation** the hotel options are the *Pilawa*, Rynek 5 (☎209-50), which also has a restaurant of sorts, and the *Podmiejski*, ul. Studzienna 8 (☎201-54). There's also a **youth hostel** (summer only) near the stations. Virtually every bar or takeaway joint in town serves at least one of the excellent beers produced by the Leżajsk brewery.

Local **buses** run to and from Rzeszów (50mins), Łańcut, Przemyśl, via Jarosław (1hr 30 min), while the train station is on the cross-country line from Sandomierz to Przemyśl.

Jarosław

Nestled at the foot of the San River valley on the main road eastwards to the Ukrainian border, the town of **JAROSŁAW** is one of the oldest in the country. An urban settlement is known to have been established here by the mid-twelfth century, on the site of a stronghold raised by a Ruthenian prince known as Jarosław the Wise some two centuries earlier. The town's strategic location at the nexus of major medieval international trade routes led to its rapid development as a commercial settlement.

In their medieval heyday the fairs held in Jarosław were second only to those of Frankfurt in size, drawing merchants from all over the continent. The most tangible reminder of the mercantile glory days is the **old market complex** at the centre of town, which has preserved the essentials of its medieval layout. Like many towns in the region Jarosław, particularly the large and dynamic local **Jewish population**, suffered badly at the hands of the Nazis.

Round the town centre

Focal point of the medieval town centre is the breezy, open central square where the fairs used to be held. Filling the centre is the Gothic **Town Hall**, a smart looking building topped by a tall spire that was burnt down, like much of the town centre, in 1625 and subsequently remodelled in Baroque and later in neo-Renaissance style, when the raised balcony was added. On several sides the square is lined with the arcaded merchants' houses: while not as grand as those in Zamość, some of the houses are impressive nonetheless, most notably the Renaissance **Osseti Mansion** on the south side. Built in the 1670s by a wealthy family of Italian merchants, the building has a beautifully decorated upper attic and a typically open, airy arcade. It's also the home of the **Town Museum** (Tues–Thurs, Sat & Sun 10am–2pm, Fri 10am–6pm), which contains an enjoyably offbeat collection of the type local museums thrive on: portraits of local priests of all denominations and the local aristocratic Potocki dynasty, period furniture and a brilliant collection of early typewriters, gramophones and polyphones make for an enjoyable tour. Looking round also gives you a chance to admire the fine original polychromy decorating several of the grand, wooden-beamed rooms.

The clearest evidence of the town's mercantile past comes from the honeycomb of **cellars** stretching out beneath the town square. Originally built as storage space for the merchants trading on the square above, the network of cellars served as an effective hide-out for local people during successive assaults on the town, most notably the Tartar raids of the fourteenth century. The cellars were gradually abandoned during later centuries, but a 150-metre long section of the (by then) flooded cellars was cleared out by miners in the early 1960s and opened to visitors a decade later.

Subject to demand, **tours** through the cellars are conducted by one of the members of staff at the museum ticket office (same opening hours as town museum). The entrance is through one of the merchants' houses on the eastern side of the square: from here you descend into the brick-walled passageways – many of the walls are original – and wind your way through the gloom down to a depth of 20-metres at the lowest point, eventually re-emerging where you started: the chill down here is explained by the ingeniously constructed ventilation system, good enough to allow meat to be kept here, and still functional.

North of the square, a short walk along the bumpy, cobbled streets is the **Parish Church,** an imposing late sixteenth-century complex surrounded by the town walls. If you are there when it's open, the *cerkiew* down the hill east of the square, a colourful eighteenth-century construction now in use again by its former Uniate occupants, is also worth a look-in. Completing the tour of religious architecture the former **Synagogue** northwest of the square on the corner of ul. Opolska, built in 1810, now a school building, is one of several that served the town's thriving Jewish population. Despite the signs warding them off, the **covered market** (*Wiata Targowa*) on ul. Grodzka, leading west of the square, is popular with Ukrainian and Russian traders from across the border, who've set up an improvised marketplace of their own out on the south side of the building.

Practicalities

The bus and train station, at the bottom of ul. Słowackiego, is a fifteen-minute walk southwest of the Old Town. As yet there's no proper tourist information office, about the best you can find being the *Turysta* office, no. 25 on the north side of the square. The **hotel** at the same address (☎22-98) is the main accomodation option in town, the others being the *Turkus*, ul. 1 Maja 5a (☎26-40), and the *City*, ul. Grunwaldzka 1 (☎35-15). All three also have restaurants: otherwise there's a scattering of cafés and snack bars in the Old Town area. For a taste of local nightlife the *Joker* on ul. Grodzka, open till midnight, is the main diversion.

Przemyśl

Overlooking the River San, just 10km from the Soviet border, with the foothills of the Carpathians in the distance, the grubby but haunting border town of **PRZEMYŚL** has plenty of potential. Climbing the winding streets of the old quarter is like walking back through history to some far-flung corner of the Hapsburg empire. As yet, it's very little visited and even by normal Polish standards has a serious dearth of accommodation, restaurants or entertainment. Access is straightforward though, with both trains and buses from Rzeszów and Łańcut.

Founded in the eighth century, Przemyśl is the oldest town in southern Poland after Kraków, and for its first few centuries its location on the borders between Poland and Ruthenia made it a constant bone of contention. Only under Kazimierz the Great did Poles establish final control of the town, developing it as a link in the trade routes across the Ukraine. Przemyśl maintained a commercial pre-eminence for several centuries, despite frequent invasions (notably by the Tartars), but as with many Polish towns economic decline came in the seventeenth century, particularly after Swedish assaults in the 1650s. Much of the town's character derives from the period after the First Partition, when Przemyśl was annexed to the Austrian empire. In 1873 the Austrians added a huge castle to the town's defences, creating the most important fortress in the eastern Austro-Hungarian Empire. During World War I this region was the scene of some of the fiercest fighting between the Austrians and Russians: throughout the winter of 1914 Russian forces besieged the town, finally bringing its surrender in March 1915, then losing it again only two months later. The devastation of both town and surrounding region was even more intense then than during the Nazi onslaught 25 years later, with only small sections of the sturdy fortifications surviving the siege.

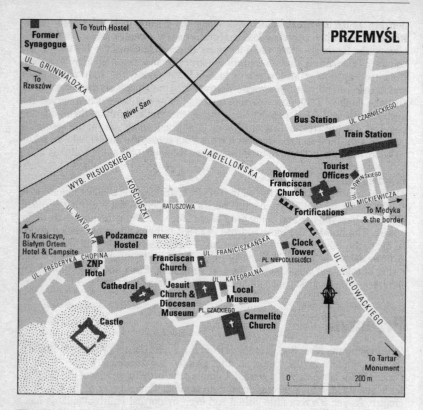

The Town

The main **train station** (Przemyśl Główny) is within walking distance of the centre. The opening up of the borders to the east of Przemyśl has turned the station area into a sort of mass cultural bazaar-cum-transit camp: at almost any time of day or night the station entrance hall is filled with former Soviet citizens – Ukrainians, Georgians and Armenians as well as Kazakhs and other Central Asian peoples – camped out on the way to or from their homelands. Exotic though the sight may appear this isn't the place to hang around at night, especially if carrying luggage: as with most of the mainline eastern border transit points along the former Soviet border, mafia-type gangs are already well established in the station area. Similar warnings apply to the **bus station**, just behind on ul. Czarneckiego.

Fragments of the **Austrian fortifications** can be seen on the approach to the Old Town, opposite the Reformed Franciscan church on the corner of ul. Mickiewicza. Ul. Franciszkańska brings you to the **Rynek**, where the **Franciscan Church** offers a demonstration of unbridled Baroque. The same goes for the **Cathedral**, further up the cobbled streets leading up to the castle – its 71-metre belltower points the way. Remnants of the first twelfth-century rotunda can be seen in the crypt, and there's a fine Renaissance alabaster *Pietà* on the main altar, but Baroque dominates the interior, most notably in the Fredro family chapel. The fourteenth-century **Castle**, home to the town theatre and currently under restoration, isn't much to look at, but the view from the ramparts makes the climb worthwhile. Of the other churches in the Old Town, the seventeenth-century **Jesuit Church*** contains an extraordinary pulpit shaped like a ship, complete with rigging. Partisans of Catholic religious paraphernalia can visit the **Diocesan Museum** in the adjacent Jesuit college (Tues–Sun 10am–4pm), which nuns take you round. The seventeenth-century **Carmelite Church** functioned as the Uniate (Greek Catholic) cathedral until 1945, when it was handed over to the Roman Catholics: the old wooden iconostasis is on display in the **local museum** (Tues–Sun 10am–2pm) over the road inside the grand old Uniate bishop's palace. The second floor heralds the museum's main attraction, an excellent collection of icons from the Uniate churches of the surrounding region. The influence of Catholic art and theology on these essentially Orthodox-derived pieces is most evident in the Madonna and Child icons, the Christ Pantocrator figures also being decidedly Roman in feel. Highlights include a mystical early eighteenth-century *Assumption of Elijah* and a fabulously earthy *Day of Judgement* from the same era, which has a team of prancing black devils facing off against a beatific angelic host.

Fifty years ago Przemyśl had much greater ethnic diversity than today: old guidebooks indicate that the area around the Carmelite church was the **Ruthenian district**. There are two **Orthodox churches** still functioning in the east of the town, both of them nineteenth-century constructions. The **Jewish Quarter** was more to the north of the old centre. Numbers 33 and 45 in ul. Jagiellońska were both synagogues before World War II, and there was another across the river – off to the left from ul. 3 Maja, now part of a garage workshop.

Out of town

For an excellent view, especially towards the Carpathians, the **Kopiec Tartarski** (Tartar Monument) on the southern outskirts of town is worth a trip: buses #28 and #28A deposit you at the bottom of the hill. Legend says the monument at the top marks the burial place of a sixteenth-century Tartar Khan who is reputed to have died nearby. For a slightly longer excursion from Przemyśl, the obvious destination is **Krasiczyn Castle**, a ten-kilometre ride west of town by bus #5. Built in the late sixteenth century for the Krasicki family by Italian architect Gallazzo Appiani, the castle is a fine example of Polish Renaissance architecture. Extensive restoration is in progress, but you can still see round most of the building, including the courtyard. The wooded **park** that shelters the castle makes a cool, relaxing spot for a stroll. When the Austrian-funded restoration is completed (1993 on current projections), Krasiczyn Castle will become a conference centre and hotel; till then the hotel and restaurant in the castle will probably remain out of action. Check out the Przemyśl tourist office for the latest details.

---

*The Jesuit Church became the focus of national attention in 1991, following the Polish-Catholic hierarchy's decision to hand the building over to the sizeable local Greek Catholic (Uniate) population, hitherto deprived of their own place of worship. The move sparked a wave of local protest, with parishioners blockading the church and refusing to hand it over. Catholic defiance was quickly met with equally spirited opposition, and for a while the situation looked as if it might develop into a serious confrontation, with disturbing ethnic undertones and old Ukrainian-Polish scores and prejudices coming to the fore. After several weeks of tense negotiations, the Catholics finally gave in and agreed to give the local Uniates free use of the building, a fact reflected in the makeshift iconostasis now in place in front of the altar.

Practicalities

The well-organised San **tourist office** across the square from the railway station at ul. Sowińskiego 4 is both an information centre and ticket office (☎56-15). The Orbis office next door is another useful resource (☎33-66).

The best **place to stay** in town – which isn't saying much – is the privately run *Pod Białym Orłem* at ul. Sanocka 8 (☎61-07); it's twenty minutes' walk west along the river from the station, or take bus #10 or #10A. Inexpensive and peacefully

---

ON TO L'VIV

There's no better illustration of the current revival of cross-border ties in Poland than the growing tourist influx to **L'VIV**, 60km across the Ukrainian border. Alongside its cultural cousin, Vilnius, L'viv (Lwów to Poles) was long one of the main eastern centres of Poland: like the Lithuanian capital, too, traditionally this was a city characterised by a diverse, **multicultural population** – three cathedrals, Armenian, Orthodox and Catholic, are still there today. In Polish terms, the city's greatest ascendancy was during the Partitions era, when it became at least as important a centre as Kraków: during the inter-war years, too, Polish culture flourished in the city. The postwar loss of the city to the Soviet Union was a cruel blow to Poles – L'viv still has a substantial Polish-speaking population – who've always remained strongly attached to the place, as evidenced by the scores of old photo albums and prewar guidebooks you can find in the bookshops these days. The recent liberalisation of border controls has led in a large influx of Polish visitors, thankfully unaccompanied by demands for the "return" to Polish control of a city that was at the forefront of the recent Ukrainian struggle for independence.

PRACTICALITIES

The short hop from Przemyśl makes a day trip to L'viv a plausible option. With travel costs minimal, the biggest outlay here is on the **visa** (currently £30 a shot) still required by the Ukrainian authorities – though reports suggest they may be on the verge of abolishing this, or at least considerably reducing the price. Obtaining a visa in Przemyśl is no problem: they can be bought either at the bus station or from one of the tourist offices grouped off the square in front of the railway station. (For once things are easier for Poles, for whom regular cross-border travel is now greatly facilitated by a straightforward voucher system.)

The best cross-border travel option is the **bus service**. Starting from around 6am PKS buses depart several times a day for L'viv from Przemyśl bus station – a two-hour journey, border formalities included. Return buses from L'viv run till the early evening, leaving you with a good half day to explore the city. Especially in summer when demand is high it's best to book your bus seat in advance. As an alternative to queuing up at the ticket counters in the bus station itself, several local **travel agencies** will make the bookings for you for a minimal fee, notably the San bureau, ul. Sowińskiego 4 (☎5615) and the next door Orbis office (☎33-66), visas included. The main disadvantage with regular **train** services that also run regularly across the border is the crowds cramming most of them, the fight to get on and off at both ends ranking with the worst Indian-style scrums. In a bid to help the beleaguered customs officials cope with the cross-border influx, the main L'viv railway station is now divided into two sections, one for domestic lines, the other for international trains. As well as long tailbacks at the main international **road** border-crossing point at MEDYKA, 9km east of Przemyśl, increasing reports of armed gangs stopping and robbing foreign vehicles along the highway on the Ukrainian side of the border mean that a **car** trip to L'viv is only for the really adventurous.

located on the edge of a wood, the hotel has a restaurant serving home-cooked specialities. The *Przemysław* (☎40-32), which is next to the tourist centre at ul. Sowińskiego 4, is a basic bed-and-breakfast place, popular with the Ukrainian "trade tourist" brigade and generally full in season. The *Sportowy* at ul. Adama Mickiewicza 30 (☎38-49), ten minutes' walk east from the station, is of similar quality but is less likely to be full. The teachers' union hostel (*Dom Nauczycielskie NZP*), close to the castle at ul. Chopina 1 (☎27-68), is inexpensive, as is the nearby *Podzamcze PTTK* at ul. Waygarta 5 (☎53-74). The **youth hostel** at ul. Lelewela 6 (☎61-45) stays open throughout the year, while the *Zamek* campsite at ul. Piłsudskiego 8a, about half a mile west of the old town, has bungalows as well as spaces for tents. If you're in a car, it's worth considering the *U Medarda pensionat* (☎18-94) in DYBAWKA, about 6km west of Przemyśl on the Krasiczyn road.

The *Białym Orłem* also comes first in the **restaurant** recommendations. If you want to eat late, there's the *Karpacka* at ul. Kościuszki 5, though you may be subjected to a local "dancing band". In the town centre the *Polonia* at ul. Franciszańska 35, the *Bałtycka* in ul. Dąbrowskiego and the *Kmiecianka* at ul. Wieniawskiego 2 will at least fill you up, while for **milk bar** fans the *Expres*, opposite the station, does the honours. If you have a car you could try the good-quality Hungarian *Eger* at ul. Grunwaldzka 134, some way out on the Rzeszów road, or the *Troika*, ul. Lwowska 18, on the border road – both are bar-restaurants.

Polish-style **fast food** is picking up in town, notably in the cafés and bars on and around Franciszkańska, a racy local pool hall on ul. Kazimera Wielkiego included.

The Sanok region

There are two good routes south from Przemyśl towards the **Bieszczady Mountains**, one direct, the other more circuitous. The first involves a two-hour train journey into and out of the **Ukraine**, ending up in **Ustrzyki Dolne** (see p285), in the foothills of the Bieszczady. If nothing else, it's a chance to travel into former Soviet territory without a visa. Trains leave once a day – currently 2.30pm – passing through several Ukrainian towns and villages without stopping. Soldiers still ride on board to ensure no-one tries any funny business. Controls used to be rigorous: in the early 1980s some Solidarity activists flushed leaflets in Russian down the toilets on the Soviet side; the train stopped and didn't move until the soldiers had recovered every single one. Nowadays the reduced troop contingent keeps a pretty low profile, but taking photos on the Ukrainian side is still not a very good idea, however innocuous you may find snapshots of passing fields and trees.

The alternative option is to go by bus through **Sanok**, sixty-odd kilometres and a two-hour ride southwest from Przemyśl. The advantage of this route is the journey through the foothills: in spring and autumn the mountains are at their most alluring, the sun intensifying the green, brown and golden hues of the beech forests. If you've the time to spare, consider stopping off at picturesque little towns such as **Bircza** or **Tyrawa Wołoska** to soak up the atmosphere; a number of villages with wooden *cerkwi* are tucked away in easy walking distance of Tyrawa.

Further east through the foothills, the village at **Arłamów**, close to the Ukrainian border, is the site of the decommissioned army HQ where president/banned Solidarity leader Lech Wałęsa was imprisoned during the early days of martial law. A luxury palatial-looking complex that used to double as a Party members' **hunting lodge** is now open to the public. Soldiers still guard the entrance, though you get the feeling that they really don't know who the place belongs to these days. The hunting facilities are currently utilised by classier holiday groups.

Sanok

Perched up on a hilltop above the San valley, **SANOK** looks a sleepy sort of place. Best known within Poland for its rubber and bus factories, whose *AutoSan* vehicles can be seen all over the country, of late the town has begun to pick up economically, largely on the back of increased cross-border trade flowing into the surrounding region. For the southbound traveller, though, the important thing about Sanok is that it's the last real town before the Bieszczady Mountains, which loom through the mists on the horizon.

The church and castle

A number of things in and around the town make it a place worth visiting in its own right, too. The reconstructed fourteenth-century **Parish Church** on the edge of the Rynek hosted the wedding of King Władysław Jagiełło in 1417. Nearby stand the remnants of the sixteenth-century **Castle**, built on the site of the original twelfth-century fortress that guarded the main highway running through the town from the southern Carpathians on into the Baltic. Much of the castle is given over to a **town museum**, and contains a collection of modern art from all over the region.

The Icon Museum

The main building to head for is the one overlooking the valley, looking like the ancestral pile of some Scottish laird. Two rooms house the fabulous Sanok **Icon Museum** (April 15–Oct 15 Tues–Sun 9am–3pm), the largest collection of Ruthenian icons in the world after the one in Moscow. Though most of the pieces date from the sixteenth and seventeenth centuries, the oldest comes from the mid-1300s, so the collection gives a clear impression of the development of the **Ukrainian school** of painting, which evolved in tandem with an autonomous and assertive local church.

Unlike Russian and Greek Orthodox iconography, however, much of the work on display here is still pretty unknown to anyone but art historians and specialists, despite its quality. The best of the early icons have both the serenity and severity of Andrei Rublev's greatest works. In contrast, later icons manifest the increasing influence of western Catholicism – which culminated in the formation of the Uniate Church in 1595 (see box on p.288) – both in their style and subject matter, with an encroaching Renaissance approach to the portraiture. In a few cases, the figures show strong Tartar influences too. Look out too for a large *Icon of Hell*, an icon of a type traditionally housed in the women's section of Orthodox churches: such lurid depictions of the torments of the underworld must have kept a few people in check.

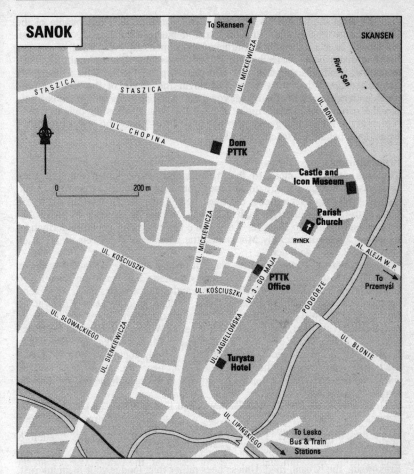

As with all such collections, the presence of these icons is related to postwar "resettlements". With many local villages deserted in the aftermath of "Operation Vistula" (again, see box on p.288), their wooden *cerkwi* neglected and falling apart, the oldest and most important icons were removed to museums. Genuine artistic concern prompted their removal, but now that local people are returning to the villages and using the churches again, it's high time for the authorities to consider handing at least some of the icons back.

The skansen
Also worth a visit is the **skansen** in the Biała Góra district, 2km north of the centre (Tues–Sun 8am–5pm, early closing off-season); if you don't want to walk, take a bus north along ul. Mickiewicza to the bridge over the river – the *skansen* is on the other side, spread along the river bank. This open-air museum, one of the best in the country, brings together examples of the different styles of all the

region's main ethnic groups – Boyks, Lemks, Dolinianie ("Inhabitants of the Valley") and Pogorzanie. (If you want detailed ethnography, an English guidebook is available at the entrance.) Specimens of every kind of country building have been carefully moved and reassembled here: smithies, inns, granaries, windmills, pigsties and churches. Up on the hillside, a couple of graceful eighteenth-century *cerkwi* nestle in the shade of the trees. In the nineteenth-century school building, you'll find some amazing old textbooks: note too the carefully preserved maps of pre-1914 Poland, showing this area as a region of the Austro-Hungarian province of Galicia – hence the portrait of Kaiser Franz Josef behind the teacher's desk.

Practicalities

The **bus station** is close to the train station, about fifteen minutes' walk southeast of the town centre; most buses from here will take you up to the main square. Of the **tourist offices**, the most helpful are the *Turysta* bureau in the hotel of the same name at ul. Jagiellońska 13, and the PTTK office a little further up the road at ul. 3-go Maja 18; if any office has maps and general information, including for the Bieszczady Mountains, the latter will. The Orbis office, at ul. Grzegorza 2, deals with tickets.

For an **overnight stay**, the best place in town is the *Turysta* (address above; ☎306-64); it is modern, soulless and quite expensive but worth the price if you can get a top-floor view over the San valley, and the downstairs bar is a weekend hang-out for the Sanok smart set. Other options are the *Dom PTTK* at ul. Mickiewicza 29 (☎314-39), some way west from the main square, which has its own modest restaurant, and the *Sports Hotel* at al. Wojska Polskiego on the banks of the River San (☎302-57), with a summer-only *Autocamping* site. The **youth hostel** is at ul. Lipińskiego 34 (☎319-80), the easterly continuation of the Lesko road. You can **camp** either in Biała Góra, near the *skansen*, or at the *AutoCamping* on al. Wojska Polskiego, situated to the east on the town side of the river.

The privately run *Bartlek* at ul. Padlewskiego 11, a side street on the way to the *skansen* (ask locals for directions), is a reasonable **restaurant**, but open erratically. The *Turysta* apart, there's also *Max*, ul. Kościuszki 24, a little way out of the centre, and a newly opened *pizzeria* halfway down central ul. 3-go Maja. Out of town there's the *Adria*, ul. Lipińskiego 58, and the *Dąbrowianka* on ul. Krakowska, the Krosno road. Unless beer rather than food is your main interest, avoid eating at the *Karpacka*, ul. Jagiellońska 24, at all costs.

Lesko and the foothills

East from Sanok the south-bound road passes through ZAGÓRZ, the hub of local rail connections, and continues a further 6km to **LESKO**, a tranquil and long-established foothills town that seems to be doing increasingly well out of its strategic tourist location. South off the approach road from Sanok is what remains of the old sixteenth-century town **Castle**, occupied by a fairly posh former miners' holiday centre (☎6268); theoretically at least the place is now open to anybody, though, typically, no one's actually yet got round to advertising the fact. If you fancy staying in what's likely to become a regular hotel, the best thing is just to turn up and ask about rooms: if the conferences the centre now hosts regularly aren't occupying the whole place, they'll happily oblige.

Lesko's other attractions relate to the town's one-time **Jewish community.** Just east off the square stands the former **Synagogue**, a solid-looking Renaissance structure with a finely sculptured facade reconstructed, like the rest of the building, after World War II, and now home of a local art gallery. Down the hill behind the building and across a stream brings you to the foot of the **Jewish cemetery**, one of the most beautiful and evocative in the whole country. Hidden from a distance by the trees covering the hillside cemetery, the steps up from the roadside – the Star of David on the gate tells you you're at the right entrance – take you up through a tangled knot of twisted tree trunks and sprawling under-growth to the peaceful hilltop cemetery site, around which are scattered 2000 odd gravestones, the oldest dating back to the early 1500s. As in other major surviving cemeteries there's a wealth of architectural styles in evidence, notably a number of ornately decorated Baroque tablets with characteristic seven branched candelabra, recurring animal motifs and often a pair of hands reaching up in prayer towards the heavens from the top of the stone: it's the setting as much as the stones that makes this cemetery so memorable, a powerful testimony to centuries of rural Jewish presence.

Castle apart, the **accommodation** options in town are the motel at ul. Bieszczadzka 4 (☎80-81) and the youth hostel (with its own restaurant) at ul. Jana Pawła 11 18 (☎269). If you're stopping off between journeys at the bus station on the square in front of the parish church the *Gyros*, a kebab takeaway on the main square, will keep the wolf from the door. If liquid refreshment is what you need the *piwiarnia Alf* just off the square will provide the necessary supplies of the honeyed *Leżajsk* brew.

South from here the bus continues through **UHERCE**, where many Polish tourists veer off towards **Jezioro Solińskie**, a fjord-like artificial lake created in the 1970s for hydroelectric power and watersports purposes. The custom-built lakeside villages of SOLINA, POLAŃCZYK and MYCZKÓW have more restaurants than anywhere else in the area, but there's little else to recommend them apart from their access to the water. In all three your best bets for accommodation now are the numerous workers' holiday houses and camping sites ranged across the water's edge. Yacht and kayak hire can be arranged with the *Bieszczady* tourist office in Solina.

Ustrzyki Dolne

Back on the main road, **USTRZYKI DOLNE**, 25km east of Lesko, is the main base for the mountains, swarming in summer with backpacking students and youth groups, many of them fresh off the afternoon train formerly known as the "Soviet Express" from Przemyśl (see p.278). Otherwise this is a small agricultural town with just a scattering of minor monuments: a synagogue (now a library), a *cerkiew* – both nineteenth century – and several memorials connected with the Ukrainian resistance (see box on p.288). **Accommodation** can be very hard to find in the hiking season. Best bets are the *Laworta* at ul. Zielona 1 (☎364), the biggest hotel in town and so most likely to have a room, the smaller *Strwiąz* off the main square at ul. Sikorskiego 1 (☎303), and the *Pensjonat Otryt* at ul. Rzeczna 26 (☎519). The **PTTK bureau** off the main square doubles up as a hostel in season (ask about **private rooms** here also), as does the *Bieszczady* office on the same street. There's plenty of **camping** space, both at the official site on ul. PCK and in the fields around the edge of town. For a meal, the *Pizzeria Romana*, just off the square, is the place local youth aim to be seen in.

Queues for **buses into the mountains** form early at the stops on the road down from the train station, and everyone has to shove their way on board. Before leaving, stock up in the shops around the station area; supplies of anything edible are unpredictable beyond here.

Krościenko

Nine kilometres north of Ustrzyki Dolne is the village of **KROŚCIENKO**, last train stop before the Soviet border (local buses run there too). The Bieszczady region is full of surprises, and this is one of them. Following the outbreak of civil war in Greece, a small community of Greek partisans and their families escaped to Poland in 1946 and settled in this area. The monument in the village centre is to **Nikos Balojannis**, a Greek resistance hero executed by the generals in Athens soon after his return in 1949. Not expecting to stay long they never made much effort to do up their houses, hence the shabby look of the place. Only a few Greeks remain these days, the younger generation having mostly elected to return to the home country. There's a fine eighteenth-century **cerkiew** in the village too, and another older one a little further north in the Wolica district.

The Bieszczady Mountains

The valleys and slopes of the **Bieszczady Mountains** were cleared of their populations – a mix of Boyks, Lemks and Ukrainians – in "Operation Vistula", following the last war (see box, p.288). Today, these original inhabitants and their descendants are coming back, but the region remains sparsely populated and is largely protected as national park or nature reserves. The reserves are carefully controlled to protect the wildlife, but are open to the public – quite a change from a decade ago, when the Communist Party elite still maintained various sections for its own high-security hunting lodges. Ecologically, the area is of great importance, with its high grasslands and ancient forests of oak, fir and, less frequently, beech. Among the rarer species of fauna inhabiting the area you may be lucky enough to sight **eagles**, **bears**, **wolves**, **lynx** and even **bison**, introduced to the Bieszczady in the 1960s. Even the highest peaks in the region, around 1300 metres, won't present many **hiking** problems, as long as you're properly kitted out. Like all mountain regions, however, the **climate** is highly changeable throughout the year: on the passes over the *połonina*(meadows) for example, the wind and rain can get very strong. The best time to visit is late autumn: here, as in the Tatras, Poles savour the delights of the "Golden October". Mountain temperatures drop sharply in winter, bringing excellent skiing conditions.

Ustrzyki Dolne to Ustrzyki Górne

The main road out of **Ustrzyki Dolne** winds south through the mountain valleys towards **Ustrzyki Górne**, a ninety-minute journey by bus. If you've developed an enthusiasm for the wooden churches of this area, and you've time to spare, you could consider a diversion a few kilometres east off the road to the border villages of JAŁOWE, BANDARÓW NARODOWY and MOCZARY (the first two are reachable by bus) to see the fine examples there. Back on the main road, you'll also find wooden churches at HOSZÓW, CZARNA GÓRNA, SMOLNIK, and – on a road off to the east – at BYSTRE and MICHNIOWIEC (bus from Czarna Górna).

BIESZCZADY REGION

Coming over the hill into **LUTOWISKA** you'll see makeshift barracks and drilling rigs, signs of the oil industry that has developed here sporadically since the last century. Locals insist that the Soviets for years blocked full development of the region's resources, fearing Polish economic independence. The grubby roadside restaurant in the village caters mainly for the oil workers.

Ustrzyki Górne

USTRZYKI GÓRNE has a wild, end-of-the-world feel, spread out along the bottom of a peaceful river valley and surrounded by the peaks of the Bieszczady. The holiday development at the north end of the village may change things in time, but for the moment Ustrzyki is little more than a few houses, a shop and a clutch of takeaway stands. The main accommodation is provided by a **PTTK hostel** at the southern end of the village; like most others in the region, it is pretty basic but it guarantees to find you at least some floor space, however crowded it gets. For **campers** there's no problem putting up your tent next to the hostel, or even elsewhere in the valley, as long as you don't make a mess. Nearby, a *baza studentowa* (student camp) operates in the summer months: you can probably get a mattress in a tent here, though as always this is easier if you've got some Almatur vouchers. A costlier but more comfortable alternative is to ask around for **private rooms** in the houses up the hill on the other side of the road from the PTTK.

Besides the smoky dive of a restaurant across from the PTTK hostel, the only **food** options in Ustrzyki are a couple of stand-up places by the main road. The wooden hut just up from the PTTK, on the same side of the road, has very rudimentary food but plentiful supplies of *Leżajsk*: a small but devoted band of locals seem to spend most of their time camped round the bar, joined in the early evening by hard cases off the Ustrzyki Dolne bus, which draws up here. Anglers might note that the stream running through Ustrzyki is prime trout-fishing territory – not that it's seen on local menus; signs on the river banks warn that fishing rights are controlled by the angling club, but permission should be easy to get.

Hiking in the Bieszczady

Walking and winter skiing are the main reasons for coming to the Bieszczady region. From Ustrzyki there are a number of **hiking options,** all of them attractive and accessible for anyone reasonably fit; times given below are reckoned for an average walker's speed, including regular stops and landscape gazing. **Skiers** will need to bring along all equipment and be prepared for minimum facilities: there are lifts at just three villages: Ustrzyki Górne, Cisna and Polańczyk. The best **map** is the *Bieszczady Mapa Turystczyna* (1:75,000).

THE BIESZCZADY BY HORSE – OR BIKE

Walking and wintertime skiing aside, there are now (at least) two other ways of exploring the wilder parts of the Bieszczady region. Traditionally the plateaux and high paths of the region have been the natural habitat of *hucule*, an ancient breed of **wild horses** found throughout the Carpathians and named after the equally temperamental people of the eastern stretches of the mountains. Up above the village of **POLANA,** a few kilometres off the main road west of Czarna Górna, a couple of dedicated local enthusiasts have set up a *hucule* stable, currently boasting a stock of around 50 pure-bred horses. In recent summers they've begun offering riding holidays in the mountains, mostly in the beautiful **Otryt range** stretching south of the village. If the idea of riding bareback through the mountains appeals, this is the one to go for – first-hand reports suggest it's an exhilirating experience. The stable's already proving a success, so anyone seriously interested should write in advance to: *Stadnina Koni Huculskich "Tabun"*, 38-709 Polana, Poland. Otherwise, if you have your own transport you could try turning up for a day or two's riding on the off chance there's a horse free. Finding your way there is impossible without help, so ask anyone in the village for the way and they'll point you in the right direction. If you do come for a period, the owners will also be able to help you find **private accommodation** in the village. Alongside the wooden *cerkiew* now used by Catholics, an additional curio in Polana is *U Żyda* – literally "At the Jew's place" – the local **pub,** which has a painting of a Jew outside, a reminder of the fact that this, like many country inns in Poland, was run by Jews up until World War II.

The other less conventional but equally exciting way of exploring the tops is on **mountain bikes** (*rowerów górskich*). In **DWENICZEK,** a little hamlet off the main road past Smolnik at the southern end of the Otryt range, a local couple have bought up 30 good-quality mountain cycles and set themselves up as a small guest house. If the idea of bombing up and down the slopes on a bike appeals – unsurprisingly, fitness is at a premium, by all accounts – they can be contacted via the main Sanok PTTK office (Sanok ☎301-13/23).

East to Tarnica and the Ukrainian border

There are two initial routes east from Ustrzyki, both leading to the high Tarnica valley (1275m). The easier is to follow the road to the hamlet of WOŁOSATE (there's a **campsite** just beyond at BESKID, right on the border) then walk up via the peak of Hudow Wierszek (973m) – about four hours all in. Shorter but more strenuous is to go cross-country via the peak of Szeroki Wierch (1268m), a three-hour hike. **Tarnica peak** (1346m) is a further half-hour hike south of the valley.

From Tarnica valley you can continue east, with a stiff up-and-down hike via **Krzemien** (1335m), **Kopa Bukowska** (1312m) and **Halicz** (1333m; 3hr) to **Rozsypaniec** (1273m), the last stretch taking you over the highest pass in the range. This would be a feasible day's hike from the Beskid campsite; the really fit could do an outing from Ustrzyki to Krzemien and back in a day.

Adventurous walkers could consider trekking into the region to the north of Tarnica valley in search of the **abandoned Ukrainian villages** and tumbled-down *cerkwi* scattered along the border (delineated by the River San). Some, like BUKOWIEC and TARNAWA WYZNIA, are marked on the map, but others aren't, so you have to keep your eyes peeled. Many villages were razed to the ground, the only sign of their presence being their orchards. The Polish **border police** who shuttle around the area in jeeps are nothing to worry about as long as you're carrying your passport, and have a plausible explanation of what you're up to. The Ukrainians who watch this area are a different proposition, though, so don't on any account wander into Ukrainian territory – police detention of hikers in L'viv has been known.

West towards the Slovak border

There are some easy walks west to the peak of **Wielka Rawka** (1307m), flanked by woods on the Slovak border. One option is to go along the Cisna road and then left up the marked path to the summit (3hr). Another is to head south to the bridge over the Wołosate river, turn right along a track, then follow signs to the peak of Mała Szemenowa (1071m), from where you turn right along the border to the peaks of Wielka Szemenowa (1091m) and Wielka Rawka (4hr).

Northwest of Ustrzyki

The best-known walking areas of the Bieszczady are the **połonina** or mountain meadows. These desolate places are notoriously subject to sudden changes of weather: one moment you can be basking in autumn sunshine, the next the wind is howling to the accompaniment of a downpour. The landscape, too, is full of contrasts: there's something of the Scottish highlands in the wildness of the passes, but wading through the tall rustling grasses of the hillsides in summer you might imagine yourself in the African savannah. Walking the heights of the passes you can also begin to understand how Ukrainian partisans managed to hold out for so long up here (see box on previous page); even for the most battle-hardened Polish and Soviet troops, flushing partisan bands out from this remote and inhospitable landscape must have been an onerous task.

Note that you can save walking time in this region by taking a **bus** from Ustrzyki Górne though Wetlina, Dołzyca and Cisna. If you've only got a very short time, you could take just a brief detour off the road north from Ustrzyki Górne to Ustrzyki Dolne. Take the bus a couple of kilometres west to the **Przelec**

BOYKS, LEMKS AND UNIATES

Up until World War II, a large part of the population of southeast Poland was classified officially as **Ukrainian**. For the provinces of L'viv, Tarnopol and Volhynia, in the eastern part of the region (all in the Ukraine today), this was accurate. However, for the western part, now Polish border country, it was seriously misrepresentative, as this region was in fact inhabited by **Boyks** (Boykowie) and **Lemks** (Lemkowie). These people, often collectively called "Rusini", are historically close to the Ukrainians but have their own distinct identities, both groups being descendants of the nomadic shepherds who settled in the **Bieszczady** and **Beskid Niski** regions between the thirteenth and fifteenth centuries.

For centuries these farming people lived as peacefully as successive wars and border changes allowed. Their real troubles began at the end of World War II, when groups of every political complexion were roaming around the ruins of Poland, all determined to influence the shape of the postwar order. One such movement was the **Ukrainian Resistance Army (UPA)**, a group fighting against all odds for the independence of their perennially subjugated country. Initially attracted by Hitler's promises of an autonomous state in the eastern territories of the Third Reich, by 1945 the UPA were fighting under the slogan "Neither Hitler nor Stalin", and had been encircled by the Polish, Czech and Soviet armies in this corner of Poland. For almost two years small bands of partisans, using carefully concealed mountain hideouts, held out against the Polish army, even killing the regional commander of the Polish army, General Karol Swierczewski, at Jabłonki in March 1947.

This is where the story gets complicated. According to the official account, UPA forces were fed by a local population more than happy to help the "Ukrainian fascists". The locals give a different account, claiming they weren't involved with the UPA, except when forced to provide them with supplies at gunpoint. The Polish authorities were in no mood for fine distinctions. In April 1947 they evacuated the entire population of the Bieszczady and Beskid Niski regions in a notorious operation code-named **"Operation Vistula"** (Akcja Wisła). Inhabitants were given two hours to pack and leave with whatever they could carry, then were "resettled" either to the former German territories of the north and west, or to the Soviet Union.

From the Gorlice region of the Beskids, a traditional Lemk stronghold, an estimated 120,000–150,000 were deported to the Soviet Union and a further 80,000 were scattered around Poland, of whom about 20,000 have now returned. The first arrived in 1957, in the wake of Prime Minister Gomułka's liberalisation of previously hard-line policy. (Rumour has it that this was Gomułka's way of thanking the

Wyzniańska pass, the first stop, from where a marked path leads up through the woods on the right-hand side of the road to the **Połonina Caryńska** (1107m) – a steep climb of roughly 45 minutes. You'll have time to walk along the pass a short way to get a feel for the landscape, and then get back down to catch the next bus on.

For a more extended trip from Ustrzyki Górne, take the steep trail marked in red and green north through the woods up to the eastern edge of the **Połonina Caryńska**, and walk over the top to the western edge (1297m; 2hr 30min). Continue down the hill to the village of BRZEGI GÓRNE where there's a **campsite** near the road. From here you can either take a bus to Ustrzyki Górne

Lemks who had helped him personally during the war.) The trickle of returnees in the 1960s and 1970s has, since the demise of communist rule, become a flow, with Lemks and Boyks reclaiming the farms that belonged to their parents and grand-parents. This return to the homeland is bringing a new level of political and cultural self-assertion. In the June 1989 elections, Stanisław Mokry, a Solidarity candidate from near Gorlice, openly declared himself a Lemk representative. In tandem with the country's sizeable **Ukrainian minority** likewise dispersed to the north and west in the postwar period, they have begun to call for some form of redress for historical injustices. In tandem with the Union of Polish Ukrainians, Boyks and Lemks have pressed for, among other things, official condemnation of the postwar deportations – a demand partially met by the Senate in August 1990 when it passed a resolution condemning "Operation Vistula", though the Sejm failed to follow suit – material compensation for property confiscated in the 1940s and 1950s, the return of some currently state-owned property, particularly the communal woodlands seized in 1949, and the passing of a national minorities law. Like other minorities in Poland, Lemks and Boyks want their own schools, language teaching and the right to develop their own culture.

But the question of self-identity is entangled by the religious divisions within the community. Like their Ukrainian neighbours, in the seventeenth century many previously Orthodox Boyks and Lemks joined the **Uniate Church**, which was created in 1595 following the Act of Union between local Orthodox metropolitans and Catholic bishops. The new church came under papal jurisdiction, but retained Orthodox rites and traditions – including, for example, the right of priests to marry. Today the majority of Lemks in the Bieszczady and Beskid Niski classify them-selves as Uniate (or "Greek Catholic", as Poles know them). Encouraged both by the pope's appointment of a Polish Uniate bishop and political changes in the Ukraine, where Uniates are finally coming into the open after years of persecution, Lemk Uniates are tentatively beginning to adopt a higher religious profile.

The Uniates' revival in Poland is still hampered, however, by the vexed question of restitution of property confiscated in the wake of "Operation Vistula", in particu-lar the 250-odd churches in the region taken away from the Uniates and mostly given to the Roman Catholics and Orthodox. The dispute over the Carmelite Cathedral in Przemyśl that broke out in spring 1991 was resolved only after a nasty local dispute with distinctly anti-Ukrainian undertones, and a row that temporarily threatened to jeopardise newly developing Polish-Ukrainian political relations. The Uniates have still not recovered most of their former church property. A further twist is added in the case of Orthodox-occupied buildings – the church in Rzepedz (see p.291) is a good example – since like Ukrainians the Lemk and Boyk communi-ties are divided between the two faiths.

(or on to Sanok), or take the red-marked path which takes you up the wooded hill to the right to the all-year PTTK **hostel** on the eastern edge of the **Połonina Wetlińska** (1228m; 1hr 30min from Brzegi) – the views from this windswept corner are spectacular. Sleeping arrangements are basic and comprise mattresses in ten-person rooms; theoretically you should bring your own food, but the young couple who run the place will probably be happy to feed you from the communal pot.

Beyond the hostel there's an excellent walk over the Połonina Wetlińska to **Przełec Orłowicza** (1075m), where the path divides in three. A sharp left takes you down the hill to WETLINA (2hr 30min from the hostel), where there's a larger

PTTK hostel and **campsite** (open all year), a restaurant and a bus stop for journeys north to Sanok or south to Ustrzyki Górne. The middle path goes to **Smerek** (1222m) and down through the woods to the bus stop in SMEREK village (2hr). The right-hand path is for the long-distance hike via Wysokie Berdo (940m), Krysowa, Jaworzec, Kiczera, Przerenina and Fałówa to DOŁŻYCA (7hr; PTTK hostel), or even further on to the villages of Jabłonki and Baligród (see below).

West of Dołzyca: the forest railway

Continuing west from Dołzyca brings you to **CISNA**, a smallish village that saw some bitter fighting during the 1945-47 civil war, when the UPA (see box, p.288) had one of their main bases nearby, a struggle commemmorated by the statue in the middle of the village. There's a reasonable supply of accommodation, including a motel, a (summer only) youth hostel and a couple of old workers' holiday homes. A kilometre to the southwest is **MAJDAN**, little more than a couple of houses but the site of an open-air rail museum and the main boarding point for the **narrow-gauge railway** running west through the forests along the Slovak border.

A product of the days when the Bieszczady region was little more than a backwoods of the Austro-Hungarian empire, the 25-kilometre long forest railway line between Majdan and **Rzepedz**, with a short additional connecting track to **Nowy Łupków**, was built as part of a scheme to connect the Austrian army regional headquarters in Majdan with the main Przemyśl–Budapest rail line. In addition to carrying passengers, these days the line forms part of a network of tracks through the forest which are used by the local forestry industry for wood transportation.

The train leaves Majdan daily at 6.30am on weekdays, arriving in Rzepedz around 11am: at midday it sets off on the downhill return run, arriving at 2.50pm: on weekends the corresponding times are: depart Majdan 9.30am, arriving around 12.30: depart again 1.00pm, arriving around 4.20pm. Though these timetables are pretty established, you'd be advised to check them beforehand – they're posted at both end-stations; alternatively the forest railway (*Osródek Transportu Leśnego*) head office is in Komańcza (☎33). If you're only making the northward leg of the journey, buses and PKP trains take you the twenty-odd kilometres onward to Zagórz and Sanok.

The majority of this memorable and out-of-the-way route passes through uninhabited hillside forests filled with a gloriously rich and diverse flora, the beautiful views over the valleys adding a touch of mountain thrill to the experience. The train's steam engine puffs away at a snail's pace for much of the journey, which is all it can manage on the steep hills it has to negotiate at regular intervals. You can pick the train up at several points along the way, and the driver can usually be persuaded to stop for a while *en route* if anyone wants to take a longer look at the scenery. At weekends the train is liable to be joined by contingents of local drinkers who spend the journey getting absolutely plastered, in many cases falling off the train at regular intervals and clambering drunkenly back on again.

A more salubrious highlight are the gleaming natural **forest lakes**, which local legends hold were created by the Devil when he crashed to the ground on a ball of fire: scientists say it's quite possible they were created by meteorites. If you're lucky you may also catch sight of rare black storks along the stretch of track up near the Slovak border.

Roughly halfway along the journey an additional stretch of track branches off to **NOWY ŁUPKÓW**, a tiny place whose name is familiar to Poles for the nearby internment camp, to which many prominent Solidarity leaders were consigned during martial law. If you have access to transport, there is an interesting Uniate *cerkiew*, now a Roman Catholic church, which is worth a visit at the village of SMOLNIK, just to the east.

Out of the mountains

There is a choice of routes out of the western Bieszczady back to Sanok. The main one runs **from Nowy Łupków through Komańcza** and a series of tiny Uniate villages such as **Rzepedź**. The other is a more obscure, winding road north from **Cisna**, via **Jabłonki** and **Baligród**. Buses run along both roads, while trains serve only the main route.

Komańcza and Rzepedź

North from Nowy Łupków, buses and PKP trains take you north to the village of **KOMAŃCZA**, whose two churches illustrate graphically the religious tensions of the region. Near the main road is a modern building recently constructed by the majority **Uniate** population, while hidden away in the woods on the edge of the hill is a nineteenth-century *cerkiew*, used by the small **Orthodox** community. In 1980 the Uniates petitioned the local authorities for their own place of worship but the *cerkiew* was given instead to the Orthodox worshippers – a good example of the divide and rule tactics used to manipulate the smaller religious groupings. At the other end of the village, uphill to the left, the **Nazarene Sisters Convent** is something of a shrine for Polish tourists: it was here that Cardinal Wyszyński, the redoubtable ex-Primate of Poland, was kept under house arrest in the early 1950s during the Stalinist campaign to destroy the independence of the Catholic Church. The **PTTK hostel** down the hill will put you up for the night, as might the convent.

You could have a fascinating time searching the Komańcza area for *cerkwi*: modern maps of the region mark them clearly. (Uniate buildings are identified in the key as "churches in ancient orthodox churches".) There's a particularly fine and typically Lemk Uniate church just beyond at **RZEPEDŹ**, roughly fifteen minutes on foot from the railway stataion. Nestled away on a hillside surrounded by tranquil clusters of trees, the church merges into the landscape – a common quality in *cerkwi* that may explain how they escaped the destruction of Bieszczady villages in the wake of "Operation Vistula" (see p.288). The interior of the church gives a sense of the twin strands of Uniate worship: on the one hand Western Madonnas and insipid oil paintings; on the other the Eastern iconostasis, the absence of an organ (in the Orthodox tradition the choir provides all the music), the pale blue Ukrainian saints, and Ukrainian-script wall inscriptions. If you're planning on staying here, the *Bieszczady Hotel* is at hand in the village.

North from Cisna

From **Cisna**, buses head to Lesko and Sanok, through a region which was the scene of some of the heaviest fighting between the Polish Army and the Ukrainian resistance. At **JABŁONKI** there's a monument to **General Karol**

Swierczewski, the veteran Spanish Civil War commander killed here in March 1947, while further north at the larger village of **BALIGRÓD** a monument commemorates the Polish soldiers who fell – but not, as yet, the Ukrainians. This was the headquarters of the Polish Army during the conflict, and if you root around in the hills you'll see fortifications and the sites of various villages cleared in 1947.

THE WOODEN CHURCHES OF THE POLISH CARPATHIANS

Despite a modern history characterised by destruction and neglect, both the Bieszczady and neighbouring Beskid Niski regions still have a significant number of villages that boast the wooden Uniate churches – *cerkiew* (plural, *cerkwi*) as they and Orthodox places of worship are known in Polish – traditional to this part of Europe.

Some of the most remarkable date from the eighteenth century, when the influence of Baroque was beginning to make itself felt, even among the carpenter architects of the Carpathians. The simpler constructions with a threesome of shingled onion domes also encountered in the Bieszczady region – a structure common to most Uniate churches – have their origin in the later, **Boyk**-derived architectural styles. Finally in the Lemk-inhabited districts of the Beskid Niski you'll often encounter grander, showier structures wth a marked Ukrainian influence, built in the 1920s and 1930s at the height of Ukrainian self-assertion within Poland.

Without your own transport, the possibility of reaching many of the churches in situ is limited, though several of the small towns mentioned in this chapter have *cerkwi* within reasonable walking distance. The easiest way of having a close look is to visit the *skansens* at Sanok or Nowy Sącz, both of which contain complete churches. If, on the other hand, you do make it out to some of the more remote villages you'll need to ask around for the key (*klucz*), which is more likely than not to be in the hands of the local priest (*ksiądz*) or the person living nearest the building.

The dark and intimate **interior** of a Uniate church is divided into three sections from west to east: the narthex or entrance porch, the main nave, and the naos or sanctuary. Even the smallest of the Uniate churches will boast a rich iconostasis all but cutting off the sanctuary, which will contain the familiar icons of (working from left to right) Saint Nicholas, the Madonna and Child, Christ Pantocrator and, lastly, the saint to whom the church has been dedicated. Above the central door of the iconostasis (through which only the priest may pass) is the representation of the Last Supper, while to the left are busy scenes from the great festivals of the church calendar – the Annunciation, the Assumption and so on. The top tier of icons features the Apostles (with Saint Paul taking the place of Judas). Typically, the Last Judgement covers the wall of the narthex, usually the most gruesome of all the depictions, with the damned being burned, boiled and decapitated with macabre abandon.

Locations of a number of *cerkwi* are indicated throughout the chapter. The current pattern of ownership varies: following the expulsions of "Operation Visula", many buildings were taken over by Roman Catholics and some by Orthodox. Despite the recent upsurge in Uniate activity, Catholics still retain many of these buildings. Some have been returned – grudgingly you feel – to the Uniates, others are shared by both branches of Catholicism, while a good many still remain abandoned.

The Beskid Niski

West from Sanok the main road, closely tracked by the slow rail line, heads towards Gorlice through the Wisłok valley: a pleasant pastoral route, with a succession of wooden villages set back in the hills of the **Beskid Niski** to the south. There's not a great deal to detain you, though, until you get west of Krosno, to the medieval town of **Biecz** and on to Gorlice, the centre for Beskid Niski hikes.

Also covered in this section is **Dukla**, an isolated old town that has long controlled the Przelec Dukielska pass into Czechoslovakia – the most important crossing point in the east of the country.

Krosno

At the heart of the country's richest oil reserves, **KROSNO**, the regional capital, is also the petroleum centre of Poland, but for the moment the resource is under-exploited, and the town seems more rooted in the past than expectant of future riches. Prior to the discovery of oil, which helped the town grow fairly wealthy in the late 1800s, Krosno had quite a record of mercantile prosperity. In particular, the town's favourable position on the medieval trade routes east meant it rapidly became one of the wealthiest Renaissance-era towns in the country, as evidenced by the plush burghers' mansions lining the square. If you're heading west towards Kraków, then this bustling, pleasantly situated town is worth the stopoff.

Around the centre

At the core of the busy modern town is the hilltop Old Town centre, a sizeable and reasonably well-preserved area with an attractive, compact-looking **Rynek** at its centre. Ranged round it are the Italianate merchants' houses fronted by arcaded passages – reconstructed in the nineteenth century in this case – characteristic of several towns in the southeast, notably the early sixteenth-century **Wojtówska Mansion** (no. 12) on the southwest side of the square, which boasts a finely decorated Renaissance portal that underscores the town's mercantile Italian connections. South of the Rynek on ul. Franciszkańska is the brick-facaded late Gothic **Franciscan Church**, notable features being some Renaissance tombstones of various local dignitaries, and on the left of the building the Baroque **Oświęcim family chapel**, a sumptuously ornate piece designed by Italian architect Falconi.

South from the Rynek along ul. Sienkiewicza, a statue on pl. Konstytucji 3 Maja commemorates **Ignacy Łukasiewicz**, the local boy who sunk what's claimed to be the world's first oil well in 1854 in the village of **Bóbrka**, 10km south of town – the pioneering Pole's drilling derrick and oil shaft are in an open-air museum there, twenty minutes away by local bus. North of the square along ul. Piłsudskiego, the main shopping street, is the **Parish Church**, a large Gothic structure with an overlay combining Renaissance and Baroque decoration to impressive effect, including a notable set of richly carved choir stalls and some fine polychromy above the nave. Unsurprisingly the **Regional Museum** (Tues–Sun 10am–3pm), in the sixteenth-century former bishops' palace at the top of the street, is mostly devoted to the local oil mining trade, the highlight being a lovingly polished collection of early kerosene lamps, the revolutionary device of which Łukasiewicz was the inventor.

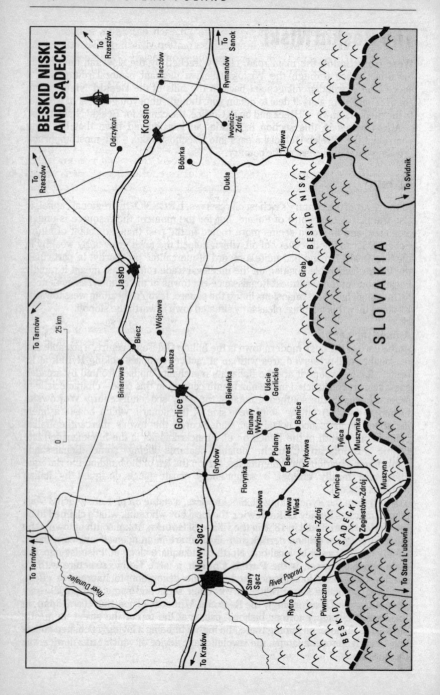

The main bus and train stations are next to each other, ten minutes' walk northwest of the Old Town. For **tourist information** visit the PTTK office at ul. Staszica 2 or Orbis at ul. Blich 1. **Accommodation** includes two modest hotels: the *Polonia*, near the centre at ul. Piłsudskiego 18 (☎220-34), and the seasonal *Bliźniak*, ul. Czajkowskiego 43 (☎218-79). There's also the expensive, three-star *Krosno-Nafta*, ul. Lwowska 21 (☎220-11), and, for anyone with a car, the *Motel Moderówka* (☎17-96) at Moderówka, 8km west on the Gorlice road. Krosno also has a **youth hostel**, well north of the centre at ul. Konopnickiej 5 (July & Aug; ☎210-09), and the *Bieszczady* tourist office may also be able to help fix up **private rooms**. Best of the **restaurants** is the *Stylowa*, in the *Krosno-Nafta* hotel. On the main square, the *Wojtowska* at Rynek 12 is a decent eatery and *piwnica* with a nice squareside location. Genuine greasy spoons are located on ul. Sienkiewicza and Franciszkańska, just off the main square.

Around Krosno

If you feel like venturing round the Krosno area, the ruins of the fourteenth-century **Castle Kamieniec**, one of the oldest fortresses in the Carpathian Mountains, can be seen at **ODRZYKOŃ**, 8km north (occasional buses).

At **HACZÓW**, 12km east (again occasional buses), a medieval town settled by Swedes and Germans in the fourteenth century, there's a beautiful mid-fifteenth-century **cerkiew**, the oldest wooden church in the country, as well as some fine timber houses.

IWONICZ-ZDRÓJ, 11km southeast of Krosno (occasional buses) off the main Sanok road, is one of the most agreeable of a succession of pleasant little spa towns nestled in the valleys coursed by tributaries of the Wisłok River. The town's strategic setting also makes it a good base for **walks** in the scenic surrounding *beskidy* (hills), with a couple of good hilltop routes leading westwards to Dukla (see below), some 6km away from town.

The main town thoroughfare leading off from the only road into town is a genteel promenade filled in season by crowds of holidaymakers, many of them staying in the plentiful *pensjonat* available for takers of the supposedly healthy local waters. The **tourist office** at the north end of the promenade will help you with finding accommodation, which given the wealth of options even in season shouldn't pose too much of a problem.

Dukla

DUKLA, 24km south of Krosno, was for centuries the main mountain crossing-point on the trade route from the Baltic to Hungary and central Europe. The location has also ensured an often bloody history, the worst episode occurring in the last war, when more than 60,000 Soviet soldiers and 6500 Czechoslovaks died in an attempt to capture the valley from the Germans.

Today, rebuilt after comprehensive damage in the fighting, Dukla is a windy, quiet and rather bleak place – every bit the frontier town with its eerie, stage-set main square. There are no real sights, save for a Rococo parish church and a local **Museum** (Tues–Sun 10am–4pm), housed in the surviving parts of the former Mniszech family palace, which gives chilling details of the wartime fighting in the "Valley of Death" to the south.

For an overnight **stay** it's a choice between the PTTK **hostel** at number 25 on the main square (☎46), the **youth hostel** at Trakt Węgierski 14 (☎8; summer only), or **private rooms** (ask at the PTTK hostel). For food and drink, check out the *Basztowa*, opposite the squat town hall in the main square, or the slightly better *Granicze* round the corner on ul. Kościuszki.

West of Dukla, one or two buses a day cover the backwoods route **to Gorlice**, taking you along the edge of the hills. If you have transport, or have time to hike, the tiny roads leading south into the Beskid Niski are well worth exploring.

Biecz

BIECZ is one of the oldest towns in Poland and was the conduit for nearly all the wine exported north from Hungary in medieval times. This thriving trade in the early equivalents of *Bull's Blood* continued until the middle of the seventeenth century, when the "Swedish Deluge" flattened the economy – but fortunately not the town.

Trains and buses both stop near the centre, with the Old Town a short walk up on the top of the hill. The **Rynek** here is dominated by the fifty-metre tower of the late Renaissance **Town Hall**. Nearby, the large **Parish Church**, complete with fortified belltower, contains Renaissance and Gothic pews, as well as a fine seventeenth-century pulpit decorated with musicians. Over the road on ul. Kromera, the local **Museum** (May–Sept Tues–Sun 9am–4pm; Oct–April closes 3pm), housed in a burgher's home that used to be part of the fortifications, has an intriguing collection of artefacts, featuring Baroque musical instruments, carpenters' tools and the entire contents of the old pharmacy – sixteenth-century medical books, herbs and prescriptions included. For the record, guides inform you that Biecz once had a school of public executioners. They were kept busy: in 1614, for example, 120 public executions took place in the square. For an overnight stay there are two options, the *Adrianka* **hotel**, ul. Świerczewskiego 35 (☎157), and the **youth hostel** (with its own restaurant) at ul. Parkowa 1 (☎14). About the only places to eat are the *Max* restaurant and a *kawiarnia*, both on the edge of the main square.

Churches around Biecz
Several villages in the vicinity of Biecz have beautiful wooden churches. In the woods at **LIBUSZA**, 9km south, off the Gorlice road, the sixteenth-century chapel still retains some of its Renaissance polychromy. Two kilometres to the east, the church at **WÓJTOWA**, another sixteenth-century specimen, is similarly splendid.

If you've got time for only one sortie though, go to **BINAROWA**, 5km north of Biecz (local bus or taxi). Constructed around 1500, the timber **church** here has an exquisitely painted interior, rivalling the better-known one at Debno in the Podhale (see Chapter Four); the polychromy is part original, part eighteenth-century additions, and all meriting close attention. If you can find him around, and you can speak Polish,you should try to get a tour with the local priest, an entertaining commentator who declares that King Kazimierz the Great, who was very fond of visiting Biecz, often stopped off at the Binarowa church on his way home.

Gorlice

GORLICE is a curious base for the Beskid Niski, the westerly extension of the Bieszczady: you'll know when you're approaching the town by the suddenly foul air. Like Krosno, the town has for a century been associated with the oil industry, Ignacy Łukasiewicz having set up the world's first refinery here in 1853. If you want further doses of petroleum history, the Local Museum on ul. Wąska (Tues–Sun 10am–4pm) is devoted to Łukasiewicz and the oil industry generally. That aside, there's not a lot to be said – Gorlice is not the most beautiful of towns.

The bus and train stations are both close to the centre on the northern side of town. The train station is the terminus of the Krosno line – trains to Tarnów and on to Kraków leave from Gorlice Zagorzany, 2km up the line (frequent train and bus connections). Tourist information is available at the PTTK office, ul. Tysiąclecia 3, and the IT bureau in the rudimentary *Wiktoria* hostel at ul. 1 Maja 1b (✶206-44). Accommodation options are the *Parkowa* hotel (✶214-60) in the Park Miejski, the *Dom Nauczyciela* teachers' hostel at ul. Wróblewskiego 10, and the youth hostel at ul. Michałusa 16 (✶225-58; July & Aug). For food try the *Magura*, ul. Waryńskiego 16 (closes 8pm), or the *Gorlicka*, ul. Słoneczna 6, both designated "category 1" restaurants. For a snack try the *kawiarnia* in the town hall basement.

South of Gorlice: walks in the Beskids

The Beskid Niski are a hilly rather than mountainous range, less dramatic than the Bieszczady, but nevertheless excellent walking country. The people – predominantly Lemks (see box p.288) – provide a warm welcome to the few hikers who do get to this area, and many of their settlements have fine examples of the region's characteristic wooden churches. As a rule you'll find these deliberately tucked away amid the trees, their rounded forms and rustic exteriors seeming almost organic to the landscape. The earliest date from the fifteenth century, most from the eighteenth and beyond. In the Gorlice area, a noticeable feature of most church cemeteries are the international names on the tombstones, a legacy of an Austro-Hungarian battle against the Russians in 1915, which left 20,000 dead.

Details of all hill walks are given in the PTSM youth hostel handbook (see *Basics*), and should be provided by the tourist offices in towns such as Krosno and Gorlice. A good local map will greatly increase your enjoyment of this region, though the best one, *Beskid Niski i Pogorze*, is out of print; you might find one in a shop or tourist office. The most ambitious route, marked in blue on the *Beskid Niski i Pogorze* map, runs some 80km from GRYBOW, 12km west of Gorlice, along the Czech border to KOMAŃCZA (see "The Bieszczady Mountains", p.284). Youth hostels (July & Aug) are strategically placed at twenty- or thirty-kilometre intervals at USCIE GORLICKIE and HAŃCZOWA (day 1), GRAB (day 2), BARWINEK (day 3) and RZEPEDZ (day 4), all with bus stops nearby.

Bielanka

The physical return of the Lemk and Boyk minorities to their roots has been accompanied by a revival of interest in their cultural and linguistic traditions. BIELANKA, 10km southwest of Gorlice, is the base of the *Lemkyownya* music and dance ensemble, which has already toured the Ukraine, Canada and the USA. Turn up in Bielanka on a Thursday evening and you may catch them rehearsing in the village hall.

The Beskid Sądecki

West from Gorlice the hills continue through a range known as the **Beskid Sądecki**, another low-lying stretch of border slopes sheltering a sizeable and expanding Lemk population. **Nowy Sącz**, the regional capital, is the obvious base for the area, which otherwise comprises very small market towns, scattered villlages and traditional peasant farms.

Nowy Sącz

NOWY SĄCZ, the main market town of the Beskid Sądecki, nestles on the banks of the River Dunajec, an out-of-the-way place these days and ideal as a base for exploring the hills. It was once better known, having bèen a royal residence from the fourteenth to the seventeenth centuries, and in the fifteenth century having seen the birth of the **Kraków-Sącz School** of painters, the first recognised Polish "school".

The Town

There are two **train stations**: the Miasto station, near the Old Town, handles Kraków trains; the Dworzec Główny station, 2km south of town, all other destinations. Local buses shuttle between the Dworzec Główny and town centre, via the **bus station** on ul. Staszica.

The centre of the spacious Rynek, in the Old Town, is occupied by the incongruous neo-Gothic **Town Hall**, which hosts occasional chamber music concerts as well as council meetings. The Gothic parish church of **St Margaret** (św. Małgorzata), off the east side of the square, has the familiar Baroque overlay, two Renaissance altars excepted. It and many of the burghers' houses lining the square are looking a lot less shabby as a result of the systematic and extensive programme of restoration which is currently being pursued around the Old Town.

Over the road on ul. Lwowska, the sixteenth-century Canonical House contains the **Town Museum** (Tues–Thurs, Sat & Sun 10am–2.30pm, Fri 10am–6pm), which displays those few pieces from the Kraków-Sącz school that haven't been taken off to the national museums in Kraków and Warsaw. Other rooms hold a collection of icons gathered from *cerkwi* in the surrounding region – not as extensive as that in Sanok but amply demonstrating the distinctive regional style of icon painting. There's plenty of folk art on show too, including some typically Polish *Christus Frasobliwy* sculptures, showing a seated Christ propping his mournful face on one hand. Finally there's an interesting collection of works by the Lemk artist Nikifors (1895–1968), known locally as the "Matejko of Krynica". Bearing inscriptions in spidery, childlike handwriting (Nikifors didn't learn to write until late in life), several of the pictures are reminiscent of Lowry's scenes of industrial northern England.

The seventeenth-century **Synagogue** on ul. Berka Joselewicza, in the ghetto area north of the Rynek, houses a contemporary art gallery (Wed–Sun 10am–2.30pm); the building has been so well modernised that there's nothing visibly Jewish left. Further up on the northern edge of the Old Town, the ruins of the **Castle**, built during Kazimierz the Great's reign, give a good view over the valley below. After being used for mass executions of local civilians, the castle was blown up by the Germans in 1945. For the adventurous shopper the daily

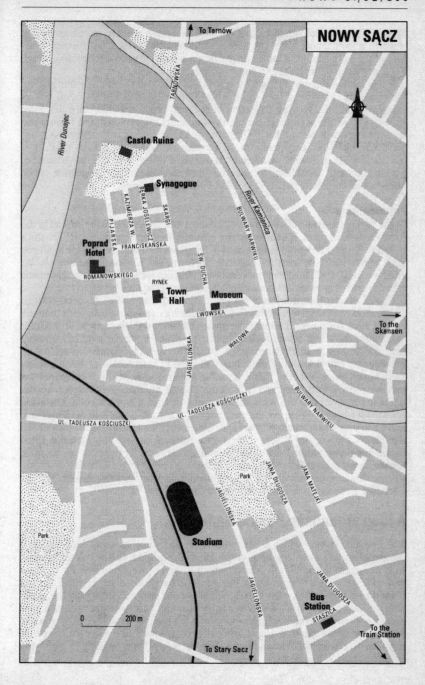

NOWY SĄCZ

To Tarnów

River Dunajec

TARNOWSKA

River Kamienica

BULWARY NARWIKU

Castle Ruins

Synagogue

BERKA JOSELEWICZ

KAZIMIERZA W.

SKARGI

PIJARSKA

Poprad
Hotel

FRANCISKAŃSKA

ROMANOWSKIEGO

RYNEK

Town
Hall

ŚW. DUCHA

Museum

LWOWSKA

To the
Skansen

WALOWA

JAGIELLOŃSKA

BULWARY NARWIKU

UL. TADEUSZA KOŚCIUSZKI

UL. TADEUSZA KOŚCIUSZKI

Park

JANA DŁUGOSZA

JANA MATEJKI

JAGIELLOŃSKA

Park

Stadium

JAGIELLOŃSKA

JANA DŁUGOSZA

Bus
Station

STASZICA

To the
Train Station

0   200 m

To Stary Sącz

Russian market, known locally as Red Square across the river on ul. Lwowska, is worth a look. There are some permanent kiosk-type setups, but the real deals can be found on the long tables or plastic dropcloths spread out on the ground. Keep an eye on your wallet and you may find some bargains.

A few kilometres east of town by bus #14 or #15 from the train or bus station, the **skansen** (May–Sept Tues–Fri 9.30am–4pm, Sat & Sun 9.30am–5pm) has an extensive and still growing collection of regional peasant architecture. If you've already visited the *skansen* at Sanok, the buildings in the Lemk and Pogorzanie sections here will be familiar. What you won't have seen before, however, are buildings like the fragments of a Carpathian Gypsy (*Cyganie*) hamlet – realistically situated some distance from the main village – and the assortment of manor houses, including a graceful seventeenth-century specimen from Małopolska, complete with its original interior wall paintings.

Practicalities

Of the various **tourist offices** in town, the most helpful are the Artus bureau in the *Hotel Panorama* on ul. Romanowskiego, just off the main square, the PTTK office at Rynek 9, and the Poprad bureau at ul. J. Długosza 21. Each will be able to fill you in on festivals and summertime events in the town. The *European Cultural Centre*, ul. Szwedska 2 (☎237-24), is also worth checking out for local events and contacts with the town's growing community of US and European students.

Choice of **accommodation** is not great. The *Panorama* at ul. Romanowskiego 4a (☎218-78) is the preferable hotel, central, cheaper and more congenial than the Orbis *Beskid Hotel* near the main station at ul. Limanowskiego 1 (☎207-70). Other options are the small *Zajazd Sądecki* hostel, ul. Król. Jadwigi 67 (☎267-17), a standard PTTK hostel at ul. Jamnicka 2 (☎227-23), and the **youth hostel** on ul. Batorego 72 (☎232-41; July & Aug; buses #14 and #15 stop outside). For **camping** there's tent space near the PTTK hostel in summer. Ask at the PTTK office for **private rooms**: when demand is high the Poprad bureau (see above) doles out sleeping places around the town. **Restaurants**, though, are pretty good. The cookery-school-assisted *Bona*, on the east edge of the main square in ul. Kościelna, serves an appetising range of local specialities such as *płacek* (potato pancakes), though it's only open till 9pm. Other reasonable places are the *Panorama* and *Beskid* hotel restaurants, the *Imperial* and the *Stylowa*, both south of the main square on ul. Jagiellońska. Milk bars, *kawiarnia* and assorted drinking dives are all over town, especially in the busy shopping area around the Rynek. Try the Cechowa, Rynek 11, a favourite with young locals.

A loop around the Beskid Sądecki

The **Poprad River** – which feeds the Dunajec just south of Nowy Sącz – creates the broadest and most beautiful of the **Beskid Sądecki valleys**. A minor road runs its length to the Slovak border, which it then proceeds to trail for the best part of 25km. Meandering along this route is as good an experience of rural Poland as you could hope for, through fields where farmers still scythe the grass, with forests covering the hills above. Tracks lead off to remote hamlets, ripe for a couple of hours' church-hunting, while along the main body of the valley you can boost your constitution at Hapsburg-looking spa towns like **Krynica**. North of Krynica, the road follows another valley to Nowy Sącz, making a satisfying circuit.

Stary Sącz

Nowy Sącz's smaller cousin town of **STARY SĄCZ**, 10km south (bus #8, #9, #10, #21 or #24; or train on the Krynica line), was first recorded in 1163 and is the oldest urban centre of the region. It's situated on a hill between the Dunajec and Poprad rivers, whose confluence you pass soon after leaving Nowy Sącz.

Like its modernised neighbour, the town's cobbled **Rynek** has an expansive feeling to it, the main difference being in the height of the buildings – none of the eighteenth-century houses round the Stary Sącz square has more than two storeys. Even in a town this small, though, you still find two thirteenth-century churches: a fortified Gothic **Parish Church** south of the square, and the convent **Church of the Poor Clares**, to the east, relieved by sixteenth-century murals. The **Town Museum** on the square (Tues–Sun 10am–1pm) will kill half an hour.

Accommodation is limited to basic rooms at the *Szalas* (☎600-77), the **youth hostel** (July & Aug) at ul. Kazimierza Wielkiego 14, and the *Poprad* **campsite** on ul. Bylych Wiezniow Politycznych. The Poprad tourist office in Nowy Sącz may also be able to find **private rooms** in or around town. The only real **restaurant** is the *Staromeijska* on the Rynek (closes 9pm), while the tallest of the Rynek's houses has a good *kawiarnia* upstairs, the *Maryszenka*. **Tourist information** is available from the Kinga bureau on the Rynek.

The Poprad valley

By local train or bus it's a scenic two-hour ride along the deep, winding Poprad valley from Stary Sącz to Krynica, and if you're not in too much of a hurry, there are one or two places worth breaking your journey at before you reach the terminus.

At **RYTRO**, 16km down the line, there are ruins of a thirteenth-century castle, and lots of hiking trails up through the woods into the mountains; there's a hotel here too. Radziejowa summit (1262m), which is reached by following a ridge path to the southwest, is one of the more popular destinations, about two hours' walk from the village. The stretch of the river after nearby **PIWNICZNA** forms the border between Poland and Slovakia, and is one of the most attractive parts of the valley, with trout-filled water of crystalline clarity. If you're not hoping to catch the fish yourself, call in at the *Poprad* restaurant in **ZEGESTIÓW-ZDRÓJ**, a lovely spa town further down the valley, for excellent poached trout. The old village, some distance uphill from the station, makes for an enjoyable, leisurely post-lunch stroll.

MUSZYNA, next along the valley, has sixteen mineral springs, spa buildings, and the ruins of a thirteenth-century castle, just north of the train station. The town museum (Wed–Sun 9.30am–3pm), installed in a seventeenth-century tavern, focuses on local woodwork, agricultural implements in particular. From Muszyna the Poprad runs south and the railway heads off to the north towards Krynica, passing through the village of POWROZNIK, with its fine seventeenth-century *cerkiew*.

Krynica

If you only ever make it to one spa town in Poland, **KRYNICA** should be it. Redolent of *fin-de-siècle* central Europe, its combination of woodland setting, rich mineral springs and moderate altitude (600m) have made it a popular resort for over two centuries. In winter the hills (and a large skating rink) keep the holiday trade coming in.

At the northern end of the promenade, past a statue of Mickiewicz, a **funicular train** (summer daily 9am–midnight) ascends a 741-metre hill for an overview of town. Ranged below you is a fine array of **sanatoria**, including an old-fashioned pump room, assorted "therapeutic centres", and mud-bath houses.

The **pump room** is the place to try the local waters. Rent or buy a tankard from the desk here before heading for the taps, where the regulars will urge you to try the purply-brown *Zuber*. Named after the professor who discovered it in 1914, it is reckoned to be the most concentrated mineral water in Europe – certainly it's the worst-smelling. *Zdroj Główny*, a mixture of three or four different waters, is one of the more palatable brews.

Krynica hasn't yet worked out how to deal with foreigners. **Accommodation** is difficult to track down, and the singularly unhelpful PTTK tourist office at ul. Kraszewskiego 6, off the southern end of the promenade, seems to have little interest in revealing what is available.

In fact, PTTK not only offer **private rooms**, but also run the *Rzymianka* **hostel** at ul. Dąbrowskiego 15 (☎22-27). Otherwise there's the *Belweder* **hotel** at ul. Kraszewskiego 14 (☎55-40); it's run by the *Jaworzyna* tourist bureau on ul. Pułaskiego, who also deal with private rooms, and a succession of former state-enterprise holiday *pensjonat*, including the *Lilliana*, ul. Piłsudskiego 13 (☎22-34), the adjoining *Stephania* (same number), the *Pogoń*, ul. Kościuszki, the *Mewa*, Bulwary Dietta 5 (☎20-51) and *Józefa*, ul. Cicha 10 (☎54-20), all located in the central spa area. There's a seasonal **youth hostel** at ul. Kraszewskiego 158 (☎442), and a campsite some way out from the centre on ul. Czarny Potok.

Restaurants are less of a struggle to track down. The *Havana* on ul. Piłsudskiego (the Nowy Sącz road) and the *Roma* at ul. Puławskiego 93 are both reasonable – though bedevilled by the usual "dancing bands". *Czarny Kot*, ul. Stara Droga, a bit out of the centre, is a good-quality joint worth the effort of seeking out. More basic are the *Dworcowa* on ul. Waryńskiego, the *Hokejowa* on ul. Sportowa, the *Cichy Kącik* at ul. Nowasadecka 100, and the *Krynicka* milk bar, ul. Dietla 15.

East from Krynica

The region **east from Krynica** is particularly rich in attractive villages and *cerkwi*, including some of the oldest in the country. Villages such as WOJKOWA, TYLICZ and MUSZYNKA, up in the hills by the Slovak border, have fine seventeenth-century examples. Local buses run occasionally from Krynica, or you could take a taxi – it won't break the bank.

North from Krynica

North from Krynica buses run to Nowy Sącz and Grybów, to the west of Gorlice. For the first 6km both routes follow the main road to KRZYKOWA, where the road divides. For Nowy Sącz you continue through the wooded groves of the Sącz Beskids, via villages such as NOWA WIES and ŁABOWA.

The **Grybów road** is an even more attractive backroads route, due north through open countryside. The village of **BEREST**, 5km north of the main Nowy Sącz road, is a real treat. Set back from the road in pastoral surroundings, it has an eighteenth-century *cerkiew*, an archetype of the harmonious beauty of this region's wooden churches. The doors, opened by a huge metal key that's kept by an ancient peasant caretaker, creak open to release a damp draft from inside;

muted scufflings from the priest's small herd of goats will probably be the only sounds to break the silence. Just a couple of kilometres up the road is **POLANY**, where a contemporary icon painter named Eugeniusz Forycki has a workshop in an old Lemk house; in summer you can visit his workshop – a sort of private *skansen*. From here to Grybów the valley is a gorgeous riverside route; if you have a car, a brief detour south to BRUNARY-WYZNE, then on to the border villages of BANICA and IZBY, is worthwhile, as all three have magnificent wooden *cerkwi*. From **GRYBÓW**, you have the choice of frequent buses and trains west to Nowy Sącz or east to Gorlice, or trains north to Tuchow and Tarnów.

travel details

Trains

Lublin to Białystok (1 daily; 9hr); Gdańsk (2 daily; 8hr); Katowice (4 daily; 6–7hr); Kielce (8 daily; 3–4hr); Kraków (4 daily; 6–8hr); Przemyśl (1 daily; 6hr); Warsaw (11 daily; 2–3hr); Zamość (4 daily; 3–4hr).

Zamość to Kraków (3 daily; 6–10 hr); Lublin (4 daily; 2–4hr); Rzeszów (1 daily; 6hr); Tarnów (3 daily; 4–8 hr); Warsaw (2 daily; 5–7hr).

Rzeszów to Gdańsk (2 daily; 11hr); Kraków (20 daily; 2––4hr); Krosno (2 daily; 3hr); Przemyśl (hourly; 1–2hr); Tarnów (20 daily; 1–2hr); Warsaw (4 daily; 5–7hr).

Łańcut to Przemyśl (15 daily; 1–2hr), via Jarosław (1hr).

Przemyśl to Kraków (15 daily; 3–6hr); Lublin (1 daily; 4hr 30min); Opole (5 daily; 7–9hr); Rzeszów (20 daily; 1–2hr); Tarnów (15 daily; 4–6hr); Warsaw (4 daily; 7–8hr); Zamość (frequent local train to Jarosław then bus; 3–4hr). Also overnight

couchettes to Wrocław and Szczecin and international trains to L'viv, Bucharest and Sofia.

Sanok to Kraków (2 daily; 7hr); Krosno (hourly; 2hr); Lublin (1 daily; 8hr); Przemyśl (2 daily; 3–4hr); Rzeszów (2 daily; 3–5hr); Tarnów (2 daily; 3–5hr); Warsaw (2 daily, including one sleeper; 10hr).

Nowy Sącz to Krynica (hourly; 2hr).

Buses

Lublin to Nałęczów, Kazimierz Dolny, Zamość, Sandomierz and Kraków.

Łańcut to Rzeszów.

Krynica to Gorlice and Nowy Sącz.

Nowy Sącz to Kraków, Rzeszów, Tarnów, Zakopane and Warsaw.

Sanok to Ustrzyki Dolne and into the Bieszczady Mountains.

Gorlice to Nowy Sącz and Kraków.

Zamość to Przemyśl, Lublin, Sandomierz and Kraków.

CHAPTER FOUR

KRAKOW, MAŁOPOLSKA AND THE TATRAS

The Kraków region attracts more visitors – Polish and foreign – than any other in the country, and the attractions are clear enough from just a glance at the map. The **Tatra Mountains**, which form the border with Slovakia, are Poland's grandest and most beautiful, snowcapped for much of the year and markedly alpine in feel. Along with their foothills, the **Podhale**, and the neighbouring, more modest peaks of the **Pieniny**, they have been an established centre for hikers for the best part of a century. And with much justice, for there are few ranges in northern Europe where you can get so authentic a mountain experience without having to be a committed climber. The region as a whole is perfect for low-key rambling, mixing with holidaying Poles, and getting an insight into the culture of the indigenous *górale*, as the highlanders are known. Other outdoor activities are well catered for, too, with raft rides down the Dunajec gorge in summer and some fine winter skiing on the higher Tatra slopes.

Kraków itself is equally popular and impressive: a city that ranks with Prague and Vienna as one of the architectural gems of central Europe, with an Old Town which retains an atmosphere of *fin-de-siècle* stateliness. A long-time university centre, its streets are a cavalcade of churches and aristocratic palaces, while at its heart is one of the grandest of European squares, the Rynek Główny. The city's significance for Poles goes well beyond the aesthetic, though, for this was the country's ancient royal capital, and has been home to many of the nation's greatest writers, artists and thinkers, a tradition retained in the thriving cultural life. The Catholic Church in Poland has often looked to Kraków for guidance, and its influence in this sphere has never been greater – Pope John Paul II was Archbishop of Kraków until his election in 1978. Equally important are the city's **Jewish roots**: until the last war, this was one of the great Jewish centres in Europe, a past whose fabric remains clear in the old ghetto area of Kazimierz, and whose culmination is starkly enshrined at the death camps of **Auschwitz-Birkenau**, west of Kraków.

For the rest, this chapter takes in an area which loosely corresponds to **Małopolska** – a region with no precise boundaries, but which by any definition includes some of the historic heartlands of the Polish state. Highlights here, in countryside characterised by rolling, open landscape, market towns and farming villages, include **Kielce**, springboard for hikes into the **Świętokrzyskie Mountains**, and the pilgrim centre of **Częstochowa**, home of the Black Madonna, the country's principal religious symbol.

KRAKÓW

KRAKÓW, the ancient capital of Poland and residence for centuries of its kings, was the only major city in the country to come through World War II essentially undamaged. Its assembly of monuments, without rival in Poland, has now been listed by UNESCO as one of the world's twelve most significant historic sites. All the more ironic, then, that the government has had to add a further tag: that of official "ecological disaster area" – for Kraków's industrial suburbs represent the communist experiment at its saddest extreme.

Up until the war, the city revolved about its **Jagiellonian University**, founded back in the fourteenth century, and its civic power was centred on the university's Catholic, conservative intelligentsia. The communist regime, wishing to break their hold, decided to graft a new working class onto the city by developing on the outskirts one of the largest steelworks in Europe, **Nowa Huta**. It was like dropping Birmingham onto the periphery of Oxford, and within a few decades its effects were apparent as the city began to crumble. Consequently Kraków is faced with intractable economic and environmental problems: how to deal with the acid rain of the steelworks, how to renovate the monuments, how to maintain jobs.

Yet the city remains a visual treat, with **Wawel Hill** one of the most striking royal residences in Europe and the old inner town a mass of flamboyant monuments. For Poles, these are a symbolic representation of the nation's historical continuity, and for visitors brought up on grey Cold War images of eastern Europe they are a revelation. Kraków's recent **political history** is also of major importance. It was at Nowa Huta – along with the Lenin Shipyards in Gdańsk – that things started to fall apart for the communist government. By the 1970s the steelworkers had become the epitome of hostility to the state, and with the birth of Solidarity in 1980 Nowa Huta emerged as a centre of trade union agitation. Working-class unity with the city's Catholic elite was demonstrated by Solidarity's call to increase the officially restricted circulation of *Tygodnik Powszechny*, a Kraków Catholic weekly which was then the only independent newspaper in eastern Europe. It was in Kraków, as much as anywhere in the country, that the new order was created.

A brief history

The origins of Kraków are obscure. An enduring legend has it that the city was founded by the mythical ruler **Krak** on Wawel Hill, above a cave occupied by a ravenous dragon. Krak disposed of the beast by offering it animal skins stuffed with tar and sulphur, which it duly and fatally devoured. In reality, traces of human habitation from prehistoric times have been found in the city area, while the first historical records are of **Slavic peoples** settling along the banks of the Wisła here in the eighth century.

Kraków's position at the junction of several important east–west trade routes, including the long haul to Kiev and the Black Sea, facilitated commercial development. By the end of the tenth century it was a major market centre and had been incorporated into the emerging **Polish state**, whose early **Piast** rulers made Wawel Hill the seat of a new bishopric and eventually, in 1038, the capital of the country. Subsequent development, however, was rudely halted in the mid-thirteenth century, when the Tartars left the city in ruins. But the urban layout established by **Prince Bolesław the Shy** in the wake of the Tartar invasions, a geometric pattern emanating from the market square, remains to this day.

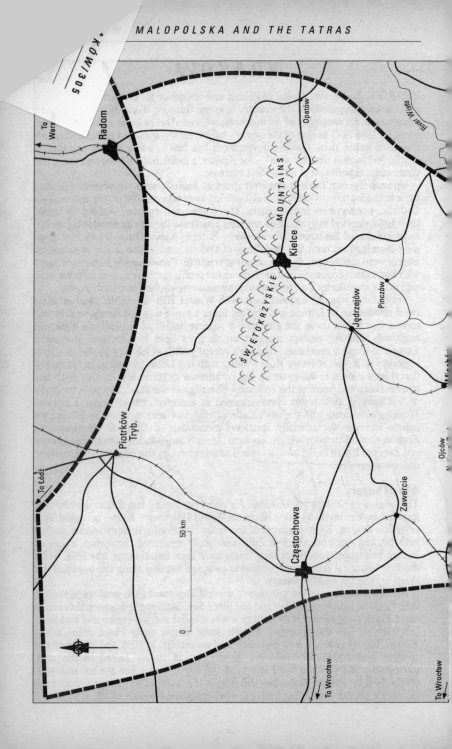

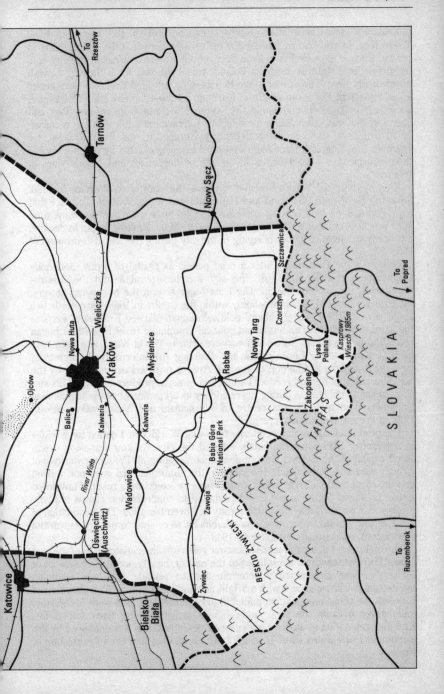

Kraków's importance was greatly enhanced during the reign of **King Kazimierz**. In addition to founding a **university** here in 1364 – the oldest in central Europe after Prague – Kazimierz rebuilt extensive areas of the city and, by giving Jews right of abode in Poland, paved the way for a thriving **Jewish community** here. The advent of the Renaissance heralded Kraków's emergence as an important European centre of learning, its most famous student (at least, according to local claims) being the young **Nicolaus Copernicus**. Part and parcel of this was a reputation for religious tolerance at odds with the sectarian fanaticism then stalking sixteenth-century Europe. It was from Kraków, for example, that King Zygmunt August assured his subjects that he was not king of their consciences – bold words in an age of despotism and bloody wars of religion.

King Zygmunt III Waza's decision to **move the capital to Warsaw** in 1596, following the Union of Poland and Lithuania, was a major blow. The fact that royal coronations (and burials) continued to take place on Wawel for some time after was little compensation for a major loss of status. Kraków began to decline, a process accelerated by the pillaging of the city during the Swedish invasion of 1655–57.

Following the **Partitions**, after a brief period as capital of a tiny, notionally autonomous republic (1815–46), the city was incorporated into the **Austro-Hungarian** province of Galicia. The least repressive of the occupying powers, the emperor granted Galicia autonomy within the empire in 1868, the prelude to a major revival. The relatively liberal political climate allowed Kraków to become the focus of all kinds of underground political groupings: **Józef Piłsudski** began recruiting his legendary Polish legions here prior to World War I, and from 1912 to 1914 Kraków was **Lenin**'s base for directing the international communist movement and the production of *Pravda*. **Artists and writers** attracted by the new liberalism gathered here too. Painter Jan Matejko produced many of his stir-ring paeans to Polishness during his residency as art professor at the Jagiellonian University, and the city was centre of Wyspiański and Malczewski's **Młoda Polska** (Young Poland) movement.

The brief interlude of independence following World War I ended for Kraków in September 1939 when the **Nazis** entered the city. Kraków was soon desig-nated capital of the Central Government, incorporating all Polish territories not directly annexed to the Reich. Hans Frank, the notorious Nazi governor, moved into the royal castle on Wawel Hill, from where he exercised a reign of unbridled terror, presaged by the arrest and deportation to concentration camps of many professors from the Jagiellonian University in November 1939. The elimination of the **Kraków ghetto**, most of whose inhabitants were sent to nearby Auschwitz (Oświęcim), was virtually complete by 1943.

The main event of the immediate postwar years was the construction of the vast **Nowa Huta steelworks** a few miles to the east of the city, a daunting symbol of the communist government's determination to replace Kraków's Catholic, intellectually orientated past with a bright new industrial future. The plan did not succeed: the peasant population pulled in to construct and then work in the steel mills never became the loyal, anti-religious proletariat the Party hoped for. Kraków's reputation as a centre of conservative Catholicism was enhanced by the election of **Pope John Paul II** in 1978, who until then had been Archbishop of Kraków.

An unforeseen consequence of the postwar industrial development is one of the highest **pollution** levels in Europe: dangerously high toxic levels are wreaking havoc with the health of the local population as well as causing incalculable damage to the ancient city centre. If you find yourself feeling exhausted or dizzy after a few days here – a common experience – then blame it on Nowa Huta, and the fumes blown in from the Katowice region. After years of prevarication, cleaning up the city is now a major local political issue, and in 1989 Kraków actually elected a Green mayor for a period.

Since 1989 and the transition to democratic rule, the city centre has been rapidly transformed by an influx of private capital – local and foreign – with Western-style shops, cafés and restaurants springing up in abundance, lending parts of the Old Town a cosmopolitan, decidedly affluent feel that confirms the city's return to the place proud Kraków residents have always maintained it belonged, in the heartlands of central Europe. Pollution notwithstanding, the historic ensemble of the square and its immediate surroundings are also undergoing a thorough clean-up for the first time in decades, allowing both locals and tourists to appreciate buildings such as the Sukiennice in their natural pristine beauty.

Orientation and transport

Kraków is bisected by the **River Wisła**, though virtually everything of interest is concentrated on the north bank. At the heart of things, enclosed by the **Planty** – a green belt following the course of the old ramparts – is the **Stare Miasto**, the Old Town, with its great central square, the **Rynek Główny**. Just south of the Stare Miasto, looming above the river bank, is **Wawel**, the royal castle hill, beyond which lies the old Jewish quarter of **Kazimierz**.

Thanks to the lack of wartime damage, the **inner suburbs** have more character than usual, the modern blocks being interspersed with the odd villa and nineteenth-century residential area. The more recent outer suburbs are no more characterful than usual. If you come in from the east, you'll see and smell the steelworks at **Nowa Huta**, their chimneys working overtime on acid rain production.

The main points of arrival are all fairly convenient.

● **Kraków Główny**, the central **train station**, is within walking distance of the Stare Miasto. All principal lines run to here. Left luggage is open twenty-four hours a day. Some trains (overnight services particularly) arrive at the southern **Płaszów** station: to get to the city centre from here, catch either a local commuter train or tram #3 #6, #9, #13 or #24.

● **Dworzec PKS**, the main **bus station**, is sited opposite the train station.

● **Arriving by car**, major roads from all directions are well signposted, though once in the centre, you'll need to cope with trams, narrow streets, heavy daytime traffic, and in much of the centre, heavily enforced parking restrictions.. There are official car parks on pl. św. Ducha and pl. Szczepański; and, although they are technically for hotel guests only, you could also try the *Cracovia*, *Holiday Inn* and *Wanda* hotels.

● **Balice airport** handles both domestic and international flights. It is half an hour west of the city, connected with the main bus station by bus #208; taxis are always available, too, and pretty reasonable at around £5–8.

Getting around

The central area of Kraków is compact enough to get around on foot; recently introduced restrictions mean that much of the **Stare Miasto** – including the Rynek – are car-free.

Exploring further afield, **trams** are plentiful, start early and run till late at night. Tram routes radiate out from the Planty to the suburbs; useful services are detailed as relevant in the text. **Buses** can also be useful, complementing the trams and keeping similarly long hours, with night buses taking over from around 11pm to 5am; they provide the main links with outer suburbs such as Tyniec and Nowa Huta, and local towns such as Wieliczka. **Local train** services can be handy for trips out of the city centre, such as to Płaszów.

Taxis are still affordable for Westerners, though as elsewhere in the country they are highly priced for the local economy. There are ranks around the centre of town   at pl. św. Ducha, Mały Rynek, pl. Dominikański, pl. Szczepański, pl. Wszysłkich Świętych, ul. Sienna (by the main post office) and at the main train station.

Information and maps

Possibly in response to the sheer volume of visitors, Kraków's city tourist office is far and away the best organised of any Polish city. The **main office**, run by *Wawel Tourist*, is just down from the station at ul. Pawia 8 (Mon–Fri 8am–4pm, Sat 8am–noon), with all the maps and brochures you could want. The **Almatur** office at Rynek Główny 7/8 is also worth a call; it handles student accommodation and is good for advice on nightlife and alternative events. As usual, **Orbis** also have information points in their hotels as well as a central office at Rynek Główny 41. They organise city tours and day excursions to Tyniec, Wieliczka, Ojców park and Pieskowa Skała castle, Oświęcim (Auschwitz), Zakopane and the Dunajec gorge; details from the main office or the information points in the *Cracovia* or *Holiday Inn* hotels. *Welcome to Krackow*, an English-language monthly available from the tourist office, Orbis hotels and certain bookshops, is a useful source of up-to-date information and current **listings**, for concerts, theatre and so on. For comprehensive listings, consult the weekly *Tydzień w Krakowie*, available from all *ruch* kiosks, or the weekend section of the Krakow edition of *Gazeta Wyborcza* newspaper, or the local *Gazeta Krakowska*.

The **maps** we've printed should be functional enough for most purposes. If you plan a longer stay, or are staying out in the suburbs, it might be worth investing in the fold-out **plan miasta** – available (if stocks have been printed recently) at the tourist offices, the *Ruch*, bookshops or street vendors.

> The Kraków telephone code is ☎012.

Accommodation

Kraków is turning into one of Europe's prime city destinations – so you should book hotels ahead in summer. If you don't, be prepared to try your luck with a private room, which, as ever, may well be some way out from the centre. **Prices** for hotels are higher than in most Polish cities but nevertheless marginally lower than Warsaw's. The cheapest places come out at around £10–15 for a double;

moderate ones at around £20–40; Orbis hotels from around £50–70. Private rooms run at around £10–12 for a double.

Hotels
During office hours the tourist office will help you book a room; otherwise you need to call the hotels direct – ideally in advance. Listings are in ascending order of price.

CHEAPER HOTELS (£10–15)
PTTK Dom Turysty, ul. Westerplatte 15/16, near the station (☎229-566). Few singles, lots of doubles as well as eight-person dormitories. Popular student venue, nearly always crowded in season; double rooms are small but decent. Recently renovated restaurant and pricey bar.

Saski, ul. Sławkowska 3 (☎214-222). Useful central location and again popular with students – Polish and foreign.

Korona, ul. Kalwaryiska 9/15 (☎666-511). Located out in the southern Podgorze district, on the edge of the wartime ghetto area, this is a cheap, lesser-known sports hotel.

Wisła, ul. Reymonta 22 (☎334-922). Another sports hotel, set in a pleasant park in the western Czarna Wieś district, next to the main football stadium. Bus #144 (from the main bus station) passes close by.

Chałupnik, ul. Kochanowskiego 12 (☎337-501). Cheap, smallish privately run overnighter in reasonable walking distance west of the Old Town.

Tramp, ul. Koszykarska 33 (☎560-229). Large hostel-type place well east of town in Płaszów district. Bus #108 passes close by.

Garnizonowy, ul. św. Gertrudy 29 (☎213-50). Cheaper part of former military hotel – ordinary soldiers this time – next to *Royal*.

MODERATE HOTELS (£20–40)
Warszawski, ul. Pawia 6 (☎220-622). Good location close to the train station – but noisy.

Polonia, ul. Basztowa 25 (☎221-233). Ditto.

Europejski, ul. Lubicz 5 (☎220-911). Ditto.

Motel Krak, ul. Radzikowskiego 99 (☎372-122). Well outside the city – see "Campsites", below, for transport details. Its advantages are a swimming pool and bungalows.

Pollera, ul. Szpitalna 30 (☎221-044). New name and (private) management; calm, central location and increasingly popular.

Krakowianka, ul. Zywiecka (☎664-191). A last resort – well south of the centre. Also has bungalows and campsite.

Monopol, ul. św. Gertrudy 6 (☎227-666). A bit more expensive than most in this category, but worth it for better-quality rooms.

Polski, ul. Pijarska 17 (☎221-144). Higher end of the price scale, again a very central and quiet location, though rather marred by a shabby selection of rooms.

Pod Kopcem, al. Waszyngtona (☎230-355). Housed in an old fortress on a hill west of the centre, this is a delightfully peaceful hotel – well worth the higher than average prices. Increasingly popular, not least for the view over the city.

Pod Różą, ul. Floriańska 14 (☎229-399). Venerable place, now taken over by the crowd using its much-advertised casino. Simple decent-quality rooms, though the street below can be noisy at night.

Piast, ul. Radzikowskiego 109 (☎364-600). Newish privately run hotel with lots of rooms but well south of town, beyond the *Motel Krak*.

Royal, ul. św. Gertrudy 26 (☎214-661). Newly renovated former officers' hotel close to Wawel. Decent-quality place popular with small tour groups.

EXPENSIVE HOTELS (£50–70)

The upmarket hotels remain dominated by Orbis, who own most of those listed below.

Cracovia, al. Puszkina 1 (☎228-666). Oldest and best-located of the Orbis hotels, a tram ride (#15 or #18) west of the centre.

Forum, ul. Konopnickiej 28 (☎669-50). Luxury Western-style business travellers' haunt, a block south of Wawel near the river. Much used by tour groups.

Francuski, ul. Pijarska 13 (☎225-122). Elegant old hotel, recently renovated. A long-established favourite with upper-crust travellers.

Holiday Inn, ul. Armii Krajowej 11 (☎375-044). Luxury international hotel favoured by the tourist jet set, well out of the city centre on the main Balice–Katowice road.

Wanda, ul. Armii Krajowej 9 (☎371-677). Not quite up to the mark of its neighbour, the *Holiday Inn*.

Demel, ul. Głowackiego 109 (☎364-448). New private hotel with all the facilities but well out of the centre.

Grand, ul. Sławkowska 5–7 (☎217-255). The newest luxury hotel in town, in a good central location. Run by Orbis.

Private rooms

The office next door to the main tourist information, at ul. Pawia 6 (Mon–Fri 8am–9pm, Sat 10am–3pm; ☎221-921) organises **private rooms**, which can be a good bet during the summer. Ask carefully about addresses, which tend to be a long way out.

Student hotels and youth hostels

Student hotels run throughout the summer months (June–Sept). Details of locations (which change each year) are available from the **Almatur** office on the main square at Rynek Główny 7/8 (☎226-352), as well as the main tourist office. A fairly dependable bet is the *Letni* students' hostel (open July–Sept), ul. Jana Pawła 82 (☎482-027), quite a distance east of town on the edge of Nowa Huta which has twin bedded rooms as well as dormitories. Take bus A or trams #4, #5, #10, or #44 from the central station, direction Nowa Huta.

There are three regular **youth hostels**.

Ul. Oleandry 4 (☎338-920). The main hostel is a huge concrete construction behind the *Cracovia* hotel – but despite this still manages to get full up during the summer. Open all year.

Ul. Kościuszki 88 (☎221-951). A smaller place, housed in a former convent overlooking the river (trams #1, #2, #6, #21). Open all year.

Ul. Złotej Kielni 1 (☎372-441). Open July & Aug only.

Campsites

Krak Camping, ul. Radzikowskiego 99, near the motel of the same name (see "Moderate Hotels", above), in the northwest of the city and with own restaurant. The most popular camping site. Buses #118, #173, #208, # 218 and #223 pass the motel.

Krakowianka, ul. Żywiecka Boczna. Part of Krakowianka hotel complex usefully located on Zakopane road. Includes bungalows and a restaurant.

Ogrodowy, ul Królowej Jadwigi 223. Decent privately run campsite well west of the centre on the road to Balice airport. Buses #B, #102, #134.

Smok, ul. Kamedulska 18. Another privately run site to the west of town on Oświęcim road. Bus #109, #229 and all lines west towards Bielany run close by.

The City

The area covered in this section is basically the city centre: with the Rynek Główny as a starting point, almost everything is within half an hour's walk. The heart of the district is the **Stare Miasto**, the Old Town, bordered by the greenery of the **Planty**. Within this area, a broad network of streets stretches southwards to the edge of **Wawel Hill**, with its royal residence, and beyond to the Jewish quarter of **Kazimierz**. Across the river, on the edge of the **Podgórze** suburb, is the old wartime ghetto. And finally, a little further out to the west, **Kościuszko's Mound** offers an attractive stretch of woods and countryside, just a ten-minute bus ride from the centre.

Rynek Główny

The **Rynek Główny** was the largest square of medieval Europe: a huge expanse of flagstones, ringed by magnificent houses and towering spires. Long the marketplace and commercial hub of the city, it's an immediate introduction to Kraków's grandeur and stateliness. By day things can get obscured by the crowds, but venture into the square late at night and you can immerse yourself in the aura of the city in its *fin-de-siècle* heyday and of the great events played out here, like the rallying call to national independence made by revolutionary leader Tadeusz Kościuszko (see box pp.332–33) in 1794. In this atmosphere the echoes of the *hejnał* – the trumpet call played each hour from the Mariacki Church (see p.316) – become an achingly mournful sound. By either day or night, too, it's equally worth exploring the network of passageways and atmospheric, often recently restored, Italianate courtyards leading off from the front of the square, many of them enlivened by the welter of cafés and restaurants that have colonised the area in the past few years.

The square is more open today than it used to be. Until the last century much of it was occupied by market stalls, a tradition maintained by the flower sellers and ice cream vendors, and by the stalls in the **Sukiennice**, the medieval cloth hall (see p.315) at the heart of the square that divides it into west and east sections, the latter of which is dominated by the Mariacki Church.

Around the square

In the east section, the focus is a statue of the romantic poet **Mickiewicz** (see box p.66), a facsimile of an earlier work destroyed by the Nazis, and a favourite meeting point. To its south is the copper-domed **St Adalbert's** (św. Wojchecha), the oldest building in the square and the first church to be founded in Kraków. The saint was a Slav bishop, reputed to have preached here in around 995 before heading north to convert (and get martyred by) the Prussians. Go down into the basement – reconstructed in the eighteenth century – and you can see the foundations of the original tenth-century Romanesque building. Traces of an even earlier wooden building, possibly a pre-Christian temple, and an assortment of archaeological finds are also on display.

Many of the **mansions** ranged around the square are associated with artists, writers and wealthy local families, though these days most of them are in use as shops, offices or museums. The eastern side of the square has some of the oldest in the city. The **Grey House** (no. 6) on the corner of ul. Sienna, for example,

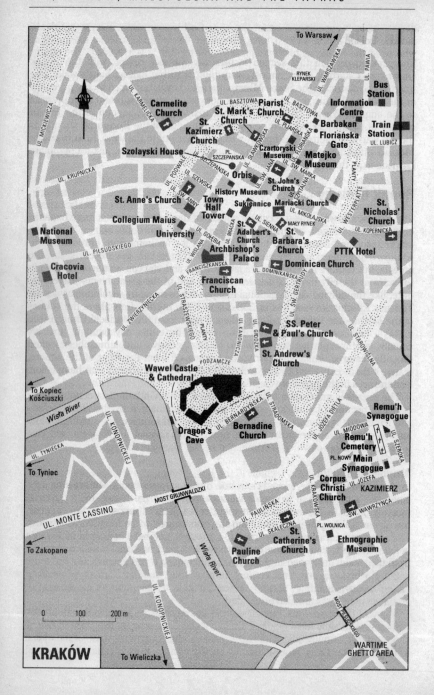

To Warsaw

RYNEK
KLEPARSKI

Bus
Station

Information
Centre

Train
Station

UL. PAWIA

UL. WARSZAŃSKA

UL. LUBICZ

UL. BASZTOWA

Carmelite
Church

UL. KARMELICKA

UL. BASZTOWA

Piarist
Church

St. Mark's
Church

St.
Kazimierz
Church

Barbakan

Floriańska
Gate

UL. MICKIEWICZA

Szolayski House

PL.
SZCZEPAŃSKA

Czartoryski
Museum

Matejko
Museum

UL. POGWALE

UL. SZEWSKA

UL. ŚW. JANA

UL. ŚW. MARKA

Orbis

St. John's
Church

UL. KRUPNICZA

History Museum

St. Anne's Church

UL. ŚW. ANNY

Town
Hall
Tower

Sukiennice

Mariacki Church

UL. MIKOŁAJSKA

St.
Nicholas'
Church

UL. KOPERNICKA

Collegium Maius

MAŁY RYNEK

University

UL. GOŁĘBIA

St.
Adalbert's
Church

UL. SIENNA

St.
Barbara's
Church

UL. WESTERPLATTE

National
Museum

UL. BRACKA

Archbishop's
Palace

Dominican Church

PTTK Hotel

UL. PIŁSUDSKIEGO

UL. FRANCISZKAŃSKA

UL. DOMINIKAŃSKA

UL. ŚW. GERTRUDY

Cracovia
Hotel

UL. WIŚLNA

Franciscan
Church

UL. STRASZEWSKIEGO

SS. Peter
& Paul's Church

UL. KANONICZA

UL. GRODZKA

PLANTY

St. Andrew's
Church

UL. STAROWIŚLNA

UL. ZWIERZYNIECKA

PODZAMCZE

Wawel Castle
& Cathedral

To Kopiec
Kościuszki

Wisła River

Remu'h
Synagogue

UL. JÓZEFA DIETLA

UL. MIODOWA

Remu'h
Cemetery

UL. SZEROKA

UL. KONOPNICKIEJ

UL. BERNARDYŃSKA

UL. STRADOMSKA

Dragon's
Cave

Bernadine
Church

PL. NOWY

Main
Synagogue

UL. TYNIECKA

To Tyniec

Corpus
Christi
Church

UL. JÓZEFA

KAZIMIERZ

MOST GRUNWALDZKI

UL. KRAKOWSKA

ŚW. WAWRZYŃCA

UL. MONTE CASSINO

UL. PAULIŃSKA

PL. WOLNICA

To Zakopane

UL. SKAŁECZNA

St.
Catherine's
Church

Ethnographic
Museum

Pauline
Church

0   100   200 m

UL. KONOPNICKIEJ

Wisła River

MOST PODGÓRSKI

KRAKÓW

To Wieliczka

WARTIME
GHETTO AREA

despite its later appearance, has many of its Gothic rooms intact; its ex-residents include Poland's first elected king, Henri de Valois, and Tadeusz Kościuszko, who used the house as his headquarters during the 1794 Uprising. The neighbouring **Montelupi House** (no. 7), with a monumental Renaissance portal, was the site of the country's first-ever post office, established by its Italian owners in King Zygmunt August's reign. The Gothic **Boner House** (no. 9) was for some time the home of the Kraków writer and painter Stanisław Wyspiański. The **Wierzynek Mansion** (no. 15) in the southeast corner is home to the city's oldest and most famous restaurant, founded in 1364 and claiming an unbroken culinary tradition. It also holds the original charter from King Kazimierz the Great. Political heavyweights who've dined here in recent years include presidents de Gaulle, Nixon, Mitterrand and Bush.

Moving anticlockwise, around to the west section of the square, the **Potocki Palace** (no. 20), with a small courtyard with loggias at the back, is a good example of a classical Kraków mansion, while the **Pod Baranami** (no. 27) is another aristocratic home, constructed from four adjacent burghers' houses in the sixteenth century. The nucleus of nineteenth-century social life, it's nowadays a cultural centre (see "Entertainment and nightlife", p.340). Further around the square, an orderly collection of shopfronts and restaurants, added on to the old burghers' houses, ends at the **Krzysztofory Palace** (no. 35) on the corner of ul. Szczepańska, another well-preserved mansion created by fusing burghers' houses into a single building with a fine courtyard at the back. These days it's part of the **Kraków History Museum** (Wed–Sun 9am–3pm, closed first Sat & Sun of the month). The museum is not very inspired, focusing on the development of the city's defences, with an offbeat display of military objects, including armour, cannons and swords; the top floor houses a large, jumbled collection of clocks and other timepieces.

The tall **Tower** – facing the Pod Baranami – is all that remains of the original, fourteenth-century **Town Hall**, pulled down in the 1820s by the authorities as part of a misguided improvement plan. It's worth the climb for an excellent overview of the city. The top floor features occasionally illuminating local exhibitions (Wed–Sun 9am–3pm); the Gothic vaults below are currently occupied by the *Teatr Satyry*, a popular satirical cabaret outfit (see "Entertainment and Nightlife" p.340).

The Sukiennice

The medieval **Sukiennice**, rebuilt in the Renaissance, is one of the most distinctive sights in the country: a vast cloth hall, topped by a sixteenth-century attic dripping with gargoyles. Its commercial traditions are perpetuated by a **covered market**, which bustles with tourists and street sellers at almost any time of year. Inside, the stalls of the darkened central arcade display a hotch-potch collection of junk and genuine craft items from the Podhale region. Popular buys include amber jewellery, painted boxes in every shape and size and thick woollen sweaters from the mountains; prices are inevitably inflated, so if you're travelling on to the south, it's better to wait until you get to the market at Nowy Targ (see "South to Zakopane", below). The **terrace cafés** on either side of the hall are classic Kraków haunts, where locals idle away the afternoon over tea and *sernik*.

The **Art Gallery** on the upper floor of the Sukiennice (Thurs noon–6pm, Fri–Mon 10am–4pm) is worth a visit for its collection of works by nineteenth-century Polish artists, among them Matejko, Malczewski, Gierymski and Chełmonski. The Matejkos here include two political heavyweights, the *Homage of Prussia* and the stirring *Kościuszko at Racławice*. As usual with Matejko, the impact is heightened if you appreciate the historical reference points, in this case the homage of the Teutonic Knights in 1525 (see "Malbork", in Chapter Two) and the Polish peasant army's victory over the Russians in 1794.

Mariacki Church and Square

Mariacki Church (St Mary's) was founded in 1222 and destroyed during the mid-century Tartar invasions. The current building, begun in 1355 and completed fifty years later, is one of the finest Gothic structures in the country – the taller of its towers, a late fifteenth-century addition, is topped by an amazing ensemble of spires, elaborated with a crown and helmet.

Legend has it that during one of the early Tartar raids the watchman positioned at the top of this tower saw the invaders approaching and took up his trumpet to raise the alarm; his warning was cut short by a Tartar arrow through the throat. The legend lives on, and every hour on the hour a lone **trumpeter** plays the sombre *hejnał* melody, halting abruptly at the precise point the watchman was supposed to have been hit. The national radio station broadcasts the *hejnał* live at noon every day and Polish writers are still apt to wax lyrical on the symbolism of the trumpet's warning.

First impressions of the **Church** are of a cavernous, somewhat gloomy expanse. What little light there is comes from the high windows at each end, the ancient altar window facing the stained glass of the west end, an Art Nouveau extravaganza by Kraków artist Stanisław Wyspiański. Walking down the nave, you'll have to pick your way past devotees kneeling in front of the fifteenth-century **Chapel of Our Lady of Częstochowa,** with its copy of the venerated image of the Black Madonna. Locals claim that this is actually older than the original.

Continuing down the high Gothic nave, under arched stone vaulting enhanced in blue and gold, the walls – like those surrounding the high altar – are decorated with **Matejko friezes**. Separating the nave from the aisles are a succession of buttressed pillars fronted by Baroque marble altars. The aisles themselves lead off to a number of lavishly ornamented chapels, fifteenth-century additions to the main body of the building. Focal point of the nave is the huge stone **crucifix** attributed to Veit Stoss (see opposite), hanging in the archway to the presbytery.

The biggest crowds are drawn by the majestic **high altar** at the far east end. Carved by the Nuremberg master craftsman Veit Stoss (Wit Stwosz, as he's known in Poland) between 1477 and 1489, the huge limewood polyptych is one of the finest examples of late Gothic art. The outer sides of the folded polyptych feature illustrations from the life of the Holy Family executed in gilded polychromy. At noon (Sundays and saints' days excluded) the altar is opened to reveal the inner panels, with their reliefs of the Annunciation, Nativity, Adoration of the Magi, Resurrection, Ascension and Pentecost; for a good view, arrive at least a quarter of an hour before the opening. These six superb scenes are a fitting backdrop to the central panel – an exquisite **Dormition of the Virgin** in which the graceful figure of Mary is shown reclining into her final sleep in the arms of the watchful Apostles. Like most of the figures, the Apostles – several of them well over life-size – are thought to be based on Stoss's contemporaries in Kraków. Certainly there's an uncanny mastery of human detail that leaves you feeling you'd recognise their human counterparts if you met them in the street. Other features of note in the chancel are the Gothic stained-glass windows, the Renaissance tabernacle designed by Giovanni Maria Mosca, and the exuberant early Baroque stalls.

VEIT STOSS

As with Copernicus, the issue of the nationality of the man who carved the Mariacki altar – unquestionably the greatest work of art ever created in Poland – was long the source of a rather sterile dispute between Polish and German protagonists. Although his early career remains something of a mystery, it now seems indisputable that the sculptor's original name was **Veit Stoss**, and that he was born between 1440 and 1450 in Horb at the edge of the Black Forest, settling later in Nürnberg, where a few early works by him have been identified. He **came to Kraków** in 1477, perhaps at the invitation of the royal court (the Polish queen was an Austrian princess), though more likely at the behest of the German merchant community, a sizeable but declining minority in the city, who worshipped in the Mariacki and paid for its new altar by subscription.

Despite being his first major commission, the **Mariacki altarpiece** is Stoss' masterpiece. It triumphantly displays every facet of late Gothic sculpture: the architectural setting, complete with its changing lights, is put to full dramatic effect; there is mastery over every possible scale, from the huge figures in the central shrine to the tiny figurines and decoration in the borders; subtle use is made of a whole gamut of technical devices, from three different depths of relief to a graded degree of gilding according to the importance of the scene; and the whole layout is based on a scheme of elaborate theological complexity that would nevertheless be bound to make an impression on the many unlettered worshippers who viewed it. It would seem that it is mostly Stoss' own work: gilders and joiners were certainly employed, but otherwise he was probably only helped by one assistant and one apprentice.

While engaged on the altarpiece, Stoss carved the relief of *Christ in the Garden of Gethsemane*, now in the City Art Museum. That it's made of sandstone – a material he later used for the Mariacki *Crucifix* – is indicative of his exceptional **versatility with materials**. This is further apparent in consideration of the works he created after finishing the altarpiece: the tomb of King Kazimierz the Jagiellonian in the Wawel Cathedral is of Salzburg marble, the epitaph to Philippus Buonaccorsi in the Dominican church is of bronze, while his two other key Polish commissions – the episcopal monuments in the cathedrals of Gniezno and Włocławek – are both of Hungarian marble. These sculptures made Stoss a great Polish celebrity, and he rose far above his artisan status to engage in extensive commercial activities, and to dabble in both architecture and engineering. The forms of the Mariacki altarpiece and his monuments were widely imitated throughout Poland, and continued to be so for the next half century.

It therefore seems all the more curious that he **returned to Nürnberg** in 1496, remaining there until his death in 1533. His homecoming was a traumatic experience: Nürnberg was well endowed with specialist craftsmen, and Stoss was forced to follow suit, concentrating on producing single, unpainted wooden figures. Attempts to maintain his previous well-to-do lifestyle led him into disastrous business dealings, which culminated in his prostituting his artistic talent by forging a document, as a result of which he was branded on both cheeks and forbidden to venture beyond the city. He never really came to terms with the ideals of the Italian Renaissance, which took strong root in Nürnberg, nor did he show any enthusiasm for the Protestant Reformation, which was supported by nearly all the great German artists of the day, most notably his fellow-townsman, Albrecht Dürer. Yet, even if Stoss never repeated the success of his Kraków years, he continued to produce memorable and highly individualistic sculptures, above all the spectacular garlanded *Annunciation* suspended from the ceiling of the church of St Lorenz.

ST BARBARA'S CHURCH AND MARIACKI SQUARE

The side door on the south side of the chancel brings you in to **Mariacki Square**, a small courtyard replacing the old church cemetery closed down by the Austrians in the last century. On the far side of the courtyard stands the fourteenth-century **St Barbara's Church**, among its contents a remarkable late Gothic Pieta group, sculpted in stone and attributed to the anonymous local artist known as "Master of the Beautiful Madonnas". During the Partitions the ruling Austrians took over the Mariacki, so the locals were forced to use this tiny place for services in Polish. The back of the church looks onto the tranquil **Mały Rynek** whose terrace cafés make an enjoyable venue for postcard sessions or a quiet beer.

From Mały Rynek, the narrow **ul. Sienna** offers an alternative route back to the main square. On the street outside no. 5 there's normally a bunch of students touting political books and badges, alternately amusing, informative or impenetrable to the foreigner. The first floor of the building houses the local branch of the **Catholic Intellectuals Club** (KIK), an organisation that's more approachable than it sounds. Founded in the wake of the post-Stalinist political thaw of the 1950s, the KIK was for over thirty years one of the few officially sanctioned independent structures in the country, and its national network played an important part in the last decade's political events. It was to the KIK offices in Kraków, for example, that local steelworkers and farmers came for help when setting up the first Solidarity organisations in 1980. Today, a number of KIK people are now prominent politicians, ex-Prime Minister Mazowiecki included.

Around the Stare Miasto

Like the Rynek, the streets around the Stare Miasto still follow the medieval plan, while their **architecture** presents a rich central European ensemble of Gothic, Renaissance and Baroque. They are a hive of commercial activity, too, with a welter of boutiques, fast-food joints and other new privately owned shops replacing the old state enterprise outlets, and a mass of **street traders**, ranging from young Poles touting Western cassettes to Russian peasants holding up gold trinkets. West of the Rynek, the atmosphere is generated by the academic buildings and student haunts of the **university district**.

Ulica Floriańska

Of the three streets leading north off the Rynek, **ul. Floriańska** is the busiest and most striking. In amongst the myriad shops, cafés and restaurants are some attractive fragments of medieval and Renaissance architecture. At no. 5, for example, a beautiful early Renaissance stone figure of the *Madonna and Child* sits in a niche on the facade of the **Floriańska Gate**. At no. 14, **Pod Różą**, the oldest hotel in Kraków, has a Renaissance doorway inscribed in Latin, "may this house stand until an ant drinks the oceans and a tortoise circles the world" – it doesn't seem to get much attention from the moneyed revellers who flock to the hotel's re-opened casino. Famous hotel guests of the past include Franz Liszt, Balzac and the occasional czar.

Further up the street at no. 41 is the sixteenth-century **Matejko House**, home of painter Jan Matejko until his death in 1893. An opulent, slighly gloomy three-storey mansion of the type favoured by the wealthy turn-of-the-century Kraków bourgeoisie, the museum (Wed, Thurs, Sat & Sun 10am–4pm, Fri noon–6pm) housed inside comprises a range of Matejko family memorabilia, parts of the man's extensive personal art collection and a number of his own paintings and assorted other artistic outpourings.

The first-floor parlour and a couple of other rooms remain pretty much as the Matejko family kept them, attractive old fireplaces included. The second and third floors house Matejko's private art gallery, notably a number of Renaissance pictures and triptychs. The rest of the exhibition is mostly Matejko's own work, including the sketches of the windows he designed for the Mariacki Church: other sketches aside there's also a collection of old costumes and armour he used as inspiration for several of his more famous pictures, notably *Sobieski at Vienna*. Not a wildly exciting museum, it's a popular enough place with Matejko freaks, of whom there still seem to be plenty in the country.

FLORIAŃSKA GATE AND THE CITY WALLS

Floriańska Gate, at the end of the street, marks the edge of the Old Town proper. A square, robust fourteenth-century structure, it's part of a small section of fortifications saved when the old defensive walls were pulled down in the early nineteenth century. The walls lead east to the fifteenth-century Haberdashers' (Pasamoników) Tower and west to the Joiners' (Stolarska) Gate, which is separated from the even older Carpenters' (Cieśli) Gate by the arsenal. The original fortifications must have been an impressive sight – three kilometres of wall ten metres high and nearly three metres thick, interspersed with no fewer than 47 towers and bastions. The strongest-looking defensive remnant is the **Barbakan**, just beyond Floriańska Gate. A bulbous, spiky fort, added in 1498, it's unusual in being based on the Arab as opposed to European defensive architecture of the time. The covered passage linking the fort to the walls has disappeared, as has the original moat – all of which leaves the bastion looking a little stranded.

The Czartoryski Palace and Szołayski House museums

Back through Floriańska Gate and past the reproduction Pop Art collections displayed on the old walls, a right turn down the narrow **ul. Pijarska** brings you to the corner of ul. św. Jana and back down to the main square. On the way, on your right, is the Baroque monastery and church of the **Holy Transfiguration**; on your left, linked to the church by an overhead passage, is the Czartoryski Palace.

THE CZARTORYSKI PALACE

A branch of the National Museum, the **Czartoryski Palace** houses Kraków's finest art collection (normally Mon, Tues & Fri–Sun 10am–4pm, but check beforehand). Its core was established by Izabella Czartoryska at the family palace in Puławy (see Chapter Three) and was then moved to Kraków following the confiscation of the Puławy estate after the 1831 Insurrection, in which the family was deeply implicated. The family were legendary collectors, particularly from the Paris salons of the seventeenth and eighteenth centuries, and it shows, despite the Nazis' removal – and subsequent loss – of many precious items.

The **ancient art** collection alone contains over a thousand exhibits, from sites in Mesopotamia, Etruria, Greece and Egypt. Another intriguing highlight is the collection of **trophies from the Battle of Vienna** (1683), which includes sumptuous Turkish carpets, scimitars and other Oriental finery.

The **picture galleries** contain a rich display of art and sculpture ranging from thirteenth- to eighteenth-century works, the most famous being Rembrandt's brooding *Landscape Before a Storm* and Leonardo da Vinci's *Lady with an Ermine*. A double pun identifies the rodent-handler as Cecilia Gallerani, the mistress of Leonardo's patron, Lodovico il Moro: the Greek word for this animal is *galé* – a play on the woman's name – and Lodovico's nickname was "Ermelino", meaning ermine. There is also a large collection of Dutch canvases and an outstanding array of fourteenth-century Sienese primitives. As in all Polish museums you may find several galleries closed off (often the best ones), ostensibly for lack of staff; passing yourself off as an art student or amateur enthusiast may gain you admission.

THE SZOŁAYSKI HOUSE MUSEUM

On down ul. św. Jana towards the Rynek, there are more wealthy Old Town residences, like the Neoclassical Lubomirski Palace at no. 15 and the eighteenth-century Kołłątaj House at no. 20, once a meeting place for the cultured elite. Back onto the square and west along ul. Szczepańska, the modest **Szołayski House**, on the eastern edge of pl. Szczepański, houses a small but important section of the city **Art Museum** (Mon–Fri, Sun 10am–3.30pm, Tues noon–5.30pm) featuring a significant collection of Gothic and Renaissance Polish art and sculpture, much of it taken from churches in the Małopolska region. The best-known exhibit here is the fourteenth-century *Madonna of Krużlowa*, an exquisite Gothic sculpture of the "Beautiful Madonna" school: unearthed in a local village church attic, this wonderful piece depicts a typically dreamy Mary with a cheerful-looking Christ perched on her shoulder. Other pieces here include a beautiful figure of Christ riding on a donkey from 1470, used in Palm Sunday processions, an expressive cycle of late fifteenth-century altarpieces from the local Augustine and Dominican churches, and a powerful *Christ in the Garden of Gethsemane*, a sandstone relief carved by Veit Stoss for the cemetery beside the Mariacki Church, as well as a small wooden *Crucifixion* attributed to his workshop. After the joys of this superb selection of Gothic sculpture the later-era art housed on the second floor is a bit of an anticlimax, though the portraits of kings Jan Sobieski and Zygmunt August will be familiar enough to anyone who's already trailed round the Wawel collections.

Also on this square are two impressive turn-of-the-century buildings in the Viennese Secessionist style: the **Stary Teatr** to the south, and the **Palace of Arts** to the west. The latter, adorned with a mosaic frieze, features exhibitions of contemporary art.

The University district

Head west from the Rynek on any of the three main thoroughfares – ul. Szczepańska, ul. Szewska or ul. św. Anny – and you're into the **university area**. The main body of buildings is south of ul. św. Anny, the principal Jewish area of the city until the early 1400s, when the university bought up many of the properties and the Jews moved out to the Kazimierz district.

THE COLLEGIUM MAIUS

The Gothic **Collegium Maius** building, at the intersection of ul. św. Anny with ul. Jagiellońska, is the historic heart of the university complex. The university got off to something of a false start after its foundation by King Kazimierz in 1364, floundering badly after his death six years later until it was revived by King Władysław Jagiełło in the early fifteenth century, when the university authorities began transforming these buildings into a new academic centre.

Through the passageway from the street, you find yourself in a quiet, arcaded **courtyard** with a marble fountain playing in the centre: an ensemble that, during the early 1960s, was stripped of neo-Gothic accretions and restored to something approaching its original form. The cloistered atmosphere of ancient academia makes a enjoyable break from the city in itself, though actually getting into the building is not so easy. Now renamed and known as the **University Museum**, the Collegium is open to guided tours only (Mon–Sat noon–2pm), for which you need to book places at least a day in advance (☎220-549). If you just turn up without having booked, you might be able to talk your way onto a tour, but in summer they're full more often than not. You could assess your chances at the shop in the courtyard arcade, which seems to have caught onto the logo craze, selling mugs, pens, sweatshirts and anything else you can think of sporting the Jagiellonian University crest.

Inside, **tours** proceed through the **ground-floor** rooms, which retain the mathematical and geographical murals once used for teaching; the **Alchemy Room**, with its skulls and other wizard's accoutrements, was used according to legend by the fabled magician Doctor Faustus. Stairs up from the courtyard bring you to an elaborately decorated set of **reception rooms**. The principal assembly hall has a Renaissance ceiling adorned with carved rosettes and portraits of Polish royalty, benefactors and professors; its Renaissance portal carries the Latin inscription *Plus Ratio Quam Vis* – "Wisdom rather than Strength". The professors' common room, which also served as their dining hall, boasts an ornate Baroque spiral staircase and a Gothic bay window with a replica statuette of King Kazimierz. In the **Treasury** the most valued possession is the copper Jagiellonian globe, constructed around 1510 as the centrepiece of a clock mechanism and featuring the earliest known illustration of America – labelled "a newly discovered land". If you find old scientific instruments interesting, ask the guide if you can see the other old laboratories and globe rooms.

THE REST OF THE DISTRICT

Several other old buildings are dotted round this area. The Baroque university church of **St Anne**, on the street of the same name, was designed by the ubiquitous Tylman of Gameren (see "Warsaw"). The **Collegium Minus**, just round the corner on ul. Gołębia, is the fifteenth-century arts faculty, rebuilt two centuries later; Jan Matejko studied and later taught here. On the corner of the same street stands the outsize **Collegium Novum**, the neo-Gothic university administrative headquarters, with an interior modelled on the Collegium Maius. The **Copernicus statue**, in front of the Collegium Novum; on the edge of the Planty, commemorates the university's most famous supposed student – some local historians doubt that he really did study here.

In term time the university district's **cafés** and **restaurants** are usually lively (see "Eating, drinking and entertainment", p.336), while the graffiti-sprayed southern section of **ul. Jagiellońska** and adjoining **ul. Gołębia** are invariably lined with students hawking books, posters and, of course, Solidarity badges – though that's mainly for the tourists these days. Student artwork, however, remains a fount of political comment: Lech Wałęsa is now as much the butt of jokes as his communist predecessors used to be.

The Nowy Gmach Modern Art Museum

For anyone interested in the development of modern Polish art there's a further section of the city **art museum** worth exploring. Housed in a large concrete block on the corner of al. 3 Maja, a couple of bus stops west of the university district along ul. Piłsudskiego, just beyond the *Crakovia* hotel, the **Nowy Gmach** (new building) **gallery** (Wed noon–5.30pm, Thurs–Sun 10am–3.30pm) features permanent exhibitions of a wide selection of painting and sculpture from the 1890s and beyond. The turn-of-the-century *Młoda Polska* movement is particularly well represented here, with a number of notable works by Wyspiański, including the designs for his windows in Wawel Cathedral, as well as a number of other major Polish artists including Mehoffer, Witkiewicz and Ślewiński. The museum also presents a diverse range of roving exhibitions, some of them, like the large "Jews of Poland" exhibition, major national cultural events, so it's always worth checking up what's on currently in the local listings.

The route to Wawel Hill

The traditional route used by Polish monarchs when entering the city took them through the Floriańska Gate, down ul. Floriańska to the Rynek, then southwards down ul. Grodzka – part of the old trade route up through Kraków from Hungary – to the foot of **Wawel Hill**. Ulica Grodzka's first crossing is with the tram lines circling the city centre at plac Dominikańska, across which stands the large brick-work basilica of the thirteenth-century **Dominican Church and Monastery**. It was badly damaged by fire in the 1850s, but the rather sombre cloisters retain sections of the Romanesque walls; **exhibitions** by local artists and students are often held here, featuring the kind of works that only a few years ago were still considered politically sensitive.

On the opposite side of the square is the equally ancient **Franciscan Church**, whose monks arrived in Kraków from Prague in 1237. Also victim of fires in the last century, its darkened interior was done up in suffocating neo-Gothic, an effect enhanced by a set of paintings by Wyspiański, who was also the creator of the stained-glass windows in the choir and chancel. On down ul. Grodzka, past the gilded stone symbol of a lion above the **Podelwie House** (no. 32), the oldest such emblem in the city, turn into ul. Poselska to find the house (no. 12) where novelist **Joseph Conrad** spent his childhood: a commemorative plaque in the corner carries a quotation from his work.

Back down Grodzka there's a last run of churches before you reach the hill. The first, **SS. Peter and Paul's**, a little way back from the street, is fronted by imposing statues of the two Apostles, actually copies of the pollution-scarred originals, now kept elsewhere for preservation's sake. Modelled on the Gesù in Rome, it's the earliest Baroque building in the city, commissioned by the Jesuits when they came to Kraków in the 1580s to quell Protestant agitation. Next comes the Romanesque **St Andrew's**, remodelled in familiar Polish Baroque style, where the local people are reputed to have holed themselves up and successfully fought off marauding Tartars during the invasion of 1241; it looks just about strong enough for the purpose. A little further on, **St Martin's**, built in the seventeenth century on the site of a Romanesque foundation, now belongs to Kraków's small Lutheran community. For the final haul to Wawel, the most atmospheric route is to cross the small plac Wita Stwosza opposite the church, and turn south down ul. Kanonicza, a largely unrestored Gothic street. At the end of the street, you emerge opposite the main path up to the castle.

Wawel Hill: the Castle and Cathedral

For over five hundred years the country's rulers lived and governed on **Wawel Hill**, whose main buildings stand pretty much as they have done for centuries. Even after the capital moved to Warsaw, Polish monarchs continued to be buried in the cathedral, and it's at Wawel that many of the nation's venerated poets and heroes lie in state. As such, Wawel represents a potent source of Polish national and spiritual pride: unusually in Kraków, there are always far greater crowds of Poles than foreigners looking around.

The cobbled path up Wawel negotiates lines of souvenir touts, silhouette artists and horoscope sellers. At the top, a typically dramatic statue of Tadeusz Kościuszko – a copy of the one destroyed by the Nazis – stands before the sixteenth-century Waza Gate. As you emerge, the cathedral rears up to the left, with the castle and its outbuildings and courtyards beyond. Directly ahead is a huge, open square, once the site of a Wawel township, but cleared by the Austrians in the early nineteenth century to create a parade ground.

Official **opening hours** are 10am to 3pm (Tues–Sun) for the cathedral, and 10am to 3pm (Tues, Thurs, Sat & Sun) or noon to 6pm (Wed & Fri) for the castle. However, times do vary so it's a good idea to check beforehand at one of the tourist offices or in the local listings (see p.310 "Information and Maps"). Keep in mind, too, that Wawel is extremely popular at all times of year – at the busiest periods, you need to turn up at least an hour and a half before opening for any chance of a ticket. **Tickets** for the cathedral and royal chambers are bought separately at the respective entry points. Guides for small groups are available for hire from the PTTK counter opposite the ticket office; Orbis also arrange tours of the Stare Miasto and castle, complete with tickets, as do a number of other local tourist offices.

The Cathedral

"The sanctuary of the nation . . . cannot be entered without an inner trembling, without an awe, for here – as in few cathedrals of the world – is contained a vast greatness which speaks to us of the history of Poland, of all our past." So was Wawel Cathedral evoked by former Archbishop Karol Wojtyła of Kraków. As with Westminster Abbey or St Peter's, the moment you enter Wawel, you know you're in a place overloaded with history.

The first cathedral was built here around the time King Bolesław the Brave established the Kraków bishopric in 1020. Fragments of this building can still be seen in the west wing of the castle and the courtyard between the castle and the cathedral, while the St Leonard's crypt survives from a second Romanesque structure. The present brick and sandstone basilica is essentially Gothic, dating from the reigns of Władysław the Short (1306–33) and Kazimierz the Great (1333–70), and adorned with a mass of side chapels, endowed by just about every subsequent Polish monarch and a fair number of the aristocratic families too.

The view down the nave of the cathedral, with its arched Gothic vaulting, is blocked by the **shrine of Saint Stanisław**, an overwrought seventeenth-century silver sarcophagus commemorating the bishop who was murdered by the king in 1079 for his opposition to royal ambitions. Beyond it stands the Baroque **high altar** and choir stalls. However, most people are drawn immediately to the outstanding array of side chapels which punctuate the entire length of the building.

THE CHAPELS

All bar four of Poland's forty-five monarchs are buried in the cathedral, and their tombs and side chapels are like a directory of the central European architecture, art and sculpture of the last six centuries.

Beginning from the right of the entrance, the Gothic **Holy Cross Chapel** (Kaplica Świętokrzyska) is the burial chamber of King Kazimierz IV Jagiełło (1447–92). The boldly coloured Byzantine-looking paintings on the walls and ceiling were completed by artists from Novgorod, while the king's marble tomb is the characteristically expressive work of Veit Stoss, of Mariacki fame. Two carved Gothic altars and a beautiful triptych of the Holy Trinity in the side panels round off a sumptuously elegant masterpiece.

Moving down the aisle, the next two chapels celebrate aristocratic families rather than kings: the **Potocki** (a Neoclassical creation) and **Szafraniec** (a Baroque ensemble at the foot of the Silver Bells tower). They are followed by the majestic **Waza** chapel, a Baroque mausoleum to the seventeenth-century royal dynasty, and the **Zygmuntowska** chapel, whose shining gilded cupola – its exterior regularly replated owing to the corrosive effects of pollution – dominates the courtyard outside. Designed for King Zygmunt the Old by the Italian architect Bartolomeo Berrecci, it's an astonishing piece of Renaissance design and ornamentation, with intricate sandstone and marble carvings, and superb sculpted figures above the sarcophagi of the king, his son Zygmunt August and his wife

---

THE ITALIAN RENAISSANCE IN KRAKÓW

Poland's long history of contacts with Italy was particularly fruitful in the artistic sphere, and an amazingly high proportion of the country's principal monuments were created by Italians who were enticed there by lucrative commissions offered by the royal court and the great rural magnates. One consequence of this is that Poland, and Kraków in particular, possesses some of the finest Renaissance architecture to be found outside Italy itself. Although the architects remained true to the movement's original classical ideals, they nonetheless modified their approach to suit the local climate and tradition. The result is a distinctive national Renaissance style which is purer than the derivatives found anywhere else north of the Alps.

The Renaissance was introduced to Poland as a direct result of the Jagiellonians' short-lived dynastic union with Hungary. **Franciscus Italus** (d.1516, and tentatively identifed as Francesco della Lora), who had been employed at the Hungarian court since the 1480s, was summoned to Kraków to reconstruct the royal palace which had been badly damaged by fire in 1499. Work on this occupied him until his death, but it was far from complete by then, as King Zygmunt subsequently decided on a complete rebuild.

The present appearance of the complex is due mainly to Franciscus' fellow-Florentine and successor as the royal architect, **Bartolomeo Berrecci** (c.1480–1537), who seems to have invented the highly original form of the courtyard. Its first two storeys are reminiscent of the celebrated Palazzo Strozzi in Florence, but the third tier is at twice the normal height, with the columns, which are moulded into bulbous shapes at the normal position of the capital, rising straight to the huge overhanging wooden roof, omitting the usual entablature in between. In his other key commission, the Zygmuntowska chapel in the Wawel Cathedral, Berrecci showed similar ingenuity. The basic shape he chose – a cube divided internally by paired pilasters, and surmounted by a dome, octagonal outside and cylindrical inside, with eight circular windows – represents the Italian ideal. Yet the overall

Queen Anna. The two altarpieces are spectacular, too: the silver *Altar of the Virgin* was designed by craftsmen from Nürnberg and includes Passion paintings by George Pencz, a pupil of Dürer.

Venerable fourteenth-century bishops occupy several subsequent chapels, while the Gothic red Hungarian marble **Tomb of King Kazimierz the Great**, immediately to the right of the high altar, is a dignified tribute to the revered monarch. The fourteenth-century **St Mary's** chapel, directly behind the altar and connected to the castle by a passage, was remodelled in the 1590s to accommodate the austere black marble and sandstone tomb of King Stefan Batory (1576–86). The **Tomb of King Władysław the Short** (1306–33), on the left-hand side of the altar, is the oldest in the cathedral, completed soon after his death; the reclining, coronation-robed figure lies on a white sandstone tomb edged with expressive mourning figures.

THE TREASURY, TOWER AND CRYPTS

The highlights of the cathedral **Treasury** (in the northeast corner, behind the sacristy) include a collection of illuminated texts and some odd items of Polish royal and ecclesiastical history – Saint Maurice's spear (a present to King Bolesław the Brave from Emperor Otto III), an eighth-century miniature of the four Evangelists, and King Kazimierz the Great's crown. An ascent of the **Zygmuntowska Tower** (access again from the sacristy) gives a far-reaching

---

appearance, with its profuse furnishings in a wide range of materials and elaborate surface decoration filling every available space on the walls, is totally unlike anything to be found in Italy. Berrecci built nothing else of significance, as his life was cut short by an assassin's knife.

Many other Italian craftsmen worked on the interior of the Zygmuntowska chapel, the most prominent being **Giovanni Maria Mosca** (c.1495–1573), generally known as "Il Padovano" on account of having been born in Padua. The recruitment of Mosca was seen as a major artistic coup, as he had already extablished a formidable reputation for himself in his native city and in Venice. Primarily a sculptor, it is probable that he was entrusted with carving the effigy of Zygmunt himself; he also made the two memorials to bishops in the chantry chapels of the east end. In addition, he struck four royal medals, carved the tabernacle in the Mariacki, and made many other funerary monuments in Kraków and elsewhere, notably those of the Tarnowskis in Tarnów cathedral. As an architect, his main work was the addition of the attic and parapet to the medieval Sukiennice, giving it a pronounced Renaissance appearance in a transformation reminiscent of that wrought by Palladio on the Basilica in Vicenza just a few years before.

The outsized savage masks on the Sukiennice were carved by the Florentine **Santi Gucci** (c.1530–1600), who was also responsible for some of the tombs in the Zygmuntowska chapel. Gucci subsequently came to prominence in his own right as court artist to Stefan Batory, adapting the Wawel's Lady Chapel into a lavish chantry in his honour. He also seems to have built a number of country houses; not all of those documented have survived, but he is thought to have been responsible for the most spectacular one remaining intact, that at Baranów Sandomierski. By the time of his death, Italian Renaissance architects had been dominant in Kraków for exactly a century. The style was to remain popular elsewhere in Poland for a considerable time yet, but in Kraków it was supplanted by the Baroque — introduced, once again, by Italians.

panorama over the city and close-up views of the five medieval bells. The largest, known as Zygmunt, is two and a half metres in diameter, eight in circumference, and famed for its deep, sonorous tone, which according to local legend scatters rain clouds and brings out the sun. These days it doesn't get too many chances to perform, as it's only rung on Easter Sunday, Christmas Eve and New Year's Eve.

Back in the cathedral, the **crypt** (in the left aisle) houses the remains of the poets **Adam Mickiewicz** and **Juliusz Słowacki**, while **St Leonard's Crypt**, part of a long network of vaults reached from near the main entrance, contains the tombs of national heroes Prince Józef Poniatowski and Tadeusz Kościuszko. The equally sanctified prewar independence leader Józef Piłsudski lies in a separate vault nearby. Standing with the crowds filing past this pantheon, you catch the passionate intensity of Polish attachment to everything connected with past resistance and independent nationhood.

Finally, as you leave the cathedral, look out for the bizarre collection of **prehistoric animal bones** – a mammoth's shinbone, a whale's rib and the skull of a hairy rhinoceros – in a passage near the main entrance. As long as they remain, so legend maintains, the cathedral will too.

The Castle

Entering the tiered courtyard of **Wawel Castle**, you might imagine that you'd stumbled on an opulent Italian palazzo. That's just the effect Zygmunt the Old intended when he entrusted the conversion of King Kazimierz's Gothic castle to a Florentine architect in the early 1500s. The major difference from its Italian models lies in the response to climate: the window openings are enlarged to maximise the available light, while to withstand snow the roofing has a distinctly northern functionalism. A spate of fires, and more recently the corrosive effects of Kraków's atmosphere, have taken their toll on the building, but it still exudes a palatial bravura.

Essentially the palace remained a grand residence for as long as the kings stuck around. The rot set in after the capital moved to Warsaw, and the castle was already in a dilapidated state when the Austrians pillaged and turned it into barracks. Reconstruction began in earnest in 1880, following Emperor Franz Josef's removal of the troops, continuing throughout the interwar years. Wawel's nadir came during World War II, when governor Hans Frank transformed the castle into his private quarters, adding insult to injury by turning the royal apartments over to his Nazi henchmen. Luckily many of the most valuable castle contents were spirited out of the country at the outbreak of war, eventually being returned to Wawel from Canada in 1961, after years of wrangling. Alongside many pieces from individual Poles at home and abroad – some of these, incidentally, items plundered by the Nazis but subsequently spotted at the big art auctions – they make up the core of today's amply stocked and well-restored collection.

The **castle** is divided into three main sections: the state rooms, crown treasury and a separate exhibition of Oriental art. The state rooms are the section to focus on if time is limited, with their art collections accumulated by the Jagiellonian and Waza dynasties.

THE STATE ROOMS AND ART COLLECTIONS

The centrepiece of the art collections is King Zygmunt August's splendid assembly of **Flanders tapestries**, scattered throughout the first and second floors. The 136 pieces – about a third of the original collection – are what remains from the depredations of czarist, Austrian and Nazi armies. Outstanding are three series from the Brussels workshops of the "Flemish Raphael", Michel Coxie, the first and most impressive of which is a group of eighteen huge Old Testament scenes, featuring a lyrical evocation of Paradise and a wonderfully detailed tapestry of Noah and family in the aftermath of the Flood. The oldest tapestry in the castle is the mid-fifteenth-century French *Story of the Swan Knight* displayed in Zygmunt the Old's first-floor bedroom.

In the northwest corner of the same floor is a remnant of the original Gothic castle, a tiny two-roomed watchtower named the **Hen's Foot Tower**. In contrast to other parts of the castle, the rooms of the north wing are in early Baroque style, the result of remodelling following a major fire in 1595. Of the luxurious apartments in this section, the **Silver Hall**, redesigned in 1786 by Domenico Merlini (of Warsaw's Łazienki Park fame), achieves a particularly harmonious blending of the old architecture with period classicism.

The **state rooms** on the top floor are amongst the finest in the building, particularly those in the **east wing** where the original wooden ceilings and wall paintings are still visible. A glance upwards at the carved ceiling of the **Audience Hall** at the southern end of the wing will tell you why it's nicknamed the "Heads Room". Executed for King Zygmunt in the 1530s by Sebastian Tauerbach of Wrocław and Jan Snycerz, only thirty of its original array of close on two hundred heads remain, but it's enough to give you a feeling for the contemporary characters they were based on – from all strata of society. The frieze by Hans Dürer illustrates *The Life of Man*, a sixteenth-century retelling of an ancient Greek legend, while the magnificent tapestries of Garden of Eden scenes are again from the Coxie workshop.

Back down the corridor is the **Zodiac Room**, ornamented by an astrological frieze – an ingenious 1920s reconstruction of a sixteenth-century fresco – as well as another series of biblical tapestries. The northeast corner towers contain the private royal apartments. The **Chapel**, rebuilt in 1602, looks onto the king's bedchamber, while the walls of the **Study**, with its fine floor and stucco decorations, are a mini-art gallery in themselves, crammed with works by Dutch and Flemish artists, among them a Rubens sketch and a painting by the younger Brueghel. The seventeenth-century **Bird Room**, named after the wooden birds that used to hang from the ceiling, leads on to the **Eagle Room**, the old court of justice, with a Rubens portrait of Prince Władysław Waza. Last comes the large **Senators' Hall** with a collection of tapestries illustrating the story of Noah and the Ark, another impressive coffered ceiling and a sixteenth-century minstrel's gallery still used for the odd concert.

THE TREASURY AND ARMOURY

If you've got the stamina, the next thing to head for is the **Royal Treasury and Armoury** in the northeast corner of the castle (entrance on the ground floor). The paucity of crown jewels on display, however, is testimony to the ravages of the past. Much of the treasury's contents had been sold off by the time of the Partitions to pay off marriage dowries and debts of state. The Prussians did most of the rest of the damage, purloining the coronation insignia in 1795, then melting down the crown and selling off its jewels. The vaulted Gothic **Kazimierz Room** contains the finest items from a haphazard display of lesser royal possessions including rings, crosses, and the coronation shoes and burial crown of Zygmunt August. The oldest exhibit is a fifth-century ring inscribed with the name MARTINVS, found near Kraków.

The prize exhibit in the next-door **Jadwiga and Jagiełło Room** is the solemnly displayed *Szczerbiec*, the thirteenth-century weapon used for centuries in the coronation of Polish monarchs. The other two exhibits here are an early sixteenth-century sword belonging to Zygmunt the Old and the oldest surviving royal banner, made in 1533 for the coronation of Zygmunt August's third wife, Catherine von Habsburg. In the following room are displayed a variety of items connected to **Jan Sobieski**, most notably the regalia of the Knights of the Order of the Holy Ghost sent to him by the pope as thanks for defeating the Turks at Vienna. Things get more military from here on. The next barrel-vaulted room contains a host of finely crafted display weapons, shields and helmets, while the final **Armoury Room** is about serious warfare, with weapons captured over five centuries from Poland's host of foreign invaders, including copies of the banners seized during the epic Battle of Grunwald.

THE ORIENT OF THE WAWEL, LOST WAWEL AND THE CAVE

The **Orient of the Wawel** exhibition, housed in the older west wing of the castle, focuses on Oriental influences in Polish culture. The first floor has an interesting section on early contacts with Armenia, Iran, Turkey, China and Japan, but the main "influences" displayed here seem to be war loot from the seventeenth-century campaigns against the Turks. The centrepiece is a collection of **Turkish tents and armour** captured after the Battle of Vienna. Other second-floor rooms display an equally sumptuous assortment of Turkish and Iranian carpets, banners and weaponry seized during the fighting – the sixteenth-century **Paradise Carpet** must have gone very nicely in the royal front room.

The **Lost Wawel** exhibition, beneath the old kitchens south of the cathedral, takes you past the excavated remains of the hill's most ancient buildings, including the foundations of the tenth-century **Rotunda of SS. Felix and Adauctus**, the oldest known church in Poland. A diverse collection of medieval archaeological finds is displayed in the old coach house.

Before leaving Wawel, take in the view over the river from the terrace at the western edge of the hill. And if you're feeling energetic, you could, instead of returning directly to town, clamber down the steps to the **Dragon's Cave** at the foot of the hill – the legendary haunt of Krak (see "A brief history", p.305) and the medieval site of a fishermen's tavern, now guarded by a tacky fire-breathing bronze dragon. From the Dragon's Cave a walk west along the bend of the river towards the **Dębnicki Bridge** is rewarded by an excellent view back over the castle. Alternatively, if you fancy a longer walk, stroll south along the river bank the kilometre or so to Piłsudski Bridge and on into Kazimierz.

Kazimierz, the ghettoes and Płaszów

South from Wawel Hill lies the **Kazimierz** district, originally a distinct town and named after King Kazimierz, who granted the founding charter in 1335. Thanks to the acquisition of royal privileges the settlement developed rapidly, trade centring around a market square almost equal in size to Kraków's. The decisive influence on the character of Kazimierz, however, was King Jan Olbracht's electing to move Kraków's already significant **Jewish population** into the area from the ul. św. Anny district in 1495.

In tandem with Warsaw, where a **ghetto** was created around the same time, Kazimierz grew to become one of the main cultural centres of Polish Jewry. Jews were initially limited to an area around modern-day ul. Szeroka and Miodowa, and it was only in the nineteenth century that they began to spread into other parts of Kazimierz. By this time there were ghettoes all over the country, of course, but descriptions of Kazimierz in Polish art and literature make it clear that there was something special about the Oriental atmosphere of this place.

The life of the area was to perish in the gas chambers of nearby Auschwitz, but many of the buildings, synagogues included, have survived. Walking round the streets today, you feel the weight of an absent culture. Yiddish inscriptions fronting the doorways, an old pharmacy, a ruined theatre: the details make it easier to picture what has gone than do the drab housing estates covering the former Warsaw ghetto.

Around the Ghetto

If you're coming from the centre of town take a tram (#3, #9, #11 or #13) down ul. Bohaterów Stalingradu and get off at the corner of ul. Miodowa. A left off ul. Miodowa into ul. Szeroka and you're into the heart of the ghetto.

The tiny **Remu'h Synagogue** at ul. Szeroka 40 is one of two still functioning in the quarter. Built in 1557 on the site of an earlier wooden synagogue, it was ransacked by the Nazis and restored after the war. It's named after Moses Isserles, also known as Rabbi Remu'h, an eminent Polish writer and philosopher and the son of the synagogue's founder. On Fridays and Saturdays the small local congregation is swelled by some of the increasing number of Jews visiting Poland these days. Behind the synagogue is the **Remu'h cemetery**, established twenty or so years earlier, and in use till the end of the eighteenth century. Many of the gravestones were unearthed in the 1950s; one of the finest is that of the still venerated Rabbi Remu'h, its stele luxuriously ornamented with plant motifs. Tombstones torn up by the Nazis have been collaged together to form a high, powerful Wailing Wall just inside the entrance.

Continuing down ul. Szeroka, no. 16 is the **Poper's Synagogue**, built in 1620 by a merchant of the same name. Restored since the war, it's now a cultural centre. Other synagogues no longer used for worship are the late sixteenth-century **Wysoka** (High Synagogue) at ul. Józefa 38, the **Ajzyk** (Isaac) synagogue nearby at ul. Jakuba 25, built in the 1630s, the 1590 **Kupa** synagogue, a little further north at ul. Warszauera 8, and the nineteenth-century **Postępowa-Tempel** synagogue at the corner of ul. Miodowa and Podbrzezie.

The grandest of all the Kazimierz synagogues was the **Old Synagogue** on ul. Szeroka, the earliest surviving Jewish religious building in Poland. Modelled on the great European synagogues of Worms, Prague and Regensburg, the present Renaissance building was completed in 1557 after a fire destroyed much of the area. The synagogue's story is entwined with the country's history: it was here, for example, that Kościuszko came to rally the Jews in 1794, a precedent followed by the Kazimierz rabbi Ber Meissels during the uprisings of 1831 and 1863. Since the war it's been carefully restored and turned into a **museum** of the history and culture of Kraków Jewry (Mon & Tues 9am–3pm, Wed, Thurs, Sat & Sun 9am–3pm, Fri 11am–6pm; closed first Sat & Sun of the month). Nazi destruction was thorough, so the museum's collection of art, books, manuscripts and religious objects has a slightly cobbled-together feel to it, though there's an interesting and evocative set of photos of life in the ghetto before World War II. The wrought-iron bima in the centre of the main prayer hall is original, the masterful product of a sixteenth-century Kraków workshop.

Western Kazimierz

As the presence of several churches indicates, the western part of Kazimierz was where non-Jews tended to live. Despite its Baroque overlay, the interior of the Gothic church of the **Corpus Christi**, on the corner of ul. Bożego Ciała, retains early features including stained-glass windows installed around 1420. The Swedish king Charles Gustaf is supposed to have used the building as his operational base during the mid-seventeenth-century siege of the city. The high church looks onto **plac Wolnica**, the old market square of Kazimierz, now much smaller than it used to be, thanks to the houses built along the old trade route through it in the nineteenth century. The fourteenth-century **Town Hall**, later rebuilt, stands in what used to be the middle of the square, its southern extension an overambitious nineteenth-century addition. It now houses the largest **Ethnographic Museum** in the country (Mon 10am–6pm, Wed–Sun 10am–3pm). The collection focuses on Polish folk traditions, although there's also a selection of artefacts from Siberia, Africa, Latin America and various Slav countries. A detailed survey of life in rural Poland includes an intriguing section devoted to ancient folk customs and an impressive collection of costumes, painting, woodcarving, fabrics and pottery – an excellent introduction to the fascinating and often bizarre world of Polish folk culture.

Two more churches west of the square are worth looking in on. On ul. Skałeczna stands fourteenth-century **St Catherine's**, founded by King Kazimierz for Augustine monks imported from Prague. The large basilican structure is a typical example of Kraków Gothic, though the interior has suffered everything from earthquakes to the installation of an Austrian arsenal. Further down the road is the **Pauline church and monastery**, perched on a small hill known as Skałka (the Rock). Tradition connects the church with Saint Stanisław, the bishop of Kraków, whose martyrdom by King Bolesław the Generous in 1079 is supposed to have happened here. An altar to him stands in the left aisle of the remodelled Baroque church, and underneath you can see the block on which he's supposed to have been beheaded. Underneath the church is a **crypt** cut into the rock of the hill, which was turned into a mausoleum for famous Poles in the late nineteenth century. Eminent artists, writers and composers buried here include Kraków's own Stanisław Wyspiański, composer Karol Szymanowski and the medieval historian Jan Długosz.

The Wartime Ghetto

Following an edict from Hans Frank, in March 1941 the entire Jewish population of the city was crammed into a tiny **ghetto** over the river, south of Kazimierz, in the area around modern-day pl. Bohaterów Getta. It was sealed off by high walls and anyone caught entering or leaving unofficially was summarily executed. After waves of deportations to the concentration camps, the ghetto was finally liquidated in March 1943, thus ending seven centuries of Jewish life in Kraków. The area is the setting of Thomas Keneally's novel *Schindler's Ark*, which re-creates life in the ghetto from the stories of survivors saved by the German industrialist Oskar Schindler.

If you know what you're looking for, it's still possible to detect signs of past Jewish presence in what is now a quiet, rather run-down suburban district. The most obvious is the **Apteka Pod Orłem** on the southwest corner of pl. Bohaterów: the old ghetto pharmacy, this is now a museum (10am–4pm, closed Sat). Its wartime proprietor Dr Pankiewicz was the only non-Jewish Pole permitted to live in the ghetto, and the exhibition touches on the sensitive question of

Polish wartime aid to Jews, as well as life in the ghetto area. No. 6, on the other side of the square, was the headquarters of the **Jewish Combat Organisation** (ŻOB) which continued operating until the ghetto's liquidation.

At the bottom of ul. Lwówska, which runs southeast of the square, there's a fragment of the **ghetto wall**. West of the square on ul. Węgierska is the burnt-out shell of what looks like an old Jewish theatre, while around the corner on ul. Jozefinska, the state mint turns out to be the former **Jewish bank**. Careful hunting round the area may produce other traces: if you want a break first, however, the coffee shop on the corner of ul. św. Benedykta and Limanowskiego is a restful place, with a gallery next door that often features Jewish artists (Mon–Fri 10am–5pm).

Płaszów concentration camp

As well as imprisoning people in the ghetto, the Nazis also relocated many Jews to the **concentration camp at Płaszów**, built near an old Austrian hill fort a couple of kilometres south of Kazimierz. Levelled after the war, the camp's desolate hilltop site is now enclosed by fields and concrete residential blocks. Although none of the local guidebooks mention the site, it is marked on the large *Kraków: plan miasta* city map by two "Pomnik Martyrologii" symbols, just above the junction of ul. Kamienskiego and ul. Wielicka.

To **get there**, take a local train (Tarnów direction) to Płaszów station, walk down to ul. Wieliczka and cross over. From here it's about ten minutes' walk west to the site: the large hilltop monument is clearly visible from the main road below. Like all concentration camps the site has an eerie, wilderness atmosphere, all the more so for the lack of buildings. Scratch beneath the surface of the grass-covered mounds and you'll find shards of pottery, scraps of metal and cutlery – telltale evidence of its wartime use.

The Kościuszko Mound and beyond

This three-hundred-metre-high hill stands a short distance west of the city centre, capped by a memorial mound erected in the 1820s in honour of Poland's greatest revolutionary hero, **Tadeusz Kościuszko**. A veteran of the American War of Independence, Kościuszko returned to Poland to lead the 1794 insurrection against the Partitions. With the failure of this uprising, he was imprisoned for two years in St Petersburg, then – after returning for a while to America to promote Polish independence – lived the rest of his life in exile in France and Switzerland. For Poles he is the personification of the popular insurrectionary tradition that involved peasants as well as intellectuals.

The mound is quite an oddity, having been added onto the hill by the citizenry of Kraków, using earth from Kościuszko's battle sites – both from Poland and (reputedly) from the United States. Access to this section of the hill is only possible via an effusive **museum** of Kościuszko memorabilia (Tues–Sat 10am–4pm). It's worth the few złotys' admission for the view alone. Lower down the hill, the deer roaming about the hillside are a surprising sight so close to a city centre, but the polluted grass can't do them much good. There is also a nineteenth-century Austrian **fort** and an upmarket **hotel and restaurant**, the *Pod Kopcem*.

From the city centre (plac Matejki) bus #100 runs to the hotel, but if you feel like a walk out of town you can cross the **Błonia** – a green belt west of the Stare Miasto – and then, crossing a couple of roads, follow one of the overgrown pathways up the slopes.

TADEUSZ KOŚCIUSZKO (1746–1817)

What Adam Mickiewicz is to the Polish literary Romantic tradition, **Tadeusz Kościuszko** is to its heroic military counterpart. Swashbuckling leader of armed national resistance in the early Partition years, Kościuszko was also a noted radical whose espousal of the republican ideals of the French Revolution did little to endear him to fellow aristocrats, but everything to win over the hearts and minds of the oppressed Polish peasantry. As the US towns and streets named after him testify, Kościuszko is also almost as well known in the **USA** as within Poland itself on account of his major role in the **American War of Independence**, in thanks for which he was made both an honorary American citizen and brigadier general in the US Army.

The bare bones of Kościuszko's life story revolve round a fabulously contorted series of battles, insurrections, revolutions and impossible love affairs. An outstanding student from the start, after fleeing to Paris in 1776 to escape from the general whose daughter he tried to elope with, Kościuszko continued on to America, where he joined up with the **independence forces** fighting the **British**. In the following five years he was right in the thick of things, helping amongst other things to bring about the capitulation of the British forces under General Burgoyne at Saratoga (October 1778) and conducting both the important Battle of the Ninety-Six and the lengthy blockade of Charleston (1781).

Returning to Poland in 1784, after a lengthy period out in the political cold he finally gained military office in 1789, simultaneously failing (again) to win the consent of a general whose eighteen-year-old daughter he had fallen in love with. Kościuszko's finest hour, though, came in 1792 with the czarist army's invasion of Poland following the enactment of internal reforms intended to free the country from Russian influence. After the bloody **Battle of Dubienka** (July 1792), Kościuszko was promoted to general by King Stanisław Poniatowski, also receiving honorary French citizenship from the newly established revolutionary government in Paris. From enforced exile in Saxony, Kościuszko soon returned to the country at the request of the expectant insurrectionary army, swearing his famous **oath of**

Las Wolski

For a more extended bout of countryside, you could take an hour's walk west from the mound to the wonderful stretch of woodland known as **Las Wolski**. At its centre there's a restaurant, a zoo and another mound – this one erected, in emulation of Kościuszko's, to the 1920s ruler Józef Piłsudski. Bus #134 runs from the city centre to the mound.

The university conference centre

Continuing west of town along the main road, ul. Księcia Józefa, a kilometre or so on a turn up ul. Jodłowa and the steep climb of the hill north through the woods takes you up to the main university conference centre, the first building you encounter being the elegant palatial structure the city's Nazi wartime ruler Hans Frank planned to convert into his personal residence. Round the back of the main building there's a bar – decent snacks are available too – that's understandably popular among students as a summer evening drinking spot, the main balcony offering a superb vantage point from which to take in the tranquil rural surroundings over a beer or two. In good weather the views south are fantastic – it's hard to believe you're still relatively close to the city centre – with the Tatras

national uprising before a huge crowd assembled on the square in Kraków in March 1794.

The immediate results of Kościuszko's assumption of leadership were spectacular. A disciplined army largely comprising scythe-bearing peasants won a famous victory over Russian forces at the **Battle of Racławice** (April 1794). In a bid to gain more volunteer peasant recruits Kościuszko issued the **Połaniec Manifesto** (May 1794), offering amongst other things to abolish serfdom, a radical move resisted by aristocratic supporters. Retreating to Warsaw, the embattled Polish forces held out for two months against the combined might of the Prussian and Russian armies, Kościuszko himself leading the bayonet charges at a couple of critical junctures. After inciting an insurrection in the Wielkopolska region that forced Prussian forces to retreat temporarily, Kościuszko was finally beaten and taken prisoner by the Russians at Maciejowice, an event that led to the collapse of the national uprising.

Imprisoned in St Petersburg and by now seriously ill, Kościuszko was freed in 1796 and returned to the USA to an enthusiastic reception in Philadelphia, soon striking up what proved to be a lasting friendship with Thomas Jefferson. The last decades of Kościuszko's life were marked by a series of further disappointments. He revisited France in 1798 in the hope that Napoleon's rise might presage a revival of Polish hopes, but refused to participate in Napoleon's plans, having failed to gain specific political commitments from Bonaparte with regard to Poland's future. Remaining studiously aloof from French advances, after Bonaparte's fall in 1814 Kościuszko was again approached for support, this time from the unlikely quarter of the Russian Emperor Alexander I, who atttempted to gain his approval for the new Russian-ruled **Congress Kingdom** established at the Congress of Vienna (1815). Uncompromising republican to the last, not surprisingly the radical conditions he put forward met with no response. Embittered, Kościuszko retired to Switzerland, where he died in 1817. Two years later the legendary warrior's remains were brought to Kraków and buried among the monarchs in the vaults of Wawel – reviving a pagan Polish burial custom, the people of the city raised the **memorial mound** to him you see today.

visible in the distance on a really clear summer's day. Unless you have your own transport you'd have to rely on a taxi to get here – if the driver doesn't know the way, saying "Instytut Badań Polonijnych" should do the trick; the cost of the journey (approximately £5 each way at current rates) is more than justified by the experience.

The Outskirts

If Wawel Hill and the main square are quintessential old Kraków, the steel mills, smokestacks and grimy housing blocks of **Nowa Huta**, 10km to the east of the city, are the embodiment of the postwar communist dream, and any Cracovian will want to show them to you.

South of the city, a fifteen-kilometre bus ride offers a glimpse at an earlier industrial past in the form of the medieval **Wieliczka salt mine**, a beautiful, UNESCO-listed site that demands a visit. **Tyniec**, 15km southwest of the city, out along the river, is a fine Benedictine abbey, which holds organ recitals during the summer.

Nowa Huta

Raised from scratch in the late 1940s on the site of an old village, the vast industrial complex of **NOWA HUTA** now has a population of over 200,000, making it by far the biggest suburb, while the vast steelworks accounts for more than fifty percent of the country's production. It's worth visiting for the insights it offers into the working-class culture of postwar Poland and the immense ecological problems facing the country.

From Kraków city centre it's a forty-minute tram journey (#4, #9, #15 or #22) to **plac Centralny**, the main square, now bereft of its statue of Lenin, which was replaced in 1990 by a small replica of the Gdańsk Crosses. From here, seemingly endless streets of residential blocks stretch out in all directions. East along the main road are the mills known until recently as the **Lenin Steelworks**, now renamed the SendzimirWorks but still belching out the thick smoke that covers the whole area with layers of filth. What to do with this vast monster of an industrial complex is something of a political hot potato for the Kraków city authorities. While it's clear that the place can't keep going indefinitely on its current heavily state-subsidised footing, shutting down all or even parts of the plant – "restructuring" is the latest buzzword – would mean major losses for a local economy already badly hit by the austerity measures of the post-Communist era. On a more upbeat note, a new Industrial Management jointly financed by the French and Polish governments has recently been set up in Kraków to examine this and other industrial issues.

In keeping with the anti-religious policies of the postwar government, churches were not included in the original construction plans for Nowa Huta. After years of intensive lobbying, however, the ardently Catholic population eventually got permission to build one in the 1970s. The **Church of the Ark**, in the northern Bienczyce district, is the result – an amazing ark-like concrete structure encrusted with mountain pebbles. Go there any Sunday and you'll find it packed with steel workers and their families decked out in their best, a powerful testament to the seemingly unbreakable Catholicism of the Polish working class. The other local church, the large **Maximilian Kolbe** church in the Mistrzejowice district, was consecrated by Pope John Paul II in 1983, a sign of the importance the Catholic hierarchy attaches to the loyalty of Nowa Huta. Kolbe, canonised in 1982, was a priest sent to Auschwitz for giving refuge to Jews; in the camp, he took the place of a Jewish inmate in the gas chambers. Trams #1, #16 and #20 from plac Centralny all pass by the building.

Tyniec

Within easy striking distance of the city centre, 15km along the river, is the village of **TYNIEC**. City bus #112 takes you there, as do excursion boats in summer, a nice trip provided you don't inspect the water too carefully.

The main attraction here is **Tyniec Abbey**, an eleventh-century foundation that was the Benedictines' first base in Poland. Perched on a white limestone cliff on the edge of the village, the abbey makes an impressive sight from the riverbank paths. The farm plots and traditional wooden cottages dotted around the village lend the place a rural feel at odds with its location so close to the city centre; it's a popular place for a Sunday afternoon stroll.

The original Romanesque abbey was rebuilt after the ·Tartars destroyed it during the 1240 invasion, and then completely remodelled in Gothic style in the fifteenth century, when the defensive walls were also added. The interior of the church subsequently endured the familiar Baroque treatment, but bits of the Gothic structure are left near the altar and in the adjoining (but usually off-limits) cloisters. From June to August the church holds a series of high-quality **organ concerts** during which the cloisters are opened.

In the village, the *Srebrna Góra* on ul. Benedyktyńska is a famed fish **restaurant** that Cracovians drive out to for the evening in droves.

Wieliczka

Fifteen kilometres south of Kraków is the salt mine at **WIELICZKA,** a unique phenomenon described by one eighteenth-century visitor as being "as remarkable as the Pyramids and more useful". Salt deposits were discovered here as far back as the eleventh century and from King Kazimierz's time onwards local mining rights and hence income were strictly controlled by the crown. As mining intensified over the centuries a huge network of pitfaces, rooms and tunnels proliferated – nine levels in all, extending to a depth of 327m with approximately 300km of tunnels stretched over an area some 10km wide. Scaled-down mining continues today, and there's a sanatorium 200m down, to exploit the supposedly healthy saline atmosphere.

To **get to Wieliczka** take a local train – there are plenty of them – or bus #FB from the main Kraków–Płaszów station. Both drop you off a little way from the mine, but it isn't difficult to locate the pit's solitary chimney and squeaky conveyor belt.

Down the mine

Entrance to the mine (Tues–Sun 8am–6pm) is by guided tour only, in groups of thirty or so; in summer there are some French-, German- and English-speaking guides around; if you turn up you might strike lucky, otherwise book in advance with Orbis. Be prepared for a bit of a walk – the tour takes two hours, through nearly two miles of tunnels.

A clanking lift takes you down in complete darkness to the first of the three levels included in the **tour,** at a depth of 135m. The rooms and passageways here were hewn between the seventeenth and nineteenth centuries, and whereas the lower sections are mechanised, horses are still used to lug things around on the top three levels. Many of the first-level chambers are pure green salt, including one dedicated to Copernicus, which he is supposed to have visited.

The further you descend, the more spectacular and weird the chambers get. As well as underground lakes, carved chapels and rooms full of eerie crystalline shapes, the second level features a chamber full of jolly salt gnomes carved in the 1960s by the mineworkers. The star attraction, **Blessed Kinga's Chapel**, comes on the bottom level: everything in the ornate fifty-metre-long chapel is carved from salt, including the stairs, bannisters, altar and chandeliers. The chapel's acoustic properties – every word uttered near the altar is audible from the gallery – has led to its use as a concert venue. A **museum**, also down at the lowest level, documents the history of the mine, local geological formations, and famous visitors such as Goethe, Balzac and the Emperor Franz Josef.

FLOODING AND CLOSURE

The future of the Wieliczka salt mines is uncertain following a serious bout of **flooding** in September 1992, when a huge river of salty water began pouring into the complex through an abandoned mine passageway some 170m underground – too much for the mine pumps to handle. So far none of the decorated chambers have been damaged, but the mine authorities have warned that some may be in danger from the floods. The town of Wieliczka, much of which is built over the mines, has also been badly affected: walls have collapsed, cracks have appeared in the fabric of the local monastery, and the train tracks running through the centre of town have shifted and twisted, causing all train services to be suspended. The EC has now provided an emergency grant towards the cost of shoring up what's recognised as a unique medieval treasure. It's not the first time there's been a shutdown – major flooding also occurred in the early 1970s, and miners are aware of scores of other small leaks in the passageways. The mine is currently closed, however, and all visits have been suspended. How long this will go on for is unclear, though it could well be some time if past experience is anything to go on. Tourist offices in Kraków will fill you in on the latest situation.

Eating, drinking and entertainment

Kraków's tourist status has given rise to a decent selection of **restaurants**, with new places springing up every week. For the moment, however, keep in mind that demand is also high and for the better places booking is essential. In general, you'll need to turn up early, too: this is not a late-night city, its life instead revolving around a central European café culture of afternoon and early evening socialising. There is, however, a good deal happening on the **cultural front**, with one of the best **theatre** groups in Europe, a long-established **cabaret** tradition and numerous **student events**. The compact size of Kraków's city centre and the presence of the university gives a general buzz that's largely absent in, say, Warsaw.

For local **listings** and general information, the weekly magazine *Tyozień w Krakowie* is invaluable, as is the newspaper *Gazeta Krakowska*.

Restaurants and snack bars

Kraków's Jewish past seems to have rubbed off on some of the better restaurants, with dishes like jellied carp and various versions of *gefillte fisch* appearing on menus. Otherwise it's pretty much a case of traditional Polish fare tempered by splashes of European cuisine – western and eastern – plus the new (for Poland) phenomenon of fast food and snacks. Recommendations within the restaurant section are in roughly ascending order of price.

Restaurants

Pani Stasia's, ul. Mikołajska 18. A small, privately owned fast-food joint, east of the Rynek. Popular with students and the like, with home cooking including great *pierogi* (cabbage pancakes). It's hidden from the street but queues are conspicuous. Lunchtime only.

Cechowa, ul. Jagiellońska 11. Handy if you're in the university area, with excellent pancakes and a fast lunchtime service.

Hawełka, Rynek Główny 34. Popular, noisy haunt serving *kasha i zrasy* (buckwheat with rolled meat) and traditional fortified *miody pitne* wines.

Myśliwska, pl. Szczepański 7. Good straightforward Polish food.

Kurza Stopka, pl. Wiosny Ludów. Cheap, clean and has a good reputation among locals.

Balaton, ul. Grodzka 37. Good but cramped Hungarian restaurant; be prepared for a wait, especially in summer.

Polski, ul. Pijarska 17. Cheap and basic hotel restaurant (pork with sauerkraut, etc), close to the city centre. Live music in the evenings.

PTTK Hostel, ul. Westerplatte 15–16. Recently tarted-up restaurant offering large portions of solid, no-nonsense meat and veg. Near the train station.

Grodzka, pl. Dominikański 6. Frequented by tourist groups but still worth a visit for dishes like *sztuka mięsa chrzanowy* (beef with horseradish sauce). Live music in the evenings; speedy lunchtime service.

Ermitage, ul. Karmelicka 3. Regular Polish cuisine and dinner-dancing till late.

Dniepr, ul. 18 Stycznia 55. Big modern place near *Pewex*. Ukrainian specialities – and dancing.

Cyganeria, ul. Szpitalna 38. Art Deco interior, gypsy music and old-style Polish cuisine pull in the city's nouveaux riches.

Staropolska, ul. Sienna 4. Deservedly popular Old Town venue with an emphasis on traditional pork and poultry dishes. Booking essential in the evening (☎225-821).

Kuchcik, Jagiellońska 12. Down-to-earth, good-quality Polish cuisine (the *bigos* and *pierogi* are recommended) in enjoyable centre-of-town location. Closes 6pm.

Hawelka, Rynek Główny 34. Reopened after complete overhaul, now transformed into posh first-floor restaurant (*Tetmajerowska*) complete with *fin-de-siecle* interior decoration by artist of same name; attached cafe, bar and self-service cafeteria on the ground floor.

Almayer, Rynek Główny 30. Smartish Chinese eaterie in a backsquare courtyard. Reservations advisable in summer (☎223-224). Open 11pm, also night bar (till 4am).

Da Pietro, Rynek Główny 17. Best of the new Italian restaurants in town, in a medieval cellar below a courtyard off the main square. Reasonably priced pasta and salads. Open till midnight.

Orbit, ul. Wrocławska 78A. Traditional Polish cuisine, large portions at moderate prices. The *barszcz* is excellent. Open to 10pm (midnight Sat).

Pod Kopcem, al. Waszyngtona. Restaurant of the elegant hotel below the Kościuszko Mound, specialising in fish from the Tatras. Reservations essential in season (☎220-311/355).

Cracovia, al. Puszkina 1. A pricey but good hotel restaurant in striking distance of the centre, with a resident dance band. Reservations advisable, especially at weekends (☎228-666). Open until midnight.

Pod Różą, ul. Floriańska 14. Another excellent hotel restaurant.

Leonard's, Rynek Główny 25. Smart new French cellar restaurant clearly aimed at the wealthy. If you want to blow money, for atmosphere you're better off at *Wierzynek*.

Wierzynek, Rynek Główny 15. This stately place is Kraków's most famous restaurant. On a good night it's one of the best in the country with specialities like mountain trout and the house *wierzynek* dish. For Westerners prices remain very reasonable at around £15 a head; to have any chance of a table booking is essential (☎221-035). Open till 11pm.

Grand, ul. Sławkowska 19. The city's newest luxury hotel has an excellent, if also rather pricey, restaurant.

Milk bars, snacks and fast food

You'll have no trouble picking up a hamburger or snack in the city centre – Western-style **fast-food joints** (including a number of big-league franchises) have moved in on the Old Town area in a major way. In among the new-look

Western setups there are a number of places specialising in more traditional Polish dishes, notably *pierogi*, and generally worth hunting out.

Na Rogu, ul. Karmelicka 17. Old-style milk bar with good selection of *pierogi*, takeaway included.

Pod Zegarem, ul. Basztowa 12. Regular lunchtime milk bar on the northern edge of the Planty.

Akademicki, ul. Podwale 5. Good, cheap student milk bar in the university district. No meat.

Da Luigi, Rynek Główny 44. Decent Polish-style pizza, generous portions.

Monika, Rynek Główny 33. Snack bar in passageway just off main square. Good place for a quick lunch.

Beirut., ul. Floriańska 1. Top corner of the street. Popular takeaway joint, decent falafels and kebabs.

Kabul, ul. Karmelicka 45a. Afghan-influenced snacks – kebabs, "Afghan" pierogi and the like.

Pizzeria Piccolina, ul. Floriańska 38. Basic pizza, also takeaways. The *Dixie Chicken* franchise is in the same building.

Tunis Grill, pl. Dominikański 1. North African grill cum snack bar with a tasty range of ethnic dishes.

Svensson, ul. Długa 12. Swedish-owned takeaway, good for a lunchtime Scandinavian *pierog* or salad.

Żywiec, ul. Floriańska 19; **Pod Basztą**, ul. Floriańska 55. Two reliable snack bars in a street (just north of the Rynek) that offers plenty of cheap places to eat. **Florian** at no. 7 is distinctly rougher – frequented by hustlers and prostitutes in the early morning for revitalising vodka and herrings.

Piccolo Pizza, ul. Szewska 14a. Useful pizza parlour, again in the university district.

Grodzki, ul. Grodzka 47. A basic self-service place, just south of the Rynek.

Giermek, ul. Karmelicka 57. Similar to the above on a street to the west of the Planty.

Chimera, ul. św. Anny 3. Deservedly popular cellar salad/snack bar in university district. Occasional live music. Open till 10pm.

Grace Pizzeria, ul. św. Anny 7. One of the best of the new pizzeria joints (also takeaways), with prices to match. Open till 10pm.

Cafés and bars

Cafes proliferate on and around the city centre, almost all those on the square adding on an impromptu outdoor terrace section in summer (regulation-issue plastic chairs and Western-brand name sunshades in all but the older-established places). Especially in the evenings these make nice places in which to soak up the square atmosphere, with the additional distraction of the assortment of roving buskers vying for the tourist zloty. An additional recent development are the myriad standup bars, mostly of the youthful, trendier variety now making major inroads in the Old Town area. You can always get a drink at one of the larger hotels until around midnight, while a growing number of nightclubs keep going through to around 3 or 4am.

Cafés

Alvorada, Rynek Główny 30 (opposite the State Bank). Mouthwatering cakes at this café on the main square, once the centre for black-market moneychangers and invaded by Western beers.

Antyczna, Rynek Główny (near the corner with ul. Sławkowska). A cosy haunt with a splendid Art Nouveau interior; the coffee's better than usual too.

Rio, ul. Floriańska 45. Stand-up café-bar with excellent coffee, frequented by actors and literary types.

Jama Michalika, ul. Floriańska 45. Famous and atmospheric old café cum cabaret, opened in 1895 – worth dropping in at for the furnishings alone (see also "Theatre and cabaret", overleaf).

Staromiejska, Mały Rynek. Nice place to sit out and enjoy the atmosphere of this attractive square. The **Pasieka** next door is rather grander.

U Zalipianek, ul. Szewska 24. Traditionally decorated, serving a range of herbal teas to a trendy crowd.

Literacka, ul. Pijarska 7. A lovely Art Deco café with marble tables and fine brews.

Zigi, ul. Grodzka 6. One of the more stylish stand-up coffee bars that are increasingly coming into fashion in the city. **Pod Pawiem**, situated on the same street, is a good second if the *Zigi* is full.

Hetmański, Rynek Główny 17. One of the nicest cafes on the south side of the Old Town.

U Pugetów, ul. Starowiślna 13. Excellent little cafe off the southern side of the Old Town.

Europejska, Rynek Główny 34. Smart modern café, good for terrace views onto the square.

Pod Baranami, Rynek Główny 27. Terrace cafe in front of the city cultural centre.

Behemot, ul. Bracka 4. Smart cafe with a good line in cakes and gateaux in pleasant courtyard off the main square; popular with foreigners. Open late.

Malmer, Rynek Główny 26. Swish squareside cafe, with a good line in *espresso*.

Bars

Harris, Rynek Główny. 28. New, upmarket Western-style piano bar already popular with Kraków yuppies. Lush decor, Foster's on tap. Open till 1am.

Shakesbeer, ul. Gołébia 2. Kraków's version of the Irish-style pubs now in vogue across the country. Billiard hall upstairs. Open late at weekends.

Tavern, Rynek Główny 25. Another posh new bar on the square. Open till 11pm.

Pod Baranami, Rynek Główny 27. Cellar bar inside cultural centre (see overleaf).

Basket, ul. Tomasza 11. Trendy basketball-theme joint with disco and pool table, ideal for late-night drinkers – open till 7am.

Pod Beczkami, ul. Dietla 46. South of Wawel in the Stradom district. Standing-room only (there are no seats) in Kraków's first beer hall joint, already a well-established haunt with local swillers. Huge selection of beers, Polish and imported. Open till 9pm.

Bacchus, ul. św. Marka 21. Cosy, popular little bar to the north of the square. Open until 1am.

Ogródek Muzyczny, ul. Jagiellońska 6. Popular university-district joint with outdoor courtyard – strictly piped Muzak though. Open till 2am.

ZPAF Photographers' Club, ul. św. Anny 3. The gallery has a basement dive across the courtyard at the back that's a trendy student hang-out.

Pod Strzelnicą, ul. Królowej Jadwigi 184. Small, private *kneipe;* snacks, beer and vodka.

Feniks, ul. Jama 2. Traditional drinking bar, open till late.

Maxime, ul. Floriańska 32. Old established bar, again open late.

Gay life

The local chapter of the national gay organisation *Lambda* is the central contact point for gays visiting town: contact them by writing (there's no openly available phone number) at Lambda Kraków, PO Box 249, 30-960 Kraków 1. A couple of places in town worth cruising are the *Club 91* bar, pl. Szczepański 7 (closes early), the *Café Club*, pl. Mariacki 7 (open till 10pm) and the *Jama Michalika* café (see listings above).

Entertainment and nightlife

Even if you don't speak the language, some of Kraków's **theatrical events** are well worth catching: in addition to consulting *Krak* or *Tydzień w Krakowie* magazines, look in at the **Pod Baranami** at Rynek Główny 27, which serves as the city's main cultural centre and a clearing house for information and tickets (room 37). It's as well to bear in mind that during the summer months everything sells out fast. For **rock** or vaguely alternative events, check the listings mentioned earlier or consult the Almatur office on the Rynek.

Theatre and cabaret

Ever since Stanisław Wyspiański and friends made Kraków the centre of the **Młoda Polska** movement at the beginning of this century, many of Poland's greatest actors and directors have been closely identified with the city. Until his death in December 1990 the most influential figure on the scene was avant-garde director **Tadeusz Kantor**, who used the **Cricot 2** theatre (ul. Kanonicza 5) as the base for his visionary productions; at the time of writing, the company's future is uncertain.

The **Stary Theatre** currently perform at three different sites: a main stage at ul. Jagiellońska 1 (☎228-566), and studio stages located in a basement at ul. Sławkowska 14 and Starowiślna 21. They place a strong emphasis on the visual aspects, making the productions that they offer (mostly reinterpretations of Polish and foreign classics) unusually accessible; they have built up an international following from appearances at the Edinburgh Festival and other such jamborees.

Of the city's other fifteen or so theatres, the splendid **Teatr im J. Słowackiego** on pl. św. Ducha, modelled on the Paris Opéra, is the biggest and one of the best known, with a regular diet of classical Polish drama and ballet, plus occasional opera. Check too, for the latest productions at places like the **Miniatura** (pl. św. Ducha), the **STU** (al. Krasińskiego 18) and the **Bagatela** (ul. Karmelicka 6). Ewa Demarczyk, "the Polish Edith Piaf", has her own theatre at ul. Floriańska 55.

Cabaret is also an established feature of Kraków. Two of the best-known venues are the **Jama Michalika** café on ul. Floriańska (an old Młoda Polska haunt), and the popular **Teatr Satyry**, beneath the town hall tower on the Rynek. The **Pod Baranami** (see above) also has a cabaret venue – considered the best in Poland – in its cellar.

Classical music

For classical concerts, the **Filharmonia Szymanowskiego**, ul. Zwierzyniecka 1, is home of the Kraków Philharmonic, one of Poland's most highly regarded orchestras (box office 9am–noon & 5–7pm). Sadly a major fire gutted the building in December 1991, destroying the main concert hall and its valuable organ in the process. For the moment, the famous resident orchestra is being forced to play elsewhere in town – the cultural centre in Nuwa Huta is one popular venue. For the latest details on where the Filharmonia are playing call ☎220-958 or consult the local listings.

The **Capella Cracoviensis**, the city's best-known choir, gives fairly regular concert performances at churches and other venues around the city – check the local listings for details.

Jazz and student clubs

The city's growing nightlife scene is well represented in the host of **student clubs** operating around the city – unpredictable, not always easy to find but generally worth the effort. Apart from the regular selection of live events and performances, they offer the additional bonus of some of the cheapest **drinking** in town. Listed below is a selection of the best ones around: a couple of nights in town hanging out in any of these places and you'll pick up on which ones are currently buzzing.

Pod Jaszczurami, Rynek Główny 7/8. Large, famously smoky club, inevitably the most popular in town on account of its main square location. Regular discos usually packed out in summer months with a combination of locals and foreign students. Live jazz every Tuesday night (again check local listings for details). Vodka and orange juices all round is the standard order in the downstairs bar. Open 8pm to 3am(☎220902 for concert/event information).

Pod Przewiązka, ul. Bydgoska 19B (☎374-502). Popular student hang-out, well west of the centre – trams #4, #8, #12, #13 or #44 pass close by. Discos till midnight on weekends (Fri included), with a small cover charge. Live jazz every Wed, rock bands on Thurs, as well as other occasional live acts and a CD club. Don't always publish programme in advance, so it's best just to turn up.

Rotunda, ul. Oleandry 1 (☎333-538). Next to a student dormitory, a short hop west of the centre, not far north of the *Cracovia* hotel. Popular student club, particularly the weekend discos, minimal cover charge, running to 2am on Saturdays (midnight otherwise). Also film club, occasional live acts.

Zaściane, ul. Reymonta 75. Hidden away in downtown student dormitory land west of town – definitely the hardest to find. Largish dance floor, weekend discos (till midnight) and an alternative music night – live bands and assorted happenings every Friday, till 2am.

Cafe Maraska, ul. Na Błoniach 7, on the edge of Błonia park. Popular dance place, not student-orientated but guaranteeing a good time (open till 2am).

Shopping

The city centre's inexorable return to the moneyed heart of central Europe is eloquently expressed in the range of **shops** in the centre, with several commerce-oriented streets, notably ul. Floriańska, gradually acquiring the affluent-looking boutiques and other consumerist hallmarks of your average western European city. Even by Polish standards, though, opening hours are a bit eccentric: most places don't open till 10 or 11am, closing around 7pm (bakeries

---

FESTIVALS

June is the busiest month for festivities, with three major events: the **Kraków Days** (a showcase for a range of concerts, plays and other performances), the **Folk Art Fair** and the **Lajkonik Pageant**. The last, based on a story about a raftsman who defeated the Tartars and made off with the khan's clothes, features a brightly dressed Tartar figure leading a procession from the Salwator Church in the western district of Zwierzyniec to the Rynek. Over the **Christmas** period, a Kraków speciality is the construction of intricately designed Nativity scenes or *szopki* : you can see some of the oldest fourteenth-century *szopki* all year round in St Andrew's Church.

On the cultural front, there are **organ concerts** at Tyniec (see "The Outskirts") from June to August, and at various of the city's churches in April. The **Graphic Art Festival**, held from May to September in even-numbered years, is a crowd-puller, too. And finally, on a rather smaller scale, there's an annual **International Short Film Festival** (May–June).

are usually an exception), so if you're planning shopping tours check your opening times first.

For a taste of a more customary postwar Polish style of shopping, the street trader's market, it's worth making your way into the **Kleparz** district north of the Old Town area. Rynek Kleparski, just across ul. Basztowa, is a barrow boy's (and girl's) paradise, with a mixed jumble of Poles and former Soviet citizens touting an imaginative variety of wares, anything from home-picked fruit and veg to books, bootleg cassettes, Soviet army uniforms, moonshine and dubiously antique bric-a-brac. Heading towards the north along shop-lined ul. Długa brings you to the larger pl. Nowy Kleparz, surrounded by an array of cheap second-hand and cut-price shops.

Listings

Airlines *LOT*, ul. Basztowa 15 (☎225-076/227-078).

Airport information ☎116-700/113-327.

Banks National Bank (*Bank Narodowy*), ul. Basztowa 20; *PeKaO*, Rynek Główny. 31.

Billiards The latest local pastime. If you fancy hitting the tables try *Billiards*, Rynek Główny 9 (pasaż Bielaka), or *Billiard*, ul. Karmelicka 10.

Bookshops Plenty of useful bookshops to choose from. Ones to look out for include *Garmond*, ul. Stolarska 1 and the *PTTK* shop, ul Jagiellońska 4, which has a good selection of photo albums and postcards, with the additional plus of a bar in the back on a courtyard. In amongst the theology *Znak*, ul. Sławkowska 1, has a good stock of albums. *Antykwariat* worth exploring are at ul. Szpitalna 19, ul. Szewska 25 and ul. Sławkowska 10.

Bus tickets are available in advance from Orbis at ul. św. Marka 25. Buying international tickets in summer can involve hours of queueing.

Car repairs *Polmozbyt* offices are at al. Pokoju 81 (Mon–Fri 6am–10pm, Sat & Sun 10am–6pm; ☎480-034), on ul. Kawiory (daily 7am–10pm; ☎375-575) and al. 29 Listopada 90 (daily 6am–10pm; ☎116-044). There are now plenty of private places too – ask at the tourist offices, hotels, cafés or the big garages themselves.

Chemists ul. Starowiślna 77, ul. Floriańska 15, Rynek Główny 13, 42 & 45, ul. Grodzka 15, ul. Karmelicka 23.

Cinemas Check local listings for details of current programmes. A selection of the more important cinemas includes the *Apollo*, ul. św. Tomasza 11, *Kijów*; al. Krasińskiego 3; *Mikro*, pl. Invalidów; *Rotunda*,;ul. Oleandry and *Wanda*, ul. św. Gertrudy 5.

Clothes ul. Szewska is a good street for boutiques as well as more traditional Polish clothes shops.

Consulates *France*, ul. Stolarska 15 (☎223-390); *Russia*, ul. Westerplatte 11 (☎228-388); *USA*, ul. Stolarska 9 (☎277-793); *Germany*, ul. Stolarska 7 (☎218-473). There is no UK representation.

Crime On the increase. Avoid the mostly unlit eastern section of the Planty at night.

Emergency Fire: 999, Ambulance: 998, Police 997.

Express mail and parcels Post office opposite the main station.

Football Wisła Kraków are one of the oldest clubs in the country, six times league champions, but these days in and out of the first division. They play out at the Wisła stadium, ul. Reymonta, in the western Czarna Wieś district (bus #144 passes close by).

Foreign newspapers All the major Orbis hotels, also some kiosks and bookshops in the city centre.

Galleries Among the numerous Stare Miasto galleries, you might check out: *Sztuka Polska*, ul. Floriańska 34; *Krzysztofory*, ul. Szczepańska 2; *Desa*, ul. św. Jana 3; and the exhibitions in the *Pod Baranami* on the Rynek.

Guarded parking Several in the central city area including: pl. św. Ducha, ul. Karmelicka, ul. Królewska, ul. Powiśle, pl. Szczepański

Health food (*Zdrowa zywność*). ul. Szlak 5.

Night shops (Most open 24hr a day.) *Cymes*, ul. Szewska 10 (delicatessen); *Amara* Szewska 15 (off licence); *U Francuza*, ul. Mazowiecka 24; *Delicje*, Rynek Kleparski 5; *Monopolowy*, ul. Kalwaryjska 26; *Jubilat*, ul. Zwierzyniecka 50.

Opticians *Foightt*, ul. Floriańska.

Petrol stations 24hr stations (some with unleaded) are to be found on: ul. Wielicka; ul. Podgórska; ul. Jasnogórska; ul. Kamienna; ul. Powst. Wielkopolskich os. Strusia; ul. Zakopiańska; and ul. Kazimierza Wielkiego.

Post office Main office is at ul. Wielopole 2, including poste restante and 24hr phone services.

Radio The local *RMF* station (70,06FM), eastern Europe's first independently owned radio setup, based inside the *Pod Kopcem* hotel, broadcasts throughout southern Poland. English-language news bulletins five times a day from Monday to Saturday (8.30am, 10.30am, 3.30pm, 5.30pm and 9pm), with BBC news at 9pm on Sundays.

Rent a car *Hertz*, ul. Armii Krajowej 15 (☎371-120). Airport delivery on request. Orbis, ul. Koniewa 9, by the *Holiday Inn*: Budget, ul. Radzikowskiego 99 (☎370-089) (inside Hotel *Krak*).

Sightseeing tours *Universal* (☎221344); round the city, also Wieliczka, Auschwitz. *Intercrac* Rynek Główny 14. (219-858); same destinations, but in minibuses instead of usual coaches. *Point*, inside *Holiday Inn* (375-044); local excursions.

Swimming pool The most central is at the *Hotel Cracovia*, al. 3 Maja; non-residents can get in for a small fee.

Taxis Currently 500 times metered figure unless otherwise stated. To call a cab try *Wawel taxi*, 666-666; *Radio Taxi*, 445-555 or *Tele Taxi*, 365-252.

Train tickets are available from the Orbis office at Rynek Główny 41 and in the train station. Expect queues at the international ticket desk.

MAŁOPOLSKA

The name **Małopolska** – literally "Little Poland" – in fact applies to a large swathe of the country, for the most part a rolling landscape of traditionally culti-vated fields and quiet villages. It is an ancient region, forming with Wielkopolska the early medieval Polish state, though its geographical divisions, particularly from neighbouring Silesia, are a bit nebulous. The bulk of Małopolska proper sits north of Kraków, bounded by the Świętokrzyskie Mountains to the north and the broad range of hills stretching down from Częstochowa to Kraków – the so-called Eagles' Nests trail – to the west.

Kielce, a largish industrial centre and the regional capital, provides a good stepping-off point for forays into the **Świętokrzyskie Mountains**, really no more than high hills but enjoyable walking territory. **Częstochowa**, the only other city of the region, is famous as the home of the Black Madonna, which draws huge crowds for the major religious festivals and annual summer pilgrimages from all over the country. Pope John Paul II is a native of the region, too, and his birth-place at **Wadowice** has become something of a national shrine, while the Catholic trail continues to the west at **Kalwaria Zebrzydowska**, another pilgrim-age site.

West of Kraków at **Oświęcim** is the **Auschwitz-Birkenau** concentration camp, preserved more or less as the Nazis left it.

Oświęcim: Auschwitz-Birkenau

When you go in there's a sign in five languages that says, 'There were four million'.

I broke down about halfway round Auschwitz, walking away from the wall against which 20,000 people were shot. There's a shrine there now; schoolgirls were laying flowers and lighting candles.

But it wasn't that particular detail that got to me. And it wasn't the stark physical evidence in earlier blocks of the conditions in which people had lived, sleeping seven or nine together on straw in three-high tiers the size of double beds.

It wasn't the enormous glass-fronted displays in which, on angled boards sometimes dozens of feet long, lay great piles of wretchedly battered old boots, or children's shoes. It wasn't the bank of suitcases, their owners' names clumsily written on them in faded paint, or the heaps of broken spectacles, of shaving brushes and hairbrushes.

It wasn't the case the length of a barrack room in the block whose subject was the 'Exploitation of Corpses', the case filled with a bank of human hair, or the small case to one side of that, showing the tailor's lining that was made from it.

It wasn't the relentless documentary evidence, the methodical, systematic, compulsive bureaucracy of mass murder.

And it wasn't the block beside the yard in which the shrine now stands, in whose basement are the 'standing cells' used to punish prisoners, measuring ninety by ninety centimetres. People were wedged together into these bare brick cubicles, and left to starve or suffocate pinned helplessly upright. In other cells in the same basement, the first experiments with Zyklon B as a means of mass extermination were conducted.

It was all these things cumulatively crushing you, a seeping of evil from every wall and corner of the place, from every brick of every block, until you reach your limit and it overwhelms you. For a short while I found myself crying, leaning against the wire. Like they tell you — the birds don't sing.

In paintings and drawings by Auschwitz inmates, the guards are shown leering and jeering at the suffering of their victims — enjoying themselves.

On the morning of the October day that England qualified for Italia '90 [the World Cup football tournament], a small group of Englishmen were seen by some of the sports press at Auschwitz, laughing and posing as they took pictures of each other – doing the Nazi salute.

From Pete Davies's *All Played Out* (Heinemann, 1990).

Seventy kilometres west of Kraków, **OŚWIĘCIM** would in normal circumstances be a nondescript industrial town – a place to send visitors on their way without a moment's thought. The circumstances, however, are anything but normal here.

Some history

Following the September 1939 Nazi invasion of Poland, Oświęcim and its surrounding region were incorporated into the domains of the Third Reich and the town's name changed to **Auschwitz**. The idea of setting up a concentration camp in the area was mooted as soon as late 1939 by the Breslau (Wrocław) division of the SS, the official explanation being the overcrowding in existing prisons in Silesia combined with the political desirability of a campaign of mass-arrests throughout German-occupied Poland to round up all potentially "troublesome" Poles. After surveying the region the final choice of location fell on an abandoned Polish army barracks in Oświęcim, then an insignificant rural town well away from major urban settlements – and prying eyes – on the borders of Silesia and Małopolska: as Himmler himself was later to explain, Auschwitz was chosen on the clinically prosaic grounds that it was a "convenient location as regards communication, and because the area can be easily sealed off".

Orders to begin work on the camp were finally given in April 1940, the fearsome **Rudolf Hoess** appointed its commander, and in June of that year the Gestapo sent the first contingent of 700-odd prisoners to the new camp – Jews in the main – from nearby Tarnów. As the number of inmates swelled rapidly so too did the physical size of the camp as Auschwitz was gradually but methodically transformed from a detention centre into a full-scale **death camp**. The momentum of destruction was given its decisive twist by Himmler's decision in 1941 to make Auschwitz the centrepiece of Nazi plans for the **"Final Solution"**, the Nazis' attempt to effect the elimination of European Jewry by systematically rounding up, transporting and murdering all the Jews in Reich territories. To this end a second camp, **Birkenau**, was set up a couple of kilometres from the main site, with its own set of gas chambers, crematoria and eventually even its own railway terminal to permit the "efficient" dispatch of new arrivals to the waiting gas chambers.

By the end of 1942 **Jews** were beginning to be transported to Auschwitz from all over Europe, many fully believing Nazi propaganda that they were on their way to a new life of work in German factories or farms—the main reason, it appears, that so many brought their personal valuables with them. The reality, of course, couldn't have been more different: after a train journey of anything up to ten days in sealed goods wagons and cattle trucks the dazed survivors were herded up the station ramp, whereupon they were promptly lined up for inspection and divided into two categories by the SS: those deemed "fit" or "unfit" for work. People placed in the latter category – up to 75 percent of all new arrivals, according to Hoess' testimony at the Nürnberg trials – were told they would be permitted to have a bath: they were then ordered to undress, marched into the "shower room" and gassed with **Zyklon B** cyanide gas sprinkled through special ceiling attachments. In this way up to 2000 people were killed at a time (the process took 15–20 minutes), a murderously efficient method of dispatching people that continued relentlessly throughout the rest of the war. The greatest massacres occurred from 1944 onwards after the special railway terminal had been installed at Birkenau to permit speedier "processing" of the victims to the gas chambers and crematoria. Compounding the hideousness of the operation, before incinerating the bodies SS guards removed gold fillings, earrings, finger rings and even the hair—subsequently used, amongst other things, for mattresses—from the mass of bodies. The cloth from their clothes was processed into the material for army uniforms, their watches given to troops in recognition of special achievements or bravery.

The precise **numbers** of people murdered in Auschwitz-Birkenau between the camp's construction in 1940 and final liberation by Soviet forces in spring 1945 has long been a subject of dispute, often for reasons less to do with a concern with factual accuracy than "revisionist" neo-Nazi attempts to deny the historical reality of the Holocaust. Though the exact figure will never be known, in reputable historical circles it's now generally believed that somewhere between 1.5 and 2 million people died in the camp, the vast majority (85–90 percent) of whom were Jews, along with sizeable contingents of Romanies (Gypsies), Poles, Soviet POWs and a host of other European nationalities.

The physical scale of the Auschwitz-Birkenau camp is a shock in itself. Most visitors, though – whose numbers, as at all the concentration camps, have dropped significantly in recent years, due largely to the demise of officially sponsored group visits from the ex-communist world – see only the main Auschwitz section of the complex. This, however, was only one component of the hideous network of barracks, compounds, factories and extermination areas: it is only in visiting Birkenau, roughly 3km down the road from Auschwitz, that you begin to grasp the full enormity of the Nazi death machine.

Practicalities

To get to Auschwitz-Birkenau from Kraków, you can take either of the regular bus or train services to Oświęcim station, an hour and a half's journey. From there it's a short bus ride to the gates of Auschwitz; there's no bus service to Birkenau, but taxis are available. Otherwise it's best to walk there. If you decide to make the journey on foot, the route to Birkenau, some 2km on from Auschwitz – though in the same direction from the train station – adds significantly to the walking distance. Rather grotesquely, there's a hotel and a large cafeteria inside the Auschwitz camp.

Auschwitz-Birkenau is unfathomably shocking. If you want all the specifics on the camp, you can pick up a detailed guidebook (in English and other languages) with maps, photos and an horrendous array of statistics. Alternatively, you can join a guided group, often led by former inmates. It's perhaps best to go with friends rather than alone – mutual support and emotional back-up is extremely helpful. Children under thirteen are not admitted to Auschwitz.

Auschwitz

Most of the Auschwitz camp buildings, the barbed-wire fences, watchtowers, and the entrance gate inscribed *Arbeit Macht Frei* ("Work Makes Free") have been preserved as the **Museum of Martyrdom** (daily Jan, Feb & late Dec 8am–3pm; March & Nov–Dec 15 8am–4pm; April & Oct 8am–5pm; May–Sept 8am–6pm). What you won't find here any longer, though, are the memorial stone and succession of plaques placed in front of and around the camp by the postwar communist authorities claiming that 4 million people died in a place officially described as an "International Monument to Victims of Fascism"; in a symbolic intellectual clean-up both the inflated numerical estimates and the lack of references to the central place of **Jews** in the genocide carried out in Auschwitz-Birkenau were removed in 1990.

The **cinema** is a sobering starting point: the film was taken by the Soviet troops who liberated the camp in May 1945 – its harrowing images of the survivors and the dead aimed at confirming for future generations what really happened. The board outside lists timings for showings in different languages. The bulk of the **camp** consists of the prison cell blocks, the first section being given over to "exhibits" found in the camp after liberation. Despite last-minute destruction of many of the **storehouses** used for the possessions of murdered inmates (there were thirty-five of them in all) there are rooms full of clothes and suitcases, toothbrushes, dentures, glasses, a huge collection of shoes, and a huge mound of women's hair – 154,322 pounds of it. It's difficult to relate to the scale of what's shown.

Block 11, further on, is where the first experiments with Zyklon B gas were carried out on Soviet POWs and other inmates in 1941. And between two of the blocks stands the flower-strewn **Death Wall**, where thousands of prisoners were summarily executed with a bullet in the back of the head. As in the other concentration camps, the Auschwitz victims included people from all over Europe – over twenty nationalities in all. Many of the camp barracks are given over to **national memorials**, moving testimonies to the sufferings of inmates of the different countries – Poles, Russians, Czechs, Slovaks, Norwegians, Turks, French, Italians . . .

Another, larger barrack is labelled simply **"Jews"**. The atmosphere here is one of poignant, quiet reverence, in which the evils of Auschwitz are felt and remembered rather than detailed or observed. On the second floor there's a section devoted to Jewish resistance both inside and outside the camp, some of which was organised in tandem with the Polish AK (*Armia Krajowa*; Home Army), some entirely autonomously.

Despite the strength and power of this memorial, some still find it disconcerting to find it lumped in among the others, as if Jews were just another "nationality" amongst many to suffer at the hands of the Nazis – despite other recent changes in the way events in Auschwitz are officially presented, this is one aspect of the old-style presentation of the Jewish dimension of the camp that you may feel has still not been fully addressed.

The prison blocks terminate by the **gas chambers** and the ovens where the bodies were incinerated. "No more poetry after Auschwitz", in the words of the German philosopher Theodor Adorno.

Birkenau

The **Birkenau camp** (same hours) is much less visited than Auschwitz, though it was here that the majority of captives lived and died. Covering some 425 acres, the Birkenau camp at its height comprised over three hundred buildings, of which over sixty brick and wood constructions remain; the rest were either burnt down or demolished at the end of the war, though in most instances you can still see their traces on the ground. Walking through the site, rows of barracks – mostly built without foundations onto the notoriously swampy local terrain – stretch into the distance, barracks in which tens of thousands (over 100,000 at the camp's peak in August 1944) lived in unimaginably appalling conditions. Not that most prisoners lived long. Killing was the main goal of Birkenau, most of it carried out in the huge **gas chambers** at the back of the camp, damaged but not destroyed by the fleeing Nazis in 1945. At the height of the killing, this clinically conceived machinery of destruction gassed and cremated sixty thousand people a day.

Most of the victims arrived in closed **trains** – cattle trucks mostly – to be driven directly from the railway ramp into the gas chambers. Railway line, ramp, sidings – they are all still there, just as the Nazis abandoned them. In the dark, creaking huts the pitiful bare bunks would have had six or more shivering bodies crammed into each level: wander round the barracks and you soon begin to imagine the absolute terror and degradation of the place. A monument to the dead, inscribed in ten languages, stares out over the camp from between the chambers.

POLES, JEWS AND THE CONCENTRATION CAMPS

The general issue of Polish-Jewish relations, both historical and current, is an emotive and sensitive area and what follows can be no more than a brief sketch of its contours.

The immediate context for the glaring omission of the Jewish perspective in official communist-era Polish guidebooks and tours of the concentration camps was straightforwardly political. For Poland's postwar communist regime, like those in other east European countries, the horrors of World War II were a constant and central reference point. Following the official Soviet line, the emphasis was on the war as an anti-fascist struggle, in which good (communism and the Soviet Union, represented by the new postwar governments) had finally triumphed over evil (fascism and Nazi Germany).

This interpretation provided an important legitimising prop for the new regimes: the Soviet Union, aided by loyal national communists, were the people who had liberated Europe from Hitler, and as inheritors of their anti-fascist mantle the newly installed communist governments sought to portray themselves as heirs to all that was noble and good. In this schematic view of the war there was no room for details of the racial aspects of Nazi ideology. People were massacred in the camps because fascists were butchers, not because the victims were Jews or Poles or Romanies. Hence the camps were opened up first and foremost as political monuments to the victims of fascism rather than to the Holocaust.

Recognising the sensitivities that continue to surround these issues, when it comes to presenting the history of the death camps Poland's post-communist authorities have shown a greater willingness than their predecessors to acknowledge the specifically anti-Semitic dimensions of Nazi devastation; along with "revised" figures for the numbers of deaths at Auschwitz, for the first time official guidebooks to the camp now state clearly that the vast majority of the victims were Jews, a marked departure from the communist-era practice of covering all Auschwitz inmates with the anonymous catch-all phrase "victims of fascism".

Despite these symbolically important changes, however, the broader issue of anti-Semitism in Poland – both historical and current – remains. There are virtually no Jews in today's Poland, yet some commentators suggest the prejudice is as current now as it ever has been. In the 1980s the debate was given a controversial focus by Claude Lanzmann's film documentary *Shoah* (1985), a relentless and shocking exploration of the Holocaust; shown only in edited form on Polish television, it was denounced by press and politicians – including President Jaruzelski – as "anti-Polish". It is not hard to see why the film caused such a stir. Lanzmann's interviews with Polish peasants in the Auschwitz region, for example, revealed deep levels of ignorance and hostility – displaying an almost medieval Catholic primitivism, they were heard to decry the Jews as Christ-killers who deserved their annihilation. Lanzmann is not alone in pointing to the Christian, and specifically Catholic historical roots of anti-Semitism in Poland – a perception, incidentally, that has led some to dub the Polish version of the prejudice "benign" (for which read "folk superstitious") in contrast to the unquestionably malignant racist variant propounded by twentieth-century fascist ideologues. The charge pursued by Lanzmann that hurt the most, though, was the implication that the Polish nation actively aided and abetted in the Nazis' destruction of the Jews and that the location of so many of the death camps inside Poland was no mere geographical coincidence.

Poles react strongly to such charges. How, they argue, were Poles supposed to help Jews when such assistance was made a capital offence? And how were farmers supposed to have resisted the acquisition of land for the camps? They also recall the many wartime instances of courageous Poles risking life and limb to save Jews, a fact testified to by the legions of ordinary Polish people commemorated in the Yad Vashem Holocaust memorial to "righteous Gentiles" established in Jerusalem in the 1950s. More generally, they point out that for several centuries Poland was home to – and in some senses a refuge for – Europe's largest Jewish community. While other European nations were persecuting and expelling their Jewish populations, the Polish-Lithuanian Commonwealth allowed its Jews unrivalled rights and political status. In everything from architecture and language to humour and cooking, Polish and Jewish cultures are deeply intertwined, and have been so for centuries.

The problem is that there are two victim nations demanding recognition: Poles and Jews. Polish indignation over charges of wartime anti-Semitism is certainly guilt-tinged – for every Pole who assisted Jews during the war there was another spotting and denouncing them – but it is also the overreaction of the fellow-sufferer. And in this context, as historian Norman Davies put it, debating who suffered most is the meanest of controversies.

The roughly 250,000 out of the prewar population of 3.5 million Polish Jews who survived the Holocaust – mostly as a result of wartime flight or deportation to the Soviet Union – returned to a country with little empathy for their specific problems, and in a couple of notorious cases, notably the 1946 **Kielce pogrom**, prone to fits of open anti-Jewish hostility. The creation of the state of Israel resulted in a significant wave of voluntary Jewish **emigration** to Palestine, a phenomenon that continued throughout the late 1940s and early 1950s, despite the communist authorities' rapidly waning enthusiasm for what they had originally hoped would prove to be a left-oriented state. Of the Jews who remained, a significant portion (some 20,000) left the country in 1968 following a viciously anti-Semitic campaign against students and intellectuals instigated by a faction within the communist party in the aftermath of the student protests which had erupted earlier that year.

The early years of post-communist rule have not been without their anti-Semitic blemishes either. Both the 1989 parliamentary election campaign and the 1990 presidential campaign were marked by startlingly chauvinistic outbursts, most notably Lech Wałęsa's populist insistence that he was a "true Pole" and his remarks that some politicians should stop "hiding behind Polish names" – a presumed reference to the Jewish origins of certain of his former Solidarity rivals, such as Adam Michnik and Bronesław Geremek. In the summer of 1989, too, a furious dispute arose over a Carmelite convent set up by Catholic nuns inside the Auschwitz camp perimeter. The nuns claimed they simply wanted to establish a place of prayer for the dead but many Jews were incensed by what they saw as a misguided attempt to "baptise" the Holocaust. The compromise proposal eventually agreed upon, whereby the nuns would move to a new centre for information, dialogue and prayer, probably at Poznań, had still not been carried out four years on, though there were signs of impending action. Cardinal Glemp in turn suggested that a world Jewish media conspiracy was being directed against the Church, a remark which provoked several noted Catholic intellectuals to publicly censure him. Wałęsa was also much criticised within Poland over his "Polish names" comments. Taken together, the incidents hint at a nasty undercurrent to Polish politics, and it's unnerving that anti-Semitism should remain a useful political tool in a country where virtually no Jews remain.

Mark Salter

Kalwaria Zebrzydowska and Wadowice

Southwest of Kraków are two places of great religious significance to Poles: **Kalwaria Zebrzydowska**, a centre of pilgrimage second only to Częstochowa, and **Wadowice**, birthplace of a certain Karol Wojtyła. From Kraków, buses are straightforward to either destination; local trains are slower.

Kalwaria Zebrzydowska

The object of pilgrims' devotions is perched on the hill overlooking **KALWARIA ZEBRZYDOWSKA**: a Bernardine church and Via Dolorosa built by the Zebrzydowski family in the early seventeenth century, following a vision of three crosses here on the family estate. Miracles followed.

The Zebrzydowskis sent an envoy to Jerusalem for drawings and models of the holy places and, on his return, began building a sequence of **chapels** across the nearby hills, many of them modelled on buildings in the city. The main **church** is a familiar Baroque effusion, with a silver-plated Italian figure of the Virgin standing over the high altar. The site always has its crowds, but they are at their most intense during August, the traditional time of pilgrimage throughout the country, and at Easter, when the Passion Plays are performed here. The heady atmosphere of collective catharsis accompanying these events offers an insight into the inner workings of Polish Catholicism: to anyone from more sober northern climes the realism (figures are tied on crosses, while spectators are dressed as Romans) can all be very perplexing, even frightening. As the *Misteria* photo album available in many bookshops around the country reminds you, however, gruesome enactments of the Crucifixion are a feature of peasant Catholic festivals throughout Europe.

Wadowice

Fourteen kilometres further down the road is the little town of **WADOWICE**, whose rural obscurity was shattered by the election of local boy Karol Wojtyła to the papacy in October 1978. Almost instantly the town became a place of pilgrimage, with the souvenir industry quick to seize the opportunities.

The **pope's birthplace** at ul. Kościelna 7, off the market square, has been turned into a shrine-like museum, while the nearby **parish church** displays the record of its most famous baptism, in 1920. For the truly devout, the local **football pitch** – where young Karol kept goal with some success – could be an additional point of pilgrimage.

Babia Góra National Park

The southwesternmost part of Małopolska forms part of the Beskid mountain chain, with by far the most notable part being the **Babia Góra** massif. It's the second smallest of Poland's national parks, though arguably the one most prized by naturalists, being of sufficient importance to be included on UNESCO's World Biosphere list. A specific characteristic is the way that the vegetation forms distinct vertical bands. Up to a height of 1150m, it's thickly wooded, particularly with beech, fir and spruce trees which then give way to spruce and rowans only. There follows a sector of dwarf mountain pines, while the highest areas have only grasses, mosses and lichen among the loose boulders. Hundreds of different plant species grow in the massif, which is also inhabited by 115 different birds and a number of wild animals, including lynxes, wolves and brown bears.

Zawoja

The gateway to the National Park is **ZAWOJA**, a straggling community situated on the banks of the River Skamica; it claims to stretch for 17km end to end, making it the longest village in Poland, and perhaps even in Europe. It isn't on a railway line, but there are direct buses from the cities of Kraków, Katowice and Bielsko–Biała, as well as from Wadowice. As a tourist resort, Zawoja has still to develop its potential: apart from private rooms, the only accommodation options are a basic **hotel**, *Hanka*, at Zawoja–Składy 2 (☎148), and a **youth hostel** at Zawoja–Wilczne (☎106); both are some way south of the "centre", on the way to Babia Góra. There are several restaurants and snack bars, all of which are stuck in a pre-market era time-warp.

Walking in the National Park

If driving, the easiest approach to Babia Góra is to go all the way to the end of the village, then continue onwards up the twisty road until you reach the car park at the easternmost end of the National Park. On foot, this can be reached by the **blue trail**, which continues gently upwards from here through the woods to the *Markowe Szczawiny* **refuge** (☎105), which serves hot meals and has dormitory accommodation. If time is limited, it's best to switch here to the **green trail**, which takes you directly up to **Diablak** (1725m), the highest peak in the range, enabling you to see a good cross-section of its scenery en route: beware that there's one place on this route where you have to make a fixed ladder ascent. From the top, which forms part of the international boundary, there's a sweeping panoramic view which stretches on (the regrettably few) clear days as far as the Tatras. It's then a comfortable descent back to the car park by the **red trail**; this offers the best views of the main peak, and should be used in both directions if you're at all wary of sheer drops. Should you have more time at your disposal, you can see the whole massif in one long day by continuing westwards from the summit of Diablak by the green trail, switching to the red to go back to the refuge, then returning to Zawoja by the black trail.

Zubrzyca Górna

It's also worth making a detour to the village of **ZUBRZYCA GÓRNA**, about 4km south of the car park, and also reachable by the green footpath. At its north-ernmost fringe is the **Ethnographical Park** (15 April–15 Sept Tues–Sun 9am–3.30pm; 16 Sept–14 April Tues–Sun 9am–2.30pm), an open-air museum of the region's traditional local architecture.

Żywiec

About 50km west of Zawoja by road – though less than half that as the crow flies – is **ŻYWIEC**, which is also readily accessible by train from any of the major cities in this corner of Poland. The town enjoys a certain international fame cour-tesy of its **brewery**, which annually produces 30 million litres of what's generally agreed to be the best beer in Poland. There are two main varieties of this – *Tatra Pils* and *Full Light*, the latter of which confusingly appears under a bewildering variety of colourful labels. Up to the end of the communist era and beyond, you were far more likely to find Żywiec beer on the shelves of a British or American supermarket than you were anywhere in Poland, most of it being exported in order to obtain desperately needed hard currency. Now, thankfully, it's widely available throughout the country. Beer aside, Żywiec is a pleasant place to while away a few hours, benefiting from a favourable location in a broad valley at the foot of three mountain chains – the Beskid Mały to the northeast, the Beskid Śląski to the north and west, and the Beskid Żywiecki to the south. A good **view** can be obtained from the shore of the often dried-up reservoir at the northern end of town.

The Town

Both the **train** and **bus stations** are located on the opposite side of the River Soła from the town centre, which is a ten-minute walk away along ul. Marchewskiego. The **Castle** (Tues, Wed, Fri & Sat 10am–2.30pm, Sun noon–3.30pm) was founded by the Dukes of Oświęcim in the fifteenth century, gaining a handsome arcaded courtyard in the Renaissance period. In the nineteenth century, it was heavily restored in a historicist manner by the Habsburgs, who also built the pristine white **Palace** opposite, currently the object of a restoration programme. The huge park to the south is well worth a stroll: it includes a whimsical eighteenth-century **Chinese tea house**.

Just to the east of the palace is the parish church of **St Mary**, which would be an unremarkable Gothic building with the standard Baroque furnishings were it not for the imperious galleried Renaissance tower, which provides a landmark from all over the town. On the main ul. Kościuszki immediately north of the church is the local **Museum** (Tues–Sat 10am–2.30pm, Sun noon–3.30pm), housed in a Baroque mansion; a little further on is one of the towers from the fortification system. The only other sight worth mentioning is the rustic wooden church of the **Holy Cross** on ul. Świętokryska, just off the western end of ul. Kościuszki.

Practicalities

Żywiec's only **hotel**, *Polonia*, is handily located at ul. Kościuszki 22 (☎41-63). The **youth hostel** is right next to the station at ul. Waryńskiego 4 (☎26-39), whereas the **campsite** *Cębina* is well to the south of town at ul. Kopernika 4 (☎48-88), near the Sporysz station. There are several decent **restaurants** along the main drag of ul. Marchewskiego and ul. Kościuszki, and another, *Ratuszowa*, at ul. Mickiewicza 1, on the corner of the market square. Every August, there's a **festival** of local folklore, while the Christmas celebrations are among the most characterful in Poland.

The Ojców Valley and the Eagles' Nests

To the northwest of Kraków, the **Ojców Valley** offers an easy respite from the pollution of the city. This deep limestone gorge of the River Prądnik has a unique microclimate and astonishingly rich variety of plants and wildlife, virtually all of it now protected by the **Ojców National Park**. It's a beautiful area for a day's trekking, particularly in September and October, when the rich colours of the Polish autumn are at their finest.

The valley also gives access to the most southerly of the **castles** built by King Kazimierz to defend the southwestern reaches of the country from the Bohemian rulers of Silesia. Known as the **Eagles' Nest Trail**, these fortresses are strung along the hilly ridge extending westwards from Ojców towards Częstochowa.

Ojców: the castle and Łokietka Cave

To get to the gorge, take a bus (direction Olkusz) to **OJCÓW**, poised above the valley 25km from Kraków. Unremarkable in itself, the village is capped by a fine, ruined **Castle**, the southern extremity of the **Eagles' Nest Trail**; it's an evocative place in the twilight hours, circled by squadrons of bats. There's not much of the castle left, though a Gothic tower houses a small **museum** devoted to the valley's flora and fauna (April 15–Oct 31 Tues–Sun 10am–5pm). Basic accommodation is provided by the *Hotel Zosia* (☎8).

From the village, you can walk down to the valley along marked trails from the bus stop. A notable feature of the gorge is its strange assortment of **caves** and other geological formations, in several of which traces of prehistoric human habitation have been discovered. The best-known is **Łokietka Cave** (daily 8am–5pm), the largest of a sequence of chambers burrowing into the cliffs outside Ojców. According to legend it was here that King Władysław the Short was hidden and protected by loyal local peasants following King Wenceslas of Bohemia's invasion in the early fourteenth century.

Halfway down the valley is the curious spectacle of a **wooden church** straddling the river on brick piles. This odd site neatly circumvented a nineteenth-century czarist edict forbidding religious structures to be built "on solid ground", part of a strategy to subdue the intransigently nationalist Catholic Church.

Pieskowa Skała

At **PIESKOWA SKAŁA**, 9km north of Ojców (45min by bus from Kraków), there's a **castle** in rather better shape, the fourteenth-century original having been rebuilt in the 1580s as an elegant Renaissance residence. As in Wawel castle, the most impressive period feature is the delicately arcaded castle courtyard, a photogenic construction that's a regular feature in the travel brochures. The castle **museum** (Tues–Sun 10am–4pm) is divided into two main exhibitions, one covering the history of the building, the other illustrating the development of European art from the Middle Ages to the nineteenth century, drawing extensively on the Wawel National Museum's collection. The roomful of Gothic pieces includes some fine carved wooden statues of the saints by unknown local artists, a fifteenth-century tapestry from Tournai and some sturdy chests from the mid-1400s. The second-floor Baroque rooms continue the period furniture theme, sumptuously decorated Flemish and Dutch tapestries lining the walls, the most notable among them depicting a series of heroic scenes from the life of Alexander the Great. To finish off a visit, head for the excellent **restaurant** at the top of one of the fortified towers. In summer they put tables out on the roof terrace, from where you can enjoy a fine view over the valley, and – if they've got it – some mouthwatering local trout.

The end of the trail

The remaining castles of the Eagles' Nest Trail are very ruined, but they're as dramatic and photogenic as their Spanish counterparts, seeming to spring straight out of the Jurassic rock formations. You really need your own vehicle to follow most of the route from here: although all castles are accessible by bus, this entails long waits and frequent detours, and it's unlikely you'd be able to find anywhere to stay. However, the most impressive of these castles are also the easiest to get to. **OGRODZIENIEC**, some 35km north of Pieskowa Skała on the main road between OLKUSZ (served by bus from Kraków) and ZAWIERCIE, preserves the substantial shell of a frontier fortress which was partly remodelled as a palace during the Renaissance.

Even more accessible is **OLSZTYN**, just a few kilometres outside the city boundaries of Częstochowa, to which it's linked by several buses an hour. The castle here is the one generally used to promote the route on tourist brochures and posters. Unusually, it's laid out in two parts, with a round watchtower crowning one outcrop of rock, and a keep on top of another; from each there's a superb view over the whole upland region.

Note that if you're travelling between Ogrodzieniec and Olsztyn by car or bike, there are other castles to see at MIRÓW, BOBOLICE and OSTRĘŻNIK.

Częstochowa

Seen from a distance, **CZĘSTOCHOWA** shows the country at its absolute worst. Its steelworks and textile factories unleash a noxious cocktail of multicoloured fumes, while the city centre is ringed by jerry-built concrete estates thrown up to accommodate a fast-growing population, currently numbering over 250,000. Yet all this is overshadowed by the city's status, courtesy of the **monastery of Jasna Góra** (Bright Mountain), as one of the world's greatest places of pilgrimage. Its famous **icon of The Black Madonna**, which has drawn the faithful here over the past six centuries, is an inescapable image: reproductions of it can be seen everywhere in Poland, with at least one adorning almost every church in the country.

The special position that Jasna Góra and its icon hold in the hearts and minds of the majority of Poles is due to a rich web of history and myth. It's not a place you can react to dispassionately, but even if you find its heart-on-sleeve fervour overbearing, an awareness of the background to it will at least make it comprehensible. Central to this is the tenuous position Poland has held on the map of Europe: at various times the Swedes, the Russians and the Germans have sought to annihilate it as a nation. Each of these traditional and non-Catholic enemies has laid siege to Jasna Góra, yet failed to destroy it, so adding to the icon's reputation as a miracle-worker – and the guarantor of Poland's very existence.

A brief history

The hill known as Jasna Góra was probably used as part of the same defensive system as the castles along the Eagles' Nest Trail, but in the fourteenth century it came under the control of **Ladislaus II**, whose main possession was the independent duchy of Opole on the other side of the Silesian frontier. In 1382 he founded the monastery here, donating the miraculous icon a couple of years later. Ladislaus spent his final years imprisoned in his own castle, having fallen into disgrace for trying to prevent the union with Lithuania. Nevertheless, the monastery quickly attracted pilgrims from a host of nations and was granted the special protection of the Jagiellonian and Waza dynasties, though it was not until the fifteenth century that a shrine of stone and brick was built.

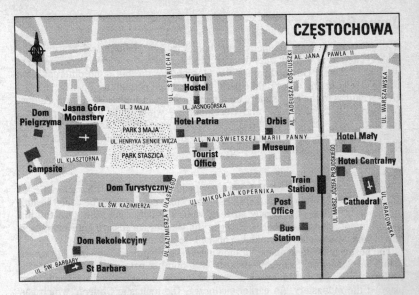

In the first half of the seventeenth century the monastery was enclosed by a modern **fortification system** as a bulwark of Poland's frontiers – and its Catholic faith – at a time of Europe-wide political and religious conflicts. Its worth was proved in the six-week-long **siege of 1655** by the Swedes, who failed to capture it in spite of having superior weapons and almost 4000 troops ranged against just 250 defenders. This sparked off an amazing national fightback against the enemy, who had occupied the rest of the country against little resistance, and ushered in Poland's short period as a European power of the first rank.

In 1717 the Black Madonna was crowned **Queen of Poland** in an attempt by the clergy to whip up patriotism and fill the political void created by the Russian-sponsored "Silent Sejm", which had reduced the nation to a puppet state. Jasna Góra was the scene of another heroic defence in 1770, when it was held by the Confederates of Bar against greater Russian forces, and retained by them until after the formal partitioning of Poland two years later. Częstochowa was initially annexed by Prussia, but after a few years as part of Napoleon's Duchy of Warsaw, it served as a frontier fortress of the Russian Empire for more than a century. It was incorporated into the new Polish state after World War I, when the icon's royal title was reaffirmed.

In 1945, Soviet troops defused bombs left by the retreating Nazis which might finally have destroyed the monastery. They later had cause to regret their actions: while Częstochowa itself developed into a model communist industrialised city, Jasna Góra became a major **focus of opposition** to the communist regime. The Church skilfully promoted the pilgrimage as a display of patriotism and passive resistance, a campaign which received a huge boost in 1978 with the election of **Karol Wojtyła** – Archbishop of Kraków and a central figure in its conception – as Pope John Paul II. His devotion to this shrine ensured worldwide media attention for Poland's plight; as a consequence, praying at Jasna Góra has become an essential photo-opportunity for the new breed of democratic politicians.

Jasna Góra

A dead straight three-kilometre-long boulevard, al. Najświętszej Marii Panny
(abbreviated as al. NMP), cuts through the heart of Częstochowa, terminating at
the foot of **Jasna Góra**. On most days, ascending the hill is no different from
taking a walk in any other public park, but the huge podium for open-air masses
gives a clue as to the atmosphere on the major **Marian festivals** – May 3, August
15, August 26, September 8 and December 8 – when up to a million pilgrims
converge here, often in colourful traditional dress. Many come on foot: every
year, for example, tens of thousands make the nine-day walk from Warsaw to
celebrate the Feast of the Assumption.

The Monastery

Although there's little of the souvenir-peddling tackiness characteristic of
Europe's other leading Marian shrines, Jasna Góra could hardly be called beautiful: its architecture is generally austere, while the defensive walls give the hill
something of a fortress-like feel. Entry is still via four successive **gateways**, each
one of which presented a formidable obstacle to any attacker.

The best way to begin an exploration is by ascending the 100-metre-high **tower**
(Mon–Sat 8am–4pm, Sun 8am–10.30am & 1–5pm), a pastiche of its eighteenth-
century predecessor, which was destroyed in one of the many fires which have
plagued the monastery. An earlier victim was the monastic **Church**, which has
been transformed from a Gothic hall into a restrained Baroque basilica. Not that
it's without its exuberant features, notably the colossal high altar in honour of the
Virgin and the two sumptuous family chapels off the southern aisle, which parody
and update their royal counterparts in the Wawel Cathedral in Kraków.

Inevitably, the **Chapel of the Blessed Virgin**, a separate church in its own
right, is the centrepiece of the monastery. It's also the only part to retain much of
the original Gothic architecture, though its walls are so encrusted with votive
offerings that this is no longer obvious. Masses are said here almost constantly
and you'll have to come very early or very late if you want much of a view of the
Black Madonna (see box overleaf). Much of the time, the icon is invisible
behind a screen, each raising and lowering of which is accompanied by a solemn
fanfare from a brass band hidden from the eyes of the believers. Even when it's
on view (normally 6am–noon, 3.30–4.40pm, 7–7.45pm & 9–9.10pm) you don't get
to see very much of the picture itself, as the figures of the Madonna and Child are
almost always decked out in crowns and robes made of diamonds and rubies. For
an idea of the impassioned reverence it inspires, on the other hand, try to coincide your visit with one of the frequent pilgrim groups, who piously hobble
around the image on bended knee.

To the north of the chapel, a monumental stairway leads to the **Knights' Hall**,
the principal reception room, adorned with flags and paintings illustrating the
history of the monastery. There are other opulent Baroque interiors, notably the
refectory, whose vault is a real tour-de-force, and the **library**. However, you'll
have to enquire at the information office by the main gateway for permission to
see them, as they are normally closed to the public.

The Museums

Jasna Góra's treasures are kept in three separate buildings. The most valuable
liturgical items can be seen in the **Treasury** above the sacristy, entered from the

southeastern corner of the ramparts (summer Mon–Sat 9–11.30am & 3.30–5.30pm, Sun 8am–1pm & 3–5.30pm; winter Mon–Sat 9–10.30am & 3.30–4.30pm, Sun 9am–12.30pm & 3.30–5pm). There's usually a long queue for entry, so be there well before it opens.

At the southwestern end of the monastery is the **Arsenal** (summer Mon–Sat 9am–noon & 2–6pm, Sun 9am–noon & 2–6pm; closes 5pm in winter), devoted to the military history of the fortress and containing a superb array of weapons, including Turkish war loot donated by King Jan Sobieski. Alongside is the **600th Anniversary Museum** (daily 11am–4.30pm), which tells the monastery's story from a religious standpoint. Exhibits include the seventeenth-century backing of The Black Madonna, which illustrates the history of the picture, and votive offerings from famous Poles, prominent among which is Lech Wałęsa's 1983 Nobel Peace Prize.

Elsewhere in town

Other than Jasna Góra, Częstochowa has very few sights, although the broad tree-lined boulevards at least give the heart of the city an agreeably spacious, almost Parisian feel. On pl. Biegańskiego, just off al. NMP, is the **District Museum** (Tues & Thurs–Sat 9am–3pm, Wed noon–6pm, Sun 10am–3pm), which has a decent archaeology section plus the usual local history displays. If you want to continue with the ecclesiastical theme, visit the small Baroque church of **St Barbara** to the south of Jasna Góra, allegedly the place where The Black Madonna was slashed. At the opposite end of town, close to the train station, is the massive neo-Gothic **Cathedral**, remarkable solely for its size.

Near the suburban station of Raków, reached by any southbound tram, is an important **Archaeology Reserve** (Tues–Sat 9am–3pm), with 21 excavated graves from the Lusatian culture of the sixth and seventh centuries BC; it's seemingly subject to random closures.

Practicalities

The well-stocked **tourist information centre** is at al. NMP 65 (Mon–Fri 9am–6pm, Sat & Sun 10am–4pm; ☎413-60 or 434-12). Other agencies worth knowing about are **Orbis**, al. NMP 40/42 (☎420-56 or 479-87), **PTTK**, al. NMP 39/41 (☎431-34), and **Juventur**, ul. Pałczyńskiego 73/77 (☎476-80).

The regular influx of pilgrims to Częstochowa means that you might have problems finding somewhere to stay: consider booking in advance, or visiting on a day trip from Kraków or Opole. Normally, the likeliest **hotel** bets are those beside the train station: *Centralny* at ul. Piłsudskiego 9 (☎440-67) and *Mały* at ul. Katedralna 18 (☎433-91); the latter is much the better bargain. Just below Jasna Góra is a luxurious Orbis hotel, *Patria*, ul. Starucha 2 (☎470-01); the three-star *Pernik* is far less conveniently sited to the northwest of the centre at ul. św. Rocha 224 (☎555-15). There are also four **motels** on the eastern outskirts of town – *Orbis*, al. Wojska Polskiego 281/287 (☎556-07 or 572-33), *PZMot*, al. Wojska Polskiego 181 (☎325-61), *Skałka*, al. Wojska Polskiego 82 (☎324-08) and *Korona*, ul. Makuszyńskiego 58 (☎522-36).

The Częstochowa telephone code is ☎034.

THE BLACK MADONNA

According to tradition, **The Black Madonna** was painted from life by **Saint Luke** on a beam from the Holy Family's house in Nazareth. This explanation is accepted without question by most believers, though the official view is kept deliberately ambiguous. Scientific tests have proved the icon cannot have been executed before the sixth century and it may even have been quite new at the time of its arrival at the monastery. Probably Italian in origin, it's a fine example of the hierarchical **Byzantine** style, which hardly changed or developed down the centuries. Incidentally, the "black" refers to the heavy shading characteristic of this style, subsequently darkened by age and exposure to incense.

What can be seen today may well only be a copy made following the picture's first great "miracle" in 1430, on the occasion of its theft. According to the official line, this was the work of followers of the Czech reformer Jan Hus, but it's more likely that political opponents of the monastery's protector, King Władysław Jagiełło, were responsible. The **legend** maintains that the picture increased in weight so much that the thieves were unable to carry it. In frustration, they slashed the Virgin's face, which immediately started shedding blood. The icon was taken to Kraków to be restored, though its condition may have precluded this. When it reappeared it had a gash (which is still visible), in confirmation of the truth of the miracle.

Sceptics have pointed out that during the Swedish siege, usually cited as the supreme example of The Black Madonna's miracle-working powers, the icon had been moved to neutral Silesia for safekeeping. Yet such was its hold over the Polish imagination that its future seemed to occasion more anguished discussion at the time of the Partitions than any other topic. In the present day, the **pope's devotion to the image** has also been a mixed blessing. It may have helped to focus the world's attention on Poland, but such emphasis on unreformed and nationalistic Catholicism as symbolised by this has also been the main reason why this charismatic religious leader has so clearly failed – in circumstances which have never been so favourable – to make a significant breakthrough towards Christian unity.

As you'd expect, there's a fair choice of **hostel** accommodation, including two outfits geared specifically to pilgrims – *Dom Pielgrzyma* at ul. Wyszińskiego 1 (☎433-02) beside the car park on the west side of the monastery and *Dom Rekolekcyjny* south of the hill at ul. św. Barbary 43 (☎411-77). There's also a *Dom Wycieczkowye* conveniently sited at ul. Pułaskiego 4 (☎445-36). Of the two seasonal **youth hostels**, much the more convenient is on Jasnogórska (☎431-21); the other is southwest of town at ul. Powstańców Warszawy 144 (☎792-29), reached on bus route #23. There's a **campsite** with a few chalets in an ideal spot directly opposite the *Dom Pielgrzyma* at ul. Oleńtiki 10/30 (☎474-95). Another is less conveniently located at the northeastern edge of the city at ul Makuszyńskiego 57.

Częstochowa is very poorly off for places to **eat** and **drink**. The top choice is, without a doubt, the *Hotel Patria*; otherwise, there's the usual clutch of snack bars and restaurants around the station, best of which is *Polonia*. Several new fast-food joints and nightspots are starting to appear on and around al. NMP. For a lively **café**, try *Adria*, about twenty minutes' walk north of the centre at al. Zawadzkiego 58.

Kielce and northern Małopolska

Most people see nothing more of the northern reaches of Małopolska than the glimpses snatched from the window of a Warsaw-to-Kraków express – a pity, because the gentle hills, lush valleys, strip-fields and tatty villages that characterise the region are quintessential rural Poland. The main town is **Kielce**, roughly halfway between Warsaw and Kraków, but the main attraction for visitors lies in rambling about in the **Świętokrzyskie Mountains** – in reality more of a hillwalkers' range.

Kielce

KIELCE, the regional capital, is nothing much to look at, having undergone the standard postwar development, but has a relaxed, down-at-heel, rural atmosphere. The pleasant main square, **pl. Partyzantów**, is lined by crumbling eighteenth- and nineteenth-century mansions, one of which (no. 3/5) houses a **regional museum** (Tues–Sun 10am–4pm), which has good local ethnography and history sections, but is silent on the ·1946 pogrom for which Kielce is notorious; the mob massacre of Jews followed the circulation of a rumour about the murder of a Christian child.

Just south on another square, pl. Zamkowy, you'll find the **Cathedral** – Romanesque, lost in later reconstruction – highlights of the murky interior being a fine Renaissance monument in red marble to a female member of the local Zebrzydowski family sculpted by Il Padovano, a sumptuous early Baroque high altarpiece from the workshops of Kraków and some elaborate Rococco decorative carvings in the choir stalls. Across the square is the early Baroque **palace** built for the bishops of Kraków, the town's owners in the mid-seventeenth century. Now a **Museum of Polish Art** (Tues–Sat 10am–4pm), the building's outstanding features are its period interiors, designed in the 1640s – in particular, the main Portrait Room which boasts a superb larchwood ceiling and a wealth of colourful polychromy. For major **religious festivals** the square east of the cathedral is packed with smartly dressed locals, many in regional folk costume, for the solemn procession round the square.

The town's **train and bus stations** are close by each other on the west side of town, a ten-minute walk down ul. Sienkiewicza into the town centre. The **PTTK** offices, upstairs at ul. Sienkiewicza 34, provide local information – though maps of the town are frequently unavailable. For **accommodation**, the dingy *Hotel Centralny* at ul. Sienkiewicza 78 (☎662-511), opposite the train station, is cheap and reasonably clean, though the same can't be said for its restaurant, which seems to be the favoured haunt of just about the entire local contingent of drunks and prostitutes. The central *Hotel Bristol*, ul. Sienkiewicza 21 (☎663-0455), is similarly priced but nicer, with a smaller but better restaurant. The reception at the *Bristol* can also arrange **private rooms**, and there is an all-year **youth hostel** at ul. Szymanowskiego 5 (☎237-35). Another alternative is the *Tysica* on ul. 3-go Maja (☎531-81), also with its own restaurant. Hotel restaurants apart, the deservedly popular *Winnica*, ul. Kryniczna 4, has some good traditional Ukrainian dishes; the *Promont*, ul. Sienkiewicza 59, is a reasonable local version of a pizzeria; and the *Prezydencka*, pl. Partyzantów 14, serves a good line in the ubiquitous *kotlet schwabowy*.

The Świętokrzyskie

In this low-lying region, the **Świętokrzyskie Mountains** stand out more than their height – 600m maximum – would suggest. Running east from Kielce, their long ridges and valleys, interspersed with isolated villages, are a popular and rugged hiking territory. During World War II the area was a centre of armed resistance to the Nazis: a grim, essentially factual account of life in the resistance here comes in Primo Levi's *If Not Now, When?*, in which he refers to the area as the Holy Cross Mountains, a literal translation of their name.

The Łysogóry

The fifteen-kilometre-long **Łysogóry** range is the most popular destination in the Świętokrzyskie. The place to head for is ŚWIĘTY KRZYŻ, one hour by bus from the main Kielce station (five departures daily, from 7am). The journey takes you along the edge of the range and eventually up a lovely mountainside road to the edge of the Świętokrzyskie National Park, stopping at a car park near Łysa Gora (Bald Mountain; 595m); across the way is the *Jodłowy Dwór*, an ugly holiday **hotel** (☎107-28) with a good restaurant.

The bus continues through the park – the only vehicle allowed to do so – but you're better off walking from here, through the protected woodland habitat of a range of birds and animals, including a colony of eagles. The path leads to a clearing – from where you can pick up the road again – then past a huge TV mast to the **Święty Krzyż abbey**, established up here by Italian Benedictines in the early twelfth century. The buildings have changed beyond recognition, about the only remnant of the original foundation being the abbey church's Romanesque doorway. The isolated mountain site, however, maintains an ancient feel: the abbey itself replaced an earlier pagan temple, traces of which were discovered nearby some years ago. On a more sombre note, the abbey buildings were turned into a prison following the enforced dissolution of the Benedictine order in 1825; it remained one right up to 1945, having been used by the Nazis as a concentration camp for Soviet POWs. Just how appalling conditions were then is indicated by photographs in the old monastery building of camp signs (in Russian and German) forbidding cannibalism.

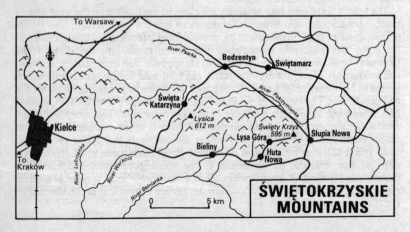

The abbey **Museum** (Tues–Sun 10am–4pm) houses one of the country's best natural history collections, covering every aspect of the area's wildlife, with exhibits ranging from butterflies and snakes to huge deer and elks. There's a good view down into the valley below the edge of the abbey, and you can also see some of the large tracts of broken stones that are a distinctive glaciated feature of the hilltops.

The path due east down the mountain leads to the village of **NOWA SŁUPIA** with its **Museum of Ancient Metallurgy** (Tues–Sun 10am–4pm), located on the site of iron ore mines and smelting furnaces developed here as early as the second century AD. For nearly a thousand years this was one of Europe's biggest ironworks. From Nowa Słupia you can take a bus back to Kielce, or you can climb back up and catch one from Święty Krzyż. If you want to stay over there's a year-round youth hostel in the village too.

The highest point of the Łyso Góry is a point known as **Łysica** (611m), a standard walking destination at the far end of the range. If you set out for Święty Krzyż early in the morning you could make it there with a good day's walk along the marked path – plenty of people do. Otherwise, catch a bus from Kielce to the village of **ŚWIĘTA KATARZYNA**, at the foot of the hills, and take the woodland path, past memorials to resistance fighters hunted down by the Nazis, to the summit – a legendary witches' meeting place and an excellent viewpoint. In Święta Katarzyna itself, there's a **convent** that's been home to an enclosed order of nuns since the fifteenth century – you can peer in at the church. For accommodation, there is a choice between a PTTK **hotel and restaurant** (☎110-111) and an all-year **youth hostel** (☎110-114).

PODHALE AND THE TATRA MOUNTAINS

Ask Poles to define their country's natural attractions and they often come up with the following simple definition: The Lakes, The Sea and The Mountains. "The Mountains" consist of an almost unbroken chain of ridges extending the whole length of the southern border, of which the highest, most spectacular and most revered are the **Tatras** – or *Tatry* as they're known in Polish. Eighty kilometres long, with peaks rising to over 2500m (8200ft), the Polish Tatras are actually a relatively small part of the range, most of which rises across the border in Slovakia. As the estimated three million annual tourists show, however, the Polish section has enough to keep most people happy: high peaks for the dedicated mountaineers, excellent trails for hikers, cable cars and creature comforts for day-trippers, and ski slopes in winter. What used to be a prime eastern bloc holiday region is now being transformed into something of a Western tourist enclave, the legions of eastern Europeans that used to descend on Zakopane rapidly being replaced by new hordes of Italians, French – and increasingly Brits – taking advantage of the low cost of holidaying in the Polish mountains.

Podhale – the Tatra foothills, beginning to the south of Nowy Targ – is a sparsely populated region of lush meadows, winding valleys and old wooden villages. The inhabitants of Podhale, the **górale**, are fiercely independent mountain farmers, known throughout Poland for their folk traditions. The region was "discovered" by the Polish intelligentsia in the late nineteenth century and the *górale* rapidly emerged as symbols of the struggle for independence, the links

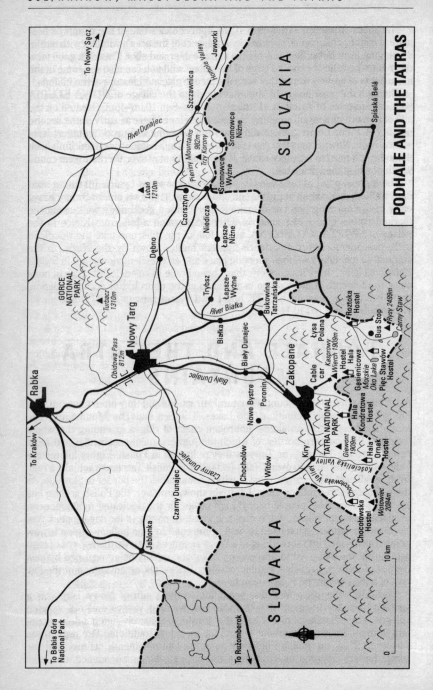

PODHALE AND THE TATRAS

forged between intellectuals and local peasants presaging the anticipated national unity of the post-independence era. As in other neglected areas of the country, the poverty of rural life led thousands of *górale* to emigrate to the United States in the 1920s and 1930s. The departures continue today, with at least one member of most households spending a year or two in Chicago, New York or other US Polish emigré centres, returning with money to support the family and, most importantly, build a house.

Since the demise of communism the traditional bonds between Podhale and the rest of the country have been shaken by what many locals see as central government's insensitivity to their specific concerns. Tensions surfaced following Solidarity's refusal to adopt a popular *górale* community leader as their main candidate in the elections of summer 1989, choosing instead a union loyalist.

Despite the influx of holidaymakers, the *górale* retain a straight-talking and highly hospitable attitude to outsiders. If you're willing to venture off the beaten track, away from the regular tourist attractions around Zakopane, there's a chance of real and rewarding contacts in the remoter towns and villages.

South to Zakopane

From Kraków the main road south – parts of it, for once, dual carriageway – heads through the foothills towards **Zakopane**, the main base for the Tatras. Approaching the mountains the road runs through a memorable landscape of gentle valleys, undulating slopes and strip-farmed fields. Along the route you'll see plenty of houses built in the distinctive pointed Podhale style – newer houses have tin roofs, the older ones are decorated wooden structures, with yellow and blue the most popular choice of colours – as well as wayside Catholic shrines and farming people dressed in the equally distinctive local costume. In addition, now, there's a sizeable contingent of new, privately run roadside restaurants and bed-and-breakfast type setups – a simple *noclegi* (rooms) is the commonest sign – established in the wake of the country's current economic transition. Most buses (and most visitors) run straight through, though it can be pretty slow going – usually around two hours – but, with a little time on your hands, it's worth considering a couple of breaks in your journey. A warning for motorists: watch out for cows – and drunks – careering out into the road: accidents are common.

Rabka and the Gorce

The climb begins as soon as you leave Kraków, following the River Raba from Myślenice to Lubień and then on, with the first glimpses of the Tatras ahead, to **RABKA**. This is a quiet little town, with a beautiful seventeenth-century **Church** at the base of the hill, now housing a small **ethnographic museum** (Tues–Sun 9am–4pm). If the idea of a stay appeals, there are a couple of decent **hotels** in town – the *Sława*, ul. Zakopiańska 2 (☎76-120) and the *Janosik*, ul Zakopiańska 16 (☎76-980) – as well as a PTTK **hostel** at ul Wąska 1 (☎77-160), by the rail station.

Surrounding Rabka is a mountainous area known as the **Gorce**, much of it national parkland. It's fine, rugged hiking country, with paths clearly signposted and colour-graded according to difficulty. There are trails to several mountain-top hostels: Luboń Wielki (1022m), Maciejowa (815m), Groniki (1027m) and – highest and best of all – Turbacz (1310m), a solid six-hour walk east of town. Before setting out, try to pick up the **map** *Beskid Makowski (Beskid Średni)*.

Nowy Targ

From Rabka the road continues over the **Obidowa Pass** (812m), then down onto a plain crossed by the Czarny Dunajec River and towards Podhale's capital, **NOWY TARG** ("New Market"). The key attraction of this squat, undistinguished town – the home of many a Polish American – is, as the name suggests, a **market**, held each Thursday on a square near the centre. This is basically a farmers' event, with horse-drawn carts lining the streets from early morning, when serious trading in animals takes place around the edges of the square. The central area is given over to stalls laden with local produce and solid, locally produced domestic appliances – tools, baskets, huge cooking pots and carved wooden plates. As with all Polish markets, there's also a lively trade in scarce or newly available consumer imports from the West. But for most visitors, the main shopping attractions are the chunky sweaters that are the region's hallmark – prices are lower and the quality generally better here than in either Kraków or Zakopane. Be prepared to haggle for anything you buy (wool and crafts especially) and arrive early if you want to get the real atmosphere. Of late the market has been invaded by droves of Russians, Ukrainians and Slovaks, the latter turning up weekly by the busload to benefit from the relatively cheaper prices of a whole host of items in Poland, their booty duly wafted through the laxly policed crossings along the Slovak border. By 10am or so, with business done, most of the farmers retreat to local greasy spoons for a hearty bout of eating and, especially, drinking.

As far as sights go, the town centre offers **St Catherine's Church**, which has a Gothic presbytery, and there's an attractive larchwood chapel across the river. The unofficial Podhale **Lenin trail** begins at the town, too: the old prison beyond the southeast corner of the main square is where he was held in 1914 on suspicion of spying – by then he'd been living in the area for nearly two years. A further Soviet connection is revealed in the local cemetery: a fierce battle for the town during the Red Army's advance in early 1945 left over a thousand Soviet soldiers dead.

If you're spending the night in town, the *Janosik*, ul. Hanka Sawickiej 8 (☎2876), is the best **hotel**, and modestly priced. The other sensible choice is the *Gorce* at 1000-lecia 74 (☎2681), a centrally located *pensjonat*. There is also a **youth hostel** at Dzielnica Nowa (☎2522; July & Aug), while **private rooms** can be arranged through the **Podhale Information Office** on pl. Pokoju. For food, there's little to choose between the *Podhalanka* and the *Dunajec*, both on pl. Pokoju, and the *Tatry*, ul. Kopernika 12.

Zakopane

South of Nowy Targ the road continues another 20km along the course of the Biały Dunajec before reaching the edges of **ZAKOPANE**, a major mountain resort, crowded with visitors throughout its summer hiking and winter skiing seasons. It has been an established attraction for Poles since the 1870s, when the purity of the mountain air began to attract the attention of doctors and their consumptive city patients. Within a few years this inaccessible mountain village of sheep farmers was transformed, as the medics were followed by Kraków artists and intellectuals, who established a fashionable colony in the final decades of Austro-Hungarian rule. A popular holiday centre ever since Poles began discover-

ing the place *en masse* in the 1920s and 1930s, in the postwar era the town grew to become one of the country's prime tourist hot-spots. In step with the growing influx of foreigners drawn by the lure of the mountains (and what remain by Western standards bargain prices), Zakopane has of late begun to acquire the hollow, overdeveloped feel of a major European tourist trap – a must for the wonderful setting and access to the peaks but little to recommend it otherwise.

The Town

The **bus** and **train stations** are both a ten-minute walk east of the main street, **ul. Krupówki**. A bustling pedestrian precinct, this is the focus of the town, given over to the traditional assortment of restaurants, cafés and souvenir shops, now spiced by the newly acquired collection of Western-style takeaway joints, delis, billiard halls and sex shops. Uphill the street merges into **ul. Zamoyskiego**, which runs on out of town past the fashionable *fin-de-siècle* wooden villas of the outskirts, while in the other direction it follows a rushing stream down towards **Gubałówka** hill (see p.369).

The **Tatra Museum** (Tues–Sun 9am–3.30pm), near the centre of ul. Krupówki, covers local wildlife, ethnography and history, including a section on the wartime experiences of the *goràle*, who were brutally punished by the Nazis for their involvement with the Polish resistance and cross-mountain contacts with the Allied intelligence. The museum is dedicated to T. Chałubinski, the doctor who "discovered" Zakopane in the 1870s. Of the number of art galleries sprouting up around town the **Hasior Gallery** (Wed–Thurs 1–7pm, Fri–Sun 9–3pm), housed in a wooden building on Jagiellońska south of the stations, is one of the most interesting, presenting the quirky but nevertheless enjoyable *oeuvre* of the contemporary artist Władysław Hasior.

In the cemetery of the **wooden church** on ul. Kościeliska you'll find the graves of many of the town's best-known writers and artists, among them that of Stanisław Witkiewicz (1851–1915) who developed the distinctive "Zakopane" architectural style based on traditional wooden building forms. There's also a commemorative tablet to his equally famous son, **Witkacy** (see box), standing by his mother's grave. Alongside the famous are the graves of old *górale* families, including well-known local figures such as the skier Helena Marusarzówna, executed by the Nazis for her part in the resistance. West of the main street is **Willa Atma**, a traditional-style villa and longtime home of composer Karol Szymanowski, now a museum dedicated to its former resident (Tues–Sun 10am–4pm).

Two Witkiewicz buildings can be visited just east of Zakopane: the **Willa Pod Jodłami** at BYSTRE and a wooden **chapel** at CHŁABÓWKA; both are on the Morskie Oko bus route. Ten minutes' walk west along ul. Kościeliska is the **Willa Koliba**, Witkiewicz's first experiment. Highlander woodcraft is famous throughout Poland, and nowhere is this skill more convincingly demonstrated than in the brace of wooden churches and chapels that can be seen in and around the town area. New churches being built demonstrate present-day design skills: two particularly worth visiting are the **Sanctuary of Our Lady of Fatima** (*Sanktuarium Matki Bożej Fatimskiej*) at **Swibówki**, a thirty-minute walk west of town along ul. Kościeliska , which also has a remarkable chapel at the rear of the main church complex, and the new church on ul. Zamoyskiego, the southern continuation of ul. Krupówki, a ten-minute walk from the town centre.

> The Zakopane area telephone code is ☎0165.

Practicalities

Zakopane has several **tourist offices**, each useful for different purposes: the *Tatry* office at ul. Kościuszki 7 is the main information centre for the whole area; Orbis at ul. Krupowki 22 helps with hotels, train and bus bookings and local trips; *Trip*, ul. Zamoyskiego 1 (☎59-47), is the most useful and best organised of the new breed of privately owned tourist offices, offering similar services but more attuned to Westerners' demands. Opening hours for the tourist offices are generally 8am to 6pm, Monday to Friday, 8am to noon on Saturdays; only the PTTK is open on Sundays.

Note that **parking** can be a bit of a problem for motorists these days in the increasingly congested town centre. Your best bets are the couple of parking lots on al. 3 Maja, directly east of ul. Krupówki. If **bikes** rather than cars is what you're interested in you can rent them from at the office at ul. Sienkiewicka 37 (☎4266).

WITKACY

Stanisław Ignacy Witkiewicz (1885–1939) – **Witkacy** as he's commonly known – is the most famous of the painters, writers and other artists associated with Zakopane. Born in Warsaw, the son of **Stanisław Witkiewicz**, the eminent painter and art critic who created the so-called **"Zakopane Style"** of primitivist wooden architecture (see opposite), it was in the artistic ferment of turn-of-the-century Zakopane that Witkacy spent much of his early life. After quitting Zakopane following his fiancée's suicide, in 1914, Witkacy joined up on an expedition to New Guinea and Australia led by a family friend, the celebrated anthropologist Bronisław Malinowski, and returned to a Europe on the verge of war. With the outbreak of World War I, as a Russian passport-holder the reluctant Witkacy was compelled to travel to St Petersburg to train as an infantry officer. In the event Witkacy's time in Russia proved influential to his artistic development. As well as experimenting with hallucinogenic drugs he began studying philosophy, a pursuit which strongly influenced the subsequent development of his work and art.

After surviving the war physically, if not mentally unscathed, in 1918 Witkacy re-established himself in Zakopane. From then on he developed his bubbling artistic talents in a host of directions, the most significant being art, philosophy, drama and novel writing. Over the following fifteen years or so Witkacy produced over a couple of dozen **plays** – his first was at the age of eight – many of which were premiered in Zakopane by his own theatre company, formed in 1925, several productions being staged in the epic surroundings of Morskie Oko lake. An exponent of an avant-gardist theory of drama that extolled the virtues of "pure form" over content, Witkacy wrote dramas that are generally bizarre, almost surrealist pieces spiced up with large dollops of sex and murder. Cold-shouldered by uncomprehending 1920s Polish audiences, the Witkacy dramatic *oeuvre* was rediscovered – and banned for some time by communist authorities – in the 1950s, since when they've consistently ranked among the most popular in the country.

Artistically Witkacy's main interests revolved around the famous **studio** he set up in Zakopane, where he churned out hundreds of portraits, many commissioned, of his friends and acquaintances from the contemporary artistic world. A dedicated drug-experimenter – Witkacy produced many of these wildly contorted images under the influence of a diverse range of narcotic substances – he habitually noted which drug he had been taking when painting in the corner of the canvas; the self-portraits in particular reveal a disturbed, restless aesthetic sensibility. Witkacy's **novels** – by common consent almost untranslatable – are similarly fantastic doom-laden excursions into the wilder shores of the writer's consciousness, a graphic example being *Nienasycenie* ("Insatiability", 1930), which revolves around an epic futuristic struggle between a Poland ruled by the dictator Kocmołuchowicz ("Slovenly") and communist hordes from China hell-bent on invading Europe from the east.

In a sense reality fulfilled Witkacy's worst apocalyptic nightmares. Following the Nazi invasion of Poland in 1939 the artist fled eastwards: on learning that the Soviets were also advancing into Poland in the pincer movement agreed under the terms of the notorious Molotov-Ribbentrop Pact, a devastated Witkacy committed suicide, a legendary act that ensured his place in the pantheon of noble patriots, as

Accommodation

All the tourist offices have **rooms** on offer, many in *pensjonat*, whose stock has greatly increased following the privatisation of many workers' holiday homes in town. Orbis run several *pensjonat*, bookable – along with other accommodation –

through the reception desk at the *Hotel Giewont*. *Tatry* operate accommodation services for groups at their main office and for individuals (mainly rooms in houses) at ul. Kościuszki 23a. Although privatisations have relieved the town's perennial accommodation problems, it's still worth booking rooms well in advance in midsummer or during the skiing season. The following **hotels and hostels** are listed in ascending order of price, which varies considerably according to season: there is also a *Tatry* **campsite** at the end of ul. Żeromskiego, on the east side of town.

Youth Hostel, ul. Nowotarska 45 (☎662-03). Open all year. Cheapest place in town – basic and fairly dirty.

Dom Turysty, ul. Zaruskiego 5 (☎3281). Cheap hotel popular with Polish students; laundry and showers on the second floor are handy.

Juventur, ul. Stołeczna 2a (☎662-53). Tour-group hotel, including many rooms without showers.

Tatry, ul. Wierchowa 4 (☎660-41). Quiet former workers' holiday home, ideally located for the bus station and town centre. Excellent views over town and mountains.

Panorama, ul. Wierchowa 6. Another decent pension, next to the *Tatry*.

Gazda, Zaruskiego 2 (☎5011); **Morskie Oko**, Krupówki 30 (☎5076); **Warszawianka**, Jagiellońska 7 (☎3261); **Imperial**, ul. Balzera 1 (☎4021). Mid-range, central hotels.

Sośnica, ul. Modrzejewskiej 7 (☎667-96). Reasonably upmarket ex-workers' pension in southern part of town with its own swimming pool, sauna and snooker room.

Giewont, Kościuszki 1 (☎2011). The town's smart hotel, right in the centre; chances of getting a room if you haven't booked are virtually zero.

Kasprowy, Polana Szymoszkowa (☎43-10). Luxury hotel west of town, looking onto the mountains.

Food and entertainment

Eating is never a problem in Zakopane. If you want a fast snack there are plenty of cafés, fast-food joints and streetside *zapiekanki* merchants to choose from. Restaurants are plentiful, too, with very good ones in the hotels *Gazda* and *Giewont*, and a very pukka one at the *Kasprowy*. The *Robber's Hut* on ul. Jagiellońska is an enjoyable recent commercial venture – a mock mountain-smuggler's den. Other choices worth considering are the *Karczma Redykołka*, at the corner of ul. Krupówki and Koscieliska, a touristy traditional-style inn with waitresses dressed in local costume; the *Empire*, further up ul. Krupówki, a newish and vaguely upmarket Chinese restaurant (a Zakopane first), and open till midnight; the nearby *Venecjia*, an Italian joint also open late; the *Watra*, ul. Zamoyskiego 2, which has live music many nights; and the reasonably priced *Obrochtówka*, ul. Kraszewskiego 10A, easily the best of the traditional-style restaurants – the *placki* (potato pancakes) in particular are excellent. A local product worth trying at least once are the bun-shaped **sheep's milk cheeses** you see on sale all over town: don't be put off by the strong smell – they're actually very tasty.

   Entertainment varies according to season. Founded in memory of the man who staged many of his own plays here, the **Teatr im. Stanisława Witkiewicza**, at ul. Chramcówki 15, north of the rail station, stages a regular variety of performances (serious and not so serious) throughout the year – check with the tourist offices for current details. The biggest cultural event, however, is the annual **International Festival of Mountain Folklore** held since the late 1960s and now occupying the prime tourist season mid-August spot. A week-long extravaganza of concerts, music competitions and street parades, alongside the sizeable contingent of local *górale* ensembles, the festival draws highlander groups from a dozen or so European countries. The timing means hefty crowds are guaranteed, but there's enough going on to keep most people happy. Along with the summer musical events in the Pieniny region further east (see p.376) you won't get a better chance to sample the tub-thumping exuberance of a *górale* choir dressed to the nines whooping their way through a string of joyous mountain melodies. Other local cultural events of note are the **Karol Szymanowski Music Days** held every July, featuring classical concerts by Polish and guest foreign artists in and around the town, and an **Art Film Festival**, held every other March.

Around Zakopane

If hiking in the Tatras proper sounds too energetic, there are a number of easy and enjoyable walks in the foothills and valleys surrounding Zakopane. For navigation purposes, the **map** to look out for is *Tatry i Podhale* (1:75,000).

Gubałówka Hill

There's an excellent view of the Tatras from the top of **Gubałówka Hill** (1120m) to the west, but everyone knows this, as you discover when you join the long queues for the **funicular from Zakopane** (follow ul. Krupówki out from the centre). From the summit, a good day reveals the high peaks to the south in sharp relief against clear blue mountain skies.

Most people linger a while over the view, browse in the souvenir shops and head back down again, but the long wooded hill ridge is the starting point of several excellent **hikes**, taking you through a characteristic Podhale landscape.

To the **west** from the top of the funicular the trails begin as a single path, which soon divides. Continue straight along the ridge and you gradually descend to the Czarny Dunajec valley, ending up at the village of WITÓW, around two hours' walking in all; buses back to Zakopane take fifteen minutes. Alternatively, take the north fork and it's a four-hour hike to the village of CHOCHOŁÓW, with its fine wooden houses and church; you can get there by two paths, either following a track (which soon becomes a road) through the village of DZIANISZ, or taking the cross-country route marked *Szlak im. Powstania Chochołowskiego* on the *Tatry i Podhale* map.

East of the funicular, the main path leads to PORONIN, on the Zakopane–Kraków road, a sleepy village distinguished by a statue of Lenin. The great man spent nearly two years here (1913–14), which used to be commemorated in a small Lenin museum, closed for the new political era. A steep climb up the marked path east of the village takes you to a hilltop area with wonderful views. Continue east from here and you come to BUKOWINA TATRZAŃSKA, a largish village with buses back to Zakopane (15min), a pension (the *Morskie Oko*; ☎7212), private accommodation office (☎7293) and restaurant.

Dolina Białego and Dolina Strążyska

For some easy and accessible valley hiking, Dolina Białego and Dolina Strążyska each provide a relaxed long afternoon's walk from Zakopane, and if you're feeling energetic you could combine the two in one day.

Leaving Zakopane to the south, along the Strążyska road, you reach **Dolina Strążyska** in around an hour. At the end of the valley (3hr) you can climb to the **Hala Strążyska**, a beautiful high mountain pasture (1303m); the **Siklawica**

waterfall, on the way, makes an enjoyable rest point, a stream coursing down from the direction of Giewont. Walk east along the meadow to the top of **Dolina Białego** and you can descend the deep, stream-crossed valley back to the outskirts of Zakopane (6–7hr in total).

Dolina Chochołowska and Dolina Kościeliska

Two of the loveliest valleys of the area are Dolina Chochołowska and Dolina Kościeliska, both a bus ride west of town. For the latter, the *Halit* inn (☎703-53) in **Kiry** (see below) makes an excellent overnight base.

Dolina Chochołowska, the longest valley in the region, follows the course of a stream deep into the hills. From the car park at the head of the valley it's a good hour's walk to the *Chochołowska* hostel, beautifully situated overlooking the meadows, with the high western Tatras and the Czech border behind. The steep paths up the eastern side lead to ridges that separate the valley from Dolina Kościeliska – one from a little way beyond the car park connects the two valleys, making a round trip possible.

Dolina Kościeliska is a classic beauty spot, much in evidence on postcards of the region. To get there take the bus to the hamlet of KIRY and set off down the stone valley track ahead. For a stiffish price a horse-drawn cart will run you down the first section of the valley to a point known as Polana Pisana, but from there on it's walkers only; the crowds diminish here, but there are always quite a few more dedicated types who carry on. A distinctive feature of Kościeliska are the **caves** in the limestone cliffs – once the haunts of robbers and bandits, legend has it. Take a detour off to the left – marked *jaskinia* (caves) – and you can visit various examples, including **Jaskinia Mroźna**, where the walls are permanently encased in ice.

Beyond Polana Pisana the narrow upper valley is a beautiful stretch of crags, gushing water and greenery reminiscent of the English Lake District, leading to the *Hala Ornak* **hostel**, a popular overnight stop with a restaurant. Two marked paths continue up beyond the hostel: the eastern route takes you the short distance to **Smreczyński Staw** (1226m), a tiny mountain lake surrounded by forest; the western route follows a high ridge over to Dolina Chochołowska – a demanding walk only for the fit.

The Tatras

Poles are serious mountaineers, with an established network of climbing clubs, and it's in the **Tatras** that everyone starts and the big names train. Most of the peaks are in the 2000–2500m range, but the unimpressive statistics belie their status, and their appearance. For these are real mountains, snowbound on their heights for most of the year and supporting a good skiing season in December and January. They are as beautiful as any mountain landscape in northern Europe, the ascents taking you on boulder-strewn paths alongside woods and streams up to the ridges, where grand, windswept peaks rise in the brilliant alpine sunshine. Wildlife thrives here: the whole area was turned into a National Park in the 1950s and supports rare species like lynx, golden eagles and brown bear – which for once you might even glimpse.

The steadily increasing volume of climbers, walkers and skiers using the slopes is having its effect on the area though, and in a bid to generate funds for local environmental protection the park authorities have now imposed a (nominal) entry charge on all visitors entering the park area, collected at booths at the main access points to the mountains. Groups of ten people or more must have an official guide, arranged, unless you're part of a pre-booked touring group, through the park offices in Zakopane (ul. Chałubińskiego 10; ☎32-03). Tussles between the conservationist-minded park authorities and local tourist developers are also holding back **skiers** – and as many see it, protecting the rich flora of the slopes – since to date the authorities have steadfastly refused to countenance the building of any further facilities, such as new ski-lifts, within the territory of the park.

Though many of the peak and ridge climbs are for experienced climbers only, much is accessible to regular walkers, with waymarked paths which give you the top-of-the-world exhilaration of bagging a peak. For skiers, despite the relative paucity of lifts and hi-tech facilities, there are some high-quality pistes, including a dry slope running down from peaks such as **Kasprowy Wierch** and Nosal.

Afraid of their citizens catching "the Polish disease" (ie Solidarity), the Czechs virtually closed this part of the border in 1980, and throughout the decade hikers were confronted with the somewhat comical sight of uniformed police sweating it over the mountain passes. Things have eased up these days, with the current editions of the *Tatry i Podhale* map showing cross-border walks in great detail, though the border police are still in evidence. Most foreigners can cross with just a passport stamp, however, and the new political climate means that exploration of the whole Tatra region is possible for the first time since the war. (See *The Rough Guide to the Czech and Slovak Republics* for cross-border details.)

Practicalities

A decent **map** of the mountains is indispensable. The best is the *Tatrzański Park Narodowy* (1:30,000), which has all the paths accurately marked and colour-coded. The often hard to obtain *Polskie Tatry* **guidebook** is likewise invaluable, giving all the main walking routes in several languages, though the English version is still awaiting a long overdue reprint.

Overnighting in the PTTK-run **huts** dotted across the mountains is an experience in itself. There are seven of them in all, clearly marked on the map (for up-to-date information on openings, check at tourist offices in Zakopane). In summer the huts are packed to the gunwales with student backpackers from all over the country: as they generally can't afford the beds they kip down on the floor, and if it's really crowded you'll probably be joining them. **Food** is basic, but pricey for Poles, most of whom bring their own; the huts are an ideal place to mix in, preferably over a bottle of vodka. Even if you don't want to lug large weights around the mountain tops, a supply of basic rations is a good idea. **Camping** isn't allowed in the National Park area, rock-climbing only with a permit – ask at the park offices (see above) for details. And for anyone attempting more than a quick saunter, the right **footwear and clothing** are, of course, essential.

Walks in the Tatras

The easiest way up to the peaks is by **cable car** from the hamlet of KUŹNICE, a 3km walk or bus journey south from Zakopane along the Dolina Bystrego. In summer the cable car is a sell-out, making advance booking at the Orbis office a virtual necessity, unless you're prepared to turn up before 8am; the only way round this – and it doesn't always work – is to buy your ticket for ten times the normal price from the touts lurking near the entrance. For the journey down, priority is always given to people who've already got tickets, so it's definitely best to buy these in advance, too. One way of avoiding the biggest queues is to make the ascent on Sunday mornings when the majority of Poles are likely to be at Mass.

Kasprowy Wierch – and descents to Kuźnice

The cable car ends near the summit of **Kasprowy Wierch** (1985m), where weather-beaten signs indicate the border. From here many day-trippers simply walk back down to Kuźnice through the Hala Gąsienicowa (an equally popular option is to walk up and return by cable car). A rather longer alternative is to strike west to the cross-topped summit of **Giewont** (1909m), the "Sleeping Knight" that overlooks Zakopane, and head down to Kuźnice through the Dolina Kondratowa past the *Hala Kondratowa* hostel. This is fairly easy going and quite feasible in a day if you start out early.

East: the Eagles' Path and Morskie Oko Lake

East of Kasprowy Wierch the walking gets tougher. From **Świnica** (2300m), a strenuous ninety-minute walk, experienced hikers continue along the **Orła Perć** (Eagles' Path), a challenging, exposed ridge with spectacular views. The *Pięc Stawów* **hostel**, in the high valley of the same name, provides overnight shelter at the end.

From the hostel you can hike back down Dolina Roztoki to **Łysa Polana**, a border crossing point in the valley, and get a bus back to Zakopane. An alternative is to continue east to the **Morskie Oko Lake** (1399m). Encircled by spectacular sheer cliff faces and alpine forest, this large glacial lake is one of the Tatras' big attractions, most frequently approached on the winding forest road from Łysa Polana, some 11km away. During the summer the paths round the

---

HIKING IN THE TATRAS

It is as well to remember that the Tatras are an alpine range and as such demand some respect and preparation. The most important rule is to stick to the marked paths, and to arm yourself in advance with a decent **map**. The weather is always changeable, and you should not venture out without waterproofs and decent foot-wear: most rain falls in the summer, when there may also be thunderstorms and even hail- and snow-showers. Even on a warm summer's day in the valleys, it can be below freezing at the peaks.

Hiking: the golden rules

• Watch the **weather forecast** (the evening forecast on the TV is easily comprehensible)

• Set out **early** (the weather is always better in the morning), and tell someone when and where you're going.

• Don't leave the **tree line** (about 2000m) unless visibility is good, and when the clouds close in, start descending immediately.

• Bring with you: a pair of **sturdy boots** to combat the relentless boulders in the higher reaches (trainers will do for the easier stretches); a **whistle** (for blowing six times every minute if you need help); and a **flask of water**

lake are packed with coach parties out for the day from Zakopane. Crumbling roads mean there's currently no bus service direct to **Morskie Oko** from Zakopane, the nearest bus stopping at Łysa Polana, east of town. If you don't feel like walking – and a fair number do – you can hire a horse-drawn buggy: at a current cost of around £6 for the round trip it's a fair bargain. The journey takes under an hour each way.

The *Morskie Oko* **hostel**,situated by the side of the lake, provides a convenient base for the ascent of **Rysy** (2499m), the highest peak in the Polish Tatras. Closer to hand on the same red-marked route is **Czarny Staw** (1580m), a lake which, if anything, appears even chillier, half an hour's walk up from Morskie Oko.

East to the Pieniny

East of the Tatras the mountains scale down to a succession of lower ranges – *beskidy* as they're known in Polish – stretching along the Slovak border. The walking here is less dramatic than in the Tatras but excellent nonetheless, and the locals are a good bunch too, including *górale* and a long-established Slovak minority. The highlights of the region are the **Pieniny Mountains**, hard by the Slovak border, and the raft run through the **Dunajec gorge**, far below.

Transport in this little-known region can be a bit of a struggle, away from the immediate vicinity of **Szczawnica**, a spa town that makes the best base for exploring the Pieniny.

The Spisz region

The road east from Nowy Targ to Szczawnica is one of the most attractive in the country, following the broad valley of the Dunajec through the **Spisz**, a backwoods region whose villages are renowned for their wooden houses, churches and folk art. Buses cover the route four or five times a day.

DĘBNO, 14km from Nowy Targ, boasts one of the best-known wooden churches in the country, a shingled, steep-roofed building with a profile vaguely reminiscent of a snail. Inside, the full length of walls and ceiling are covered with exuberant, brilliantly preserved fifteenth-century polychromy and wooden carving. Their subjects are an enchanting mix of folk, national and religious motifs, including some fine hunting scenes and curiously Islamic-looking geometric patterns. In the centre of the building fragments survive of the original roodscreen, supporting a tree-like cross, while the altarpiece triptych features an unusually militant-looking Saint Catherine.

Just to the south of the road, 12km on from Dębno, is **CZORSZTYN**, a small village with a memorable if very ruined castle. From its heights you get a sweeping view over the valley and to the castle of Niedzica (see overleaf) across the mouth of the Dunajec gorge. The valley itself is the subject of a controversial hydroelectric **dam project**, whose initial stages are already disfiguring the land below Czorsztyn. Environmentalists fear that the flooding of the Czorsztyn area will transform the Spisz into mosquito-ridden marshland, but despite strong protests and considerable technical problems the project is inching ahead, supported by the heavy industry lobby – though the government has recently promised a review of the whole project.

Niedzica – and west along the Slovak border

NIEDZICA lies just across the gorge from Czorsztyn, reachable on foot in a half-hour walk to the south and over a pedestrian bridge or, more circuitously, by road to the west of Czorsztyn; some of the Nowy Targ-to-Szczawnica buses take a detour here en route.

The village occupies a strategic position at a major confluence of the Dunajec, with a largish tributary plunging down from Slovakia. Control of this valley and the border territory explains the presence of the **castle**, perched above the river. Originally raised in the fourteenth century, it was reconstructed in its current Renaissance style in the early 1600s, and today lies under threat from the hydroelectric scheme, which some experts believe will erode its rock foundations. It today houses a **museum of Spisz folk art** (Tues–Sun 8am–5pm) and an artists' retreat. A Tintin-like folk tale associates the castle with the Incas. The wife of the last descendant of the Inca rulers allegedly lived here in the late eighteenth century, and left a hidden document detailing the legendary Inca treasure buried in Titicaca lake in Peru – a document supposedly discovered in 1946.

To the **west of Niedzica**, a little-frequented backroad winds its way towards Nowy Targ and Zakopane through the heart of the Spisz. Most villages here were effectively cut off from the outside world well into the nineteenth century, and serfdom was only abolished here in 1931. It still feels like another world, particularly in villages like TRYBSZ and ŁAPSZE with their Slovak populations. If you get the chance, visit on a Sunday morning, for the local choirs are reputedly wonderful.

Szczawnica and around

East of the Tatras there's a plethora of spa towns amid the river gorges and steep valleys of the border area. SZCZAWNICA, one-time haunt of Nobel Prize-winning novelist Henryk Sienkiewicz, is a highly picturesque example, sited on the edge of the sparkling River Dunajec below the peaks of the Pieniny. It is also by far the most visited town in the region, crowded through the summer with all types of mountain holidayers: canoeists setting off down the gorge, hikers heading off to the hills, industrial workers recuperating in the sanatoria.

Buses run here from both Nowy Targ (40km) and, on a slightly roundabout route, from Zakopane (50km), dropping you in the centre of town, by the river. From here it's a short walk up to the bustling square, and the staid health establishments of the **upper town**. In the communist era Szczawnica's alkaline spring water was consumed by miners and steelworkers, now replaced by the regular brand of health-seeking tourists, Polish and foreign; casual visitors are free to wander in and sample the waters. There's little else to see in town, unless you happen to be around during *górale* folk events. The attraction for most foreign visitors lies in getting out to explore the Pieniny and the Dunajec gorge.

There are no real hotels, but accommodation isn't a problem: in season half the town population rent out **rooms** in their homes for next to nothing and there's the usual full range of former workers' holiday *pensjonaty*, notably the *Jakubówka*, ul. Jana Wiktora 17 (☎22-39); *Pod 9*, ul. Manifestu Lipcowego 9 (☎26-76); next-door *Wiktorialis* (☎23-25); and *Szczęście*. You can arrange lodgings through the PTTK office at ul. Manifestu Lipcowego 2a, the Pieniny bureau, ul. Wygon 4a or at Orbis, on the main square at pl. Dietla 7. A more spartan alternative is the *Orlica* **PTTK hostel** at ul. Pienińska 12 (☎22-48), right on the edge of the gorge, a kilometre south along the river.

Krościenko

The small town of **KROŚCIENKO**, a ten-minute bus ride north of Szczawnica, is an alternative base for the Pieniny, located right at the edge of the mountains and starting point for hikes to the Trzy Korony (see below). It again has the possibility of **private rooms**, arranged through the **PTTK office** at ul. Jagiellońska 28 (☎3059), and an undistinguished collection of restaurants.

Dolina Homole

A short local excursion worth considering is to the **Dolina Homole**, 8km east of Szczawnica. This is a peaceful valley of wooded glades and streams, and you can walk up to the surrounding hilltops in less than two hours. There's a PTTK **campsite** up here too.

From Szczawnica it's a fifteen-minute bus ride east to the village of **JAWORKI**, starting point for the walk and an interesting example of the ethnic and religious twists characterising the eastern hill country. At first sight the late eighteenth-century **church** looks like a regular Catholic building but a glance at the iconostasis behind the altar indicates a different history. Although now Roman Catholic, it was originally a Uniate *cerkiew*, in what was the westernmost point of Lemk settlement in Poland (see Chapter Three). Today only a couple of Lemk families remain. If you find the church closed, ask for the key from the house next door. A basic **bar-restaurant** (closed Mon) in the village does fine fish dishes and *Okocim* beer.

The Pieniny

A short range of Jurassic limestone peaks, rearing above the spectacular Dunajec gorge, the Pieniny offer some stiff hill walking and the appeal of requiring no serious climbing to reach its 1000-metre summits. Jagged outcrops are set off by abundant greenery, the often humid mountain microclimate supporting a rich and varied flora. Like the Tatras, the Pieniny are an officially designated National Park and have a network of controlled paths. The detailed *Pieniński Park Narodowy* (1:22,500) **map** is useful and is available in most tourist offices and bookshops.

Trzy Korony

The main range, a 10km stretch between Czorsztyn and Szczawnica, is the most popular hiking territory, with the peaks of **Trzy Korony** (Three Crowns; 982m) the big target.

There are several routes up, the best-known leading from **Krościenko**. From the bus stop here you can follow the signs – and in summer the packs of hikers – southwards on the yellow route. The path soon begins to climb through the mountainside woods, with plenty of meadows and lush clearings on the way. Around two hours from Krościenko you'll finally reach **Okrąglica**, the highest peak of the Trzy Korony, via some chain-bannistered steps. On a clear day there's a excellent view over the whole area: the high Tatras off to the west, the slopes of Slovakia to the south, and the Dunajec gorge far below.

Many hikers take the same route back, but two alternatives are worth considering. One is to walk to Szczawnica, a two- or three-hour trip. Head back along the route you came as far as Bajków Groń (679m), about three-quarters of the way down, and from there follow the blue path across the mountains south to Sokolica and down to the river, where you can get a boat across to the *Orlica* hostel. The other, if you want to combine the walk with the Dunajec gorge, is to descend the mountain south to Sromowce Niżne, one of the two starting points for the raft trip upriver (see below).

PIENINY GÓRALE: MUSIC EVENTS

Like the Podhale, the Pieniny region is populated by *górale* highlanders who for much of the century have been migrating to the United States in great numbers; it's not uncommon to come across broad Chicago accents in the villages. To the outsider, the main distinction between the Podhale and Pieniny clans is the colours of their **costumes** – the reds, browns and blacks of the western Podhale giving way to the purple-blues of the Pieniny decorated jackets. Like their Podhale neighbours, the *górale* of the Pieniny dress up traditionally on Sundays and for other major community events – weddings, festivals and the like. The men's costume consists of tight-fitting woollen trousers decorated with coloured strips of embroidery (*parzenice*), high leather cummerbund-type bands round the waist, decorated jackets and waistcoats and a feather-topped hat. The women wear thin woollen blouses, thickly pleated skirts festooned with flowers and brightly coloured headscarves. The men also go in for thick embossed leather shoes (*kierpce*) of the type you can pick up in the tourist shops. Besides costume the clans have their own distinct **dialects**, and even Polish speakers find it hard to follow a Pieniński in full swing.

Music is the most accessible aspect of their culture. In summer you may well catch vocal ensembles at open-air folk evenings held in Szczawnica or Krościenko – a good excuse for everyone to dress up and sing their hearts out. While the harmonies and vocal style are similar in both *górale* regions, the Pieniński make more use of instruments – violins and a thumping bass in particular – to create a sound that has marked similarities to Slovak and Hungarian country styles. The visiting crowds are overwhelmingly Polish at these traditional old-time romps, and for the atmosphere alone it's well worth joining them.

The Dunajec gorge

Below the heights of the Pieniny the fast-moving Dunajec twists and turns below great limestone rockfaces and craggy peaks. The river is a magnet for **canoeists**, who shoot fearlessly through the often powerful rapids; for the less intrepid, the two-hour **raft trip** provides an enjoyable version of the experience.

The most popular **starting point** for this trip is KĄTY, a few hundred metres east of SROMOWCE WYŻNE; regular buses run to Kąty from Szczawnica and Nowy Targ. There's a second landing stage further downriver at SROMOWCE NIŻNE, easier to reach if you've been hiking in the Pieniny; this village has a largish PTTK hostel and lies across the river from the Slovak settlement and monastery of ČERVENY KLÁŠTOR, the main Slovakian starting point for raft trips.

Trips currently run from April to late August, starting at 8am and finishing around 4pm. In season, if you turn up on the day you can expect to queue a couple of hours for a place; tickets can be booked through local Orbis offices, regional hotels (in Kraków and Zakopane for example), and tourist offices, including *Tatry* and *Związek Podhalański* bureaux.

The rafts are sturdy log constructions, carrying up to ten passengers plus two navigators in traditional Pieniny costume. Here, as further east, the river forms the border with Slovakia and at several points Slovak villages face their Polish counterparts across the banks, with their own rafters and canoeists hugging the southern side of the river. After plenty of sharp twists and spectacular cliffs, the rafts end up at Szczawnica, from where buses return to Kąty up to 4pm.

travel details

Trains

From Kraków to Białystok (1 daily; 10hr); Bydgoszcz (3 daily; 7–9hr); Częstochowa (12 daily; 2–4hr); Gdańsk (3 daily; 5–11hr); Katowice (26 daily; 1hr 30min–2hr); Kielce (11 daily; 2–3hr); Krynica (8 daily; 5–6hr); Lublin (3 daily; 5–7hr); Nowy Sącz (11 daily; 3–4hr); Poznań (7 daily; 7–8hr); Przemyśl (15 daily; 3–5hr); Rzeszów (20 daily; 2–3hr); Szczecin (5 daily; 12–14hr); Warsaw (19 daily; 2hr 30min–6hr; expresses from 6–7am and 6.40–8pm); Wrocław (15 daily; 4–6hr); Zakopane (15 daily; 3–5hr). Also **international connections** to Budapest, Prague and Vienna.

From Częstochowa to Kraków (11 daily; 2–3hr); Kielce (10 daily; 2hr); Katowice (hourly; 1–2hr); Łódź (15 daily; 2–3hr); Warsaw (14 daily; 3–4hr); .

From Kielce to Kraków (8 daily; 2–3hr); Częstochowa (10 daily; 2hr); Łódź (1 daily; 4hr); Warsaw (12 daily; 3–4hr);.

From Zakopane to Kraków (15 daily; 3–5hr); Częstochowa (3 daily; 7–8hr; sleepers); Gdańsk (1 daily; 12hr; sleeper); Katowice (2–4 daily; 4–6hr); Warsaw (2 daily; 5–12hr).

Buses

From Kraków to Nowy Targ (12 daily; 1–2hr); Sandomierz (2 daily; 4–5hr); Tarnów (15 daily; 1–1hr 30min); Zamość (2 daily; 6–8hr); Zakopane (8–10 daily; 2hr 30min–3hr).

From Zakopane to Nowy Targ (hourly; 30min); Szczawnica (5 daily; 1hr); Katowice (2 daily; 4hr); Bielsko-Biata (3 daily; 2hr30min–4 hr); Nowy Sącz (3 daily; 1–2hr); Kraków (regular throughout the day; 2hr 30min–3hr); Lublin (1 daily; 8hr); Warsaw (1 daily; 8–9hr); Reszów 1 daily; 3– 4hr).

Flights

From Kraków Daily flights to Gdańsk (2hr; July & Aug) and Warsaw (50min; May–Oct). Also international flights to Köln, Frankfurt, London, Paris and Rome.

CHAPTER FIVE

SILESIA

In Poland it's known as *Śląsk*, in the Czech Republic as *Sleszko*, in Germany as *Schlesien*: all three countries hold part of the frequently disputed province that's called in English **Silesia**. Since 1945, Poland has had the best of the argument, holding all of it except for a few of the westernmost tracts, a dominance gained as compensation for the Eastern Territories, which were incorporated into the USSR in 1939 as a result of the Nazi–Soviet pact and never returned.

Silesia presents a strange dichotomy. On the one hand there's its notorious heavy industry, especially the huge **Katowice** conurbation, by far the largest unmodernised "black country" left in Europe. An even worse environmental disaster exists in **Wałbrzych**, one of the most polluted towns in the world. Similar problems, albeit on a smaller scale, also affect the province's chief city, **Wrocław**, holding back its potential to become a rival to Kraków, Prague and Budapest as one of central Europe's most enticing cosmopolitan centres.

Silesia's other face, ironically enough, is its role as a national playground, as the Sudeten mountain chain at its western extremity contains two of the most popular recreation areas in the country. Of these, the **Karkonosze National Park** offers the more rugged scenery, while the **Kłodzko Region** has a richer and more surprising range of landscapes, with the lazy ambience of its spa resorts providing a counter-attraction to bracing mountain hikes.

Along with Wielkopolska and Małopolska, Silesia was a key component of the early Polish nation. Following the collapse of the country's monarchical system, the Duke of Silesia, a member of the Piast dynasty, sometimes served as Poland's uncrowned king. However, this system fell by the wayside in the wake of the Tartar invasions in the thirteenth century, and the duchy was divided into **Lower** and **Upper Silesia**. As the succeeding dukes divided their territory among their sons, Silesia became splintered into eighteen principalities: hence what you see today is the legacy of a series of pint-sized former capitals, each with its fair share of castles, palaces, churches and other monuments.

As each line died out, its land was incorporated into **Bohemia**, which eventually took over the entire province when the Piasts were extinguished in 1675 – by which time it had itself become part of the Austrian-dominated **Habsburg Empire**. In 1740, Frederick the Great, king of the militaristic state of **Prussia**, launched an all-out war on Austria, his pretext being a dubious claim his ancestors had once had to one of the Silesian principalities. After changing hands several times, all but the southern part of the province was taken over by the Prussians in 1763, becoming part of Bismarck's Germany in 1871.

In 1921 a plebiscite resulted in the industrial heartlands of the province becoming part of the recently resurrected Polish state. A further 860,000 Silesians opted for Polish rather than German nationality when given the choice in 1945, and displaced Poles from the Eastern Territories were brought in to replace the Germans who were now evacuated from the region. Yet, although postwar Silesia has developed a strongly Polish character, people with definite family roots in the province are often bilingual and, in a situation analogous to the Scots or Welsh, consider their prime loyalty to lie with Silesia rather than Poland. To complicate the picture further, many have German ancestors, a group targeted – not without success – by right-wing political extremists in Germany bent on re-creating the prewar Reich. It was only as a result of international pressure that the German government decided not to stake a claim to Silesia as part of the unification talks; notwithstanding the November 1990 treaty confirming the borders, the issue will probably only be buried completely when Poland manages to close the gap in living standards between the two countries.

WROCŁAW AND AROUND

Lower Silesia's historic capital, **WROCŁAW**, is the fourth largest city in Poland and has an exhilarating big city feel to it, yet behind this animated appearance lies an extraordinary story of emergence from the verge of ruin. Its special nature comes from the fact that it contains the soul of two great cities. One of these is the city that has long stood on this spot, Slav by origin but for centuries dominated by Germans and generally known as **Breslau**. The other is **Lwów** (now L'viv), capital of the Polish Ukraine, which was annexed by the Soviets in 1939 and retained by them in 1945. After the war, its displaced population was encouraged to take over the severely depopulated Breslau, which had been confiscated from Germany and offered them a ready-made home.

Part re-creation of Lwów, part continuation of the tradition of Breslau, postwar Wrocław has a predominantly industrial character. However, there's ample compensation for this. The multinational influences which shaped the city are graphically reflected in its architecture: the huge Germanic **brick Gothic churches** which dominate the skyline are intermingled with Flemish-style Renaissance mansions, palaces and chapels of Viennese Baroque, and boldly utilitarian public buildings from the early years of this century. The tranquillity of the parks, gardens and rivers – which are crossed by over eighty **bridges** – offer a ready escape from the urban bustle, while the city has a vibrant cultural scene, its **theatre** tradition enjoying worldwide renown.

Wrocław is encircled by rural terrain that is rivalled within Silesia only by the far better-known – and consequently far more touristy – Karkonosze Mountains and Kłodzko Valley. After the account of Wrocław itself you'll find a rundown on the most attractive places within easy reach of the city.

Wrocław's history

The origins of Wrocław are unknown. There may well have been a community here in Roman times, but the earliest documentary evidence is a ninth-century record of a Slav market town called **Wratislavia** situated on a large island at the point where the River Odra receives three tributaries. Subsequently, this became known as **Ostrów Tumski** (Cathedral Island) in honour of the bishopric founded here in 1000 by Bolesław the Brave.

German designs on Wratislavia came to the fore in 1109, when the army of Emperor Henry V was seen off by Bolesław the Wrymouth. The site of the battlefield became known as **Psie Pole** (Dogs' Field), which today is one of the city's five administrative districts; the name supposedly arose because the

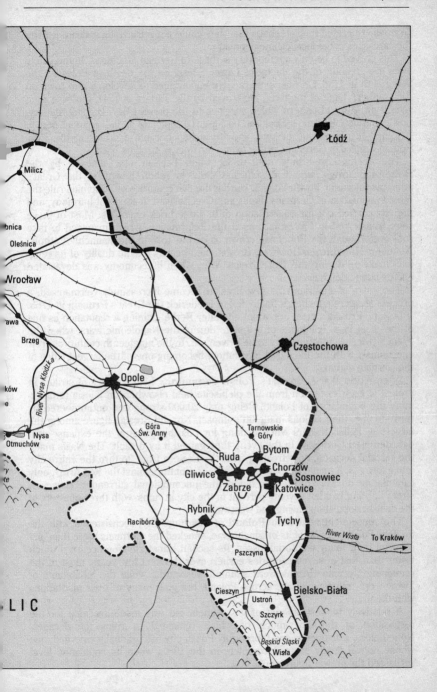

Germans retreated in such chaos that they could not retrieve their dead, leaving the carcasses to the local canine population.

This proved to be only a temporary setback to German ambitions. Immediately after the creation of the duchy of Lower Silesia on the death of Bolesław the Wrymouth in 1138, German settlers were encouraged to develop a new town on the southern bank of the river. Destroyed by the Tartars in 1241, this was soon rebuilt on the grid pattern which survives to the present day. In 1259 the city, now commonly known as **Breslau**, became the capital of an independent duchy. It joined the Hanseatic League, and its bishop became a prince of the Holy Roman Empire of Germany, ruling over a territory centred on Nysa.

The duchy lasted only until 1335, when Breslau was annexed by the **Bohemian kings**, who had sufficient clout to rebuff Kazimierz the Great's attempts to reunite it with Poland. During the two centuries of Bohemian rule the mixed population of Germans, Poles and Czechs lived in apparent harmony, and the city carried out the construction of its huge brick churches. Most of these were transferred to Protestant use at the Reformation, which managed to take root even though the Bohemian crown passed in 1526 to the staunchly Catholic **Austrian Habsburgs**. However, Breslau paid heavily for the duality of its religious make-up during the Thirty Years' War, when its economy was devastated and its population halved.

The years of Austrian rule saw Breslau become increasingly Germanised, a process accelerated when it finally fell to Frederick the Great's **Prussia** in 1763. It became Prussia's most important city after Berlin, gaining a reputation as one of the most loyal lynchpins of the state during the Napoleonic wars, when the French twice occupied it, only to be driven out. In the nineteenth century it grew enormously with the Industrial Revolution, becoming one of the largest cities of the German nation.

After World War I, Breslau's **Polish community** held a series of strikes in protest at their exclusion from the plebiscite held elsewhere in Silesia to determine the boundaries of Poland. Being only 20,000 strong and outnumbered by thirty to one, their actions made little impact. Nor did Breslau figure among the targets of Polish leaders when looking for possible gains at the expense of a defeated Nazi Germany. In the event, they gained it by default. The Nazis made the suicidal decision, on retreating from the Eastern front, to turn the entire city into a fortress. It managed to hold out for four months against the Red Army, only capitulating on May 6, the day before the unconditional surrender. However, street fighting had left seventy percent of the city in ruins, with three-quarters of the civilian population having fled westwards.

The subsequent **return to Poland** of this huge city, rechristened with the modern Polish version of its original name, shocked the Germans more than any other of their many territorial losses. Its second transformation occurred much faster than that of seven centuries earlier: over the next few years, most of the remaining German citizens were shunted westwards, while the inhabitants of Lwów were transferred here across Poland, bringing many of their institutions with them.

A relatively modest amount of government aid was made available for the restoration of the city, much of which remained in ruins for decades. Nonetheless, a distinctive and thoroughly Polish city has gradually emerged, one whose revival finally seemed complete in the 1980s when its population level surpassed the prewar figure of 625,000.

The Wrocław telephone code is ☎071.

Arrival, information and getting around

The main **train station**, Wrocław Główny – itself one of the city's sights – faces the broad boulevard of ul. Marsz. Józefa Piłsudskiego, about fifteen minutes' walk south of the centre. All international and most major domestic services stop there, but there are two other stations you may find yourself using. **Wrocław Świebodzki**, another fine structure from the railways' nineteenth-century heydays, located close to the inner ring road on pl. Sergiusza Kirowa, is used by most trains between Wrocław and Jelenia Góra, plus some of those to and from Legnica and Głogów. On pl. Staszica, well to the north of Ostrów Tumski and connected to the centre by trams #0 and #1, is **Wrocław Nadodrze**, for trains to and from Łódź, Trzebnica and Oleśnica.

At the time of writing, the main **bus station** was still at pl. Konstytucji, diagonally opposite Wrocław Główny, but was due to be moved to ul. Sucha, at the back of the train station, a terminal which is currently used by international services only. The small bus stations beside each of the other rail stations are only for destinations within the Wrocław district.

Bus #106 runs between Wrocław Świebodzki and the **airport**, which lies in the suburb of Strachowice, 10km to the southwest.

The main organisation for local tourism, **Odra-Tourist**, is at ul. Piłsudskiego 98 (Mon–Fri 9am–5pm, first Sat in month 9am–2pm; ☎44-41-01). For maps and leaflets, it's better to go to the small **tourist information office** at ul. Kazimierza Wielkiego 39 (Mon–Sat 10am–4pm; ☎44-31-11). For students, the **Almatur** office at ul. Tadeusza Kościuski 34 (☎44-30-03) is a useful contact point. The main **Orbis** offices are at Rynek 29 (Mon–Fri 8am–7pm, Sat 8am–5pm; ☎326-65 or 347-80) and ul. Piłsudskiego 62 (same times; ☎387-45 or 44-87-17). However, most services are available cheaper at new private agencies: particularly recommended is the English-speaking **Welcome-Tourist** on the first floor of the *Hotel Saigon*, ul. Wita Stwosza 22/23 (☎44-28-85).

The **trams** cover almost the entire built-up area of the city; the #0, a circular route round the central area, makes an easy introduction to the city. A pair of historic trams, known as *Jaś i Małgosia* (Hänsel and Gretel) run all summer as well.

Finding a place to stay

Wrocław has accommodation to suit every taste and pocket; the entries which follow are more or less exhaustive. Prices within each category are a good bit lower than in Warsaw, a touch lower than in Poznań, and roughly comparable to Kraków's. There is no especially busy time of year.

Cheaper hotels

Note that most of these options entail a bit of commuting, and therefore have no obvious advantages over a room in a private house (see overleaf).

Domu Kultury, ul. Kazimierza Wielkiego 45 (☎44-38-66). The only bargain hotel in the city centre, housed on the upper floors of a cultural centre. There are no single rooms.

DOSiR, ul. Wejherowska 2 (☎55-01-98). Sports hotel west of centre at terminus of bus #127.

Irys, ul. Irysowa 1 (☎25-32-78). Brand-new venture, located to the northwest of the city and reached by bus #108.

Nauczycielski, ul. Nauczycielska 2 (☎22-92-68). Intended for teachers, but open to anyone if they've got room; situated on Ostrów Tumski and reached by trams #0, #1, #2, #10 or #12. Dorm accommodation is also available.

Oficerski, ul. Adama Próchnika 130 (☎60-33-03). In the southwestern suburbs near tram routes #13, #14 and #20.

Orka, ul. Międzyleska 2 (☎67-60-51 ext. 47). Run by the same management as *Irys*; is just beyond the terminus of trams #2, #15 and #22 on the east side of town.

Śląsk, ul. Oporowska (☎61-16-11). Sports hotel in a park to the southwest of the centre, served by trams #4, #5, #1, #13, #16, #18 and #20.

Żeglarz, ul. Władysława Reymonta 4 (☎21-29-96). Near Nadodrze station on route of tram #14.

Moderate hotels

A cluster of moderately priced hotels, mostly of the two-star class, can be found in the vicinity of the main train station.

Europejski, ul. Piłsudskiego 88 (☎310-71). At the time of writing, this was in the middle of a major refurbishment which will take it into the luxury category. Pending its completion, a two-tier pricing structure will remain in operation for the modernised and unmodernised rooms.

Grand, ul. Piłsudskiego 100 (☎360-71). Does not quite live up to its name – the rooms are decidedly modest in size – but is, at least until the *Europejski*'s refurbishment is complete, the most enticing of this group of hotels.

Piast I, ul. Piłsudskiego 98 (☎300-33). A step down in class from its neighbour, a fact reflected in the lower prices.

Piast II, ul. Stawowa 13 (☎375-60). Somewhat dilapidated, but the cheapest of the hotels around the station. Being just off ul. Piłsudskiego, it also has the advantage of far less traffic noise than its neighbours.

Polonia, ul. Piłsudskiego 66 (☎310-21). Currently the most expensive of the hotels on this street, and also the liveliest, thanks in part to its casino.

Luxury hotels

The five Orbis hotels – which all have the standard international facilities, with prices to match – now have strong competition from two newly established private ventures.

Dwór Wazów, ul. Kiełbaśnicza 2 (☎44-16-33). This was originally opened as a restaurant complex (see "Eating and Drinking"), but now offers a limited number of very pricey double rooms and suites equipped with all the mod cons.

Monopol, ul. Modrzejewskiej 2 (☎370-41). Venerable old three-star Orbis hotel which has fallen into relative decay. Taking into account its character, location and lower prices, it's the best bet if you want a luxurious stay in the city.

Motel, ul. Lotnicza 151 (☎51-81-53). Orbis-run, and way to the northwest of the centre, by the terminus of trams #18, #21, #22 and #23 and on the route of #3 and #10.

Novotel, ul. Wyścigowa 35 (☎370-41). Modern four-star Orbis hotel at the extreme southern edge of the city near the terminus of tram #17.

Panorama, pl. Dominikański 8 (☎44-36-81). Another typical four-star Orbis-owned concrete box of a hostel with a much more central position on the eastern side of the city centre.

Saigon, ul. Wita Stwosza 22/23 (☎44-28-81). Brand-new Vietnamese-owned establishment, occupying the spruced-up premises of what was until recently the guesthouse of the local polytechnic. Prices are a good deal lower than in its Orbis competitors.

Wrocław, ul. Powstańców Śląskich 7 (☎61-46-51). The most prestigious and expensive of the Orbis group. Unfortunately, it's in a far from ideal situation southwest of the main railway station and on the route of trams #6, #7, #8, #13, #14 and #20.

Hostels, campsites and private rooms

The PTTK **tourist hostel** has an excellent location at ul. Szajnochy 11 (☎44-30-73). One of the city's two **youth hostels** is close to the main station at ul. Hugona Kołłątaja 20 (☎388-56); the other is at the northeastern edge of the city at ul. Kielczowska 43 (no phone), reached by bus #N. Nearby is one of the **campsites** (☎344-42), but the better one is on the east side of town near the Olympic Stadium at al. Ignacego Padarewskiego 35 (☎48-46-51) – trams #9, #16 and #17 go close. Chalets can also be rented at both sites. Information on summer **student hostels** is available at Almatur (see p.383).

Rooms in **private houses** can be booked at the *Biuro Zakwaterowania* at ul. Piłsudskiego 98 (☎44-41-01).

The City

Wrocław's central area, laid out in an approximate chessboard pattern, is delineated by the River Odra to the north and by the bow-shaped ul. Podwale – the latter following the former fortifications, whose ditch, now bordered by a shady park, still largely survives. The main concentration of shops – many housed in grandiose Stalinist buildings – and places of entertainment are found at the southern end of the centre and in the streets leading south to the train station; this is also where most of the new market traders have set up. Immediately bordering the Odra at the northern fringe of the centre is the university quarter. Beyond are a number of peaceful traffic-free islets, formerly sandbanks, linked to each other and to the mainland by graceful little bridges. The southern part of the much larger island of Ostrów Tumski, further east, is the city's ecclesiastical heart, with half a dozen churches and its own distinctive hubbub. Further north is an area of solidly nineteenth-century tenements, while the city's main green belt lies off the eastern side of the island.

The Rynek

Centre of the chessboard is occupied by the vast space of the **Rynek**. Unlike the central squares in Poland's other main cities, this is still open to traffic, though it may not remain so for much longer. No longer a place of commerce, it now has a tourist and leisure-orientated tone, being given over mainly to museums, restaurants, cafés, travel agencies and bookshops. Unfortunately, a lot of scaffolding is usually in evidence: although the historic buildings are well looked after, the pollution from local factories makes it necessary to clean them every few years.

The town hall

The magnificent **Town Hall**, symbol of the city for the last seven centuries, was originally a modest one-storey structure erected after the Tartar invasion, and was progressively expanded down the years. Its present appearance dates largely to the fifteenth-century high point of local prosperity, when the south aisle was

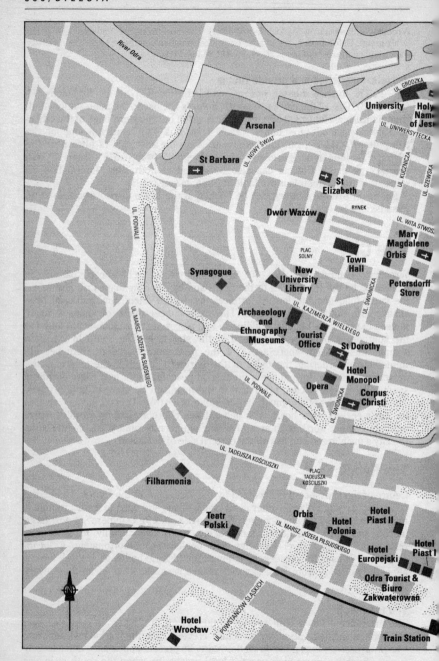

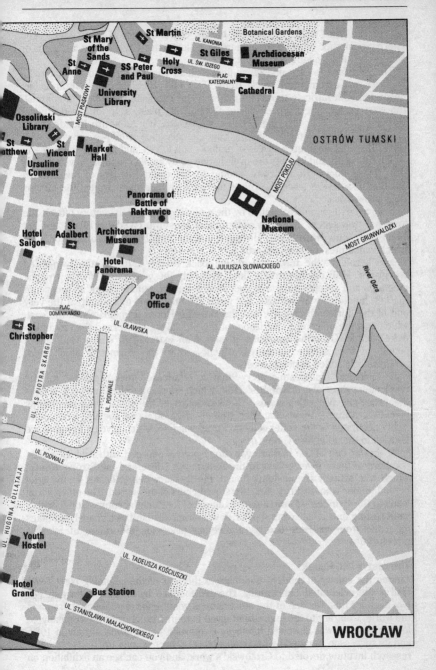

WROCŁAW

added and the whole decorated in an elaborate late Gothic style. The international mix of stylistic influences reflects the city's status as a major European trading centre at the time.

The **east facade** – the one which figures in all Wrocław's promotion material – features an astronomical clock from 1580 and an elaborate central gable, decorated with intricate terracotta patterns and exquisite pinnacles. In contrast, the west facade (the main entrance) is relatively plain, save for the octagonal Gothic belfry with its tapering Renaissance lantern. It's the **south facade** which is the real show stopper, with its huge Renaissance windows crowned with spire-like roofs, its filigree friezes of animals and foliage and its rich statuary – in which the saints and knights are overshadowed by an old crone and a yokel. This pair appear above the doorway leading to the vaulted cellars of the *Piwnica Świdnicka*, a tavern since the thirteenth century, and named after the famous beer of Świdnica.

Relieved of its municipal duties by the adjoining nineteenth-century offices, the town hall now serves as the city's **Historical Museum** (Wed–Fri 10am–4pm, Sat 11am–5pm, Sun 10am–6pm). However, it's the largely unaltered interior itself which constitutes the main attraction.

The kernel of the town hall, dating back to the 1270s, is the twin-aisled **Burghers' Hall** on the ground floor. Not only the venue for important public meetings and receptions, it also did service throughout the week as a covered market, functioning as such for 450 years. The next part to be built, at the very end of the thirteenth century, was the **Bailiff's Room** immediately to the east, which was the office and courtroom of the official who governed the city in the duke's name. Over the centuries, it gained an extravagant stellar vault and a couple of Renaissance doorways, which lead to the chambers which were progressively added as needs arose.

A tasteless nineteenth-century marble staircase goes upstairs to the resplendent three-aisled **Knights' Hall**, which supplanted the Burghers' Hall as the scene of civic celebrations. The keystones of the hall's vault are highly inventive, some of them character studies of all strata of society. Even more richly decorated is the coffer-ceilinged oriel window, which gives a Renaissance flourish to the otherwise Gothic design.

At the far end of the hall are two stone portals adorned with wild men. The southern of these gives access to the Alderman's Office and the **Strong Room**, which was actually the customs house, the treasury being located in the oriel behind, under whose wacky vault are stored coins of the period. The other portal leads to the **Princes' Room**, a pure example of fourteenth-century Gothic with a vault resting on a single central pillar. It was originally built as a chapel, but takes its name from its later use as a meeting place for the rulers of Silesia's principalities.

The rest of the Rynek

Among the cluster of modern buildings to the rear of the adjoining New Town Hall is the celebrated **Laboratory Theatre** founded by **Jerzy Grotowski**. For two decades this was one of the most famous centres for experimental drama in the world. Contrary to the impression given in tourist brochures, the company no longer exists: it was dissolved following Grotowski's emigration to Italy in 1982, and its successor, founded by his pupils, has also been wound up. In its place is a research institute devoted to Grotowski's work, and you can see an exhibition on the Laboratory Theatre if you ask at the offices down the alley to the left. The tiny studio theatre, on the second floor of the building, is still used – on average once a week – for experimental performances by visiting actors: check the billboard outside for details.

Of the mansions lining the main sides of the Rynek, those on the western side are the most distinguished and colourful. Among several built in the self-confident style of the Flemish Renaissance, no. 2, the **Griffin House** (Pod Gryfami), is particularly notable. Number 5, with a superb Mannerist facade, is known as the **Waza Court** (Dwór Wazów), in honour of the tradition that it was the place where King Zygmunt Waza stayed during secret negotiations for his marriage to Anna von Habsburg. The mansion has recently been converted into Wrocław's chief gourmet citadel (see "Eating and drinking").

Next door at no. 6 is the **House of the Golden Sun** (Pod Złotym Słońcem), behind whose Baroque frontage is a suite of Renaissance rooms containing the **Museum of the Art of Medal Making** (Tues–Sun 11am–6pm); its shop sells examples of the craft, which must be the classiest souvenirs in town. The last striking house in the block is no. 8, again Baroque but preserving parts of its Gothic predecessor; it's known as the **House of the Seven Electors** (Pod Siedmioma Elektorami), a reference to the seven grandees – one of whom was the King of Bohemia – who elected the Holy Roman Emperor.

West of the Rynek

At the southwest corner of the Rynek is a second, much smaller square, **plac Solny**. Its traditional function as a market has recently been revived, with flowers the dominant item, just as salt was in centuries past. Most of the buildings date back no further than the early nineteenth century, with pride of place taken by the Neoclassical former **Stock Exchange**, which occupies the lion's share of the southern side of the square.

Just off the northwest corner of the Rynek are two curious Baroque houses known as **Jaś i Małgosia**, linked by a gateway giving access to the close of **St Elizabeth**. Proving that brick is not an inherently dull material, this is the most beautiful of Wrocław's churches. Since the end of the fourteenth century its stately ninety-metre **tower**, which was under construction for 150 years, has been the city's most prominent landmark. Sadly, the church was burnt out under suspicious circumstances in 1976; restoration work has as yet a long way to go, and the whole close is still sealed off.

Facing the inner ring road just west of here is the only other block of old **burghers' houses** surviving in the city. Across the road and down ul. Antoniego Cieszyńskiego is the **Arsenal**, originally sixteenth century but considerably altered by the Prussians a couple of hundred years later. Most of it is dilapidated, but a restored section houses a splendidly fusty branch of the **Historical Museum** (Tues, Thurs & Fri 10am–4pm, Sat 11am–5pm, Sun 10am–6pm).

On the next street to the south, ul. Mikołaja, stands the Gothic church of **St Barbara**, which has been given to Russian Orthodox exiles from Lwów. If you come here on Saturday evening or on Sunday between 8am and 1pm you can hear their gravely beautiful sung services, which last for well over two hours. At other times, only the chapel entered from the cemetery on the north side of the church is kept open.

Two streets further to the south is the plain Baroque church of **St Anthony**, immediately to the east of which is the maze-like former **Jewish quarter**, whose inhabitants fled or were driven from their tenements during the Third Reich and were never to return. It seems that the postwar authorities have always been unsure as to how to react to this embarrassing legacy of the city's German past: a recent Polish guidebook to Wrocław makes no mention of the quarter's existence. The Neoclassical **Synagogue**, tucked away on a tiny square halfway down an alley, must once have been a handsome building, for all its shocking dereliction.*

South of the Rynek

Immediately to the east of the Jewish quarter is a part of the city built in obvious imitation of the chilly classical grandeur of the Prussian capital, Berlin. Indeed it was Carl Gotthard Langhans, designer of the Brandenburg Gate, who built the Neoclassical palace on the northern side of ul. Kazimierza Wielkiego, now the **New University Library**. He also had a hand in the monumental **Royal Palace** on the opposite side of the street. The central block of this now houses the **Archaeology Museum** (Tues, Wed & Fri 10am–4pm, Thurs 9am–4pm, Sat & Sun 10am–5pm), a dry survey of the prehistory of the region. Rather more fun is the **Ethnographical Museum** (Tues, Wed, Fri & Sat 10am–4pm, Thurs & Sun 11am–4pm) in the southern wing, a good place to visit if you have kids in tow.

The royal flavour of this quarter is continued in a different vein with the lofty Gothic church of **St Dorothy**, otherwise known as the "Church of Reconciliation". This was founded in 1351 by Charles IV, King of Bohemia and the future Holy Roman Emperor, in thanks for the conclusion of his negotiations with Kazimierz the Great, which secured Bohemia's rule over Silesia in return for a renunciation of its claim to Poland. Unlike most of Wrocław's other brick churches, this stayed in Catholic hands at the Reformation, becoming a Franciscan monastery. Its interior was whitewashed and littered with gigantic altars in the Baroque period, giving it a very different appearance from its neighbours, which still bear the hallmarks of four centuries of Protestant sobriety.

Behind St Dorothy's stands the **Opera House**, built by Carl Ferdinand Langhans in a faithful continuation of his father's Neoclassical style. Facing it is another example of fourteenth-century Gothic, **Corpus Christi** (Kościół Bożego Ciała), distinguished by the delicate brickwork of its facade porch and gable, and by the elaborate interior vaulting.

East of the Rynek

Returning to ul. Kazimierza Wielkiego and proceeding eastwards, you come to the part-Gothic, part-Renaissance church of **St Christopher**, used by the small minority of German-speaking Protestants who remain here. Behind it stretches the vast esplanade of **pl. Dominikański**. Until 1945 there was a heavily built-up quarter on this spot, but this was so badly damaged in the street fighting that it

---

*Another poignant reminder of the Judaic heritage is the **Jewish cemetery**, south of the main train station at ul. Ślęża 113, on the route of trams #9 and #19. However, although this is now officially recognised as a historical site of considerable significance, access is possible only at weekends.

had to be completely razed. There's some compensation for this loss in the unusually wide **view** of the old city which has been opened up as a result. Between here and the Rynek, at the junction of ul. Oławks and ul. Szewska, is a classic of twentieth-century design, the former **Petersdorff store** by Erich Mendelssohn. Built in 1927 and used for retail purposes ever since, it's the only one of several stores by the great German Expressionist architect to have survived, its counterparts all having fallen victim to modernising fads. The concrete and glass building relies for its effect on the interplay between the bold horizontals of the main street fronts and the dramatically projecting cylinder on the corner.

The twin-towered **St Mary Magdalene**, a block north of here, is another illustration of the seemingly inexhaustible diversity of Wrocław's brick churches: this one is unusual in having flying buttresses, giving it a French feel. A bevy of funeral plaques and epitaphs line its exterior, though the most striking adornment is the twelfth-century stone **portal** on the south side. This masterpiece of Romanesque carving (whose tympanum has been moved for conservation to the National Museum) came from the demolished abbey of Ołbin in the north of the city. At the opposite side of the church is a separate entrance to a beautifully pure Gothic chapel, now a commercial gallery.

At the northern end of pl. Dominikański are the buildings of the **Dominican Monastery**, centred on the thirteenth-century church of **St Adalbert** (św. Wojciecha), which is embellished with several lavish Gothic and Baroque chapels. A couple of blocks east, the gargantuan former **Bernardine Monastery** stands in splendid isolation; there's a particularly fine view of its barn-like church from the park beyond. The last important example of Gothic brickwork in the city, the monastery was begun in the mid-fifteenth century and finished only a few years before the Reformation, whereupon it was dissolved and the church used as a Protestant parish church. Severely damaged during the war, the church and cloisters have been painstakingly reconstructed to house the somewhat misleadingly named **Museum of Architecture** (Tues, Thurs & Fri 10am–4pm, Sat 11am–5pm, Sun 10am–6pm). In fact, this is a fascinating documentary record, using sculptural fragments and old photos, of the many historic buildings in the city which perished in the war.

Just east of here is the main post office building, with a **Museum of Posts and Telecommunications** (Mon–Sat 10am–3pm, Sun 11am–2.30pm) containing an impressive collection of stamps from the period of the Russian-controlled Kingdom of Poland; a couple of old mail coaches and all kinds of antiquated equipment are also on view.

The Racławice Panorama

Wrocław's best-loved sight, the **Panorama of the Battle of Racławice** (Tues–Sun 8am–7pm), is housed in a specially designed rotunda in the park by the Bernardine monastery. This gigantic painting, 120m long and 15m high, was commissioned in 1894 to celebrate the centenary of the defeat of the Russian army by the people's militia of Tadeusz Kościuszko near the village of Racławice, between Kraków and Kielce. Ultimately this triumph was in vain: the third and final Partition of Poland, which wiped it off the map altogether, occurred the following year. Nonetheless, it was viewed a century later by patriots of the still subdued nation as a supreme example of national will and self-sacrifice, which deserved a fitting memorial.

For a few decades, panorama painting created a sensation throughout Europe and North America, only to die abruptly with the advent of the cinema. In purely artistic terms, most surviving examples are of poor quality, but this one is an exception, due largely to the participation of **Wojciech Kossak**, one of the most accomplished painters Poland has produced. Amazingly, he and his co-worker, **Jan Styka**, completed the project in just nine months. Seven other painters were hired for the execution of details, but the vast majority of the canvas is the work of these two men.

The subsequent **history of the painting** is a remarkable saga which tells a great deal about the political situation of Poland. Despite an attempt by Polish-Americans to buy it and have it shipped across the Atlantic, it was placed on public view in Lwów, which was then part of Austria – the only one of the Partitioning powers which would have tolerated such nationalist propaganda. It remained there until 1944, when it was substantially damaged by a bomb. Although allocated to Wrocław, as the cultural heir of Lwów, it was then put into storage – officially because there were no specialists to restore it and no money to build the special structure the painting would need. The truth was that it was politically unacceptable to allow Poles to glory in their ancestors' slaughter of Russians.

That all changed with the events of 1980. Within five years the painting had been immaculately restored and was on display in a snazzy new building, with much attention being paid to natural foreground of soil, stones and shrubs, which greatly adds to the uncanny appearance of depth. Not only is it Poland's most hi-tech tourist attraction, it's also one of the most popular, an icon second only in national affection to The Black Madonna of Jasna Góra. Poles flock here in their droves, and you may have to book several hours in advance for a showing, which lasts for about 45 minutes: make sure you ask to hear the **English-language cassette** which explains all the details of the painting. Be warned that everyone is marched out as soon as the tape stops playing; you can, however, study the scale model of the battlefield downstairs at leisure.

The National Museum

At the opposite end of the park is the ponderously Prussian neo-Renaissance home of the **National Museum** (Tues, Wed, Fri & Sat 10am–4pm, Thurs & Sun 11am–6pm), which unites the collections of Breslau and Lwów. At the moment you need to come on two consecutive days to see everything: to save money, only half of the museum is open each day. However, one of the most important sections, **medieval stone sculpture**, is housed in the hall around the café and is open daily. Here you can see the delicately linear carving of *The Dormition of the Virgin* which formed the tympanum of the portal of St Mary Magdalene. The other major highlight is the poignant early fourteenth-century *Tomb of Henryk the Righteous*, one of the earliest funerary monuments to incorporate the subsequently popular motif of a group of weeping mourners.

On the first floor, one wing is devoted to an impressive display of Silesian **polychrome wood sculptures**. The most eye-catching exhibits are the colossal late fourteenth-century statues of saints from St Mary Magdalene, their raw power compensating for a lack of sophistication. More pleasing are the many examples of the "Beautiful Madonnas" which were for long a favourite subject in Central European sculpture: a particularly fine example is the one made in the early fifteenth century for the cathedral.

The **foreign paintings** in the opposite wing include only a few worth specially seeking out. Among these are Cranach's *Eve*, originally part of a scene showing her temptation of Adam which was cut up and repainted as two portraits of a burgher couple in the seventeenth century. *The Baptism of Christ* is a fine example of the art of Bartholomeus Spranger, the leading exponent of the erotic style favoured at the imperial court in Prague at the turn of the seventeenth century.

One of the star pieces in the comprehensive collection of **Polish paintings** on the top floor is the amazingly detailed *Entry of Chancellor Jerzy Ossoliński into Rome in 1633* by Bernardo Bellotto, best known for his documentary record of eighteenth-century Warsaw (see Chapter One). The other leading exhibit here is an unfinished blockbuster by Matejko, *Vows of King Jan Kazimierz Waza*. Set in Lwów Cathedral, it illustrates the monarch's pledge to improve the lot of the peasants at the end of the war against his invading Swedish kinsmen. Other works to look out for are Piotr Michałowski's *Napoleon on Horseback*, the *Fatherland Triptych* by Jacek Malczewski, and some mountain landscapes by Wojciech Gerson. A number of galleries are devoted to **contemporary arts and crafts**, much of it surprisingly daring for work executed under communist rule.

The University quarter

Wrocław's academic quarter can be reached in just a few minutes from the Rynek by ul. Kuźnicza, but the most atmospheric approach is to walk there from the National Museum along the south bank of the Odra, for a series of wonderfully peaceful **views** of the ecclesiastical quarter opposite.

Overlooking the Piaskowsky Bridge is the **Market Hall** (Hala Targowa), an early twentieth-century secular update of the idiom of the brick churches. It is piled with irresistible food and other goods, and boasts that it was equally replete even during martial law. From this point, the triangular-shaped university quarter, jam-packed with historic buildings, is clearly defined by two streets, ul. Uniwersytecka to the south and ul. Grodzka, which follows the Odra.

Along the northern side of the former are three religious houses. First is **St Vincent**, founded as a Franciscan monastery by Henryk the Pious not long before his death at the Battle of Legnica (see "Legnica", p.402). One of the grandest of the city's churches, it was severely damaged in the war and is not yet fully restored. Its Baroque monastic buildings overlooking the Odra are now used by the university. Henryk also founded the **Ursuline Convent** alongside, which served as the mausoleum of the Piasts, who ruled the city during its period as an independent duchy.

Last in the row is the fourteenth-century church of **St Matthew** (św. Macieja), containing the tomb and memorial portrait of the city's most famous literary figure, the seventeenth-century mystic poet Johann Scheffler – better known as **Angelus Silesius** ("the Silesian Angel"), the pseudonym he adopted after his conversion to Catholicism. Many of Scheffler's poems still enjoy worldwide popularity as hymns, though his epigrams (standards of any anthology of German verse) represent his finest achievement. Facing the south side of the church is the Renaissance palace of the Piasts of Opole, while across ul. Szewska is the Baroque residence of their cousins from Brzeg-Legnica; both are now used by the university.

Behind St Matthew's stands one of Wrocław's most distinguished buildings, the domed **Ossoliński Library**. Originally a hospital, it was erected in the last quarter of the seventeenth century and was designed by the Burgundian architect Jean Baptiste Mathey. The library collections are another legacy from Lwów, where they were assembled by the family whose name they still bear; among the many precious manuscripts is the original of the Polish national epic, Mickiewicz's *Pan Tadeusz*. Check on the boards outside for details of special exhibitions.

The elongated pl. Uniwersytecki begins on the southern side with a dignified eighteenth-century palace, **Dom Steffensa**, again owned by the university. Facing it is one of the most obviously Austrian features of the city, the **Church of the Holy Name of Jesus**, built at the end of the seventeenth century in the rash of Counter-Reformation religious building in the Habsburg lands. Its most arresting feature is the huge allegorical ceiling fresco by the most celebrated Austrian decorative painter of the day, Johann Michael Rottmayr.

Adjoining the church is the 171-metre-long facade of the Collegium Maximum of the **University**, founded in 1702 by Emperor Leopold I. The wide entrance portal bears a balcony adorned with statues symbolising various academic disciplines and attributes; more can be seen high above on the graceful little tower.

A frescoed staircase leads up to the main assembly hall or **Aula** (open daily 9am–3.30pm, but frequently closed). The only historic room which remains in the huge building, it's one of the greatest secular interiors of the Baroque age, fusing the elements of architecture, painting, sculpture and ornament into one bravura whole. Lording it from above the dais is a statue of the founder, armed, bejewelled and crowned with a laurel. The huge illusionistic **ceiling frescoes** by Christoph Handke show the *Apotheosis of Divine and Worldly Wisdom* above the gallery and auditorium, while the scene above the dais depicts the university being entrusted to the care of Christ and the Virgin Mary. On the wall spaces between the windows are richly framed oval portraits of the leading founders of the university, while the jambs are frescoed with *trompe l'oeil* likenesses of the great scholars of classical antiquity and the Middle Ages.

Wyspa Piasek, Ostrów Tumski and eastward

From the Market Hall, the Piaskowsky Bridge leads you out to the sandbank of **Wyspa Piasek**, about half the area of which is green, with a cluster of historic buildings crammed together in the centre. The first you come to on the right-hand side is the **University Library**, installed in an Augustinian monastery which was used as the Nazi military headquarters. Beside it is the fourteenth-century hall church of **St Mary of the Sands** (Kościół NMP na Piasku), dull on the outside, majestically vaulted inside. The aisles have an asymmetrical tripartite rib design known as the Piast vault, which is peculiar to this region. In the south aisle is the Romanesque tympanum from the previous church on the site, illustrating the dedication by its donor, Maria Włast. Across the road stands the Baroque church of **St Anne**, now used by a Uniate community from Lwów (see Chapter Three), and other parts of the Augustinian monastic complex, while at the far end of the islet are two old **mills**, known as *Maria i Feliks*.

Ostrów Tumski

The two elegant little painted bridges of Most Młyński and Most Tumski, which look as though they should belong in an ornamental garden, connect Wyspa Piasek with Ostrów Tumski. For those not already sated by medieval churches, there's a concentration of five more here, beginning just beyond Most Tumski with the fifteenth-century **SS. Peter and Paul**, behind which is the squat hexagonal **St Martin** of a couple of centuries earlier.

Far more prepossessing than these is the severe and imperious **Holy Cross and St Bartholomew**, which, with its massive bulk, giant buttresses and pair of dissimilar towers, looks like some great fortified monastery. In fact, it's really two churches, one on top of the other. The lower, dedicated to St Bartholomew, is more spacious and extensive than an ordinary crypt, but lacks the exhilarating loftiness of its partner upstairs. The complex was founded in 1288 by Duke Henryk the Righteous as his own mausoleum, but his tomb has now been removed to the National Museum. A highly elaborate Baroque **monument to St Jan Nepomuk** stands in the square outside; his life is illustrated in the column bas-reliefs.

Ulica Katedralny leads past several Baroque palaces (among which priests, monks and nuns are constantly scuttling) to the twin-towered **Cathedral**. Grievously damaged in 1945, this has been fully restored to its thirteenth-century form, but is not one of the more attractive of Wrocław's churches. The one exterior feature of note is the elaborate **porch**, though its sculptures, with the exception of two delicate reliefs, are mostly nineteenth-century pastiches. Three chapels behind the high altar make a visit to the dank and gloomy interior worthwhile. On the southern side is **St Elizabeth's Chapel**, built in the last two decades of the seventeenth century, its integrated architecture, frescoes and sculptures created by Italian followers of Bernini. Next comes the Gothic **Lady Chapel**, with the masterly Renaissance funerary plaque of Bishop Jan Roth by Peter Vischer of Nuremberg. Last in line is the **Corpus Christi Chapel**, a perfectly proportioned and subtly decorated Baroque gem, begun in 1716 by the Viennese court architect Fischer von Erlach. To see the chapels, you'll probably have to ask at the sacristy, or tag onto one of the organised groups passing through.

Opposite the northern side of the cathedral is the tiny thirteenth-century church of **St Giles** (św. Idziego), the only one in the city to have escaped destruction by the Tartars, and preserving some finely patterned brickwork. Down ul. Kanonia is the **Archdiocesan Museum** (Tues–Sun 10am–3pm), a sizeable and ramshackle collection of sacred artefacts. For a bit of relief from cultural indigestion, you can escape from the same street into the **Botanical Gardens** (Mon–Fri 8am–6pm or dusk, Sat & Sun 10am–6pm).

Ulica Szczytnicka leads eastwards to the elongated avenue of pl. Grunwaldzki, which gained notoriety in 1945 when it was converted into an airstrip to allow the defeated Nazi leaders to escape. At its southern end is the most famous of the city's bridges, **Most Grundwaldzki**, built in 1910.

East of Ostrów Tumski

Wrocław's most enticing stretch of greenery is the **Park Szczytnicki**, east of Ostrów Tumski, on the route of trams #1, #2, #4, #10 and #12. Its focal point is the **Hala Ludowa**, a huge hall built in 1913 to celebrate the centenary of the liberation of the city from Napoleon. Designed by Max Berg, the innovative municipal architect, it combines traditional Prussian solidity with a modernistic dash – the unsupported dome, with a diameter of 130 metres, is an audacious piece of engineering even by present-day standards. The hall is still used for exhibitions, sporting events and other spectaculars, but even if there's nothing on you can ask at the porter's desk to see inside. Around the Hala Ludowa are a number of striking colonnaded pavilions; these were built a few years earlier by Berg's teacher Hans Poelzig, who was responsible for making the city a leading centre of the *Deutscher Werkbund*, the German equivalent of the arts and crafts movement.

In the same park is a work by a yet more famous architect: the box-like **Kindergarten** with peeling whitewash is eastern Europe's only building by Le Corbusier. Along with the huge steel needle beside the hall, this is a legacy of the Exhibition of the Regained Territories, held here in 1948. Other delights in the park include an amphitheatre, a Japanese garden and pagoda, an artificial lake, and hundreds of different trees and shrubs – including oaks that are more than six hundred years old. Best of all is a sixteenth-century **wooden church**, brought here from Kędzierzyn in Upper Silesia. Its tower is particularly striking, especially the lower storey with its highly distinctive log construction, a form normally associated with the Ukraine. Across the road lie the **Zoological Gardens** (summer 9am–7pm, winter 9am–5pm), with the largest collection of wild animals in Poland.

Eating, drinking and entertainment

Wrocław has a good selection of places to eat and drink, most of which are within a relatively small area – the episcopal and university quarters are noticeably barren. All the Orbis hotels, plus some of those around the main station, have both a restaurant and a café, but although these are all safe bets, Wrocław is one city where you can generally eat better elsewhere. Nightlife isn't exactly a Wrocław strong point, but the city's theatre is maintaining its high reputation.

Restaurants

Dwór Wazów, Rynek 5. The "King's Restaurant" of this new complex is the best and most expensive in town, specialising in regal banquets with flambé meat dishes. Reservations recommended (☎44-16-33).

Dwór Wazów, ul. Kiełbaśnicza 6/7. The "Burghers' Restaurant", entered from the first street west of the Rynek, is just as recommendable as its pretentious stablemate, yet its prices are only marginally higher than those of the basic restaurants.

Piwnica Świdnicka, Rynek-Ratusz. This famous old restaurant under the Town Hall is a must, but beware of outrageously marked-up imported drinks which can easily double the price of a meal. Dancing in the evenings.

Saigon, ul. Wita Stwosza 22/23. The hotel restaurant appropriately specialises in Vietnamese food, expertly prepared in the traditional way.

Spiż, Rynek-Ratusz 2. At the time of writing, this new venture deserved to be regarded as the best restaurant in Wrocław. It incorporates Poland's first boutique brewery, with a strong dark beer, a light Pils and a tangy wheat beer all freshly made on the premises.

Zorba, Rynek-Ratusz. Tiny authentic Greek restaurant hidden away in the alley behind the New Town Hall. Open noon–6pm.

KDM, pl. Tadeusza Kościuszki 5/6. Much the best choice for inexpensive but hearty traditional dishes, serving Polish drinks only. Dancing in the evenings.

Bieriozka, ul. Marcelego Nowotki 13. Close to the Jewish quarter, the cuisine is supposedly Russian but there's little evidence of this.

Pod Chmielem, ul. Odrzańska 17. Beer hall serving high-quality food.

Grunwaldzka, pl. Grunwaldzki 6. Pick of the restaurants on Ostrów Tumski.

Snack bars

Kambuz, ul. Ruska 58. Excellent and reasonably priced little fish restaurant, with changing daily specials.

Pod Złoty Dzbanem, Rynek 23. Slightly upmarket snack bar.

Vega, Rynek 27a. The most conveniently sited of the city's milk bars.

Wojtus, Rynek 37. Very cheap and decent snack bar.

Pizzeria, Rynek 46/47. Specialises in pizzas, but with a range of hot snacks as well.

Miś, Kuźnicza 48. Milk bar close to the university quarter.

Wzorcowy, ul. Świerczewskiego 80. Best of the fast-food joints in the vicinity of the station.

Cafés

Dwór Wazów, Rynek 5. Situated above the restaurant, with a real palm-court atmosphere. There's also the alternative of sitting outside in the courtyard at the back.

Prospera, Rynek 28. Another first-floor café, with a predominantly young clientele.

Zak, Rynek-Ratusz 7. Has a tempting array of high-calorie desserts.

Małgosia, corner of Rynek and ul. Odrzańska. Relaxed basement café in one of Wrocław's most famous houses.

Monopol, ul. Modrzejewskiej 2. The hotel's *kawiarnia*, with its perfectly preserved Jugendstil wall paintings, carved wood and plaster mouldings, is an ideal place for a spot of relaxation.

Uni-café, pl. Uniwersytecki 11. Popular student hang-out in the shadow of the great University facade.

Tutti Frutti, pl. Tadeusza Kościuszki 1. Probably the most popular rendezvous point; frequently packed.

Pod Kalamburem, ul. Kuźnicza 29a. Beautiful Jugendstil decor, very low prices.

Saba, ul. św. Jadwigi. Housed in a splendid Baroque palace on Wyspa Piasek; one of the few refreshment spots in the episcopal quarter.

Cocktail Bar, ul. Komandorska 4a. Close to the station, with the best ice creams and milk shakes in town.

Entertainment and festivals

Outside the big hotels, lively **nightspots** in Wrocław are thin on the ground. The most obvious place to drink and dance the night away is *Winiarnia Bacchus* at no. 16 on the Rynek, which is open from 10pm to 5am. There's live music every evening at the *Rura* jazz club, ul. Łazienna 4, while the main student club, *Pałaczyk*, ul. Tadeusza Kościuszki 34, has discos each Saturday.

Despite the demise of Grotowski's famous studio, Wrocław remains a major **theatre** centre. Henryk Tomaszewski, a former associate of Grotowski, has built up an international reputation for his pantomime company, which performs in alternation with classic drama at the *Teatr Polski*, ul. Gabrieli Zapolskiej 3 (☎386-53). *Teatr Kameralny*, ul. Świdnicka 28 (☎44-63-01), is the other main venue for straight plays, while the experimental mantle has been taken up by

Kalambur, ul. Kuźnicza 29a (☎44-54-11). *Jedliniok*, a student song-and-dance ensemble decked out in colourful traditional costumes, perform at the *Teatr Gest*, pl. Grunwaldzki 63 (☎21-00-14). *Teatr Lalek*, pl. Teatralny 4 (☎44-12-17), is a celebrated puppet theatre: book well in advance for its regular weekend shows, which are invariably sold out. The city's annual **drama festivals** include one devoted to monologues in January, and a contemporary Polish play season in May and June.

There's a similarly wide choice in classical **music**. Both the *Opera*, ul. Świdnicka 35 (☎386-41), and the *Operetka Wrocławska*, ul. Pitsudskiego 67 (☎44-49-16), maintain high standards: tickets are easy to obtain and absurdly cheap by Western standards. Orchestral concerts and recitals take place regularly at the *Filharmonia*, ul. Pitsudskiego 19 (☎44-20-01).

Wrocław hosts two contrasting **international music festivals** each year: the renowned *Jazz on the Odra* in May, and *Wratislavia Cantans*, devoted to oratorios and cantatas, in September. There's also a festival of early music at the beginning of December.

Listings

Airline *LOT*, ul. Pitsudskiego 36 (☎363-76).

Bookshops Main concentration is on the Rynek, including one devoted to Russian and another to imported publications, both with many titles in English; others on ul. Świdnicka.

Car breakdown *PZMot*, ul. Jagiellończyka 18 (daily 6am–10pm; ☎981); *Polmozbyt*, pl. Grunwaldzki 47 (daily 7am–10pm; ☎954).

Car hire Orbis, Rynek 29 (☎347-80/326-65).

Petrol station The one at ul. Żmigrodzka is open 24hr and has a lead-free pump.

Post offices Head office is at ul. Zygmunta Krasińskiego 1; there's a branch at Rynek 28 and another, with a restricted 24-hr service, in the square in front of the main train station.

What's on Best source of information is the monthly *Informator Wrocławski*.

The Wrocław district

The administrative **district of Wrocław** – covering a roughly circular area, with the city itself at the centre – is predominantly rural, with the River Odra and its tributaries draining some of the most productive agricultural land in the country. Yet the scenery is very varied, ranging from an isolated massif in the southwest through several forests to a chain of small lakes in the northwest. Due to the extensive **public transport** network, Wrocław itself makes a perfectly adequate touring base, though there's a reasonable amount of basic **accommodation** elsewhere should you prefer to stay in a more tranquil location.

Ślęża and Sobótka

The flatness of the plain south of the Odra is abruptly broken some 30km from Wrocław by an isolated outcrop of rocks with two peaks, the higher of which is known as **Ślęża** (718m). One of the most enigmatic sites in Poland, Ślęża was used for pagan worship in Celtic times, and was later settled by the Slav tribe after whom the mountain – and Silesia itself – are named.

Ślęza is normally approached from **SOBÓTKA**, which is on the rail line and some bus routes to Świdnica. Between the bus terminal and the train station is the Gothic parish church, outside which stands the first of several curious ancient **sculptures** to be seen in the area – consisting of one stone placed across another, it's nicknamed *The Mushroom*. On the slopes of Ślęza there's a large and voluptuous statue of a woman with a fish, while the summit has a carved lion on it. Exactly what these carvings symbolise is not known: some certainly postdate the Christianisation of the area, but that hasn't prevented their association with pagan rites. Even though the site hasn't achieved the cult status of its English counterparts – Glastonbury, Avebury and Stonehenge – it's not exactly a place to look for quiet mystery, being enormously popular with day-trippers and often teeming with busloads of schoolkids.

Five separate **hiking trails** traverse the hillsides, some of them stony, so it's essential to wear shoes with a good grip. More than an hour is necessary for the busiest stretch, the direct ascent from Sobótka to the top of Ślęza by the route indicated by yellow signs. The summit is spoiled by a number of ugly buildings including the inevitable television tower, while the neo-Gothic chapel is a poor substitute for the castle and Augustinian monastery which once stood here. Recompense is provided in the form of the most extensive panoramic view in Silesia.

Should you wish to stay, there are a couple of **tourist hostels** in Sobótka: *Pod Misiem*, ul. Mickiewicza 7 (☎199), and *Pod Wieżycą*, ul. Żymierskiego 13 (☎147). At SULISTROWICE, 2km to the south, there's a **campsite** (☎604) with chalets. On Sobótka's main square is a bar which does very cheap meals; otherwise you'll have to stock up at the grocery shop.

Oleśnica

OLEŚNICA, 30km to the east of Wrocław, is today a market town of around 35,000 people, yet it was once the capital of a tiny principality. Some of the feel of an old ducal capital lingers on, largely owing to the **Castle** which still completely dominates the town. Raised in the fourteenth century, it was transformed in the sixteenth into a magnificent palace in the German Renaissance style for a member of the Bohemian royal family. The majority of the building is now taken up by offices, but there's also a small archaeological museum (Tues–Sun 10am–3pm).

The Gothic **Parish Church**, once the duke's chapel, is linked to the castle by a covered archway; other reminders of its ducal past are the grandiose tombs in the chancel. Oleśnica was a bastion of the Reformation, with the local Polish-speaking population seemingly as enthusiastic as their German overlords. Although the church has now been returned to the Catholics, its arrangement of wooden galleries is a legacy of the Protestant emphasis on preaching. The only other notable monument in Oleśnica is an extensive section of the **town walls**, including an impressive but unkempt gateway across from the bus station.

There are two **hotels** here: the one-star *Śląsk*, at no. 12 on the Rynek (☎20-54), and the three-star *Perla* at ul. Zawadzkiego 12 (☎35-19). Best choice for a meal is the *Piast* restaurant on the same square.

Trzebnica

TRZEBNICA, 24km north of Wrocław, is even smaller and more unassuming than Oleśnica, yet is another place with a long and distinguished history, having been granted a charter in 1202 by Duke Henryk the Bearded. It was his marriage to the German princess Saint Hedwig (known in Poland as Jadwiga) which was largely responsible for shifting Silesia towards a predominantly German culture, setting the trend for the next six centuries.

The couple established a **Cistercian convent** in the town, the sole monument of note. Built in the severe style favoured by this order – still Romanesque in shape and feel, but already with the Gothic pointed arch and ribbed vault – it was progressively remodelled and now has a predominantly Baroque appearance. A survival from the original building is the **portal**, which was found during excavation work and re-erected, half-hidden, behind the porch. Its sculptures, showing King David playing the harp to Bathsheba and a maidservant, are among the most refined European works of the thirteenth century. The northern doorway also survives, but is of a far lower standard of workmanship.

Inside the church, the main feature is the large Gothic **St Hedwig's Chapel** to the right of the choir. The princess, who spent her widowhood in the convent, was canonised in 1267, just 24 years after her death, whereupon this chapel was immediately built in her memory. In 1680, her simple marble and alabaster sepulchral slab was incorporated into a grandiose tomb, whose sides are lined with mourners. At the same time, a considerably less ostentatious memorial to her husband was placed in the choir, its entrance guarded by statues of Saint Hedwig and her even more celebrated niece, Saint Elizabeth of Hungary.

The only places to stay in Trzebnica are the three-star **motel** on ul. Prusicka (☎12-00-48) and the **campsite** (which also has chalets) at ul. Leśna 2 (☎12-12-26). There's a very basic **restaurant** opposite the convent, and a couple of even more basic snack bars in the town centre.

The Żmigród and Milicz lake district

North of Trzebnica lies a lake district with several nature reserves, centred on the small towns of ŻMIGRÓD and MILICZ, which both lie in the valley of the Barycza, a tributary of the Odra. The former is on the main rail line to Leszno and Poznań, the latter on a different northbound route.

Between Milicz and SULMIERZYCE, just over the Wielkopolska border, is one of Europe's most important **bird reserves**. Over 170 different water and moorland species breed in the area, while an even larger number use it as a stop-off point on their migration. Black and white storks, swans, herons, seagulls, cranes, cormorants and great crested grebes are among the species most likely to be seen, apart from the inevitable ducks and geese. If you're lucky, you might even be able to spot sea eagles, who spend the winter here. Autumn, as the birds prepare to leave, is the best season for a visit: they are less timid at this time and more likely to be seen in groups in the open countryside. There are marked trails throughout the area, and an observation tower at the Wzgórze Joanny (Joanna Hill) south of Milicz. Other parts of this lake district are **forest reserves**, in some of which wild boar and both red and fallow deer roam freely. Be warned, however, that the marshy soil often means that stretches of this countryside are impassable.

Until 1991, one of Poland's best-loved **narrow gauge railways** traversed the area. It started off from the tracks at the northeastern edge of Trzebnica, continued past the junction of PREDZKOWICE along the western fork to its terminus at Żmigród, before backtracking and taking the eastern fork via Milicz to the other terminus at Sulmierzyce, passing right through the bird sanctuary en route. This was long a popular trip with visiting train enthusiasts, but the line was hopelessly uneconomic to maintain, and the only surprise about its demise was how long it was delayed. There are hopes that, in the future, a preservation society will be able to revive the line for occasional excursion services: check the latest position on this with one of the tourist agencies in Wrocław.

Accommodation options are limited: Żmigród has a **tourist hostel**, *Żmigrodzianka*, at ul. Wojska Polskiego 5 (☎37-38), or alternatively a **campsite** with chalets can be found at ul. Poprzeczna 13 (☎412-15) in KARŁOWO, just south of Milicz.

Lubiąż

Set just back from the Odra, about 55km downstream from Wrocław and connected to it by fairly regular buses, the quiet village of LUBIĄŻ stands in the shadow of a **Cistercian abbey** which ranks as one of the largest and most impressive monastic complexes in central Europe. Originally founded by the Benedictines in the first half of the twelfth century, it was taken over by the Cistercians a generation later, and some medieval features survive, as is clearly apparent when viewing the abbey from the approach road.

However, the overwhelming impression is one of Baroque: the community flourished, both economically and culturally, in the aftermath of the disastrous Thirty Years' War, and was able to build itself palatial new headquarters, with over 300 halls and chambers. Silesia's greatest painter, **Michael Willmann** (see also "Krzeszów", p.416) lived here for four decades, carrying out a multiplicity of commissions for the province's religious houses. However, prosperity was short-lived: decline began in 1740, when Silesia came under the uncompromisingly Protestant rule of Frederick the Great's Prussia, and continued apace until secularisation in 1810. Since then, the complex has served as a mental hospital, stud farm, munitions factory, labour camp and storehouse, in the process drifting into a state of semi-dereliction. After the fall of communism, a foundation was established with the hope of attracting foreign capital to turn it into an international hotel and conference centre. Whether this will come to anything remains to be seen – appeals are still being made.

In the meantime, what has undoubtedly the potential to become one of Poland's leading tourist attractions has the merest trickle of visitors. The main reason for coming is to see the awesome exterior, and in particular the 223-metre-long **facade**, whose austere economy of ornament is interrupted only by the twin towers of the church. Unfortunately, the latter's interior (currently out of bounds for security reasons) was stripped of most of its rich furnishings during World War II, and a few small frescoes on the cupola of scenes from the lives of saints Benedict and Bernard are all that remain of Willmann's extensive decorative scheme. Most of the rest of the abbey is similarly inaccessible, but a few rooms in the north wing have been restored and are open as a **museum** (June–Sept Tues–Sat 10am–2pm, Sun 11am–5pm); these include the summer refectory, an elegant Baroque hall with pristine white stucco work and illusionist ceiling frescoes.

The village's parish church, **St Valentine** (św. Walentego), likewise Baroque, has an altarpiece by Willmann, *St Valentine Healing the Sick*. There's nowhere to stay, and only one café-restaurant, the very basic *Odrzanka*, located on the recently rechristened main street, ul. Willmanna.

AROUND SILESIA

Though much of the Silesian countryside is flat farmland, the scenery at the western edge of the province is its strongest draw. The **Karkonosze National Park** and the valleys around **Kłodzko** have some of Europe's best hiking country, along with a series of resorts offering everything from spa treatments to winter sports. None of the other old ducal capitals, such as **Legnica**, **Świdnica**, **Brzeg**, **Opole** and **Cieszyn**, is developed to anything like the same extent as Wrocław, and some still have an attractively small-town air. Many of the province's finest surviving monuments are to be found in these towns; other slightly less central sights are the medieval fortifications of **Paczków** and the Baroque monasteries of **Legnickie Pole** (close to Legnica) and **Krzeszów**. The southern part of the province is dominated by one of central Europe's largest conurbations, centred on **Katowice**; its heavy industry has been crucial to Poland's economy, but the failure to modernise has led to an environmental disaster which is currently one of the country's most challenging problems. A more modern economic infrastructure is emerging in **Bielska-Biała**, which lies further south in the part of Silesia which was retained by the Austrians until the end of World War I. It serves as a gateway to another mountain range popular with walkers, the **Beskid Śląski**.

Travelling by **public transport** should present few problems, but bear in mind that the varied terrain means that journeys often take even longer than usual. There's plentiful **accommodation** in the most popular areas, though choice in many other parts of the province is often restricted.

Legnica

In 1241 the Tartar hordes won a titanic battle 60km west of Wrocław against a combined army of Poles and Silesians, killing its commander, Duke Henryk the Pious. Silesia's subsequent division among Henryk's descendants into three separate duchies began a process of dismemberment which was thereafter to dog its history. One of the new capitals was **LEGNICA** , a fortified town a few kilometres from the battlefield, one of the few in the area to have escaped destruction. It remained a ducal seat until the last of the Piasts died in 1675, but by then its role as their main residence had been taken over by Brzeg.

Although often ravaged by fires and badly damaged in World War II, Legnica has maintained its role as one of Silesia's most important cities, and is nowadays a busy regional centre preserving a wide variety of monuments – admittedly interspersed with a fair amount of shoddy concrete – as evidence of its varied history.

The Town

If you're arriving at the **train station** to the northeast of the old city, or the **bus station** diagonally opposite, the main sights are best covered by a circular walk. Following either ul. Dworcowa (between the stations) or the parallel ul. Pocztowa (behind the bus station) to the right, you shortly come to the ample pl. Zamkowy, site of the early fifteenth-century **Głogów Gate** (one of only two surviving parts of the city wall) and the enormous **Castle**.

The latter is a bit of a mish-mash, and now houses administrative offices, with no interesting interiors to see. Nonetheless, it has some outstanding features, particularly the **gateway** in the form of a triumphal arch, the only surviving part of the Renaissance palace built here. Two towers survive in restored form from the earlier defensive castle, replaced by a Romantic pseudo-fortress designed by the great Berlin architect Karl Friedrich Schinkel.

Continuing down ul. Nowa, which offers the best overall view of the castle, you arrive at ul. Pantyzanow, the axis of a well-preserved Baroque quarter. On the right are the Jesuit buildings, with the church of **St John** and the college next door united in a single, sweeping facade. Protruding from the eastern side of the church, its orientation and brick Gothic architecture looking wholly out of place, is the presbytery of the thirteenth-century Franciscan monastery which formerly occupied the spot. It owes its survival to its function as the Piast mausoleum: inside you can see several sarcophagi, plus Baroque frescoes illustrating the history of Poland and Silesia under the dynasty.

Across the road stands the **Regional Museum** (Wed–Sun 11am–5pm), housed in the former mansion of the Cistercian monastery of Lubiąż. Another fine palace of the same epoch, the **Rycerska Academy**, can be found in the street immediately behind, ul. Chojnowska. Here also is the late fourteenth-century **Chojnow Tower** plus a small section of the medieval wall.

This same street runs into the elongated **Rynek**. Sadly, this has lost much of its character: the two rows of historic buildings placed back-to-back along the central part of the square are now set off by functional modern dwellings, which have transformed the Rynek from a public meeting place into a residential area. Eight arcaded Renaissance houses, all brightly coloured and some decorated with graffiti, have managed to survive. At the end of this block is the **Town Hall**, a restrained Baroque construction, while behind is the **Theatre**, built in the first half of the nineteenth century in a style reminiscent of a Florentine palazzo. There's also a fine but blackened eighteenth-century fountain dedicated to Neptune.

The far end of the square is closed by the large twin-towered brick church of **SS Peter and Paul**, with its fairytale neo-Gothic exterior, which fits very well with the monumental turn-of-the-century buildings in and around the small pl. Chopina on its south side. Two lovely fourteenth-century portals have survived: the northern one, featuring a tympanum of *The Adoration of the Magi* flanked by statues of the church's two patrons, overshadows the more prominent facade doorway with its *Madonna and Child*. The furnishings of the interior, which largely retains its original form, range from a late thirteenth-century font with bronze bas-reliefs to an elaborate Renaissance pulpit and a theatrical Baroque high altar.

Ulica Piotra i Pawła and ul. Rosenbergów both lead to pl. Mariacki, with the brick Gothic church of **Our Lady**, whose gaunt exterior brings to mind military rather than ecclesiastical architecture. Notwithstanding its dedication, it's still the place of worship of the remnant of the Protestant community, who were in a majority here until 1945.

Legnickie Pole

LEGNICKIE POLE, 9km southeast of the city, is on the site of the great battleground; it can be reached by any bus going to Jawor, or by the municipal services #9, #16, #17 and #20. Extensive repair work was carried out in 1991 on the village's monuments in conjunction with the 750th anniversary of the battle.

A church was erected on the spot where Henryk the Pious's body was found (according to tradition, his mother was only able to identify the headless corpse from his six-toed feet), and in time this became a Benedictine monastery – popularly but implausibly said to be the rustic Gothic building in the centre of the village. A Protestant parish for four centuries, the church has been secularised to house the **Museum of the Battle of Legnica** (Tues–Sun 11am–5pm), which includes diagrams and mock-ups of the conflict and a copy of Henryk's tomb (the original is in Wrocław's National Museum).

The Benedictines, who were evicted during the Reformation, returned to Legnickie Pole in the early eighteenth century and constructed the **Abbey** (Tues–Sun 11am–5pm) directly facing their alleged former premises. It was built by **Kilian Ignaz Dientzenhofer**, the creator of much of Prague's magnificent Baroque architecture. His characteristic use of varied geometric shapes and the interplay of concave and convex surfaces is well illustrated here. The interior of the church, an oval nave plus an elongated apse, is exceptionally bright, an effect achieved by the combination of white walls and very large windows. Forming a perfect complement to the architecture are the bravura **frescoes** covering the vault by the Bavarian **Cosmos Damian Asam**. Look out for the scene over the organ gallery, which shows the Tartars hoisting Henryk's head on a stake and celebrating their victory, while the duke's mother and wife mourn over his body.

Since the second dissolution of the monastery in 1810, the **monastic buildings** (currently a women's hospice) have been put to a variety of uses. For nearly a century they served as a Prussian military academy; its star graduate was Paul von Hindenburg, German commander-in-chief during World War I and president from 1925 until his death in 1934.

Practicalities

In Legnica, the only **hotel** is the four-star *Cuprum* (☎285-44) at no. 7 on ul. Skarbowa, which leads from pl. Mariacki back to the bus station; this also has the best restaurant and café in town. The other accommodation possibility is the **youth hostel** at ul. Jordana 17 (☎254-12). Alternative places to **eat** and **drink**, on the other hand, are reasonably plentiful. Recommendable **restaurants** include *Adria*, Rynek 27, *Tivoli*, ul. Złotoryjska 31, and *Polonia*, ul. Skarbowa 1; the best **cafés** are *W–Z*, ul. Wrocławska 5, and *Hortex*, ul. NMP 11. For a lively evening atmosphere, try the **nightclub** at ul. Jaworzyńska 149, which features jazz and disco music. The **Orbis** office is due east of pl. Mariacki at ul. Wrocławska 10/18 (☎229-23). Several more travel bureaux can be found around the Rynek; you should be able to pick up leaflets on the town, though most likely only in Polish.

In Legnickie Pole there's an officially designated **restaurant**, *Rycerska*, on the main square; don't expect too much from the food, though there's draught beer on tap. At the edge of the village is the only **campsite** (☎823-97) in the Legnica area; it also has chalets for rent.

Northwestern Silesia

Northwestern Silesia is little visited and contains nothing in the way of obvious tourist attractions. However, it has a few old towns which are, for very different reasons, worth a passing look.

Głogów

GŁOGÓW, 60km north of Legnica, is a name which crops up often in history books. The capital of one of the many Piast duchies, it has produced a remarkable number of influential citizens for a place whose population has never numbered more than a few thousand. These include Jan of Głogów, teacher of Copernicus; Andreas Gryphius, the greatest German poet and dramatist of the seventeenth century; and Arnold Zweig, the Jewish novelist who became a leading intellectual figure in Israel and then in the German Democratic Republic. The town was also the scene of one of E.T.A. Hoffmann's chilling fantasies on the theme of schizophrenia, *The Jesuit Chapel at G___*.

In 1945, Głogów was turned into a fortress by the retreating Nazis and completely destroyed. Visiting it today is still a shocking experience. The historic centre, which lies about ten minutes' walk to the left of the station, has never been rebuilt and stands as an overgrown wasteland, around which has sprung up a modern town with no real heart to it. An abortive attempt was made to patch up the parish church, formerly a handsome piece of brick Gothic architecture, but clearly it was too badly damaged for full restoration. However, the **Jesuit College** described in Hoffmann's story has somehow managed to survive, rising in defiance above the desolation. Inside, a photographic exhibition provides a poignant documentary record of the appearance of the town before its destruction.

There's certainly no reason for wanting to stay overnight in Głogów, but if you do find yourself needing a bed, there's a good **hotel**, *Kasztelanski*, at the edge of the destroyed old town on pl. Konstytucji 3 Maja (☎332-216). Its restaurant is the best place for a meal, while there's a pleasant café in the *Dom Kultury* on the same square, featuring live music at weekends.

Zielona Góra

The wartime experience of **ZIELONA GÓRA** , 60km northwest of Głogów, was very different. Hardly damaged at all, it has grown to become an important centre for the machine and textile industries since passing into Polish hands, and now has a population numbering some 100,000. It also has a somewhat esoteric claim to fame as being the only place in Poland where wine is produced.

Although it lacks any outstanding sights, the whole central area of Zielona Góra has a certain novelty value, full of examples of the sorts of buildings which in most other central European towns tended to fall to the bulldozers if they hadn't already been destroyed in the war. It's a patchwork of the architectural styles practised in turn-of-the-century Germany, with the solidly historicist Wilhelmine rubbing shoulders with the experimental forms of Jugendstil. There are also a few older landmarks in the midst of these, including a couple of towers surviving from the fifteenth-century ramparts, the Gothic church of St Hedwig and the much-remodelled Renaissance town hall in the centre of the Rynek. Most imposing of all is the large **Parish Church**, an eighteenth-century example of the Silesian penchant for half-timbered ecclesiastical buildings.

Practicalities

Orbis obviously think well of Zielona Góra, as they have a prestigious international **hotel**, the *Polan*, a couple of blocks east of the station at ul. Staszica

9a (☎700-91). Alternatively, there's a cheaper hotel, *Śródmiejski*, right in the town centre at ul. Żeromskiego 23 (☎44-71), and a **youth hostel**, open April to October inclusive, just to the southeast of the station at ul. Wyspiańskiego 58 (☎708-40). The Orbis travel bureau is at ul. Świerczewskiego 28 (☎659-58), while **Almatur** is at ul. Westerplatte 30 (☎728-67). Pick of the many **restaurants** in the town are *Topaz* on ul. Boharetów Westerplatte and *Ostoja* on ul. Poznańska. The best time for a visit here is September, when there are **festivals** devoted to the wine harvest and to international song and dance troupes.

Żagań

Some 40km west of Głogów, 50km southwest of Zielona Góra, and reachable from either by train, is the old ducal capital of **ŻAGAŃ**. Like Głogów it suffered badly in World War II, when it gained international notoriety as the site of the Nazi prisoner-of-war camp, Stalag VIIIC. Although it has been partially restored, it stands very much in the shadow of what was an exceptionally illustrious past for such a small town: the duchy was once conferred on Alfred von Wallenstein, the military genius who had commanded the imperial forces in the Thirty Years' War; the astronomer Johannes Kepler passed the last two years of his life there, as Wallenstein's guest; while the great French novelist Stendhal was a later resident.

Starting at the western end of the compact centre, you first see the finest of the half-dozen historic churches, **St Mary**, formerly part of an Augustinian monastery. Originally a high gabled Gothic hall church from the fourteenth century, its interior, which boasts a beautiful Renaissance altar dedicated to the Holy Trinity, was completely remodelled in the Baroque epoch. Further east is the first of two large market squares, the Old Rynek, lined with a number of sixteenth- and seventeenth-century burghers' mansions, and the Gothic **Town Hall**, to which a Florentine-style loggia was appended last century. Beyond is the larger New Rynek, with the Jesuit church on the north side. Set in a park just to the south is the **Palace**, begun in the Renaissance period by order of Wallenstein, but mostly built in an extremely Italianate Baroque style later in the seventeenth century. It was badly desecrated during World War II, when its rich interiors were destroyed; it's now used as a cultural centre.

On ul. Ilwianska in the suburb of Stary Żagan is the site of Stalag VIIIC, now designated the **Museum of Martyrology** (daily 10am–5pm). Some 200,000 prisoners from all over the world, most of them officers, were incarcerated here, and the film *The Great Escape* is based on a true episode in its history. A monument commemorates those who were murdered, while a special room displays prisoners' beds along with samples of their hair, glasses, clothes and documents, plus photographs and a plastic model of how the camp once looked.

Practicalities

Żagań has three **hotels**, of which the most recommendable is the parkside *Mylnowka*, ul. Zelazna 2a (☎30-74); alternatives are the more upmarket *Nadbrodzańki*, ul. Kilińskiego 1 (☎32-20 or 34-47), and the basic basic *Dom Turysty*, pl. Konstytucji 1 (☎34-67). The best places to **eat** and **drink** are to be found in the first two hotels; otherwise try *Staromiejska* on the Rynek or *Kaprys* in the precinct on ul. Warszawska. Each May, the Crystal Room of the Palace is put to appropriate use as the venue for the main local **festival**, the all-Polish Dance competition.

Jelenia Góra and around

JELENIA GÓRA, which lies 60km southwest of Legnica and some 110km from Wrocław, is the gateway to one of Poland's most popular holiday and recreation areas, the Karkonosze National Park. Its name means "Deer Mountain", but the rusticity this implies is scarcely reflected in the town itself, a manufacturing centre for the past five centuries. Founded as a fortress in 1108 by King Bolesław the Wrymouth, Jelenia Góra came to prominence in the Middle Ages through glass and iron production, with high-quality textiles taking over as the cornerstone of its economy in the seventeenth century. With this solid base, it was hardly surprising that, after it came under Prussian control, the town was at the forefront of the German Industrial Revolution.

The Town

Some of Jelenia Góra's present-day factories look stuck in a nineteenth-century time-warp, and pollution is a major problem. Thankfully, however, industry has always been confined to the peripheries, and the traffic-free historic centre is remarkably well-preserved. Even in a country with plenty of prepossessing central squares, the plac Ratuszowy is outstanding. Not the least of its attractions is that it's neither a museum-piece nor the main commercial centre: most of the businesses are restaurants and cafés, while the tall mansions are now subdivided into flats. Although their architecture ranges from the late Renaissance via Baroque to Neoclassical, the houses form an unusually coherent group, all having whitewashed walls and an arcaded front at street level. The latter feature, which provides protection against the harsh winter climate, is highly unusual for Poland. Occupying the familiar central position on the square is the large mid-eighteenth-century Town Hall. Its graceful tower is one of the dominant features of the skyline, while the unpainted stonework provides the best possible foil to the houses.

To the northeast of pl. Ratuszowy rises the slender belfry of the Gothic parish church of SS Erasmus and Pancras. Epitaphs to leading local families adorn the outer walls, while the inside is chock-full of Renaissance and Baroque furnishings. Yet another eye-catching tower can be seen just to the east, at the point where the main shopping thoroughfare, ul. Marii Konopnickiej, changes its name to ul. 1 Maja. Originally part of the sixteenth-century fortifications, it was taken over a couple of centuries later to serve as the belfry of St Anne's Chapel. The only other survivor of the town wall is the tower off ul. Jasna, the street which forms a westward continuation of pl. Ratuszowy.

Continuing down ul. 1 Maja, you come in a couple of minutes to the Baroque chapel of Our Lady; it's normally kept locked, but if you happen to be here on a Sunday morning you can drop in to hear the fervent singing of its Russian Orthodox congregation. At the end of the street, enclosed in a walled park-like cemetery, is another Baroque church, Holy Cross, built in the early eighteenth century by a Swedish architect, Martin Franze, on the model of St Catherine's in Stockholm. Though sober from the outside, the double-galleried interior is richly decorated with *trompe l'oeil* frescoes.

From the bustling al. 15 Grudnia, which skirts the old town to the south, ul. Jana Matejki leads to the District Museum (Tues, Thurs & Fri 9am–3.30pm,

Wed, Sat & Sun 9am–5pm), set just below the wooded Kościuszki hill. Apart from temporary exhibitions, the display space here is given over to the history of **glass** from antiquity to the present day, with due emphasis on local examples and a particularly impressive twentieth-century section.

For the best **viewpoint** in town, go westwards from pl. Ratuszowy along ul. Jasna, then cross ul. Podwale and continue down ul. Obrońców Pokoju into the woods and over the bridge. Several paths lead up the hill, which is crowned with an outlook tower that's permanently open. From the top there's a sweeping view of Jelenia Góra and the surrounding countryside.

Jelenia Góra practicalities

The main **train station** is about fifteen minutes' walk east of the centre at the far end of ul. 1 Maja. Local buses plus a few services to nearby towns leave from the bays in front, but the **bus station** for all inter-city departures is at the opposite end of town off ul. Obrońców Pokoju.

PTTK have a tourist information bureau at al. Wojska Polskiego 40 (Mon–Sat 8am–4pm; ☎220-00). English is spoken at the **Orbis** office, ul. 1 Maja 1 (Mon–Fri 8am–5pm, Sat 8am–1/2pm; ☎262-11); ask here if you want a room in a **private house** in Jelenia Góra or one of the nearby resorts. Other services available here include the hiring of mountain guides, and flights by hang-glider or helicopter (not outrageously expensive if you're in a large enough group).

Another Orbis agency is in the spanking new five-star **hotel**, *Jelenia Góra* (☎240-81), located at ul. Gen. Karola Świerczewskiego 63 at the southeastern edge of town, on the road to Kowary and Karpacz. This is one of the best-equipped hotels in Poland, with prices to match. The considerably less glamorous alternatives are *Europa* at ul. 1 Maja 16 (☎232-21) and *Spartacus*, ul. Świerczewskiego 42 (☎249-12) in the park between *Hotel Jelenia Góra* and the town centre; the park also has the only **campsite** (☎269-42). Of the two **youth hostels**, *Bartek*, ul. Bartka Zwycięzcy 10 (☎257-46), is handy for the station, whereas *Michałek* is inconveniently sited to the far north of town at ul. Wiejska 86 (☎241-55). There's also a **PTTK hostel** at ul. 1 Maja 88 (☎230-59).

On the western side of pl. Ratuszowy are three **restaurants**, *Pokusa*, *Retro* and *Pod Smokiem*, all with outside tables. The last-named, specialising in flambé dishes, is the pick of the trio, though its local nickname of "the Chinese restaurant" refers to the decor rather than to the cooking. Fiery Hungarian-style dishes are served at *Tokaj* on ul. Pocztowa, just round the corner from another good choice, *Staropolska Karczma* on ul. 1 Maja. There are plenty of **snack bars** and **cafés** in the centre, among which *Hortex* on pl. Ratuszowy is particularly good.

Cultural life centres on the Secessionist-style **Cyprian Norwid Theatre** at al. Wojska Polskiego 38 (☎232-74), whose main season is in the autumn. Jelenia Góra hosts concerts of chamber and organ music in July, while early to mid-August sees a **festival** of street theatre.

Cieplice Śląskie-Zdrój

The municipal boundaries of Jelenia Góra have recently been extended to incorporate a number of communities to the south, nearest of which is the old spa town of **CIEPLICE ŚLĄSKIE-ZDRÓJ**, 8km away. Local bus #9 passes through the centre of Cieplice; #7, #8 and #15 stop on the western side of town, enabling you to connect with buses and trains to Szklarska Poręba (see "The Karkonosze Mountains" overleaf), while #4, #13 and #14 stop on the eastern side, with bus connections to the other main resort in the range, Karpacz.

Although it has a number of modern sanatoria, along with concrete apartment blocks in the suburbs, Cieplice seems to bask in the aura of an altogether less pressurised age. To catch this atmosphere at its most potent, attend one of the regular concerts of **Viennese music** in the spa park's delightful Neoclassical **theatre**.

The broad main street of Cieplice is oddly designated as a square – plac Piatowski. Its main building is the large eighteenth-century **Schaffgotsch Palace**, named after the German grandees who formerly owned much of the town. There are also a couple of Baroque **parish churches** – the one for the Catholics stands in a close at the western end of the street and is generally open, whereas its Protestant counterpart to the east of the palace is locked except on Sunday mornings. In the Park Norweski, which continues the spa park on the southern side of the River Podgórna, is a small **Ornithological Museum** (Tues–Sun 9am–4pm).

Practicalities

At the western edge of the spa park at ul. Cervi 11 is the **hotel** *Cieplice* (☎510-41); until recently it was the most prestigious in the region though its facilities (only light meals available) hardly justify its four-star rating. There's also a **tourist hostel**, *Pod Różami*, at pl. Piatowski 26 (☎514-54). The **campsite**, *Rataja* (☎525-66), is near the Orle train station outside town to the southwest, on the routes of buses #7 and #15. In the assembly rooms beside the spa theatre is a good **café** with a cold buffet service and dancing in the evenings. The hostel has a **restaurant**, and there's a decent **milk bar** at the western end of pl. Piatowski, but you'll have to go to Jelenia Góra if you want a full meal later than 5pm.

Sobieszów

Buses #7, #9 and #15 all continue the few kilometres south to **SOBIESZÓW**. Once again, there are two Baroque **parish churches**, both located off the main ul. Cieplicka: the one built for the Protestants is appropriately plain, while that for the Catholics is exuberantly decorated. In an isolated location on the southeastern outskirts is the **Regional Museum** (Tues–Sun 9am–4pm), with displays on the local geology, flora and fauna.

From there, the red and black trails offer a choice of ascents to **Chojnik Castle** (Tues–Sun 9am–4pm), which sits resplendently astride the wooded hill of the same name. It's actually much further from town than it appears – allow about an hour for the ascent. Founded in the mid-fourteenth century, the castle is celebrated in legend as the home of a beautiful man-hating princess who insisted that any suitor had to travel through a treacherous ravine in order to win her hand. Many perished in the attempt: when one finally succeeded, the princess chose to jump into the ravine herself in preference to marriage. The castle was badly damaged in 1675, not long after the addition of its drawbridge and the Renaissance ornamentation on top of the walls. Yet, despite its ruined state, enough remains to give a good illustration of the layout of the medieval feudal stronghold it once was, with the added bonus of a magnificent **view** from the round tower.

Practicalities

The castle houses a restaurant and **tourist hostel** (☎535-35), though its isolated position makes the novelty value the sole reason for staying. Sobieszów itself has another hostel, *Nad Wrzosówką* at ul. Cieplicka 213 (☎536-27), along with a **campsite**, *Łazienkowska*, at the northern edge of the town centre on ul. Łazienkowska. Also on ul. Cieplicka are a **restaurant**, *Ostoja*, and a couple of snack bars.

Jagniątków

At the very edge of the Karkonosze, just south of Sobieszów but beyond the municipal boundaries of Jelenia Góra, is the village of **JAGNIĄTKÓW**, once home of the German novelist and playwright **Gerhart Hauptmann**, winner of the 1912 Nobel Prize for Literature. Having fallen foul of the Nazis he formerly supported, Hauptmann spent his last years in this isolated corner of his native province, staying on even when it came under Polish rule in 1945. The psychological novels he wrote here have worn less well than his earlier naturalistic works, notably his drama of Silesian industrial life, *The Weavers*. **Hauptmann's house**, a spectacular

---

HIKING IN THE NATIONAL PARK

The 1:30,000 **map** of the National Park, available from kiosks and travel offices, shows all the paths and viewpoints and is a must if you intend doing any serious walking. Special care should to be taken in winter, even though the area is patrolled by mountain rescue teams with St Bernard dogs, as many paths are impassable or dangerous for months on end; the map shows avalanche zones.

No matter what the season, the range is notorious for extremely changeable weather with an **average annual temperature of around freezing point**, so make sure you take warm clothing even on a sunny summer's day. **Mist** hangs around on about 300 days in the year, so always stick to the marked paths and if necessary stop to shelter in the refuge huts which are liberally sprinkled throughout the area. Finally, many of the trails pass sections of the **frontier** with the Czech Republic and often converge with paths coming up from the opposite side of the border. These are generally controlled by guards, but in any event resist the temptation to cross: this is still illegal and the signposts are clear enough to make any protestations of linguistic ignorance untenable as an excuse.

Some routes

Other than relatively short circular walks around Karpacz and Szklarska Poręba, there is really only one obvious hiking route which links the two; this is the main ridge route from Śnieżka west to Szrenica. Not surprisingly, this is a very well-trodden route, popular with large groups of guitar-toting students, but it is worth putting up with the crowds.

Śnieżka is most easily reached by the chair lift to Kopa but there are also various paths. The one marked with red stripes from Biały Jar follows the stream to the chair lift terminal and then forks right near the *Orlinek* hotel onto an unmade track which climbs steadily 40 minutes to a junction with a yellow path and a rather dull refuge. The path continues above the treeline and after some steeper zigzags reaches the Pod Śnieżka refuge, roughly another 40 minutes later: the refuge is less than 15 minutes above the Kopa chair lift terminal, following the black stripes. From here the side-trip east to the summit of Śnieżka takes under 20 minutes each way by the direct red path. There's also an easier route, the "Jubilee Way", marked

Jugendstil mansion with a Great Hall lined with giant murals, is now a convalescent home for child victims of industrial pollution from the Katowice conurbation. You're free to visit the memorial room, with its first editions of his major works.

The Karkonosze Mountains

The **Karkonosze** (still better known by their German name of Riesengebirge, or "Giants' Mountains") are the highest and best-known part of the chain known as the Sudeten (or Sudety) mountains, which stretch 300km northwest from the Beskids, forming a natural border between Silesia and Bohemia. Known for its raw, highly volatile climate, the predominantly granite Karkonosze range rises abruptly on the Polish side, and its lower slopes are quite heavily forested with fir, beech, birch and pine, though these are suffering badly from the "dying forest syndrome" which is so endemic in central Europe. At around 1100m, these trees give way to dwarf mountain pines and alpine plants, some of them imported. Above 1350m the summits have an unusually stark appearance for this part of Europe.

with blue stripes, which goes round the north side of the peak and reaches the top from the east.

For Szklarska Poręba take the granite-cobbled track west, marked with initially black, then blue and red stripes. After 20 minutes this reaches Spalona Strażnica, where the main track (marked with blue stripes) turns right, dropping to the big Strzecha Akademicka and Samotnia refuges, and to the Wang Chapel. The red path continues across an open plateau and past the glacial lakes of Mały Stam and Wielki Stam to the north. At the third viewpoint (25 minutes on) there is an emergency shelter; most walkers turn right soon after this to return to Karpacz, either following green markings to join the blue track, or ten minutes west (at the Słonecznik rocks) following yellow markings via the Pielgrzmy (pilgrims) outcrops.

From Słoneczik the path is almost level until it drops after half an hour to the Karkonoska pass and the Odrodzenie refuge. The huge building with car park is the Czech Spindlerovka *bouda*, with waitress service and buses down to Spindleruv Mlyn, the main resort of the Czech Krkonose (but note warnings above). The red markings continue along a broad track and then a road following the border for 30 minutes to two more Czech refuges, Moravská *bouda* and Petrova *bouda*. The track climbs for 20 minutes to the Śląskie Kamienie or Silesian Rocks, and continues fairly easily, above impressive cirques to the north and past paths down to the villages of Jagniatków and Michałowice for 50 minutes to reach the Snieżne Kotły TV tower, dwarfing what would otherwise be impressive rock outcrops.

After a further 35 minutes on a gravel road across open moorland, you can loop right (after the Trzy Świnki outcrops) to the Szrenica observatory and the upper terminal of the chair lift from Szklarska Poręba (with snack bar) and return to the red route following black markings. From here it takes 15 minutes along an even better road to drop away from the border and reach the Hala Szrenicka refuge.

To reach Szklarska Poręba from here, the red stripe markings simply follow the unmade road, forking right after 30 minutes at the Park boundary and the Kamienczyka waterfall, beautifully framed by trees and the most picturesque falls in the Karkonosze. Another quarter-hour brings you out just above the Julia Crystal works, a pleasant ten minutes' walk west of the town centre.

Primarily renowned as **hiking** terrain, these mountains formerly rivalled the Black Forest as Germany's most popular scenic region. Set beneath dramatically changing skies, its peaks often blanketed by mist, the range strongly stirred the German Romantic imagination and was hauntingly depicted by the greatest artist of the movement, Caspar David Friedrich. From the amount of German you hear spoken in the resorts, and from the turned-up *lederhosen* and feathered hats worn by so many hikers, you might think that this area still belonged to Germany. Yet the Polish tourist authorities aren't complaining at the Germanic hordes who pour in to take advantage of the low prices and in many cases to cast wistful glances at the former homes of their ancestors. The collapse of communism has depleted the system of trade union holiday homes and reduced the custom from other eastern Europeans, who are now free to travel wherever they please. As a result, even with the steady flow of BMW-drivers, the Karkonosze resorts find themselves facing the prospect of economic ruin. The easiest way to avert this, and the one currently being heavily touted, would be to develop the area's potential as a **winter sports** region; it has some facilities at the moment, but they are still fairly rudimentary.

The upper reaches of the Karkonosze have been designated as a **National Park**. Lying just outside its boundaries are two sprawling resorts, Szklarska Poręba and Karpacz, which make the most convenient centres for exploring the mountains, though Jelenia Góra and its satellites are viable alternatives. As the area is relatively compact – the total length of the Karkanosze is no more than 37km – and the public transport system good (if circuitous), there's no need to use more than one base.

Szklarska Poręba

SZKLARSKA PORĘBA lies 18km southwest of Jelenia Góra and just to the west of a major international road crossing into the Czech Republic. It can be reached from Jelenia Góra either by train, depositing you at the station on the northern heights of the town, or by bus, whose terminus is at the eastern entrance to the resort.

Whichever way you choose to arrive, make sure you walk the last few kilometres of the bus route from PIECHOWICE (which also has a train station); although not actually in the National Park, this offers some of the most beautiful scenery in the Karkonosze. The road closely follows the course of the **Kamienna**, one of the main streams rising in the mountains, which is joined along this short stretch by several tributaries, in a landscape reminiscent of the less wild parts of the Scottish highlands. Much the best vistas are to be had from the road itself, which has a lane set aside for walkers; the views from the hiking trails are obscured by trees most of the time. However, you do need to make a detour down one of the paths in order to see the **waterfall** formed by the Szklarska just before it joins the Kamienna; the point to turn off is well signposted from the bus stop and car park by the main road, and it's usually thronged with souvenir sellers.

The Kamienna slices Szklarska Poręba in two, with the main streets in the valley and the rest of the town rising high into the hills on each side. It's well worth following the stream all the way through the built-up part of the resort, as there follows another extremely picturesque stretch, with some spectacular rock formations (the **Kruce Skalny**) towering above the southern bank. Beyond, at the extreme western edge of town, is the celebrated **Huty Julia** glassworks, whose nineteenth-century core can be visited by guided tour on weekday mornings. From here, you can ascend by the black or red trails into the mountains.

Taking the **red trail**, you enter the National Park at the **waterfall** of the Kamienczyka, which is about a third of the way up the trail to **Szrenica** (1362m). Tumbling down the valley in a single slanting dive and beautifully framed by woodland, it's the most picturesque of the falls in the Karkonosze. Unfortunately, the observation platforms are currently fenced off for safety reasons.

However, the easiest and quickest way into the mountains is by **chair lift**, which goes in two stages to the summit of Szrenica. Its departure point is at the southern end of town: from the bus station, follow ul. 1 Maja, then turn right into ul. Turystyczna, continuing along all the way to the end, following green then black markings. Despite its rickety appearance, the chair lift, which generally operates between 9am and 5pm, is quite secure.

Practicalities

As you'd expect, Szklarska Poręba has a great variety of accommodation. Of the **hotels**, the best value is *Sporthotel*, by the chair lift at ul. Turystyczna 27 (☎17-30-37); other options are *Piechowice*, ul. Turystyczna 8 (☎17-36-93), *Sudety*, right in the heart of the resort at ul. Krasickiego 10 (☎17-27-36), and the motel *Relax* (☎17-26-95), at ul. Jeleniogórska 9, on the Piechowice road about 1km east of town. The Biuro Zakwaterowania across from the bus station at ul. Maja 4 (☎17 23-93) can arrange stays in **private rooms**, while the Orbis office around the corner at ul. Jedności Narodowej 13a (☎17-23-47) has access to **pensions** offering good-value, all-in deals. There are **tourist hostels** at ul. Sportowy 6 (☎17-22-37) and ul. 1 Maja 16 (☎17-27-09) and the Kochanówka PTTK hut by the Szklarska waterfall (☎17-24-00) on the road east. The **youth hostel** is a less enticing option, being out in the sticks at ul. Piastowska 1 (☎17-21-41), on the wrong side of town for the best walks. Ul. Jedności Narodowej offers the main concentration of places to **eat** and **drink**, with *Polonia* at no. 5 being the most recommendable; several alternatives can be found on ul. Turystyczna.

Karpacz

KARPACZ, 15km south of Jelenia Góra and linked to it by three trains and at least 20 buses a day, is an even more scattered community than Szklarska Poręba, occupying an enormous area for a place with only a few thousand permanent inhabitants. Much of it is built along the main road, ul. 1 Maja, which stretches and curves 3km uphill to the *Hotel Biały Jar*. This is the convergence of four hiking trails and terminus for some buses; others (at least one an hour) continue up the road to the adjoining village of BIERUTOWICE.

In the centre of Bierutowice is the most famous, not to say curious, building in the Karkonosze – the **Wang Chapel**. This twelfth-century Romanesque church, which boasts some wonderfully refined carving on its portals and capitals, stood for nearly six hundred years in a village in southern Norway. By 1840, it had fallen into such a state of disrepair that the parishioners sought a buyer for it. Having failed to interest any Norwegians, they sold it to the most powerful architectural conservationist of the day, King Friedrich Wilhelm IV of Prussia. He had the church dismantled and shipped to this isolated spot, where it was meticulously reassembled over a period of two years; the stone tower, added at the beginning of the present century, is the only feature which is not original. In deference to Friedrich Wilhelm's wishes, it's still used on Sunday mornings for Protestant worship; there are also organ recitals on alternate Sundays in summer. Otherwise, it's opened only for groups, but as these come here very frequently in season, you shouldn't have any trouble getting in.

Immediately above the Wang Chapel is one of the entry points to the National Park, from where the blue hiking trail goes up into the mountains. Faster access is by the **chair lift** midway between here and the *Biały Jar*. This ascends directly to the summit of **Kopa** (1375m); try not to be put off by the machinery, which is even more decrepit-looking than its counterpart in Szklarska Poręba. The normal hours of operation are 8am to around 5pm.

A short distance west of the chair lift is the upper of two **waterfalls** on the Łomnica river, which rises high in the mountains and flows all the way through Karpacz, defining much of the northern boundary of the town, as well as the course of ul. 1 Maja, which follows a largely parallel line. The second waterfall, below Biały Jar on a path marked in red, stands in complete contrast to the rustic charm of the first, having been altered to form a dam. However, on its northern bank there's the attraction of the pleasantly secluded wooded heights of Karpatka and a café on the waterfront.

The only other sightseeing attraction in Karpacz itself is the small **Museum of Sport and Tourism** (Tues, Wed, Fri & Sun 9am–4pm, Thurs 11am–6pm), housed in an alpine chalet on ul. Kopernika, close to the second bus stop on ul. 1 Maja. Below the museum is the valley of the Dolna, which offers a superb **view** over the National Park.

Hikes from Karpacz

The most obvious goal of any walk is the austere **Śnieżka** (Schneekoppe, or "Snow Peak"), at 1602m the highest peak in the range and normally covered with snow for half the year. Lying almost due south of Karpacz, it can be reached by the black trail in about three hours from the *Biały Jar*, or in about fifty minutes if you pick up the trail at the top of the Kopa chair lift. From the chair lift you pass through the **Kocioł łomniczki**, whose abundant vegetation includes Carpathian birch, gentian, cloves, alpine roses and monk's hood; only moss, lycopodia, alpine violets and lichen grow on the slopes of Śnieżka itself. Access to the actual summit is by either the steep and stony "Zigzag Way" (the red trail) which ascends by the most direct method, or the easier "Jubilee Way" (the blue route), which goes round the northern and eastern sides of the mountain. At the top is a large modern weather station-cum-snack bar, where you can get cheap hot meals; refreshments are also available in the refuges on Kopa and Pod Śnieżka and at the junction of the two trails.

On a clear day, the **view** from Śnieżka stretches for 80km, embracing not only other parts of the Sudeten chain in Poland and the Czech Republic, but also Wrocław, Ślęża, Legnica and the Lausitz Mountains in Germany. However, good visibility is a rarity; the more usual misty effects at least offer a highly atmospheric consolation.

The **red trail**, which passes close to the frontier in covering all the main summits in the National Park, makes the most obvious basis for a walking route. One section particularly worth seeing is that immediately to the west of Śnieżka, which runs above two glacial **lakes**, Mały Stam and Wielki Stam. If you don't want to continue onwards to Szklarska Poręba, you can then descend by the black trail, then switch to the blue, which brings you out at the Wang Chapel.

However, it is advisable to go on a bit further by the red trail, and descend by the yellow trail: this gives you the opportunity to see the most picturesque **rock formations** in the Karkonosze, the Słonecznik and the Pielgrzymy.

If the above routes seem too strenuous, a satisfyingly easy alternative is to take the blue trail from the Wang Chapel to the Samotnia refuge on the shore of Mały Staw, a round trip lasting about two and a half hours.

Practicalities

In the Dolna valley, below the museum at ul. Obrońców 5, is the Karkonosze's leading **hotel**, the luxurious and ultra-modern Orbis-run *Skalny* (☎19-721). The alternatives are the aforementioned *Biały Jar*, ul. 1 Maja 79 (☎19-319), and *Orlinek*, just before the chair lift at ul. Olimpijska 9 (☎19-548). There's a **tourist hostel** in the town centre at ul. Waryńskiego 6 (☎19-513), and another, the *Wilcza*, just across the road from the *Skalny* (☎19-789) and a basic campsite at the swimming pool. The *Liczyrzepa* **youth hostel** is at ul. Gimnazjalna 9 (☎19-290) on the corner of ul. Żeromskiego, most easily reached by following the green stripes downhill from Biały Jar. Near the northern entry to Karpacz are the railway station, the main **campsite** (☎19-316) and the **Biuro Zakwaterowania** (☎19-453) for **private rooms**, both at ul. 1 Maja 8. Information about **pensions** offering full and half board should be available from **Orbis** at no. 50 on the same street (☎19-547). A wide variety of places to **eat** and **drink** can also be found around here.

From the Karkonosze to the Kłodzko Region

In the stretch of land between the Karkonosze Mountains and Silesia's other main recreation area – the Kłodzko valley to the southeast – lie several historic towns, most of them connected with the former **Duchy of Świdnica**, which lasted only from 1290 to 1392 but exerted a profound influence on Silesian culture. The places mentioned are best visited in passing from the one holiday district to the other, or on day trips from Wrocław or the resorts themselves. Accommodation is very limited, and there's not likely to be a reason for wanting to spend the night anyway.

Kamienna Góra

Weaving became the staple craft of Silesia in the fourteenth century, and **KAMIENNA GÓRA**, which lies 38km southeast of Jelenia Góra, carries on this uninterrupted tradition with its silk, linen and clothing works. Founded as a fortress to protect Świdnica against the Bohemians, Kamienna Góra's greatest moment came in 1345, after it had fallen to the enemy, in an incident still celebrated in local folklore. Taking a leaf out of the book of the Greeks in their siege of Troy, the counter-attacking troops smuggled themselves back into the town hidden in hay carts, then emerged to rout the garrison. Not surprisingly, wars have featured strongly in the town's history: it was the scene of a rare Austrian victory over the Prussians in 1760, then in 1813 was the rallying point of the allied armies ranged against Napoleon.

The central square, **plac Wolności**, is lined with a number of fine old houses, of which no. 11 houses the **museum** (Tues & Fri–Sun 10am–4pm, Wed & Thurs

10am–3pm), devoted mainly to weaving in the region. Nearby stands the Gothic church of **SS Peter and Paul**, which seems to have never really recovered from its sacking at the hands of followers of the Czech reformer Jan Hus. Far more imposing is the **Church of Grace** on a hillock at the southern side of town, a Greek-cross design which is one of half a dozen Silesian churches specially built in the early eighteenth century for Protestant worship.

There's a **hotel**, *Karkonosze*, at ul. Świerczewskiego 33 (✿22-30) and a **tourist hostel** at no. 2 on the same street (✿22-21). The usual range of places to eat and drink can be found, but don't expect anything wonderful.

Krzeszów

The village of **KRZESZÓW**, 8km south of Kamienna Góra by regular bus, lies in the shade of a huge **Abbey** complex which ranks, historically and artistically, among the most significant monuments in Silesia. It was first settled in 1242 by Benedictines at the instigation of Anne, widow of Henryk the Pious. However, they stayed for less than half a century; the land was bought back by Anne's grandson, Bolko I of Świdnica, who granted it to the Cistercians and made their church his family's mausoleum. Despite being devastated by the Hussites and again in the Thirty Years' War, the abbey flourished, eventually owning nearly 300 square kilometres of land, including two towns and forty villages. This economic base funded the complete rebuilding in the Baroque period, but not long afterwards the community went into irreversible decline as the result of the confiscation of its lands during the Silesian Wars.

For over a century the buildings lay abandoned, but in a nicely symmetrical turn of events they were reoccupied by Benedictine monks from Prague in 1919, with a contingent of nuns joining them after World War II. Even so, this is no more than a token presence, and the unkempt appearance of the close strikes you immediately. Restoration work is well under way, but will clearly continue for some time yet.

The two churches are very different in size and feel. The smaller and plainer of the two, **St Joseph's**, was built in the 1690s for parish use. In replacing the medieval church, its dedication was changed to reflect the Counter-Reformation cult of the Virgin Mary's husband, designed to stress a family image which was overlooked in earlier Catholic theology. The magnificent **fresco cycle**, in which Joseph – previously depicted by artists as a shambling old buffer – appears to be little older than his wife and is similarly transported to heaven from his deathbed, is a prime artistic expression of this short-lived cult. Executed with bold brushwork and warm colours, it is the masterpiece of **Michael Willmann**, an East Prussian who converted to Catholicism and spent the rest of his life carrying out commissions from Silesian religious houses. On the ceiling, Willmann continued the family theme with various Biblical genealogies.

The **Monastic Church**, in the grand Baroque style, was begun in 1728 and finished in just seven years – hence its great unity of design, relying for effect on a combination of monumentality and elaborate decoration. Three altarpieces in the transept are by Willmann, but the most notable painting is a Byzantine icon which has been at Krzeszów since the fourteenth century. The nave ceiling frescoes illustrate the life of the Virgin, and thus form a sort of counterpoint to those in the parish church; that in the south transept shows the Hussites martyring the monks.

From the south transept you pass into the **Piast mausoleum** behind the high altar. This is kept open when tourist groups are around (which is quite frequently in summer); at other times you'll have to persuade a monk or nun to open it up. Focal point of the chapel is the grandiose coloured marble monument to Bernard of Świdnica, to each side of which are more modest Gothic sarcophagi of Bolko I and II. The history of the abbey is told in the frescoes on the two domes.

Other buildings in the close include the monastic quarters adjoining the church, the now derelict hostelry beside St Joseph's, a shrine which is part of a series of wayside chapels continued outside the precincts, and the former estate management offices fronting the entrance gateway. The gateway previously housed a restaurant, but this was closed at the time of writing, with the shops left as the only places to buy food.

Bolków, Jawor and Strzegom

The very name of **BOLKÓW**, 35km east of Jelenia Góra and 19km north of Kamienna Góra, proclaims its foundation by the first Duke of Świdnica, Bolko I. Although a ruin, his **Castle** (Tues–Fri 9am–4pm, Sat 8am–3pm, Sun 9am–4pm) is still an impressive sight, rising imperiously above the little town. Later converted into a Renaissance palace, it passed into the control of the monks of Krzeszów, and was finally abandoned after their Napoleonic suppression. A section of the buildings has been restored to house a small museum on the history of the town, and you can ascend the tower for a huge panoramic view.

There's little to see in the lower town, though the gaudily painted Gothic parish church and the sloping Rynek have a certain charm. On the square there's a cheap and decent restaurant, *Kosmos*. The town has one **hotel**, *Bolków*, ul. Sienkiewicza 17 (☎341); it was recently taken over and refurbished by a family who have returned here from exile in the UK – hence the English-style bar. Various special interest excursions are operated from here.

Jawor

Some 20km north, about halfway towards Legnica, lies the somewhat larger town of **JAWOR**, which was formerly the capital of one of the independent Silesian duchies. It preserves a fair number of proud Renaissance and Baroque patrician houses, many of them on the Rynek. Here also can be seen the **Town Hall**, whose neo-Renaissance bulk, dating from the end of last century, makes an odd contrast with the tower retained from its fourteenth-centrury Gothic predecessor. A somewhat later Gothic style is evident in the church of **St Martin**, a fine hall design, with varied furnishings including Renaissance choir stalls and a Baroque high altar.

From the Rynek, ul. Złotoryjska leads northwest to pl. Wolności. Here stands the town's most intriguing monument, the half-timbered **Church of Peace** (Kościół Pokoju). Its name derives from the Peace of Westphalia of 1648, which brought to an end the morass of religious and dynastic conflicts known as the Thirty Years' War, though could equally well apply to the tranquil setting outside the old town walls. The church was one of three (two of which survive) that Silesia's Protestant minority was allowed to build following the cessation of hostilities, and both the material used – wood and clay only, no stone or brick – and the location outside the town centre were among the conditions laid down by the ruling Habsburg emperor. Designed by an engineer, Albrecht von Säbisch, the church was cleverly laid out in such a way that an enormous congregation could be packed into a relatively modest space, an effect illustrated even more clearly in its counterpart in Świdnica (see opposite).

Strzegom

STRZEGOM, 15km southeast of Jawor and 20km east of Bolków on the road and train routes to Wrocław, is Silesia's oldest town, and might even be the oldest in Poland. An important centre for the extraction of granite and basalt, it has long been predominantly industrial, with few suggestions of its antiquity. The only worthwhile monument is the **parish church**, a lofty Gothic design chiefly notable for its monumental facade illustrating *The Last Judgement* and the southern porch with a tympanum of *The Dormition of the Virgin*.

Continuing onwards from Strzegom by rail, you shortly come to the junction of JAWORZYNA ŚLĄSKI, where the lines to Wrocław and Świdnica split. Train buffs should make a point of alighting here: steam engines are still in operation, and a number of historic locomotives have been parked as static displays. A preservation centre has been earmarked for here, and it's intended to run special excursion services: check locally for the latest situation.

Wałbrzych and Książ

Right up to the end of the communist period and beyond, visiting **WAŁBRZYCH** was like travelling back to the Britain of Lowry's paintings – or even of Dickens' *Hard Times*. Its five mines, its steelworks, glassworks and numerous factories combined to produce one of Europe's most polluted environments: the air was always heavy and putrid, the buildings cloaked in grime. Ironically, this bastion of outdated technology was very largely a modern creation. Although its lead and coal mines had been worked for several hundred years, the number of inhabitants numbered only a few hundred in 1800 and it was still a modest town early this century, before accelerating to its present population of 125,000 – the highest in Lower Silesia after Wrocław.

That such a place was located between two of Poland's main resort areas was unfortunate, to the say the least, the more so as the hilly landscape surroundings, the **Góry Wałbrzyskie**, are themselves picturesque. Desperate attempts are now being made to clean up Wałbrzych, and noticeable progress has already been achieved. The town centre has a few passably interesting eighteenth- and nineteenth-century buildings, best of which is the Neoclassical **Protestant church** by Carl Gotthard Langhans on pl. Marchlewskiego. Both north and south of the main commercial quarter are large public parks which afford good vantage points over the town and its surroundings.

Książ

The one obviously positive point about Wałbrzych is its proximity to **KSIĄŻ**, which lies just off the few kilometres of road leading to the smaller industrial town of ŚWIEBODZICE.

Given the surrounding environment, it's miraculous that Książ gives the appearance of being deep in rural countryside. There's even a **stud farm** offering riding holidays here; you're allowed to wander round its stables for a nominal fee.

Książ's tranquillity is disturbed only by the presence of the tourists drawn by the vast **Castle** (May–Sept Mon–Fri 9am–5pm, Sat & Sun 9am–6pm; Oct & April

Mon–Fri 9am–4pm, Sat & Sun 9am–5pm; Nov–March Mon–Fri 9am–3pm, Sat & Sun 9am–4pm), which commands a thickly wooded valley and is a magnificent sight from a distance. Close to, it's less impressive, due to the disparate styles in which it's built, taking in practically everything from the thirteenth-century Romanesque of Duke Bolko I's original fortress to nineteenth-century Romanticism. Some of it is even more modern, as work was carried out to transform it into a bomb-proof bunker for Hitler. Nonetheless, a few fine interiors remain, notably the **Maximilian Hall**, a piece of palatial Baroque, complete with carved chimneypieces, gilded chandeliers, a fresco of Mount Parnassus, and multicoloured marble panelling. The basement houses a good cheap **restaurant**, while one of the outbuildings has been converted into a fairly luxurious **hotel** (☎250-17).

Świdnica

Few adjacent towns could be less similar than Wałbrzych and ŚWIDNICA, less than 20km to the northeast and connected by numerous buses and trains. Twentieth-century growth has largely bypassed what was for centuries Silesia's second most important city, and its population today barely tops the 40,000 mark. Yet, aided by the fact that it suffered little damage in World War II, it still preserves much of the grandeur of a former princely capital and is one of the most attractive Silesian towns.

Although Świdnica's period of independent glory – which came not long after its twelfth-century foundation – was short-lived, the town continued to flourish under Bohemian rule. Not only was it an important centre of trade and commerce, it ranked as one of Europe's most renowned brewing centres, with its famous *Schwarze Schöps* forming the staple fare of Wrocław's best-known tavern and exported as far afield as Italy and Russia.

A few minutes' walk north from the **train and bus stations**, the **Rynek** is predominantly Baroque, though the core of many of the houses is often much older. Two particularly notable facades are at no. 7, known as **The Golden Cross**, and no. 8, **The Gilded Man**. In the central area of the square are two fine fountains and the handsome early eighteenth-century **Town Hall**, which preserves the tower and an elegant star-vaulted chamber from its Gothic predecessor.

SS Stanislaw and Wenceslas

Off the southwestern corner of the Rynek, the main street, ul. Staromiejska, curves gently downhill. The view ahead stretches past a number of Baroque mansions to the majestic **belfry** – the second highest in Poland – of the Gothic parish church of **SS Stanislaw and Wenceslas**. Intended as one of a pair, the tower was so long under construction that its final stages were built after the introduction of the Reformation. The church also boasts a splendidly monumental **facade**, in front of which are placed a Baroque statue of Saint Jan Nepomuk and a beautiful late Gothic relief of *St Anne, the Virgin and Child*. Around the early fifteenth-century portals, the two patrons occupy a privileged position in the group of Apostles framing the Madonna. Look also at the Bridal Doorway on the north side of the nave, so called because it was reserved for wedding ceremonies: it features chauvinistic carvings of *Samson and Delilah* and *Aristotle and Phyllis*, as a warning to the bridegroom of woman's potential for corrupting man.

During the Thirty Years' War, the church was returned to Catholic use and shortly afterwards given to the Jesuits, who subsequently erected the large college building on the south side. They also carried out a Baroque transformation of the **interior**, respecting the original architecture while embellishing it to give a richer surface effect. A massive high altar with statues of the order's favourite saints dominates the east end; the organ with its carvings of the heavenly choir provides a similar focus to the west, while the lofty walls were embellished with huge Counter-Reformation altarpieces, some of them by Willmann.

The Church of Peace

Set in a quiet walled close north of the town centre, the **Church of Peace** (Kościół Pokoju) was built in the 1650s for the displaced Protestant congregation of SS Stanislaw and Wenceslas, according to the conditions on construction applied at Jawor (see p.417) a few years before and to plans drawn up by the same engineer. Although the smaller of the two, it is the more accomplished: indeed, it is generally considered to be the greatest half-timbered church ever built. At first sight, the rusticity of the surroundings seems to be mirrored in the architecture, but it's actually a highly sophisticated piece of design: despite its compact shape, it reproduces the shape of a large cathedral. Over 3000 worshippers could be seated inside, thanks to the double two-tiered galleries, with a further 4000 standing: all would be able to hear the preacher, and most could see him.

The whole appearance of the church was sharply modified in the eighteenth century, as the Protestant community increased in size and influence after Silesia came under the rule of Prussia. A vestibule was added to the west end, a baptistery to the east, while a picturesque group of **chapels and porches** was tagged on to the two long sides of the building. The latter served as the entrances to the private boxes of the most eminent citizens, whose funerary monuments are slowly weathering away on the exterior walls. At the same time, the church was beautified inside by the addition of a rich set of **furnishings** – pulpit, font, reredos and the large and small organs.

Practicalities

Świdnica has two **hotels** – *Piast*, just off the Rynek at ul. Marksa 11 (☎230-76), and *Sportowy*, south of the centre at ul. Śląska 37 (☎225-36); beside the latter is a **campsite** with chalets. The *Piast* has a **restaurant**; other places to eat and drink can be found in and around the Rynek, including a café in the town hall. At no. 31 on the square is an **Orbis** office (☎226-74).

The Kłodzko Region

Due south of Wrocław is a rural area of rocky mountains, wooded hills, gentle valleys and curative springs that provides the perfect antidote to the heavy industry of so much of Silesia. Known as the **Kłodzko Region** after its largest town, it's surrounded on three sides by the Czech Republic, with the Sudeten mountains forming a natural frontier. This is one of the most popular holiday areas in Poland, catering for all inclinations from the sedentary to the hyperactive.

On the one hand, there are five **spa resorts** (identified by the suffix *-Zdrój*), the largest concentration in the country and a reminder of the area's long period under the rule of Germany, a nation addicted to this type of therapy. The slightly run-down appearance of these towns only adds to their appeal, their somnambulent atmosphere providing a tantalising evocation of prewar central Europe. For the people who congregate here for rest and rehabilitation, the day's most arduous activity is a meander down to the pump room to fill up their beakers with the local spring water – which is actually mild and refreshing, with not a hint of the sulphuric taste characteristic of that of so many other spas.

High above these resorts are some of Poland's best **hiking routes**, passing through marvellously varied and often bizarre landscapes. A network of marked paths covers the entire region, in which there are several separate ranges. To the northwest are the **Góry Stołowe** (Table Mountains), which give way to the **Wzgórza Lewińskie**. Further south are the **Góry Orlickie** and **Góry Bystrzyckie**, the former lying predominantly within the Czech Republic. The southeast of the area is taken up by the massif of the **Masyw Śnieżnika**, beyond which are the **Góry Bialskie**, while much of the eastern boundary is defined by the **Góry Złote** (Golden Mountains).

Many trails follow a complete circuit and take several days, but it's easy to make up your own shorter routes if you want to base yourself in one place. Some of the ascents can be quite strenuous, though if you're reasonably fit and wearing sturdy shoes you shouldn't have any problems. The *Ziemia Kłodzka* **map**, available from tourist offices and newsagents in the area, is a must if you intend doing any serious walking, but beware of occasional divergences in detail from the actual marking of the paths. **Winter sports** ensure the area attracts activity holidaymakers all year round, even if the facilities have as yet not been developed to their full potential.

Accommodation throughout the Kłodzko Region is plentiful and, with the winding down of subsidised factory vacations, is currently undersubscribed. It's possible to stay here very cheaply – the custom-built **pensions** offering half-board terms are particularly good value. For **getting around**, buses take second place to walking; picturesque rail lines hug the valleys, but the stations are usually on the outskirts of the towns.

Kłodzko

Dominated as it is by two large fortresses rising on the heights above the River Nysa Kłodzka, it's immediately obvious that **KŁODZKO** was once a place of enormous strategic importance. This becomes even clearer from a glance at a map – several rivers converge in the vicinity, giving the town control over access to a number of valleys, including what was the main trade route between Bohemia and Poland. Until the eighteenth-century Prussian takeover, Kłodzko's orientation had been towards the former, and its main Polish connection prior to 1945 was that it once belonged to the father of Adalbert, the Czech saint who was to have a crucial impact on the development of Poland (see "Gniezno", Chapter Six).

The main survivor of the medieval fortifications is the Gothic **bridge** leading into the Old Town. Its defensive function by then being obsolete, it was embellished in the Baroque period by sacred statuary, among which a *Coronation of the Virgin* stands out. Nowadays, the bridge has been taken over by the market traders, including dealers in paintings and artefacts. Before crossing over, take a look at the restrained Baroque **Franciscan church**, originally part of a Jesuit college.

On the opposite bank, impressively grand nineteenth-century mansions rise high above the river. Passing them, you ascend to the sloping Rynek, which has a number of fine old houses from various periods. Standing in the centre is the **Town Hall**, which retains the handsome Renaissance belfry of its predecessor; the rest would look very much at home in Manchester or Leeds, being a good example of the sort of self-confident architecture favoured last century by newly prosperous cities.

Just to the south, and closer to the river, is a smaller and quieter square dominated by the parish church of **Our Lady**. Like its namesake in Świdnica, this Gothic building was adapted to Baroque without being ruined in the process. Look out for the fourteenth-century tomb of the founder, Bishop Ernst of Pordolice, which somehow managed to survive the desecrations of the Hussites five centuries ago. Across from the church is the **Kłodzko Region Museum** (Mon–Fri 10am–6pm), which provides a good introduction if you're intending to see a bit more of the area.

From the Rynek, pathways ascend to the huge Prussian-built **Fortress** (Tues–Sun 9am–5pm), the more important of the two commanding the valley, now crudely adorned with the name of the town in huge letters. Its former impregnability – which enabled it to withstand a siege in 1807 by the all-conquering army of Napoleon – is still obvious, with the natural rock providing the first line of defence. To travel along the whole length of its **underground passages** would take hours; some of these are so narrow that you're virtually forced to get down on your hands and knees. As a contrast, there are superb **views** of the town and its surroundings.

Practicalities

If you're arriving by rail, get off at the Kłodzko Miasto **train station**, which is beside the **bus station** and only a few minutes' walk from the centre; this is also the best place to catch trains heading south, and to the two spa valleys to the east and west. The main station, Kłodzko Główny, is over 2km north and only worth using if you're heading to Wrocław or Jelenia Góra.

The helpful **Orbis** office, located just beside the bridge at ul. Grottgera 1 (Mon–Fri 10am–5pm, alternate Sat 10am–noon; ☎27-75 or ☎39-78), can help you find a place to stay anywhere in the region. An alternative source of information is the **tourist office** on the corner of the Rynek (Mon–Fri 10am–4pm). Although Kłodzko makes an ideal touring base, accommodation is far scarcer than in the nearby spas. Of the **hotels**, *Astoria* on pl. Jedności (☎30-35) is worth considering for convenience, being right beside the bus station. The alternatives are *Nad Młynówka* at ul. Daszyńskiego 16 (☎25-63) and an out-of-town motel, *Zosia* (☎37-37). For a cheaper deal, try for a chalet at the **campsite**, beyond the fortress on ul. Nowy Świat (☎30-31) or go to the **youth hostel**, situated south of the centre at ul. Krasickiego 8 (☎21-74).

Kłodzko is a bit short on places to **eat** and **drink**, with a couple of cafés being all the upper town has to offer. Outside the hotels, the only two restaurants are on ul. Grottgera between the bus station and Orbis office. Of these, *Wilcza Jama* is particularly recommended, with decent opening hours and excellent Czech beer; *Czardasz* across the road is acceptable enough.

The best snack bars are *Małgosia*, to the rear of the Miasto station at ul. Połabska 2, and *Kłodzka Róża*, by the park across the river from the bus station at ul. Daszyńskiego 3. Good vegetarian dishes can be had at the aforementioned motel.

Polanica-Zdrój

The nearest resort to Kłodzko is **POLANICA-ZDRÓJ**, located some 15km to the west, which was only really developed this century. Lacking any kind of commercial centre, the spa quarter is the heart of Polanica, and its gardens – ablaze with rhododendrons and azaleas in the spring – are the town's chief joy.

Lying just out of the mountains, Polanica isn't ideally placed for the best scenery, but there are still some good **walks** to be had in the immediate vicinity. Taking the black trail to the southwest brings you into the Góry Bystrzyckie; about two and a half hours are required to ascend to the first main viewpoint, **Wolarz** (850m). A similar length of time is needed to reach the other summit within easy reach, **Szczytnik** (589m), via the yellow route going northwest; this has a neo-Gothic castle and a view over the glass-making village of SZCZYTNA below.

Practicalities

Where Polanica really scores is in its choice of accommodation. The **PTTK** at ul. Zdrojowa 15 (☎312), just south of the spa quarter, will help you find a room if there isn't space in its own hostel. Both **hotels** are further south, on the way to the train station: *Polonia* is at ul. Wojska Polskiego 4 (☎500), the more luxurious *Polonica* at ul. Warszawska 14a (☎485); the latter was closed at the time of writing. The campsite and another **tourist hostel** are northeast of the spa park on ul. Sportowa. There are also at least half-a-dozen **pensions** offering bargain all-in rates: ask at PTTK or **Orbis**, ul. Zdrojowa 5 (☎412) for details. Plenty of cafés are scattered throughout the resort, but the only **restaurant**, other than those in the hotels, is *Globus*, Kłodzka 7.

Duszniki-Zdrój

Ten kilometres west of Polanica lies the far more venerable and attractive spa of **DUSZNIKI-ZDRÓJ**. Despite the short distance between the two, their climates are quite different, Duszniki's being more fluctuating and extreme, with hotter summers and harsher winters. The town is a well-known cultural centre, with a beautiful nineteenth-century theatre as a centrepiece of the spa quarter. In the first half of August each year, a **Chopin Musical Festival**, which usually manages to feature at least one world-famous pianist, is held here, commemorating the concerts given during a convalescence by the sixteen-year-old composer in 1826.

Duszniki divides into two halves, with the Old Town lying midway between the spa quarter and the train station. On the **Rynek**, Renaissance and Baroque styles are mingled in the Town Hall and the burghers' houses, one of which bears a plaque recording Chopin's stay. Down ul. Adama Mickiewicza is another fine square, pl. Warszawy, where the former **Drapers' Guild Hall** can be identified by the emblem of a lamb with the tools of the draper's trade.

Ulica Kłodzko, the oldest street in town, is dominated by the parish church of **SS Peter and Paul**, a bland example of early eighteenth-century Baroque put into the extraordinary class by two fantastically ornate **pulpits**; one of these – a unique and slightly morbid specimen – is shaped like the whale which swallowed Jonah, with the creature's mouth fixed open to form a platform for the preacher.

At the bottom of the same street is the **Museum of the Paper Industry** (Tues–Sun 10am–3pm), which occupies a large paper mill dating from the beginning of the seventeenth century. One of Poland's most precious industrial buildings, its fine half-timbering, sweeping mansard roof and delicate rosette decoration make it a handsome piece of Baroque. Following ul. Sprzymierzonych south from here, then turning left up ul. Wiejska, brings you to a tiny chapel which now houses the **Museum of the Chopin Festival** (Tues–Fri 10am–3pm, Sat & Sun 1–3pm), with photos and programmes of past events.

If you continue uphill, you reach Nawojowa (675m), one of the **viewpoints** within easy reach of the town. The other, just to the south, is Ptasia Góra (736m), which is connected by the brown trail leading back to the spa quarter. Among longer hikes, the **red trail** leads south in about three and a half hours to ZIELENIEC, the highest-lying village in the region and a winter sports centre. A short distance to its east is the **Topieliska nature reserve**, a high-altitude peat bog with tundra-like flora, including cotton grass and dwarf birch. Another worthwhile section of the red trail goes west from Duszniki, arriving after a couple of hours at the ruined thirteenth-century Lewin Castle, another fine viewpoint. The **blue trail** leads north from Duszniki into the Góry Stołowe (see opposite).

Practicalities

The **PTTK** office, at no. 14 on the Rynek (☎540), operates a room-finding service. This organisation's own **tourist hostel** is *Pod Muflonem* (☎339), just below Ptasia Góra; the **youth hostel** is far more conveniently sited in a school building at ul. Kłodzka 22 (☎255), but is open only during the summer holidays. Other options include a **hotel**, *Miejski*, just off the Rynek at ul. Karola Świerczewskiego 2 (☎504), a **pension**, *Blachownia*, in the northeastern corner of the spa quarter at ul. Wojska Polskiego 64 (☎100), and the **campsite**, close to the station at Dworcowa 6 (☎489). The only **restaurant** is *Slowianka* on the Rynek, but cafés and snack bars are dotted all round town.

Kudowa-Zdrój and the Góry Stołowe

KUDOWA-ZDRÓJ lies in a wide basin at the foot of the Góry Stołowe and Wzgórza Lewińskie, 16km west of Duszniki and a couple of kilometres before a major road crossing into the Czech Republic. More than any of the other resorts in the Kłodzko Region, Kudowa preserves much of the feel of the bygone days when it was patronised by the internationally rich and famous. Spacious nineteenth-century villas set in their own grounds give Kudowa its aristocratic air, yet it has no obvious centre other than the **spa park**. This can claim the largest sanatorium and pump room in the region, along with an extensive *jardin anglais* with over three hundred different species of tree and shrub. From here, it's a gentle ascent north to the Wzgórze Kapliczne (420m), which takes its name from the Protestant chapel on its summit.

Practicalities

Orbis and **PTTK** both have offices on ul. Zdrojowa – at no. 47 (☎266) and no. 42a (☎222) respectively. The main room-finding agency, however, is in the resort's leading **hotel**, *Kosmos* at ul. Mariana Buczka 8a (☎511). On ul. Łąkowa, just off ul. Gen. Karola Świerczewskiego (the street leading to the border crossing) are the other hotel, *OSiR* (☎627), and the **campsite** (☎627), while the **tourist hostel** *Pod Strzechą* is on ul. Słone (☎262), slightly nearer the frontier. **Pensions** include *Gwarek*, ul. Juliusza Słowackiego 10 (☎661), and *Marysieńka*, ul. 1 Maja 3. There's a wide variety of places to **eat** and **drink**, with the restaurants in the *Kosmos* and the tourist hostel probably the best bets.

Each July, Kudowa hosts a **festival** devoted to Stanisław Moniuszko, who shared the nationalist outlook of Chopin, his compatriot and contemporary, but whose music has never caught on abroad to anything like the same extent.

Into the Table Mountains

Though they seldom rise above 900m and are almost as flat as their name suggests, the **Góry Stołowe** (Table Mountains) are the most enticing range in the Kłodzko Region. The nearest base is **KARŁÓW**, 11km east of Kudowa via the so-called "road of a hundred bends". However, there's only a campsite here (plus a restaurant and a couple of bars), leaving Kudowa itself as the main alternative if you haven't a tent.

From Kudowa, the **green trail** makes a good basis for a day's walk. It leads north to the outlying hamlet of CZERMNA, where the **cemetery chapel** strikes a discordant note in this area of healthy living – its walls, ceiling and altar are gruesomely covered with the skulls and bones of the dead of the Thirty Years' War, the Silesian Wars and the Seven Years' War. The trail then goes northeast to the first of several fantastic rock formations in the range, the **Błędne Skały** (Erratic Boulders), where it twists and turns, squirming through narrow gaps between gigantic rocks. It then continues via PASTERKA to Karłów, from where a climb of nearly 800 steps leads to the **Szczeliniec Wielki**, the highest point in the range at 919m. Here the rocks have been weathered into a series of irregular shapes nicknamed "the camel", "the elephant", "the hen", and so on. There's a small entrance fee once you get to the top, then you follow the trail which goes down into and through a deep chasm, on to a viewpoint and back by a different route.

Further south, in the vicinity of LĘŻNO, the route passes the **Sawanna Afrykańska**, a remnant of the upper layer of the mountains, formed fifty million years ago when the region was similar to the African savannahs of today. Trees bent into umbrella shapes by the wind add to the uncanny impression. The green trail continues south to LEWIN, but before that you can pick up the red trail which completes a circle back to Kudowa.

As an alternative, take the more direct **red trail** from the Błędny Skałny to Karłów. This then continues eastwards to the largest and most scattered group of rocks in the area, the **Skalne Grzyby** (Rocky Mushrooms), which were formed by uneven erosion. Proceeding southwards from here, you can switch to either the yellow route to Duszniki or the blue route to Polanica; the red route itself descends in an hour or so to Wambierzyce.

Wambierzyce

If hardly worthy of the title "the Silesian Jerusalem", **WAMBIERZYCE** is nevertheless a highly distinctive place which has drawn pilgrims since the twelfth century, when a blind man was cured by praying at a statue of the Madonna and Child placed here on a lime tree.

The Baroque **Basilica**, perched above a broad flight of steps, is the fourth on the site, and retains the outer walls of its predecessor, which collapsed soon after it was built. Its monumental exterior gives no hint of the intricate layout inside, where a broad **processional way** passes a variety of chapels, grottoes and other nooks and crannies containing representations of scenes from the lives of Christ and the Virgin. The nave of the church is an octagon hung with six large altarpieces by Michael Willmann, while the oval presbytery has a cupola illustrating the fifteen mysteries of the Rosary. A magnificent silver **tabernacle** from Venice bears the miraculous image, with a profusion of votive offerings to the side.

Scattered all around the village are nearly one hundred **shrines** containing sculptures representing the minutiae of the Passion story. They are oddly grouped out of sequence, except towards the end, which culminates in the **Calvary** on the hill facing the basilica. Halfway up is the **Szopka** (April–Sept Tues–Sun 10am–5pm), a large mechanical contraption that presents biblical and everyday local scenes, laid out like miniature theatre sets.

Wambierzyce has only one very basic **restaurant**, *Turystyczny*, on the square below the basilica; the local grocery store opposite is a good enough source for putting together a picnic. The restaurant may also have rooms to let; otherwise the nearest **hotel** is *Graniczny* on the Rynek in RADKÓW, the next village to the northwest (☎26).

Bystrzyca Kłodzka

Midway down the valley south of Kłodzko, some 15km away, is **BYSTRZYCA KŁODZKA**, its peeling medieval core reminiscent of a decayed Mediterranean town. This impression is particularly strong if from the train station (for once conveniently sited), you circle the town to the left and cross the river. Bearing left, you'll shortly get a magnificent full-frontal view of the town's tier-like layout, which on a sunny day looks more Spanish than Polish.

Substantial sections of the **walls** survive, including the Kłodzko and Water gates and the Knights' Tower. The tower later became a belfry for the Protestant church, which dominates the smaller of the two central squares, the Mały Rynek. Now deconsecrated, it houses the **Museum of Fire-Making** (Tues–Sun 10am–4pm), okay if matchbox labels give you a buzz. In the middle of the main square, pl. Wolności, is the **Town Hall**, which has a nineteenth-century body tacked onto a Renaissance tower. Further uphill, the parish church of **St Michael the Archangel** is a ragbag of different styles, featuring two well-crafted late Renaissance portals and an unusual double-naved interior.

Bystrzyca is not particularly well placed for **walks**, though the yellow route to Polanica and Duszniki is one of the best long hikes in the region; taking up the better part of a day, it passes through lonely high moorland.

The only **hotel** in Bystrzyca is the *Piast* at ul. Okrzei 26 (☎11-03-22). There are a couple of **restaurants** on pl. Wolności, *Regionalna* and *Rycerska*.

The Masyw Śnieżnika

At the southeastern corner of the Kłodzko Region is the bracingly wild **Masyw Śnieżnika**, the best of whose scenery can be seen in a good day's walk. The main jumping-off point is the straggling community of **MIĘDZYGÓRZE**, 13km southeast of Bystrzyca; there's no train station, but it's served quite well by buses, which terminate in the village centre but also stop at the **hotel**, *Nad Wodospadem*

(☎20), on the western outskirts. If you alight there, you can descend to see the River Wilczka's beautiful 27-metre **waterfall**; a bridge directly above enables you to peer down at the roaring mass, while platforms at various levels on both sides of the river give a variety of downstream views.

The **red trail** leads all the way through Międzygórze, then rises steeply through lovely wooded countryside. After a couple of hours you come to the Na Śnieżniku **refuge** (☎30); though set in total isolation at over 1200m, this is actually a fully functioning post office which has dormitory accommodation and also serves cheap homely meals. It's then a much gentler ascent to the plateau-like summit of **Śnieżnik** (1425m), the highest point in the Kłodzko Region, set right on the Czech border.

You can return to Międzygórze by a variety of routes, but it's better to descend northwards by the yellow trail in the direction of KLETNO, which will bring you in about an hour to the **Bear's Cave** (Jaskinia Niedźwiedzia). Discovered in 1966 during quarrying, the cave takes its name from the bear fossils that predominate among the 24 species of prehistoric animal bones discovered there. As yet, no trace of human habitation has been found, but only a small part of the cave has so far been excavated. The extraordinary **stalactites and stalagmites** in the section of the cave opened to the public have been given nicknames like "the palace", "the corridor", "the Madonna and Child" and "the bat". Visits are by guided tour only; as opening hours are very variable and admissions tightly controlled, it's best to check the current position with a local tourist office before setting out, or at least to make sure you arrive by the early afternoon.

The nearest bus stop to the Bear's Cave is some 3km further north; even cars have to be left over 1km away. The yellow walking trail continues to the glass-making town of STRONIE ŚLĄSKIE, terminus of a train line from Kłodzko. A further 5km north is Lądek-Zdrój.

Lądek-Zdrój

LĄDEK-ZDRÓJ is an eastern competitor to the three valley resorts west of Kłodzko, of which it most resembles Duszniki, having an historic centre as a counterbalance to the spa quarter. According to tradition, the waters here were known for their healing properties as early as the thirteenth century, when the bathing installations were allegedly destroyed by the Tartars. They have certainly been exploited since the beginning of the sixteenth century, and have attracted visitors as august as Goethe and Turgenev.

Centrepiece of the pompous Neoclassical **spa buildings** – the most grandiose in the Kłodzko Region – is the main sanatorium, a handsome domed building with extravagantly sculpted porticoes. In the older part of town, a sixteenth-century **bridge** over the River Biała Lądecka, a tributary of the Nysa Kłodzka, can still be seen. The **Rynek** is largely Baroque, with a number of fine gabled houses, above which soars the octagonal tower of the Town Hall.

The Masyw Śnieżnika is close enough to Lądek to be a goal for adventurous **walks**. However, the curiously named **Góry Złote** (Golden Mountains) immediately to the east of the town make a more obvious excursion. Following the blue trail southeast, you ascend within an hour to the ruined medieval castle on **Karpień** (776m) via a series of fantastically weathered rocks, so typical of the region. You can see another group of these by transferring to the green trail north to LUTYNIA, before circling back to Lądek.

Practicalities

PTTK have an office at ul. Kościuszki 36 (☎255), between the Old Town and the spa quarter. The only two **restaurants**, *Pod Filarami* and *Ratuszowa*, are both on the Rynek; the first is particularly good. **Pensions** offering full or half board include *Złoty Łan*, ul. Żwirki Wigury 14 (☎243), *Maskiewicz*, ul. Wolności 10 (☎767), and *Watra*, ul. Brzozowa 14 (☎609). There's a **youth hostel** in the outlying hamlet of STÓJKÓW (☎540) to the south.

North of the Kłodzko Region

If you're travelling between Kłodzko and Wrocław by either road or rail, there are a trio of places on the way well worth stopping at for an hour or two.

Ząbkowice Śląskie

The market town of **ZĄBKOWICE ŚLĄSKIE**, 20km north, has been dubbed "the Silesian Pisa" on account of its fourteenth-century **leaning tower**, just off the Rynek. By the 1400s the ground on which it was built had shifted so much that a storey was added perpendicular to the ground to try to straighten it. The opposite happened, and the thing now leans about five feet out of true. From the tower's appearance, you would think that it was a defensive structure, but it's actually the detached belfry of the church of **St Anne**, which stands in a peaceful garden behind.

A few blocks south is the shell of the **Castle**. Built at the end of the thirteenth century by Bolko I of Świdnica, it was transformed around 1530 into a palace for the Bohemian royal family by Benedict Rieth, who had previously designed the dazzling interiors of Prague's royal palace. Sadly, Ząbkowice's castle was burnt out in the Thirty Years' War and, although the remains are substantial, there's little to hint at their former splendour.

Ziębice

The former ducal capital of **ZIĘBICE** lies 16km east of Ząbkowice (connected by bus) and on the direct rail line between Kłodzko and Wrocław. Its historic core is surrounded by significant sections of the medieval **fortifications**, the most impressive survival being the Paczków Gate.

Ziębice's skyline is dominated by its pride and joy, the parish church of **SS Mary and George**, which was begun soon after the town was founded in the early thirteenth century. The sturdy tower of roughly hewn masonry stands in stark contrast to the brickwork of the rest of the facade, which is divided into paired sections, each with its own portal and elaborate gable. This mirrors the interior arrangement of the nave, which is divided down its axis by a row of columns, a feature characteristic of Bohemia but rarely encountered elsewhere. In the fifteenth century, the airy, late-Gothic aisled chancel was added, its arcades facing down each half of the divided nave, producing highly unusual spatial effects.

Henryków

Just a few kilometres north lies **HENRYKÓW**, which can be reached from both Ziębice and Ząbkowice by either bus or rail; trains are more frequent, but the station is more than 2km from the village. In 1220, the first **Cistercian abbey** in Silesia was founded here by Duke Henryk the Bearded, who immodestly named it after himself. Half a century later, the abbot, a man named Piotr, compiled a chronicle in which appears the earliest written sentence in the Polish language – a fact which has bestowed on Henryków a special place in the national consciousness.

In the late seventeenth and early eighteenth centuries, the monastery was greatly expanded in the monumental Baroque style then in vogue. These buildings still dominate the village, which, since the monastery's suppression, has been left with the problem of how to make full use of them. The architecture of the **church**, whose plain Gothic style reflects the Cistercians' ascetic principles, has survived largely intact, though its interior is swamped with Baroque furnishings, including much fine woodwork and several altarpieces by the ubiquitous Michael Willmann. The church is normally kept locked, so you may have to search out a priest to show you round.

Paczków to Nysa

Leaving the Kłodzko Region to the east, you immediately cross into the almost unrelievedly flat plateau of Upper Silesia, which stretches down to the Beskid Mountains. The route runs through a string of small fortified towns associated for most of their history with the bishops of Breslau/Wrocław, who ruled an independent principality here from 1195 until its dissolution by Prussia in 1810. For covering this stretch, buses have the edge on trains for both convenience and frequency of service.

Paczków

In contrast to its neighbours, the quiet little market town of **PACZKÓW**, 30km east of Kłodzko, has preserved its medieval fortifications almost intact – hence its designation as "the Polish Carcassonne". In reality, Paczków is hardly in that league, but has the advantage of being untouched by the hands of romantically inclined nineteenth-century restorers. In few other places does it require so little imagination to visualise how it must have looked in the Middle Ages.

Nowadays, the mid-fourteenth-century **ramparts** form a shady promenade in the centre of the town; their visual impact is diminished by the enveloping later buildings, though it's a wonder that the town managed to grow so much without their demolition. As it is, nineteen of the twenty four towers survive, as do 1200 metres of the original 1350 metres of wall, pierced by three gateways: the square Wrocław Gate of 1462 and the cylindrical Ząbkowice and Kłodzko gates from around 1550.

The area within the walls, set on a gentle slope, consists of just a handful of streets, but is centred on a **Rynek** as large as that of a big city. In the familiar off-centre position is the **Town Hall**, so comprehensively rebuilt last century that only the belfry of its Renaissance predecessor is left; ask inside for permission to ascend for the best view of the town.

Rearing up behind the Rynek is the awesome parish church of **St John**, a strongly fortified part of the town's defences. Begun soon after the completion of the walls, it was under construction for a century, with the crenellated attic not added until the Renaissance period. A section was lopped off the tower in the early eighteenth century, and a Baroque helmet put in its place. Inside, the box-like geometry of the design is particularly evident, with the chancel the same length as the main nave. The furnishings are almost all neo-Gothic, giving a fusty, nineteenth-century feel to the interior.

Practicalities

Paczków's sole **hotel**, *Zacisze*, ul. Wojska Polskiego 31 (☎62-77), lies outside the ramparts but on a street leading directly off the east side of the Rynek; it is over-priced for its tacky condition, and doesn't serve meals. With that in mind, the **youth hostel**, which is even closer to the Rynek at ul. Kołłątaja 9 (☎64-41), is a better bet. There's also a **campsite** just southeast of the centre at ul. Jagiellońska 5 (☎65-09). Currently the only **restaurant** is *Kameralna* at ul. Wrocławska 11 which, although acceptable and very cheap, stops serving meals in the early evening. There are cafés on ul. Wojska Polskiego and the Rynek, the latter bearing the inevitable name of *Carcassonne*.

Otmuchów

OTMUCHÓW, 14km east of Paczków, nestles between two artificial lakes formed by the damming of the River Nysa Kłodzka. The original capital of the prince-bishopric, it's nowadays a sleepy backwater which springs to life only with the summer influx of watersports enthusiasts.

Dominating the town is the **Castle**, originally twelfth-century Romanesque, which guarded an extensive fortification system that has vanished but for one ruined gateway. It was transformed into a palace in the sixteenth century, and in 1820 was sold to Wilhelm von Humboldt, founder of the University of Berlin and architect of Prussia's educational system. He lived here in retirement, the liberal views he had championed having fallen from official favour. Nowadays, it's a sana-torium; there's unrestricted access to the courtyard, but you'll have to ask for permission to climb the tower, which commands a fine view.

On the Rynek is the Renaissance **Town Hall**, adorned with a beautiful sundial. The square slopes upwards to a well-kept floral garden and the **Parish Church**, a very central European-looking Baroque construction with a rhythmical twin-towered facade. Its ample interior is richly decorated with stucco work by Italian craftsmen and large painted altarpieces, including several by Michael Willmann.

Practicalities

The only places to stay are the **campsites** to the west of town, the nearer being at ŚCIBÓRZ (☎53-93), the other a few kilometres on at SARNOWICE (☎52-25). Each village has two **restaurants**. In Otmuchów itself there are the café-restaurant *Zamkowa* on the Rynek and the snack bar *Bażant* on ul. Świerczewskiego.

Nysa

The name of **NYSA,** 12km east of Otmuchów, has become synonymous with the trucks made there for export all over eastern Europe. Yet industry is a relative newcomer to this town which, in spite of the devastation of 1945, still preserves memories of the days when it basked in the fanciful title of "the Silesian Rome", a reference to its numerous religious houses and reputation as a centre of Catholic education. It came to the fore when the adoption of the Reformation in Breslau forced the bishops to reside outside the city; they then built up Nysa, the capital of their principality for the previous couple of centuries, as their power base.

The Town

Both the **bus** and **train stations** are at the eastern side of the town; from there, bear right along the edge of the park, then turn left into ul. Kolejowa which leads in a straight line towards the centre. On the way, you pass the fourteenth-century **Wrocław Gate**, an unusually graceful piece of military architecture now left stranded by the demolition of the ramparts. It's a tantalising reminder of Nysa's long role as a border fortress: first fortified in the twelfth century by Bolesław the Wrymouth in his struggles against his Bohemian-backed brother Zbigniew, it remained an important stronghold until World War II. The only other remnant of the fortifications is the **Ziębicka Gate** on ul. Krzywoustego further down to the right, a severe brick tower lightened by the insertion of a marble carving of a lion.

Nysa's vast **Rynek** presents a very sorry appearance, having lost its town hall and all its old houses during the war. Only the jolly seventeenth-century **Weigh House**, which looks as if it belongs somewhere in the Low Countries, has been rebuilt. The sides of the square are now lined with concrete monstrosities.

Off the northeastern side of the Rynek is the huge church of **St James** (św. Jakuba), which long served as the cathedral of the exiled bishops. Put up in just six years in the 1420s, it's a fine example of the hall church style, with nave and aisles of equal height – a design much favoured in Germany but rare in Poland. It's also unusual for this part of the world in having been very little altered, the only modifications being the reconstruction in Renaissance or Baroque style of three of the chapels. Entering through the graceful double portal, it's the spareness of the vast interior which makes the strongest impression. So crushing is the weight of the vault that many of the octagonal pillars, adorned with statues of the Apostles, have sagged under the strain. The chapels provide the only intimate note: fenced off by elegant grilles, they overflow with funerary plaques and monuments to the bishops and local notables. The squatness of the church's detached **belfry** is explained by the fact that it was abandoned after fifty years' work.

South of St James' lies the well-preserved Baroque episcopal quarter. The **Bishops' Palace**, reached down ul. Jarosławka, is now fitted out as a surprisingly good local **museum** (Tues, Wed & Fri 10am–3pm, Sat 11am–3pm, Sun 11am–4pm), with well-documented displays on the history of Nysa, including impressive fragments from demolished buildings.

From here turn right into ul. Grodzka, where the **Bishops' Residence**, which was built right up against the ramparts, stands forlorn and neglected. Further up the street, the complex of **Jesuit buildings** has survived in better shape. The white-walled church is in the plain style favoured by the order, though its austerity is softened by some recently discovered ceiling frescoes and a beautiful eighteenth-century silver tabernacle at the high altar. Adjoining it is the famous **Carolinum** college, whose luminaries included the Polish kings Michał Korybut Wiśniowiecki and Jan Sobieski.

South of the Rynek is the only other reminder of "the Silesian Rome" in the shape of the **Monastery of the Hospitallers of the Holy Sepulchre** (Klasztor Bożogrobców). This order moved to Nysa from the Holy Land at the end of the twelfth century, but the huge complex you see today dates from the early eighteenth century. It's now a seminary, and you'll probably have to ask at the reception on ul. św. Pawła to get into the resplendent Baroque church on the parallel ul. Bracka. This features a reproduction of the Holy Sepulchre in Jerusalem and a cycle of highly theatrical frescoes by the brothers Christoph Thomas and Felix Anton Scheffler.

Practicalities

Nysa has only one **hotel**, the three-star *Piast* opposite the Ziębicka Gate at ul. Krzywoustego 14 (☎40-84). Otherwise, there's a **motel** on the outskirts of town at ul. Świerczewskiego 1a (☎34-17) – only practicable if you've got a car – a *Dom Wycieczkowy* at ul. Świerczewskiego 42 (☎21-35) and a **youth hostel** close to the station at ul. Warszawy 7 (☎37-31). Best **restaurants** are the one in the hotel, *Warszawianka* at no. 25 on the same street and *Pod Starą Wagą* on the Rynek; the last also has a café. **Orbis** are at ul. Wrocławska 14 (☎41-69).

Brzeg

Situated about 40km from both Wrocław and Opole, the old ducal seat of **BRZEG** is an easily manageable and agreeable market town, with an impressive array of monuments that make it a good stopping-off point for a few hours. Originally a fishing village on the bank (*brzeg*) of the Odra, Brzeg was documented in the early thirteenth century as having a castle of a branch of the Piast dynasty. In 1311 it became a regional capital in the continuing subdivision of Silesia, and ousted Legnica as the main residence of the court. The Piasts remained there until 1675 when this family, a prominent dynasty throughout the recorded history of Poland, finally died out.

The Palace

Brzeg's most historic area lies close to the river in tranquil isolation from the commercial centre, at the opposite end of town from the train and bus stations. Seen from its spacious square, the **Palace** is a bit of a jumble: predominantly Renaissance, with the Gothic presbytery of St Hedwig's (the mausoleum of the Piasts), plus various misjudged later additions. Badly damaged by Frederick the Great's troops in 1741, the palace was relegated for the next century and a half to the status of an arsenal. Only in the last decade has restoration returned parts of the structure to something like their former glory, which, in the case of the Renaissance sections, is something special. Built in the 1530s by a team of Italian masons, Brzeg became the prototype for a whole series of palaces in Poland, Bohemia, northern Germany and Sweden.

The **gateway**, modelled on Dürer's woodcut of a triumphal arch in honour of Emperor Maximilian, is extravagantly rich. Above, in a shameless piece of self-glorification, are portrait figures of Duke George II and his wife, Barbara von Brandenburg. At the same level are pairs of knights whose coats of arms include those of Brzeg, Legnica and the Jagiellonian monarchs of Poland – the last, given that Silesia had not been a part of Poland for the past three centuries, being an expression of unrequited loyalty. Two tiers of busts above the windows trace the duke's genealogy, beginning with the peasant Piast at the upper left-hand corner.

To some extent, the three-storey **courtyard** resembles the Wawel palace in Kraków, above all in the lofty arcades. However, its carved decoration ultimately gives it a different character, with the heraldic motif continued on the more modest interior gate and antique-style medallions to the sides of the arcades. To the southwest corner of the courtyard rises the Lwów Tower, a survival of the medieval castle, along with part of its fortifications.

The halls of the second floor have been adapted to house the **Piast Museum** (Wed 10am–6pm, Thurs–Sun 10am–4pm). At the time of writing, exhibits from the

National Museum in Wrocław were on view here, including an impressive array of devotional sculptures and a magnificent group of canvases, including a hauntingly powerful series of *The Four Doctors of the Church* by Michael Willmann.

The rest of the town

Across from the palace stands the **Piast College**, which was built some thirty years later. It has suffered even more from the vagaries of time, but once more a school is functioning behind the great portal. Directly opposite is the former Jesuit church of the **Holy Cross**, which dates back to the turn of the eighteenth century. Sober enough from the outside, its single interior space is encrusted with Rococo decorations.

Back towards the centre is the **Town Hall**, which belongs to the same architectural school as the palace, and again is an adaptation of an older structure, from which the tall belfry survives. It consists of two long parallel buildings, each terminating in a tower crowned by a bulbous Baroque steeple, joined together by the galleried facade. Further on towards the stations is the market square, centred on the very German-looking fourteenth-century church of **St Nicholas** (św. Mikołaja). Its exterior was marred by a heightening of the towers last century – the builders lacked the wit to use bricks of matching colour. However, the interior is pleasingly spacious and boasts a varied collection of memorial plaques of prominent families. If you come around the Mass times, you may get to see the Gothic wall paintings recently uncovered in the sacristy.

Practicalities

Brzeg has only one **hotel**, *Piast*, situated just a couple of minutes' walk from the station on the way to the town centre at ul. Piastowska 14 (☎20-27), though there's also a motel, *U Rybiorza*, on ul. Obwodnica (☎34-73) at the edge of town on the way to Opole. The only other accommodation option is the **youth hostel** on ul. Świerczewskiego, south of the centre and west of the station, but this is only open for a few weeks in summer. Classiest **restaurant** by far is the *Ratuszowa* in the town hall cellars, which is excellent and surprisingly inexpensive. In the cultural centre on ul. Armii Krajowej is *Ambrozja*, a popular **café-bar** by day, a disco from 10pm each evening. The **Orbis** office is at ul. Staromiejska 14 (☎22-91), while **PTTK** is at ul. Piastowska 2 (☎21-00). In late May, Brzeg's Schloss, Town Hall and churches are put to impressive use for a four-day-long international **festival** of classical music.

Opole and around

If you're planning on spending a fair amount of time in Silesia, chances are you'll end up in **OPOLE** sooner or later. Situated in the very heart of the province, midway down the train line between Wrocław and Katowice, and within easy reach of Nysa, the Kłodzko Region and Częstochowa, the city makes a convenient touring base. Though ravaged by over twenty fires throughout its history, the centre presents a well-balanced spread of old and new, ringed by a green belt and with the more unsightly industry banished to the outskirts.

One of Opole's main assets is its setting on the banks of the Odra. The river divides to form an island, the **Wyspa Pasieka**, which was inhabited in the ninth century by a Slavic tribe called the Opolanes. Bolesław the Brave established the island as a fortress, but subsequently became divorced from its mother country, serving as the capital of a Piast principality from 1202 until this particular line died out in 1532.

The city and the highly productive agricultural land around were understandably coveted by the Polish state after World War I, but Opole voted to remain part of Germany in the plebiscite of 1921, subsequently becoming the capital of the German province of Upper Silesia. In contrast to most other places ceded to Poland after World War II, the Opole region retained a sizeable **German minority**, and is the prime focus of German political troublemakers.

The City

The hub of Opole has long moved from the Wyspa Pasieka to the right bank of the Odra, where the central area is laid out on a grid-iron pattern. Nonetheless, the island in many ways makes the best place to begin an exploration, and can be reached in a few minutes from the main **train** and **bus** stations at the southern end of town via ul. Wojciecha Korfantego.

The waterfront

Of the four bridges crossing the arm of the river, look out for the second, one of several structures in Opole built around 1910 in the Secessionist style. Arched like a bridge in a Japanese garden, this steel construction was made so cheaply that it became known as the **Groschen Bridge** after the smallest coin then in circulation. It bears the curious coat of arms of the city, showing half an eagle and half a cross: the local Piasts allowed one side of the family's traditional blazon to be replaced by a symbol of the city's acquisition of a relic of the True Cross.

Of the medieval Piast **Castle**, almost nothing is left save a gaunt round tower, now partly hidden behind functional 1930s administrative buildings; in summer you can climb to the top for a view of the city. The grounds have been converted into a park with a large artificial lake and an open-air amphitheatre, the setting for a **Festival of Polish Song** held each June. Continuing northwards along ul. Piastowa, you get a good view of the Old Town on the opposite bank, and in particular of the former **wharf** directly opposite, with a picturesque jumble of buildings rising directly from the river.

The city centre

Returning across the Odra by ul. Zamkowa, you soon arrive at the **Franciscan church**, a much-altered Gothic construction chiefly remarkable for the richly decorated Chapel of St Anne off the southern side of the nave. Endowed by the local Piasts to serve as their **mausoleum**, it has an exquisite star vault studded with keystones of the family eagle and painted with floral and heraldic motifs. The two magnificent double tombs were carved around 1380 by a member of the celebrated Parler family. Although he was still alive, an effigy of Duke Bolko III was made to accompany that of his recently deceased wife, with a similar monument created in belated memory of his two ancestral namesakes. The retable is from a century later, and shows Bolko I offering a model of this monastery to Saint Anne, while Ladislaus II presents her with a model of the great church of Jasna Góra in Częstochowa.

If you ring at any reasonable time at the door of the **Franciscan monastery** just around the corner on ul. Koraszewskiego, a monk will escort you round the

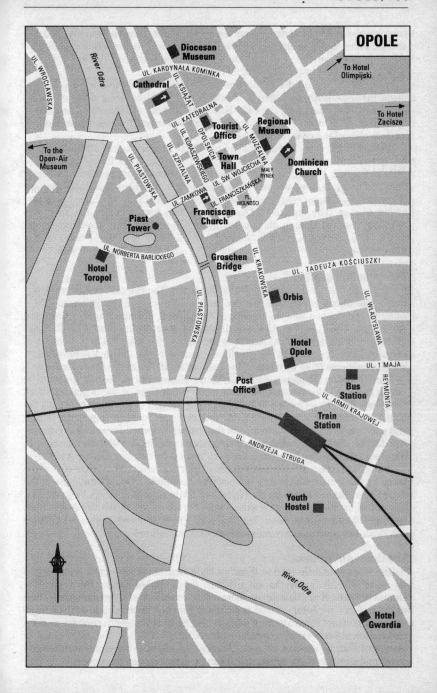

complex and will light up the chapel – a necessity for seeing it properly. You will also be taken down to the catacombs, which contain the unadorned coffins of other members of the dynasty and a number of fourteenth-century frescoes, notably a faded but tragically powerful *Crucifixion*.

Immediately beyond the Franciscan monastery is the **Rynek**, whose cheerful mansions were badly damaged in World War II, but have been deftly restored. The **Town Hall** dates from the early Nazi years and is a self-conscious pastiche of the Palazzo Vecchio in Florence, yet its unrelieved severity is suggestive more of a prison than of the civic headquarters.

Housed in the former Jesuit college on ul. św. Wojciecha just off the Rynek is the **District Museum** (Tues & Thurs–Sun 10am–3pm, Wed 10am–5pm), whose main strength is the archaeology section, with exhibits from prehistoric to early medieval times. A steep stairway then ascends to a hill where Saint Adalbert (see "Gniezno", in Chapter Six) used to preach as Bishop of Prague, Opole being part of his diocese. The church of **Our Lady**, which now occupies the spot, was originally Gothic, though this is hardly apparent from the neo-Romanesque facade and Baroque interior decorations. Beyond are the tower of the fourteenth-century fortress and remains of the sixteenth-century town wall.

The cathedral quarter

From the Rynek, ul. Książąt Opolskich leads past the eye-catching Secessionist **Bank Rolników**, which was founded by the local Polish population in 1911 – along with a newspaper – as a gesture of nationalist defiance. Further down the street you come to the **Cathedral**, mixing fourteenth-century Gothic and nineteenth-century imitation. Raised to the status of a cathedral only a couple of decades ago, the church is chiefly famous for the allegedly miraculous, jewel-encrusted icon to the right of the main altar, known as the *Opole Madonna*.

The **Diocesan Museum** (Tues & Thurs 10am–noon & 2–5pm, first Sun in month 2–5pm) is located in a block of modern buildings at the beginning of ul. Kardynała Kominka. Opened in 1987 largely as a result of voluntary effort, it's the object of considerable local pride as the first non-state museum in postwar Poland and one whose display techniques put the nationally owned collections to shame. Ask for the leaflet in English which describes the exhibits, all from churches in the Opole region. On the ground floor are several outstanding Gothic sculptures, including an *Enthroned Madonna* in the Parler style. Upstairs, pride of place is taken by the fourteenth-century reliquary made to house Opole's fragment of the True Cross; there's also a lovely *Virgin and Child* attributed to Fra Filippo Lippi. The small room next door features gifts to adorn the *Opole Madonna* from worthies ranging from King Jan Sobieski to the present pope. Imaginative exhibitions of contemporary religious art are also featured.

The Open-Air Museum

By the side of the main road to Wrocław, 8km west of the city centre and reached by buses #5, #19 or #A, is an excellent **Open-Air Museum** (Muzeum Wsi Opolskiej; Tues–Sun 10am–5pm). Some sixty examples of the rural architecture of the region have been erected here, many grouped in simulation of their original environment. Particularly notable is the early seventeenth-century wooden church from Gręboszów, a typical example of what is still the main place of worship in many Silesian villages. Another highlight is an eighteenth-century water mill in full working order, which can be demonstrated on request.

Opole practicalities

The **tourist office** on ul. Książąt Opolskich (Mon–Fri 9am–5/6pm, Sat 10am–3pm) has maps and booklets on Opole in Polish and German. **Orbis** is at ul. Krakowska 31 (☎363-36), while **Almatur** is at pl. Kopernika 1 (☎377-36).

The best accommodation bets are the **sports hotels** – *Toropol*, ul. Norberta Barlickiego 13 (☎366-91) on the Wyspa Pasieka, and *Gwardia*, ten minutes' walk south of the station at ul. Kowalska 4 (☎364-29). Cheapest of the other **hotels** are *Zacisze*, just east of the historic quarters at Grundwaldzka 28 (☎395-33), and *Zajadz Kastelański*, well to the west of the city centre at ul. Koszyka 29 (☎743-028) but close to over a dozen bus routes, including #2, #4, #5, #7, #8 and #9. The leading hotel is *Opole*, across from the station at ul. Krakowska 59 (☎386-51), a three-star place catering mainly to affluent German tourists, with prices to match. Similarly luxurious is the motel *Olimpijska*, not far from the northern suburban station of Opole-Wschodnie at ul. Oleska 86 (☎263-51); from the centre take bus #3, #11, #C, #D or #N. The **youth hostel** is to the rear of the main train station at ul. Struga 16 (July & Aug; ☎333-52). Another summer possibility is the **student hotel**, *Zygzak*, north of the motel at ul. ZSP 10 (☎262-57). Opole has no camping facilities.

Prices in the *Hotel Opole*'s **restaurant**, the *Hotelowa*, are bargain basement in comparison with the accommodation, but the quality isn't outstanding. Alternative choices for a full meal are *Europa*, pl. Wolności 1, and *Festiwalowa*, ul. Kościuszki 3. More adventurous menus are on offer at *Karczma Słupska*, ul. Książąt Opolskich 6, specialising in huge pork knuckles, and the Hungarian *Czardasz*, to the east of the centre at ul. Ozimska 63, which has dancing in the evenings.

If you're after something less fancy, there's the **milk bar** *Krówka*, ul. Krakowska 11, and a snack bar for fish dishes: *Rybny*, ul. Władysława Reymonta 9. Among the many **cafés** are two on the Rynek, *Pod Arkadami* and *Melba*, and a couple more on ul. Krakowska, *Ptyś* and *Teatralna*.

Góra Świętej Anny

Forty kilometres southeast of Opole, conspicuous on its 410-metre-hill, is the village of **GÓRA ŚWIĘTEJ ANNY**. Associated with the cult of Saint Anne, mother of the Virgin Mary, it's one of the most popular places of **pilgrimage** in Poland and is the scene of colourful processions on July 26 each year. Outside major church festivals, however, it's a moribund little place, the antithesis of the relentlessly busy Jasna Góra. For that, it can thank its relatively isolated situation: getting here by public transport is problematic, and is best done by taking a train from Opole to ZDZIESZOWICE, then covering the remaining 6km on foot or by bus. It's worth bringing a picnic, as the village has only a café and some tacky snack bars which aren't always open.

Although the cult of Saint Anne is long established in Silesia, Góra Świętej Anny's status as a major pilgrimage shrine dates back only to the mid-seventeenth century, when a **Franciscan monastery** was built to replace a modest Gothic votive chapel. As is the case with Jasna Góra, its popularity is intimately associated with Polish nationalism, fanned by the fact that the monks have been expelled three times (as a result of the policies of Napoleon, Bismarck and Hitler). For five days in May 1921, the village was the scene of bitter fighting following the Upper Silesia plebiscite, which left it in German hands. Ill-feeling has persisted: it was only in 1989 that the outlawing of Masses in German, introduced when the monks returned in 1945 in retaliation for previous bans on Polish services, was rescinded.

The **Church**, decorated in a restrained Baroque style, houses the source of the pilgrimage, a tiny miraculous statue of *St Anne with the Virgin and Child*, high above the main altar. An unassuming piece of folksy Gothic carving, it's usually decked out in gorgeous clothes. Below the monastery buildings is the mid-eighteenth century **Calvary**, an elaborate processional way with 33 chapels and shrines telling the story of the Passion. A large and less tasteful **Lourdes grotto** was added as the centrepiece in 1912.

The Katowice conurbation

Poland's main industrial area consists of an almost continuously built-up conurbation of about a dozen towns, beginning around 65km southeast of Opole. Two million inhabitants make this the most densely populated part of the country, with 350,000 in the largest city, **KATOWICE**.

Since the beginning of the *glasnost* era, the region has attracted worldwide attention because of the horrendous **pollution** of its outdated factories. It's officially classified as an environmental disaster area by the Polish Academy of

THE UPPER SILESIA DISPUTE OF 1918–22

In the aftermath of World War I, the dispute between Poland and Germany over the ownership of Upper Silesia represented the first reasonably successful attempt by the international community at providing an enduring, if not permanent, solution to a potentially explosive problem by means of mediation rather than through military force.

Following Germany's wartime defeat, the Allies at first intended to transfer the whole of Upper Silesia to the newly resurrected Poland, which would otherwise have been a poor agricultural country with no industrial base. Polish spokesmen stressed their **historical claim** on the territory and on its **demographic make-up**, although the latter couldn't be quantified exactly. Strongly partisan support for the transferral of sovereignty came from France, which wished to weaken Germany as much as possible and establish a strong ally to its east. This rather unnerved the British, ever anxious about the balance of power in Europe and concerned at the potential danger of French hegemony. They gradually came to back the ferocious German backlash against the proposed change in ownership, believing that it was in Europe's best interests for industries to be left in the hands of the nation that had developed them, rather than being handed over to a new country with no business experience: Prime Minister Lloyd George went so far as to suggest that allocating Upper Silesia to Poland was like giving a clock to a monkey.

As the Allies dragged their feet on the issue, Upper Silesia remained the one unresolved question on the now much-changed map of Europe. Frustrated at the lack of progress, the Poles staged **insurrections** in 1919 and 1920. Eventually, the Allies decided to test popular feelings by means of a **plebiscite**, which was held in March 1921. This was won by the Germans by 707,000 votes to 479,000, but the result was discredited by the fact that a large number (thought to be around 180,000) of former citizens were temporarily shipped back from their new homes

Sciences and many of its inhabitants are constantly subjected to severe health hazards, as the large number of disease-ridden children testifies. Similarly, the effect on buildings goes beyond turning local stonework a delicate shade of spearmint green: the dispersion of the pollution is responsible for the severe damage caused to Kraków, some 70km to the east.

The region's rich mineral seams have been extensively mined since the Middle Ages, but it wasn't until the nineteenth-century **Industrial Revolution** that the area became urbanised. In 1800, Katowice had just 500 inhabitants. Fifty years later, its population was a still modest 4000 before Upper Silesia mushroomed into the powerhouse of the Prussian state, in tandem with the broadly similar Ruhr at the opposite end of the country.

With a population composed almost equally of Germans and Poles (and with many of mixed blood), the fate of the area became a hot political issue after World War I – and one that was to be of far more than local significance (see box). In the communist period, the conurbation maintained its high-profile position, thanks to the ideological stress placed on heavy industry. Workers here enjoyed a privileged position; mining wages, for example, were three times the national average income. However, the failure to modernise plant and machinery is now taking its toll; on top of health and environmental problems many enterprises have been shut down in the past couple of years, resulting in high unemployment and a very uncertain future for the region.

---

elsewhere in Germany. Support for continued German sovereignty was strongest in the industrial communities closest to Poland, making the solution of partition seemingly intractable, particularly as it was taken for granted that the conurbation could not be divided satisfactorily .

In May 1921, a third insurrection led to the occupation of the territory by the Polish army. Realising the need for a quick solution, the Allies referred the matter to the **League of Nations**, the body newly established to promote world peace. The neutral observers who were assigned to the task decided that partition was the only fair solution, and used the plebiscite returns as the basis for determining the respective shares of the carve-up. By the **Geneva Convention on Upper Silesia** of 1922, which ran to 606 articles, the Germans retained two-thirds of the land and three-fifths of the population, but an international boundary was cut through the industrial conurbation, leaving Poland with the vast majority of the coal mines and blast furnaces. However, in what was itself a radical and previously untried experiment, the area was kept as an economic unit, with guarantees on the movement of goods, material and labour, the provision of public services and the rights of individuals who found themselves living under an alien flag.

Despite dire predictions to the contrary, the agreement endured for the full fifteen years it was scheduled to operate. The Poles proved perfectly capable of running what had previously been German industrial concerns, and the presence of an international frontier did not impede the conurbation's productivity. Admittedly there was a persistent flow of grievances, mostly from the Germans, who conveniently forgot that they had managed to hold on to a good deal of valuable territory which they'd come close to losing. However, the country's new democratic leaders felt duty bound to stop short of calling for a return of the lost portion, and, had it not been for the advent of Hitler, the League's highly imaginative solution might well have survived indefinitely.

Katowice

Katowice is not a place you'll want to go out of your way to see, but if you do find yourself there for any reason, there are a number of places – and in particular a surprising amount of greenery – where you could kill some time.

The city centre sprawls in all directions around the train station, with the main commercial area lying straight ahead of the main entrance to the north. A few blocks to the east is the long ul. Wojciecha Korfantego, where at no. 3 is the **Silesian Museum** (Muzeum Śląskie; Tues–Fri 10am–5pm, Sat & Sun 11am–4pm). This features changing exhibitions plus a variety of contemporary paintings downstairs, while the upstairs gallery has an entertaining selection of Polish art from 1800 to World War II. Major names such as Piotr Michałowski, Jan Matejko and Stanisław Wyspiański are here, but the most intriguing work is a highly accomplished *Self-Portrait* by Stanisław Ignacy Witkiewicz, better known for his brilliantly original novels and plays. Continuing down the street to the end, you come to an enormous roundabout (known simply as the Rondo) with a sports hall reminiscent of a flying saucer. In front stands the **Monument to the Silesian Uprisings**: three tall shapes in the form of clipped wings, symbolising each of the attempts to gain freedom from German rule.

Any tram going from the roundabout westwards towards CHORZÓW will bring you to Katowice's main recreation area, the **Wojewódzki Park**, whose main attraction is a big wheel similar to the famous Prater in Vienna, which offers a grandstand view if you have the stomach to undertake the giddy ride. Somewhat less terrifying is the triangular-shaped chair lift circuit round the park, which is good fun if rather pointless. Behind the huge football stadium (four stops after the big wheel), and technically over the municipal boundary into Chorzów, is the **Górnośląski Park** (May–Sept Tues–Fri 10am–5pm, Sat & Sun noon–7pm). If you don't have a chance to go into the mountains, the wooden buildings brought here from nearby rural communities will give you a fair idea of what you're missing.

From the rear of the train station, ul. Jana Kochanowskiego leads uphill towards the **Cathedral of Christ the King**. Begun in 1927 and finished in 1955, it offers a modernist reinterpretation of the classical idiom, the most successful feature being the vast central space of the interior, set under a huge dome. The striking stained glass windows, embroideries and sculptures are proof of the continued vibrancy of religious art in present-day Poland. A block to the west, ul. Kościuszki continues on to the **Kościuszko Park**, which has another noteworthy commemorative monument, this time to the victims of World War II and the Holocaust. It's a reminder of the parachute tower formerly occupying the site, where people learnt how to jump; the Nazis continued to put it to use – having taken the parachutes away. At the southern end of the park is a walled close containing an early seventeenth-century **wooden church** and its detached belfry, brought here from the village of Syrnia.

Practicalities

There are three cheap **hotels**, of the run-down two-star class, in the immediate vicinity of the station. *Centralny*, a couple of minutes' walk east of the main entrance at ul. Dworcowa 9 (☎53-90-41), seems to be almost permanently full, but there are normally vacancies at *Śląski*, a few minutes' walk further on at ul. Mariacka 15 (☎53-70-11), and *Polonia*, just to the rear of the station at ul.

Kochanowskiego 3 (☎51-40-51). A step up in class are *Budowlani*, further east of *Śląski* at ul. Maja 3 (☎58-60-81), and *Sprotowy*, across from the Kościuszko Park at ul. Ceglana 68 (☎51-00-93). These are followed by the two places on ul. Korfantego: *Katowice* at no. 9 (☎59-80-21) and *Olimpijski*, beyond the Rondo at no. 35 (☎58-22-82). Top of the range are the two four-star Orbis hotels with all the usual luxuries: *Silesia*, right in the heart of the shopping district at ul. Piotra Skargi 2 (☎59-62-11), and *Warszawa*, east of the Rondo at ul. Rożdzieńskiego 16 (☎59-60-11). The **youth hostel**, about fifteen minutes' walk east from the rear of the station at ul. Graniczna 27a (☎51-94-57), is one of the most welcoming in Poland. There's also a lakeside **campsite** to the southwest of the city centre at Adamieckiego 6 (☎51-87-84), reached by buses #4, #673 or #E1.

Several of the best **restaurants** are in the hotels, notably *Polonia* and both Orbis establishments. *Kaczma Słłupska*, ul. Mariacki 1, offers traditional Polish food, while *Hungaria*, across the street at no. 6, is well known locally for its Hungarian-style dishes – and as a gay hang-out. On ul. Stawowa, the pedestrian precinct opposite the station, you'll find two of the most popular new eateries: the good and authentic *Restauracja Chińska*, and the fast-food *Best*; other newcomers are *As*, a couple of blocks east on the unprepossessing Rynek, and *Corner*, across the tracks on ul. 27 Go-Styczni. *Krysztatowa*, a real olde-worlde central European **café** at ul. Warszawska 5, is by far the best choice for coffee, cakes or ice-cream.

There's a municipal **tourist office** right beside the station at ul. Młyńska 11 (☎53-95-66). **Orbis** is at ul. Wojciecha Korfanty 2 (☎58-75-32), **PTTK** at ul. św. Jana 12 (☎58-87-00) and **Almatur** at ul. 3 Maja 7 (☎59-88-58). Katowice has a lively cultural scene. Regular **concerts** are given by the Silesian Philharmonic, ul. Sokolska 2 (☎52-62-61), and the Symphony Orchestra of Polish Radio and Television, pl. Sejmu Śląskiego 2 (☎57-13-84). The *Teatr Stanisława Wyspiański* on the Rynek (☎59-89-76) presents high-quality **drama** productions, though its fame is eclipsed by the *Teatr Zagłębia* in the adjacent town of SOSNOWIEC. Regular **football** matches are held at *GKS Katowice*'s stadium at the southwestern corner of Wojewódzki Park. The conurbation has several other top-flight teams, including the one with the best record in Poland, *Górnik* of ZABRZE.

Tarnowskie Góry

From a tourist point of view, the only worthwhile town in the area is **TARNOWSKIE GÓRY**, at the far northern end of the conurbation and reached from Katowice in about an hour by train. It's a place with a far more venerable history: silver and lead deposits were discovered in the thirteenth century and it was given an urban charter and mining rights in the sixteenth by the Dukes of Opole. Some idea of its underground wealth is given in a document dated 1632, listing 20,000 places where minerals could be exploited.

There are two **historic industrial sites** in Tarnowskie Góry, which make a fascinating alternative to the famous salt mines of Wieliczka (see Chapter Four). Probably the best approach is to telephone the Friends of Tarnowskie Góry Association for a **guided tour** (daily 7.30am–3.30pm; ☎85-49-96), or to ask a tourist office to do it for you; they have guides who speak German plus a little English and French. Otherwise, you can just turn up at the sites and wait to tag on to the next organised group passing through; these are frequent in summer and at weekends. Warm clothing and shoes with a good grip are essential.

The first of the sites is the **Sylvester Mine and Museum** (9am–2pm; closed Tues). From Tarnowskie Góry station, take any bus going to BYTOM: if an express service, get off at the first stop; if a normal service, at the third. Alternatively, it can be reached directly from Katowice by taking express bus #A as far as Osada Janas. Dating back to medieval times, the mine was formerly worked for silver, lead and copper. In the small museum you can see the old equipment, plus models of how the mine was worked and the water levels controlled.

A large wall map explains the connection between the levels of the mine and the **Black Trout Shaft** (Sztolnia Czarnego Pstrąg; daily 8.30am–dusk), 3km away. If you've booked a tour, the guide will accompany you from the Sylvester mine; by public transport the easiest approach is to return to the station, then take bus #19 as far as the hospital; the way is then signposted through the park. Here you make a spooky journey by boat along one of the former drainage channels through rock-hewn "gates". Each has a different name, with a legend attached: at one point, for instance, any woman wanting to find a husband within the year is invited to rap on the wall. At the end of the trip, wait until the water becomes still – the reflection from the ceiling creates the uncanny illusion that the water has disappeared.

Each September, Tarnowskie Góry hosts a costume **festival** in honour of the visit of King Jan Sobieski, who stopped off in 1683 on his way to relieve Vienna from the Turks.

South of Katowice

Just beyond the southern end of the Katowice conurbation, about forty minutes from the city by train, is the small town of **PSZCZYNA**. It's best known for its particularly unpronounceable name, which features in a favourite Polish tongue-twister. On a more serious note, it holds an honoured place in the nation's history for having provided the leadership of the first Upper Silesian Uprising in 1919, and it was duly incorporated into Poland after the plebiscite.

However, the main claim on your attention is likely to be the **Palace** (May–Oct Wed 9am–5pm, Thurs & Fri 9am–3pm, Sat & Sun 10am–3pm; Nov–April Wed 10am–4pm, Thurs & Fri 10am–2pm, Sat & Sun 10am–2pm). The building's chequered history mirrors the area's turbulent past. A Piast hunting lodge from the twelfth century, it was successively expanded and rebuilt in the Gothic and Renaissance styles before gaining its largely Baroque appearance following a fire; other parts were added in the nineteenth century. It contains many tasteful period furnishings, some of them brought from other Polish stately homes. On the first and last Sunday of the month, chamber concerts are held in the beautiful Baroque ballroom – tickets available at the booking office on the day of performance. The English-style **park** (free access) has a lake with water lilies and a wooden bridge straight from a Monet painting.

The handsome late eighteenth-century **Rynek** in front of the palace is lined with fine mansions and a sober Baroque Protestant church. At no. 18, look out for the bison sign which gives the *Pod Zubrem* its name. On ul. Parkowa, a block north of ul. Dworcowa, the road between the town centre and the station, is the only other attraction worth mentioning, a small **skansen** (Wed–Sun 10am–3pm) of reassembled rural buildings.

A few places to **eat** and **drink** can be found on the Rynek and the nearby ul. Piastowska. **PTTK** have an office at no. 3 on the Rynek (☎35-30); the same organisation runs a **tourist hostel**, located at ul. Bogedalnia south of the town centre.

Bielsko–Biała

A further 25km south of Pszczyna, at the foot of the Beskid Śląski and Beskid Mały ranges, lies **BIELSKO–BIAŁA**, which, as its name suggests, was formerly two separate towns, united as recently as 1951. The parts now form one seamless whole with the River Biała, which formerly divided them, appearing as an insignificant stream in the city centre. This makes it all the more extraordinary that the two towns spent most of their history in different countries – Bielsko belonged to the duchy of Cieszyn, which in due course became part of Bohemia, whereas Biała was part of the Oświęcim duchy, which fell to the Polish crown in the fifteenth century. Even though both were under Austrian rule during the Partitions, Bielsko formed part of its small Silesian province, whereas Biała was in Galicia.

Both towns flourished in the late nineteenth century, thanks to their high-quality textile products, and the cityscape today, like its northern English counterparts, is dominated by the supremely self-confident buildings of this period, with many in the Viennese Secessionist style. The present-day city still ranks among the most prosperous in Poland, and has one of the country's soundest economic infrastructures. Car manufacturing, under licence from Fiat, is a key industry, with the new award-winning Cinquecento having quickly established itself as one of Europe's best small motors.

Bielsko centre

Arriving at the main bus or train stations in the northern part of Bielsko, it's a fifteen-minute walk to the centre down ul. 3 Maja, a broad boulevard lined with turn-of-the century tenements so characteristic of the city. It ends at pl. Bolesława Chrobrego, above which stands the **Castle** (Tues, Wed & Fri 10am–3pm, Thurs 10am–6pm, Sat 9am–3pm, Sun 9am–2pm), an eclectic structure dating back to the Gothic period but whose present appearance is largely the result of a mid-nineteenth-century rebuild. Inside, a few surprisingly modest rooms are open, with displays of works of art and furnishings from the Middle Ages onwards.

West of the castle is a labyrinth of hilly, twisting streets and alleys which lost its function as a town centre when Bielsko united with Biała, and now has a down-at-heel feel. Nonetheless, the strange early twentieth-century church of **St Nicholas**, a couple of blocks south of the small Rynek on ul. Schodowa, was recently given a boost by being raised to the status of a cathedral. The tall belfry, flanked by two smaller towers, is a somewhat surrealistic re-interpretation of the Italian Renaissance, providing the city with its most visually striking landmark. Inside are a number of imposing Secessionist stained glass windows. North of the Rynek are several reminders of the historical strength of Protestantism in these parts: the **plac Luthra** features the only statue of Martin Luther to be found in Poland and a neo-Gothic church which is one of three still-functioning Lutheran places of worship in Bielsko–Biała – a Polish record. The ensemble is completed by the peaceful cemetery situated a couple of blocks to the north.

Biała centre

Biała's centre is just a few minutes' walk east of pl. Bolesława Chrobrego. The dominant building is the bulky neo-Renaissance **Town Hall**, whose tower provides a suitably secular counterfoil to that of St Nicholas across the river. From here, walk north to pl. Wojska Polskiego, a pleasant square on whose northeastern corner stands the town's prettiest Secessionist building, the **Frogs' House** (Pod Żabami), a former wine restaurant that takes its name from its amusing carvings.

On ul. Targowa immediately to the east is the Neoclassical **Lutheran Church**, a traditional late eighteenth-century preaching hall with a large number of nineteenth-century embellishments, which include a fine organ and a pulpit in the shape of a boat. An even more eye-catching pulpit of this type is the ornate Rococo creation, complete with Jonah emerging from the mouth of the whale, which can be seen in the twin-towered **Church of Providence** (Kościół Opatrzności Bożej) at the extreme southeastern end of central Biała, itself an excellent example of the opulent Baroque architecture favoured in the Habsburg domains.

The Outskirts

In the formerly separate village of MIKUSZOWICE at the extreme southeastern edge of the urban area, reached by bus #2, #5 or #55, is the wooden church of **St Barbara**, one of the finest examples of this distinctive form of vernacular architecture to be found anywhere in Poland. Apart from those examples in open-air museums, it's rare to find such a structure in an urban setting, though the rustic location in a walled close by the River Biała seems a world away from the city centre. Built at the end of the seventeenth century, the church is strikingly geometric, with a square tower and nave and a hexagonal chancel, while its skyline, with its bulbous bell turrets and steeply pitched shingle roofs, is aggressively picturesque. The interior was adorned a generation after its construction with a series of naive wall paintings illustrating the legend of its patron saint. There's also a lovely fifteenth-century carving of the Madonna and Child in the left aisle.

For a taste of the mountains which form the backdrop to Bielsko-Biała, take bus #8 to its terminus at the southwestern extremity of the city. From here, you can ascend **Szyndzielna** (1026m) for a sweeping panoramic view. It's about three hours' walk up by the red trail, or you can go up in less than fifteen minutes by cable car (Jan, Feb, Oct & Dec 9am–4.30pm; March–May & Nov 9am–5.30pm; June–Aug 9am–6.30pm).

Practicalities

There are two **hotels** in the city centre – the venerable three-star *Prezydent*, ul. 3 Maja 12 (☎272-11), and the two-star *Pod Poczta*, ul. 1 Maja 4a (☎260-37). Of the cheaper options, *Olimp* is just south of the centre of Biała and near the Lipnik suburban station at ul. Rychlińskiego 13 (☎475-09); *Budolwlani* is by the sports stadium in the far southern suburbs, near the terminus of buses #1, #14 and #24; *Konsul* is at the far west of town at ul. Zapora 3 (☎255-64), and reached by bus #16; while *ZIAiDZ* is on the road towards the cable car at ul. Brygadzistów 170 (☎421-79), shortly before the terminus of bus #8. The most luxurious hotel in the city is *Magura*, a standard four-star Orbis concrete box in the southern part of Biała at ul. Żywiecka 93 (☎465-45), on the route of buses #2, #5, #9, #11 and #55. There's also a motel, *Ondraszek*, to the north of Bielsko at ul. Warszawska 185 (☎220-37), reached by bus #58.

The **youth hostel** has a handy location in the northern part of central Biała at ul. Komorowicka 25 (☎274-66), while the **PTTK hostel** is a few minutes' walk southwest of the main train station at ul. Krasińskiego 38 (☎238-18). **Campsites** can be found just north of the cable car station at ul. Karbowa 15 (☎460-80) and in the foothills to the west, past the terminus of bus #26, at ul. Pocztowa 43 (☎464-25).

Among the places to eat and drink, special mention must go to the aforementioned *Prezydent*. Another good choice for traditional Polish fare is *Teatralna*, ul. 1 Maja 4, while *Patria*, ul. Wzgórze 19, is one of a number of elegant **cafés** in the immediate vicinity of the castle. There are also some adventurous new eateries, such as *Pizzeria Capri*, ul. 3 Maja 13, which makes pizzas in the proper Italian way, and the lively bistro *Starówka*, pl. Smolki 5. For an evening's entertainment, it's worth checking on the programmes at the two **theatres** – *Teatr Polski*, ul. 1 Maja 1 (☎284-51), and *Banialuka*, ul. Mickiewicza 20 (☎210-46). The latter is the national puppet theatre, and in May of even-numbered years presents a world **festival** of this genre.

The **tourist office** for the Beskid Śląski area, **In-Tour**, is across from the station at ul. Piastowska 2 (☎224-06). **Orbis** are at ul. 3 Maja 9 (☎279-06), **PTTK** at ul. Wzgórze 7 (☎236-48). Finally, note that a number of **bus** routes in the region, including that to Cieszyn, have been privatised and do not leave from the bus station any longer, but from a stand across the road, just north of the train station.

The Beskid Śląski

Immediately south of Bielsko–Biała lies the Silesian section of the **Beskid Mountains**. It's an archetypal central European landscape, characterised by thickly wooded slopes and an uncompromisingly rural way of life. Within Poland, it's a popular holiday area: the prolonged and heavy snowfalls make it ideal for winter sports, while there are good hiking opportunities in summer. As yet, Western tourists are still very rare, largely because of the dearth of quality hotels (or indeed of any kind of accommodation easily bookable in advance), but the irony is that there's actually a huge variety of **places to stay**. Most of these are fairly basic (and correspondingly cheap) – there are many refuges in the mountains themselves, while the resorts usually have at least a campsite and some kind of hostel. There's also an abundance of rooms in private houses (identified by signs saying *Noclegi* or *Pokoje*); most of these will provide meals for a nominal amount, or allow you to do your own catering. If you're after a bit more luxury, there are plush Alpine-style holiday homes for rent: a number of these can be booked beforehand in the UK (see *Basics* for details). If you're planning on doing any serious walking, it's essential to get hold of the map *Beskid Śląski i Żywiecki* (1:75,000), which is readily available locally.

Szczyrk and around

The main resort in the Beskid Śląski is **SZCZYRK**, set in the valley of the River Żylica about 15km southwest of Bielsko–Biała with regular bus connections. It ranks second to Zakopane as the most popular ski centre in the country, and has an international-class downhill route which is generally considered to be superior to that of its rival. In winter, the skiing seems to be as much a social activity as anything else, and the party atmosphere should compensate for the frustrations of waiting in long queues for the ski-lifts. Accommodation options include an unusually large number of rooms in **private houses**, plus a **youth hostel**, ul. Sportowa 2 (☎933), the *Dom Turysty* **PTTK hostel**, ul. Górska 7 (☎578), and the *Skalite* **campsite**, ul. Kempingowa 4 (☎760).

All year round, a cable car runs from Szczyrk to the summit of **Skrzyczne** (1257m), the highest peak in the range; the energetic alternative is to walk up by either the blue or the green trail. The latter continues southwards to **Barania Góra** (1220m), enabling you to visit the spring on its slopes forming the source of the **River Wisła** (or Vistula). This, Poland's greatest waterway, subsequently winds a serpentine 1090km course through Oświęcim, Kraków, Warsaw and Toruń before disgorging itself into the Baltic just east of Gdańsk.

Wisła and around

From Barania Góra, there's a choice of marked descents to the town of **WISŁA**, which can also be reached by bus from Szczyrk via the spectacular main road which makes a looping circuit through the valleys and passes of the range. There's an even more circuitous rail link with Bielsko–Biała, the latter stages of which closely hug the banks of the Wisła, which has already metamorphosed from a mountain stream to a significant river. The best **hike** from here is southwest via the blue then the yellow trail to **Stożek** (978m), a fine vantage point which forms part of the border with the Czech Republic. Among the places to stay in Wisła are two cheap **hotels**, *Piast*, ul. 1 Maja 47 (☎35-78), and *Centrum*, ul. 1 Maja 57 (☎35-77); the *Nad Zaporą* **PTTK hostel**, ul. Czare 3 (☎24-11); and the *Joniało* **campsite** on ul. Wyzwolenie (☎28-20).

Ustroń Brenna and around

USTROŃ, a few kilometres downstream from Wisła and likewise on the rail line to Bielsko–Biała, stands just to the west of one of the most popular peaks in the Beskids, **Równica** (884m). This can be reached by the red trail, but it's actually even more fun to ascend by car or bus via a tortuous mountain road. A second recommended hike in the area is southwest from Ustroń by the blue route to **Czantoria** (995m), another summit right on the Czech frontier. Accommodation possibilities in Ustroń include a basic **hotel**, *Równica*, ul. 22 Lipca 63 (☎24-27); the *Motel*, ul. Baranowa (☎25-46), and *Czantoria*, ul. 1 Maja 99 (☎34-68), both in the outlying village of POLANA; and a **youth hostel** (☎35-01) in the hamlet of JASZOWIEC below Równica.

On the eastern side of Równica, on the bank of the River Brennica, lies **BRENNA**, the most secluded resort in the range. The course of the river has been terraced here, and there are good opportunities for bathing; there's also an open-air theatre which is used for regional song and dance events on weekends throughout the summer. Accommodation includes a simple **hotel**, the *Beskid*, at no. 760 (☎553).

Cieszyn

If you missed out on Berlin when it still had the Wall, then **CIESZYN**, some 30km west of Bielsko–Biała, will give you an idea on a smaller scale of the realities of life in a place arbitrarily divided by a line drawn on a map. Following the break-up of the Habsburg Empire after World War I, it was claimed by both

Czechoslovakia and Poland, each of which had large numbers of resident nationals. In the event, the 1920 Conference of Ambassadors decided on using the River Olza as the frontier, meaning the right-bank part of town became Polish and the opposite side (known as Český Těšín) Czech. However, no attempt was made to rationalise the nationality problem, with chaotic results. Until recently, ethnic Poles living on the Czech side could cross over to work each day using special passes, whereas Polish nationals were only entitled to cross in the other direction if armed with an official invitation and a visa. The exception was All Saints' Day, when the border was thrown open. Despite the demise of communism, border controls remain strict in an attempt to thwart traders out to exploit price divergencies in the two countries. The result is often long, slow-moving queues of people waiting for hours to cross what in normal circumstances would be no more than a town-centre bridge.

Cieszyn, having somehow escaped the war damage which blighted so many Silesian towns, is a pleasing place of somewhat faded streets of Baroque, Neoclassical and Jugendstil houses. The central Rynek, with the eighteenth-century Town Hall, stands at the highest point of the central area, about ten minutes' walk west of the bus and train stations. Just off the southwest corner of the square is the Gothic church of **St Mary Magdalene**, containing the mausoleum of the Piast dukes who established an independent principality here in 1290.

The main street, ul. Głębocka, lined with some of the most imposing mansions, sweeps downhill from the Rynek towards the river. If you take ul. Sejmowa to the left and then the first turning right, you'll find yourself on ul. Trzech Braci ("Street of the Three Brothers"). Here stands the **well** associated with the legend of the town's foundation. In the year 810 the three sons of King Leszko III of Poland met up at this spring after a long spell wandering the country. They were so delighted to see each other again that they founded a town here named "I'm happy" (cieszyć się). From the foot of ul. Głębocka, it's only a few paces along ul. Zamkowa to the Most Przyjazni, the pedestrian **frontier post** for crossing over to the Czech part of town. The return in the opposite direction is via the Most Wolności, about 700m upstream.

On the west side of ul. Zamkowa rises a hill crowned by a Gothic **clock tower** (daily April–Oct 9.30am–5pm, Nov–March 9.30am–3pm), the only surviving part of the Piast palace. From the top, there's a superb view over both sides of the town. Alongside stands one of the oldest surviving buildings in Poland, the **chapel of St Nicholas**, a beautiful Romanesque rotunda dating back to the eleventh century. Also on the hill are a Neoclassical hunting palace and a "ruined" Romantic folly among the trees.

Practicalities

Orbis have a four-star **motel** about 2km north of the town centre at ul. Motelowa 93 (☎204-51). A much more conveniently sited **hotel** is *Pod Jeleniem*, Rynek 20 (☎201-40), but this was closed at the time of writing, leaving the sports hotel *Piast*, just south of the Most Wolności crossing point at al. Jana Łyska 1 (☎220-44), as the only alternative. Further south, at al. Jana Łyska 12 (☎208-33), is the *Olza* **campsite**. Places to **eat** and **drink** are few and far between: try *Centralna*, ul. Mennicza 1, or *Zamkowa*, ul. Głęboka 64. There's a **PTTK tourist office** at ul. Głębocka 56 (☎211-86), while the **Orbis** office is at Rynek 19 (☎212-40).

travel details

Trains

Wrocław to Białystok (2 daily; 10hr 30min–13hr; couchettes); Bydgoszcz (7 daily; 4–5hr); Częstochowa (6 daily; 3–4hr); Gdańsk (6 daily; 6hr–7hr 30min; couchettes); Jelenia Góra (19 daily; 2hr 30min–3hr); Kalisz (3 daily; 2hr–2hr 30min); Katowice (21 daily; 3–4hr); Kielce (3 daily; 5hr–6hr 30min); Kłodzko (7 daily; 2hr 30min); Kołobrzeg ((3 daily; 8–10hr); Kraków (17 daily; 4–6hr); Legnica (22 daily; 1hr); Leszno (27 daily; 1hr–1hr 30min); Lublin (3 daily; 8hr 30min–9hr 30min; couchettes); Łódź (14 daily; 4–6hr); Olsztyn (2 daily; 7hr 30min–10hr; couchettes); Opole (42 daily; 1hr–1hr 30min); Poznań (26 daily; 2hr–3hr 30min); Przemyśl (5 daily; 8hr 30min; couchettes); Rzeszów (6 daily; 7hr; couchettes); Słupsk (2 daily; 9–10hr); Szczecin (11 daily; 6hr–7hr 30min; couchettes); Świnoujście (3 daily; 7–8hr); Wałbrzych (20 daily; 1hr 30min); Warsaw (16 daily; 6–7hr; couchettes); Zakopane (1 daily; 8hr 30min; couchettes); Zielona Góra (10 daily; 2–3hr). Also **international connections** to Görlitz, Dresden and Prague.

Jelenia Góra to Bydgoszcz (1 daily; 8hr; couchettes); Częstochowa (2 daily; 6hr); Gdańsk (1 daily; 10hr; couchettes); Kalisz (4 daily; 5–6hr 30min); Katowice (6hr 30min–8hr); Kielce (1 daily; 8hr; couchettes); Kłodzko (4 daily; 2hr); Kraków (2 daily; 4–5hr; couchettes); Leszno (3 daily; 4–5hr); Lublin (1 daily; 11hr 30min; couchettes); Łódź (4 daily; 6hr 30min–9hr); Opole (4 daily; 4hr–4hr 30min); Poznań (4 daily; 5hr–6hr 30min); Szczecin

(1 daily; 9hr; couchettes); Wałbrzych (23 daily; 1hr; couchettes); Warsaw (4 daily; 8hr 30min–9hr 30min); Wrocław (18 daily; 2hr 30min); Zielona Góra (2 daily; 4hr 30min–5hr 30min).

Katowice to Białystok (2 daily; 6–8hr; couchettes); Bydgoszcz (6 daily; 5–7hr; couchettes); Częstochowa (34 daily; 1hr 30min–2hr); Gdańsk (8 daily; 6hr 30min–9hr; couchettes); Jelenia Góra (3 daily; 7hr); Kielce (11 daily; 2hr 30min–3hr 30min); Kołobrzeg (2 daily; 10hr 30min–1hr 30min; couchettes); Kraków (40 daily; 1hr 30min–2hr); Legnica (7 daily; 4–7hr); Leszno (7 daily; 4hr 30min–5hr); Lublin (5 daily; 6–7hr); Łódź ((8 daily; 3hr 30min–5hr); Olsztyn (2 daily; 8hr 30min–11hr); Opole (23 daily; 2hr); Poznań (15 daily; 5–7hr); Przemyśl (7 daily; 5hr 30min); Rzeszów (8 daily; 4–5hr); Słupsk (2 daily; 10–13hr; couchettes); Szczecin (7 daily; 9–10hr); Świnoujście (3 daily; 10hr–1hr 30min); Wałbrzych (3 daily; 6hr); Warsaw (17 daily; 3hr 30min–5hr); Wrocław (23 daily; 3–4hr); Zakopane (3 daily; 5–7hr; couchettes); Zamość (2 daily; 8–10hr); Zielona Góra (4 daily; 5–6hr).

Buses

Wrocław to Kłodzko, Legnica, Oleśnica, Sobótka, Świdnica, Trzebnica.

Jelenia Góra to Bolków, Kamienna Góra, Karpacz, Kłodzko, Legnica, Szklarska Poręba.

Kłodzko to Kudowa-Zdrój, Lądek-Zdrój, Międzygórze, Paczków–Otmuchów–Nysa–Opole.

Katowice to Cieszyn, Pszczyna.

CHAPTER SIX

WIELKOPOLSKA AND POMERANIA

Wielkopolska and **Pomerania**, the two northwest regions of the country, constitute a large swathe of modern Poland. Despite their proximity, however, the feel and history of each is highly distinct. Wielkopolska formed the core of the original Polish nation and has remained identifiably Polish through subsequent centuries; Pomerania, by contrast, bears the imprint of the Prussians, who ruled this area from the early eighteenth century through to 1945 – the province only became Polish after 1945, and "Lower Pomerania", to the west of Świnoujście, remains German territory.

In **Wielkopolska** the chief interest is supplied by the regional capital **Poznań**, an attractive city famed within Poland for the 1956 riots which were the first major revolt against communism. **Gniezno**, the ancient capital of the first Piast monarchs and the normal seat of the Primate of Poland, is a big church centre, full of seminaries and trainee priests. Out in the countryside, the outstanding attractions are the **Wielkopolska National Park** and the Iron Age village of **Biskupin**, Poland's most ancient preserved settlement.

Pomerania is dominated by the Baltic, with ports such as **Szczecin** playing a crucial role in the country's economy, in tandem with a network of seaside resorts that pulls in large numbers of Polish and foreign tourists. The Baltic may be not quite the Med, but temperatures climb high enough for summer swimming and the **beaches** sweep far enough for escapes from the crowds. Among the towns, the architectural high points are **Stargard Szczeciński**, with some of the finest examples of the brick Gothic buildings so typical of the Baltic lands, and **Kamień Pomorski**, an old lagoon settlement with a wonderful cathedral. The region has wildlife appeal, too, with a rich variety of animal and bird life in the **Słowiński National Park** and a bison reserve in the forested **Woliński National Park**. Inland, the Pomeranian **lakeland** is less known than its counterpart in Mazury, but offers enjoyable, low-key pursuits for canoeists and hikers.

WIELKOPOLSKA

Much of the landscape of **Wielkopolska** is dull, but its human story is an altogether different matter, as its name – "Great Poland" – implies. This area has been inhabited continuously since prehistoric times, and it was here that th Polish nation first took shape. The names of the province and of Poland its derive from a Slav tribe called the **Polonians**, whose leaders – the **Piast** fami were to rule the country for five centuries. Their embryonic state emerged u

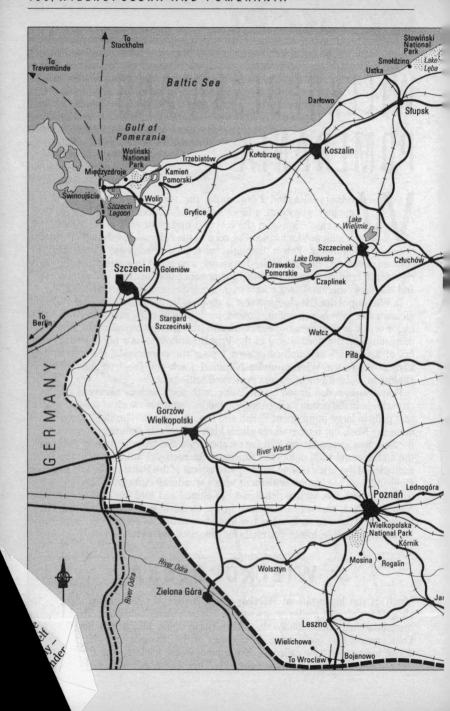

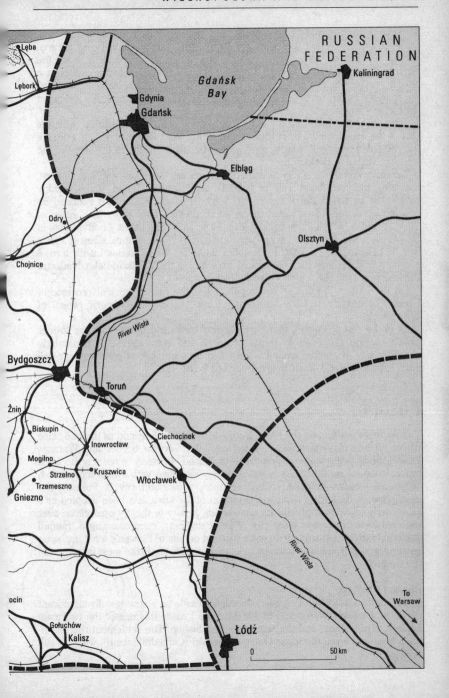

Mieszko I in the mid-tenth century, but the significant breakthrough was achieved under his son, Bolesław the Brave, who gained control over an area similar to that of present-day Poland, and made it independent from the German-dominated Holy Roman Empire. Though relegated to the status of a border province by the mid-eleventh century, Wielkopolska remained one of the indisputably Polish parts of Poland, fighting the Germanisation which swamped the nation's other western territories.

The major survival from the early Piast period is at **Lake Lednica**, which is part of the established tourist trail known as the Piast Route; strangely enough, the region's prehistoric past is represented far more vividly, in the form of the Iron Age village of **Biskupin**.

Gniezno was the first city to achieve dominance, but soon went into decline, accepting the consolation role of Poland's ecclesiastical capital. It was quickly supplanted as the regional centre by nearby **Poznań**, which has retained its position as one of Poland's leading commercial cities. Even older than either of these is **Kalisz**, which dates back at least as far as Roman times. Another town in the province which has played an important part in Polish culture, albeit at a later date, is **Leszno**, once a major Protestant centre. Yet this is predominantly a rural province, and perhaps its most typical attraction is the **Wielkopolska National Park**, epitomising the region's glaciated landscape.

On the eastern border of Wielkopolska lies the minute ancient province of **Kujawy**; it has a few fairly interesting towns, notably the historic capital of **Włocławek**.

As in the rest of Poland, there are plentiful trains and buses, with the former usually having the edge in terms of speed and convenience. A particularly diverting way of getting around is provided by a number of narrow-gauge rail lines, the most useful of which are described in the text.

Poznań

Thanks to its position on the Paris–Berlin–Moscow rail line, and as the one place where all international trains stop between the German border and Warsaw, POZNAŃ is many visitors' first taste of Poland. In many ways it's the ideal introduction, as no other city is more closely identified with Polish nationhood. "Posnania elegans Poloniae civitas" (Poznań, a beautiful city in Poland), the inscription on the oldest surviving depiction of the town, has been adopted as a local catchphrase to highlight its unswerving loyalty to the national cause over the centuries. Nowadays it's a city of great diversity, encompassing a tranquil cathedral quarter, an animated centre focused on one of Europe's most imposing squares, and a dynamic business district whose trade fair is the most important in the country.

Poznań's history
In the ninth century the Polonians founded a castle on a strategically significant island in the River Warta, and in 968 Mieszko I made this one of the two main centres of his duchy, and the seat of its first bishop. The settlement that developed here was given the name **Ostrów Tumski** (Cathedral Island), which it still retains.

Although initially overshadowed by Gniezno, Poznań did not follow the latter's decline with the transference of the court to Kraków in the mid-thirteenth century. Instead, it became the undisputed capital of Wielkopolska and the main bastion of Poland's western border. The economic life of the city then shifted to the west bank of the river, which was laid out in a chessboard pattern around a market square – an arrangement preserved today. Poznań's prosperity soared as it profited from the union of Poland and Lithuania and the decline of both the Teutonic Order and the Hanseatic League, becoming a key junction of European trade routes as well as a leading centre of learning.

Along with the rest of the country, decline inevitably set in with the Swedish wars of the seventeenth and eighteenth centuries. Revival of sorts came during the Partitions period, when Poznań became the thoroughly Prussian city of Posen; sharing in the wealth of the Industrial Revolution, it also consolidated its reputation as a rallying point for **Polish nationalism**, resisting Bismarck's Germanisation policy and playing an active role in the independence movements. A rising in December 1918 finally forced out the German occupiers, ensuring that Poznań would become part of the resurrected Polish state. A university was founded in the following year, with the annual trade fair established two years after that.

Poznań's rapid expansion during the interwar period has been followed by accelerated growth, doubling in population to its present level of almost 600,000, and spreading onto the right bank of the Warta. The city's association with the struggle against foreign hegemony – this time Russian – was again demonstrated by the **food riots of 1956**, which were crushed at a cost of 74 lives. These riots are popularly regarded as the first staging post towards the formation of Solidarity 24 years later.

> The Poznań telephone code is ☎061.

Arrival, information and rooms

The main **train station**, Poznań Główny, is southwest of the historic quarter; the front entrance, not immediately apparent, is situated between platforms 1 and 4. Tram #5 goes from the viaduct above to the city centre. The **bus station** is five minutes' walk to the east along ul. Towarowa. Buses #59 and #77 serve the **airport** in the western suburb of Ławica.

The main **tourist office** is at Stary Rynek 59 (Mon–Fri 9am–5pm, Sat 10am–2pm; ☎52-61-56). An alternative source of information is the **PTTK** bureau at no. 90 on the same square (☎52-37-56). International rail tickets can be purchased from the **Orbis** office at al. Karola Marcinkowskiego 21 (☎53-20-52). The **Almatur** office for students can be found at al. Aleksandra Fredry 7 (☎52-36-45).

Accommodation
Because of the trade fair, Poznań has plenty of accommodation, but hotel prices consequently tend to be Western rather than Polish. Staying here on a tight budget shouldn't present any real problems, however, as the city has a better than average supply of hostels.

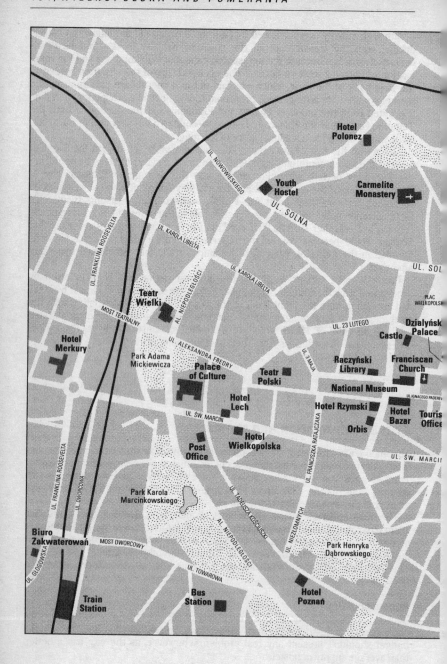

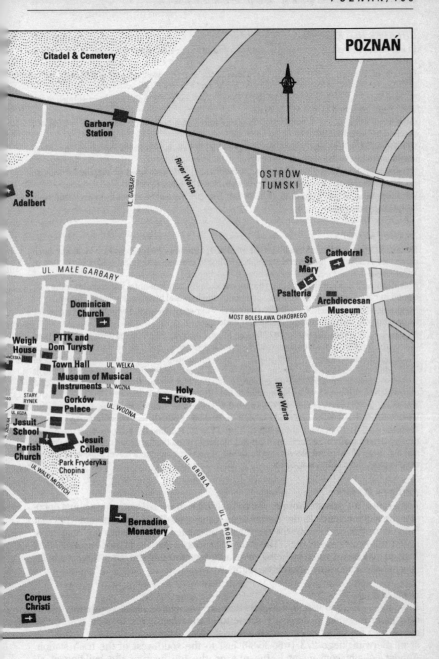

POZNAŃ

Citadel & Cemetery

Garbary
Station

River Warta

OSTRÓW
TUMSKI

St
Adalbert

UL. GARBARY

UL. MAŁE GARBARY

St
Mary

Cathedral

Psalteria

Archdiocesan
Museum

Dominican
Church

MOST BOLESŁAWA CHRÓBREGO

Weigh
House

PTTK and
Dom Turysty

ANCESKA

Town Hall   UL. WELKA

Museum of Musical
Instruments   UL. WOZNA

River Warta

STARY
RYNEK

Holy
Cross

GO

Gorków
Palace   UL. WODNA

UL. KOZIA

Jesuit
School

Jesuit
College

Parish
Church

Park Fryderyka
Chopina

UL. WALKI MŁODYCH

UL. GROBLA

Bernadine
Monastery

UL. GROBLA

Corpus
Christi

CHEAPER HOTELS

Lech, ul. św. Marcin 74 (☎53-01-51). One of a pair of long-established three-star hotels right in the heart of the commercial district.

Ławica, ul. Wichrowa 100 (☎14-35-01). Motel at the extreme western end of the city's limits, in the same suburb as the airport, and reached by bus #59 or #77.

Naramowice, ul. Naramowicka 150 (☎22-70-11). Two-star hotel in the northern suburb of the same name, reached by bus #67 or #105.

Olimp, ul. Warmińska 1 (☎458-21). Two-star hotel, situated northwest of the centre and reached by tram #9 or #11.

POSiR, ul. Marcina Chwiałkowskiego 34 (☎33-05-11). Sports hotel with an unusually convenient location just to the south of the centre.

Rzymski, al. Karola Marcinkowskiego 22 (☎52-81-21). Old-fashioned two-star hotel with an excellent location just a couple of minutes' walk from the Stary Rynek.

Wielkopolska, ul. św. Marcin 67 (☎52-76-31). Directly across the street from *Lech*, and similar to it in every respect.

LUXURY HOTELS

Bazar, al. Karola Marcinkowskiego 10 (☎512-51). Famous historic hotel which has been closed for renovation for several years; according to current schedules, it should re-open in 1995.

Meridian, ul. Litenska (☎41-12-01). Brand-new and privately run hotel in a tranquil setting by a pond in Park Sołacki. Its restaurant is currently the best and most expensive in Poznań.

Merkury, ul. Franklina Roosevelta 20 (☎408-01). Four-star Orbis hotel which is convenient for its proximity to the train station and the fair buildings.

Novotel, ul. Warszawska 64/66 (☎77-00-11). Plush Orbis motel on the eastern approach road to the city, but still on various tram routes, including #6, which goes to the station.

Park, ul. Majakowskiego 77 (☎79-40-81). New German-owned hotel on the southern bank of Lake Maltańskie. Prices for rooms and food are comparable with its Orbis rivals, but it surpasses them in quality. Not very practical if you don't have a car, though buses #55, #57 and #66, which each connect with one or other of the city centre trams, pass by.

Polonez, al. Niepodległości 54/68 (☎39-91-41). Another four-star Orbis establishment; located to the north of the centre, it's quieter and not so expensive as its counterparts.

Poznań, pl. Gen. Henryka Dąbrowskiego 1 (☎33-20-81). Pending the re-opening of the *Bazar*, this high-rise block is the flagship of Orbis's modern concrete alternatives. Even if you're not staying there it's a useful place to know about, as services include a travel bureau and a car rental office, and English is spoken.

PRIVATE ROOMS

For a room in a **private house**, you could try the *Biuro Zakwaterowana*, just opposite the side entrance to the station at ul. Głogowska 16 (Mon–Fri 9am–7pm, Sat 9am–3pm; ☎66-63-13), but they're mainly interested in long stays and may have nothing for short-term rent. The inflated prices at the Orbis office in the *Hotel Poznań* may mean you'd be better off in a budget hotel. At the latter there's a hefty surcharge for stays of one and two nights.

HOSTELS

In summer, Poznań usually has between five and eight official **youth hostels** in operation; as some of these are prone to change from year to year, it's best to check the current situation with the tourist office. The handiest of the regulars is at ul. Berwiniskiego 2/3 (☎66-36-80) just to the southwest of the train station. Almost equally convenient is the one on the top floor of the building at al.

Niepodległości 32/40 (☎52-49-25). If you don't mind staying far out, the new hostel at ul. Biskupińska 27 (☎22-10-63), 7km west in the suburb of Strzeszyn, is well spoken of; take bus #68 from the station to the terminus, then change to bus #60 or walk on for 10 minutes. The largest hostel of the group is inconveniently situated 10km southeast of the city at Głuszyna 127 (☎78-84-61); take a suburban train to Starołęka, then bus #58.

In total contrast, the final possibility for dormitory accommodation, the **tourist hostel** *Dom Turysty*, has an ideal location at Stary Rynek 91 (☎52-88-93).

CAMPSITES

Both **campsites** are far from the centre of things but offer the consolation of relaxing lakeside settings. *Maltańska*, ul. Krańcowa (☎76-60-11), is at the northeastern end of the eponymous lake; bus #402 passes fairly close. *Strzeszynek*, ul. Koszalińska 15 (☎48-31-29), lies about 9km to the northwest of the city and is reached by bus #95; chalet-type accommodation is available here as an alternative to pitching a tent.

The City

In spite of its size, most of Poznań's attractions are grouped in clusters which are no great distance from one another. Walking is the only way of getting to grips with the city, considerable parts of which are free from traffic. The trams, though forced to circumnavigate the most historic areas, do pass through the busy shopping streets to the west, and are also of use if you want to escape to the green belt.

The Stary Rynek

For seven centuries the grandiose **Stary Rynek** has been the hub of life in Poznań, even if these days it has lost its position as the centre of political and economic power. Archetypally Polish, with the most important public buildings sited in the middle, it was badly damaged during the last war, subsequently gaining the sometimes overenthusiastic attentions of the restorers. Their work has now been mellowed – successfully, in a bizarre sort of way – by the effects of pollution.

THE TOWN HALL

The **Town Hall** is in every way predominant. Originally a two-storey Gothic brick structure, it was radically rebuilt in the 1550s by Giovanni Battista Quadro of Lugano, whose turreted facade gives it a quasi-military feel. Every day at noon, the effigies of two rams emerge onto the platform of the **clock** and butt their heads twelve times. This is in honour of the best-known local legend, which narrates that the two animals locked horns on the steps of the town hall, and thereby drew attention to a fire which had just begun there, so saving the city from yet another conflagration. In thanks, the rams were immortalised in the local coat of arms, as well as by this timepiece. Other sides of the building are inscribed with the words of Polish Renaissance sages, to which the restorers were forced to add extracts from the communist constitution.

The interior is now the **Museum of the History of Poznań** (Mon, Tues & Fri 10am–4pm, Wed noon–6pm, Sun 10am–3pm); though this is less didactic than it sounds, the main reason for entering is to see the building itself. Surviving from the Gothic period are the vaulted **cellars**, transformed into the prison in the sixteenth century; they now contain the earliest objects in the display, notably items excavated on Ostrów Tumski and the medieval pillory. However, the show-stopper is the Renaissance **Great Hall** on the first floor, formerly the scene of council meetings. Its coffered vault bears polychrome bas-reliefs which embody the exemplary civic duties and virtues through scenes from the lives of Samson, King David, Venus and Hercules. The southern section shows astrological figures, while the marble busts of Roman emperors around the walls are reminders of the weighty tradition of municipal leadership.

ELSEWHERE: PALACES AND MUSEUMS

Outside the town hall stands a fine but horribly blackened Rococo **fountain**, alongside a copy of the **pillory**, in its traditional location. Further to the south are the colourful **Houses of the Keepers**, once home of the market traders, many of whom sold their wares in their arcaded passageway. The present structures, though very heavily restored, date from the sixteenth century and are thus the oldest in the square.

At the back is the **Weigh House** (Waga Miejska), the second most important public building in this great trading centre; what you see today is a reproduction of the original, again the work of Quadro. Round the corner from here is the sternly Neoclassical **Guardhouse** (Odwach), built for "defence and decoration"

HENRYK SIENKIEWICZ (1846–1916)

Outside Poland, **Henryk Sienkiewicz's** reputation has rested largely on *Quo Vadis?*, an epic on the early Christians in the decadent days of the Roman Empire, which won him the 1905 **Nobel Prize for Literature** and quickly became a favourite subject with movie moguls. Yet the huge popular success of this led, after the author's death, to the almost total international neglect of the remainder of his colossal oeuvre, which, even in hopelessly inadequate translations, had marked him out as Poland's answer to Dickens. The sudden interest in all things Polish which followed the collapse of communism has already spawned new English translations of several of his other books, which should help to restore his literary status to its rightful place.

Born in the Podlasie region to a minor aristocratic family of Tartar origin, Sienkiewicz began his career as a **journalist** and **short story writer**, the culmination of which was a trip to the United States in 1876–77, where he worked in a short-lived Polish agricultural commune in California. Here he wrote *Letters from America* (containing vivid descriptions of such diverse subjects as New York City and the Indian campaigns), and the burlesque novella *Charcoal Sketches*, a satire on rural life in Russian Poland. On his return home, he drew on his experiences of emigré life in *American Stories*, which includes his one work in this genre which frequently turns up in literary anthologies, *The Lighthouse Keeper*. These were followed by the despairing novella *Bartek the Conqueror*, the finest of a number of works set in the Poznań region – which, being under Prussian control, made a safer medium for the nationalist message of an author subject to Russian censors.

Thereafter, Sienkiewicz changed tack, reviving what was then regarded as the outmoded form of the **historical epic**. His vast trilogy *With Fire and Sword*, *The Deluge* and *Fire in the Steppe* is set against the heroic backdrop of Poland's

of the city in the 1780s – just before the whole Polish state crumbled. In recent years, a museum of the history of the working-class movement has been housed here, but this looks like being a casualty of the backlash against the communist years. Between here and the Houses of the Keepers are two ugly structures which add the only discordant notes to the square – communist legacies which should be disowned even more urgently. One of them is now the **Wielkopolska Museum of Arms** (Tues noon–6pm, Wed & Fri 10am–4pm, Sat & Sun 10am–3pm), a moderately interesting display of weaponry in the province from the Middle Ages onwards.

Many a medieval and Renaissance interior lurks behind the Baroque facades of the **gabled houses** lining the outer sides of the Stary Rynek, most of them shops, restaurants, cafés or public offices. Particularly fine are those on the eastern side, where no. 45 is the **Museum of Musical Instruments** (Tues 11am–5pm, Wed & Fri 10am–4pm, Sat 10am–5pm, Sun 10am–3pm), the only collection of its kind in Poland. Its exhibits range from folk instruments from all over the world, through Chopin memorabilia to a vast array of violins. The last is a reminder that every five years the city hosts the Wieniawski International Violin Competition, one of the most prestigious events for young virtuosi.

The western side of the square is almost equally imposing, above all because of the massive green and white **Działyński Palace** at no. 78, which was one of the headquarters of the nineteenth-century struggles to keep Polish culture alive.

---

seventeenth-century wars with the Cossacks, Swedes and Turks. It is remarkable for its sure sense of structure, employing a permanent set of characters – whose language is skilfully differentiated according to their class and culture – with plentiful genealogical digressions and romantic interludes to break the unfolding of the main plot. Historical realism, however, was sacrificed in favour of Sienkiewicz's own Catholic, nationalist, chivalrous and anti-intellectual outlook. *Quo Vadis?*, which followed the trilogy, is his only novel without a Polish setting, although it has always been regarded as a fable about the country's oppression under the Partitions, emphasised by the fact that two of the leading characters are Lygians – inhabitants of what subsequently became the heartlands of Poland. Ironically, it is really one of Sienkiewicz's weaker works, irredeemably marred by its maudlin sentimentality, for all its mastery of narrative, description and characterisation. He showed a greater concern for historical accuracy in his final epic, *The Teutonic Knights*, in which Poland's plight was reflected in the clearest and most relevant parallel from the past.

Sienkiewicz also produced a couple of novels with contemporary settings, *Without Dogma* and *The Połaniecki Family*. These helped increased his cult status in **nationalist circles**, and political activity, boosted by the international celebrity status bestowed by *Quo Vadis?*, became increasingly important to him after the turn of the century. At the same time, his creative powers began to wane: he abandoned a planned trilogy on the life and times of King Jan Sobieski, though the excellent children's novel, *In Desert and Wilderness*, showed his continuing versatility. On the outbreak of World War I Sienkiewicz moved to Switzerland where, along with the pianist Ignacy Jan Paderewski, he was instrumental in setting up the **Polish National Committee**, which in due course came to be recognised by the Western allies as a provisional government. However, he did not live to play the direct political role that might otherwise have fallen to him when Poland was resurrected at the end of the war.

The houses at the extreme ends of this side were the homes of prominent Poznań personalities. Number 71 belonged to Jan Chróściejewski, twice the mayor of the city around 1600 and the author of the first book on children's diseases. Giovanni Battista Quadro lived in no. 84, whose facade has been painted with scenes narrating his life. Its interior houses the **Henryk Sienkiewicz Literature Museum** (Mon–Fri 10am–5pm). Although Poland's most celebrated novelist (see box on pp.458–59) had only a rather tenuous connection with Poznań, this is the most important museum dedicated to his life and works.

West of the Stary Rynek

Just to the west of the Stary Rynek stands a hill with remnants of the inner circle of the medieval walls. This particular section guarded the **Castle** (Zamek Przemysława), which was the seat of the rulers of Wielkopolska. Modified down the centuries, it was almost completely destroyed in 1945 but has been partly restored to house the **Museum of Decorative Arts** (Tues & Sun 10am–5pm, Wed, Fri & Sat 10am–4pm). This features an enjoyable enough collection from medieval times to the present day, while the Gothic cellars are used for changing displays of posters, an art form taken very seriously in Poland.

Below the hill is the Baroque **Franciscan Church**, its transepts formed by sumptuous chapels dedicated to the Virgin and Saint Francis. Its decoration, including the ornate stalls and high altar, was executed by the Franciscan brothers (in both senses of the word) Adam and Antonin Swach, the former a painter, the latter a sculptor and stuccoist. On the interior of the west wall you can see examples of a uniquely Polish art: portraits of nobles painted on sheet metal, which were placed on the deceased's coffin.

From here it's only a short walk round the corner to the vast elongated space of **plac Wolności**, which formerly bore the name of Napoleon, then Kaiser Wilhelm, only gaining its present designation – Victory Square – after the Wielkopolska uprising in 1918. The **Bazar Hotel**, a favourite meeting place of Polish patriots throughout the Partitions period, was where Paderewski lodged when he led the rebellion against the German garrison. Diagonally opposite stands another seminal centre of the fight to preserve Polish culture, the **Raczyński Library**. Architecturally, it's one of the most distinguished buildings in the city, erected in the 1820s in the grand style of the Louvre.

THE NATIONAL MUSEUM

Directly facing the Raczyński Library is the ponderous **National Museum** (Tues noon–6pm, Wed, Fri and Sat 10am–4pm, Sun 10am–3pm), on the first floor of which is one of the few important displays of old master paintings in Poland. The **Italian** section begins with panels from Gothic altarpieces by artists such as Bernardo Daddi and Lorenzo Monaco, and continues with Renaissance pieces such as Bellini's tender *Madonna and Child with Donor*, Bassano's *Venus in Vulcan's Forge*, Bronzino's *Cosimo de' Medici* and the fascinating *Game of Chess* by Sofonisba Anguisciola, one of the few celebrated woman painters of the period.

Dominating the gallery's small but choice **Spanish** section is the prize exhibit, Zurbarán's *Madonna of the Rosary*. This Counter-Reformation masterpiece was part of a cycle for the Carthusian monastery at Jerez, and features actual portraits of these silent monks. By the same artist is *Christ at the Column*, a sharply edged work from the very end of his career, and there are also a couple of notable works by his contemporary Ribera. In the extensive display of the **Low Countries**, high-lights are a *Madonna and Child* attributed to Massys and the regal *Adoration of the Magi* by Joos van Cleve.

The **Polish** canvases are an anticlimax, but look out for the room dedicated to the versatile Jacek Malczewski, the historical scenes by Jan Matejko, the land-scapes of Wojciech Gerson, and the subdued portraits of Olga Boznańska. Also hung in this section is Bellotto's huge *Election of Stanisław August*, a fascinating documentary record of the way a Polish king was chosen.

BEYOND PLAC WOLNOŚCI

Moving into the business thoroughfares which branch out west from pl. Wolności, you shortly come to the **Theatr Polski** on ul. 27 Grudnia. Erected in the 1870s by voluntary contributions, this was yet another major cultural institu-tion during the Partitions period: the uphill nature of this struggle is reflected in the inscription on the facade – "the nation by itself". Overlooking the busy junc-tion at the end of the street is the city's most distinguished postwar building, the **Dom Tomarowy** department store. Built in the mid-1950s, it's an imposing ten-storey cylinder constructed round a hollow core in which are three spiral stair-cases. On ul. św. Marcin, a block to the south, are more eye-catching pieces of modern architecture – three tall, well spaced-out glass blocks put up at the end of the 1960s.

An insight into the curious dichotomy of life during the Partitions is provided by the large buildings standing further to the west, which reflect the self-confidence of the German occupiers in the first decade of this century. Ironically, many of these cultural establishments and administration offices were taken over just a few years after they were built by an institution with very different values, the new University of Poznań. The most imposing of the group, the huge neo-Romanesque **Kaiserhaus**, had an even more dramatic change of role. Built in imitation of the style favoured by the Hohenstaufen emperors of early medieval Germany, it was intended to accommodate the Kaiser whenever he happened to be in town. Instead, it has become a Palace of Culture with a distinctively populist stamp. In the park beyond are two huge crosses bound together, forming a **monument** to the victims of the Poznań food riots and also celebrating the birth of Solidarity. It was put up on the 25th anniversary of the former event in 1981 – during martial law.

South and east of the Stary Rynek

Returning to the Stary Rynek and continuing along ul. Wodna soon brings you to the **Górków Palace**, which still preserves its intricate Renaissance portico and sober inner courtyard. The mansion now houses the **Archaeology Museum** (Tues–Fri 10am–4pm, Sat 10am–6pm, Sun 10am–3pm), where the displays are short on aesthetic appeal but commendably thorough. They trace the history of the region from the time of the nomadic hunters who lived here between 15000 and 8000 BC, all the way to the early feudal society of the seventh century AD.

Down ul. Świętosławska is a complex of former Jesuit buildings, the finest examples of Baroque architecture in the city. The end of this street is closed by the facade of what's now generally known as the **Parish Church** (Kościół Frany), completed just forty years before the expulsion of the Jesuits in 1773. Its interior is all coloured columns, gilded capitals, monumental sculptures, large altarpieces and rich stuccowork, in the full-blown Roman manner. Over the high altar is a painting illustrating a legendary episode from the life of Saint Stanisław. Then a bishop, he was accused by King Bolesław the Generous of not having paid for a village he had incorporated into his territories. In order to prove his innocence, the saint resurrected the deceased former owner of the land to testify on his behalf.

Across the road is the **Jesuit School**, now one of Poland's main ballet academies; try to see its miniature patio, an architectural gem. To the east of the church is the front section of the **Jesuit College**, currently the seat of the city council. The Jesuits have returned to Poznań, though they were unable to reclaim the buildings they created. Instead, they now occupy the oldest left-bank building, the **Dominican Church** to the northeast of the Stary Rynek. Despite a Baroque recasing, this still preserves original Romanesque and Gothic features, as well as a stellar-vaulted Rosary Chapel.

The late Baroque church of the **Holy Cross** (Kościół Wszystkich Świętych), almost due east of the Stary Rynek, is the epitome of a Lutheran church, with its democratic central plan layout and overall plainness. Yet although it survives as an almost complete period piece, the exodus of virtually all the Protestants this century means that it's now used for Catholic worship, as is evidenced by the jarring high altar.

At no. 25 on the adjacent ul. Grobla is the lodge of the freemasons, now the **Ethnographical Museum** (Tues, Wed, Fri and Sat 10am–4pm, Sun 10am–3pm). Further south is the very different Baroque church of the **Bernardine monastery**, which has been gleamingly restored by the monks who repossessed it following its wartime use as a workshop for the opera house. At the southern extremity of the old town is **Corpus Christi** (Kościół Bożego Ciała), a soaring fifteenth-century Gothic church that once belonged to a Carmelite monastery.

North of the Stary Rynek

The northern quarters are best approached from plac Wielkopolski, a large square now used for daily markets. From here ul. Działowa passes two churches facing each other on the brow of the hill. To the right is the Gothic **St Adalbert** (św. Wojciecha), chiefly remarkable for its stumpy little seventeenth-century belfry, the only piece of wooden architecture left in the city. Opposite, the handsome Baroque facade of the **Carmelite monastery** makes a highly effective contrast. Further uphill are the most exclusive cemetery in Poznań, reserved for people deemed to have made a valuable contribution to the life of Wielkopolska, and a monument to the defenders of the city in 1939.

Beyond, al. Niepodległości ascends to the vast former **Citadel**. This Prussian fortress was levelled after the war to make a public park, albeit one whose main appeal is to necrophiles. There's a cemetery for the 6000 Russians and Poles who lost their lives in the month-long siege which led to its capture, while to the east are the graves of British and Commonwealth soldiers.

Ostrów Tumski and the right bank

From the left bank the bridge Bolesława the Great (Most Bolesław Chrobrego) crosses to the holy island of **Ostrów Tumski**, a world away in spirit, if not in distance, from the hustle of the city. (Trams #4, #8, #16 and #17 go over the bridge.) Only a small portion of the island is built upon, and a few priests and monks comprise its entire population. Lack of parishioners means that there's not the usual need for evening Masses, and after 5pm the island is a ghost town.

The first building you see is the late Gothic **Psalteria**, characterised by its elaborate stepped gable. It was erected in the early sixteenth century as a residence for the cathedral choir. Immediately behind is an earlier brick structure, **St Mary's** (Kościół Panny Marii); this lofty and unusually graceful chapel was given controversial but effective stained glass and murals after the war. Across the street is the **Archdiocesan Museum** (Mon–Fri 9am–3pm, Sat & Sun 1–3pm), with a homely spread of paintings, sculptures, textiles and treasury items from the Middle Ages to the present day.

THE CATHEDRAL

The streets of the island are lined by handsome eighteenth-century houses, all very much in the shadow of the **Cathedral**. Over the centuries, the brickwork of the church was progressively hidden under Baroque and Neoclassical remodellings. When much of this was stripped away by wartime devastation, it was decided to restore as much of the Gothic original as possible. However, the lack of documentary evidence for the eastern chapels meant that their successors had to be retained. The Baroque spires on the two facade towers and the three lanterns around the ambulatory, which give a vaguely eastern touch, were also reconstructed.

Inside, the **crypt**, entered from below the northern tower, has been extensively excavated, uncovering remains of the pre-Romanesque and Romanesque cathedrals which stood on the site, as well as parts of the sarcophagi of the first two Polish kings, Mieszko I and Bolesław the Brave. Their current resting place is the **Golden Chapel** on the axis of the ambulatory. Miraculously unscathed during the war, this luscious creation, representing the diverse if dubious tastes of the 1830s, is the antithesis of the plain architecture all around it. Its decoration is a curious cooperation between mosaic artists from Venice (who created the patterned floor and the copy of Titian's *Assumption*) and a painter and a sculptor from the very different Neoclassical traditions of Berlin.

Of the many other **funerary monuments** which form one of the key features of the cathedral, the finest is that of Bishop Benedykt Izdbieński, just to the left of the Golden Chapel. This was carved by Jan Michałowicz, the one native Polish artist of the Renaissance period who was the equal of the many Italians who settled here. The other outstanding tomb is that of the Górka family, in the Holy Sacrament chapel at the northern end of the nave, sculpted just a few years later by one of these itinerant craftsmen, Hieronimo Canavesi. Other **works of art** to look out for are the late Gothic carved and painted high altar from Silesia, the choir stalls from the same period, and fragments of sixteenth-century frescoes, notably a cycle of the Apostles.

ŚRÓDKA

Crossing Most Mieska I brings you to the right-bank suburb of **Śródka**, the second oldest part of the city, whose name derives from the word for Wednesday – market day here in medieval times. Though there's nothing special to see, something of the atmosphere of an ancient market quarter survives. Just beyond is another distinct settlement, known as **Komandoria** after the commanders of the Knights of Saint John of Jerusalem, who founded it towards the end of the twelfth century. The late Romanesque church of this community, **St John's**, survives with Gothic and Baroque additions and now stands in splendid isolation beside one of the busiest traffic intersections in the city.

Just south of here is the western end of **Lake Maltańskie**, the city's most popular playground. This artificial stretch of water, more than 2km in length, has excellent watersports facilities, along with restaurants, a campsite and two motels. Beyond its eastern edge is a wooded park with a cluster of small lakes, criss-crossed by marked walking trails. Here also is the **Zoo** (daily 9am–dusk), which is connected to St John's by a **narrow-gauge railway** (hourly services, May–Sept only) specially designed for children.

Eating, drinking and entertainment

In choosing somewhere to eat and drink, the **hotels** (see p.456) should always be borne in mind. Each of the Orbis establishments has a restaurant and café with prices which, although a bit higher than elsewhere in town, are still reasonable value. Better still are the restaurants at the two non-Orbis luxury hotels, *Meridian* and *Park*. Otherwise, the gastronomic situation is in more of a state of flux than in almost any other city in Poland, with the majority of the restaurants, and nearly all the milk bars, having closed down since the fall of communism. A number of Chinese and Italian-style eateries, plus a host of Westernised fast-food joints and trendy café-bars, have emerged instead, sometimes as direct replacements. Another snag is that what there is tends to be heavily concentrated in and around the Stary Rynek, with other quarters, notably Ostrów Tumski, having nowhere to eat at all. Note that Poznań is a major brewing centre, and that its **beers**, *Ratusz* and (especially) *Lech*, are not the inferior products their price tags would suggest.

Restaurants and snack bars

Adria, ul. Głogowska 14. Just across from the station, and with its own nightclub.

Avanti, Stary Rynek 76. A spaghetti house which is probably the cheapest and most popular snack bar in town.

Club Elite, Stary Rynek 2. Despite the misleading name, this is a good place to sample traditional Polish cuisine.

Krakus, ul. św. Marcin 25. Much the best of the new private restaurants, with a varied menu of Polish and international dishes.

Panda, ul. Karola Libelta 37. Perhaps the pick of the Chinese restaurants which are starting to spring up all over town.

Pizzeria Capriccio, Stary Rynek 95. Unusual in Poland in serving genuine pizza, as opposed to the imitations which have become such a national craze.

Pod Arkadami, pl. Cyryla Ratajskiego 10. The only milk bar surviving in the central area.

Smakosz, ul. 27 Grudnia 9. Open a bit later than most other restaurants, but can get crowded.

Tai-Paw, ul. Ogrodowa 10. Features a mixed menu of Oriental and European dishes.

Tivoli, ul. Wroniecka 13. Decent and cheap trattoria which has deservedly become popular.

U Dylla, Stary Rynek 37. Serves good and reasonably priced food in an ideal setting, with a choice of Western and Polish drinks.

W-Z, ul. Aleksandra Fredry 12. Has long opening hours because of the nightly dances, for which there's a compulsory surcharge.

Cafés and café-bars

Café Focus, ul. Ignacego Paderewskiego 7. New café-bar mainly patronised by the younger set; open till 5am.

Eliksiv, Stary Rynek 61. Has an array of irresistible gooey puddings.

Sukiennicza, Stary Rynek 98. Superb coffee, cakes and ice cream dishes in an unhurried setting, complete with resident pianist, reminiscent of central Europe's pre-communist days.

Trocadero, ul. 3 Maja. Bar which is particularly popular with college students.

U Rajców, Stary Rynek 93. Tea house, with a sideline in mead.

Winiarnia Ratuszowa, Stary Rynek 55. A conventional enough café at ground-floor level, with a wonderfully atmospheric wine bar in the medieval cellars.

Nightlife and culture

Nightspots in Poznań are rare, unless you count the cabaret scene in the Orbis hotels and the restaurants around the station. Best chance of some action is to ask around the university buildings about **student clubs**: the largest, *Odnowa*, is at ul. św. Marcin 80/82. The lively *Bratniak* peace and environmentalist group meets in building B on ul. Dożynkowa to the north of the centre, reached by tram #4 or #16.

There's a far better choice if you want highbrow **culture** in the evening. The *Teatr Polski*, ul. 27 Grudnia 7 (☎52-56-27), presents classic plays, while the *Teatr Nowy*, ul. Jarosława Dąbrowskiego 5 (☎48-12-41), specialises in modern fare. **Opera** is performed at the *Teatr Wielki*, ul. Aleksandra Fredry 9 (☎52-82-91), and the *Polski Teatr Tańca*, ul. Kozia 4 (☎52-42-41), offers varied **dance** programmes. Classical concerts are held at the *Filharmonia Poznańska*, ul. św. Marcin 81. Musicals are put on at the *Teatr Animacji*, ul. Niezłomnych 1a (☎52-17-86), while puppet shows are among the attractions at the *Teatr Lalki i Aktora* in the *Pałac Kultury* at the corner of ul. św. Marcin and al. Niepodległości (☎52-88-16).

Listings

Airlines *LOT*, ul. św. Marcin 69 (☎549-85); *British Airways*, ul. Dąbrowskiego 5 (☎48-88-88).

Bookshops Can be found on Stary Rynek, ul. Ignacego Paderewskiego, pl. Wolności, and at the corner of ul. 27 Grudnia and ul. Gwarna.

British Council Ul. Franciszka Ratajczaka at the corner with ul. 27 Grudnia.

Car hire Office in *Hotel Poznań*, pl. Gen. Henryka Dąbrowskiego (☎33-02-21).

Consulate USA, ul. Fryderyka Chopina 4 (☎52-95-86). There is no UK consulate.

Festivals Main folklore event is the *Jarmarkt Świętojański* (St John's Market) held during the International Trade Fair in the second week of June. There's a festival of boys' choirs every February, and the Wieniawski International Violin Competition will next be staged in November 1995.

Football *Lech Poznań*, currently among Poland's best teams, play at the *Lech* stadium, west of the city centre on ul. Grunwaldzki, reached by tram #13.

Petrol station 24-hr station on ul. Warszawska, with a lead-free pump; another on ul. Serbska.

Post offices Head office is at ul. Kosciuśki 77.

What's on A free monthly programme in Polish and an English abridgement, both known as *iks*, are available from tourist information points.

Around Poznań

It's simple to escape from the big-city feel of Poznań, as its outskirts soon give way to peaceful agricultural villages set in a lake-strewn landscape. Within a 25-kilometre radius of the city is some of the finest scenery in Wielkopolska, along with two of Poland's most famous castles, each of which makes a relaxing day or half-day excursion.

Kórnik

KÓRNIK, site of one of the great castles of Wielkopolska, is 22km southeast of Poznań on the east bank of lakes Skrzynki and Kónickie, the first two in a long chain of six. There are regular services from the main bus station and from the terminus at Rondo Rataje; don't go by train, as the station is 4km from the village.

Somewhat run-down, Kórnik has an appealing rural feel to it, consisting essentially of one very long street, ul. Poznańska (where you'll find the best of the three restaurants, *Turystyczna*). This street culminates in a market square, dominated by the red-brick **Parish Church**, originally Gothic but heavily rebuilt last century. It contains tombs of the Górka family, the first owners of the town, though these are poor relations of their monument in Poznań Cathedral.

The Górkas built their **Castle** at the extreme southern edge of the village in the fifteenth century. A fragment of the original survives, as does the medieval layout with its moat, but the castle was rebuilt in neo-Gothic style last century by the German architect Karl Friedrich Schinkel, best known for his Neoclassical public buildings in Berlin. However, his designs were considerably modified, and credit for the final shape of the castle is due to the owner, Tytus Działyński, whose aim was as much to show off his collection of arms and armour, books and *objets d'art* as to provide a luxurious home for himself.

In contrast to the plain grandeur of the exterior, with its mock defensive towers and battlements, the **interior** (April 15–Oct 15 Tues–Fri & Sun 9am–3pm, Sat 9am–2pm; rest of year closes 1hr earlier) is for the most part very intimate, and creates the impression of trespassing into a private residence of a century or more ago. The one really theatrical gesture is the spacious **Moorish Hall** on the first floor, which mimics the most spectacular of Arab palaces, the Alhambra in Granada. Ask to borrow the leaflet in English which describes all the exhibits.

To see all sides of the castle's exterior, you have to visit the **Arboretum** (May–Oct daily 9am–6pm). Originally in the formal French style, this was transformed in the seemingly arbitrary manner of a *jardin anglais*. There are over 2000 species of trees and shrubs, from all corners of the world. The lakeside offers an even more pleasant stroll, particularly the western bank with its fine distant views.

Rogalin

With your own transport, it's easy to combine a visit to Kórnik with the castle in the hamlet of **ROGALIN**, 11km to the west on the road to Mosina (see opposite). Unfortunately, only three buses pass this way in each direction, and the timetables don't work out for seeing both monuments on the same day, unless you're prepared to walk or take a chance on hitching.

The **Palace** (Wed–Sun 10am–4pm, last admission 3pm; May–Sept open until 6pm on Sat) was the seat of another eminent Poznań family, the Raczyńskis. In contrast to Kórnik, it's a grand country residence built in a style which shows the Baroque melting into Neoclassicism, and it forms the axis of a careful layout of buildings and gardens. At the time of writing, the palace was in the middle of a long-term restoration with the central block closed. In the meantime, you can visit the recently restored small rooms in the two wings, and the **art gallery** off the northern side; most of its paintings are second-division, but there's a marvellous exception, Monet's *Landscape at Pourville*.

Fronting the palace courtyard is a long forecourt, to the sides of which are the stables and **coach house**, the latter crammed with old carriages once used by owners of this estate, along with the last horse-drawn cab to operate in Poznań. Passing outside the gates, a five-minute walk brings you to the **Mausoleum** of the Raczyński family. Set peacefully at the side of the road, this is a slightly reduced copy of one of the best-preserved monuments of classical antiquity, the Maison Carrée in Nîmes, built in a startlingly pink sandstone.

At the back of the main palace is an enclosed formal garden, now desperately in need of a gardener or two. More enticing is the English-style park beyond, laid out on the site of a primaeval forest. This is chiefly remarkable for its **oak trees**, three of the most ancient of which have been fenced off for protection. Among the most celebrated natural wonders of Poland, they are at least 1000 years old – and thus of a similar vintage to the Polish nation itself. They are popularly known as Lech, Czech and Rus, after the three mythical brothers who founded the Polish, Czech and Russian nations; with all due modesty, the largest is designated as Rus.

If you intend to be here around lunchtime, it's best to bring your own picnic, though there's a **restaurant**, *Pod Dębami*, about 1km away from the palace, and another, *Na Skarpie*, in ROGALINEK, 3km to the west.

The Wielkopolska National Park

The only area of protected landscape in the province, the **Wielkopolska National Park** occupies an area of some 100 square kilometres to the south of Poznań. Formed in geologically recent times, it's a glacial and post-glacial landscape of low moraines, gentle ridges and lakes, several of them very substantial. Half the park is taken up by forest, predominantly pine and birch planted as replacements for the original hardwoods.

Although the scenery in the park is hardly dramatic, it is unspoiled by any kind of development and warrants a day's exploration. By public transport the main point of access to Poznań is **MOSINA**, a small, straggling rural community on the Poznań–Wrocław rail line, served by all except the express trains. The sole **hotel** and restaurant is Moreno (☎13-27-46), close to the park on the main road to **STĘSZEW**. The latter, 13km to the west on a regular bus route, and on the rail line between Poznań and Wolsztyn, is the other possible base if you want to stay in the area, as it has a **campsite** (☎13-40-61), set on the banks of Lake Lipno just to the northeast. On the Rynek there's a restaurant, *Broniszanka*, along with the **Regional Museum** (Tues–Sun 9am–1pm).

For a day trip, however, the most convenient point of entry is OSOWA GÓRA, a station apparently serving nowhere, just to the west of Mosina at the end of a separate line from Poznań; it passes along the shore of one of the finest of the lakes, Budzyńskie.

Alternative approaches are the twin villages of **PUSZCZYKÓWKO** and **PUSZCZYKOWO**, on the left bank of the snaking River Warta immediately north of Mosina. Each has one restaurant, and the latter also has a couple of snack bars and a cheap hotel, *Sadyba*, ul. Brzozowa 15a (☎13-31-28). Situated on the opposite side of the rail line from Puszczykowo proper is a **Museum** (Tues–Sat 10am–3pm, Sun 10am–4pm) with displays on the evolution of the region's landscape.

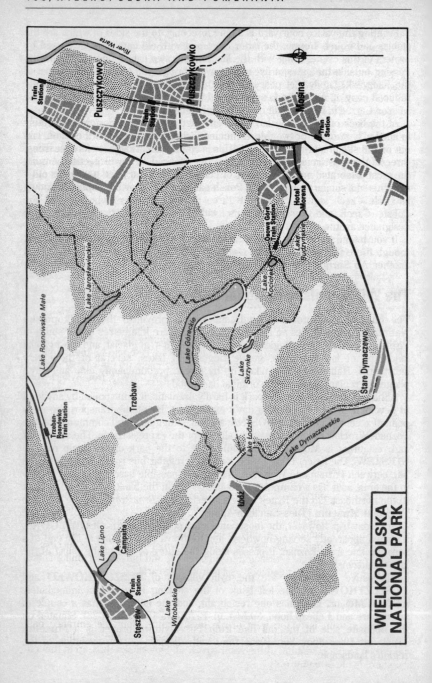

WIELKOPOLSKA NATIONAL PARK

Walks in the park

When exploring the park, it's best to stick to the three official **hiking paths**, which are generally well marked and unstrenuous. Each takes several hours to cover its entire length, though it's easy enough to switch from one to the other – the best idea if you're restricted for time.

Walking **from Osowa Góra** gets you into the best of the terrain quickly. From the car park above the station (which offers one of the park's few panoramic views), the **blue trail** leads round the small heart-shaped Lake Kociołek, which is beautifully shaded by trees, then continues through the forest to the southern end of Lake Góreckie. It then climbs through thick woods before passing through open countryside to Lake Łódźkie, on the far side of which – off the trail but on the main road – is the hamlet of ŁÓDŹ, clustered around a seventeenth-century wooden church. The route then leads along the northern shore of Lake Witobelskie to Stęszew.

The **red trail** from Osowa Góra passes Lake Kociołek, then travels circuitously uphill, skirting the small Lake Skrzynka just before crossing the blue trail. It arrives at the bend in the sausage-shaped Lake Góreckie, from where there's a view across to an islet with a ruined castle – a former fortress of the Działyński family, and a meeting point for the Polish insurgents of 1863. The path then leads about halfway round the perimeter of the lake as far as JEZIORY, where there's another car park plus a restaurant and café. Two separate red paths proceed to Puszczykówko, while a third follows the long northerly route to Puszczykowo via Lake Jarosławieckie.

The **black trail** begins at the station of **Trzebaw-Rosnówko**, then traverses the fields to the hamlet of TRZEBAW, before continuing through the woods to Lake Łódźkie. It then follows the eastern bank of this lake and its much longer continuation, Lake Dymaczewskie – which together make up the largest stretch of water in the park – before ending at STARE DYMACZEWO, from where you can take a bus to Mosina or Steszew.

Leszno and around

The last notable stop in Wielkopolska before Silesia is **LESZNO**, which lies some 90km south of Poznań. Nowadays a bustling market town, it hardly hints at the glittering role it has played in Poland's history. Its entire early story is bound up with one of the country's most remarkable dynasties, the Leszczyński family, who founded Leszno in the late fourteenth century. The last of the male line, **Stanisław Leszczyński**, deposed the hated Augustus the Strong of Saxony to become King of Poland in 1704, only to be overthrown by the same rival six years later. He briefly regained the throne in 1733, but met with far more success in exile in France, marrying his daughter to Louis XV, and himself becoming Duke of Lorraine and gaining a reputation as a patron of the arts.

The Town

The **train station** is to the west of the town centre; from the entrance hall continue straight ahead until you come to an underpass on the left; this brings you out on to the beginning of the main street, ul. Słowiańska. Just up to the left from here is the **bus station**.

THE BOHEMIAN BRETHREN

Along with many other Polish grandees, the Leszczyńskis enthusiastically adopted the Reformation, though Stanisław, like Augustus the Strong, was forced to convert to Catholicism in order to launch his bid for the crown. In the first half of the seventeenth century Leszno became a refuge for the Bohemian Brethren, Czech Protestants who were forced to flee their homeland by the religious intolerance of the Thirty Years' War. The academy these exiles founded in Leszno developed into one of Europe's great centres of learning, thanks to the leadership of Jan Amos Komeński, known as **Comenius**. Creator of the first illustrated textbook, he was called to put his educational theories into practice in England, Sweden, Hungary and Holland, and even received invitations from the Protestant-loathing Cardinal Richelieu in France and from Harvard University, which wanted him as its president. Though Comenius and his colleagues were eventually forced to leave Leszno by the Swedish Wars of the 1650s, the town remained a major educational centre into the last century. The Brethren were later transformed into the Moravian Church, a body which continues to have an influence out of all proportion to its size, particularly in the USA.

Heading straight ahead brings you to the pedestrianised **Rynek**, one of Poland's most handsome squares. It's predominantly Baroque, having been rebuilt after the Swedish Wars, which left Leszno in ruins. The colourist approach favoured by the architects – prominent among whom was the Italian Pompeo Ferrari – is shown to best effect in the red, yellow and white **Town Hall**, which occupies the usual central position, its tall belfry serving as the main local landmark.

Just south of the Rynek, the exterior of the large church of **St Nicholas** (św. Mikołaja) strikes a more sombre note. Its interior, on the other hand, has some extravagant Rococo furnishings, the most eye-catching being the huge monuments to the Leszczyńskis. A fascinating contrast with this richness is provided by the clean, sober lines of the **Holy Cross** (św. Kryża), a couple of minutes' walk to the southwest on pl. Metziga. On the same square is the **Museum** (Tues & Thurs 2–7pm, Wed & Fri 9am–2pm, Sat & Sun 10am–2pm), a miscellaneous local collection, featuring a room devoted to Comenius of the Bohemian Brethren.

A few streets east of here, off ul. Bolesława Chrobrego, is the church of **St John**, aesthetically unremarkable but semi-interesting as the place where the Bohemian Brethren held their services.

Practicalities

There are two good and cheap **hotels** on ul. Słowiańska – *Leszno* at no. 11 (☎20-22-17) and *Centralny* at no. 30 (☎20-22-10). The latter has a café only, whereas the former, whose rooms were closed for renovation at the time of writing, boasts one of the better **restaurants** in town. A wide variety of other places to eat and drink can be found down the same street and on the Rynek; the only other hotel in town is *Junior*, ul. Strzelecka 7 (☎20-56-66). The **Orbis** office is at ul. Słowiańska 29 (☎20-25-65).

If you want an overnight stay with some panache, you could head for the palace designed by Pompeo Ferrari for the Sułkowski family – who bought Leszno from the Leszczyńskis – at RYDZYNA, 9km to the southeast and reached by regular buses; it has been coverted into a **hotel** and restaurant (☎20-58-47).

NARROW-GAUGE RAILWAYS IN WIELKOPOLSKA

The best-known narrow-gauge line in Wielkopolska, the Biskupin Railway between Gąsawa and Żnin, is described on pp.479–80. However, this is essentially a tourist facility, as opposed to other such lines in the province which still serve the needs of local communities.

A highly recommended example of these runs from STARE BOJANOWO, 18km south of Leszno on the main line to Wrocław, to WIELICHOWA, 15km to the north-west. The poor state of repair of the tracks suggest that closure may be imminent, but modern, immaculately maintained little diesels are in operation. Strung out along the route are a number of small communities, many of which have hardly changed in centuries, while a few others have been transformed by recent political and economic reforms – as the new German cars parked beside some of the farms testify.

Another line worth sampling starts at ŚRODA WIELKOPOLSKA, 30km south-east of Poznań, and runs southwest through 12km of pleasant pastoral scenery to its terminus at ZANIEMYŚL.

Wolsztyn

If you have a nostalgia for the days of **steam**, head 50km northwest from Leszno to the little lakeside town of **WOLSZTYN**, where steam engines can be seen shunting throughout the day. You may even make the journey by steam, but double-decker commuter diesels are more common.

The town centre has a few fine buildings, notably a Neoclassical palace and a Baroque church with an impressive frescoed vault. On the main street, ul. Piątego Stycznia, is the **Marcin Rożek Museum** (Tues–Fri 9am–4pm, Sat & Sun 10am–2pm), occupying the home of this artist, one of the best Poland ever produced, who was murdered in Auschwitz. It's his sculptures which stand out, notably the large reliefs on the rear of the house and the classically inspired portrait busts in the garden – mostly replicas of works destroyed by the Nazis.

Taking the back exit from here brings you to the shore of Lake Wolsztyn. If you follow its perimeter back towards the railway, then continue away from the town, you shortly come to an **open-air museum** of traditional farm buildings; it's always accessible through an unlocked gate. The only possibility for accommodation is the railwaymen's hostel which welcomes visiting enthusiasts; enquire at *Dispozyto* office in engine shed just east of the station.

Kalisz and around

At the extreme southeastern corner of Wielkopolska, 130km from Poznań, lies the heavily industrialised town of **KALISZ**. Almost universally held to be Poland's oldest city, it was referred to as Calissia by Pliny in the first century and was described in the second century as a trading settlement on the "amber route" between the Baltic and Adriatic. Though apparently inhabited without interruption ever since, it failed to develop into a major city. Despite its history, Kalisz is not worth a special journey, but it makes a convenient stopover if you're passing this way, and is the obvious place from which to approach the palace at **Gołuchów**.

Kalisz town

Both the **train** and **bus** stations are to be found at the southwestern end of the city. To reach the centre, take bus #19, #101 or #102: no buses run within the old quarter, which is situated between the rivers Prosna and Bernardynka. The only reason for enduring the long straight walk down ul. Górnośląska and ul. Śródmiejska is to take a close look at the two space-age churches which shoot up from parallel boulevards – potent symbols of the key role of Catholicism in modern Poland. If you do decide to walk, you can turn down ul. Tadeusza Kościuszki (on the left as you approach the Old Town) to see the **Kalisz Museum** at no. 12 (Tues, Thurs, Sat & Sun 10am–2.30pm, Wed & Fri noon–5.30pm), which contains material from the many archaeological excavations carried out in the area.

Ulica Śródmiejska terminates at the unprepossessing Rynek, with its large Baroque town hall. Down ul. Kanonicka at the northwestern end of the square is the brick Gothic church of **St Nicholas** (św. Mikołaja), which has been subject to a fair amount of neo-Gothic tinkering, though for once this is not entirely to its disadvantage. Inside, the prize item is the altarpiece of *The Descent from the Cross*, brought here from Rubens' workshop in Antwerp. Located just off the southeastern corner of the Rynek is a smaller square which lies in front of the **Franciscan Church**, an older and simpler example of Gothic brickwork, but with generous Baroque interior decorations, including a pulpit in the shape of a boat.

From here, it's just a short walk to ul. Kolegialna, which defines the eastern perimeter of the Old Town. This is dominated by the long facade of the **Jesuit College**, a severe Neoclassical composition incorporating a Renaissance portal. The only part of the building that visitors are allowed to enter is the church, which follows the plain Mannerist style of the Jesuits' most important church, the Gesù in Rome. Immediately beyond the college, standing beside the surviving fragment of the city's ramparts, is the single-towered **Collegiate Church**, a more adventurous example of Baroque which includes parts of its Gothic predecessor. The interior bristles with works of art, the most notable of which is a Silesian polyptych from around 1500 – but unfortunately only the vestibule is normally kept open.

Kalisz practicalities

Kalisz is reckoned prestigious enough to warrant its own luxury Orbis **hotel**, *Prosna*, ul. Górnośląska 53/55 (☎33-921), about a third of the way down the road from the bus station to the town. A better bet, though, is the *Europa*, al. Wolności 5 (☎720-31) – it's a classy place with a much better location by the river, but won't break the bank. Less convenient is the PTTK sports and tourist hotel, *Dom Wycieczkowy* (☎746-50), by the stadium to the east of the Old Town, the end of bus route #101. There's also a **youth hostel** in a small park east of the *Europa*, with the reception nearby at ul. Częstochowska 17 (☎726-36).

For **eating** and **drinking**, the hotels are probably the best choice. Pick of the other options are *Adria*, ul. Piekarska 13 due east of the Rynek, and *U Barbary i Bogumiła*, ul. Górnośląska 69, just up from the bus station; there are more basic alternatives in and around the Rynek.

Orbis have an office at Śródmiejska 1 (☎738-16); the Rynek's information office has been closed down.

Gołuchów

Twenty kilometres away on the main road to Poznań, and reached by frequent inter-city buses or by local bus #A, lies the village of **GOŁUCHÓW**, a nondescript place were it not for its **Palace**, the one outstanding monument in the Kalisz area.

It began as a small defensive castle, built for Rafał Leszczyński of the famous Leszno family in 1560. Early the following century, his son Wacław completely transformed it into a palatial residence worthy of a man who had risen to be Royal Chancellor. Like the Polish state itself, it gradually fell into ruin. In 1853 it was bought by Tytus Działyński, the owner of Kórnik, as a present for his son Jan, who married Izabella, daughter of the formidable Adam Czartoryski. While her husband languished in exile for his part in the 1863 Uprising, Izabella devoted herself to re-creating the glory of the castle, eventually opening it as one of Poland's first museums. Rather than revert to the Italianate form of the original, she opted for a distinctively French touch – with its steeply pitched roofs, prominent chimneys, towers and graceful arcaded courtyard, the palace looks as if it has been transported from the Loire Valley.

The small **apartments** (tours Wed–Sat 10am–4pm, Sun 11am–5pm; leaflet in English available) are crammed with paintings and *objets d'art*. Highlight of the display are some magnificent antique vases – just part of an assembly whose other items are now kept in the National Museum in Warsaw. After the guided tour, you can wander off to the two rooms under the stairway, in which changing exhibitions from the castle's collection of engravings are held. If you ask the English-speaking curator, you might get to see rooms not included on the tour, such as the tiny library and the upstairs guest rooms.

Gołuchów's **park** is cultivated for serious scientific purposes, and contains a **Museum of Forestry** (Tues–Sun 10am–3pm); you'll also come across Izabella's neo-Gothic funerary chapel. For refreshments, there's a café in the park and a restaurant in the village.

If you want to stay, the sole possibility is the **campsite**, which is well signposted from the main road.

Gniezno and around

Despite the competing claims of Poznań, Kruszwica and Lednica, **GNIEZNO** is generally credited as the first capital of Poland, a title based on the dense web of myth and chronicled fact which constitute the story of the nation's earliest years. Normally Poland's ecclesiastical capital, with an unhurried atmosphere in keeping with the dominance of churchly affairs, the town is situated 50km east of Poznań and reached in an hour by express train, or in at least two hours by bus.

Gniezno lies on the **Piast Route** (Szlak Piatowski), a tourist trail between Poznań and Inowrocław which, as the name implies, offers constant reminders of the Piast dynasty. The first major sight east of Poznań is **Lake Lednica**, which is most easily reached from Gniezno and has therefore been included in this section.

Gniezno's history

Lech, the legendary founder of Poland, supposedly came across the nest (*gniazdo*) of a white eagle here; he founded a town on the spot, and made the bird the emblem of his people, a role it still maintains. Less fancifully, it's known for sure that Mieszko I had established a court here in the late tenth century, and that in the year 1000 it was the scene of one of the landmarks in the country's history.

The catalyst for this, ironically enough, was a Czech, **Saint Adalbert** (Wojciech), the first Bishop of Prague. Unable to cope with the political demands of his office, he retired to a monastery, but later bowed to pressure from Rome to take up missionary work. In 997 he set out from Gniezno to evangelise the Prussians, a fierce Baltic tribe who lived on Poland's eastern borders – and who quickly dispatched him to a martyr's death. In order to recover the body, Mieszko I's son, **Bolesław the Brave**, was forced to pay Adalbert's weight in gold, an astute investment as it turned out. At the pope's instigation, Emperor Otto III made a pilgrimage to Gniezno, bringing relics with him which would add to the site's holiness. Received in great splendour, he crowned Bolesław with his own crown, confirming Poland as a fully fledged kingdom and one which was independent of the German-dominated Holy Roman Empire. Furthermore, Gniezno was made the seat of Poland's first archbishopric; Adalbert's brother was the first to be appointed to the post.

Gniezno was soon replaced as capital by the more secure town of Kraków, and although it made a partial recovery in the Middle Ages, it never grew very big. Nevertheless, it has always been important as the official **seat of the Primate of Poland**. Throughout the period of elected kings, the holder of this office functioned as head of state during each interregnum, and it is still one of the most prestigious positions in the land. In recent times, the Gniezno archbishopric has been coupled to that of Warsaw, with the Primate tending, for obvious reasons, to spend far more time in the latter city. The pressures this caused led in 1992 to Gniezno losing its historic role as the Primate's seat in return for its own full-time archbishop, though it will permanently regain the honour on the retirement or death of the present incumbent, Cardinal Glemp.

The City

The compactness of Gniezno is immediately evident: arriving at either the **train** or **bus station**, side by side to the south of the centre, it's only a couple of minutes' walk straight down ul. Lecha to the main thoroughfare, ul. Bolesława Chrobrego. The shabby streets off it, particularly to the left, twist and turn in a medievally haphazard manner, though few buildings date back further than last century. Even the **Rynek**, normally the showpiece of a Polish city, is distinctly run-down.

There are, however, three Gothic churches worth a quick look. Just off the southern side of the Rynek is the **Holy Trinity** (św. Trójcy), partly rebuilt in the Baroque style following a fire, beside which stand the only surviving remains of the city walls. Off the opposite side of the Rynek towers the Franciscan church, while further to the north is **St John's**. The latter, a foundation of the Knights Templar, preserves fourteenth-century frescoes in its chancel and has carved bosses and corbels depicting virtues and vices.

The Cathedral

Downhill from the Rynek lies Gniezno's episcopal quarter, presenting an altogether smarter appearance than the commercial centre. A flourishing seminary is the main focus of activity, but the most important monument is the

Cathedral, beside which stands a statue of Bolesław the Brave. Strongly reminiscent of Poznań Cathedral, the basic brick structure was built in the fourteenth century in the severest Gothic style, but was enlivened in the Baroque period by a ring of stone chapels and by the addition of steeples to the twin facade towers. Not surprisingly, memorials to Saint Adalbert dominate the interior. At the entrance to the sanctuary, in the shadow of a fifteenth-century limewood crucifix, is his red marble **tomb**, carved around 1480 by Hans Brandt of Gdańsk. Another craftsman from the same city, Peter van Rennen, made the silver **shrine** above the high altar, to which one's eye is drawn down the whole length of the building. Surrounded by figures representing the different social classes, this features – like the tomb – an imaginary portrait of the saint, along with depictions of the chief events of his life.

An inevitable influence on van Rennen was the magnificent pair of **bronze doors** at the beginning of the southern aisle. Cast around 1170, these are among the finest surviving examples of Romanesque decorative art, and are unique in Poland. Adalbert's life from the cradle to beyond the grave is illustrated in eighteen scenes, going up the right-hand door and then down the left, all set within a rich decorative border. Quite apart from their artistic quality, the doors are remarkable as a documentary record: even the faces of the villainous Prussians are based on accurate observation. If you pass through the doorway, you can see the beautiful **portal** on the other side. Though its tympanum of *Christ in Majesty* is orthodox enough, the carvings of animals and the prominent mask heads give it a highly idiosyncratic flavour.

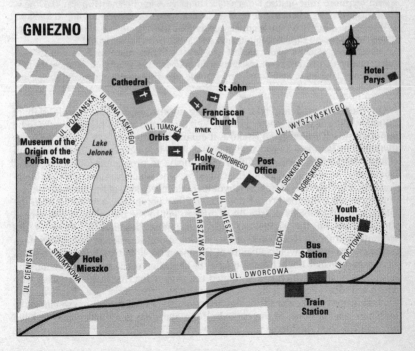

CARDINAL STEFAN WYSZYNSKI (1901–81)

In the history of communist Europe, there is nothing remotely comparable to the career of Stefan Wyszyński, who adapted the traditional powers of the Primate of Poland to act as spokesman and regent of his people in a strikingly novel way. Not only did he function as a permanent and high-profile opposition leader to the communist regime; he was also seen as a powerful and influential figure in his own right.

Wyszyński's early ministry was centred in Włocławek, where he was ordained in 1924, quickly establishing a reputation in the social field. He spent the war years in the **underground resistance movement**, having been saved from the German concentration camps which accounted for most of his colleagues in Włocławek through the prompt action of his bishop, who had ordered him to leave the town. He returned as head of the Włocławek seminary in 1945, and then had a meteoric rise, being appointed Bishop of Lublin the following year, before his elevation to the archdiocese of Gniezno, with Warsaw added as well, and the title of **Primate of Poland**, in 1948.

The elimination of Poland's formerly substantial Jewish, Orthodox and Protestant minorities as a result of World War II and its aftermath meant that **nearly 98 percent of the population professed Catholicism**, as opposed to the prewar figure of 75 percent. At the same time, however, organised religion came under threat from the atheist communist regime which was imposed on the country. Matters came to a head with the Vatican's worldwide decree of 1949, which ordered the withholding of sacraments to all communist functionaries and sympathisers: this caused particular tensions in Poland, where the new administration, particularly in rural areas, was dependent on practising Catholics. Wyszyński reached a **compromise agreement** with the government the following year whereby the affairs of church and state were clearly demarcated.

This cosy relationship did not last long: a wave of **Stalinist repression** in 1952–3 led to the end of religious instruction in schools, the usurption of most of the Church's charitable activities, and to the imprisonment and harassment of

On the west wall are two outstanding **monuments**. The marble slab of Zbigniew Oleśnicki is a masterpiece by Veit Stoss, and one of his few works to be found outside Nürnberg and Kraków. It contrasts with the nervy line of the brass memorial to Jakub ze Sienna that stands alongside, made earlier in the fifteenth century by Flemish artisans. Other monuments to prominent local clerics and laymen can be seen throughout the cathedral. One which has to catch your attention is that to **Primate Stefan Wyszyński**, in the north side of the ambulatory.

Directly opposite the bronze doors is another porch only accessible from the interior. You'll probably need a bit of guile to get to see the manuscripts kept in the **archive** on the right-hand side. The most beautiful of these is the eleventh-century *Golden Codex*, made for Gniezno at Reichenau in southwestern Germany, the most inventive centre of European book illumination at the time. A far simpler gospel book from a couple of centuries earlier has annotations by Irish missionaries, which has prompted the suggestion that it was the Irish who converted the Polish tribes. Other valuable treasures are kept in the **Archdiocesan Museum** (Tues–Sat 10am–4pm), housed in one of the cluster of buildings on the north of the cathedral; the star item is a chalice said to have belonged to Saint Adalbert.

thousands of priests. As a culmination, the Bishop of Kielce was sentenced to twelve years' imprisonment on charges of espionage. Wyszyński's protests led to his own **arrest**, and he was confined to the monastery of Komańcza in the remote Bieszczady Mountains. The detention of a man widely regarded as possessing saintly qualities had the effect of alienating the regime even further from the bulk of the populace, and Wyszyński acted as the symbolic figurehead to the unrest which reached crisis proportions in 1956.

Wyszyński was **released** later that year as part of the package – which also included the return of Gomułka to power – forestalling the Soviet invasion which would almost certainly have ensued had a political breakdown occurred. From then on, the communists were forced to accept the **special status** of the Catholic Church in Polish society, and they were never afterwards able to suppress it: in 1957, Wyszyński was allowed to travel to Rome to receive the Cardinal's hat he had been awarded five years previously. Under his leadership – which, from a theological point of view, was extremely conservative – Poland came to be regarded as **the most fervently Catholic nation in the world**, with the Jasna Góra pilgrimage promoted as the central feature of national consciousness. Wyszynski's sermons, often relayed from every pulpit in the country, became increasingly fearless and notable for such pronouncements as his celebrated claim that "Polish citizens are slaves in their own country".

Although Wyszyński did not live to see the collapse of the communist regime against which he had fought so doggedly, his last years were ones of unbridled triumph. The standing to which he had raised Poland within the Roman Catholic faith was given due reward in 1978, when his right-hand man, Karol Wojtyła – once courted by the communists as a potentially more malleable future Primate – leapfrogged over him to become the first-ever Polish pope. Then, at the very end of his life, the government was forced to yield to him as a powerbroker at the heart of the **Solidarity crisis**. When Wyszyński died, he was rewarded with a **funeral** matched in postwar Europe only by those of the victorious war leaders, Churchill and de Gaulle; the country came to a standstill as even his communist opponents were prominent in paying their last respects.

Lake Jelonek

Just west of the cathedral is Lake Jelonek, a peaceful spot with a wonderful view of the town. Overlooking its far bank, but best approached via the main road, is a large modern building containing a college and the **Museum of the Origins of the Polish State** (Tues–Sun 10am–5pm). This contains archaeological finds from various Wielkopolska sites, along with changing art exhibitions. There's also a video show on the early history of Poland, with screenings in English on request.

Gniezno practicalities

There's little evidence to show that Gniezno is expecting foreign tourists. Both **Orbis** and **PTTK** have offices on the Rynek, but neither has any tourist information.

There are three **hotels**, top of the range being *Mieszko*, beside the sports stadium above Lake Jelonek (☎46-25); this is on the model of an expense-account motel, but with prices about a quarter of what they would be in the West. Its bistro is one of the livelier nightspots in a town which is generally quiet of an evening. Cheaper alternatives are *Parys*, ul. Roosevelta 53 (☎56-70), and *Orle Gniazdo*, ul. Wrzesinska 25 (☎36-18). The **youth hostel** is conveniently close to the stations at ul. Pocztowa 11 (☎13-23).

The best **restaurant** in the centre of town is *Gwarna* at the corner of ul. Mieszka I and ul. Bolesława Chrobrego; others worth a try are the *Teatralno,* also on ul. Bolesława Chrobrego, and *Robotnicza,* which is situated at the corner of ul. Mieszka I and ul. Dąbrówki. There are, in addition, several **cafés** on and around the Rynek.

Lake Lednica

One of the key places in the early life of Poland is the long, narrow **Lake Lednica**, 18km west of Gniezno and easily reached by bus. The place to get off is across from the entrance to the **Wielkopolska Ethnographic Park** (April 15–Oct 31 Tues–Sun 9am–5pm), by the turn-off to DZIEKANOWICE. Laid out in an exhilarating location by the side of the lake, this open-air museum consists of about fifty traditional rural buildings from the last 250 years or so, mostly originals – including three working windmills, a Baroque cemetery chapel with all its furnishings, and several farmsteads.

From here, continue on to the village, bear left along the main street, then right at the grocery store; it's then a walk of twenty minutes or so to the disparate tourist complex known as the **Museum of the First Piasts at Lednica** (same hours). Entered through an impressive wooden gateway, whose upper storey turns out to be a snack bar, this features a few more rural buildings, a craft shop in yet another windmill, a small collection of archaeological finds, and over-life-sized statues of Polish warriors of a millennium ago. More importantly, it's the departure point for **Ostrów Lednicki**, the largest of the three islands in Lake Lednica, which can easily be reached in a couple of minutes by the chained ferry.

This unlikely site, uninhabited for the last six centuries, was once a royal seat equal to Poznań and Gniezno in importance – Bolesław the Brave was born here, and it may also have been where his coronation by Emperor Otto III took place, rather than in Gniezno. It began life in the ninth century as a fortified town covering about a third of the island and linked to the mainland by a causeway. In the following century a massive **palace** was constructed, along with a church: the excavated remains only hint at its former grandeur, but the presence of stairways prove it must have been at least two storeys high. The buildings were destroyed in 1038 by the Czech Prince Brzetysław, but the church was rebuilt soon afterwards, only to gradually fall into disuse, along with the town itself. For centuries the island served as a cemetery, only to be lulled out of its sleep by tourism.

Biskupin

The Iron Age village of **BISKUPIN**, 30km north of Gniezno, is one of the most evocative and exciting archaeological sites in Europe. Though the area has long been a fruitful source for excavations, its full significance only became apparent in 1933, when the local schoolmaster noticed some hand-worked stakes standing in the reeds at the edge of Lake Biskupin. He also learned from a landowner that other artefacts had been found during peat cutting. Experts from Poznań soon pronounced that the site had been a **fortified village** of the Lusatian culture, founded around 550 BC and destroyed in tribal warfare some 150 years later. The subsequent uncovering of the settlement has thrown fresh light on the tribal life of the period, enabling the solution of many previously unresolved questions.

The only way to reach Biskupin by public transport is to take a bus to **GĄSAWA**, 2km south of Biskupin, then switch to the **narrow-gauge steam train** which stops right in front of the site up to five times daily. Unlike most of the many other historic lines in Poland, it exists solely for tourist purposes and runs only when the site is open. Nonetheless, the open-windowed red and yellow carriages are sufficiently unkempt to seem authentic and add a distinctive note to the otherwise monotonously green landscape. (For more on the railway, see overleaf.)

The Site

In contrast to the overcautious approach which makes so many famous archaeological sites disappointing to non-specialists, it was decided to reconstruct the original appearance of a section of the village. The price to be paid for this approach is evident at the entrance to the **Archaeological Park** (daily mid-April to end Sept 8am–7pm; Oct 8am–6pm subject to weather), where ramshackle snack bars, tacky souvenir shops and amusement booths are overrun by endless busloads of schoolkids in early summer. There's also a small tourist office which sells an excellent booklet to the site in English.

From the entrance, it's best to go straight ahead past a re-erected old farmhouse to the **Museum**, which contains all manner of objects dug up here – tools, household utensils, weapons, jewellery, ornaments and objects for worship. Piecing together the evidence, archaeologists have been able to draw a picture of a society in which hunting had been largely superseded by arable farming and livestock breeding. Their trade patterns were surprisingly extensive – their iron seems to have come from Transylvania, and there's a fascinating group of exhibits imported from even further afield, the most exotic being some Egyptian beads. Most remarkable of all was the tribe's prowess in building, as can be seen in the model reconstruction of the entire village. Beyond the museum buildings is an enclosure for tarpans, miniature working horses which have evolved very little since the time of the settlement.

Returning to the farmhouse, it's only a couple of minutes' walk down the path to the right to the **excavations**. The foreground consists of the uncovered foundations of various buildings, some from as late as the thirteenth century; of more interest are re-creations of the Iron Age buildings – although only a section of each has been built, and not exactly on their former site, it requires little imagination to picture what the whole must have looked like. For the best view of the settlement, take a **cruise** on the old steamer which chugs round the lake throughout the day: departure times are posted on the jetty, and the cost is nominal.

The **palisade** was particularly ingenious: it originally consisted of 35,000 stakes grouped in rows up to nine deep and driven into the bed of the lake at an angle of 45°. It acted both as a breakwater and as the first line of the fortifications. Immediately behind was a circular **wall** of oak logs guarded by a tall watchtower: the latter is the most conjectural part of the whole restoration project. Inside the defences were a ring road plus eleven symmetrical streets, again made of logs and filled in with earth, sand and clay; the **houses** were grouped in terraces ranged from east to west to catch the sun. An entire extended family would live in each house, so the population of the settlement probably numbered over 1000. As you can see from the example open for inspection, each house had two chambers: pigs and cattle – the most important privately owned objects – were kept in the lobby, while the main room, where the family slept in a single bed, was also equipped with a loft for the storage of food and fuel.

The Biskupin Railway

Next stop after Biskupin on the narrow-gauge railway is **WENECJA**, which is itself well worth a visit. This hamlet's name is the Polish word for Venice, fancifully justified by the fact that it is almost surrounded by water, lying as it does between two lakes. Nearby communities are equally improbably styled "Rome", "Paris" and "Scotland". To the right of the station are the remains of the fourteenth-century **Castle** of Mikołaj Nałęcz, a notorious figure known by the nickname of "the Bloody Devil of Wenecja". Only the lower parts of the walls survive, admittedly in good shape, but to see inside you have to take a leaf out of the book of a medieval attacker and scale them. On the opposite side of the tracks is the open-air **Museum of Narrow-Gauge Railways** (daily 9am–5pm), which has a collection of engines and rolling stock from all over Europe.

The terminus of the twelve-kilometre route is **ŻNIN**, a small town again set between two lakes, part of a long north–south chain. In the centre of its Rynek stands the remarkable and forlorn tower of the demolished fifteenth-century **Town Hall**, whose interior has been fitted out as the local museum (Tues–Fri 9am–4pm, Sat 9am–3pm, Sun 10am–3pm). There are several restaurants, cafés and bars here, and a couple of **accommodation** options if you fancy a night in a quiet location – *Hotel Brda*, ul. 700 Lecia 1 (☎207), and a campsite (☎76) by Lake Mały Żnin to the south.

It's easy to move on from Żnin: in addition to mainline and narrow-gauge trains, it's also well served by buses on the main road between Gniezno and Bydgoszcz.

Trzemeszno to Inowrocław

Sixteen kilometres east of Gniezno, the Piast Route winds through **TRZEMESZNO**, a straggling little lakeside community that was founded, according to tradition, by Saint Adalbert. It can be reached either by bus or Baltic-bound train – the latter involving a fairly long walk through the fields to the town.

The ancient church which Adalbert is said to have established was succeeded by a Romanesque structure, parts of which are incorporated in the Baroque **Basilica** which dominates the town. From the outside it appears austere, but the interior is lavishly decorated from the tiled pavement to the frescoed dome. In the main square is a monument to the local hero, the shoemaker Jan Kiliński, who played a leading role in the 1794 Insurrection (see "Warsaw"; Chapter One). Next to the church is the *Hotel Czeremcha* (☎380), which also has the town's only restaurant.

Mogilno

A further 16km northeast is **MOGILNO**, again set on the bank of a lake. Here the railway splits, with a branch slowly and circuitously following the Piast Route, offering an alternative to the more regular buses. Mogilno itself isn't a place you'll want to hang around for long, but it does have a couple of worthwhile churches, the Gothic St James and the eclectic St John the Evangelist, both by the lakeside on the opposite side of town from the stations. The latter preserves its Romanesque crypt and apse, complete with carved frieze, though the building was heavily transformed in both the Gothic and Baroque epochs.

Strzelno

The Piast Route's most important artistic treasures are found 17km east of Mogilno in the archetypally Polish rural town of **STRZELNO**. Both the bus and train stations are set at the western fringe of town; from there, walk straight ahead, turning left at the *Hotel Dom Wycieczkowy* on pl. Duszyńskiego (☎237) – at the end of this street is the rather run-down main square. Continuing down to the right brings you to the far end of town. Enclosed in a precinct – a haven of peace when the tour groups aren't there – are two outstanding Romanesque buildings.

The monastery of the **Holy Trinity** is a typically Polish accretion: brick Gothic gables reminiscent of the Baltic ports and a monumental Baroque facade sprout from a dignified late twelfth-century Romanesque shell. After the war, some of the interior encrustations were removed to reveal, in well-nigh perfect condition, four original nave **pillars**. Two of these, adorned with figurative carvings set in a foliage surround, are crafted with a delicacy found in few other European sculptures of the period; a third is reminiscent of Arab art in its geometrical shapes. Another column of almost equal quality forms the sole support of the beautiful vault of the Chapel of St Barbara, to the right of the chancel.

Beside the monastery church stands the slightly older little red sandstone rotunda of **St Procopius**. In contrast to its neighbour, this has preserved the purity of its original form, its round tower perfectly offset against the protruding apses. It's normally kept locked, but you should be able to gain access if you ask in Holy Trinity or the buildings alongside.

Incidentally, the churches are not the earliest evidence of worship on this site: the large stone block in front of them is thought to have been used for pagan rites.

Kruszwica

As the Piast Route moves on to sleepy **KRUSZWICA**, 16km northeast of Strzelno by road but much further by rail, it enters the tiny province of Kujawy. Standing at the head of the pencil-slim **Lake Gopło**, the largest of all western Poland's lakes, Kruszwica is enshrined in Polish folklore as the cradle of the Piast dynasty.

Both the **bus** and **train stations** are located at the northwestern fringe of the town. From here, walk ahead to the main street, ul. Niepodległości, where you'll find the only **restaurant** worth mentioning, the inevitably named *Piatowska*. Continuing down the street, you come to the spacious but unremarkable Rynek, just east of which is a bridge over the lake.

THE LEGEND OF THE FOUNDATION OF THE PIAST DYNASTY

The legend goes that the descendants of Lech were ousted as the nation's rulers by the evil Popiel family. To ensure there was no competition for his succession, the last King Popiel killed all his male kin except his own children, then established himself at a castle in Kruszwica, where he subjected his people to a reign of terror. One day, saints John and Paul came in the guise of poor travellers, but the king refused them hospitality and they were forced to lodge with a peasant named Piast. They baptised him and his family, and predicted that he would be first in a long line of monarchs, whereupon they vanished. Shortly afterwards, the Poles rose up against their evil ruler. He took refuge in his castle tower, where he was eventually devoured by rats. The people then chose the worthy Piast as his successor.

The shady tree-lined peninsula immediately to the south of this is a popular tourist spot, as evidenced by the presence of a PTTK information point and a number of snack stands. It's dominated by a brick octagon known as the **Mouse Tower** (Mysia Wieża). Allegedly, this was where the rodent feast took place; in fact, ironically enough, it was part of a castle built by the last of the Piast dynasty, Kazimierz the Great. During the summer season, you can climb to the top for a sweeping view down the length of Lake Gopło.

Kruszwica's only other historic monument is the early twelfth-century **Collegiate Church**, situated on the eastern shore of the tip of the lake which lies north of the bridge. A grim granite basilica with three apses, it has been stripped of most of its later accretions, except for the brick Gothic tower. Supposedly occupying the miraculous site of Piast's cottage, it served as a cathedral for the first half-century of its life, but was then supplanted by Włocławek.

Inowrocław

The end of the Piast Route comes 15km north of Kruszwica at **INOWROCŁAW**. Here the main monument is the **Church of the Assumption**, a contemporary of the Romanesque basilicas in Strzelno and Kruszwica, albeit one somewhat devalued by remodelling carried out early this century. It occupies a pleasantly landscaped position in a park, a few minutes' walk east of the big roundabout which lies between the compact commercial centre and the bus and train stations, which are respectively ten and fifteen minutes' walk to the north. In the heart of the Old Town is **St Nicholas** (św. Mikołaja), a Gothic parish church with Renaissance and Baroque additions. Around the time this was being built in the fifteenth century, underground salt springs were discovered in the area, but it was not until the 1870s that Inowrocław became a popular **spa**, with thermal establishments built to the west of the Old Town. The prosperity this brought is reflected in the grand turn-of-the-century buildings erected along the town's main axis, ul. Królowej Jadwigi, which are now re-emerging from decades of neglect in their full colourful pomp. Unfortunately, although the baths are still in use, the modern town has harnessed the waters as the basis of a chemical industry which has led to heavy pollution and the mushroom growth of concrete suburbs whose only saving grace is the fact that they're spaced out with plenty of greenery.

Given the current appearance of Inowrocław, it's not likely to rate as an overnight stop. If you do want to use it as a touring base, then there are two **hotels** on ul. Królowej Jadwigi: *Bast* at no. 35 (☎728-88 or 720-24) is the nicer of them, and will be even more so when its refurbishment is complete; *Pod Lwem* at no. 1

(☎720-01) is fairly basic, and a bit cheaper. The former's **restaurant** is the best among a very limited range of options of places to eat and drink.

Inowrocław offers a wide choice of connections onwards to Toruń and Bydgoszcz, or else back to Gniezno either directly or via Żnin.

Włocławek and Ciechocinek

The only other places of interest in Kujawy lie to the east, on or near the River Wisła – the province's historic capital, **Włocławek**, and the highly distinctive spa town of **Ciechocinek**. If continuing onwards from the Piast Route, it's best to go there by bus; otherwise they are readily accessible by train from either Płock (see Chapter One) or Toruń (see Chapter Two).

Włocławek

Situated some 60km southeast of Inowrocław, **WŁOCŁAWEK** is nowadays predominantly an industrial town, with a huge paper mill fed by the neighbouring forests, though it's best known for its production of one of Poland's favourite tourist souvenirs – glazed earthenware, hand-painted with brown floral motifs. Włocławek's early development owed much to its strategic position on the River Wisła; it has been the seat of a bishop since the mid-twelfth century, and it remains an important episcopal centre – the formidable Stefan Wyszyński (see "Gniezno"), scourge of successive communist governments, spent most of his early priesthood there. For long the town operated a rigid anti-Semitic policy, with Jews prohibited from settling until the eighteenth century.

Around town

Arriving at either the **bus** or **train stations**, situated together at the southwestern end of the centre, ul. Tadeusza Kościuszki leads to pl. Wolności, a characterless large square forming the hub of the modern business district, which has migrated here from its original position overlooking the Wisła. The Rynek, several blocks north along ul. 3 Maja, now has a certain dilapidated charm, looking more like the centrepiece of a rural village than of a sizeable town. Its historic houses range in date from the seventeenth to the nineteenth centuries; a fine Baroque example on the east side now contains the **District Museum** (Tues 10am–6pm, Wed, Fri & Sat 10am–3pm, Thurs 10am–noon & 3–6pm, Sun 10am–2pm), with displays on the archaeology, history, art and folklore of Kujawy. On the north side of the square is the parish church of **St John**, originally Gothic but heavily remodelled in the Baroque period.

A short distance to the west lies the brick Gothic **Cathedral**, which was begun in 1340, a few years after a fire which completely destroyed its predecessor along with much of the rest of the town. At the end of last century, it was ruthlessly restored and embellished – notably by the addition of the fantastical spires, whose brickwork rather jars with that of the lower parts of the towers. Just as the silhouette now has a predominatnly Romantic flavour, so too does the interior, which was given a heavy painted decoration. Far more interesting are the chapels, particularly that dedicated to Saint Joseph on the north side. Regrettably, this is very dark and kept locked, but you can peek in to see the **tomb** of Bishop Piotr Moszyński, beautifully carved in Hungarian marble by Veit Stoss (see "Kraków",

Chapter Four): it adopts a highly individual but subsequently much imitated arrangement, featuring a full-length relief carving of the deceased on the sloping lid of the sarcophagus. In the same chapel is a fine funerary monument to Monsiegneur Karnowski by another, this time anonymous, sculptor from Nürnberg. Also of note is the late Renaissance **mausoleum of the Tarnowski family**, which protrudes showily from the south side of the cathedral, its coloured marble exterior adorned with sundials, its interior richly furnished with statues and busts.

It's well worth crossing the impressive modern cantilever bridge over the Wisła, which is here dotted by a number of sandbanks; from the northern side you're rewarded with an excellent **view** over the town and the river.

Practicalities

Orbis have an office just off the eastern side of pl. Wolności at ul. Zduńska 8 (☎252-28 or 230-21). There's a reasonable choice of accommodation, beginning with two mid-range **hotels**, of which the old coaching inn *Zajazd Polski*, pl. Wolności 5 (☎250-51) scores in atmosphere over the functional modern *Kujawy*, ul. Kościuszki 18/20 (☎262-31). There's also a **sports hotel**, *Delfin*, southeast of the centre at al. Fryderyka Chopina 12 (☎260-00), and reached by bus #15; the seasonal **youth hostel** is a few blocks east of pl. Wolności at ul. Chmielna 24 (☎273-63). For **eating** and **drinking**, the hotels are just about the only options in the centre, except for the uninspiring snack bars in the vicinity of the station.

Ciechocinek

CIECHOCINEK, a town with its own microclimate, and with rather more life about it than the normal run of spas, lies slightly back from the Wisła, about half-way between Włocławek and Toruń. It can be reached directly from either city by bus; if travelling by train, alight at ALEKSANDRÓW KUJAWY, from where there are fairly regular services down a seven-kilometre-long branch line terminating at what must be a strong contender for the title of Poland's most salubrious and elegant train station.

Straight ahead from here is the **Park Zdrojowy**, with floral gardens, tree-lined avenues and the usual spa buildings – pump room, concert hall and bandstand. Far more intriguing, however, is the **Park Tężniówy** on the opposite side of the railway tracks from the town. Here, in three separate sections stretching for over 1.5km, is the mass of wooden poles and twigs which make up the **saltworks**, begun in 1824 but not completed until several decades later. It's an extraordinary sight – undoubtedly one of the most impressive industrial monuments to be found anywhere in Europe – and is all the more remarkable in that it can still be seen functioning as originally intended. The technology behind it is very simple: water from the town's saline springs is pumped to the top of the structure, from where it trickles back down through the twigs. This not only concentrates the salt, it also creates a wondrously healthy atmosphere in the covered space below. Formerly, patients would walk through the saltworks, breathing in deeply as they went, but, for conservation reasons, this is unfortunately no longer permitted.

As Ciechocinek is still geared to those attending recuperative programmes in the sanatoria, there's no real reason for anyone else to want to stay over, but, if you do, a small office at the corner of the train station can arrange **rooms**. There are a few restaurants in the town centre, plus several cafés here and in the parks.

POMERANIA (POMORZE)

Pomerania's long, sandy coastline is its major attraction, and a couple of days holed up on the Baltic here is one of the most pleasant ways of unwinding that the country can offer. Less known but equally appealing, though, is the inland forested lake district, with its market towns, Prussian peasant houses and marvellous Gothic brick churches.

A BRIEF HISTORY OF POMERANIA

In prehistoric times the southern Baltic coast was inhabited by the Celts, who were later displaced by a succession of Germanic tribes. By the end of the fifth century they too had been ousted by Slav people known as the **Pomorzanie**, relics of whose settlements are preserved on Wolin island, in the west of the region. The lands of the Pomorzanie were in turn conquered by the Piast **King Mieszko I**, who took Szczecin in 979 – a campaign which is cited by the Poles in support of their claim to ownership of this often disputed territory. Thereafter the picture gets more complicated. Throughout the medieval era Pomerania evolved as an essentially independent dukedom ruled by a local Slav dynasty commonly called the **Pomeranian princes**, who nonetheless owed loyalty to the Polish monarch. Eastern Pomerania was conquered by the Teutonic Knights in 1308, and was later known as Royal Prussia; this part of the region returned to the Polish sphere of influence under the terms of the 1466 Treaty of Toruń and is described in Chapter Two.

The ethnic mix of the region played a dominant part in governing its allegiances. While a Slav majority retained its hold on the countryside, heavy German colonisation of the towns inexorably tilted the balance of power to the territorially ambitious Brandenburg margraviate. In line with the westward drift, the Pomeranian princes finally transferred formal allegiance to the Holy Roman Empire in 1521, and the inroads of the Reformation further weakened the region's ties with Catholic Poland, which anyway was more interested in its eastern borderlands than its western terrains. In 1532, the ruling Gryfit dynasty divided into two lines, and their territory was partitioned along a line west of the Odra delta: the larger eastern duchy was henceforth known as Hinter Pomerania; the small one to the west as Lower or Hither Pomerania. None of the latter's territory has ever subsequently formed part of Poland.

Control of the region was fiercely disputed during the **Thirty Years' War**, with the Swedes taking over all of Lower Pomerania, plus some of the coastline of Hinter Pomerania. The Treaty of Westphalia of 1648 formalised the division of the latter, whose capital, Szczecin/Stettin, thereby became part of Sweden. Following the departure of the Swedes in the 1720s, **the Prussians** re-united Lower and Hinter Pomerania into a single administrative province, and during the Partitions were able to join it up with their territories to the east by the annexation of Royal Prussia. Their control over the region was undisturbed until after the Versailles Treaty of 1919, when a strip of Pomerania's eastern fringe was ceded to Poland, some of it forming part of the notorious "Polish Corridor". Nearly all of the territory of the old duchy of Hinter Pomerania was **allocated to Poland** in 1945, as part of the compensation deal for loss of the Eastern Territories to the Soviet Union. Mass emigration of the area's German population, which started during the final months of the war, gathered apace after the transfer of sovereignty; in their place came displaced Polish settlers, mostly from the east.

Bydgoszcz, a major industrial city with a small historic centre, serves as the gateway to the **lakes** to the north. For these, the best base is **Czaplinek**, on the shores of **Lake Drawsko**, as attractive a stretch of water as any in Mazury. On the coast there are plenty of resorts to choose from: **Łeba** combines beaches with the **Słowiński National Park**; the old port of **Darłowo** preserves a distinctively Pomeranian character; while to the west many of the finest beaches are found around **Kołobrzeg** and on the islands of **Wolin** and **Uznam**. Just inland, **Kamień Pomorski** warrants a visit, whether for its cathedral or the summer music festival. All places are readily accessible from the great port of **Szczecin**, Pomerania's largest city and historic capital, while nearby **Stargard Szczeciński** offers several of the province's architectural highpoints.

Transport links within Pomerania are good: there's a reasonable train service that runs parallel to the coast on the Gdańsk–Szczecin line, with local connections up to the coastal resorts and buses for excursions into the countryside.

Bydgoszcz

BYDGOSZCZ is a sprawling industrial city, developed around a fortified medieval settlement strategically located on the River Brda, shortly before its confluence with the Wisła. Its growth towards its present size began towards the end of the eighteenth century when, as the Prussian town of Bromberg, it became the hub of an important waterway system as the result of the construction of a canal linking the Wisła to the Odra via the rivers Brda, Noteć and Warta. Unlike much of the region to the north, it has been Polish since 1920, when it was ceded by Germany and incorporated into the province of Poznań. During World War II, the city suffered particularly badly at the hands of the Nazis: mass executions of civilians followed its fall, and by the end of the war over 50,000 people – a quarter of the population – had been murdered, with many of the rest deported to labour and concentration camps.

The City

Strangely enough, the fabric of the city suffered far less from wartime damage than many others in this part of Poland. Even if the centre – which nows seems very small-scale, particularly in the light of the doubling of the population in the postwar period – has nothing of outstanding interest, it has plenty of character, with an attractive waterfront dividing the Old Town on the south bank from the grandly self-confident Prussian streets opposite.

As ever, the focal point of the medieval centre is the Rynek, on which stands a typical communist-style **Monument** to the victims of Nazism. There are also a few Baroque and Neoclassical mansions, notably no. 24, which contains the municipal library. These are rather overshadowed by the vast bulk of the **Jesuit College**, which closes the west side of the square, with another fine frontage along ul. Jezuicka. Begun at the end of the seventeenth century, this was for long the town's leading educational establishment, but it is now used for the municipal offices.

In a secluded corner just to the north is the redbrick fifteenth-century **Parish Church** (Kościół Farny). This has recently been raised to the status of a co-cathedral, though its dimensions and appearance are more modest than those of many a village church. Nonetheless, its exterior is graced by a fine Gothic gable, while inside, among the usual Baroque ornamentation, is the sixteenth-century high altar of *The Madonna with the Rose*. The church overlooks what is fancifully styled the "Bydgoszcz Venice", the banks on either side of the island formed by two arms of the Brda. On the peninsula at the edge of this island are an old **Granary** and **Mill**; the latter is designated as a museum, but was closed at the time of writing.

The south side of the main **waterfront** is dominated by two, much larger half-timbered granaries of the eighteenth century. One of these contains the **Historical Museum** (Tues–Sat 10am–4pm, but closed for restoration at the time of writing), with displays on the history of the town, including archive material on the Nazi atrocities. From the quay outside, **boats** regularly depart in summer for excursions along the Brda.

Crossing over to the northern bank, you come to the former **Convent Church** of the Poor Clares (Kościół Klarysek), a curious amalgam of late Gothic and Renaissance, with later alterations. Its conventual buildings now contain the **District Museum** (Tues–Sat 10am–4pm), which is mostly given over to the work of the eclectic local artist Leon Wyczółkowski. This marks the start of al. 1 Maja, the main commercial axis of the modern part of town, along which are a number of turn-of-the-century buildings currently being restored to their colourful former state.

Five blocks east of here is a historical curiosity which rewards the short detour – the **Basilica of St Vincent de Paul**, a vast circular brick church self-consciously modelled on the Pantheon in Rome and capable of accommodating 12,000 worshippers. Its construction was a direct result of the town's change in ownership from Protestant Prussia to Catholic Poland, which necessitated a much larger space for the main feast days than the small existing churches were able to provide.

Practicalities

Both the **bus** and **train stations** are located to the northwest of the city centre: a 15-minute walk straight down ul. Dworcowa brings you out at al. 1 Maja, the lazy alternative being to take tram #1, #2, #4 or #8. There's a **tourist office** (Mon–Sat 7am–3pm; ☎22-53-50) just across from the station at ul. Zygmunta Augusta 10.

The best **hotel** is the Orbis-run *Pod Orlem*, al 1 Maja 14 (☎22-18-61), which has recently been lovingly restored to its *fin de siècle* elegance. Another attractive option is *Ratuszowy*, which occupies a Baroque mansion two blocks south of the Rynek at ul. Długa 37 (☎22-88-61). In comparison with these, *Brda*, the huge concrete skyscraper at ul. Dworcowa 94 (☎22-56-55), seems unenticing and poor value, though the slightly run-down *Centralny*, ul. Dworcowa 85 (☎22-88-76), is worth considering if you want to save money; its reception is supposed to be able to find rooms in private houses. The **youth hostel** is also handily placed, being likewise just a couple of minutes' walk from the station at ul. Józefa Sowińskiego 5 (☎22-75-70).

Each of the first three hotels listed has a good **restaurant**; other options include *Śródmiejska*, ul. Dworcowa 19, *Rybna*, al. 1 Maja 22, and *Kaczma Słupska*, al. 1 Maja 28. A few decent **milk bars** still survive, such as *Dworcowy*, ul. Dworcowa 75, and *Ratuszowy*, ul. Długa 27.

For an evening's entertainment, the *Filharmonia Pomorska*, just east of ul. 1 Maja at ul. Karola Libelta 16, is the main **musical** venue; as well as regular concerts, it features a fortnight-long classical festival each September. The main **theatre** is the nearby *Teatr Polski*, al. Mickiewicza 2.

The Pomeranian Lakeland

The **Pomeranian Lakeland** lies over to the northwest of Bydgoszcz, centred on the resort town of **Szczecinek**. A marshy, green area, with quiet, tree-lined roads and small market towns, it is dotted with over one thousand lakes which are connected by a trellis of east–west and north–south waterways – making it possible to travel all over the area by boat. There is very little tourist infrastructure as yet, though many Poles have holiday *dachas* on the lakesides. Perhaps the most attractive area to make for is around **Lake Drawsko**, with its relaxed little town of **Czaplinek**.

Although some train lines weave their way across the district, **buses** are the best way of getting into the heart of the lakeland – either from Bydgoszcz, Szczecin or Gdańsk, or from the coastal resorts. If you want to walk, or have a **car**, you can get well off the beaten track to lakes that haven't made it into this section – or into any of the Polish tourist literature, in which Pomerania remains oddly played down. In the remoter reaches, the tradition of Polish hospitality compensates for the lack of formal **accommodation**: turn up at a bar and ask, and someone can usually arrange a room for the night.

Chojnice and around

Some 50km north of Bydgoszcz, near Lake Charzykowskie, lies **CHOJNICE**, a quiet, unpretentious place with a dusty, open square – the setting for its main bit of animation, a weekly market, when the streets are filled with horse-drawn carts. Architecturally, the town has a few reminders of its past as the last Polish stronghold of the Teutonic Knights. The most impressive of these buildings is the Gothic **Parish Church**, a sturdy brick construction whose high tower dominates the town centre. Sections of the town **walls** have also survived the battering of the centuries, most notably the five-storey **Czuchołow Gate** (Brama Czuchołowoska), off the western edge of the Rynek.

Few foreign visitors will want to stay in Chojnice. Should you need to do so, the Orbis ofice at pl. Bojownikow 3 can provide information on private rooms and **hotels**. At present there are just two rather basic places – the *Olimp*, ul. Kościerska 9 (☎36-29), and the *Turystyczny*, ul. Myśliboja 5 (☎51-89) – and a summer **youth hostel** at ul. 31 Stycznia 21/23 (☎50-39).

Lake Charzykowskie and the Tucholski Forest

A few kilometres north of Chojnice, a series of lakes and waterways extends for an unbroken sixty kilometres towards the edges of Kashubia (see Chapter Two). The place to start out at is **Lake Charzykowskie**, approached from the village of CHARZYKOW, a five-kilometre bus ride to the north of town. East of Chojnice stretches the huge **Tucholski Forest** (Bory Tucholski), a dense expanse of woodland punctuated by lakes and crisscrossed by streams and rivers, the largest being the Brda, flowing north from Bydgoszcz. In the heart of the forest are a string of peasant villages and, on the banks of the Brda, a few holiday centres.

Odry stone circles

Just outside the village of **ODRY**, 20km northeast of Chojnice (served by sporadic buses), a wooded nature reserve hides a well-preserved megalithic site.

A sequence of irregular **stone circles** and overgrown burial mounds, it covers an area about half the size of a football pitch. It has been dated to the first or second century, though little is known of its origins.

To find the clearing in which it stands isn't easy, adding to the enjoyment of the site when you finally arrive; before setting out from the village ask directions for the *Kręgi Kamieniece*. Most of the year, you're likely to be on your own, though at the midsummer solstice the circle draws in the local Gdańsk chapter of hippies, alternatives and New Agers.

Szczecinek and Lake Drawsko

One of the most popular lakeland bases is **SZCZECINEK**, due west of Chojnice. A modern and rather over-functional holiday centre, it stands a kilometre back from the enticing **Lake Wielimie**. As you'd expect, there's plenty of watersport facilities, with an increasing number of rental places for the general demand.

Accommodation in town is provided by the **hotels** *Zamek*, ul. Mickiewicza 2 (☎420-74), *Pomorski*, ul. Bohaterów Warszawy (☎409-51), and *Fala*, ul. Kilińskiego 7 (☎401-11), or the all-year **youth hostel** at pl. Wazów 1 (☎4336). There's also a **camping site**, the *Leśny*, at ul. Kościuszki 76 (☎401-02).

Czaplinek and Lake Drawsko

The best-known lake area is the Drawskie region, 40km west of Szczecinek. **Lake Drawsko**, the centre of the district, is one of the largest Pomeranian lakes, a tranquil expanse of deep, clear water some ten kilometres in length. In summer you'll find groups of Polish canoeists powering their way through the area: if you feel like joining them, there are hire facilities in town. Walking is wonderful, too, with paths rambling off through the lakeside woods for miles in all directions.

On the banks of Drawsko is **CZAPLINEK**, an early Slav stronghold eventually incorporated into the Brandenburg domains. The town has a drowsy charm about it, with eighteenth-century wooden houses adding character to the modern centre, and tourism doesn't yet seem to have much affected the easy-going life of the place. Despite the popularity of the lake, **accommodation** is limited to two basic *Dom Wycieczkowe* – the *Pomorski*, ul. Jagiellońska 11 (☎454-44), and the *Czapla*, ul. Piaskowa 1 (☎452-55) – and a lakeside **campsite**, ul. Drawska 79 (☎451-68).

Łeba and around

Northwest of Gdańsk the hills of Kashubia merge into the lush wooded coastline of eastern Pomerania. The easternmost resort is **ŁEBA**, an attractive old fishing village at the mouth of the river of the same name; it's 90km from Gdańsk with reasonable train and bus connections via Lebork – which is also the route taken by trains from Słupsk, Koszalin (see p.493) and points west. Buses from Gdańsk take the main roads; if you're coming by car, a more appealing approach is on the backroads, taking you through the tiny hamlets and along the delightful tree-lined avenues that characterise this part of the country. To avoid getting lost you'll really need the *Pobrzeze Bałtyku mapa turystyczna*, which marks all the minor roads.

The **village** itself is set some way back from the sea: dunes and beaches cover the original site of the village, which was forced to move inland in the late sixteenth century because of shifting sands and erosion. Both bus and train drop you just off ul. Kościuszki, the street running down the middle of the village. Lined with attractively gabled fishermen's houses, the street bustles in summer with tourist traffic heading for the long sandy **beaches** just to the north, which are widely regarded as among the cleanest on the Baltic coast. Poles aren't the only people who have enjoyed the bracing location: wandering through the park that provides the main approach to the beaches you'll pass the summer house used by Nazi propaganda chief Josef Goebbels. Closer to the sea, the ruins of a Gothic church loom from the sand dunes, a lone reminder of the village's former location.

Even in season, **accommodation** shouldn't be too much of a problem here. There's a welter of former workers' holiday homes on or around ul. Nadmorska, the main route east of the town and in striking distance of the sea: the *Przymorze* **tourist office**, ul. Tyrystyczna 3 (☎661-360), or the PTTK bureau at ul. 1 Maja 6 just east of the train station can help out with these. In town the obvious options for staying the night include the *Morski*, ul. Morska (☎661-468) close to the seafront, the *Pensjonat Angela*, pl. Dworcowy 2a (☎662-647), a stone's throw from the central bus and train stations, the *Wodnik*, ul. Nadmorska 10 (☎661-466), and the PTTK hostel at ul. 1 Maja 6 (☎661-324). For **campers** – and there are plenty of them in summer – there are several sites along ul. Turstyczna and Nadmorska, all in striking distance of the beaches, a number of them with the additional bonus of wooden bungalows to rent. Best of the numerous tourist **restaurants** is the *Karczma Słowińska* on ul. Kościuszki – decent menu plus excellent local *Hewelius* beer.

The Słowiński National Park

West of Łeba are the lakes and sand dunes of the **Słowiński National Park**, one of the country's strangest but most memorable natural attractions, special enough to be included in UNESCO's list of world Biosphere Reserves. The park gets its name from the **Slovincians**, a small ethnic group of Slav origin who, like their neighbours the Kashubians, have retained a distinctive identity despite centuries of Germanisation.

This area is an ornithologist's paradise, with over 250 **bird** species either permanently inhabiting the park or using it as a migratory habitat. Geomorphically speaking this is an unusual region: the shallow lagoons covering the central part of the park once formed an inland sea gulf, which the insistent pounding of the sea and wind eventually separated from the main body of the sea. Between them a narrow spit of land emerged roughly 2000 years ago, whose dense original covering of oak and beech forests was gradually eroded by intensive animal grazing and tree felling, the forests disappearing under the desert-like sand dunes that eventually swallowed up the thirty-odd kilometre spit. Abandoned to the elements by its few original human inhabitants, during World War II the expanse of shifting, undulating sand provided an ideal training ground for units of Afrika Corps, who drilled here in preparation for the rigours of Rommel's North African Campaigns. In the latter stages of the war the park was turned into one of several launch sites for the fearsome V1 and V2 rockets that bombarded London – you can still see the remains of some of the rocket installations a couple of kilometres west of Łeba.

FAUNA IN THE PARK

Birds in the park are classified into three main groups: nesting, migratory and wintering species. Nesters include such rare species as the white-tailed eagle, black stork, crane, ruff and eagle-owl. During the late autumn migration period you'll see large flocks of wild **geese** winging over the lakes, and in winter you'll find ducks and other fowl from the far north of Europe sheltering here on the warmer southern shores of the Baltic – velvet scoters, mergansers, auks and whooper swans included. Mammals are numerous too, the shores of the lakes harbouring deer and boar, with elks, racoons and badgers in the surrounding woods.

Access to the park is from **RĄBKA**, a small holiday village on the shores of **Jezioro Łebsko**, the largest and best-known of the lagoons, a bus ride or twenty-minute walk west of Łeba. The shores are covered with thick reeds, making access to the water difficult but providing ideal cover for the birds: sanctuaries at several points protect the main breeding sites. Though it is possible to skirt some of the southern edge, most visitors continue along the **northern** side, on a road into the dune territory that is the park's distinguishing feature. From July to August tourist buses from Łeba and Rąbka run west to the edge of the sands; at any other time of year you'll have to walk the whole way. Most people are content to venture a kilometre or so beyond where the bus finishes, returning either with the bus or by a parallel path running along the coast, but if you're feeling up to a sterner challenge you could walk on to the village of Smołdzino (see below) – 12km from where the bus stops. You could then return to Łeba by a roundabout bus route in the evening, or even stay overnight.

Even a brief hike will give you the flavour of the terrain, though. A short distance out of the lakeside woods, huge dunes are piled up to 30m high; dried by the sun and propelled by the wind, they migrate over 10m per year on average, leaving behind the broken tree stumps you see along the path. Out in the middle of the dune area there's a desert-like feeling of desolation with the sands rippling in the wind, giving an unsettling sense of fluidity as the dunes change their form around you.

Smołdzino

SMOŁDZINO is the site of the park's **Natural History Museum** (Tues–Sat 9am–5pm), which contains an extensive display of the park's flora and fauna; the park offices here can provide you with detailed information about the area, including advice on bird-watching around the lake. Just to the west of the village is **Rowokół** hill, whose observation tower at the top affords a panoramic view over the entire park area. There's a summer youth hostel and a farm hostel in the village as well.

Kluki

Five kilometres east of Smołdzino, on the western edge of Lake Łebsko and at the end of a minor road, is the little village of **KLUKI**, which is served by occasional buses from Smołdzino and more frequent ones from Słupsk. Entirely surrounded by woods, Kluki has an enjoyable *skansen* of Slovincian wooden architecture (May–Sept Tues–Sun 9am–4pm; Oct–April 9am–2pm), providing a flavour of the traditional way of life of these tough seafaring and fishing people.

Słupsk and the central coast

Continuing west, the next place of any significance is **SŁUPSK**, 20km beyond the nondescript town of LEBORK on the main road and rail line. An early Slav settlement, ruled by Pomeranian princes and Brandenburg margraves for much of its history, Słupsk was completely wrecked in 1945. Faceless postwar developments now dominate the town, which is probably best known in Poland for its annual **piano festival**, held in September. Of late it's been in the news as the centre of industrial unrest against the Solidarity government, with Słupsk rail workers helping to paralyse the rail network of the northwest in protest at the austerity policies. It's not a place to detain you, but it can be useful as a base for exploring the Słowiński National Park, to which the **Orbis** office at ul. Wojska Polskiego 1 (☎236-14) organises summer excursions.

What little there is worth seeing in the town centre can be covered in an hour or two. On the banks of the river, the Renaissance castle houses a **Regional Museum** (Tues–Sun 10am–4pm); alongside displays of local ethnography, there's a large collection of modern Polish art, most notably a series of canvases by Stanisław Ignacy Witkiewicz. The old castle **Mill** is one of the earliest specimens of its kind in the country, while the reconstructed Gothic **Dominican Church** has a fine Renaissance altarpiece and the tombs of the last Pomeranian princes.

This scattering of historic sites aside, the town's main attractions are two highly reputable **restaurants**, the *Karczma Słupska* at ul. Wojska Polskiego 11 and the *Pod Kluką* at ul. Kaszubska 22 – both in the centre, both offering a spread of traditional Polish cuisine with a sprinkling of regional specialities.

Accommodation is provided by the passable *Przymorze* **motel**, ul. Szwedka 41 (☎308-52), the *Piast* **hotel**, ul. Jednosci Narodowej 2 (☎252-86), and the *Zamkowy* hotel, ul. Dominikańska 9 (☎252-94). **Private rooms** are arranged by the *Biuro Zakwaterowania*, ul. Dominikańska 9 (Mon–Sat 7.30am–3.30pm).

Ustka

USTKA, 20km northwest of Słupsk by bus or local train, is a one-time member of the Hanseatic League that's been a popular holiday resort for well over a century. The town itself has little character, the old fishing village having long been replaced by a nondescript modern harbour. The main attraction, though, is the surrounding beaches, as good as any on the Baltic coast, especially those east of town stretching along towards the Słowiński National Park, generally less crowded than the major resorts further west. If the idea of a seaside stopover here appeals, there are a couple of useful **accommodation** options in and around the town, including the *Bałtycki*, ul. Grunwaldzka (☎144-048), and the *Koga*, ul. Kochanowskiego 14 (☎145-548), both situated east of town. For **campers** there's a good site at Przewlowka, a couple of kilometres southeast of town.

Darłowo and Darłówko

A more attractive proposition than Ustka is **DARŁOWO**, 40km further west and a couple of kilometres inland on the River Wieprza, though here the drawback is the difficulty of public transport – trains from Słupsk involve a change at Sławno, and buses take nearly two hours.

The beaches north of the town, around the resort of DARŁÓWKO, are as popular as any, but what makes Darłowo special are the buildings of the old Hanseatic fishing centre. The **Rynek**, still a marketplace, is dominated by a gracefully reconstructed Baroque town hall, complete with its Renaissance doorway. On one side of the Rynek sits the Gothic **St Mary's** church, an attractive brick building with a relatively restrained Baroque interior overlay; in amongst a clutch of royal tombs is that of the notorious Scandinavian ruler King Erik VII (1397–1459), a relative of King Kazimierz the Great, who was deposed in 1439 and lived out the last years of his life in exile here. Further out from the centre you'll find parts of the fifteenth-century **walls**, including the town gate, just beyond which is **St Gertrude's**, another impressive Gothic structure with an unusual twelve-sided ambulatory. On the other side of town, the well-preserved fourteenth-century castle of the Pomeranian princes now houses an extensive **Regional Museum** (Tues–Sun 8am–4pm), focusing on the town's maritime past.

The **information office** by the town gate might be able to sort out **private rooms**, but they're more likely to direct you to the PTTK *Dom Wycieczkowy* (☎27-56) in Darłówko. This basic hotel-restaurant is well located in a quiet spot by the river, the peace broken by holiday-time discos at the bar across the sound. Other options include the basic *pensjonat* at ul. Marynarska 36 (☎21-92), not far from the beach, as well as a number of former workers' holiday homes, now opened up to tourists – current details from the tourist office. There's also a camping place at ul. Courada 20 (☎28-72) near the sea.

West from Darłowo

If you've a car and time on your hands, it's worth taking the backroads west from Darłowo, which pass through an attractive open landscape of fields, woods and quiet old Pomeranian villages. The sturdy German farm buildings are still standing, as in several cases are the Gothic brick churches, often in better condition than those in the major towns. A characteristically beautiful example is at **IWIĘCINO**, a tiny village stuck in the middle of nowhere halfway between Darłowo and Koszalin. The fourteenth-century structure has a beautifully decorated wooden ceiling, painted sixteenth-century pews, a delicate Renaissance altarpiece and a splendid late Baroque organ.

Koszalin

As even the determinedly upbeat tourist brochures tacitly admit, KOSZALIN, the bustling provincial capital 25km west of Darłowo, isn't the sort of place that gets the crowds shouting. The onetime seat of a local line of Pomeranian prince-bishops, who were eventually replaced in the mid-seventeenth century by Pomerania's Brandenberg rulers, like so many towns in this region, the Old Town was badly damaged during 1945, and postwar reconstruction of the newly vacated German city was more about residential blocks and intensive industrial development than aesthetic statements. That said, the town's historic core has at least retained the basics of its regular medieval layout, including the rectangular central **Rynek**, a large area effectively built from scratch after World War II. Just south of the square is **St Mary's Church**, an imposing oft-remodelled Gothic structure with a few pieces of original decoration, notably a large fourteenth-century crucifix and a scattering of Gothic statuary, originally from the main altarpiece and now incorporated into the stalls, pulpit and organ loft. A sizeable chunk of the town's medieval fortifications survived wartime destruction, mostly on the northern edge of the Old Town area bordering the banks of the River Dzierzécinka that connects Lake Jamno, some ten kilometres north of town, with

Lake Lubiatowo, a similar distance southwards. The nineteenth-century water-mill facing the walls from the corner of ul. Mlynska houses the **Regional Museum** (Tues–Sun 10am–4pm) with a varied collection of folk art, archaeological finds and other regional miscellany. The most interesting part is the mini-*skansen* next to the building, which contains a number of examples of the sturdy peasant architecture characteristic of the Pomeranian coastal region. Back into the centre is the old sixteenth-century **Town Executioner's House** on ul. Grodzka, rebuilt to serve as a local theatre, while a short walk south of the Rynek stands the octagonal **St Gertrude's Chapel**, just next to another theatre and the town's main surviving Gothic structure.

Practicalities

For **information** the local tourist office at ul. Dworcowa 10, just across from the bus and train stations, and the next-door Orbis bureau will provide everything you need to know. The few **accommodation** options are the plush *Arka*, ul. Zwycięstwa 20/24 (☎235-58) next to Orbis – a Western holidaymakers' favourite – the *Sportowy*, ul. Fałata 34 (☎513-17), a considerably more basic sports hotel east of the centre, the *Za Lasem*, ul. Morska 152 (☎232-26) on the main Kołobrzeg road north of town, and an all-year **youth hostel**, ul. Gnieźnieńska 3 (☎260-68), south of town; there are also a couple of fairly spartan summer-only youth hostels – details from the tourist office. Best of the town's restaurants are the *Balaton*, in the *Arka* hotel, the nearby *Bałtyk*, ul. Zwycięstwa 28, and the *Ratuszowa* on the Rynek.

North of Koszalin

For Polish holidaymakers, Koszalin is mainly known as a convenient access point for the spread of beaches along the coast to the north of town. The most popular resort is **MIELNO**, a half-hour bus ride (#1 from the main bus station) some 12km northwest of town (local trains also run from Koszalin during the summer season). The town was an early Slav stronghold and fishing settlement that used to serve as the main port for Koszalin. If you feel like mingling with the holiday crowds – despite the growing popularity of many coastal resorts with Germans and Scandinavians, this is still Polish holiday territory in the main – you could do worse than stop off at this smallish coastal resort for a relaxing night or two. Places to stay are the *MOSiR* hostel, ul. Słoneczna no.5 (☎362), and the campsite at ul. Orła Białego 1 (☎240) near the main beach. Alternatively there's **UNIEŚCIE**, another smaller resort a couple of kilometres' bus ride west of Mielno on the sandy spit of land separating Lake Jamno from the sea. The main **accommodation** here is the *Agawa*, ul. Róży Wiatrów 38 (☎18-96-76). The lake is a popular yachting area, and even in high summer you can probably hire boats at the waterside – best booked in advance through the tourist office in Koszalin.

Kołobrzeg

Beyond Darłowo the next coastal town of any size is **KOŁOBRZEG**, a largish town clumped around the mouth of the River Parsęta, a forty-kilometre bus or train ride west of Koszalin. With one and a half million visitors annually, it's one of the country's busiest seaside resorts, with a decent collection of holiday-orientated amenities integrated into its otherwise drab landscape.

The paucity of ancient buildings belies the town's history. One of the oldest Pomeranian settlements, it grew on the economic foundations of the **salt works** that were established here in the seventh century. By the mid-800s a decent-sized fortified town had developed, and in 1000 Bolesław the Brave founded one of the early Piast bishoprics in what was becoming a significant port. A steady influx of German merchants and sailors eventually led to its incorporation into the Hanseatic League in the mid-thirteenth century. Badly hit by the Thirty Years' War, in 1655 it passed into the control of the Brandenburg Margraves, who established a fortress here. A change of emphasis came two centuries later when a new spa resort began to develop, attracting crowds from all over the Baltic region. The Germans defended the town to the last in 1945, leaving the place a ruin by the time the Polish and Russian armies arrived in March. A band of the liberators gathered on the beach to swear an oath that this ancient Piast town would thenceforth be Polish forever, sealing the vow in suitably dramatic style by hurling a wedding ring into the sea – "Poland's Reunion with the Sea", as the event came to be known.

The town and the beach

Architecturally, the only remotely interesting bit of Kołobrzeg is the Old Town, situated ten minutes' walk southeast of the bus and train stations. The **Collegiate Church of St Mary** was originally built as a simple Gothic hall, but was extended in the fifteenth century with the addition of star-vaulted aisles which add enormously to the impression of depth and spaciousness. A particularly striking effect was achieved with the facade, whose twin towers were moulded together into one vast solid mass of brick. Many of the furnishings perished in the war, but some significant items remain, notably several Gothic triptychs and a fourteenth-century bronze font. To the north stands the other key public building, the **Town Hall**. A castellated Romantic creation incorporating some of its fifteenth-century predecessor, it was built from designs provided by the great Berlin architect Karl Friedrich Schinkel. In the surrounding streets you'll find a number of Gothic burghers' houses – look out in particular for the Dom Schlieffenów on ul. Gierczak – but otherwise there's really nothing to look at.

It's the sand that the visitors come for, and throughout the summer you'll find throngs of Polish holidaymakers soaking up the sun on the main strand a short walk north of the station. Like many of the Pomeranian resorts the beach has a slightly downbeat, old-fashioned feel, with wicker chairs, weather-beaten hot-dog stands and tawdry snack bars. And it's long enough for a decent stroll, with a pier and a seafront parade edging an attractive park. Beyond the pier at the western end there's a tall brick lighthouse and a stone monument marking the spot where Kołobrzeg married the ocean.

Practicalities

The main **information** office is the Orbis bureau at ul. Dworcowa 4, in the centre of town. The most obvious central **accommodation** options are the *Monika pensjonat*, ul. 22 Lipca 18a (☎232-32), the Orbis-run *Solny*, ul. Fredry 4 (☎224-01), and the similarly upmarket *Skanpol*, ul. Dworcowa 10 (☎234-11). The radical shake-up of the tourist industry engendered by post-communist privatisation means there's also now a wealth of other **accommodation** available, again principally the droves of workers' holiday homes and sanatoria that fill the streets between the sea front and the railway station. Though many are still enjoying their usual roaring summer trade, there are enough rooms currently available for you to be virtually guaranteed a place to stay. **Private rooms** can be arranged by the *Bałtywia* office at ul. 1 Armii Wojska Polskiego 5 (Mon–Sat 7am–3pm), and there is in addition a summer **youth hostel** at ul. Łopuskiego 13 (☎21-31). The town campsite, the *Bałtywia*, is at ul. IV Dywizji WP 1 (☎45-69). Best **restaurants** in town are the *Fregata*, ul. Dworcowa 12, and those in the *Solny* and *Skanpol* hotels.

Along the Hanseatic Route

Moving onwards from Kołobrzeg, the choice is between continuing westwards along the coastal area by bus, or heading southwest towards Szczecin, a journey more conveniently made by train. If the former is the more obviously attractive option, the latter offers the chance to see three more towns which were members of the Hanseatic League in its heyday. For all their former prosperity, of which their churches and fortifications offer a tantalising reminder, each is now very decayed and can readily be appreciated in a short stopover.

Trzebiatów

By far the most attractive of the trio is **TRZEBIATÓW**, which lies on the banks of the Baltic-bound River Rega, just under 30km from Kołobrzeg. It's a place where time seems to have gone backwards, transforming a well-heeled trading town into a straggling agricultural village with a pronounced rural air. Certainly a good deal of imagination is required to visualise this sleepy Polish backwater as it was in the sixteenth century when it played a key role in the Reformation: Johannes Bugenhagen, who spent nearly two decades as rector of its Latin School, became one of Luther's leading lieutenants, returning in 1534 to persuade the Pomeranian assembly which had specially convened here to adopt the new faith throughout the province.

Trzebiatów's skyline is dominated by the magnificent tower of **St Mary**, one of the most accomplished Gothic churches of the Baltic region, crowned with the unusual combination of a brick octagon and a lead spire. In it hang two historic bells – one, named Gabriel, is from the late fourteenth century; the other, known as Mary, dates from the early sixteenth century. The building's interior is chiefly notable for its clear architectural lines and uncluttered appearance which, like the German epitaphs on the walls, are evidence of the four centuries it spent in Protestant hands.

Just up the hill from the church is the Rynek, in the centre of which stands the **Town Hall**, constructed in the sober Baroque style favoured in northern German lands. A few restored Gothic houses line the square, though their appearance is diminished by the presence of so many undistinguished newer buildings. Just off the southern side is the **Chapel of the Holy Ghost**, another brick Gothic structure, and the setting for the assembly which decided to introduce the Reformation into Pomerania. Substantial sections of the **town walls** also survive, particularly along the Rega, where you can see an impressive tower, the Kaszana Baszta.

Practicalities

Both the **bus** and **train stations** are located outside the built-up part of town, about ten minutes' walk to the east. There's one **hotel**, the very basic *Rega*, just off the Rynek at ul. Wojska Polskiego 37 (☎725-07). Choice among **restaurants** is between *Bałtyka*, Rynek 25, and *Kaszana Baszta*, ul. Wojska Polskiego 19.

Gryfice

About 20km up the Rega from Trzebiatów is **GRYFICE**, a slightly larger town with a decidedly more urban feel to it. German commentators on Pomerania are readily stirred to anger at the mere mention of its name: the town was taken undamaged by the Red Army in 1945, only to be set ablaze soon afterwards, and was later used as the site of a penal camp in which a large number of civilians were detained.

The Gothic church of **St Mary** is a copybook example of the Baltic style, notable chiefly for its sturdy single western tower and its finely detailed portals; inside are some good Baroque furnishings, notably the pulpit and the high altar. The surviving parts of the **fortifications** – the Stone Gate, the High Gate and the Powder Tower – can be seen towards the river to the east.

Gryfice's sole **hotel**, *Światowid*, is at ul. Kościuszki 13 (☎22-68), on the same street as the bus station and a couple of minutes' walk east of the train station. The only obvious place to **eat** is *Gryfiszanka*, just by the church at pl. Zwycięstwa 10.

Goleniów

The largest and liveliest town of the group is **GOLENIÓW**, 55km southwest of Gryfice. It's an important rail junction, the meeting-point of the line between Kołobrzeg and Szczecin with those to Kamień Pomorski and Świnoujście. Not the least of its assets is its situation in the middle of the **Puszcza Goleniowska**, a vast forested area, most of it wilderness, which stretches almost all the way up to Wolin – a particularly scenic journey by train.

Goleniów's main church, **St Catherine**, is less imposing than its counterparts in Trzebiatów and Gryfice, largely because of extensive remodelling last century, when the tower was added. Amends are made by the **town walls**, whose surviving towers and gateways make a nicely varied group, with the showpiece being the **Wolin Gate**, the largest to be found anywhere in Pomerania. Also worth a look is the half-timbered eighteenth-century **granary** on the banks of the River Ina.

Again, there's just the one **hotel**, *Słowianin*, ul. Jedności Narodowej 34 (☎22-01). **Restaurants** include *Ina*, ul. Jedności Narodowej 4, and *Miłła*, ul. Wojska Polskiego 7.

Kamień Pomorski

Some 60km west of Kołobrzeg lies the quiet little waterside town of **KAMIEŃ POMORSKI**, an atmospheric Pomeranian centre which demands a visit for its fine cathedral. For public transport from Trzebiatów you'll have to rely on buses to take you across country; there are no train connections along this bit of the coast, only northwards from Szczecin. Travelling on the main routes it's easy to miss this town, since it's not on the major coastal road to Świnoujście, and getting there by any means of transport involves a detour.

The town's history starts in the ninth century, when a port was established here on the River Dziwna, a short stretch of water connecting the huge Szczecin lagoon (Zalew Szczeciński) with the smaller Kamień lagoon (Zalew Kamieński) – all of which are part of the delta formed by the Odra as it nears its mouth at the Gulf of Pomerania. By the late twelfth century Kamień was significant enough to be appointed the seat of the bishopric of West Pomerania, a position it kept for nearly 400 years, while by the late 1300s it felt rich enough to join the Hanseatic League. The Swedes seized the town during the Thirty Years' War, but by the late seventeenth century it had been appropriated by the Brandenburg rulers, not coming under Polish control until after World War II. Despite extensive wartime damage, Kamień Pomorski seems to have come out better than most towns in the area: concrete blocks fill in the huge gaps between the occasional burghers' mansions, yet there's enough of the older architecture to retain a sense of times past.

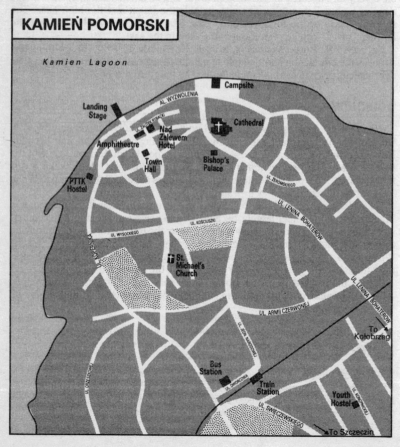

KAMIEŃ POMORSKI

Kamien Lagoon

Campsite

Landing Stage

AL. WYZWOLENIA

Cathedral

UL. ZAMKUPIACKA

Nad Zalewem Hotel

Amphitheatre

Town Hall

Bishop's Palace

PTTK Hostel

UL. ŻEROMSKIEGO

UL. LENINA BOHATERÓW

UL. KOŚCIUSZKI

UL. WYSOCKIEGO

UL. OKRZEI

St. Michael's Church

UL. ARMII CZERWONEJ

To Kołobrzeg

UL. LENINA BOHATERÓW

UL. GEN. NARBORZA

Bus Station

UL. PRZECZNA

UL. SWOROCYWA

Train Station

Youth Hostel

UL. KOSZALIŃSKA

UL. ŚWIECZEWSKIEGO

To Szczecin

The Town

All Kamień's sights are some way north of the bus and rail stations, on and around the **Rynek**, where proximity to the lagoon lends a maritime feel. The fifteenth-century **Town Hall**, in the middle, is a careful reconstruction, its solid symmetrical brick archways rising to the familiar stepped gables at each end. Parts of the walls ringing the Old Town have survived, notably the **Brama Wolińska** west of the square, an imposing Gothic gateway, surrounded by apartment blocks.

East of the square stands the magnificent **Cathedral**, one of the finest Romanesque structures in the country, made yet more startling by its backwater location. Construction of the brick and granite basilica began in the 1170s, following the creation of the Kamień bishopric, with many subsequent additions over the following centuries. Entrance to the building is through the fine Romanesque portal of the southern transept, adorned with weathered mid-thirteenth-century statues of the saints. Inside the cathedral you're enveloped by majestic Gothic vaulted arches; the presbytery is older, and is covered with flowing early thirteenth-century decoration. Other sections of the earliest polychromy are tucked away in corners around the transept, including a stern *Christ Pantocrator* and a fine *Crucifixion* that was uncovered in the 1940s. The focus of attention, though, is the superb fifteenth-century triptych gracing the altar, the most outstanding of many such Gothic pieces in the building – the rest are in the **Sacristy Museum**. A central *Coronation of Mary* is surrounded by scenes from the lives of the saints, most notably John Chrysostom, to whom the building is dedicated. To the right of the altar is another finely sculpted Romanesque portal, leading to the sacristy.

The cathedral's most famous feature, however, is its massive Baroque organ, at the back of the building, its forest of silver pipes and exuberant detail crowned by a procession of dreamy gilded saints. As you approach from the nave, a portrait of the instrument's creator, a local bishop by the name of Bogusław de Croy i Archot, stares down on the congregation from a cherub-encircled frame. From June to August the cathedral hosts an international organ and chamber music festival, with concerts every Friday – details from tourist offices throughout the region.

To complete the ensemble, across pl. Katedralny is the **Bishop's Palace**, a stately, late Gothic structure with a finely carved attic.

Practicalities

In summer the tourist **information point** on plac Katedralny dispenses maps and information; otherwise try the Orbis office on the Rynek. Best **accommodation** option is the *Nad Zalewem*, Zaułek Rybacki 1 (☎208-17), just off the Rynek with a view of the lagoon. Otherwise there's the less salubrious *Dom Pracy Twórczej* at ul. H. Sawickiej 1 (☎207-49), the PTTK *Dom Wycieczkowy* at ul. Słowackiego (☎202-41), a summer **youth hostel** at ul. Konopnickiej 19 (☎207-84), and a **campsite** by the lagoon on ul. Wyzwolenia (☎212-80). The only halfway decent **restaurants** are the *Steńka*, ul. Rejtana 25, and the *Pod Muzami* on the Rynek.

Wolin

Across the water from Kamień Pomorski is **WOLIN**, the first of two large, heavily indented islands which separate the Szczecin lagoon from the Gulf of Pomerania. The gap dividing Wolin from the mainland is at times so narrow that it's sometimes described as a peninsula rather than an island; indeed, roads are built directly over the River Dziwna in two places – near its mouth at DZWINÓW, some 12km from Kamień, and at **Wolin town** towards the island's southern extremity, where it is also forded by the railway between Szczecin and the border town of **Świnoujście** at the western extremity of Wolin. From Kamień, you can choose to approach by either of these two roads, the only ones of significance on the island. They converge at the seaside resort of **Międzyzdroje**, before continuing onwards to Świnoujście.

Wolin, which is 35km long and between 8km and 20km across, offers a wonderfully contrasted landscape of sand dunes, lakes, forest, meadows, moors and both ground and terminal moraines. Part of its dramatic **coastline** – undoubtedly its most memorable feature – has attracted crowds of holidaymakers since last century; it is likely to be heavily developed in the future, but in the meantime it remains relatively unspoilt. A sizeable portion of the island is under protection as a national park, and you really need to take time to hike if you want to appreciate it to the full.

Wolin Town

The town of **WOLIN** occupies the site of one of the oldest Slav settlements in the country. According to early chronicles, a pagan tribe known as the Wolinians established themselves here in the eighth century, developing one of the most important early Baltic ports. A temple to Trzygłów and to Światowid, a triple-headed Slav deity, existed here until the early twelfth century, and was presumably destroyed by the Christian Poles only when they captured the stronghold.

Echoes of the town's pagan past are present in the totem-like reconstructed wooden figures dotted around close to the water, all depicting Slav gods. The desolate ruins of a medieval church just up from the main square only add to the haunted atmosphere of the place. Recent excavations have uncovered plentiful evidence of the Wolinian settlement: you can see their discoveries in the local **Museum** (Tues–Sun 10am–4pm) on the main road through town.

For an overnight stay there's one rudimentary **hotel**, the *Wineta* on the main road (☎618-84), a summer **youth hostel** at ul. Mickiewicza, and a camping space right by the water's edge, popular with anglers and sailors.

Międzyzdroje

By far the best base for exploring the island is **MIĘDZYZDROJE**, which offers easy access to the best hiking trails in addition to a wonderful beach. A favourite Baltic resort with the prewar German middle class, it went downmarket with its transferral to Poland. Now, in a shockingly quick about-turn since the fall of communism, it looks as though Międzyzdroje is in the process of selling out to Western developers. Already it is dominated by the huge white bulk of a luxury hotel rapidly thrown up by the seashore at the northeastern end of town, whose car park is regularly full to the brim with BMWs and Mercedes from Germany, Denmark and Sweden. This seems to belong to another world from the tatty trade-union holiday homes and flats which make up the rest of the resort's accommodation.

Międzyzdroje's **promenade** stretches for all of 4km, the focal point being the inevitable pier, beside which is a bandstand. If you want to find out more about the island's flora and fauna, visit the **National Park Museum** (Tues–Sun 10am–3pm) at ul. Niepodległości 3 in the town centre. Best vantage point for a view of the town and the coast is the hump known as **Kawcza** ("Coffee Hill") at the resort's northeastern extremity.

Practicalities

The **train station** is at the southeastern fringe of town, albeit little more than ten minutes' walk from the beach; the **bus station** is closer to the centre, on ul. Niepodległości. If you want to stay in unbridled comfort, the aforementioned **hotel**, *Amber Baltic*, ul. Bohaterów Warszawy 26a (☎808-00), charges standard international prices for its facilities, which include golf, bowling, tennis and surfing, plus an outdoor swimming pool which seems somewhat superfluous beside such an outstanding beach. Other accommodation options for independent travellers are limited, though this should soon change. In the meantime, there's a **PTTK hostel** by the train station at ul. Kolejowa 2 (☎803-82), a seasonal **youth hostel** at ul. Leśna 17 (☎806-11), and a **campsite** on the west side of town at ul. Polna 10a (☎802-75). For the latest information on places to stay, contact the **tourist office**, ul. Światowida 19 (☎807-70) or **Orbis**, ul. Kolejowa 20 (☎800-15).

The Woliński National Park

The **Woliński National Park** is an area of outstanding natural interest: apart from its richly varied landscapes, it is the habitat of over 200 different types of bird – the sea-eagle is its emblem – and numerous animals such as red and fallow deer, wild boar, badgers, foxes and squirrels. It would take several days to cover all its many delights, but a good cross-section can be seen without venturing too far from Międzyzdroje. Alternatively, take a bus or train going in the direction of Wolin town, or a bus going towards Kamień or Kołobrzeg, and alight at any stop: you'll soon find signs enabling you to pick up one of the colour-coded trails. Before setting out to do any serious hiking, make sure you pick up a copy of the detailed local map, *Zalew Szczeciński – Mapa żeglarsko–turystyczna* (1:75,000), which has all the paths clearly marked; it's readily available from kiosks and bookshops throughout Pomerania.

The Trails

By far the most spectacular scenery in the park is to be seen by following the **red trail** along its eastward stretch from Międzyzdroje, which passes for a while directly along the beach. You soon come to some truly awesome-looking tree-crowned **dunes**, where the sand has been swept up into cliff-like formations up to 95m in height – the highest to be seen anywhere on the Baltic. Quite apart from its visual impact, much of this secluded stretch is ideal for a spot of swimming or sunbathing away from the crowds. After a few kilometres, the markers point the way upwards into the forest, and you follow a path which skirts the tiny Lake Gardno before arriving at the village of **WISEŁKA**, whose setting has the best of both worlds, being by its eponymous lake, and above a popular stretch of beach. Here you will find a restaurant, snack bars, an excellent ice cream kiosk and several shops. The trail continues eastwards through the woods and past more small lakes to its terminus at **KOŁCZEWO**, set at the head of its own lake and the only other place along the entire route with refreshment facilities. From either here or Misełka, you can pick up a bus back to Międzyzdroje.

Also terminating at Kołczewo is the **green trail**: if you're prepared to devote a very long day to it, you could combine this with the red trail in one circular trip. You pick up the path near Międzyzdroje's train station, then ascend gently through the woods to a small **bison reserve** (closed Mon), set up a couple of decades ago to reintroduce the animals to this habitat. The trail continues its forest course, emerging at a group of glaciary lakes around the village of WARNOWO (which can also be reached directly by train), where there's another reserve, this time for mute swans. Five lakeshores are then skirted en route to Kołczewo.

The third route, the **blue trail**, follows a southward course from Międzyzdroje's train station, again passing through wooded countryside before arriving at the northern shore of the Szczecin lagoon. Following this in an easterly direction, you traverse the heights of the Mokrzyckie Góry, then descend to the town of Wolin.

Finally, the western section of the **red trail** follows the coast for a couple of kilometres, then cuts straight down the narrow peninsula at the end of the island to the shore of the islet-strewn Lake Wicko Wielkie, before cutting inland to Świnoujście.

Świnoujście

The bustling fishing port, naval base and frontier post of ŚWINOUJŚCIE is one of the most popular entry points into Poland, thanks to the passenger ships which sail there from Sweden, Denmark and Germany. Its international ferry terminal, together with both the bus and train stations (of which the latter is a dead end), are stranded at the end of the island of Wolin. The town centre, reached by regular car ferries on which pedestrians travel free, lies on a quite separate island across the River Świna, another part of the Odra delta, just before it opens out into the Gulf of Pomerania.

In Poland, this island is known as **Uznam**, but it's far better known by its German name of *Usedom*. In 1945 the victorious Allies decided to allocate all of Świnoujście to Poland, rather than use the more obvious river boundary, with the result that the town was left as a tiny enclave at the end of an otherwise German island. At the time of writing, the ludicrous border situation of the communist epoch still prevailed, whereby the only means of driving to the German resort of AHLBECK, just a couple of kilometres away, is to make a 100km detour via Szczecin. Hopefully this position will change before long, and in the meantime it is possible to cross the border on foot. Despite its heavy volume of foreign tourists, Świnoujście is almost entirely devoid of sights: the town was very badly damaged in the war and now has a nondescript commercial centre which is nonetheless noticeably more prosperous looking than the Polish norm. Beyond it lies the spacious **spa park**, which stretches all the way up to the one big attraction, the lovely white sandy **beach**.

Practicalities

If you fancy a few days by the sea, Świnoujście has the best choice of accommodation along the Pomeranian coast. Overlooking the harbour at ul. Armii Krajowej 5 (☎23-91) is most expensive of the **hotels**, the medium-priced *Bałtyk*. Close to the beach are *Albatros*, ul. Kasprowicza 2 (☎23-35), and *Atol*, ul. Orkana 3 (☎30-10). Young people can stay cheaply at the nearby *Almatur*, ul. Żeromskiego 17

(☎58-50), situated in the same building as the helpful travel bureau of the same name. The **campsite**, *Relax*, is a few blocks further east at ul. Słowackiego 1 (☎39-12), whereas the **youth hostel** is inconveniently sited at the southern end of town at ul. Gdyńska 26 (☎59-61). For **private rooms**, ask at the Biuro Zakwaterowań by the waterfront at ul. Armii Krajowej 14a (☎39-93). There's little to get excited about in the way of places to **eat** and **drink**: it's probably best to stick to the hotels.

The main **Orbis** office at ul. Świerczewskiego 24 (☎44-11) has plenty of maps and information; they also organise excursions into the Woliński National Park. In summer **ferries** operate along the coast to Kołobrzeg, Darłowo, Ustka and other ports: details and bookings from the Wasów marine terminal (☎30-06) or the Orbis office. There's also supposed to be a hydrofoil service across the lagoon to Szczecin, but this has been discontinued indefinitely. For services to Scandinavia, ask at the international terminal, or contact the *Polferries* office in Szczecin at ul. Kardynała Wyszyńskiego 28 (Mon–Sat 11am–4.30pm; ☎342-38 or 359-45).

Szczecin

The largest city in northwestern Poland, with 400,000 inhabitants, **SZCZECIN** sprawls around the banks of the Odra in a tangle of bridges, cranes and dock machinery: a sort of Polish Newcastle. *Szczecin zawsze Polski* – "Szczecin, for ever Polish" – proclaims the hoarding on the main road approach, betraying a certain nervousness about the ownership of this longtime German city.

The Slav stronghold established here in the eighth century was taken by the first Piast monarch, Mieszko I, in 967 – a point much emphasised in Polish histories. From the early twelfth century Szczecin became the residence of a local branch of Piast princes, rulers of Western Pomerania, but German colonists were already present in force by the time the city joined the Hanseatic League in the mid-thirteenth century. The next key event was the port's capture by the Swedes in 1630, after which it was held by them for nearly a century. Sold to the Prussians in 1720, it remained under Prussian rule until 1945, when it became an outpost on Poland's newly established western frontier. With the border just west of the city limits and Berlin – for which Stettin/Szczecin used to be the port – only a couple of hours away by car or train, the German presence is still palpable.

Wartime pummelling destroyed most of the old centre, which never received quite the same restorative attention as some less controversially Polish cities. Despite the city's size, there isn't that much to take in – a full day is enough to cover all the main sights.

> The Szczecin telephone code is ☎091.

Arrival, information and accommodation

The central **train station** and the nearby **bus terminal** are located near the water's edge, from where it's a fifteen-minute walk or a quick tram ride up the hill to the town centre. For details of the comprehensive **bus and tram** routes you'll need to get hold of a copy of the *Szczecin: plan miasta*.

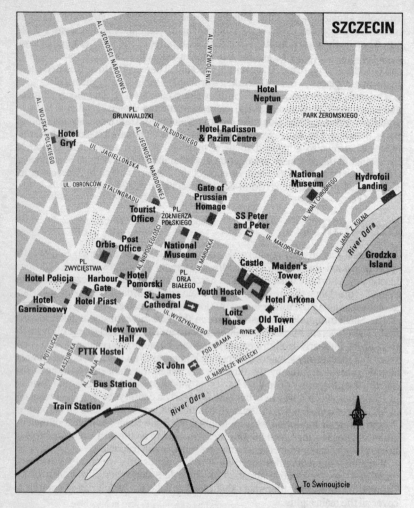

Szczecin **airport** – chiefly dedicated to internal flights but with some international services – is in fact located at Goleniów (☎18-27-08), 45km north of the city, with bus services to and from the *LOT* office at al. Wyzwolenia 17 (☎33-99-26).

The municipal **tourist office** is at al. Jedności Narodowej 1 (☎392-53 or 425-81). An alternative source of information is the **Pomerania** tourist bureau, pl. Brama Portowa 4 (☎472-08 or 345-61), which can help with accommodation arrangements throughout the province. **Almatur**, ul. Bohaterów Warszawy 83 (☎22-31-18), will be able to tell you where the international student hotels are operating – locations are changeable. **Orbis**, pl. Zwycięstwa 1 (☎34-51-54), is mainly of use for train tickets.

Finding a place to stay

There's a fair spread of **accommodation** in town, ranging from the most luxurious international class hotels to very basic hostels, and even in high summer you shouldn't have too much trouble finding a bed for the night.

CHEAP HOTELS

Dom Marynarza, ul. Malczewskiego 10 (☎22-24-61). Basically a seamen's hotel, but is open to everyone, and has been reported clean and safe for female travellers.

Dom Turysty PTTK, pl. Batorego 2 (☎34-58-33). Close to the station; noisy and crowded.

Garnizonowy, ul. Potulicka 1/3. Former barracks privatised to form a basic hotel right in the heart of town.

Kolarski, al. Wojska Polskiego 246 (☎709-71 or 764-01). Sports hotel well to the northwest, on the route of trams #1 and #9.

Pogon, ul. Twardowskiego 12 (☎782-78). Basic overnighter, run by a sports club, in the district of Pogodne, northwest of the centre, close to the suburban station of the same name; trams #5 and #7 go closest.

Policja, corner of pl. Zwycięstwa and ul. Potulicka (☎51-31-91). Unnumbered, and marked simply as "Hotel", this former police residence has been converted into a no-frills hotel which is particularly good value, given its central location.

Wodojewódzkiego Domu Sportu, ul. Unisławy 29 (☎22-28-56). Sports hotel just to the north of the city centre; take tram #2, #3 or #12 to pl. Witosa.

MODERATE HOTELS

Gryf, al. Wojska Polskiego 49 (☎33-45-66). West of the centre; nicest of the mid-range bunch, with colourfully furnished rooms, but not always with private bathrooms.

Piast, pl. Zywcięstwa 3 (☎33-66-62). Unspectacular rooms in busy central location.

Pomorski, pl. Brama Portowa 4 (☎33-61-51). Cheaper alternative in same part of town.

Szmaragd, ul. Kopalniana (☎61-31-32). The hotel to go for if you want to stay somewhere more reminiscent of the countryside than the city: it's right by the Emerald Lake in the suburb of Zdroje, a 15-minute walk west of the suburban station of that name.

EXPENSIVE HOTELS

Arkona, ul. Panieńska 10 (☎33-93-07). Concrete Orbis block just behind the old town hall, and below the castle.

Neptun, ul. Matejki 18 (☎24-01-11). Luxury Orbis joint on the west side of Park Żeromskiego.

Radisson, pl. Rodła 10 (☎59-55-95). Gleaming custom-built luxury hotel opened at the end of 1992. Has its own casino, nightclub, fitness centre and swimming pool along with all the other facilities expected by pampered business people. One for the expense-account classes only; guaranteed to make any old-style communist *apparatchik* turn in his grave.

Reda, ul. Cukrowa 2 (☎82-24-61). The third Orbis hotel, rather inconveniently sited well to the southwest of town; take bus #61 or #70.

HOSTELS AND CAMPSITES

Ul. Unisławy 26 (☎232-566). Main hostel, on top floor of a school building; open all year. Take tram #2 or #3 to pl. Kilińskiego, north of the centre.

Ul. Grodzka 22 (☎894-24). In the centre; open July & first half of Aug only.

Ul. Monte Cassino 19a (☎224-761). Situated just north of the centre; trams #1 and #9 go nearest.

PTTK Camping, ul. Przestrzenna 24 (☎613-264). In Dąbie, 3km east of town – take the local train to Szczecin-Dąbie station. Open May–Sept; tent space and bungalows available.

The City

The medieval Old Town, laid out on a slope on the left bank of the Odra, was heavily bombed in the last war. Restoration work on the showpiece buildings went on until the 1980s, with the gaps filled by drab modern housing. In the interim, commercial life shifted to the New Town further uphill, which had survived in far better shape. It was laid out towards the end of last century in the Parisian manner, with broad boulevards radiating out from pl. Grunwaldzki.

The commercial centre

Ascending ul. Dworcowa from the train station, you soon see some of the massive late nineteenth- and early twentieth-century Prussian buildings so characteristic of the heart of the city. Commanding the heights is the bulky redbrick frame of the neo-Gothic **New Town Hall**, now the seat of the maritime authorities. In the square below is a fountain in the form of an anchor, symbolising Szczecin's indebtedness to the sea; unfortunately, the allegorical female figure which formerly stood aloft was a casualty of the war. Across the street, steps lead up to the former **Savings Bank**, a dream-like Jugendstil fantasy whose slender tower and decorative facades seem to echo just about every architectural style.

At the top of ul. Dworcowa is the traffic-engulfed square named after the **Harbour Gate** (Brama Portowa), a stately Baroque archway built by the Prussians in 1725 to mark their purchase of the city. This is exuberantly adorned with relief carvings, including a depiction of the god of the Odra leaning on the jug from which the waters of the river flow. Immediately to the west of the gateway is the largest and busiest of the squares, pl. Zwycięstwa, on which stand a couple of turn-of-the-century churches which have successively served the local garrison. Ahead stretches al. Niepodległości, the city's main axis, on whose western side successively stand two more of the big Prussian public buildings – the Post Office, still fulfilling its original function, and the administration building of the Pomeranian district, which has been taken over by the displaced Savings Bank.

On pl. Rodła, an intersection on al. Wyzwolenia, the northern continuation of al. Niepodległości, the **Pazim Centre**, a hotel, shopping, banking and business complex of steel-framed, blue glass buildings, has been thrown up since the fall of communism, officially opening on the last day of 1992. Maybe this is an early example of the way Poland will start to look in the years to come, but something which so blatantly smacks of Chicago or Detroit feels like a very discomfiting intruder.

The cathedral and around

Downhill from the Harbour Gate, ul. Kardynała Wyszyńskiego leads to the **Cathedral of St James** (św. Jakuba), a massive Gothic church grievously damaged in 1945, and the subject of a painstaking restoration programme which was only completed in 1982, an event celebrated by its elevation to the seat of a bishop the following year. The oldest parts of the church date back to the fourteenth century and are the work of Hinrich Brunsberg, the finest of the specialist brickwork architects of the Baltic lands; the hall design he used here is notable for its consummate simplicity. In the middle of the following century, the single massive **tower** was constructed to replace the previous pair; this is now only half of its prewar height of 120m, having been rebuilt minus the tapering spire which for long dominated the city's skyline. Its five-and-a-half-ton bell now stands outside, as does a memorial to Carl Loewe, one of the great ballad composers and singers of last century, who was for several decades the church's organist and the municipal music director. To the rear of the church are its dependencies, including a pretty little Gothic rectory.

On pl. Orła Białego, the square on the northwest side of the cathedral, is the Baroque **Pod Globusem Palace**, originally built for the ruler of the Prussian province of Pomerania and now used as the medical academy. Across from it stands an intriguing covered **fountain** adorned with satyrs and an eagle, which began life in the eighteenth century as an outlet of the municipal waterworks. Hidden among the trees a few paces away is another piece of Baroque frippery, a statue of the goddess Flora.

The lower town

Down ul. Wyszyńskiego towards the waterfront, you come on the right-hand side to ul. Pod Bramą, on which stands the oldest surviving building in Szczecin, the Franciscan monastery of **St John** (św. Jana), part of which dates back to the thirteenth century. It's mainly of note for showing that medieval builders could and did get their calculations wrong, and is full of geometric inconsistencies: the chancel is in the shape of an irregular decagon, yet has a seven-part vault, while the later nave adjoins at an oblique angle, its off-centre vaulting a vain attempt to align the bays with the aisle windows.

Far more distinguished is the attractively gabled **Old Town Hall**, now rather lost in the concrete surroundings of the Rynek. It's an artful reconstruction of the fourteenth-century original, probably designed by Hinrich Brunsberg, which was flattened in the war; the restorers opted to return it to something like its original appearance, preserving only one Baroque gable as a reminder of the successive modifications it had undergone. These days the building serves as a small **Museum of Local History** (Tues–Sun 10am–4pm).

The only burgher's mansion now still standing in Szczecin is the mid-sixteenth-century **Loitz House**, just uphill at the corner of ul. Kurkowa, a tower-type residence of a prominent local banking and trading dynasty. Further down the same street are two other rare medieval survivors, a barn and the municipal weigh-house. Of the once formidable fifteenth-century fortification system, almost nothing remains save the appropriately graceful **Maiden's Tower**, now stranded in a park to the north of the Rynek in the lee of the spaghetti junction just before the waterfront.

The Castle

North from St James's along ul. Grodzka takes you to the **Castle** of the Pomeranian princes, commanding the river from its hillside perch. A Slav fortified settlement on this spot was replaced in the mid-fourteenth century by a stone structure, the oldest section of the current building. The whole thing was given a Renaissance enlargement in the late sixteenth century, and again remodelled in the 1720s. Princes and dukes aside, the building has been used as a brewery, office block, barracks and anti-aircraft emplacement – the last function being the direct cause of its flattening in an air raid in 1944. Reconstruction continued into the 1980s, since when it's been turned into a museum and cultural centre. Much of the building is closed to the public, the **Museum** (Tues–Sun 10am–4pm) occupying scattered parts of the castle.

The chapel on the ground floor of the north wing is now a concert hall, while the upper floor has several spartan exhibition rooms, the main source of interest being a smattering of contemporary Polish art. The main exhibition rooms are in the three-storey west wing, and contain a forgettable display of paintings and *objets d'art*. In the east wing, much of the decoration has been carefully reworked; most of this section is now occupied by a theatre and other cultural facilities. Renaissance tin sarcophagi and the decorated burial vaults of the Pomeranian princes still occupy the cellars, one of the few parts to survive the war intact.

After a visit to the castle café – a popular rendezvous point, lined with pictures of prewar Szczecin – it's worth climbing the **Belltower** for the view over the city, port and surroundings. If you're here in summer, you might get to hear an open-air concert in the castle square.

The rest of the centre

Immediately to the west of the castle is ul. Farna, where the residence of the commandant formerly stood. This was the birthplace in 1729 of Sophie von Anhalt-Zerbst, a princess of a very minor German aristocratic line who has gone down in history as **Empress Catherine the Great of Russia**. A character of extreme ruthlessness – she deposed her own husband, and was probably behind his subsequent murder – her reputation has always been a matter of controversy. Among her "achievements" was a considerable imperialistic expansion, one manifestation of which was a leading role in the three Partitions which wiped Poland off the map. That her native city is now Polish is a truly delicious irony.

A couple of blocks further west is ul. Staromłyńska, at the corner of which rises an elegant Baroque palace, formerly the Pomeranian parliament and now home of a section of the **National Museum** (Tues & Thurs 10am–5pm, Wed & Fri 9am–3pm, Sat & Sun 10am–4pm). On the ground floor is an impressive display of medieval Pomeranian sculpture. Highlights include the thirteenth-century columns, topped with delicately carved capitals, from the monastery of Kołbacz; a monumental wooden Crucifix of the same period from Kamień Pomorski, and a huge and expressive carved and painted mid-fifteenth century polyptych from Stargard Szczeciński. Later sections upstairs emphasise Polish painters, with a perhaps token German work thrown in occasionally. Works from the nineteenth century and onwards are displayed in the annexe across the street. The ground floor features several important Polish artists, most notably Waliczewski, Merkel and the broodingly introspective Jacek Malczewski. Upstairs there's plenty of 1970s Polish sci-fi art by popular artists like Ryszard Szymański, alongside an evocative collection of paintings by local artists on sea-based themes. There's also a quite staggering display of **Renaissance jewellery** – among the finest to be seen anywhere in Europe – offering the most potent surviving proof of the wealth and splendour of the court of the Pomeranian princes.

Across the broad open space of pl. Żołnierza Polskiego is the Baroque **Gate of Prussian Homage** (or Royal Gate), whose sculpted arches, with reliefs of military trophies, echo those of the Harbour Gate. Its interior is now used for changing exhibitions of the work of contemporary painters and photographers. Facing it to the east is the beguiling fourteenth-century **SS Peter and Paul**, a Gothic church built on the site of one established by Polish missionaries in the early twelfth century. In a rich ensemble of original ornamental detail the most striking elements are the seventeenth-century memorial tablets, the German inscriptions reminding you of the city's Teutonic heritage.

On the north side of the church, ul. Małopolska leads to **Wały Chrobrego**, a showpiece boulevard lined with towering prewar German public buildings. One of these houses a branch of the **National Museum** (same times), this one devoted mainly to maritime history, notably the seafaring culture of the early Pomeranian Slavs; there's also an unexpected section on African ethnology. A block to the north lies the **Park Żeromskiego**, the only significant bit of park in the centre.

The Harbour

Szczecin is one of the largest ports on the Baltic, with a highly developed shipping industry, and you'll appreciate the essence of the city more fully if you take a **boat trip** round the port and harbour. Excursions, lasting just over an hour, leave from the **Dworzec Morski** terminal, northeast of Wały Chrobrego. Ask here about the boat and hydrofoil services across the vast Szczecin Lagoon to Świnoujście; these were suspended in 1992, but may be reinstated. The border with Germany cuts across the middle of the lagoon, but the demise of the GDR means this isn't the source of tension it used to be for local sailing enthusiasts. It's also worth crossing the Odra to **Łasztownia**, a free port constructed at the end of last century, which still preserves many grandly self-confident buildings of that epoch.

The Outskirts

Despite the heavily built-up character of its centre, Szczecin has plenty of stretches of greenery, which are ideal for a quick break from the urban bustle, particularly on summer evenings. Just to the north of the centre is the **Park Kasprowicza**, which can be reached by tram #1 or #9. It's best known for the huge triple eagle monument made to commemorate the fortieth anniversary of the outbreak of World War II, symbolising the three generations of Poles who lost their lives. Across the narrow Lake Rusałka is the **Dendrological Garden**, which contains over 200 species of trees and shrubs, including a host of exotic varieties. Continuing on either on the same trams to the terminus, you arrive at **Park Głębokie**, centred on the sausage-shaped lake of the same name, a small part of which is developed, the rest preserved in rustic tranquillity.

The most distinctive park in the city is that in the eastern suburb of Zdroje, reached either by a slow train, or bus #A or #B. Here you'll find a number of hiking trails, a couple of restaurants, and the **Emerald Lake** (Jezioro Szmaragdowe), which was created in the 1920s by flooding a former quarry; you can go for a swim there, or simply admire the play of light on its deep green waters.

One train stop further east is **DĄBIE**, for centuries a separate town, and one formerly prosperous enough to have been a member of the Hanseatic League. It's set at the mouth of the River Regalica, part of the Odra's delta, at the head of the Dąbie lagoon, a miniature version of the Szczecin lagoon immediately to the north. The attractive waterfront is a hugely popular sailing area, while the town centre boasts the Gothic church of St Mary, an archetypal example of Baltic brickwork, and the Renaissance Princes' Palace.

Eating, drinking and entertainment

The gastronomic situation in Szczecin has improved enormously since the fall of communism. At least for the time being, the city has the best of both worlds, as some good old-fashioned milk bars, snack bars and restaurants have managed to survive alongside a host of new ventures (not all of which can be expected to last), including a number of ethnic eateries plus the ubiquitous Westernised fast-food joints. There's certainly no longer the old problem about eating late, as many places stay open until midnight. If you discount the ghastly hotel nightspots, bars are in shorter supply, but the students in town provide some term-time action.

Restaurants

Argentyna, al. Wojska Polskiego 39. Plush new establishment specialising in huge grilled steaks, Argentine-style.

Balaton, pl. Lotników 3. Respectable and very reasonably priced offerings of Hungarian food and wine.

Bistro 2000, al. Wojska Polskiego 21. Extremely popular with the younger crowd; has a varied and esoteric menu featuring French, Italian and Chinese dishes, plus yummy desserts.

Chief, ul. Świerczewskiego 16. Probably the single most recommendable restaurant in Szczecin, with tasteful decoration, a good ambience, and a wide selection of sea and river fish specialities, plus a limited choice of other fare.

Gryf, al. Wojska Polskiego 49. Reasonable hotel restaurant.

Hai-Phong, ul. Szarotki. Vietnamese restaurant at the far northeastern corner of Park Żeromskiego, just a couple of minutes' walk from the ferry terminal.

Imola, ul. Parkowa 12. The pasta and pizzas here act like magnets to the young in-crowd.

Pod Muzami, pl. Żołnierza Polskiego 2. Long-established restaurant in the heart of the shopping area.

Riga, al. Piastów 15. Latvian restaurant, with old Polish and Lithuanian dishes also on offer.

Snack bars

Jedyna, al. Jedności Narodowej 42. Decent and very cheap milk bar.

Rybarex, ul. Obrońców Stalingradu 5a. Fish bar with a wide and adventurous selection of dishes: ideal for fast lunchtime service.

Turysta, ul. Obrońców Stalingradu 6. Milk bar with a large menu of classic homely Polish food.

Bars and cafés

Bajka, ul. Niepodległości 30. Boozy local nightspot.

Duet, ul. ks. Bogusława 1/2. Relaxing café with wide choice of teas, cakes and ice creams.

U Wyszaka, pl. Rzepichy. Trendy upmarket hang-out in the old town hall cellars.

Royal Pub, ul. Mariacka 26. Something of a rarity in Poland: a self-conscious imitation of a London tavern.

Zamkowa, ul. Rycerska. *Kawiarnia* inside the castle.

Nightlife

There are a number of **student clubs**, the top venues being the *Pod Wieża* at ul. Rybacka 1, and the *Kontrasty* at ul. Wawrzyniaka 7; details of where the current action is can be had from the Almatur office. Trendiest **disco** is the perversely named *Miami Nice*, ul. Bohaterów Warszawy 35.

The *Filharmonia Szczecińska*, pl. Armii Krajowey 1 (☎22-12-52), has a regular programme of **classical music** concerts, while operas and operettas are sometimes performed in the castle (☎888-02 for information). Main **theatre** is the *Teatr Polski*, ul. Swarożyca 5 (☎22-16-21), while puppet shows are held at the *Teatr Lalek Pieciuga*, ul. Kaszubska 9 (☎452-74).

Stargard Szczeciński

Some 25km southeast of Szczecin lies **STARGARD SZCZECIŃSKI**, the town which replaced it as capital of Pomerania for the duration of the Swedish occupation of the western part of the province. Situated on the River Ina, a tributary of the Odra, Stargard owed its early development to its position on the old trade routes to and from the Baltic; nowadays primarily an industrial centre, it suffered severe damage in World War II, but most of the principal monuments of the medieval Old Town survived. Carefully restored, they give ample evidence of a prosperous past, and are of sufficiently outstanding quality to warrant a detour, despite being surrounded by a depressing number of modern concrete buildings.

The Old Town

Arriving at the train station, or the bus station to its rear, it's just a few minutes' walk east down ul. Kardynała Wyszyńskiego to the Old Town. This nestles behind fifteenth-century brick **walls** some 4m thick, of which substantial sections remain, including five towers and four gateways. The shady Park Chrobrego has been laid out as a promenade along the western side, the longest surviving portion. Another uninterrupted stretch can be seen round to the north, at the back of the severe-looking Gothic church of **St John**, whose 90m tower is now the highest in Pomerania, given the reduced height at which St James' in Szczecin was rebuilt. Following ul. Chrobrego from here, you come to the Ina, where stands the most impressive part of the fortification system, the **Mill Gate** (Brama Młyńska). This is a covered bridge under which boats could pass, protected by a mighty pair of battlemented octagonal towers topped with sharply pointed steeples.

The Rynek, which occupies an unusually off-centre location towards the southeastern end of the Old Town, has a number of impressive reconstructed burghers' houses. At the corner stands the **Town Hall**, a plain Gothic structure whose character was changed out of all recognition by the addition of a spectacularly curvaceous late Renaissance gable adorned with polychromed terracotta tracery. Next to it is the **Guard House**, whose open arcades and loggia suggest the Mediterranean rather than the Baltic. Together with the Weigh House next door, it houses the local museum (Tues & Fri 10am–4pm, Wed & Sat 10am–3pm, Fri 1–7pm, Sun 10am–2pm).

Fine as all these buildings are, they are outclassed by the magnificent church of **St Mary**, which rears up behind the Rynek. One of the most original and decorative examples of the brickwork Gothic style to be found anywhere in the Baltic lands, it was begun around 1400, probably by Hinrich Brunsberg. The two towers, with their glazed green and white ceramics, can be seen from all over the town: the southern one, topped with a fancy gable, resembles a great tower-house; its higher northern counterpart is a truly bravura creation, topped by four chimney-like turrets and a great central octagon, itself crowned in the Baroque era with a two-storey copper lantern. As a fittingly small-scale contrast, the east end and the protruding octagonal chapel dedicated to the Virgin show off the full decorative possibilities of brick, so often wrongly regarded as an intransigent material. The stately interior seems very sober by comparison; the extravagant vaults were only added in the seventeenth centruy. An offbeat sense of humour is revealed in the long-mouthed figures in the Lady Chapel, counterpointing the po-faced saints and other worthies on the ceiling bosses.

Practicalities

For **tourist information**, try the Orbis office on the main square, Rynek Staromeijski 5 (☎77-26-45). **Accommodation** options are very limited: the PTTK hostel at ul. Kuśnierzy 5 (☎77-31-91) was closed at the time of writing, while the new hotel by the Mill Gate, a conversion of a block of flats, falls short both on cleanliness and security. Otherwise, there's only a sports hotel, *Błękitni*, ul. Cegalna 1 (☎77-20-19). Places to **eat** and **drink** are similarly few and far between in the central area – try *Basztowa*, ul. Chrobrego 7a, or *Pomorzanka*, on the west side of Park Chrobrego at ul. Czarnieckiego 3.

travel details

Trains

Poznań to Białystok (1 daily; 10hr 30min; couchettes); Bydgoszcz (12 daily; 2hr–2hr 30 min); Częstochowa (8 daily; 4–6hr); Gdańsk (7 daily; 4hr); Gniezno (hourly; 1hr); Inowrocław (12 daily; 2hr); Jelenia Góra (5 daily; 5–6hr); Kalisz (5 daily; 2hr 30min–3hr 30min); Katowice (15 daily; 5–6hr); Kołobrzeg (5 daily; 5hr); Kraków (8 daily; 7hr); Leszno (34 daily, 1hr–1hr 30min); Łódź (7 daily; 4–5hr); Olsztyn (4 daily; 4hr 30min–6hr); Opole (9 daily; 3hr 30min–4hr 30 min); Przemyśl (3 daily; 11–13hr; couchettes); Rzeszów (3 daily; 10–11hr; couchettes); Słupsk (4 daily; 5–7hr); Szczecin (18 daily; 3–4hr); Świnoujście (7 daily; 4–5hr); Toruń (8 daily; 2hr 30min–3hr); Wałbrzych (4 daily; 4–5hr); Warsaw (20 daily; 4–5hr); Wrocław (26 daily; 2hr–3hr 30 min); Zakopane (2 daily; 11–13hr; couchettes); Zielona Góra (6 daily; 2hr 30min–3hr). Also **international connections** to Berlin, Moscow, Riga and St Petersburg.

Kalisz to Białystok (1 daily; 8hr); Jelenia Góra (4 daily; 5–6hr 30min); Legnica (5 daily; 4hr 30min–5hr 30 min); Leszno (3 daily; 2hr 30 min); Lublin (3 daily; 7hr); Łódź (25 daily; 1hr 30min–2hr); Poznań (6 daily; 2hr 30min–3hr 30 min); Szczecin (2 daily; 6hr); Wałbrzych (4 daily 4–5hr); Warsaw (11 daily; 3hr–4hr 30min); Wrocław (14 daily; 2hr–3hr 30min); Zielona Góra (3 daily; 4–5hr).

Leszno to Białystok (1 daily; 12hr); Bydgoszcz (5 daily; 3hr 30min–4hr 30min); Gdańsk (6 daily; 5hr 30min–6hr 30min); Jelenia Góra (4 daily; 4hr–4hr 30min); Kalisz (3 daily; 3hr 30min); Katowice (6 daily; 4hr 30min–5hr 30min); Kraków (4 daily; 6hr 30min); Łódź (3 daily; 4hr); Olsztyn (2 daily 6–8hr; couchettes); Opole (9 daily; 2hr 30min–3hr 30min); Poznań (36 daily; 1hr–1hr 30min); Przemyśl (1 daily; 10hr 30min; couchettes); Rzeszów (1 daily;

9hr; couchettes); Słupsk (2 daily; 7hr 30min–8hr 30min; couchettes); Szczecin (7 daily; 5–6hr); Świnoujście (1 daily; 6hr); Toruń (2 daily; 3–4hr); Wałbrzych (4 daily; 3–4hr); Warsaw (2 daily; 6hr); Wrocław (26 daily; 1hr 30min–2hr); Zakopane (1 daily; 10hr; couchettes); Zielona Góra (2 daily; 2hr).

Bydgoszcz to Częstochowa (5 daily; 5–6hr); Gdańsk (hourly; 2hr); Kołobrzeg (8 daily; 5hr); Kraków (3 daily; 7–8hr); Łódź Kaliska (11 daily; 3–4hr); Poznań (11 daily; 2–4hr); Szczecin (2–3 daily; 4–6hr); Toruń (hourly; 40min); Warsaw (6 daily; 4–5hr).

Słupsk to Gdańsk (12 daily; 2–4hr); Kołobrzeg (4 daily; 2–2hr 30min); Koszalin (hourly; 1hr); Szczecin (9 daily; 3–4hr); local trains to Ustka (via Sławno) and Darłowo.

Kołobrzeg to Bydgoszcz (6 daily; 5hr); Gdańsk (4 daily; 4–5hr); Koszalin (9 daily; 1hr); Szczecin (4 daily; 4–5hr); Warsaw (8 daily; 8–10hr).

Kamień Pomorski to Szczecin (1 daily; 2hr 30min).

Świnoujście (all via Szczecin) to Kraków (2 daily; 12–13hr; sleeper); Poznań (7 daily; 4–5hr); Szczecin (18 daily; 2–2hr 30min); Warsaw (3 daily; 8–10hr; sleeper).

Szczecin to Bydgoszcz (3 daily; 4–5hr); Gdańsk (7 daily; 5–6hr); Kołobrzeg (6 daily; 3–4hr); Kraków (6 daily; 10–11hr); Łódź (4 daily; 6–7hr); Poznań (20 daily; 3–4hr); Słupsk (9 daily; 3–4hr); Świnoujście (20 daily; 2hr–2hr 30min); Warsaw (7 daily; 5–8hr; sleeper).

Szczecinek to Czaplinek (8 daily; 1hr); Kołobrzeg (4 daily; 2hr–2hr 30min).

Buses

Poznań to Kórnik/Rogalin/Mosina, Gniezno and Kalisz.

Gniezno to Gąsawa (for Biskupin), Mogilno, Żnin/Bydgoszcz.

Leszno to Gołuchów/Kalisz.

Bydgoszcz to Toruń, Chojnice and Szczecinek.

Szczecinek to Czaplinek, Słupsk and Szczecin.

Łeba to Słupsk and Gdańsk.

Słupsk to Darłowo, Ustka and Koszalin.

Kołobrzeg to the coast (Sarbinowo, Mielno), Kamień Pomorski and Świnoujście.

Kamień Pomorski to Świnoujście, Wolin, Szczecin and Kołobrzeg.

Świnoujście to Wolin, Międzyzdroje, Szczecin, Kołobrzeg and Trzebiatów.

Szczecin to Stargard Szczeciński, Wolin and Świnoujście.

PART THREE

THE
CONTEXTS

THE HISTORICAL FRAMEWORK

No other European country has had so chequered a history as Poland. At its mightiest, it has been a huge commonwealth stretching deep into what is now the CIS; at its nadir, it has been a nation that existed only as an ideal, its neighbours having on two occasions conspired to wipe it off the map. Yet, for all this, a distinctive Polish culture has survived and developed without interruption for more than a millennium.

THE BEGINNINGS

The great plain that is present-day Poland, stretching from the River Odra (or Oder) in the west all the way to the Russian steppes, has been inhabited since the Stone Age. For thousands of years it was home to numerous tribes – some nomadic, others settlers – whose traces have made Poland a particularly fruitful land for archaeologists. Lying beyond the frontiers of the Roman Empire, it did not sustain anything more socially advanced than a tribal culture until a relatively late date.

The exact period when this plain was first settled by **Slav** tribes is uncertain, but it may have been as late as the eighth century. Although diffuse, the various Slav groups shared a common culture – certainly to a far greater extent than is true of the Germanic tribes to the west – and the Polish language can be said to have existed before the Polish state.

It was the **Polonians** (the "people of the open fields"), based on the banks of the River Warta between Poznań and Gniezno, who were ultimately responsible for the forging of a recognisable nation, which thereafter bore their name. From the early ninth century, they were ruled by the **Piast dynasty**, whose early history is shrouded in legend but emerges into something more substantial with the beginnings of recorded history in the second half of the tenth century.

In 965, the Piast **Mieszko I** married the sister of the Duke of Bohemia and underwent public baptism, thus placing himself under the protection of the papacy. Mieszko's motives appear to have been political: Otto the Great, the Holy Roman Emperor, had extended Germany's border to the Odra and would have had little difficulty in justifying a push eastwards against a pagan state. By 990, Mieszko had succeeded in uniting his tribal area, henceforth known as Wielkopolska (Great Poland), with that of the Vistulanian tribe, which took the name of Małopolska (Little Poland). Silesia, settled by yet another Slav tribe, became the third component of this embryonic Polish state.

Mieszko's policies were carried to their logical conclusion by his warrior son **Bolesław the Brave**. In 1000 the Emperor Otto III was despatched by the pope to pay tribute to the relics of the Czech saint Adalbert, which Bolesław had acquired. During his stay, the emperor crowned Bolesław with his own crown, thus renouncing German designs on Polish territory. Subsequently, Bolesław established control over Pomerania, Kujawy and Mazovia; he also gained and lost Bohemia and began Poland's own easterly drive, pushing as far as Kiev. The name "Poland" now came into general use, and its status as a fully fledged kingdom was underlined by Bolesław's decision to undergo a second coronation in 1022.

PIAST POLAND

By the middle of the eleventh century, Małopolska had become the centre of the nation's affairs and Kraków had replaced Gniezno as capital, owing to Wielkopolska's vulnerability to the expansionist Czechs and

Germans. Political authority was in any case overshadowed by the **power of the Church**: when Bishop Stanisław of Kraków was murdered in 1079 on the orders of Bolesław the Generous, the clergy not only gained a national saint whose cult quickly spread, but also succeeded in dethroning the king.

In the early twelfth century, centralised monarchical power made a comeback under **Bolesław the Wrymouth**, who regained Pomerania – which had become an independent duchy – and repulsed German designs on Silesia. However, he undid his lifetime's work by his decision to divide his kingdom among his sons: for the rest of the century and beyond, Poland lacked central authority and was riven by feuds as successive members of the Piast dynasty jostled for control over the key provinces. Pomerania fell to Denmark, while Silesia began a long process of fragmentation, becoming increasingly Germanic.

In 1225 Duke Konrad of Mazovia, under threat from the heathen Prussians, Jacwingians and Lithuanians on his eastern border, invited the **Teutonic Knights**, a quasi-monastic German military order, to help him secure his frontiers. The Knights duly based themselves in Chełmno, and by 1283 they had effectively eradicated the Prussians. Emerging as the principal military power in mainland Europe, the Knights built up a theocratic state defended by some of the most awesome castles ever built, ruthlessly turning on their former hosts in the process. They captured the great port of Gdańsk in 1308, renaming it Danzig and developing it into one of Europe's richest mercantile cities. At the same time, German peasants were encouraged to settle on the fertile agricultural land all along the Baltic. Poland was left cut off from the sea, with its trading routes severely weakened as a result.

If the Teutonic Knights brought nothing but disaster to the Polish nation, the effects of the **Tartar invasions** of 1241–42 were more mixed. Although the Poles were decisively defeated at the Battle of Legnica, the Tartars' crushing of the Kiev-based Russian empire paved the way for Polish expansion eastwards into White and Red Ruthenia (the forerunners of Belarus and Ukraine), whose principalities were often linked to Poland by dynastic marriages. On the down side, the defeat spelt the beginning of the end for Silesia as part of

Poland. It gradually split into eighteen tiny duchies under the control of Bohemia, then the most powerful part of the Holy Roman Empire.

KAZIMIERZ THE GREAT

It was only under the last Piast king, **Kazimierz the Great** (1333–70), that central political authority was firmly re-established in Poland. Kraków took on some aspects of its present appearance during his reign, being embellished with a series of magnificent buildings to substantiate its claim to be a great European capital. It was also made the seat of a university, the first in the country and before long one of the most prestigious in the continent. Kazimierz's achievements in **domestic policy** went far beyond the symbolic: he codified Poland's laws, created a unified administrative structure with a governor responsible for each province, and introduced a new silver currency.

With regard to **Poland's frontiers**, Kazimierz was a supreme pragmatist. He secured his borders with a line of stone castles and formally recognised Bohemia's control over Silesia in return for a renunciation of its claim to the Polish crown. More reluctantly, he accepted the existence of the independent state of the Teutonic Knights, even though that meant Poland was now landlocked. To compensate, he extended his territories eastwards into Red Ruthenia and Podolia, which meant that, although the Catholic Church retained its prominent role, the country now had sizeable Eastern Orthodox and Armenian minorities.

Even more significant was Kazimierz's encouragement of **Jews**, who had been the victims of pogroms all over Europe, often being held responsible for the Black Death. A law of 1346 specifically protected them against persecution in Poland and was a major factor in Poland's centuries-long position as the home of the largest community of world Jewry.

THE JAGIELLONIANS

On Kazimierz's death, the crown passed to his nephew Louis of Anjou, King of Hungary, but this royal union was short-lived, as the Poles chose Louis' younger daughter **Jadwiga** to succeed him in 1384, whereas her sister ascended the Hungarian throne. This event was important for two reasons. First, it was an assertion of power on the part of the aristocracy and the beginnings of the move towards an elected monarchy. Second, it led soon afterwards to the most important and enduring alliance in Polish history – with **Lithuania**, whose Grand Duke, **Jagiełło**, married Jadwiga in 1386. Europe's last pagan nation, Lithuania, had resisted the Teutonic Knights and developed into an expansionist state which now stretched from its Baltic homeland all the way to the Crimea.

After Jadwiga's death in 1399, Jagiełło ruled the two nations alone for the next 45 years, founding the Jagiellonian dynasty – which was to remain in power until 1572 – with the offspring of his subsequent marriage. One of the first benefits of the union between the two countries was a military strength capable of taking the offensive against the Teutonic Knights, and at the **Battle of Grunwald** in 1410, the Order was defeated, beginning its long and slow decline. A more decisive breakthrough came as a result of the **Thirteen Years' War** of 1454–66. By the Treaty of Toruń, the Knights' territory was partitioned: Danzig became an independent city-state, run by a merchant class of predominantly German, Dutch and Flemish origin, but accepting the Polish king as its nominal overlord; the remainder of the Knights' heartlands around the Wisła (Vistula) became subject to Poland under the name of Royal Prussia; and the Order was left only with the eastern territory thereafter known as Ducal Prussia or East Prussia, where it established its new headquarters in the city of Königsberg.

Towards the end of the fifteenth century, Poland and Lithuania began to face new dangers from the east. First to threaten were the Crimean Tartars, whose menace prompted the creation of the first Polish standing army. A far more serious threat – one which endured for several hundred years – came from the **Muscovite czars**, the self-styled protectors of the Orthodox faith who aimed to "liberate" the Ruthenian principalities and rebuild the Russian empire which had been destroyed by the Mongol Tartars. The Jagiellonians countered by building up their power in the west. The Bohemian crown was acquired by clever politicking in 1479 after the religious struggles of the Hussite Wars; that of Hungary followed in 1491. However, neither of these unions managed to last.

THE RENAISSANCE AND REFORMATION

The spread of **Renaissance** ideas in Poland – greatly facilitated by the country's Church connections with Italy – was most visibly manifested in the large number of Italianate buildings constructed throughout the country, but science and learning also prospered under native Polish practitioners such as Nicolaus Copernicus.

This period saw a collective muscle-flexing exercise by the Polish nobility (*szlachta*). In 1493, the parliament or **Sejm** was established, gaining the sole right to enact legislation in 1505 and gradually making itself an important check on monarchical power.

The **Reformation** had a far greater impact on Poland than is often admitted by Catholic patriots. Its most telling manifestation came in 1525, with the final collapse of the Teutonic Order when the Grand Master, Albrecht von Hohenzollern, decided to accept the new Lutheran doctrines. Their state was converted into a secular duchy under the Polish crown but with full internal autonomy – an arrangement that was to be disastrous for Poland in the long term but which removed any lingering military strength from the Order. Lutheranism also took a strong hold in Danzig and the German-dominated cities of Royal Prussia, while the more radical Calvinism won many converts among the Lithuanian nobility. Poland also became home for a number of refugee sects: along with the acceptance already extended to the Jewish and Orthodox faiths, this added up to a degree of religious tolerance unparalleled elsewhere in Europe.

THE REPUBLIC OF NOBLES

Lacking an heir, the last of the Jagiellonians, **Zygmunt August**, spent his final years trying to forge an alliance strong enough to withstand the ever-growing might of Moscow. The result of his negotiations was the 1569 **Union of Lublin**, whereby Poland, Royal Prussia, Livonia (subsequently part of Latvia) and Lithuania were formally merged into a commonwealth. In the same year the Sejm moved to Warsaw, a more central location for the capital of this new agglomeration; its capital status became official in 1596.

On the death of Zygmunt August in 1572, the Royal Chancellor, Jan Zamoyski, presided over negotiations which led to the creation of the so-called **Republic of Nobles** – thenceforth kings were to be elected by an assembly of the entire nobility, from the great magnates down to holders of tiny impoverished estates. On the one hand this was a major democratic advance, in that it enfranchised about ten percent of the population, by far the largest proportion of voters in any European country; but on the other hand it marked a strengthening of a **feudalistic social system**. Capitalism, then developing in other European countries, evolved only in those cities with a strong German or Jewish burgher class (predominantly in Royal Prussia), which remained isolated from the main power structures of Polish society.

In 1573, the Frenchman Henri Valois was chosen as the first elected monarch, and, as was the case with all his successors, was forced to sign a document which reduced him to a managerial servant of the nobility. The nobles also insisted on their **Right of Resistance** – a licence to overthrow a king who had fallen from favour. The Sejm had to be convened at two-yearly intervals, while all royal taxes, declarations of war and foreign treaties were subject to ratification by the nobles.

Although candidates for the monarchy had to subscribe to Catholicism, the religious freedom which already existed was underpinned by the **Compact of Warsaw** of 1573, guaranteeing the constitutional equality of all religions. However, the Counter-Reformation left only a few Protestant strongholds in Poland: a large section of the aristocracy was re-converted, while others who had recently switched from Orthodoxy to Calvinism were persuaded to change allegiance once more. The Orthodox Church was further weakened by the schism of 1596, leading to the creation of the Uniate Church, which recognised the authority of Rome. Thus Poland gradually became a fervently Catholic nation once more.

The Republic of Nobles achieved some of its most spectacular successes early on, particularly under the second elected king, the Transylvanian prince **Stefan Bathory**. Having carried out a thorough reform of the army, he waged a brilliant campaign against the Russians in 1579–82, neutralising this particular threat to Poland's eastern borders for some time to come.

THE WAZA DYNASTY AND ITS AFTERMATH

The foreign policy of the next three elected monarchs, all members of the Swedish **Waza** dynasty, was less fortunate. Zygmunt August Waza, the first of the trio, was a Catholic bigot who soon came into conflict with the almost exclusively Protestant population of his native land and was deposed in 1604. Though his ham-fistedness meant that Poland now had a new (and increasingly powerful) enemy, he continued as the Polish king for the next 28 years, having fought off a three-year-long internal rebellion.

In 1618, Poland's situation became even more precarious, as John Sigismund von Hohenzollern inherited Ducal Prussia as well as the Electorate of Brandenburg. A couple of decades later, the Hohenzollerns inherited much of Pomerania as well, with another section being acquired by Sweden. Poland managed to remain neutral in the calamitous series of religious and dynastic conflicts known as the **Thirty Years' War**, from which Sweden emerged as Europe's leading military power.

The reign of the third of the Wazas, **Jan Kazimierz**, saw Poland's fortunes plummet. In 1648, the year of his election, the Cossacks revolted in the Ukraine, eventually allying themselves with the Russian army, which conquered eastern Poland as far as Lwów. This diversion inspired the Swedes to launch an invasion of their own, known in Polish history as the "Swedish Deluge", and they soon took control of the remainder of the country. An heroic fightback was mounted, ending in stalemate in 1660 with the Treaty of Oliwa, in which Poland recovered its former territories except for Livonia. Three years earlier, the Hohenzollerns had wrested Ducal Prussia from the last vestiges of Polish control, merging it with their other territories to form the state of Brandenburg-Prussia (later shortened to Prussia).

As well as the territorial losses suffered, these wars had seen Poland's population reduced to four million, less than half its previous total. A further crucial development of this period had been the first use in 1652 of the **liberum veto**, whereby a single vote against a measure was enough to cancel it. In principle, the nobility governed the republic as a sort of collective conscience in a wholly disinterested manner – and thus would be expected to act with unanimity. The first time someone objected to a measure, there was some debate as to whether his veto was sufficient to override the will of the majority: once it had been ruled that indeed it was, the practice soon became widespread in the protection of petty interests, and Poland found itself on the slippery slope towards ungovernability. This process was hastened when it was discovered that one dissenter was constitutionally empowered to object not only to any particular measure, but to dissolve the Sejm itself – and in the process repeal all the legislation it had passed. Meanwhile, the minor aristocracy gradually found themselves squeezed out of power, as a group of a hundred or so great **magnates** gradually established a stranglehold.

JAN SOBIESKI

Before repeated use of the *liberum veto* led to the final collapse of political authority, Poland had what was arguably its greatest moment of glory in international power politics – a consequence of the **Ottoman Turks'** overrunning of the Balkans. They were eventually beaten back by the Poles, under the command of **Jan Sobieski**, at the Battle of Chocim in 1673 – as a reward for which Sobieski was elected king the following year. In 1683 he was responsible for the successful **defence of Vienna**, which marked the final repulse of the Turks from western Europe.

However, Poland was to pay a heavy price for the heroism of Sobieski, who had concentrated on the Turkish campaign to the exclusion of all other issues at home and abroad. His relief of Vienna exhausted Poland's military capacity while enabling Austria to recover as an imperial power; it also greatly helped the rise of the predatory state of Prussia, which he had intended to keep firmly in check. His neglect of domestic policy led to the *liberum veto* being used with impunity, while Poland and Lithuania grew apart as the nobility of the latter engaged in a civil war.

THE DECLINE OF POLAND

Known as "Augustus the Strong" owing to his fathering of over 300 children, Sobieski's successor, **Augustus Wettin**, was in fact a weak ruler, unable to shake off his debts to the Russians who had secured his election. In 1701 Friedrich III of Brandenburg-Prussia openly defied him by declaring Ducal Prussia's right to be regarded as a kingdom, having himself crowned in Königsberg. From then on, the Hohenzollerns plotted to link their territories by ousting Poland from the Baltic; in this they were aided by the acquisition of most of the rest of Pomerania in 1720. Augustus's lack of talent for power politics was even more evident in his dealings with Sweden, against whom he launched a war for control of Livonia. The conflict showed the calamitous decline of Poland's military standing, and the victorious Swedes deposed Augustus in 1704, securing the election of their own favoured candidate, **Stanisław Leszczyński**, in his place.

Augustus was reinstated in 1710, courtesy of the Russians, who effectively reduced Poland to the role of a **client state** in the process. The "Silent Sejm" of 1717, which guaranteed the existing constitution, marked the end of effective parliamentary life. The Russians never hesitated to impose their authority, cynically upholding the Republic of Nobles as a means of ensuring that the liberal ideals of the Age of Reason could never take root in Poland and that the country remained a buffer against the great powers of western Europe. When Leszczyński won the election to succeed Augustus the Strong in 1733, they intervened almost immediately to have him replaced by the deceased king's son, who proved to be an even more inept custodian of Polish interests than his father. Leszczyński was forced into exile, spending the last thirty years of his life as the Duke of Lorraine.

In 1740 Frederick the Great launched the **Silesian Wars**, which ended in 1763 with Prussia in control of all but a small part of the province. As a result, Prussia gained control over such parts of Poland's foreign trade as were not subject to Russia. The long-cherished ambition to acquire Royal Prussia and thus achieve uninterrupted control over the southern coast of the Baltic was Frederick's next objective.

When the younger Augustus Wettin died in 1763, the Russians again intervened to ensure the election of **Stanisław-August Poniatowski**, the former lover of their empress, Catherine the Great. However, Poniatowski proved an unwilling stooge, even espousing the cause of reform. Russian support of the Orthodox minority in Poland led to a growth of Catholic-inspired nationalism, and by obstructing the most moderately liberal measures, Russian policy led to an outbreak of revolts. By sending armies to crush these, they endangered the delicate balance of power in eastern Europe.

THE PARTITIONS

Russia's Polish policy was finally rendered impotent by the revolt of the **Confederacy of Bar** in 1768–72. A heavy-handed crackdown on these reformers would certainly have led to war with Prussia, probably in alliance with Austria; doing nothing would have allowed the Poles to reassert their national independence. As a compromise, the Russians decided to support a Prussian plan for the **Partition of Poland**. By a treaty of 1772, Poland lost almost thirty percent of its territory. White Ruthenia's eastern sectors were ceded to Russia, while Austria received Red Ruthenia plus Małopolska south of the Wisła – a province subsequently rechristened Galicia. The Prussians gained the smallest share of the carve-up in the form of most of Royal Prussia, but this was strategically and economically the most significant.

Stung by this, the Poles embarked on a radical programme of reform, including the partial emancipation of serfs and the encouragement of immigration from the three empires which had undertaken the Partition. In 1791, Poland was given the first **codified constitution** in Europe since classical antiquity and the second in the modern world, after the United States. It introduced the concept of a people's sovereignty, this time including the bourgeoisie, and adopted a separation of powers between executive, legislature and judiciary, with government by a cabinet responsible to the Sejm.

This was all too much for the Russians, who, buying off the Prussians with the promise of Danzig, invaded Poland. Despite a tenacious resistance under **Tadeusz Kościuszko**, erstwhile hero of the American War of Independence, the Poles were defeated the following year. By the **Second Partition** of 1793, the constitution was annulled; the Russians annexed the remaining parts of White and Red Ruthenia, with the Prussians gaining Wielkopolska, parts of Mazuria and Toruń in addition to the star prize of Danzig. This time the Austrians held back and missed out on the spoils.

In 1794, Kościuszko launched a national **insurrection**, achieving a stunning victory over the Russians at the Battle of Racławice with a militia largely composed of peasants armed with scythes. However, the rebellion was put down, Poniatowski forced to abdicate, and Poland wiped off the map by the **Third Partition** of 1795. This gave all lands east of the Bug and Niemen rivers to Russia, the remainder of Małopolska to Austria and the rest of the country, including Warsaw, to Prussia. By an additional treaty of 1797, the Partitioning powers agreed to abolish the very name of Poland.

NAPOLEON AND THE CONGRESS OF VIENNA

Revolutionary France was naturally the country that Polish patriots looked to in their struggle to regain national independence, and Paris became the headquarters for a series of exiles and conspiratorial groups. Hopes eventually crystallised around **Napoleon Bonaparte**, who assumed power in 1799, but when three Polish legions were raised as part of the French army, Kościuszko declined to command them, regarding Napoleon as a megalomaniac who would use the Poles for his own ends.

Initially, these fears seemed unfounded: French victories over Prussia led to the creation of the **Duchy of Warsaw** in 1807 out of Polish territory annexed by the Prussians. Although no more than a buffer state, this seemed an important first step in the re-creation of Poland and encouraged the hitherto uncommitted **Józef Poniatowski**, nephew of the last king and one of the most brilliant military commanders of the day, to throw in his lot with the French dictator. As a result of his successes in Napoleon's Austrian campaign of 1809, part of Galicia was ceded to the Duchy of Warsaw.

Poniatowski again played a key role in the events of 1812, which Napoleon dubbed his "Polish War" and which restored the historic border of Poland-Lithuania with Russia. The failure of the advance on Moscow, leading to a humiliating retreat, was thus as disastrous for Poland as for France. Cornered by the Prussians and Russians near Leipzig, Poniatowski refused to surrender, preferring to lead his troops to a heroic, suicidal defeat. The choice faced by Poniatowski encapsulated the nation's hopeless plight, and his act of self-sacrifice was to serve as a potent symbol to Polish patriots for the rest of the century.

The **Congress of Vienna** of 1814–15, set up to organise post-Napoleonic Europe, decided against the re-establishment of an independent Poland, mainly because this was opposed by the Russians. Instead, the main part of the Duchy of Warsaw was renamed the **Congress Kingdom** and placed under the dominion of the Russian czar. The Poznań area was detached to form the **Grand Duchy of Posen**, in reality no more than a dependency of Prussia. Austria was allowed to keep most of Galicia, which was governed from Lwów (renamed Lemberg). After much deliberation, it was decided to make Kraków a city-state and "symbolic capital" of the vanished nation.

THE ARMED STRUGGLE AGAINST THE PARTITIONERS

The most liberal part of the Russian Empire, the Congress Kingdom enjoyed a period of relative prosperity under the governorship of **Adam Czartoryski**, preserving its own parliament, administration, educational system and army. However, this cosy arrangement was disrupted by the arch-autocrat Nicholas I, who became czar in 1825 and quickly imposed his policies on Poland. An attempted **insurrection** in **November 1830**, centred on a botched assassination of the czar's brother, provoked a Russian invasion. Initially, the Polish army fared well, but was handicapped by political divisions (notably over whether the serfs should be emancipated) and lack of foreign support, despite the supposed guarantees provided by the Vienna settlement. By the end of the following year, the Poles had been defeated; their constitution was suspended and a reign of repression began. These events led many to abandon all nationalist hopes: the first great wave of Polish **emigration**, principally to America, began soon after.

An attempted insurrection against the Austrians in 1846 also backfired, leading to the end of Kraków's independence with its re-incorporation into Galicia. This setback was a factor in Poland's failure to play an active role in the European-wide revolutions of 1848–49, though by this time the country's plight had attracted the sympathy of the emergent socialist movements. Karl Marx and Friedrich Engels went so far as to declare that Polish liberation should be the single most important immediate objective of the workers' movement. The last major uprising, against the Russians in 1863–64, attracted the support of Lithuanians and Galicians but was hopelessly limited by Poland's lack of a regular army. Its failure led to the abolition of the Congress Kingdom and its formal incorporation into Russia as the province of "Vistulaland". However, it was immediately followed by the **emancipation of the serfs**, granted on more favourable terms than in any other part of the czarist empire – in order to cause maximum ill-feeling between the Polish nobility and peasantry.

CULTURAL AND POLITICAL RESISTANCE

Following the crushing of the 1863–64 rebellion, the Russian sector of Poland entered a period of quiet stability, with the abolition of internal tariffs opening up the vast Russian market to Polish goods. For the next half-century, Polish patriots, wherever they lived, were concerned less with trying to win independence than with keeping a distinctive **culture** alive. In this they were handicapped by the fact that this was an era of great empires, each with many subjugated minorities whose interests often conflicted: Poles found themselves variously up against the aspirations of Lithuanians, Ukrainians and Czechs. They had the greatest success in Galicia, because they were the second largest ethnic group in the Habsburg Empire, and because the Habsburgs had a more lax attitude towards the diversity of their subjects. The province was given powers of self-government and, although economically backward and ruled by a reactionary upper class, flourished once more as a centre of learning and the arts.

Altogether different was the situation in Prussia, the most efficiently repressive of the three Partitioning powers. It had closely followed the British lead in forging a modern industrial society, and Poles made up a large percentage of the workforce in some of its technologically most advanced areas, notably the rich minefields of Upper Silesia. The Prussians, having ousted the Austrians from their centuries-long domination of German affairs, proceeded to exclude their rivals altogether from the **united Germany** they created by 1871, which they attempted to mould in their own Protestant and militaristic tradition.

For the Poles living under the Prussian yoke, the price to be paid for their relative prosperity was a severe clampdown on their culture, seen at its most extreme in the **Kulturkampf**, whose main aim was to crush the power of the Catholic Church, with a secondary intention of establishing the unchallenged supremacy of the German language in the new nation's educational system. It misfired badly in Poland, giving the clergy the opportunity to whip up support for their own fervently nationalistic brand of Catholicism.

Meanwhile, an upturn in political life came with the establishment, in response to internal pressure, of representative assemblies in Berlin, Vienna and St Petersburg. Towards the end of the century, this led to the formation of various new Polish **political parties and movements**, the most important of which were: the Polish Socialist Party (PPS), active mainly in the cities of Russian Poland; the Nationalist League, whose power base was in the peripheral provinces; the Peasant Movement of Galicia; and the Christian Democrats, a dominant force among the Silesian Catholics.

THE RESURRECTION OF POLAND

World War I smashed the might of the Russian, German and Austrian empires and allowed Poland to rise from the dead. Desperate to rally Poles to their cause, both alliances in the conflict made increasingly tempting offers: as early as August 1914 the Russians proposed a Poland with full rights of self-government, including language, religion and government, albeit one still ultimately subject to the czar.

When the German and Austrian armies over-ran Russian-occupied Poland in 1916, they felt obliged to trump this offer, promising to set up a **Polish kingdom** once the war was over. The foundations of this were laid immediately, with the institution of an interim administration – known as the Regency Council – and the official restoration of the Polish language. Even though carried out for cynical reasons, these initial steps were of crucial importance to the re-launch of a fully independent Poland, a notion which had soon gained the support of the US President Woodrow Wilson and of the new Bolshevik government in Moscow.

Meanwhile two bitter rivals had emerged as the leading contenders for leadership of the Polish nation. **Józef Piłsudski**, an impoverished noble from Lithuania and founding member of the PPS, had long championed a military solution to Poland's problems. During the war, his legions fought on behalf of the Germans, assuming that the defeat of the Russians would allow him to create the new Polish state on his own terms. In this, he favoured a return to the great tradition of ethnic and religious diversity of centuries past. **Roman Dmowski**, leader of the Nationalist League, represented the ambitions of the new middle class and had a vision of a purely Polish and staunchly Catholic future, in which the Jews would, as far as possible, be excluded. He opted to work for independence by exclusively political means, in the hope that victory over Germany would lead the Western allies to set up a Polish state under his leadership.

In the event, Piłsudski came out on top: the Germans, having held him in internment for well over a year, released him the day before the **armistice of November 11, 1918**, allowing him to take command of the Regency Council. He was sworn in as head of state three days later. Dmowski had to accept the consolation prize of head delegate to the Paris Peace Conference, though his associate, the concert pianist Ignacy Jan Paderewski, became the country's first Prime Minister.

POLAND REDEFINED

The new Poland lacked a defined territory. Initially, it consisted of the German and Austrian zones of occupation, centred on Warsaw and Lublin, plus Western Galicia. Wielkopolska was added a month later following a revolt against the German garrison in Poznań, but the precise frontiers were only established during the following three years on an *ad hoc* basis. Yet, though the Paris Conference played only a minor role in all this, it did take the key decision to give the country access to the sea by means of the **Polish Corridor**, a strip of land cut through the old Royal Prussia, which meant that East Prussia was left cut off from the rest of Germany. Despite intense lobbying, it was decided to exclude Danzig from the corridor, on the grounds that its population was overwhelmingly German; instead, it reverted to its former tradition as a city-state – an unsatisfactory compromise which was later to have tragic consequences.

The **Polish-Soviet War** of 1919–20 was the most significant of the conflicts that crucially determined the country's borders. Realising that the Bolsheviks would want to spread their revolution to Poland and then to the industrialised West, Piłsudski aimed to create a grouping of independent nation-states stretching from Finland to Georgia to halt this new expansionist Russian Empire. Taking advantage of the civil war between the Soviet "Reds" and the counter-revolutionary "Whites", his army marched deep into Belarus and the Ukraine. He was subsequently beaten back to Warsaw, but skilfully regrouped his forces to pull off a crushing victory and pursue the Russians eastwards, regaining a sizeable chunk of the old Polish-Lithuanian Commonwealth's eastern territories in the process, an acquisition confirmed by the Treaty of Riga of 1921.

At the very end of the war, Piłsudski seized his home city of Wilno (Vilnius), which had a predominantly Polish population but was wanted by the Lithuanians – who had opted for independence rather than a revival of the union. The grudge borne by Lithuania over this proved costly to them, as they became dependent on, and were later annexed by, the Soviet Union. Other border issues were settled by **plebiscites** organised by the League of Nations, the new international body set up to resolve such matters. In the most significant of these Germany and Poland competed for Upper Silesia. The Germans won, but the margin was so narrow that the League felt that the distribution of votes justified the partition of the province. Poland gained most of the Katowice conurbation, thus ensuring that the country gained a solid industrial base.

THE INTER-WAR YEARS

Although the Polish state managed to develop coherent political, economic and educational institutions, plus a transport and communications network, all were essentially fragile creations, as became obvious when Piłsudski refused to stand in the **1922 presidential elections** on the grounds that the office was insufficiently powerful. Worse, the victor,

Gabriel Narutowicz, was hounded by the Nationalists for having won as a result of votes cast by "non-Poles", and was assassinated soon afterwards. For the next few years, Poland was governed by a series of weak governments presiding over hyper-inflation, feeble attempts at agrarian reform and a contemptuous army officer class.

In May 1926, Piłsudski staged a military coup, ushering in the so-called **Sanacja** regime, named after a slogan proposing a return to political "health". Piłsudski functioned as the state's commander-in-chief until his death in 1935, though he held no formal office after an initial two-year stint as Prime Minister. Parliamentary life continued, but opposition was emasculated by the creation of the so-called Non-Party Bloc for Co-operation with the Government, and disaffected groups were brought to heel by force if necessary.

Having a country led by Stalin on one frontier was bad enough; when Hitler seized power in Germany in 1933, Poland was a sitting target for two ruthless dictators, despite managing to sign ten-year non-aggression pacts with each. Hitler had always been open about his ambition of wiping Poland off the map again, regarding the Slavs as a race who were fit for no higher role than to be slaves of the Aryans. His foreign policy objectives were quickly put into effect by his annexation of Austria in 1937 and of parts of Czechoslovakia – with British and French connivance – in 1938. As Hitler's attentions turned towards Poland, his foreign minister Joachim von Ribbentrop and his Soviet counterpart Vyacheslav Molotov concluded the notorious **Nazi-Soviet Pact** in August 1939, which allowed either side to pursue any aggressive designs without the interference of the other. It also included a secret clause which agreed on a full partition of Poland along the lines of the Narew, Wisła and San rivers.

WORLD WAR II

On September 1, 1939, Hitler **invaded Poland**, beginning by annexing the free city of Danzig, thereby precipitating World War II. The Poles fought with great courage, inflicting heavy casualties, but were numerically and technologically in a hopeless position. On September 17 the Soviets invaded the eastern part of the country, claiming the share-out agreed by the Nazi-Soviet Pact. The Allies, who had guaranteed to come to Poland's defence, initially failed to do so, and by the end of the first week in October the country had capitulated. A government-in-exile was established in London under **Władysław Sikorski**.

Millions of civilians – including virtually every Jew in Poland – were to be slaughtered in the Nazi **concentration camps** that were soon being set up in the occupied territory. And as this was going on, Soviet prisoners were being transported eastwards to the **Gulag**, while wholesale murders of the potentially troublesome elements in Polish society were being carried out, such as the massacre of Katyn, where 4500 officers were shot.

With the Nazi disavowal of the 1939 Pact and the invasion of the Soviet Union in June 1941, the Polish resistance, led by the **Home Army** (AK), no longer had to fight on two fronts, as it prompted Stalin to make an alliance with Sikorski. The Soviet victory at Stalingrad in 1943 marked the beginning of the end for the Nazis, but it enabled Stalin to renege on his agreement with the government-in-exile. At the **Tehran Conference** in November, he came to an arrangement with Britain and America with regard to future spheres of influence in Europe, making it almost inevitable that postwar Poland would be forced into the Soviet camp. He also insisted that the Soviet Union would retain the territories it had annexed in 1939. Allied support for this was obtained by reference to the current border's virtual coincidence with the so-called "Curzon Line", which had been drawn up by a former British Foreign Secretary in 1920 in an unsuccessful attempt at mediation in the Polish-Soviet War.

During the **liberation of Poland** in 1944, any possibility of reasserting genuine Polish control depended on the outcome of the **uprising in Warsaw** against the Nazi occupiers. On July 31, with the Soviets poised on the outskirts of the city, the Home Army was forced to act. The Red Army lay in wait during the ensuing bloodbath. When the insurgents were finally defeated at the beginning of October, Hitler ordered that the city be razed before leaving the ruins to the Red Army. In early 1945, as the Soviets pushed onwards through Poland, the Nazis set up last-ditch strongholds in Silesia, but these were overrun by the time of the final armistice in April.

No country suffered so much from World War II as Poland. In all, around 25 percent of the population died, and the whole country lay devastated. Moreover, although the Allies had originally gone to war on its behalf, it found itself **reduced in size** and **shifted westward** across the map of Europe by some 200 kilometres, with its western frontier fixed at the lines of the Odra and Nysa rivers. Stalin had in effect achieved his twin aims of moving his frontiers and his sphere of influence well to the west.

The losses in the east – including Lwów and Wilno, both great centres of Polish culture – were painful, and involved the transfer of millions of people across the country in the following two years. There were compensations, however: Pomerania and the industrially valuable Silesia were restored after a gap of some seven centuries; and the much-coveted city of Danzig, which had been detached since its seizure by the Teutonic Knights, was also returned – and as Gdańsk, it was later to play a major role in the formation of postwar Poland.

THE RISE OF POLISH COMMUNISM

The Polish communists took power, not through popular revolution – as their Soviet counterparts had – nor even with significant public support – as the Czech communists had – but through the military and political dictate of an occupying force. Control was seized by the **ZPP** (Union of Polish Patriots), an organisation formed by Stalin in 1943 from Polish exiles and Russian placemen with polonised names. As the Red Army drove the Germans westward, the ZPP established a Committee for National Liberation in Lublin, under the leadership of **Bolesław Bierut**. This was to form the core of the Polish government over the next few years.

Political opposition was fragmented and ineffectual. From the government in exile, only a single prominent figure returned to Poland after 1945 – Stanislaw Mikolajczyk, leader of the prewar Peasants' Party. He was to leave again in 1947, narrowly avoiding imprisonment.

The Polish communists and socialists who had remained in Poland during the war now regrouped. The communists, though suspicious of Moscow, joined the ZPP to form the Polish Workers' Party under general-secretary

POLAND 1938

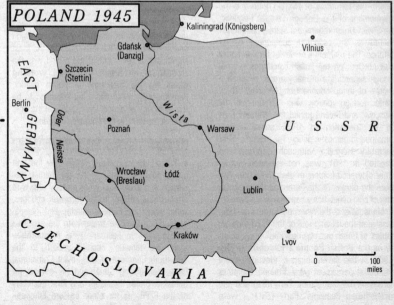

POLAND 1945

Władysław Gomułka, as the socialists attempted to establish a separate party. Meanwhile the Soviets ran the country as an outlying province, stripping factories of plant and materials, intimidating political opponents, and orchestrating the brutal suppression of a nationalist uprising in the Western Ukraine by the Polish army, in what is referred to as the **Civil War** (1945–47).

The economic and political framework of Poland was sealed by the elections of 1947. The communists and socialists, allied as the **Democratic Bloc**, won a decisive victory over their remaining opponents through an extended campaign of political harassment and manipulation. After the forcible merger of the socialists and communists in 1948 as the **PZPR** (Polish United Workers' Party), it only remained for the external pressures of the emerging Cold War to lock Poland completely into the Soviet sphere of influence and the Soviet model of economic and political development.

THE TRANSFORMATION OF POLAND

Polish history from 1947 to 1955 must be understood against the backdrop of an emergent Cold War. After the Berlin Blockade (1948), the formation of NATO (1949) and the rearmament of the German Federal Republic, the Soviet Union regarded a stable, communist Poland as an essential component of its defence. The realpolitik of Soviet foreign policy was not lost on the Polish communists, who, though subordinate in many areas, retained a degree of independence from Moscow. Thus, while foreign policy was determined by Moscow, and Poland joined the Warsaw Pact on its formation in 1955, some leeway remained in domestic policy. For example, First Secretary Gomułka, although deposed and arrested in 1951, was not executed, unlike other disgraced leaders in eastern Europe. Nor were the purges of the Party and the suppression of civil opposition as savage as elsewhere.

Nonetheless, the new constitution of 1952 enshrined the leading role of the PZPR in every aspect of Polish society, designating the country as the **Polish People's Republic (PPR)**. Further, while the trappings of elections and a two-house parliament were retained, the other parties – the Democratic Party (SD) and the reconstituted Peasants' Party (ZSL) – were under the effective political control of the PZPR. Real power lay with the Politburo, Central Committee, and the newly formed economic and administrative bureaucracies. Only the Catholic Church, although harassed and extensively monitored by the authorities, retained a degree of independent political and cultural organisation – a defiance characterised by the Primate, **Cardinal Wyszyński**, arrested in 1953 for "anti-state" activities and imprisoned for three years.

Nationalisation continued throughout this period, accelerated through the first **Three Year Plan** (1947–50) and the first **Six Year Plan** (1950–1956). Although the former retained some emphasis on the role of private ownership, the thrust of both was towards the collectivisation of agriculture and the creation of a heavy industrial base. Collectivisation proved impossible in the absence of the sort of force used by Stalin against the Kulaks: the programme slowed in the mid-Fifties and was tacitly abandoned thereafter. Industrially the plans proved more successful: major iron and steel industries were established, mining extensively exploited in Silesia and an entire shipbuilding industry developed along the Baltic coast – most notably in Gdańsk. There were, inevitably, costs: standards of living remained almost static, food was scarce, work was long, hard and often dangerous, and unrestrained industrialisation resulted in terrible pollution and despoilation of the land. Perhaps the most significant achievement of the period was the creation of an **urban industrial working class** for the first time in Polish history. Paradoxically, these very people proved to be the backbone of almost every political struggle against the Party in the following decades.

1956 – THE POLISH OCTOBER

In Poland, as in Hungary, **1956** saw the first major political crisis of the communist era. Faction and dissension were already rife, with intellectuals calling for fundamental changes, splits within the Party leadership and increasing popular disenchantment with the excesses of Stalinism. In February 1956 **Khrushchev** made his famous "secret" speech to the Twentieth Congress of the Soviet Communist Party, denouncing Stalin and his crimes: for Bolesław Bierut, President and First Secretary of the PZPR, as for other eastern European leaders, the speech was a bombshell, unmasking the lie of the absolute correctness of Stalin's every act. Reform-minded members of the Party in Poland were the first to make copies available in the west, but for Bierut and the hardline leadership it was the end: Bierut died directly after the congress, many suspecting that he had committed suicide.

Then in June workers in Poznań took to the streets over working conditions and wages. The protest rapidly developed into a major confrontation with the authorities, and in the ensuing street battles with the army and security police up to eighty people were killed and many hundreds of others wounded. Initial government insistence that "imperialist agents" had instigated the troubles gave way to an admission that some of the workers' grievances were justified and that the Party would try to remedy them.

The Poznań riots further divided an alarmed and weakened party. Hardliners pushed for defence minister General Rokossowski to take over the leadership, but it was Gomułka, with his earnest promises of reform, who carried the day. In October the Party plenum elected Gomułka as the new leader, without consulting Moscow. An enraged Khrushchev flew to Warsaw to demand an explanation of this unprecedented flouting of Moscow. East German, Czech and Soviet troops were mobilised along Poland's borders, in response to which Polish security forces prepared to defend the capital. Poland held its breath as Gomułka and Khrushchev engaged in heated debate over the crisis. In the end, Gomułka assured Khrushchev that Poland would remain a loyal ally and maintain the essentials of communist rule. Khrushchev returned to Moscow, Soviet troops withdrew, and four days later Gomułka addressed a huge crowd in Warsaw as a national hero. The Soviet invasion of Hungary to crush the national uprising there in early November 1956 provided a clear reminder to Poles of how close they had come to disaster.

The **Polish October**, as it came to be known, raised high hopes of a new order, and initially those hopes seemed justified. Censorship was relaxed, Cardinal Wyszyński was released and state harassment of the Church and control over the economy eased. But the impetus for reform quickly faded, and the 1960s saw a progressive return to centralised planning, a stagnant economy and steadily increasing levels of political control.

1970-79: FROM GOMUŁKA TO GIEREK

The final days of the Gomułka years were marked by a contrast between triumph in foreign policy and the harsh imposition of economic constraint. Pursuing his policy of Östpolitik, Willy Brandt – SPD Chancellor of the German Federal Republic – visited Poland in December 1970 and laid to rest some of the perennial concerns of postwar Polish foreign policy. In signing the Warsaw Treaty, West Germany recognised Poland's current borders and opened full diplomatic relations. And in an emphatic symbolic gesture, Brandt knelt in penance at the monument to those killed in the Warsaw Uprising.

A few days later, on December 12, huge food price rises were announced, provoking a simmering discontent that was to break out in strikes and demonstrations along the Baltic coast, centring on Gdańsk. When troops fired on demonstrators, killing many, the protests spread like wildfire, to the point of open insurrection. A traumatised central committee met five days before Christmas, hurriedly bundling the moribund Gomułka into retirement and replacing him as First Secretary with **Edward Gierek**, a member of the Party's reformist faction in the 1960s. Price rises were frozen and wage increases promised, but despite a Christmas calm, strikes broke out throughout January 1971, with demands for free trade unions and a free press accompanying the more usual economic demands. Peace was only restored when Gierek and the Minister of Defence, General **Wojciech Jaruzelski**, went to the Gdańsk shipyards by taxi to argue their case and admit their errors to the strikers.

The Gierek period marked out an alternative route to social stability. Given access to western financial markets by Brandt's reconciliation, the Gierek government borrowed heavily throughout the early Seventies. Food became cheaper and more plentiful as internal subsidies were matched by purchases from the West and the Soviet Union. Standards of living rose and a wider range of consumer goods became more freely available. However, the international economic recession and oil crises of the mid-Seventies destroyed the Polish boom at a stroke. Debts became impossible to service, new loans harder to obtain, and it became apparent that earlier borrowing had been squandered in unsustainable rises in consumption or wasted in large-scale projects of limited economic value.

By 1976, the wheel had turned full circle with remarkable rapidity. The government announced food price rises of almost treble the magnitude of those proposed in the early Seventies. This time the ensuing strikes were firmly repressed and many activists imprisoned, and it is from this point that one can chart the emergence of the complex **alliance between Polish workers, intellectuals and the Catholic Church**. In response to the imprisonment of strikers, the KOR (Committee for the Defence of Workers) was formed. Comprising dissident intellectuals, it was to provide not only valuable publicity and support for the opposition through Western contacts, but also new channels of political communication through underground *samizdat* publications, plus a degree of strategic sophistication that the spontaneous uprisings had so far lacked.

But perhaps even more decisive was the election of **Karol Wojtyła**, Archbishop of Kraków, as **Pope John Paul II** in 1978. A fierce opponent of the communist regime, he visited Poland in 1979 and was met by the greatest public gatherings that Poland had ever seen. For the Polish people he became a symbol of Polish cultural identity and international influence, and his visit provided a public demonstration of their potential power.

1980–89: SOLIDARITY

Gierek's announcement of 100 percent price rises on foodstuffs in July 1980 led to more strikes, centring on the **Gdańsk shipyards**. Attempts by the authorities to have a crane operator, Anna Walentynowicz, dismissed for political agitation intensified the unrest. Led by a shipyard electrician, **Lech Wałęsa**, the strikers occupied the yards and were joined by a hastily convened group of opposition intellectuals and activists, including future prime minister Tadeuz Mazowiecki. Together they formulated a series of demands – the so-called **Twenty-one Points** – that were to serve not only as the principal political concerns of the Polish opposition, but to provide an intellectual template for every other oppositional movement in eastern Europe.

Demands for popular consultation over the economic crisis, the freeing of political prisoners, freedom of the press, the right to strike, free trade unions and televised Catholic Mass were drawn up along with demands for higher wages and an end to party privileges. Yet the lessons of Hungary in 1956 and Czechoslovakia in 1968 had been learnt, and the opposition was careful to reiterate that they "intended neither to threaten the foundations of the Socialist Republic in our country, nor its position in international relations".

The Party caved in, after protracted negotiations, signing the historic **Gdańsk Agreements** in August 1980, after which free trade unions, covering over 75 percent of Poland's 12.5 million workforce, were formed across the country, under the name *Solidarność* – **Solidarity**. Gierek and his supporters were swept from office by the Party in September 1980, but the limits of Solidarity's power were signalled by an unscheduled Warsaw Pact meeting later in the year. Other eastern European communist leaders perceptively argued that Solidarity's success would threaten not only their Polish counterparts' political futures, but their own as well. Accordingly, Soviet and Warsaw Pact units were mobilised along Poland's borders. The Poles closed ranks: the Party reaffirmed its Leninist purity, while Solidarity and the Church publicly emphasised their moderation.

Throughout 1981 deadlock ensued, while the economic crisis gathered pace. Solidarity, lacking any positive control over the economy, was only capable of bringing it to a halt, and repeatedly showed itself able to do so. General Jaruzelski took control of the Party in July 1981 and, in the face of threats of a general strike, continued to negotiate with Solidarity leaders, but refused to relinquish any power. A wave of strikes in late October 1981 were met by the imposition of **martial law** on December 12, 1981: occupations and strikes were broken up by troops, Solidarity was banned, civil liberties suspended and union leaders arrested. However, these measures solved nothing fundamental, and after a second visit by Pope John Paul II in 1983 martial law was lifted.

The period 1984 to 1988 was marked by a final attempt by the Jaruzelski government to dig Poland out of its economic crisis. The country's debt had risen to an astronomical $39 billion, wages had slumped, and production was hampered by endemic labour unrest. In 1987 Jaruzelski submitted the government's programme of price rises and promised democratisation to a referendum. The government lost, the real message of the vote being a rejection not merely of the programme but of the notion that the Party could lead Poland out of its crisis. As the Party's route lay blocked by popular disenchantment, the opposition's opened up after major strikes in May 1988.

Jaruzelski finally acknowledged defeat after a devastating second wave of strikes in August of that year and called for a "courageous turnaround" by the Party, accepting the need for talks with Solidarity and the prospect of real power sharing – an option of political capitulation probably only made possible by the accession of Gorbachev to the Kremlin.

1989-90: THE NEW POLAND

The **round-table talks** ran from February to April 1989, the key demands being the absolute acceptance of the legal status of Solidarity, the establishment of an independent press and the promise of what were termed semi-free elections. Legalisation of Solidarity was duly agreed, opposition newspapers were to be allowed to publish freely and all 100 seats of a reconstituted upper chamber, the Senate, were to be freely contested. In the lower house of parliament, the Sejm, 65 percent of seats were to be reserved for the PZPR and its allied parties, with the rest openly contested.

The communists suffered a humiliating and decisive defeat in the consequent **elections** held in **July 1989**, whereas Solidarity won almost every seat it contested. Thus while the numerical balance of the lower chamber remained with the PZPR, the unthinkable became possible – a Solidarity-led government. In the end, the parties which had previously been allied to the PZPR broke with their communist overlords and voted to establish the journalist **Tadeusz Mazowiecki** as prime minister in August 1989, installing the first non-communist government in eastern Europe since the war. Subsequently the PZPR rapidly disintegrated, voting to dissolve itself in January 1990 and then splitting into two notionally social democratic currents.

The tasks facing Poland's new government were formidable: economic dislocation, political volatility and a rapidly changing foreign scene in the rest of eastern Europe. For the most part, the government retained a high degree of support in the face of an **austerity programme** far stiffer than anything proposed under the communist regime.

INTO THE NINETIES – TRANSFORMATION?

Lech Wałęsa, long out of the main political arena, forced the pace in the **presidential election of 1990**, calling for the removal of Jaruzelski, a faster pace of reform and a concerted effort to remove the accumulated privileges of the senior Party men. Against him stood Prime Minister Mazowiecki and the previously unknown Jan Tymiński, a Canadian-Polish businessman employing free-market rhetoric and Western-style campaigning techniques. Although clearly in the lead in the first round of voting in December 1990, Wałęsa was required to face a second round against Tymiński. Mazowiecki, having finished a disappointing third, then resigned as prime minister, taking the whole government with him. Wałęsa won the second round comfortably.

In January 1991 he appointed as prime minister Jan Krzysztof Bielecki, a leading intellectual force within Solidarity. This appointment was symptomatic of the country's changing political and social climate: a business-oriented liberal from Gdańsk (as opposed to the hitherto dominant school of Warsaw intellectuals), Bielecki represented the new technocratic elite already making rapid headway in the "new Poland". Significantly, Bielecki retained the services of Leszek Balcerowicz as finance minister (and deputy prime minister), a move indicative of the new government's commitment to continuing along the path of economic reform followed by the Mazowiecki administration.

Throughout 1991 the **economy** – specifically the government's commitment to persevering with a tough **austerity programme** – continued to dominate the national agenda, with steadily rising prices, rocketing unemployment (up to 11% by November 1991) and continued government spending cuts making heavy inroads into the pockets and lives of ordinary Poles. Internationally, however, Balcerowicz's tough policies gained the support of the Western financial institutions, a fact that found practical expression in a landmark agreement with the Paris club of the International Monetary Fund (IMF) on a fifty-percent reduction of Poland's estimated 33 billion dollars of official debt (providing the country continues to pursue IMF-approved economic policies, including keeping the budget deficit at under five percent of GDP).

Elections – the first fully free ones since World War II – were slated for the spring of 1991 but eventually postponed until October; preparations were hampered by continuing rows over the precise form of electoral system to be used. The election campaign itself was a fairly tame affair, the most notable feature being the spectacular array of parties (nearly seventy in total) taking part, including everyone from national minorities like the Silesian Germans to the joke "Beer Lovers' Party" as well as a bewildering array of old-time opposition factions, religiously based parties, nationalists and one-off independents.

The **"hyper proportional" system** (with no percentage entry hurdles) finally agreed for the elections during the autumn, however, was a recipe for political factionalism and fragmentation in the time-honoured Polish mould: 29 parties entered the new Sejm, the highest scorer, the Democratic Union (UD), gaining a meagre 14 percent of the alarmingly low (43 percent) turnout. Bielecki resigned, and a two-month period of confusion followed during which he tried in vain to cobble together a new and workable governing coalition. In the end Wałęsa ended the disarray by inviting **Jan Olszewski**, a lawyer and prominent former dissident, to form a new coalition government.

One issue that remained unresolved at the end of 1991 was the vexed question of **withdrawing Soviet troops.** Deadlocked negotiations and strong resistance from the Soviet and subsequently Russian authorities meant that unlike Czechoslovakia and Hungary, Poland still had no firm timetable for the removal of the 50,000 or so combat troops stationed in the country over two years on from the demise of communist authority. The decisive breakthrough came during Wałęsa's high-profile official visit to Moscow in May 1992, when the Polish president signed a treaty with his Russian counterpart Boris Yeltsin confirming that all Russian troops were to be withdrawn by end of 1993. Troop withdrawals proceeded apace, and in October 1992 the last Soviet combat forces pulled out of Poland, marginally ahead of schedule, leaving behind just a few support units to get out before the process is completed.

Abandoning Bielecki's emphasis on economic reform, the new centre-right coalition government put together by Olszewski adopted an aggressively confrontational emphasis on those elements of political reform – notably the highly-charged issue of "**decommunisation**" – which it believed the previous two administrations had ignored. The most explosive of these proved to be a government-sponsored parliamentary motion in May 1992 envisaging the production of a list of public figures suspected of having collaborated with the security services during the communist era. A political crisis blew up rapidly over what became known as the **lustration** issue. A no-confidence vote in the Sejm at the beginning of June 1992 led to Olszewski's enforced ouster as prime minister. Despite Wałęsa's best efforts the president's initial candidate to assume the premiership, the youthful Waldemar Pawlak of the Peasants' Party (PSL), failed to muster the necessary parliamentary support. After some ten weeks of bargaining, **Halina Suchocka** of the Democratic Union was nominated as Poland's **first woman prime minister**. Her new cabinet embraced everyone from the Catholic rightists of the Christian National Association (ZChN) to members of her own left-liberal-inclined UD, a consummate piece of political bargaining and compromise that surprised many observers accustomed to the infighting and posturing that at times still appears to be endemic to Polish political life.

To date the Suchocka government has proved surprisingly successful and cohesive. Domestically its most important achievement so far has been the **social pact** over wage increases, concluded between government and trade unions (the remnants of declining Solidarity included) in autumn 1992 after a major wave of strikes – a temporary resolution, at least, of an issue which has regularly threatened to derail Poland's post-communist reform project. On the darker side, the increasingly powerful role of **the Church** in Poland's political and social life has come to the fore, above all in the heated national debate sparked by government moves to **criminalise abortion**, a move supported strongly by the Catholic Church but opposed by many within the country, not least women, as well as by western institutions like the Council of Europe. Internationally, the most significant long-term development under the Suchocka government to date has been the **EC Association Agreement** signed in January 1992 and formally ratified by the Sejm in the autumn, amid loud accusations of a sell-out to the West from conservative, nationalistically minded forces fearful of the tacit acceptance of liberal secularism they see implied by European integration.

Into 1993 the question of large-scale **privatisation** remains a contentious, and still unresolved, issue. In March the Sejm threw out a bill designed to privatise over 600 major state enterprises, with members of government coalition parties voting against Suchocka in a characteristically defiant display of Polish independent-mindedness. In contrast to the country's ailing, debt-ridden state industries the flourishing private sector, now reckoned to account for almost fifty percent of national output, appears to be doing well, providing the basis for the economic upturn generally reckoned to be underway in the country.

MONUMENTAL CHRONOLOGY

1500 BC	Iron Age tribes of Lusatian culture.	Fortified settlement of **Biskupin**.
10C	Creation of Polish state.	Ruins of palace at **Ostrów Lednicki**, St Mary on the Wawel, **Kraków**.
11–12C	Poland under the early Piasts.	**Romanesque** architecture – cathedrals of **Gniezno** (bronze doors only survive) and **Kraków** (crypt); Collegiate church, **Kruszwica**; Premonstratensian monastery, **Strzelno**.
Early 13C	Monasticism spreads to Poland; Teutonic Knights invited into the country.	**Transitional** style introduced by Cistercians – monasteries at **Trzebnica** and **Henryków**. Fully fledged **Gothic** first appears in Dominican and Franciscan churches in **Kraków**. First Teutonic buildings – castle of **Kwidzyn**, beginning of construction of fortress at **Malbork**.
14C	Teutonic Knights establish a Baltic state; reign of Kazimierz the Great (1333–70); Bohemian control of Silesia recognised.	Great century of Gothic building, particularly of brick, in the Teutonic territories. Middle Castle, **Malbork**; castle at **Lidzbark Warmiński**; town hall and churches of St Mary and St John, **Toruń**; town hall, Great Mill, St Mary, **Gdańsk**; cathedral, **Frombork**. **Kraków** adorned with Gothic buildings – Sukiennice (cloth hall), churches of Corpus Christi and St Catherine, suburb of Kazimierz. Laying out of new town of **Kazimierz Dolny**; stone castles of the **Eagles' Nest Trail**; cathedrals of **Gniezno** and **Poznań** rebuilt. Series of brick churches in **Wrocław** (Breslau) – cathedral, Holy Cross, St Mary of the Sands; fortifications of **Paczków**.
Late 14C, 15C	Poland under the Jagiellonians; Silesia officially part of Bohemia.	**Late Gothic** buildings – university and town gates, **Kraków**; town hall and further brick churches, **Wrocław**; St James, **Nysa**.
16C	Last of Jagiellonian dynasty; creation of Republic of Nobles (1572).	Italian architects bring **Renaissance** to Poland, introduced at Wawel Castle, **Kraków**. In same city, Zygmuntowska Chapel in Wawel Cathedral, rebuild of Sukiennice, Old Synagogue. Palaces at **Brzeg** and at **Krasiczyn**; rebuild of town hall at **Poznań**. **Late Renaissance** and **Mannerist** styles practised from 1570s until around 1610. Layout of planned town of **Zamość**, including town hall, collegiate church and synagogue, by Bartolomeo Morandi. Beginning of construction of Royal Palace, **Warsaw**. Armoury and Golden House, **Gdańsk**; other town mansions in **Kraków**, **Kazimierz Dolny**, **Sandomierz** and **Wrocław**.

1587–1668	The Waza dynasty.	Early **Baroque** style of the Jesuits introduced with SS Peter and Paul, **Kraków**. Rebuilding of monastery of Jasna Góra, **Częstochowa** and palace of **Łańcut**. Waza Chapel in Wawel Cathedral, **Kraków**, marks Polish debut of full-blooded Baroque.
Late 17C	Turkish Wars; Poland at height of its international prestige.	Extensive building in **Warsaw**, including palace of Wilanów, the more restrained Krasiński and Radziwiłł palaces and Church of Holy Sacrament. All except the first designed by Tylman of Gameren, architect also of St Anne, **Kraków**, and the palace of **Nieborów**.
Late 17C, early 18C	Poland under the Saxon kings; Silesia part of Habsburg Empire.	Italianate Baroque in parish church, **Poznań**; town hall and churches, **Leszno**. Additions to Royal Palace, **Warsaw**. Buildings by Baroque architects from Vienna and Prague in Silesia: Ossoliński Library, Elector's Chapel in cathedral, Church of Holy Name and university, **Wrocław**; St Joseph and Monastery Church, **Krzeszów**; monastery of **Legnickie Pole**.
1764–1795	Reign of Stanisław-August Poniatowski; Silesia under Prussian rule.	**Neoclassicism** appears in additions to Royal Palace and in Łazienki Palace, **Warsaw**. Period of great country houses, including **Arcadia** and **Rogalin**. More severe version of Neoclassical style is adopted in Silesia – university library and royal palace, **Wrocław**; fortress at **Kłodzko**.
1795–1914	Poland under Partition.	Late Neoclassical buildings include Raczyński Library, **Poznań**, and theatre, **Wrocław**. Neo-Gothic of Berlin architect Karl Friedrich Schinkel in palace of **Kórnik** and castle of **Legnica**; castle in **Lublin** is in similar vein. Grandiose, derivative styles characteristic of the nineteenth century best illustrated in Polish Bank and Grand Theatre in **Warsaw** and in factories and houses of **Łódź**. In early twentieth century, notable public works in **Wrocław** – Grunwaldzki Bridge and Max Berg's Hala Ludowa. Also **Jugendstil** and **Secessionist** styles in then German cities such as Zielona Góra and Opole.
1918–present	Resurrection of Polish state; World War II; Poland under communism; democracy restored.	**Nazi** architecture in German lands, notably Wolf's Lair, **Gierłoz**. Postwar concentration on factories and housing estates, with occasional showpieces, such as Palace of Culture, **Warsaw**. After an initial ban, spectacular modern churches built: two of the finest are in Kraków suburb of **Nowa Huta**.

POLAND'S ENVIRONMENT

The following piece, which examines the current state of the Polish environment in the aftermath of the heavy-industry oriented communist era, is by David Goldblatt, a political analyst and researcher with the Open University who has recently completed a Phd on the history and politics of the environment movement in Britain. Thanks are also due to Iza Kruszewska of Greenpeace and the Environmental Service Agency, Warsaw, for some of the background material to the article.

THE COMMUNIST LEGACY

Perhaps, of all the heavy legacies that forty-five years of state socialism have left the Polish people, the environmental legacy is the most onerous. Capitalist societies, as we know, have hardly proved environmentally benign. However, few societies have matched the environmental devastation wrought by Polish communism. The path of economic modernisation pursued after World War II, when combined with the institutional failures of a centrally planned economy and an authoritarian polity, has yielded an almost unparalleled record of environmental degradation. It seems that only parts of the ex-Soviet Union – where the same conditions operated in an even more extreme fashion – can match this.

The heart of the problem has been the peculiarly lopsided structure of the Polish economy. Pursuing an inappropriate Soviet model of economic development after the Second World War, Poland embarked on the **rapid expansion** of its energy and heavy industries: coal mining, electricity production, steel, concrete, shipbuilding. The country is still dependent on domestically produced coal, especially the brown coal lignite, which has created a particularly damaging mix of energy and industry. These facts alone would have ensured rising levels of atmospheric, aquatic and soil **pollution**. However, the institutional structures of state socialism made matters considerably worse. The inefficiency of the Polish economy meant that older and more polluting plant was kept running for longer and in worse condition; investment in new technologies was blocked by a desperate lack of foreign exchange; and pollution regulations were rarely enforced – all in a political climate where any threat of local or national protest was repressed. The only saving grace of technological lag and the scarcity of capital is that Poland has never seriously embarked upon a nuclear programme, although both the communists and the post-communist governments have contemplated it.

THE STATE OF POLISH CITIES

The environmental consequences of state socialism have fallen most heavily upon some of Poland's cities, the most seriously affected area being Upper Silesia in the southwest corner of the country. At its heart is the sprawling industrial conurbation of **Katowice**, the industries and households of which consume a vast quantity of locally mined coal for production and heating. In addition, zinc and lead ores are mined and smelted, and the region receives significant atmospheric pollution from Northern Bohemia in the Czech Republic and Saxony in eastern Germany. Together these areas form "**The Black Triangle**", producing a phenomenal cocktail of sulphur dioxide, nitrogen oxides, dust and particulates, smog and ozone. Twenty-five percent of total atmospheric emissions are generated in this two percent of the country, and that's not including the range of carcinogenic chemicals produced and released by factories into local communities and water courses. The mining industry has left widespread subsidence and discharges untreated saline waste into the Oder and Vistula rivers.

The consequences of these emissions are predictable, if no less horrific for that. People are ill more often and more seriously, and die in greater numbers after shorter lives; **life expectancy** for adults in the region is three years less than the Polish average. Infant mortality is running at the rate of twenty deaths per 1,000 births, which is around double the western European average. In the Bytom area it is almost three times that rate. The number of children born with **congenital defects** sixty percent higher than Poland as a whole, child leukaemia rates are double an already high national average and bronchial illness and circulatory problems are widespread.

To the east of Katowice and downwind of much of its atmospheric pollution lies Kraków. Here the story is just as grim: on top of imported pollution, the city houses the infamous **Nowa Huta steelworks**, still the largest factory in Poland and already out of date by the time it went into operation in the 1940s. Designed in the previous decade, Nowa Huta was based on a steel plant in Pittsburgh, the plan of which was stolen from the Americans by the Soviets, who passed it on to the Poles. Producing steel at a price that almost no one will buy, the plant consumes vast amounts of coal, electricity and iron ore with the result that iron dust, cadmium, zinc and lead deposits envelop the city in a stationary cloud of smog for over a hundred days a year. Not surprisingly, adults in Kraków have four times as many colds as other Poles and three times as much asthma; lung cancer and degenerative bone diseases are also widespread. Also, the sulphur dioxide emitted from both Nowa Huta and the power stations that supply it are rapidly eating away at the very stone fabric of both old and new parts of the city; the faces have been wiped from statues; stained glass is destroyed. It is proving easier to raise international funding to save the buildings of Kraków – a United Nations' world heritage site – than to ease the plight of its inhabitants.

AGRICULTURE AND THE COUNTRYSIDE

Outside of the cities, in Poland's extensive rural areas, the situation is bad but less serious. Agriculture is a major contributor to both water and soil pollution. Compared to Western farming methods, Poland uses significantly less fertiliser and pesticide, but poor techniques and antiquated chemicals mean that more of these substances are leached into the environment with more **toxic effects**. In addition, ill-conceived, large-scale drainage programmes orchestrated by the communists have caused the loss of valuable wetlands.

More significantly, pollution from Poland's industrial cities has seeped into the countryside. It is estimated that nearly eighty percent of the land has acidic soils, whilst those areas near non-ferrous metal-smelting industries have recorded extremely dangerous levels of heavy metal contamination. These heavy- metals find their way into vegetables and cereals, leading people in the worst-affected areas to turn to their own allotments and gardens.

At the same time, however, Poland has some of the most untouched and unique landscapes in the whole of Europe: the pristine primeval forest of Białowieża on the Belarus border; the mountain forests of Carpathia; the untouched bogs and peatlands of the Biebrza swamps that teem with birdlife; the south-eastern steppe lands. The result is an abundance of rare fauna, including bears, lynx, wild-cats and golden eagles, though – along with 25 percent of all Polish vertebrates and 28 percent of flowering plants – these are sadly in **danger of extinction**.

In 1989 the United Nations Environment Programme estimated that 5–10 percent of Poland's forests were damaged. More accurate unofficial estimates suggest a figure nearer 75 percent. The **Sudetan Mountains** in the south are especially threatened. In many areas only blackened tree stumps remain, the result of destruction by acid rain blown north over the border from the Czech Republic and south from Silesia. Not only are the trees dying, but the remaining acidified soil is being washed into the Odra River basin, nowadays threatened with regular flooding.

Most under-reported of Poland's rural environmental problems is the quiet crisis of rural sanitation and health. If a partially organic agriculture and extensive wilderness are the environmental benefits of underdevelopment, then its underside is the minimal provision for sewerage, clean water and safe waste disposal that Poland's rural population continues to endure. Over half of community and privately owned wells have water unfit for human consumption. Few villages have any collective facilities for the collection and disposal of waste, so that ditches and forests all over the countryside are littered by thousands of untreated and unregulated dumps.

POLAND'S RIVERS AND THE BALTIC SEA

Poland's rivers and lakes are in no better state than its land. According to the government's own system of classification, less than twenty percent of rivers are fit for consumption and two-thirds are already so badly polluted that they are unsuitable to receive industrial wastes.

Most of the effluents are carried by the Wisła and the Odra rivers. Both flow northwards from Upper Silesia, adding its pollution to that of western and eastern Poland, and then into the Baltic. According to the Polish Ministry of the Environment the Baltic is now the **most polluted sea in Europe**, although the Poles have been generously helped in making it so by the twelve other nations with Baltic coastlines.

The Baltic Sea is a particularly fragile ecosystem because it is so shallow and so little of its polluted waters can escape into the North Sea. Many of Poland's Baltic beaches have been closed to the public owing to health risks, the coastlines around Gdańsk and Szczecin being worst affected. In addition the leaching of nitrogen and phosphorous compounds from agriculture to rivers and then to the sea is causing an excessive growth of algae in the Baltic. The dead algae accumulates on the sea floor, concentrating pollutants and creating large areas of dead sea without oxygen – approximately 100,000 square miles to date.

ENVIRONMENTAL POLITICS AND POLICIES

Despite the widespread abuse of civil liberties under the communists and their draconian repression of all dissident political activity, a small **environmental movement** did emerge to challenge the wave of environmental degradation engulfing Poland in the late 1970s and early 1980s. This included groups like the National Conservation League (LOP) and Polski Klub Ekologiczny (PKE) founded in Kraków in 1980. In the early 1980s the movement, in close cooperation with Solidarity, forced the publication of secret government reports acknowledging the catastrophic state of the Polish environment and the cosmetic nature of environmental policy and legislation, plus the closure of the heavily polluting Skawina aluminium plant.

Since 1989, environmental pressure groups and research institutes have proliferated in Poland and a **Green party** has been formed, although it failed to win any seats at the parliamentary election in December 1991. While post-communist governments have proved more receptive to environmental issues and a great deal more open about the state of the Polish environment, there have been considerable conflicts.

Current government policy is addressing itself to global and national environmental problems, the establishment of strict environmental standards and the creation of adequate enforcement agencies. However, as the Polish Green movement has sharply pointed out, capitalist democracy is not, as yet, proving to be that much more effective at curbing environmental degradation than its socialist predecessor. The social costs of environmentally restructuring Polish industry are enormous. There is little chance of domestic lignite being replaced by imported fuels. Clean technologies are available but expensive. Above all, the market is proving as environmentally problematic as central planning. The arrival of capitalism has brought the familiar detritus of Western economic growth: the rise of the car and the demise of public transport, the proliferation of unrecyclable and wasteful packaging. However, these developments have not as yet got out of control. It is not inconceivable that with a degree of foresight and international assistance and finance, the Poles may both deal with the legacy that state socialism has left them and circumvent some of the worst aspects of the West's poor environmental record. If they are able to do so it will be an achievement every bit as great as the peaceful revolution of 1989.

WOMEN IN POLAND

In 1990–91 Małgorzata Tarasiewicz worked as Women's Officer for Solidarity, a position she eventually resigned from following disagreements with the trade-union leadership over the controversial issue of abortion and the question of democracy within the movement. Currently president of the Polish section of Amnesty International and active in grassroots organisations, for many years she was a leading member of Wolność i Pokój (Freedom and Peace), an oppositional movement with close connections with Western peace groups such as European Nuclear Disarmament (END). The following article, which offers a personal perspective on the issues facing women in post-communist Poland, was originally published in *Feminist Review* (no. 39), winter 1991.

WOMEN IN POLAND: CHOICES TO BE MADE

Some people say: let us first establish our democracies and then we can work out the details (meaning the rights of women). But if these two things do not go hand in hand, not only will women remain second-class citizens but also our societies will remain backward civilisations, limiting themselves only to talk about democracy. Without the participation of women in changes in Poland and without their being involved in political, social and economic life, democracy will never be achieved. The new situation creates new conditions in all spheres of life. Economic competition and new routes to political posts mean new opportunities for women, opportunities to take positions in which they will have a chance to influence the society they live in.

Eastern Europe is in a **transitional period**. This period is marked by a struggle of ideas, which is especially important since whichever ideas emerge as dominant are going to influence the lives of more than one generation.

Some years ago, an unofficial organisation in Poland received a letter from somebody who had a paint sprayer and wanted to write slogans on walls but did not know what to write, so asked for advice. It is a present-day reality in Poland that where government positions are at stake, the only groups that can make any gains are those that are well organised and experienced in using **political pressure**. Women are definitely not such a group. They are like the person with the paint sprayer; their problem is how to exert their rights.

Over the past forty years women's organisations were treated instrumentally, and though the legal system could have been considered pro-feminine, in Poland, as in other eastern European countries, there was a great discrepancy between the legal system and social reality. "Front" women's organisations, with a conformist membership, have created a destructive and demoralising image of what a women's organisation is like. The stereotype that originated in this way is now very much predominant within the society. So new attempts to establish a women's group are often discredited as the second Women's League, as the communist organisation was named. Moreover, issues like abortion are used instrumentally during political turning points like the parliamentary elections in the spring of 1989 or the presidential elections in the autumn of 1990. All the major political forces are playing on the issue of abortion for their own ends. Catholic fundamentalists reject any kind of discussion of the topic and support the criminalisation of abortion. Ex-communists, surrounded by some remnants of the Women's League, advocate the right to choose. The alliance with the Church makes it rather awkward for other major forces to speak up about this issue. Because of this, popular consciousness identifies pro-choice attitudes with the corruption of the past 45 years. The strong influence of the Catholic Church makes society stick to the traditional vision of the female role, limited to a wife and mother stereotype.

The political climate is dominated by traditional values. With the growth of unemployment there are government plans to send women home from their jobs in order to improve the situation on the labour market. Moreover, women see staying at home as new and progressive (Rosen, 1990). The only point of reference for Poland is the prewar period, which is the only model of the social organisation of an independent Polish nation. It is viewed with nostalgia and among other things it provides the image of what a family should be like and what the feminine role is. Polish prewar society, dominated by Catholic ideals, definitely cannot be a model for a completely different post-totalitarian country aspiring to a free market economy, with all the setbacks and benefits that such a situation brings about. The most visible advantage consists in transforming the image of work. In the communist period, work was not considered to be a source of independence. **Low wages** became a kind of substitute for social welfare. In the new situation women will probably develop a new attitude towards gaining professional skills. The most common danger that women, like the rest of society, will have to face is unemployment.

By the end of October 1990, women formed 51 percent of the one million unemployed. It's important to stress that among young people more women than men remained unemployed. By the end of October 1990 there were 37.3 percent **unemployed women** for one vacancy compared with 9.5 percent men. In six regional districts there were over a hundred women for one job vacancy (and in one district as many as 1,398). For 97.3 percent of registered unemployed women there was no offer of a job at all. Women, because of their double duties, cannot compete with men on the labour market. Women's situation will get even worse with time and advances of restructuring in those branches of industry – like the textile industry – that employ mainly women. At the moment, employment in some textile enterprises is kept stable but, in order to avoid mass redundancies, women are sent on unpaid leave or work only two days a week, earning 500,000zł, which is well below the poverty level.

Economic recession and the urge to cut costs has led to degradation of the value of women's work. According to data from 1988, almost two-thirds of Polish women worked outside the home. However, the motivation for most of them was not the hope of fulfilling career ambitions or the intentions of being financially independent but a much more mundane need to make ends meet. This situation led to mass participation of women in the labour market. Since all consumer goods were scarce in eastern Europe women had a second full-time job running the household. The difficulty of obtaining goods forced many women to take part-time jobs. Now it is often this kind of

a job that disappears first. Polish women are also less qualified than men and as such are easier to dismiss. Another reason for dismissing women is a **cultural** one: it seems to be generally accepted in Poland that a man needs a job more than a woman.

In an opinion poll carried out at the end of 1990, 45 percent of working women's husbands thought that women should not work outside their homes. The same opinion was shared by 53 percent of men whose wives did not work professionally, by 35 percent of working women and by 47 percent of housewives.

It was a common belief that as soon as we got rid of communist rule the aid and investment would start pouring in from the Western countries. This turned out not to be true. The majority of Western businessmen interested in eastern Europe are interested in quick profits only. They do create some jobs, but on their own conditions: **no trade unions**, no complaints about work conditions, low wages. That is why few men want to work there; women have no choice no matter how big the **health hazards** are. Women's cooperatives and the training of women managers are discussed both in the Ministry of Labour and the trade unions, but as funding is insufficient and women are not adequately organised it only remains in the domain of wishful thinking. The conditions of work that are offered to unskilled workers are often unacceptable and the pay too low for men.

A woman's position on the labour market is perceived as more flexible due to the predominant image of woman as wife and mother whose main life goal is to support the family. Escaping the social pressure to become a mother of the traditional type and "**finding alternative forms of female identity**" are among the most important women's issues in Poland. This adds to the problem of unemployment. The traditional role models determine women's position in public life, resulting in male domination in all spheres of social and political activity. Women's internalised negative view of themselves leads many women to reject institutions aimed against existing inequalities. Recently, hearing about the possibility of creating a **Ministry of Women's Affairs**, one woman was shocked and said she felt human first and foremost so why should such an institution be needed at all?

Besides an internalised negative view of themselves, there is another factor responsible for women's denial of the existence of discrimination in our society. This other factor is pride in being a Polish mother and in preserving the **patriotic values** of the Polish nation. That is why women's problems are crucial in the transition period in Poland and eastern Europe. George Konrad, a writer from Hungary, in his book *Anti-Politics* explains how, during the last forty years, the private sphere was the only place where people could retain their soul and resist the intrusiveness of the state. The importance of the **private sphere** which was mainly women's domain made the role essential to all forms of resistance to the communist system. Now the uniqueness of the private sphere is much diminished as the civil society establishes itself. When men join public life women are left in a less valued sphere of life. Long associated with the home, women are simply not seen as part of the new civil society.

In the immediate future, the main things to be achieved for women's benefit will lie in two spheres. The first is concerned with the better circulation of information between eastern bloc countries, so that particular solutions can be found together. The experience of Western countries is equally valued, as it can be applied to Polish conditions so that we do not have to break through an open door. The information should cover such questions as ways of retraining women, of creating new jobs and legislative problems. The other sphere of activity consists of what may seem to be more abstract, that is, changing the stereotype of a woman. This would involve a broad range of activities including work with the mass media and revision of educational systems. In this respect, too, we will need extensive support from our more experienced peers.

REFERENCES

Małgorzata Dobraczynska *Dilemmas of Polish Women – Let's Work?* Paper given at CSCE Women's Conference, Berlin, November 1990.
Ruth Rosen "Women and Democracy in Czechoslovakia – an interview with Jirina Siklova" in *Peace and Democracy News* (Campaign for Peace and Democracy, New York), Fall 1990.

GAYS AND LESBIANS IN POLAND

In a country where official Catholic attitudes to gender, morality and sex continue to exercise a powerful influence on national life, social attitudes to gays and lesbians are imbued with a specific complex of prejudices and dilemmas. The following article by Lucy Kimbell, a US citizen living and working in Poland, provides an insight into the situation of gays and lesbians in contemporary Poland. The article originally appeared in *The Warsaw Voice*, to which thanks are due for permission to reproduce it.

NOT SO ROSY

We meet in a trendy bar in the centre of Warsaw. We talk in English and, although it is unlikely that many of the people around us will understand what we are saying, we keep our voices low. Piotr (not his real name), a teacher aged 28, tells me his story concisely over a dish of cream and fruit. He is happy to talk to someone – it gives some perspective – but he is not optimistic about what the future holds for him and many others. When one of us mentions the h-word (homosexual), we automatically flinch as if someone at another table has overheard.

Poland has relatively liberal laws regulating sexual behaviour in comparison with, for example, the United Kingdom. The Criminal Code of 1963 does not even mention, let alone criminalise, homosexual activity and the **age of consent** for sex is 15 across the board, without specifying whether heterosexual or homosexual. Gays and lesbians have more legislative freedom in Catholic post-communist Poland than in that bastion of freedom, the United States, where in some states homosexual relations are banned, or in Britain, where the age of consent for men is 21.

But in North America – and nearer to this Warsaw bar – in Germany or Britain, while there may be legislative restrictions through which the state polices sexual behaviour, there is such a thing as a lesbian and gay subculture, even a **"pink" counter-culture**. There are

lesbian and gay studies programmes at universities, there are TV programmes catering for the lesbian and gay audience. There is certainly lesbian and gay politics.

Gays and lesbians in Poland, like any other minority group, are sensitive about the language used to describe what defines their difference. Piotr corrects himself when he says "homosexual" when he means "gay". The word "homosexual" was originally a nineteenth-century medical category which sought to identify – and treat – a pathology. The h-word differs from "gay" or "lesbian" in the assumptions behind it. Homosexuality is almost a condition: being lesbian or gay is just one of those things.

The words are pretty much the same in many languages. Slang varies, of course, expressing on a more fundamental level each society's attitudes. Polish slang for gay or queer is **pedał**, literally a pedal, but close to *pederasta*, with all the condemnation invested in it.

In the West, lesbian and gay activists have been reclaiming the g-word since the beginning of **Gay Liberation** in the early 1970s, a movement which learned its lessons from the Civil Rights Movement. During the last twenty years in the West, despite legislative and organisation difficulties in some countries, a distinct culture of liberation has developed – liberation and celebration, evidenced in the annual June Gay Pride marches in cities throughout the world. In Poland we keep our voices low and Piotr asks me not to use his real name in the article.

Lesbian and gay activists say that it is important to draw a distinction between a gay (as opposed to gay and lesbian) community that is literally **underground** – men meeting in stations, hotel bars and public toilets – and a community of lesbian and gay activists. The history of lesbian and gay activism in Poland is brief.

After the defeat of communism in Poland, it seemed that many minority groups would be able to develop their communities without the hindrances the former authorities put in their way. Democracy is supposed to recognise difference. But the spark that was lit in the Polish gay scene never became the roaring, warming fire that it might have. "People are not interested in gays at all here," Piotr says.

He doesn't look so interested himself. His bowl of cream glows a sickly yellow in the artificial light.

Poland's first gay **magazine**, *Filo*, published in Gdańsk by a nucleus of activists who later became the city's **Lambda group**, started publishing six years ago when the communist authorities were still in power. That it was allowed to publish is significant, as is the fact that its circulation was restricted to a hundred copies. The first Polish lesbian and gay organisation, Polish Lambda, was not allowed to register formally until February 1990 after several attempts.

Lambda groups were set up around the country in all the major cities, and more magazines were founded by private companies. The Lambda groups had dozens of members – some actively campaigning, others just there to meet people. At its high point, the Warsaw Lambda group had over 200 members.

Warsaw's first openly **gay disco** with a capacity of 500, Café Fiolka, opened in September 1990, linked with Poland's first lesbian and gay information agency, **Pink Service**. A British TV company came to make a documentary about the lesbian and gay scene in Poland for Channel 4. The Warsaw Lambda group got coverage in the national press and radio, and with the help of this publicity more people got in touch through the box number.

A community of activists began developing and adopted the slogans of pride and liberation and personal identity politics from the West. The Warsaw Lambda group set up an informal café staffed by volunteers, providing somewhere to meet and information about safer sex and the dangers of **HIV and AIDS**. It was possible to meet people elsewhere than in public toilets or at stations – if you knew the right people and got to hear about what was happening.

As with the gay movements elsewhere in the world, more men than women were involved. No one is able to offer a simple explanation as to why **lesbians** are more invisible than gay men in Poland. Ania who is 19 and still at school is reluctant to explain her opinion. "We go to meetings but the men talk about things that don't really interest us. We want to set up a group for lesbians in Warsaw." I ask the question that is begging to be asked: Where can a young lesbian or gay man have

sex since most young people live with their parents into their twenties or older?

Ania shrugs: "I am lucky because my mother knows about me, and she lets my girlfriend come and stay at our flat. But for most people it is impossible. . . . You have to stay with friends, wait for your parents to go out. . . . I don't know anyone whose mother is as understanding."

However, despite the burgeoning gay activism, during the **presidential election campaign** last autumn – an ideal time for all minority groups to draw attention to themselves – the subject of sexuality remained closed. The newsletter *Warsaw Gay News*, printed in English by Pink Service, undertook a survey of the candidates' opinions about homosexuality and homosexuals.

The conversations with the various candidates or their spokespeople provide an interesting perspective on what for most Poles seems to be barely an issue.

Former Prime Minister Tadeusz Mazowiecki's spokesman said, "It would be wiser not to touch the subject." Sexual politics often confuses the traditional alignments across the political spectrum. Leszek Moczulski of the **Confederation for an Independent Poland** claimed that "the question of sexuality is a very individual issue. Everyone has a right to choose how, where, and with whom. . . . We have to protect one's privacy. The legal system should be focused on this issue."

Stan Tymiński's assistant fell in with more predictable attitudes when he said that "this problem is not a good one to discuss during his campaign. . . . We are not interested in minorities." **Lech Wałęsa**'s press office was also reluctant to discuss it, declaring that he was not interested in this issue. In answer to the question as to how, if he became president, he would treat the minority, he said: "I don't know yet whether I will treat them as outcasts of society. It is hard for me to answer this question now. We'll see after the elections. . . ."

The staunchly Catholic Wałęsa had been the focus of foreign interest earlier in the year when it was reported at the **International Lesbian and Gay Association** (ILGA) conference in Stockholm that he had said that drug users and homosexuals should be eliminated. Western journalists – in particular the **gay press** – were quick to pick up on the story.

However, the apparent source of the alleged comments, the editor of *Filo* magazine, said that he had not heard the statement himself. There were no records of any statement on the subject in the minutes of Solidarity's second conference at which the comments were alleged to have been made.

Wałęsa's press spokesman, Andrzej Drzycimski, said that they had received a lot of letters about the alleged comments. He suggested that for the Polish gay activists it was a way to get attention from the international gay community and general public opinion.

The altercations around Wałęsa's alleged comments, and the initial enthusiasm displayed by (admittedly mostly young, mostly well-educated) urban lesbians and gays, could have provided a sound basis for a movement similar to, and linked by ILGA with, lesbian and gay liberation movements elsewhere in the world. Café Fiolka was busy every Friday night and Pink Service was making money. Poland even had a publicly gay man, **Sławek Starosta**, pop star and director of Pink Service, who refused to compromise and keep his sexual orientation secret.

In April 1991 there was a **big meeting** of all the Polish lesbian and gay groups, new businesses and publications held over a weekend at Café Fiolka. But somehow, the initial post-communist euphoria had gone. The energy for organising, for activism along the lines common in the West, dissipated.

Activists began slipping away. The 24-year-old chairman of the Warsaw Lambda group died tragically of a heart attack and the vice-chairman assumed his responsibilities without an election. The group lost its office at the university, and without this focus, lost much of its energy. Some of the new magazines went out of business after only a few issues. Even after the long summer break during which one expects activity to quieten down, things did not pick up. The spark really had gone out. What happened to the energy?

Irek Krzemiński, assistant professor of sociology at Warsaw University and a former Solidarity activist, makes reference to ideas of democracy in his analysis of what put out the spark. His was the **generation of '68** which experienced the transition from traditional Polish patterns to the idea that individuality –

including sexual individuality – was connected with freedom. "In the 1970s, Polish society was changing in this direction – openness toward sex in general and accepting all minorities. Now it is quite different. . . . Society is changing in an unpleasant direction. It is paradoxical that at the beginning of the 1990s we have in some senses more of a closed mind, a **more traditional**, more collectivist attitude than we had during the last ten years of communism in Europe."

To develop a campaign, a movement needs more than enthusiasm. It needs to be able to organise and it needs money, and above all it needs to come from within a community. According to Sławek Starosta of Pink Service, those involved in setting up Lambda made a lot of mistakes. "We were really isolated from the existing gay community. We looked around and we didn't see it. We were young and inexperienced and the people from the gay community didn't want any kind of group set up so they didn't help."

According to Krzemiński, another factor in the dampening of activism is the **Church**, which always plays a special role in Poland. "The Church had a big, big role in the defeat of Communism. . . . In contrast to the soldiers on the streets, there was the visible freedom of the Church. But now the Church has the idea of continuing to have a political role in the state."

The Church is traditionally antagonistic to sexual freedom of any kind. As Polish society continues to negotiate the major readjustments of the last two years, the Church carries on clinging onto the fiercely traditional values which are being undermined. Krzemiński sums them up: "Women should be at home, men should be out working hard for their families, gays are dreadful. . ."

The Church's attitude toward lesbians and gays, and particularly to lesbian and gay organising, is one element of a general **hostility** to "other", to the very concept of strangers. According to Krzemiński, as Poland continues down the path of reform and transformation, both political, economic and social, the kinds of frustrations that people are experiencing are the ideal vehicle for developing hostility to "other". The racism and xenophobia now rampant in Germany provide a **warning** of how the energies unleashed by the post-communist changes can be channelled. "It's only during the past few years that I have begun to feel in personal danger because of my sexuality," he adds, somewhat ominously.

In Starosta's opinion, there is little sign that the current trend in Polish lesbian and gay activism will reverse. "People are now very much involved in their lives – trying to survive – and they don't have the time or the money to do things for other people. I don't see any signs of change."

Café Fiolka may have to close in the spring since although it is busy every Friday night, no one goes the other nights it is open and it is losing money. Pink Service is still expanding and the newly founded erotic gay men's magazine it publishes, *Men*, is doing well, but other magazines have closed.

While the Church continues to have a prominent role in society and people are not prepared to put energy into organising, things are unlikely to change. In those quiet conversations in trendy Warsaw bars, it is the h-word that you will hear, not the word "gay". It is desperation you will sense, not celebration.

Attitudes in Poland are likely to remain distinct from those experienced by gays and lesbians elsewhere in Europe or in the United States. Levels of "queerbashing" have forced gay groups to organise **protection** for visitors to bars and clubs and to protect the community since the police often won't.

In Poland, while there is always the possibility of violence, for example from the gangs who occasionally lie in wait outside Fiolka, it is an indifferent hostility. It is not the sort that makes you feel the attackers wish you weren't there, but the sort that says you really don't matter.

BOOKS

A vast amount of writing both from and about Poland is available in English, and the quantity looks set to increase at an accelerated pace with the advent of the post-communist regime.

Most of the books listed below are in print, and those that aren't should be easy enough to track down in second-hand bookshops; where two publishers are given, the first is British, the second US. In Britain, the best sources for specialist books are *Colletts International Bookshop*, 40 Great Russell St, London WC1B 3PJ (☎071 580-7538) and the Polish-run *Orbis Books*, 66 Kenway Rd, London SW5 ORD (☎071 370-2210), which also stocks a large selection of photo albums (many out of print) from Poland itself. Another way of getting hold of out-of-print titles is by joining the library of the School of Slavonic and East European Studies, University of London, Malet St, London WC1 (☎071 637-4934). With a reference, non-students pay a £35 deposit for borrowing rights. The library also has a wide selection of magazines and journals from Poland and eastern europe generally.

TRAVEL

Karl Baedeker *Northern Germany, Southern Germany and Austria, Russia* (all o/p, but staple finds in second-hand shops). The old nineteenth- and early twentieth-century Baedekers are always fascinating, but never more so than in the case of Poland, which was then under Partition. A strong German bias is evident in the first two books, with Polish elements often ignored or glossed over; even in the later editions there's not the slightest anticipation of Poland's possible re-emergence as a nation.

Joram Kagan *Poland's Jewish Heritage* (Hippocrene). New guidebook providing a useful summary of the Jewish sites of Poland, along with an outline history.

Alfred Döblin *Journey to Poland* (I.B. Tauris/ Paragon House). Döblin, best known for his weighty Expressionist novels, visited the newly resurrected Polish state in 1923, primarily to seek out his Jewish roots, though he himself was non-practising, and was later to convert to Catholicism. The result is a classic of travel literature, full of trenchant analysis and unnervingly prophetic predictions about the country's future, interspersed with buttonholing passages of vivid descriptive prose.

Denis Hills *Return to Poland* (Bodley Head, o/p). Hills, a peripatetic British lecturer who had a brief period as an international celebrity when condemned to death by Idi Amin, paid a return visit to Poland (where he had worked half-a-century before) in 1985. His deportation as a result of official suspicion about the motives behind his trip and his previous sojourn forms the highpoint of a mildly entertaining travelogue which somehow never quite catches fire.

Hillaire Belloc *Return to the Baltic* (Constable, o/p). Whimsical account of Belloc's travels through Denmark, Sweden and Poland – he clearly felt more at home among his fellow-Catholics in Warsaw and Kraków than in Lutheran Scandinavia.

Tim Burford *Hiking Guide to Poland and Ukraine* (Bradt Publications). Thoroughly researched guide to hiking in the region.

HISTORY

Adam Zamoyski *The Polish Way* (John Murray/ Watts). The most accessible history of Poland, going right up to the 1989 elections. Zamoyski is an American emigré Pole, and his sympathies – as you would expect in a member of one of Poland's foremost aristocratic families – are those of a blue-blooded nationalist.

Norman Davies *The Heart of Europe: A Short History of Poland* (OUP). A brilliantly original treatment of modern Polish history, beginning with the events of 1945 but looking backwards over the past millennium to illustrate the author's ideas. Scrupulously gives all points of view in disentangling the complex web of Polish history.

Norman Davies *God's Playground* (2 vols; OUP/Columbia UP). A masterpiece of erudition, entertainingly written and pretty much definitive for the pre-Solidarity period.

Norman Davies *White Eagle, Red Star: The Polish Soviet War, 1919–20* (Orbis Books/Hippocrene). Fascinating account of a little-known but critically important episode of European history, at a time when Lenin appeared ready to export the Soviet Revolution into Europe.

Norman Davies and **A. Polonsky** (eds) *Jews in Eastern Poland and the USSR 1939–49* (Macmillan). Meticulously researched and well-written account of the fate of eastern Europe's largest Jewish population in time of war.

Oskar Halecki *History of Poland* (Routledge, UK). An alternative to Davies if you want a manageable chronological account of Polish history, but its nationalistic bias puts it at a severe disadvantage.

Neal Ascherson *The Struggles for Poland* (Pan/Random). Ascherson's book was designed to accompany the Channel 4 TV series and its focus is squarely on the twentieth century, with just a thirty-page chapter on the previous thousand years. For most general readers, though, this is the best possible introduction to modern Polish history and politics.

Józef Piłsudski *Memoirs of a Polish Revolutionary and Soldier* (Faber & Faber, o/p/ AMS Press). Lively stuff from Lech Wałęsa's hero, who – after a dashing wartime career – was Poland's leader from 1926 to 1934.

Wacław Jedrzejewicz *Piłsudski – a Life for Poland* (Hippocrene). Comprehensive biography of the enigmatic military strongman.

Antony Polonsky *Politics in Independent Poland, 1921–39* (OUP, o/p). Somewhat academic review of the period.

Patrick Brogan *Eastern Europe: The Fifty Years War, 1939–89* (Bloomsbury). Useful summaries of the eight European communist nations (plus the Baltic republics) from conception to collapse.

Chimen Abramsky, Maciej Jachimczyk and Antony Polonsky (eds) *The Jews in Poland* (Basil Blackwell). Historical survey of what was for centuries the largest community of world Jewry.

WORLD WAR II AND THE HOLOCAUST

Józef Garlinski *Poland in the Second World War* (Macmillan/Hippocrene). General history by a UK-based émigré, from a partisan standpoint.

Jan Ciechanowski *The Warsaw Uprising of 1944* (CUP). Compelling, day-by-day account – the best of many on this subject.

Gustaw Herling *A World Apart* (OUP/Arbor House, o/p). Account of deportation to a Soviet labour camp, based on the author's own experiences.

Jan Nowak *Courier for Warsaw* (Collins Harvill). Racily written memoir of the Polish underground resistance.

Martin Gilbert *The Holocaust* (Fontana). The standard work, providing a trustworthy overview on the slaughter of European Jewry – and the crucial role of Poland, where most Nazi concentration camps were sited.

The Warsaw Ghetto (Interpress, Warsaw). Official state publication, issued in several languages, that documents the destruction of the capital's Jewish population.

Richard C. Lukas *The Forgotten Holocaust* (Hippocrene). Detailed study of Nazi atrocities against Polish Gentiles which, in the author's view, was every bit as barbaric as against their Jewish counterparts.

Dan Kurzman *The Bravest Battle* (Pinnacle, o/p/ Putnam, o/p). Detailed account of the 1943 Warsaw Ghetto Uprising, conveying the incredible courage of the Jewish combatants.

Alan Adelson and Robert Lapides *The Łódź Ghetto – Inside a Community under Siege* (Penguin). Scrupulously detailed narrative of the 200,000-strong ghetto, with numerous personal memoirs and photographs.

Primo Levi *If This is a Man* and *The Truce*; *Moments of Reprieve*; *The Drowned and the Saved*; *The Periodic Table*; *If Not Now, When?* (all Abacus). An Italian Jew, Levi survived Auschwitz because the Nazis made use of his training as a chemist in the death-camp factories. Most of his books, which became ever bleaker towards the end of his life, concentrate on his experiences during and soon after his incarceration in Auschwitz, analysing the psychology of survivor and torturer with extraordinary clarity. *If Not Now, When?* is the story of a group of Jewish partisans in occupied Russia and Poland: giving plenty of insights into eastern European anti-Semitism, it's a good corrective to the mythology of Jews as passive victims.

Janina Bauman *Winter in the Morning* (Pan/ Free Press); *A Dream of Belonging* (Virago/ Trafalgar Square). Bauman and her family survived the Warsaw Ghetto, eventually leaving the country following the anti-Semitic backlash of 1968. *Winter* is a delicate and moving account of life and death in the ghetto. Less dramatic but equally interesting, *Belonging*, the second volume of her autobiography, tells of life in the Communist Party and disillusionment in the early postwar years.

Betty Jean Lifton *Janusz Korczak: The King of the Children* (Chatto/Farrar, Srauss & Giroux). Biography of the Jewish doctor who died in Treblinka with the orphans for whom he cared. He was the eponymous subject of Andrzej Wajda's latest film.

Art Spiegelman *Maus* (Penguin/Pantheon). Spiegelman, editor of the cartoon magazine *Raw*, is the son of Auschwitz survivors. *Maus* is a brilliant comic-strip exploration of the ghetto and concentration camp experiences of his father, recounted in flashbacks. The story runs through to Art's father's imprisonment at Auschwitz; subsequent chapters of the sequel – covering Auschwitz itself – have been printed in recent editions of *Raw*.

Rudolf Höss *Kommandant at Auschwitz* (o/p). Perhaps the most chilling record of the barbarity: a remorseless autobiography of the Auschwitz camp commandant, written in the days between his death sentence and execution at Nürnberg.

Saul Rubinek *So Many Miracles* (Penguin, UK). Rubinek's interviews with his parents about their .early life in Poland and survival under Nazi occupation make a compelling piece of oral history, and one that paints a blacker than usual picture of Polish-Jewish relations.

Carl Tighe *Gdańsk: National Identity in the German-Polish Border Lands* (Pluto). Alternatively titled "Gdańsk: the Unauthorised Biography", an apt description of a fascinating history of a city that Poles and Germans have tussled over for centuries. Studiously avoiding the pro- or anti-Polish/German dichotomy that bedevils many interpretations, the author sets out to capture the unique story of the Gdańsk/

Danzig citizenry, arguing that claims of real Polish or German identity tell us more about the needs of latterday nationalists than the cultural complexities of the past.

Krystyna Olszer (ed) *For Your Freedom and Ours: Polish Progressive Spirit from the 14th Century to the Present* (Ungar, US). Fascinating anthology of uncompromising statements, essays and manifestoes by Poles from over the centuries – everyone's here, from Kościuszkio, Mickiewicz and Piłsudski to the 1980 Gdańsk Agreements that marked the founding of Solidarity.

POLITICS AND SOCIETY

Timothy Garton Ash *The Polish Revolution: Solidarity 1980–82* (Cape/Random); *The Uses of Adversity* (Granta/Penguin/Random); *We The People: The Revolution of 89* (Granta/Penguin/Random). Garton Ash has been the most consistent and involved Western reporter on Poland in the Solidarity era, displaying an intuitive grasp of the Polish mentality. His *Polish Revolution* is a vivid record of events from the birth of Solidarity – a story extended in the climactic events of 1989, documented as an eyewitness in Warsaw, Budapest, Berlin and Prague.

Jan Josef Lipski *A History of KOR – The Committee for Workers' Self-Defence* (University of California Press). Detailed history of key 1970s opposition movement that is regarded as one of Solidarity's main inspirations. A resistance veteran and leading light in KOR, Lipski shows how it developed ideas and strategies of non-violence and an "independent civil society" as a response to totalitarianism. A demanding but worthwhile read.

Grazyna Sikorska *Jerzy Popiełuszko, a Martyr for Truth* (Fount/Eerdmans, o/p). Hagiographic biography of the murdered Catholic priest and national hero.

Mark Frankland *The Patriots' Revolution* (Sinclair Stevenson). After Tim Garton Ash, the best of the snap reports on the eastern European revolutions.

Misha Glenny *The Rebirth of History: Eastern Europe in the Age of Democracy* (Penguin). One chapter deals with Poland, homing in on the economic and political difficulties of post-communist reconstruction.

Grupa Publikacyjna Forum *Forum Polek: Polish Women's Forum* (available from POSK, 238–246 King St, London W6 ORF). Highly worthwhile anthology – in English and Polish – of essays, memoirs, fiction and poetry by London-based émigré (and second generation émigré) writers.

Stewart Steven *The Poles* (Collins Harvill/ Macmillan, o/p). Excellent journalistic account of all aspects of society in early 1980s Poland.

Paul Latwski (ed) T*he Reconstruction of Poland 1914–23* (Macmillan). Wide-ranging set of academic essays focusing on the lead-up to the country's (re)achievement of independence, and subsequent struggles with newfound state-hood, particularly the sensitive question of minorities. Useful annex of period documents.

ESSAYS AND MEMOIRS

Adam Michnik *Letters From Prison* (University of California Press). Collection of writings by prominent opposition intellectual and editor of the *Gazeta Wyborcza*, once Solidarity's house newspaper, now critical of (and disowned by) Wałęsa. The essay "A New Evolutionism" is a seminal piece of new political writing, and the more historical pieces are fascinating, too.

Adam Zagajewski *Solidarity, Solitude* (Ecco Press, US). One of Poland's finest contemporary poets responds in essay form to recent (published 1990) events.

Josef Tischner *Solidarity* (Harper & Row). Essays by leading Solidarity activist and priest. Illuminating on the movement's essentially religious philosophy of the 1980s.

Kazimierz Brandys *Warsaw Diary 1977–81* (Chatto/Random, o/p). This account by a major Polish journalist and novelist brilliantly captures the atmosphere of the time, and especially the effect of John Paul II's first papal visit in 1979. During martial law, possession of this book carried an automatic ten-year sentence.

Teresa Toranska *Oni: Poland's Stalinists Cross-Examined* (Collins Harvill/Harper Collins). Interviews with Polish communists and Party leaders from the Stalinist era carried out during the Solidarity era by investigative journalist Toranska. The result is a fascinating insight into how Stalin established Soviet control over eastern Europe, and Poland in particular.

Lech Wałęsa *An Autobiography: A Path of Hope* (Pan/H. Holt). Ghostwritten, it would seem, by a Solidarity committee, in the years before Lech split the party and created his own role as "axe-wielding" president.

Tim Sebastian *Nice Promises* (Chatto). Former Warsaw BBC correspondent's reflections on the early 1980s in Poland. Chatty, anecdotal stuff, but plenty of insights into the politics and spirit of the times.

Adam Czerniawski *Scenes from a Disturbed Childhood* (Serpent's Tail). Uplifting, entertainingly written account of a childhood spent escaping the traumas of World War II – to Turkey and an Arab school in Palestine, before ending up with his impoverished upper-class family in southeast England. A welcome addition to wartime émigré memoir literature.

Toby Nobel Fluek *Memoirs of my Life in a Polish Village 1930–39* (Hamish Hamilton). Touching memoir of a young Jewish girl growing up in a village near Lwów in the 1930s. Plenty of insights into the tradional prewar Polish rural way of life, enhanced by the author's simple but evocative illustrations.

Barbara Porajska *From the Steppes to the Savannah* (Ham). Simply written yet informative memoir of one of the hundreds of Poles deported to Kazakhstan and other parts of Soviet Asia following the Soviet annexation to eastern Poland in 1939. Like many others, too, the author finally made it to Britain, via adventures in Iran and East Africa.

Hans Magnus Enzensberger *Europe, Europe* (Picador/Pantheon). A tour de force from the German anarchist, delving outside the mainstream to answer the question "What is Europe?". The section on Poland is a wonderfully observant roam around the main cities in 1986.

Lynne Jones *States of Change – A Central European Diary* (Merlin, UK). Highly personal account, wandering mainly through Poland and paying special attention to the alternative scene of punks, greens, anarchists, peaceniks, etc.

Granta 30: New Europe! (Penguin, UK). Published at the beginning of 1990, this state-of-the-continent anthology includes Neil Ascherson on the eastern Polish borderlands and a series of brief reactions to events from a dozen or so European intellectuals.

Czesław Miłosz *The Captive Mind* (Penguin/Random). Penetrating analysis of the reasons so many Polish artists and intellectuals sold out to communism after 1945, with four case-studies supplementing a confession of personal guilt. Also *Native Realm* (Penguin/University of California Press). An unorthodox autobiography of the years before Miłosz defected to the West; especially illuminating on the Polish–Lithuanian relationship.

Ryszard Kapuscíński *The Soccer War* (Granta, UK). For many years Kapuscíński was the only full-time Polish foreign correspondent, and he's best known for his trilogy on the dictators of Iran, Angola and Ethiopia. His latest book, a collection of sketches of Third World politics, offers many wry insights into his native land.

CULTURE, ART AND ARCHITECTURE

Jan Kott (ed.) *Four Decades of Polish Essays* (Northwestern University Press). Culture-based anthology – on art, literature, drama, plus politics – that features most of the major intellectual names of postwar Poland.

The Polish Jewry: History and Culture (Interpress, Warsaw). Wide-ranging collection of essays and photographs on all aspects of culture – from customs and family life to theatre, music and painting. A beautiful production.

David Buxton *The Wooden Churches of Eastern Europe* (CUP). Wonderful illustrations of Poland's most compelling architectural style. Well worth hunting out in libraries: it will make you want to traipse around Silesia, the Bieszczady Mountains and Czech borderlands.

Polish Realities *The Arts in Poland 1908–89* (Third Eye Centre, Glasgow). Excellent anthology of essays on all aspects of cultural life in Poland in the 1980s – architecture and youth culture alongside the obvious pieces on film, literature and theatre – which accompanied a major season of events in Glasgow under the same title. A testimony to the city's special links with Poland.

Roman Vishniac *Polish Jews – A Pictorial Record* (Schocken Books). Haunting selection of pictures by the legendary photographer, evoking Jewish life in the *shtetls* and ghettoes of Poland

immediately before the outbreak of World War II. A good introduction to the great man's work if you can't get hold of *A Vanished World* (Penguin, o/p), the acclaimed album that brings together most of the 2000 or so photos from Vishniac's travels through Jewish Poland.

Tomasz Wisniewski *Synagogues and Jewish Communities in the Białystok Region: Jewish Life in Eastern Europe before 1939* (David). Encyclopaedic survey of the wealth of pre-Jewish architecture in the eastern borderlands, much of it destroyed but with a significant number of buildings still surviving. Only available in Poland so far – a useful companion to any trip through the region.

Les Icones de Pologne (Editions de Cerf/ Arkadia, o/p). Good reproductions of most of the major icons from Poland's regional museums. Scour the *antiquariats* of the big cities for a copy.

Huit Siecles d'Eglises Polonaises: le Cas du Ermland (Romain Pages Editions). Beautifully photographed French album of the distinctive church architecture of the Warmia region of northeast Poland, including useful background text. An English-language edition is supposed to be due out soon, which you should be able to pick in the area.

Reise nach Masuren (Rautenberg Verlage). One of the large series of photo albums based on East Prussian memorabilia, produced by the German Rautenberg publishing house. Despite some dubious *alte Heimat* politics that occasionally steer dangerously close to straightforward revanchism, these volumes are nevertheless infused with a clear love of the old East Prussian territories, and the photographs of the region are some of the best around.

POLISH FICTION

Joseph Conrad *A Personal Record* (with *The Mirror of the Sea*, OUP). An entertaining, ironic piece of "faction" about Conrad's family and his early life in the Russian part of Partition Poland, addressing the painful subjects of his loss of his own country and language.

Tadeusz Konwicki *A Minor Apocalypse* (Faber/Random); *A Dreambook for our Time* (Penguin, o/p); *The Polish Complex* (Farrar, Strauss & Giroux). A convinced Party member in the Fifties, Konwicki eventually made the break with Stalinism; since then a series of highly respected novels, films and screenplays have established him as one of Poland's foremost writers. Describing a single day's events, *A Minor Apocalypse* is narrated by a character who constantly vacillates over his promise to set fire to himself in front of the Party headquarters. *Dreambook* is a hard-hitting wartime tale, while *The Polish Complex* is a fascinating, often elusive exploration of contemporary life in Poland. Like Miłosz and many others who grew up in Wilno, now the capital of Lithuania, Konwicki betrays a yearning for a mystic homeland.

Czeslaw Miłosz *The Seizure of Power* (Faber/Farrar, Strauss & Giroux); *The Issa Valley* (Carcanet). *The Seizure of Power*, the first book by this Nobel Prize-winning writer, is a wartime novel, while the semi-autobiographical *Issa Valley* is a wonderfully lyrical account of a boy growing up in the Lithuanian countryside.

Jerzy Andrzejewski *Ashes and Diamonds*(o/ p in UK/Northwestern). Spring 1945: resistance fighters, communist ideologues and black marketeers battle it out in small-town Poland. A gripping account of the tensions and forces that shaped postwar Poland, and the basis for Andrzej Wajda's film of the same title.

Tadeusz Borowski *This Way for the Gas, Ladies and Gentlemen* (Penguin). These short stories based on his Auschwitz experiences marked Borowski out as the great literary hope of communist Poland, but he committed suicide soon after their publication, at the age of 29.

Ida Fink *A Scrap of Time* (Penguin/Schocken). Haunting vignettes of Jews striving to escape the concentration camps – and of the unsung Polish Gentiles who sheltered them.

Stanisław Ignacy Witkiewicz *Insatiability* (Quartet/Salem House). Explicit depiction of artistic, intellectual, religious and sexual decadence against the background of a Chinese invasion of Europe. The enormous vocabulary, complicated syntax and philosophical diversions don't make an easy read, but this is unquestionably one of the most distinctive works of twentieth-century literature.

Witold Gombrowicz *Ferdydurke* (Penguin); *Pornografia* (Penguin); *The Possessed* (Boyars). The first two experimentalist novels concentrate on humanity's infantile and juvenile obsessions, and on the tensions between urban life and the traditional ways of the countryside. *The Possessed* explores the same themes within the more easily digestible format of a gothic thriller.

Pawel Huelle *Who Was David Weiser?* (Bloomsbury). Well-translated first novel by a young Gdańsk-born writer, centring on an enigmatic young Jewish boy idolised by his youthful contemporaries: author's themes and style show an obvious debt to fellow Danziger Günter Grass.

Janusz Korczak *King Matty the First* (Hippocrene). Written by the famous Jewish doctor who died, along with his orphans, at Treblinka, this long children's novel, regarded as the Polish counterpart of *Alice in Wonderland*, appeals also to adults through its underlying sense of tragedy and gravitas.

Wiesław Myśliwski *The Palace* (Peter Owen). Imaginative novel by controversial (i.e. former Party-linked) peasant-born writer: shepherd discovers secrets of abandoned aristocrats' palace as World War II closes in.

Isaac Bashevis Singer *The Magician of Lublin* (Penguin/Fawcett); *The Family Moskat* (Penguin/Farrar, Strauss & Giroux); *Collected Stories* (Penguin/Farrar, Strauss & Giroux); *The Slave* (Penguin/Avon); *Satan in Goray* (Penguin/ Fawcett); *The King of the Fields* (Penguin/Nal Dutton). Singer, who emigrated from Poland to the USA in the 1930s, writes in Yiddish, so his reputation rests largely on the translations of his novels and short stories. Only a selection of his vast output is mentioned here. *The Magician of Lublin* and *The Family Moskat*, both novels set in the ghettoes of early twentieth-century Poland, are masterly evocations of life in vanished Jewish communities. *The Slave* is a gentle yet tragic love story set in the seventeenth century, while *Satan in Goray* is a blazing evocation of religious hysteria in the same period. His penultimate work, *The King of the Fields*, re-creates the early life of the Polish state, and is his only novel without a Jewish emphasis.

Israel Joshua Singer *The Brothers Ashkenazi* (o/p in UK Carroll & Graf,). In contrast to his younger brother, I.J. Singer was a non-believer and was happiest writing in the grand manner, as in this epic of the rise and fall of a Jewish family in Łódź..

Shmuel Yozef Agnon *A Simple Story* (Schocken); *Dwelling Place of My People* (Scottish Academic Press). Agnon, Polish-born Nobel Prize-winner and father-figure of modern Hebrew literature, sets *A Simple Story* in the Jewish communities of the Polish Ukraine, belying its title by weaving an unexpected variation on the traditional Romeo-and-Juliet-type tale of crossed lovers. In *Dwelling Place* he recalls his childhood in Poland, in a series of highly refined stories and prose poems.

Asher Barash *Pictures from a Brewery* (Peter Owen). Depiction of Jewish life in Galicia, told in a style very different from the mythic, romantic approached favoured by Agnon.

Jan Potocki *Tales from the Saragossa Manuscript: Ten Days in the Life of Alphonse von Worden* (Dedalus/Hippocrene). A self-contained section of a huge unfinished Gothic novel written at the beginning of the nineteenth century by a Polish nobleman: a rich brew of picaresque adventures, dreams, hallucinations, eroticism, philosophical discourses and exotic tales.

Henryk Sienkiewicz *Quo Vadis?* (Alan Sutton/Hippocrene); *Charcoal Sketches and Other Tales* (Angel/Dufour); *With Fire and Sword*; *The Deluge*; and *Fire in the Steppe* (all Copernicus/Hippocrene). Sienkiewicz's reputation outside Poland largely rests on *Quo Vadis?* (which won him the Nobel Prize), treating the early Christians in Nero's Rome as an allegory of Poland's plight under the Partitions. Until recently, Sienkiewicz's other blockbusters existed only in inadequate and long out-of-print translations, but the Polish-American novelist W.S. Kuniczak has recently rendered the great trilogy about Poland's seventeenth-century wars with the Swedes, Prussians, Germans and Turks into English in a manner which at last does justice to the richly crafted prose of the originals. If the sheer size of these is too daunting, a more than adequate taste of the author's style can be had from the three novellas in the *Charcoal Sketches* collection, which focus on the different classes of nineteenth-century Polish rural society with a wry wit and a sense of pathos.

Władysław Reymont *The Peasants*; *The Promised Land* (both o/p). Reymont won the Nobel Prize for *The Peasants*, a tetralogy about

village life (one for each season of the year), but its vast length has led to its neglect outside Poland. *The Promised Land*, which was filmed by Wajda, offers a comparably unromanticised view of industrial life in Łódź.

Andrzej Szczypiorski *The Beautiful Mrs Seidemann* (Abacus). Best-selling novel by prominent contemporary Polish writer who survived both the Warsaw Uprising and subsequently the concentration camps. The story centres around a Jewish woman who uses her wits – and beauty – to survive the Nazis. Stirringly written, though the fatalistic historical musings (he's obviously got a foreign audience in mind) become increasingly oppressive as the book progresses.

Bruno Schulz *Street of Crocodiles* & *Sanitorium under the Sign of the Hourglass* (Picador/Viking Penguin). These kaleidoscopic, dream-like fictions, vividly evoking life in the small town of Drohobycz in the Polish Ukraine, constitute the entire literary output of their author, who was murdered by the SS.

Marek Hłasko *The Eighth Day of the Week*; *Killing the Second Dog* (single Minerva paperback in UK; Greenwood Press and Cane Hill Press respectively); *Next Stop – Paradise & the Graveyard* (Heinemann). Poland's "Angry Young Man", Hłasko articulated the general disaffection of those who grew up after World War II, his bleak themes mirrored in a spare, taut prose style.

Aleksander Wat *Lucifer Unemployed* (Northwestern University Press). Comic reversals of religion, politics and culture by Poland's leading Futurist: an attempted revolution in England peters out into a football match; a Jew becomes pope; the Devil comes to terms with unemployment in the face of Europe-wide depravity. Slightly dated, but still hilarious.

Stanisław Lem *Return from the Stars*; *Tales of Pirx the Pilot*; *His Master's Voice* (Mandarin/ Harcourt Brace). The only recent Polish writing to have achieved a worldwide mass-market readership, Lem's science fiction focuses on the human and social predicament in the light of technological change.

Janusz Anderman *Poland Under Black Light* (Readers International, US); *The Edge of the World* (Readers International, US). Stark, highly cinematic stories and sketches of life in Poland under martial law, with more than a dash of black humour in the second collection.

Henia Karmel-Wolfe *The Baders of Jacob Street* (Lippincott, o/p). Kraków-set tale of the impact of Nazi occupation on a Jewish family.

Adam Gillon (ed.) *Introduction to Modern Polish Literature* (Orbis/Hippocrene). An excellent anthology of short stories and extracts from novels, many of them (eg Reymont's *The Peasants*) out of print in English.

Bolesław Prus *"Pharaoh"* (Polonia). This late nineteenth-century epic, set in ancient Egypt, offers a trenchant examination of the nature of power in a society which was of more than passing relevance to Partition-era Poland.

POLISH POETRY

Adam Mickiewicz *Pan Tadeusz* (Everyman, o/p; parallel text published by the Polish Cultural Foundation/Hippocrene); *Konrad Wallenrod & Grażyna* (University Press of America). Poland's national epic, set among the gentry of Lithuania at the time of the Napoleonic invasion, is here given a highly effective verse translation. In contrast to the self-delusion about Polish independence shown by the characters in *Pan Tadeusz*, *Konrad Wallenrod* demonstrates how that end can be achieved by stealth and cunning; like *Grażyna*, its setting is Poland-Lithuania's struggle with the Teutonic Knights.

Karol Wojtyła *Easter Vigil and Other Poems* (Hutchinson/Random, o/p). Pope John Paul II followed a sideline career in poetry throughout his priesthood. This selection casts light on the complex private personality of a very public figure.

Tadeusz Różewicz *Conversations with the Prince* (Anvil Press, UK). These uncompromising verses, rooted in everyday speech, are among the most accessible examples of modern Polish poetry.

Anna Swir *Fat Like the Sun* (Women's Press). Selection from a leading feminist poet.

Adam Zagajewski *Tremor* (o/p in UK/Farrar, Strauss & Giroux). The early poems here belong to the "angry generation" of 1968; the later, more metaphysical work sometimes focuses on the poet's native city of Lwów.

Czesław Miłosz *Collected Poems* (Penguin/Ecco Press). A writer of massive integrity,

Miłosz in all his works wrestles with the issues of spiritual and political commitment; this collection encompasses all his poetic phases, from the surrealist of the 1930s to the émigré sage of San Francisco.

Zbigniew Herbert *Selected Poems* (Carcanet/Ecco Press); *Report from the Besieged City* (OUP/Ecco Press). Another fine contemporary poet, with a strong line in poignant observation; intensely political but never dogmatic.

Czesław Miłosz (ed) *Polish Postwar Poetry* (University of California Press). Useful anthology selected and mostly translated by Miłosz, with an emphasis on poetry written after the thaw of 1956. The closer you get to the 1980s the grittier and more acerbic they become, as befits the politics of the era.

Adam Czerniawski (ed) *The Burning Forest* (Bloodaxe/Dufour). Selected by one of Poland's leading contemporary poets, this anthology covers Polish poetry from the laconic nineteenth-century verses of Cyprian Norwid, through examples of Herbert, Różewicz and the editor, up to young writers of the present day.

Susan Bassnett and Piotr Kuhiwczak (eds) *Ariadne's Thread: Polish Women Poets* (Forest Books/Three Continents). Poems by eight distinctive contemporaries, ranging from re-interpretations of classical myth to the horrors of torture.

S. Barańczak & C. Cavanagh (eds) *Spoiling Cannibal's Fun: Polish Poetry of the Last Two Decades of Communist Rule* (Northwestern University Press). Representative anthology of recent Polish poetry with informative introductory essay by co-editor and translator Stanisław Barańczak, one of the country's pre-eminent émigré literary figures whose poems are also featured in this volume.

Wisława Szymborska *People on the Bridge* (Forest). Recent volume of poems by one of the country's most distinctive modern (female) voices, translated by fellow poet, Adam Czerniawski.

Aleksander Wat *Selected Poems* (Penguin). Dating from Wat's middle and later years, these wide-ranging poems, with their predominant tone of despair at the century's excesses, make a fascinating contrast to the Futurist short-story fantasies he wrote in the interwar period.

POLISH DRAMA

Juliusz Słowacki *Mary Stuart* (Greenwood Press). Słowacki ranks second only to Mickiewicz in Polish esteem, but his reputation hasn't travelled. Nonetheless, this is a fine example of Romantic drama, set against the backdrop of the murders of David Rizzio and Mary's husband, Henry Darnley.

Stanisław Ignacy Witkiewicz *The Madman and the Nun, The Water Hen & The Crazy Locomotive* (Applause, UK). Witkiewicz created a Theatre of the Absurd twenty years before the term came into common use through the work of Ionesco and Beckett. This volume makes the ideal introduction to the versatile avant-garde painter, novelist and playwright.

Witold Gombrowicz *The Marriage; Operetta; Princess Ivona* (all Boyars/Northwestern University Press). Three plays exploring similar themes to those found in Gombrowicz's novels.

Sławomir Mrożek *Tango* (Cape, o/p); *Vatzlav* (Applause/Grove Weidenfeld); *Striptease, Repeat Performance & The Prophets* (Applause, UK). Mrożek is the sharpest and subtlest satirist Poland has produced, employing nonsensical situations to probe serious political issues.

Tadeusz Różewicz *The Card Index, The Interrupted Act & Gone Out; Marriage Blanc & The Hunger Artist Departs* (all Boyars). The best works by an unremittingly inventive experimentalist.

Tadeusz Kantor *Wielopole/Wielopole* (Boyars). One of the most successful products of Poland's experimental theatre scene, complete with a lavish record of its production plus the author/director's rehearsal notes.

Solomon Anski *The Dybbuk* (in *Three Great Jewish Plays*, Applause). Written by a prominent member of the Jewish socialist movement, this drama of divine justice is the masterpiece of Yiddish theatre. Also included in the anthology is a work on a similar theme, *God of Vengeance* by Scholem Asch.

LITERATURE BY FOREIGN WRITERS

E. T. A. Hoffmann *The Jesuit Chapel at G___* (in *Six German Romantic Tales*, Angel, UK); *The Artushof* (in *Tales of Hoffmann*, Penguin). Hoffmann began writing his masterly stories of the macabre while a bored civil servant in Prussian Poland; these are two with a specifically Polish setting.

Gerhart Hauptmann *The Weavers* (Eyre Methuen/Ungar). Set against the background of an heroic but inevitably futile mid-nineteenth-century uprising by the Silesian weavers against the mill owners, this intense drama gained its reputation as the first "socialist" play by having a collective rather than a single protagonist.

Isaac Babel *Red Cavalry* (in *Collected Stories*, Penguin/NAL Dutton). A collection of interrelated short stories about the 1919–20 invasion of Poland, narrated by the bizarrely contradictory figure of a Jewish Cossack communist, who naturally finds himself torn by conflicting emotions.

John Hersey *The Wall* (Random House, US). Tale of Jewish resistance to the Nazis.

Günter Grass *The Tin Drum* (Picador/Random); *Dog Years* (Picador/Harcourt Brace); *Cat and Mouse* (Picador/Ameron). These three novels, known as the "Danzig Trilogy", are one of the highpoints of modern German literature. Set in Danzig/Gdańsk, where the author grew up, they hold up a mirror to the changing German character this century. His latest novel, *The Call of the Toad* (Secker & Warburg/HBJ), provides a satirical commentary on post-communist Polish and German attitudes towards the same city's past.

Leon Uris *Mila 18* (Corgi /Bantam). Stirring tale of the Warsaw Ghetto Uprising – Mila 18 was the address of the Jewish resistance militia's HQ.

James Michener *Poland* (Corgi/Fawcett). Another of Michener's blockbusters, larded with highly symbolic peasants and aristocrats. Characterisation is wooden and schematic, but a lot of research went into it, and it's no bad introduction to the intricacies of Polish history.

Thomas Keneally *Schindler's Ark* (Coronet/ Viking Penguin). Based on the life of Oskar Schindler, a German industrialist who used his business operations to shelter thousands of Jews, this powerful novel – the subject of an upcoming Spielberg film – won the 1982 Booker Prize.

Piers Paul Read *Polonaise* (Alison/Avon). Aristocratic family saga, set partly in Poland.

Brian Moore *The Colour of Blood* (Paladin NAL Dutton). Superb thriller of ecclesiastical and state manoeuvrings, set in unnamed Poland in the early 1980s.

John Simpson *A Fine and Private Place* (Robson/St Martin). A Kraków location and oddments of history and politics add spice to this espionage thriller by the BBC's former eastern European correspondent.

FILM

Brian McIlroy *World Cinema: Poland* (Flicks Books/H. Holt). In-depth study of the contemporary film scene including interviews, biographies and plenty of black and white stills.

Andrzej Wajda *Double Vision: My Life in Film* (Faber, UK). Autobiography of Poland's most famous director; rather more rewarding than some of his recent celluloid creations.

Krzysztof Kieślowski and Krysztof Piesiewicz *Decalogue* (Faber, UK). Transcripts of the internationally acclaimed series of fims, set in a Warsaw housing estate, featuring tales of breaches of the Ten Commandments.

MAGAZINES AND PERIODICALS

There's a wide range of specialist publications relating both to Poland and to east-central Europe generally. One of the most useful is *East European Reporter*, a bi-monthly journal (£5 an issue) which regularly carries useful in-depth coverage of current political and social developments, including translations of articles by journalists, politicians and other analysts from within the region. Similarly useful for background material is the *RFE/RFL Report*, published by the US government-financed Radio Free Europe based in Munich. Despite the original Cold Warrior profile, this is actually one of the most valuable current sources of information on developments in the region. *East European Reporter* can be obtained through academic bookshops or at those specialising in eastern Europe whereas *RFE/RFL Report* is available in many university libraries, or on subscription (a hefty 270DM yearly; 150DM for students) — libraries can provide details.

LANGUAGE

Polish is one of the more difficult European languages for English speakers to learn. Even so, it is well worth acquiring the basics: not only is Polish beautiful and melodious, but a few words will go a long way. This is especially true away from the major cities where you won't find a lot of English spoken. (Knowledge of German, however, is quite widespread.)

The following features provide an indication of the problems of Polish grammar. There are three genders (masculine, feminine and neuter) and no word for "the". Prepositions (words like "to", "with", "in" etc) take different cases, and the case changes the form of the noun. Thus, "miasto" is the Polish for "town", but "to the town" is "do miasta" and "in the town" is "w mieście". You don't have to learn this sort of thing off by heart, but it can be useful to be able to recognise it.

Such grammatical complexity is a product of Polish history. During the periods when Poland didn't even exist as a nation, Polish was taught as virtually a foreign language, and the teachers were determined that nothing should be lost. Hence the "conservative" retention of so many archaic features.

Finally, a brief word on how to address people. The familiar form used among friends, relations and young people is "ty", like French "tu" or German "du". However, the polite form which you will usually require is "Pan" when addressing a man and "Pani" for a woman (literally "Sir" and "Madam"). ALWAYS use this form with people obviously older than yourself, and with officials.

PRONUNCIATION

While Polish may look daunting at first, with its apparently unrelieved rows of consonants, the good news is that it's a phonetic language – ie it's pronounced exactly as spelt. So once you've learnt the rules and have a little experience you'll always know how to pronounce a word correctly.

Stress:

Usually on the penultimate syllable, eg Warszawa, przyjaciel, matka

Vowels:

a: as "u" in "run".
e: "e" in "neck".
i: "i" in "Mick", never as in "I".
o: "o" in "lot", never as in "no" or "move".
u: "oo" in "look".
y: unknown in Standard English; cross between "e" and Polish "i", eg the "y" in the Yorkshire pronunciation of "Billy".

Three **specifically Polish** vowels:
ą: nasalised – like "ong" in "long" or French "on".
ę: nasalised – like French "un" (eg Lech Wałęsa).
ó: same sound as Polish "u".

Vowel combinations:

ie: pronounced y-e, eg "nie wiem" (I don't know): ny-e vy-em (not nee-veem).
eu: each letter pronounced separately as above, eg "E-u-ropa" (Europe).
ia: rather like "yah", eg "historia" (history): histor-i-yah.

Consonants

Those which look the same as English but are different:
w: as "v" in "vine", eg "wino" pronounced "vino" (wine).
r: trilled (as in Scottish pronunciation of English r).
h: like the "ch" in Scottish "loch".
Some consonants are pronounced differently at **the end of a word** or syllable: b sounds like p, d like t, g like k, w like f.

Specifically Polish consonants:

ć = ci: "ch" as in "church".
ł: "dark l" sounding rather like a "w".

ń = ni: "soft n", sounding like "n-ye", eg "koń" (horse): kon-ye.

ś = si: "sh" as in "ship".

ź = zi: like the "j" of French "journal".

ż = rz: as in French "g" in "gendarme". (Note that the dot over the z is sometimes replaced by a bar through the letter's diagonal.)

Consonantal Pairs

cz: "ch" (slightly harder than "ć" and "ci").

sz: "sh" (ditto "ś", "si").

dz: "d" as in "day" rapidly followed by "z" as in "zoo", eg "dzwon" (bell): d-zvon. At the end of a word is pronounced like "ts" as in "cats".

dż: "d-sh", eg "dżungla" (jungle): d-shun-gla.

dź: sharper than the above; at the end of a word is pronounced like "ć" (ch).

szcz: this fearsome-looking cluster is easy to pronounce – "sh-ch" as in "pushchair", eg "szczur" (rat): sh-choor.

A POLISH LANGUAGE GUIDE

BASIC WORDS

Tak	Yes	Teraz	Now	Więcej	More
Nie	No/not	Później	Later	Mniej	Less
Proszę	Please/you're welcome	Otwarty	Open	Mało	A little
		Zamknięty	Closed/shut	Duzo	A lot
Proszę bardzo	More emphatic than "proszę"	Wcześniej	Earlier	Tani	Cheap
		Dosyć	Enough	Drogi	Expensive
Dziekuję, dziekuję bardzo	Thank you	Tam	Over there	Dobry	Good
		Ten/ta/to	This one (masc/ fem/neuter)	Zły/niedobry	Bad
Gdzie	Where			Gorący	Hot
Kiedy	When	Tamten/	That one	Zimny	Cold
Dlaczego	Why	tamta/tamto		Z	With
Ile	How much	Wielki	Large	Bez	Without
Tu; tam	Here; there	Mały	Small	W	In
				Dla	For

BASIC PHRASES

Dzień dobry	Good day; hello	Co to znaczy po polsku?	What's the Polish for that?
Dobry wieczór	Good evening		
Dobra noc	Good night	Jestem tu na urlopie	I'm here on holiday
Cześć!	"Hi!" or "'Bye" (like Italian "ciao")	Jestem Brytyjczykiem/ Brytyjka	I'm British (male/ female)
Do widzenia	Goodbye	Irlandczykiem/Irlandką	Irish
Przepraszam	Excuse me (apology)	Mieszkam w . . .	I live in . . .
Proszę Pana/Pani	(ditto) requesting information	Dzisiaj	Today
		Jutro	Tomorrow
Jak się masz?	How are you? (informal)	Pojutrze	Day after tomorrow
Jak się Pan/Pani ma?	(ditto: formal male/female)	Wczoraj	Yesterday
		Chwileczkę	Moment! Wait a moment
Dobrze	Fine		
Czy Pan/Pani mówi po angielsku?	Do you speak English?	Rano	In the morning
		Po południu	In the afternoon
Rozumiem	I understand	Wieczorem	In the evening
Nie rozumiem	I don't understand	Gdzie jest . . .	Where is . . . ?
Nie wiem	I don't know	Jak dojechać do . . . ?	How do I get to . . . ?
Proszę mówić trochę wolniej	Please speak a bit more slowly	Która (jest) godzina?	What time is it?
		Jak daleko jest do . . . ?	How far is it to . . . ?
Nie mówię dobrze po polsku	I don't speak Polish very well		

ACCOMMODATION

Hotel	Hotel	*To drogo*	That's expensive
Noclegi	Lodgings	*To za drogo*	That's too expensive
Czy jest gdzieś tutaj hotel?	Is there a hotel nearby?	*Czy to obejmuje śniadanie?*	Does that include breakfast?
Czy Pan/Pani ma pokój?	Do you have a room?	*Czy nie ma tańszego?*	Do you have anything cheaper?
Pojedynczy pokój	Single room		
Podwójny pokój	Double room	*Czy mogę zobaczyć pokój?*	Can I see the room?
Będziemy jedną dobę	For one night (doba: 24 hours)	*Dobrze, wezmę*	Good, I'll take it
Dwie noce	Two nights	*Mam rezerwację*	I have a booking
Trzy noce	Three nights	*Czy możemy tu rozbić namioddy?*	Can we camp here?
Tydzień	A week		
Dwa tygodnie	Two weeks	*Czy jest gdzieś tutaj camping?*	Is there a campsite nearby?
Pokój z łazienką	With a bath		
Z prysznicem	With a shower	*Namiot*	Tent
Z balkonem	With a balcony	*Schronisko*	Cabin
Z ciepłą wodą	Hot water	*Schronisko młodziezowe*	Youth hostel
Z bieżącą wodą	Running water	*Proszę o jadłospis*	The menu, please
Ile kosztuje?	How much is it?	*Proszę o rachunek*	The bill, please

TRAVELLING

Auto	Car	*W jedną stroną*	Single
Samolot	Aircraft	*Proszę z miejscówką*	I'd like a seat reservation
Rower	Bicycle	*Kiedy odjeżdża pociąg do Warszawy?*	When does the Warsaw train leave?
Autobus	Bus		
Prom	Ferry	*Czy muszę się przesiadać?*	Do I have to change?
Pociąg	Train		
Dworzec, samochód, stacja	Train station	*Z jakiego peronu odjedzie pociąg?*	Which platform does the train leave from?
Autobusowy	Bus station	*Ile to jest kilometrów?*	How many kilometres is it?
Taksówka	Taxi	*Ile czasu trwa podróż?*	How long does the journey last?
Autostop	Hitchhiking		
Piechotą	On foot	*Jakim autobusem do . . ?*	Which bus is it to . . . ?
Prosze bilet do . . .	A ticket to . . . , please	*Gdzie jest droga do . . . ?*	Where is the road to . . . ?
Bilet powrotny	Return	*Następny przystanek, proszę*	Next stop, please

SOME SIGNS

Wejście; wyjście	Entrance; exit/way out	*Peron*	Platform
Wstęp wzbroniony	No entrance	*Kasa*	Cash desk
Toaleta	Toilet	*Stop*	Stop
Dla panów; męski	Men	*Granica międzynarodowa*	Polish state frontier
Dla pan; damski	Women	*Rzeczpospolita Polska*	Republic of Poland
Zajęty	Occupied	*Uwaga; baczność*	Beware, caution
Wolny	Free, vacant	*Uwaga; niebezpieczeństwo*	Danger
Przyjazd; odjazd	Arrival; departure (train, bus)	*Policja (formerly: milicja)*	Police
Przylot; odlot	(ditto for aircraft)	*Informacja*	Information
Remont	Closed for renovation/ stocktaking	*Nie palić; palenie wzbronione*	No smoking
Ciągnąć; pchać	Pull; push	*Nie dotykać*	Do not touch
Nieczynny	Out of order; closed (ticket counters, etc)		

DRIVING

Samochód, auto	Car	*Benzyna*	Petrol/gas
Na lewo	Left	*Stacja benzynowa*	Petrol/gas station
Na prawo	Right	*Olej*	Oil
Prosto	Straight ahead	*Woda*	Water
Parking	Parking	*Naprawić*	To repair
Objazd	Detour	*Wypadek*	Accident
Koniec	End (showing when a previous sign ceases to be valid)	*Awaria*	Breakdown
		Ograniczenie prędkości	Speed limit
Zakaz wyprzedzania	No overtaking		

DAYS, MONTHS AND DATES

Poniedziałek	Monday	*Kwiecień*	April	*Poniedziałek, pierwzy*	Monday, 1st
Wtorek	Tuesday	*Maj*	May	*Kwiecień*	April
Środa	Wednesday	*Czerwiec*	June	*. . . drugi Kwiecień*	. . . 2nd April
Czwartek	Thursday	*Lipiec*	July	*. . . trzeci Kwiecień*	. . . 3rd April
Piątek	Friday	*Sierpień*	August	*Wiosna*	spring
Sobota	Saturday	*Wrzesien*	September	*Lato*	summer
Niedziela	Sunday	*Październik*	October	*Jesień*	autumn
Styczeń	January	*Listopad*	November	*Zima*	winter
Luty	February	*Grudzień*	December	*Wakacje*	holidays
Marzec	March			*Święto*	bank holiday

NUMBERS

Polish	Num	Polish	Num	Polish	Num	Polish	Num
Jeden	1	*Jedenaście*	11	*Trzydzieści*	30	*Czterysta*	400
Dwa	2	*Dwanaście*	12	*Czterdzieści*	40	*Pięćset*	500
Trzy	3	*Trzynaście*	13	*Pięćdziesiąt*	50	*Sześćset*	600
Cztery	4	*Czternaście*	14	*Sześćdziesiąt*	60	*Siedemset*	700
Pięć	5	*Piętaście*	15	*Siedemdziesiąt*	70	*Osiemset*	800
Sześć	6	*Szesnaście*	16	*Osiemdziesiąt*	80	*Dziewięćset*	900
Siedem	7	*Siedemnaście*	17	*Dziewięćdziesiąt*	90	*Tysiąc*	1 000
Osiem	8	*Osiemnaście*	18	*Sto*	100	*Milion*	1 000 000
Dziewięć	9	*Dziewietnaście*	19	*Dwieście*	200		
Dziesięć	10	*Dwadzieścia*	20	*Trzysta*	300		

Polish	Num
Dwadzieścia pięć	25
Sześćset dziewięćdziesiąt cztery	694
Trzy tysiące dwieściesiedemdziesiąt osiem	3278

GLOSSARIES

GENERAL TERMS

ALEJA Avenue (abbreviation al.).

BESKIDY Range of hills, eg Beskid Niski.

BIURO ZAKWATEROWANIA Accommodation office.

BRAMA Gate.

CERKIEW (pl. CERKWIE) Orthodox church, or a church belonging to the Uniates, a church loyal to Rome but following Orthodox rites.

CMENTARZ Cemetery.

DOLINA Valley.

DOM House.

DOM KULTURY Community arts and social centre, literally a "Cultural House".

DOM WYCIECZKOWY Cheap, basic type of hotel.

DROGA Road.

DWORZEC Station.

GŁÓWNY Main – as in Rynek Główny, main square.

GÓRA (pl. GÓRY) Mountain.

GRANICA Border.

JEZIORO Lake.

KANTOR Exchange office.

KAPLICA Chapel.

KAWIARNIA Café.

KATEDRA Cathedral.

KLASZTOR Monastery.

KOŚCIÓŁ Church.

KSIĄDZ Priest.

KSIĄŻĘ Prince, duke.

KSIĘGARNIA Bookshop.

KRAJ Country.

LAS Wood, forest.

MASYW Massif.

MIASTO Town. (Stare Miasto – old town; Nowe Miasto – new town.)

MOST Bridge.

NARÓD Nation, people.

NYSA River Neisse.

ODRA River Oder.

OGRÓD Gardens.

PAŁAC Palace.

PIWNICA Pub.

PLAC Square.

PLAŻA Beach.

POCZTA Post office.

POGOTOWIE Emergency.

POKÓJ (pl. Pokóje) Room.

POLE Field.

PROM Ferry.

PRZEDMIEŚCIE Suburb.

PRZYSTANEK Bus stop.

PUSZCZA Ancient forest.

RATUSZ Town Hall.

RESTAURACJA Restaurant.

RUCH Kiosk.

RYNEK Marketplace, commonly the main square in a town.

RZEKA River.

SEJM Parliament.

SKAŁA Rock, cliff.

SKANSEN Open-air museum with reconstructed folk architecture and art.

STOCZNIA Shipyards.

ŚWIĘTY Saint (abbreviation św.).

STAROWIERCY (Old Believers) Traditionalist Russian Orthodox sect, small communities of which survive in east Poland.

STARY Old.

ULICA Street (abbeviation ul.).

WOJEWÓDZTWO Administrative district.

WIEŚ (pl. WSIE) Village.

WIEŻA Tower.

WINIARNIA Wine cellar.

WISŁA River Vistula.

WODOSPAD Waterfall.

WZGÓRZE Hill.

ZAMEK Castle.

ZDRÓJ Spa.

ZIEMIA Region.

ART/ARCHITECTURAL TERMS

AISLE Part of church to the side of the nave.

AMBULATORY Passage round the back of the altar, in continuation of the aisles.

APSE Vaulted termination of the altar end of a church.

BAROQUE Exuberant architectural style of the seventeenth and early eighteenth centuries, characterised by ornate decoration, complex spatial arrangement and grand vistas. The term is also applied to the sumptuous style of painting of the same period.

BASILICA Church in which nave is higher than the aisles.

BLACK MADONNA National icon, an image of the Virgin and Child housed in the Jasna Góra monastery in Częstochowa.

CAPITAL Top of a column, usually sculpted.

CHANCEL Section of the church where the altar is situated, usually the east end.

CHOIR Part of church in which service is sung, usually beside the altar.

CRYPT Underground part of a church.

FRESCO Mural painting applied to wet plaster, so that colours immediately soak into the wall.

GOTHIC Architectural style with an emphasis on verticality, characterised by pointed arch and ribbed vault: introduced to Poland in the thirteenth century, surviving in an increasingly decorative form until well into the sixteenth century. The term is also used of paintings and sculpture of the period.

HALL CHURCH Church design in which all vaults are of approximately equal height.

JUGENDSTIL German version (encountered in western Poland) of Art Nouveau, a sinuous, highly decorative style of architecture and design from the period 1900–15.

MANNERISM Deliberately over-sophisticated style of late Renaissance art and architecture.

MŁODA POLSKA (Young Poland) Turn-of-the-century cultural movement centred on Kraków.

NAVE Main body of the church, generally forming the western part.

NEOCLASSICAL Late eighteenth- and early nineteenth-century style of art and architecture returning to classical models as a reaction against Baroque and Rococo excesses.

RENAISSANCE Italian-originated movement in art and architecture, inspired by the rediscovery of classical ideals.

ROCOCO Highly florid, light and graceful style of architecture, painting and interior design, forming the last phase of Baroque.

ROMANESQUE Solid architectural style of the late tenth to mid-thirteenth centuries, characterised by round-headed arches and geometrical precision. The term is also used for paintings of the same period.

ROMANTICISM Late eighteenth- and nineteenth-century movement, rooted in adulation of natural world and rediscovery of the country's rich historic heritage, strongly linked in Poland to the cause of national independence.

SECESSIONIST Style of early twentieth-century art and architecture, based in Germany and Austria, which reacted against academic establishments.

STUCCO Plaster used for decorative effects.

TRANSEPT Arms of a cross-shaped church, placed at ninety degrees to nave and chancel.

TRANSITIONAL Architectural style between Romanesque and Gothic.

TRIPTYCH Carved or painted altarpiece on three panels.

TROMPE L'OEIL Painting designed to fool the onlooker into believing that it's actually three-dimensional.

HISTORICAL AND POLITICAL GLOSSARY

AUSTRO-HUNGARIAN EMPIRE Vast Habsburg-ruled domain incorporating most of Central Europe, enlarged to include Polish province of Galicia during the Partition period.

BALCEROWICZ, LESZEK Finance minister since the 1989 elections; responsible for introducing the current programme of radical, free market economic reform.

BIELICKI, JAN Solidarity adviser and young technocrat, based in Gdańsk; was prime minister from December 1990 to November 1991.

CENTRE AGREEMENT Political grouping formed by Lech Wałęsa in 1990, and subsequently estranged from him, critical of the supposedly slow pace of government reforms.

CHRISTIAN NATIONAL UNION (ZChN) Most important of the Catholic-based political parties formed in the early post-communist era.

CITIZENS MOVEMENT-DEMOCRATIC ACTION (ROAD) Coalition of intellectuals and former Solidarity activists formed to oppose Wałęsa's Centre Agreement. Key figures included the then Prime Minister Mazowiecki, Adam Michnik, Zbigniew Bujak and Bronisław Geremek. Became *Democratic Union* in 1991.

COMMONWEALTH Union of Poland, Lithuania, Royal Prussia and Livonia (Latvia); formed by Lublin Union (1569), it lasted until the Third Partition of 1795.

CONGRESS KINGDOM OF POLAND Russian-ruled province of Poland established in 1815, following the Congress of Vienna.

DEMOCRATIC UNION (UD) Currently one of the major political parties with strong support among former Solidarity intellectuals. Prime Minister Halina Suchocka is a member.

DUCAL PRUSSIA (East Prussia) The eastern half of the territory of the Teutonic Knights, converted into a secular duchy in 1525 and divided in 1945 between Poland and the Soviet Union.

GALICIA Southern province of Poland including Kraków incorporated into Austro-Hungarian Empire during the Partition period, granted autonomy in latter half of nineteenth century.

GEREMEK, BRONISŁAW Medieval historian at Warsaw University who acted as adviser to Wałęsa and the Solidarity movement. Elected leader of the Solidarity group in parliament after the June 1989 elections but resigned in November 1990.

GIEREK, EDWARD Leader of the Communist Party in the 1970s, until removed following the strikes of summer 1980.

HABSBURG The most powerful imperial family in medieval Germany, operating from a power base in Austria.

HANSEATIC LEAGUE Medieval trading alliance of Baltic and Rhineland cities, numbering about 100 at its fifteenth-century peak. Slowly died out in seventeenth century with competition from the Baltic nation-states and rise of Brandenburg-Prussia.

HOLY ROMAN EMPIRE Name of the loose confederation of German states (many now part of Poland) which lasted from 800 until 1806.

JAGIELLONIAN Dynasty of Lithuanian origin which ruled Poland-Lithuania from 1386 to 1572.

JARUZELSKI, WOJCIECH General of the armed forces, called in by the Party in 1981 to institute Martial Law and suppress Solidarity. His subsequent flexibility and negotiating skill helped to usher in democracy and he became president after the June 1989 elections, until the election of Wałęsa in December 1990.

KULTURKAMPF Campaign launched by German Chancellor Bismarck in the 1870s, aimed at suppressing Catholic culture (including the Polish language) inside German territories.

KUROŃ, JACEK Veteran opposition activist and key figure in Solidarity movement; served as minister of labour in the Mazowiecki government returning to the same position in the Suchocka administration.

LUSTRATION Vexed controversy during the Olszewski premiership surrounding the question of prominent politicians supposed to have collaborated with the communist-era security services.

MARTIAL LAW Military crackdown instigated by General Jaruzelski in December 1981 and remaining in effect until summer 1983.

MAZOWIECKI, TADEUSZ Catholic lawyer and journalist and longtime adviser to Solidarity. Country's first post-communist prime minister who ran unsuccessfully for president against Wałęsa in December 1990.

MICHNIK, ADAM Warsaw academic and leading Solidarity theoretician and activist. Currently chief editor of the independent daily *Gazeta Wyborcza*.

NAZI–SOVIET PACT (or MOLOTOV–RIBBENTROP PACT) 1939 agreement between Nazi Germany and the Soviet Union, which contained a secret clause to eliminate Poland from the map.

ODER-NEISSE LINE Western limit of Polish territory set by Yalta Agreement, 1945.

OLSZEWSKI, JAN Combative former dissident and lawyer who become prime minister at the end of 1991, his leadership floundering six months later (June 1992) over the **lustration** issue (see above).

PARTITION PERIOD Era from 1772 to 1918, during which Poland was on three occasions divided into Prussian, Russian and Austrian territories.

PIASTS Royal dynasty which forged the Polish state in the tenth century and ruled it until 1370; branches of the family continued to hold principalities, notably in Silesia, until 1675.

POLISH UNITED WORKERS PARTY (PZPR) Former communist party who disbanded themselves in January 1990, the majority forming a new Social Democratic Party.

POLONIANS Slav tribe which formed the embryonic Polish nation.

PRUSSIA Originally a Slavic Eastern Baltic territory, now divided between Poland and the Russian Federation. It was conquered by the

Teutonic Knights in the thirteenth century and acquired in 1525 by the Hohenzollerns, who merged it with their own German possessions to form Brandenburg-Prussia (later shortened to Prussia).

ROUND TABLE AGREEMENT Pathbreaking bi-partisan agreement between Jaruzelski's communist government and the Solidarity opposition in spring 1989, leading to the elections in June of that year.

ROYAL PRUSSIA (West Prussia) Territory centred on the Wisła delta, originally the easternmost sector of Pomerania, renamed after its capture from the Teutonic Knights in 1466.

RUTHENIA A loose grouping of principalities, part of which formed Poland's former Eastern Territories.

SOLIDARITY (Solidarność) The eastern bloc's first independent trade union, led by Lech Wałęsa, suppressed under martial law and relegalised in 1989, before forming the core of the new democratic government. Now irrevocably split into pro- and anti-Wałęsa factions.

SUCHOCKA, HALINA Lawyer from Poznań chosen as Poland's first ever woman prime minister in summer 1992. A popular, if somewhat aloof figure.

TARTARS Mongol tribe who invaded Poland in the thirteenth century, some settling subsequently.

TEUTONIC KNIGHTS Quasi-monastic German military order who conquered parts of the eastern Baltic, establishing their own independent state 1226–1525.

WAŁĘSA, LECH Shipyard electrician who led strikes in the Gdańsk shipyards in 1980, leading to the establishment of the independent trade union, Solidarity, of which he became chairman. In this role, he opposed the communist government throughout the 1980s, and led negotiations in the Round Table Agreement of 1989. Following the June 1989 elections, he parted company with many of his former Solidarity allies, forcing a presidential contest, which he won in December 1990. Awarded the Nobel Peace Prize in 1983.

WAZA (Vasa) Swedish royal dynasty which ruled Poland 1587–1668.

WORKERS' DEFENCE COMMITTEE (KOR) Oppositional group formed in the mid-1970s, regarded by many as a precursor to Solidarity.

YALTA AGREEMENT 1945 agreement between the victorious powers which established Poland's (and Europe's) postwar borders.

AN A–Z OF STREET NAMES

The stars from the pantheon of Polish communist iconography after whom many streets were named after World War II have now largely disappeared. Since the Solidarity election victory of 1989 a systematic renaming of streets has been carried out, though in classic Polish style it took local authorities a lot longer to agree on new names than in, say, neighbouring Czechoslovakia, the whole process being held up by interminable local infighting. It's not the first time such a process has occurred either: nineteenth-century Russian and German street names were replaced by Polish ones after World War I, which themselves came down following the Nazi wartime occupation. Many older streets have simply reverted to their prewar names, the new ones showing a marked preference for Catholic identification. Remember that street names always appear in their genitive or adjectival form, eg Franciscan Street is Franciszkańska, Piłsudski Street is Piłsudskiego and Mickiewicz Street Mickiewicza.

General Władysław Anders (1892–1970) Renowned military figure who led the Polish troops was exiled to Siberia at the start of World War II and later returned to fight on the Allied side in the Middle East, then in Europe.

Józef Bem (1794–1850) Swashbuckling military figure who participated in the 1848 "Springtime of the Nations" in both Austria and Hungary.

General Zygmunt Berling (1896–1980) First Commander-in-Chief of communist-sponsored Polish forces in the Soviet Union

Bohaterów Getta Literally "Heroes of the Ghetto", in memory of the April 1943 Warsaw Ghetto Uprising against the Nazis.

Władysław Broniewski (1897–1962) Early socialist adherent of Piłsudski's World War I Legions, revolutionary poet and famously unreformed drunkard.

Fryderyk Chopin (1810–49) (also sometimes spelt "Szopen" in Polish). Celebrated Romantic-era composer and pianist, long a national icon (see p.102).

Chrobrego Refers to Bolesław the Great, first king of Poland and the man who established the country as a definite independent state.

Maria Dąbrowska (1889–1965) Fine modern Polish writer best known for her epic novels.

Aleksander Fredro (1793–1876) Popular dramatist, especially of comedies.

Grunwald Landmark medieval battle (1410) where combined Polish-Lithuanian forces thrashed the Teutonic Knights.

Jan Kasprowicz (1860–1926) Popular peasant-born Neo-Romantic poet and voluminous translator of Western classics into Polish.

Jan Kochanowski (1530–84) Renaissance-era poet, the father of the modern Polish literary canon.

Maksymilian Kolbe (1894–1941) Catholic priest martyred in Auschwitz, canonised by Pope John Paul II.

Tadeusz Bór-Komorowski (1895–1966) Commander of AK (Home Army) forces during the 1944 Warsaw Uprising.

Maria Konopnicka (1842–1910) Children's story writer of the nineteenth century, adherent of the "Positivist" School which developed in reaction to the traditional national preference for Romanticism.

Mikołaj Kopernik (1473–1543) Indigenous name of the great astronomer known elsewhere as Copernicus, who spent much of his life in the Baltic town of Frombork.

Tadeusz Kościuszko. (1746–1817) Dashing veteran of the American War of Independence and leader of the 1794 Insurrection in Poland (see p.331).

Armii Krajowej (AK) The Home Army, forces of the wartime Polish Resistance.

Józef Ignacy Krasicki (1735–1801) Enlightenment-era poet-Bishop of Warmia, dubbed the "Polish Lafontaine".

Zygmunt Krasiński (1812–59) Author of *Nieboska Komedia*, one of the trio of Polish Romantic messianic greats.

Józef Kraszewski (1812–87) Hugely popular historical novelist. His novels (over 200 of them) cover everything from the early Piasts to the Partition era.

6 Kwietnia Battle of Racławice (1794) where Kościuszko's largely peasant army defeated the Czarist forces.

11 Listopada (11 November) Symbolically important post-World War I Polish Independence Day.

29 Listopada Start of (failed) November 1830 Uprising against the Russians.

1 Maja Labour Day.

3 Maja Famous democratic Constitution of 1791.

9 Maja Polish "V" Day – the Russian-declared end of World War II – one day after Britain and other western European countries.

Jan Matejko Patriotic *fin-de-siècle* painter closely associated with Kraków, where he lived most of his life.

Adam Mickiewicz (1798–1855) *The* Romantic Polish poet, a national figure considered kosher by just about every one, former communist leaders included (see p.66).

Stanisław Moniuszko Romantic composer, popular in Poland but little known elsewhere.

Gabriel Narutowicz (1865–1922) First President of the Second Polish Republic, assassinated a few days after his nomination.

Ignacy Paderewski (1860–1941) Noted pianist and composer who became the country's first prime minister post-World War I and the country's regaining of independence.

Jan Paweł II. The incumbent Catholic pontiff and Polish national hero. Many streets are now renamed after Pope John Paul.

Józef Piłsudski (1867–1935) One of the country's most venerated military-political figures, key architect of the regaining of independence after World War I, and national leader in the late 1920s and early 1930s.

Józef Poniatowski (1767–1813) Nephew of the last Polish king who fought in numerous Polish and Napoleonic campaigns: an archetypal Polish military-Romantic hero.

Jerzy Popiełuszko Radical Solidarity-supporting priest murdered by the Security Forces in 1984, and since elevated to the ranks of national martyrs.

Bolesław Prus (1847–1912) Positivist writer, best known for quasi-historical novels such as *Pharoah* and *Lalka* (The Doll).

Kazimierz Pułaski (1747–79) Polish-American hero of the US War of Independence.

Mikołaj Rej So-called "Father of Polish Literature", one of the first to write in the language.

Władysław Reymont (1867–1925) Nobel Prize-winning author of *The Peasants* and *The Promised Land*.

Władysław Sikorski (1881–1943). Prewar Polish prime minister and wartime commander-in-chief of Polish forces in the West.

Marie Skłodowska-Curie (1867–1934) Nobel Prize-winning scientist and discoverer of the radioactive elements radium and polonium.

Juliusz Słowacki (1809–49) Noted playwright and poet, one of the three Polish Romantic greats.

Henryk Sienkiewicz (1846–1916) Stirring historical novelist who won the Nobel Prize for his epic *Quo Vadis*.

Jan Sobieski (1635–96) Quintessentially Polish king famous for his celebrated rescue of Vienna (1683) from the Ottoman Turks.

15 Sierpnia Date of the battle of Warsaw (August 1920) that halted the Soviet offensive against Poland, popularly known as the "miracle on the Vistula".

Bohaterów Stalingradu "Heroes of Stalingrad", a reference to the turning point in the defeat of Nazi Germany; less common than it was, but one of the few communist names to survive.

22 Stycznia Date of the start of January Uprising of 1863 against the Russians.

Karol Świerczewski One of the few commmunist figures to survive the post-1989 street name clearout (not everywhere though), a fact probably explained by his role in the controversial 1947 "Operation Vistula" (see p.291).

Świętego Ducha. Literally "Holy Spirit", generally used in square names.

Świętej Trójcy Holy Trinity – another self-explanatory Catholic favourite.

Karol Szymanowski (1882–1937) Noted modern Polish classical composer, a long-time Zakopane resident.

Kazimierz (Przerwa) Tetmajer (1865–1940) Turn-of-the-century Neo-Romantic poet, part of the Kraków-based Młoda Polska school.

Westerplatte The Polish garrison whose attack by the Nazis in September 1939 signalled the start of World War II.

Wszystkich Świętych Literally "All Saints" – a popular Catholic festival.

Stanisław Ignacy Witkiewicz (1885–1939) Maverick modernist artist and writer whose plays anticipated postwar Theatre of the Absurd.

Stanisław Wyspiański (1867–1907) Renowned *Młoda Polska* era poet, playwright and painter best known for his plays *Wesele* (The Wedding) and *Wyzwolenie* (Liberation).

Wilsona After US President Woodrow Wilson, who supported the cause of Polish independence at the Versailles Conference (1919).

1 Września Start of World War II – the September 1939 Nazi invasion of Poland.

Kardynał Stefan Wyszyński (1901–81) Tenacious postwar Catholic Primate of Poland, figurehead of popular resistance to communism.

Stefan Żeromski (1864–1925) One of the most renowned Polish novelists, a Neo-Romantic writer best known for his historical novel *Popioły* (The Ashes).

TOWN NAMES

Because Poland's borders have changed so often, many of its towns, including virtually all which were formerly German, have gone under more than one name. What follows is a checklist of names most of which can now be regarded as historical. The letters in parenthesis identity the language of the non-Polish form: G=German, OS=Old Slav, C=Czech, R=Russian, U=Ukrainian, L=Lithuanian E=English.

Barczewo Wartenburg (G)
Biała Biala (G)
Bielsko Bielitz (G)
Bierutowice Brückenberg (G)
Bolków Bolkenhain (G)
Braniewo Braunsberg (G)
Brzeg Brieg (G)
Brześć Brest (E), Briest (R)
Brzezinka Birkenau (G)
Bydgoszcz Bromberg (G)
Bystrzyca Kłodzka Habelschwerdt (G)

Chełmno Kulm (G)
Chmielno Ludwigsdorf (G)

Chojnice Kornitz (G)
Cieplice Śląskie-Zdrój Bad Warmbrunn (G)
Cieszyn Teschen (G)
Czaplinek Tempelburg (G)

Daręóko Rügenwaldermünde (G)
Darłowko Rügenwalde (G)
Dąbie Altdamm (G)
Dobre Miasto Guttstadt (G)
Duszniki-Zdrój Bad Reinerz (G)

Elbląg Elbing (G)
Ełk Lyck (G)

Frombork Frauenburg (G)

Gdańsk Gyddanyzc (OS), Danczik, Dantzig,
Danzig (G), Dantsic (E)
Gdynia Gdingen (OS), Gottenhafen (G)
Gierłoż Görlitz (G)
Giżycko Lötzen (G)
Głogów Glogau (G)
Gniezno Gnesen (G)
Goleniów Gollnow (G)
Góra Świętej Anny Sankt Annaberg (G)
Grudzidz Graudenz (G)
Grunwald Tannenberg (G)
Gryfice Greifenberg (G)

Hel Hela (G)
Henryków Heinrichau (G)

Inowrocław Hohensalza (G)
Iwięcino Eventin (G)

Jagniątków Agnetendorf (G)
Jawor Jauer (G)
Jelenia Góra Hirschberg (G)

Kadyny Cadinen (G)
Kamienna Góra Landeshut (G)
Kamień Pomorski Cammin (G)
Karłów Karlsberg (G)
Karpacz Krummhübel (G)
Kartuzy Karthaus (G)
Katowice Kattowitz (G)
Kętrzyn Rastenburg (G)
Kluki Klucken (G)
Kłodzko Glatz (G)
Kołczewo Kolzow (G)
Kołobrzeg Kolberg (G)
Koszalin Kösel (G)
Kraków Cracow (E), Krakau (G)
Kruszwica Kruschwitz (G)

Krzeszów Grüssau (G)
Książ Fürstenstein (G)
Kudowa-Zdrój Bad Kudowa (G)
Kwidzyn Marienwerder (G)

Lądek-Zdrój Bad Landeck (G)
Legnica Liegnitz (G)
Legnickie Pole Wahlstatt (G)
Leszno Lissa (G)
Lidzbark Warmiński Heilsberg (G)
Lubiąż Leubus (G)
Lwów Lemberg (G), Lvov (R), Ł'viv (U)
Łeba Leba (G)
Łódź Litzmannstadt, Lodsch (G)

Malbork Marienburg (G)
Międzygórze Wölfesgrund (G)
Międzyzdroje Misdroy (G)
Mikołajki Nikolaiken (G)
Milicz Militsch (G)
Morąg Mohrungen (G)
Mrągowo Sensburg (G)

Nysa Neisse (G)

Oleśnica Oels (G)
Oliwa Oliva (G)
Olsztyn Allenstein (G)
Olsztynek Hohenstein (G)
Opole Oppeln (G)
Orneta Wormditt (G)
Oświęcim Auschwitz (G)
Otmuchów Ottmachau (G)

Paczków Patschkau (G)
Pasłęk Preussich Holland (G)
Polanica-Zdrój Bad Altheide (G)
Poznań Posen (G)
Pszczyna Pless (G)

Reszel Rössel (G)
Ruciane Nida Niedersee (G)

Słupsk Stolp (G)
Smołdzino Schmolsin (G)
Sobieszów Hermsdorf (G)
Sobótka Zobten (G)
Sopot Zoppot (G)
Sorkwity Sorquitten (G)
Stargard Szczeciński Stargard (G)
Strzegom Striegau (G)
Strzelno Strelno (G)
Szczecin Stettin (G)

Szczecinek Neustettin (G)
Szklarska Poręba Schreiberhau (G)
Sztutowo Stutthof (G)
Świdnica Swidnitz, Schweidnitz (G)
Święta Lipka Heiligelinde (G)
Świnoujście Swinemünde (G)

Tarnowskie Góry Tarnowitz (G)
Toruń Thorn (G)
Trzebiatów Treptow (G)
Trzebnica Trebnitz (G)
Trzemeszno Tremessen (G)

Ustka Stolpmünde (G)

Wałbrzych Waldenburg (G)
Wambierzyce Albendorf (G)
Warszawa Warsaw (E), Warschau (G)
Węgorzewo Angerburg (G)
Wilkasy Wolfsee (G)
Wilno Vilnius (L), Vilna (R)
Wisełka Neuendorf (G)
Wisła Weichsel (G)
Włocławek Leslau (G)
Wolin Wollin (G)
Wrocław Breslau (G), Wratislavia (OS), Vratislav (C)

Ząbkowice Śląskie Frankenstein (G)
Zielona Góra Grünberg (G)
Ziębice Münsterberg (G)

Żagań Sagan (G)
Żmigród Trachenberg (G)
Żukowo Zuckau (G)
Żywiec Saybusch (G)

ACRONYMS AND ORGANISATIONS

ALMATUR Official student organisation and travel office.

IT (Informator Turystyczny) Tourist information office.

NBP (Narodowy Bank Polski) Polish National Bank.

ORBIS State travel agency; abroad, Orbis offices are called POLORBIS.

PKO (Polska Kasa Oszczędności) State savings bank.

PKP (Polskie Koleje Państwowe) State railways.

PKS (Polska Kommunikacja Samochodowa) State bus company.

PTTK (Polskie Towarzystwo Turystyczno-Krajoznawcze) Tourist agency – literally Polish Tourism and Nature Lovers' Association.

PZMot (Polski Związek Motorowy) National motorists' association.

PZPR (Polska Zjednoczona Partia Robotnicza) Polish Communist Party – now defunct.

INDEX

HELP US UPDATE

We've gone to a lot of effort to ensure that this edition of *Poland: The Rough Guide* is up-to-date and accurate. However, things are changing at an extraordinary speed in Poland, with new businesses cropping up daily and prices in a continual state of flux – so any suggestions, comments or corrections would be much appreciated.

We'll credit all contributions, and send a copy of the next edition (or any other Rough Guide if you prefer) for the best letters. Please write to:

Mark Salter and Gordon McLachlan, The Rough Guides, 1 Mercer Street, London WC2H 9QJ.

THE ROUGH GUIDES

The complete series of Rough Guides are available from all good bookshops but can be obtained directly from Penguin by writing to: *Penguin Direct, Penguin Books Ltd, Bath Road, Harmondsworth, West Drayton, Middlesex UB7 ODA; or telephone our credit line on 081 899 4036 (9am - 5pm)* and ask for Penguin Direct. Visa, Access and Amex accepted. Delivery will normally be within 14 working days.

Title	ISBN	Price				
Amsterdam	1858280184	£6.99	Mexico	0747101493	£6.95
Barcelona and Catalunya	0747102716	£7.99	Morocco	1858280648	£7.99
Berlin	1858280338	£8.99	New York	1858280737	£6.99
Brazil	0747101272	£7.95	Nothing Ventured	0747102082	£7.99
Brittany & Normandy	1858280192	£7.99	Paris	1858280389	£7.99
Bulgaria	1858280478	£8.99	Peru	0747102546	£7.95
California	1858280575	£9.99	Poland	1858280346	£9.99
Canada	185828001X	£10.99	Portugal	1858280222	£7.99
Crete	1858280494	£6.99	Prague	185828015X	£7.99
Cyprus	185828032X	£8.99	Provence/Cote d'Azur	1858280230	£8.99
Czech and Slovak Republics	185828029X	£8.99	Pyrenees	1858280524	£7.99
Egypt	1858280028	£9.99	San Francisco	0747102589	£5.99
Europe	1858280273	£12.99	Scandinavia	1858280397	£10.99
Florida	1858280109	£7.99	Sicily	1858280370	£8.99
France	1858280508	£9.99	Spain	1858280079	£8.99
Germany	1858280257	£11.99	St. Petersburg	1858280303	£8.99
Greece	1858280206	£9.99	Thailand	1858280168	£8.99
Guatemala & Belize	1858280117	£7.99	Tunisia	074710249X	£8.99
Holland, Belgium, Luxembourg	1858280036	£8.99	Turkey	1858280133	£8.99
Hong Kong & Macau	1858280761	£6.99	Tuscany and Umbria	1858280559	£8.99
Hungary	1858280214	£7.99	U.S.A.	1858280281	£12.99
Ireland	1858280516	£8.99	Venice	1858280362	£8.99
Italy	1858280311	£12.99	West Africa	1858280141	£12.99
Kenya	185828063X	£7.99	Women Travel	1858280710	£7.99
Mediterranean Wildlife	0747100993	£7.95	Zimbabwe & Botswana	1858280060	£8.99

The availability and published prices quoted are correct at the time of going to press but are subject to alteration without prior notice.
Penguin Direct ordering facilities are only available in the UK.